Lecture Notes in Computer Sci

Commenced Publication in 1973
Founding and Former Series Editors:
Gerhard Goos, Juris Hartmanis, and Jan van Leeuwen

Pierre Fraigniaud (Ed.)

Distributed Computing

19th International Conference, DISC 2005
Cracow, Poland, September 26-29, 2005
Proceedings

 Springer

Volume Editor

Pierre Fraigniaud
Université Paris-Sud
CNRS, LRI
91405 Orsay Cedex, France
E-mail: Pierre.Fraigniaud@lri.fr

Library of Congress Control Number: 2005932827

CR Subject Classification (1998): C.2.4, C.2.2, F.2.2, D.1.3, F.1.1, D.4.4-5

ISSN   0302-9743
ISBN-10   3-540-29163-6 Springer Berlin Heidelberg New York
ISBN-13   978-3-540-29163-3 Springer Berlin Heidelberg New York

Springer is a part of Springer Science+Business Media

springeronline.com

© Springer-Verlag Berlin Heidelberg 2005
Printed in Germany

Typesetting: Camera-ready by author, data conversion by Scientific Publishing Services, Chennai, India
Printed on acid-free paper   SPIN: 11561927   06/3142   5 4 3 2 1 0

Preface

DISC, the International Symposium on Distributed Computing, is an annual forum for presentation of research on all facets of distributed computing, including the theory, design, analysis, implementation, and application of distributed systems and networks. The nineteenth edition of DISC was held on September 26–29, 2005, in Cracow, Poland.

There were 162 fifteen-page-long (in LNCS format) extended abstracts submitted to DISC this year, and this volume contains the 32 contributions selected by the Program Committee among these 162 submissions. All submitted papers were read and evaluated by at least three Program Committee members, assisted by external reviewers. The final decision regarding every paper was taken during the Program Committee meeting, which took place in Paris, July 1–2, 2005.

The Best Student Award was split and given to two papers: the paper "General Compact Labeling Schemes for Dynamic Trees", authored by Amos Korman, and the paper "Space and Step Complexity Efficient Adaptive Collect", co-authored by Yaron De Levie and Yehuda Afek.

The proceedings also include 14 two-page-long brief announcements (BA). These BAs are presentations of ongoing works for which full papers are not ready yet, or of recent results whose full description will be soon or has been recently presented in other conferences. Researchers use the brief announcement track to quickly draw the attention of the community to their experiences, insights and results from ongoing distributed computing research and projects. The BAs included in this proceedings were selected among 30 BA submissions.

DISC 2005 was organized in cooperation with Warsaw University and Jagiellonian University. The support of the University of Liverpool, INRIA, CNRS, and the University of Paris Sud (LRI) is also gratefully acknowledged. The review process and the preparation of this volume were done using CyberChairPRO.

July 2005

Pierre Fraigniaud
DISC 2005 Program Chair

Organization

DISC, the International Symposium on Distributed Computing, is an annual forum for research presentations on all facets of distributed computing. The symposium was called the International Workshop on Distributed Algorithms (WDAG) from 1985 to 1997. DISC 2005 was organized in cooperation with the European Association for Theoretical Computer Science (EATCS).

Program Chair:
Pierre Fraigniaud, CNRS and University of Paris Sud

Organizing Chair:
Dariusz Kowalski, Warsaw University and University of Liverpool

Steering Committee Chair:
Alex Shvartsman, University of Connecticut

Organizing Committee:
Krzysztof Diks, Warsaw University
Kazimierz Grygiel, Warsaw University
Dariusz Kowalski, Warsaw University and University of Liverpool (Chair)
Krzysztof Szafran, Warsaw University
Marek Zaionc, Jagiellonian University

Steering Committee:
Alex Shvartsman, University of Connecticut (Chair)
Paul Vitanyi, CWI and University of Amsterdam (Vice-Chair)
Hagit Attiya, Technion
Faith Fich, University of Toronto
Pierre Fraigniaud, CNRS and University of Paris Sud
Rachid Guerraoui, EPFL
Roger Wattenhofer, ETH Zurich

Program Committee

Lenore Cowen	Tufts University
Panagiota Fatourou	University of Ioannina
Hugues Fauconnier	University of Paris VII
Pierre Fraigniaud	CNRS and University of Paris Sud (Chair)
Roy Friedman	Technion
Yuh-Jzer Joung	National Taiwan University
Dariusz Kowalski	Warsaw University and University of Liverpool
Victor Luchangco	Sun Microsystems Laboratories
Maged Michael	IBM T.J. Watson Research Center
David Peleg	Weizmann Institute
Greg Plaxton	University of Texas at Austin
Sergio Rajsbaum	National Autonomous University of Mexico
Sylvia Ratnasamy	Intel Research Laboratory
Nicola Santoro	Carleton University
Sebastiano Vigna	University of Milan
Jennifer Welch	Texas A&M University

Sponsoring Organizations

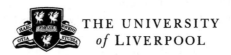

Referees

Maha Abdallah
Saurabh Agarwal
Marcos K. Aguilera
Stefan Amborg
Emmanuelle Anceaume
Filipe Araujo
Hagit Attiya
Elad Barkan
Denis Barthou
Paolo Boldi
Costas Busch
Po-An Chen
Pu-Jen Cheng
Bogdan Chlebus
Gregory Chockler
Cheng-Fu Chou
Piotr Chrzastowski
John Chuang
Bruno Codenotti
Reuven Cohen
Michele Colajanni
Massimo Coppola
Artur Czumaj
Shantanu Das
Carole Delporte
Ned Dimitrov
Shlomi Dolev
Feodor F. Dragan
Keith Duddy
Pascal Felber
Faith Ellen Fich
Matthias Fitzi
Pierre Francois
Keir Fraser
Felix C. Freiling
Eli Gafni
Jie Gao
Juan Garay
Maris Gardinariu
Leszek Gasieniec
Cyril Gavoille
Chryssis Georgiou
Bastian Pochon
Eric Goubault

Leszek Gryz
Rachid Guerraoui
Danny Hendler
Lisa Higham
Polly Huang
David Ilcinkas
Prasad Jayanti
Jehn-Ruey Jiang
Colette Johnen
Thomas Fahringer
Alexandru Jugravu
Erez Kantor
Brad Karp
Idit Keidar
David Kempe
Alex Kesselman
Gabi Kliot
Lukasz Kowalik
Piotr Krysta
Eyal Kushilevitz
Aleksandar Kuzmanovic
Mikel Larrea
Emmanuelle Lebhar
Chih-Yu Lin
Zvi Lotker
Dahlia Malkhi
Petros Maniatis
Charles Martel
Jean Mayo
Hurfin Michel
Ethan L. Miller
Neeraj Mittal
Mark Moir
Shlomo Moran
Pat Morin
Marcin Mucha
Alfredo Navarra
Robert Nikolajew
Sotiris Nikoletseas
Nicolas Nisse
Daniel Nussbaum
Alina Oprea
Katarzyna Paluch
Alessandro Panconesi

Evaggelos Papapetrou
Boaz Patt-Shamir
Andrzej Pelc
Stefan Petters
Scott Pike
Bastian Pochon
Giuseppe Prencipe
Michel Raynal
Michael Reiter
Laurent Rosaz
Sergio Ruocco
Eric Ruppert
Jared Saia
Rahul Sami
Piotr Sankowski
Elad Schiller
Michael Scott
Mordechai Shalom
Dennis Shasha
Scott Shenker
Ioannis Stamatiou
Rob van Stee
Paul Stodghill
Michal Strojnowski
Mitul Tiwari
Sebastien Tixeuil
Olga Tkachyshyn
Francisco J. Torres-Rojas
Panos Vassiliadis
Giovanni Vigna
Roman Vitenberg
Berthold Voecking
Da-Wei Wang
Hsinping Wang
Adam Warski
Mirjam Wattenhofer
Peter Widmayer
Avishai Wool
Pawel Wrzeszcz
Aleksandr Yampolskiy
Haifeng Yu
Shmuel Zaks
Xi Zhang
Aaron Zollinger

Table of Contents

Invited Talks

Digital Fountains and Their Application to Informed Content Delivery
over Adaptive Overlay Networks
    Michael Mitzenmacher 1

Securing the Net: Challenges, Failures and Directions
    Amir Herzberg.. 2

Regular Papers

Coterie Availability in Sites
    Flavio Junqueira, Keith Marzullo 3

Keeping Denial-of-Service Attackers in the Dark
    Gal Badishi, Amir Herzberg, Idit Keidar 18

On Conspiracies and Hyperfairness in Distributed Computing
    Hagen Völzer 33

On the Availability of Non-strict Quorum Systems
    Amitanand Aiyer, Lorenzo Alvizi, Rida A. Bazzi 48

Musical Benches
    Eli Gafni, Sergio Rajsbaum 63

Obstruction-Free Algorithms Can Be Practically Wait-Free
    Faith Ellen Fich, Victor Luchangco, Mark Moir, Nir Shavit 78

Efficient Reduction for Wait-Free Termination Detection in a
Crash-Prone Distributed System
    Neeraj Mittal, Felix C. Freiling, S. Venkatesan,
    Lucia Draque Penso... 93

Non-blocking Hashtables with Open Addressing
    Chris Purcell, Tim Harris...................................... 108

Computing with Reads and Writes in the Absence of Step Contention
    Hagit Attiya, Rachid Guerraoui, Petr Kouznetsov 122

Restricted Stack Implementations
Matei David, Alex Brodsky, Faith Ellen Fich 137

Proving Atomicity: An Assertional Approach
Gregory Chockler, Nancy Lynch, Sayan Mitra, Joshua Tauber 152

Time and Space Lower Bounds for Implementations Using k-CAS
Hagit Attiya, Danny Hendler 169

(Almost) All Objects Are Universal in Message Passing Systems
Carole Delporte-Gallet, Hugues Fauconnier, Rachid Guerraoui 184

Ω Meets Paxos: Leader Election and Stability Without Eventual
Timely Links
Dahlia Malkhi, Florin Oprea, Lidong Zhou 199

Plausible Clocks with Bounded Inaccuracy
Brad T. Moore, Paolo A.G. Sivilotti 214

Causing Communication Closure: Safe Program Composition with
Non-FIFO Channels
Kai Engelhardt, Yoram Moses 229

What Can Be Implemented Anonymously?
Rachid Guerraoui, Eric Ruppert 244

Waking Up Anonymous Ad Hoc Radio Networks
Andrzej Pelc 260

Fast Deterministic Distributed Maximal Independent Set Computation
on Growth-Bounded Graphs
Fabian Kuhn, Thomas Moscibroda, Tim Nieberg,
Roger Wattenhofer 273

Distributed Computing with Imperfect Randomness
Shafi Goldwasser, Madhu Sudan, Vinod Vaikuntanathan 288

Polymorphic Contention Management
Rachid Guerraoui, Maurice Herlihy, Bastian Pochon 303

Distributed Transactional Memory for Metric-Space Networks
Maurice Herlihy, Ye Sun 324

Concise Version Vectors in WinFS
Dahlia Malkhi, Doug Terry 339

Adaptive Software Transactional Memory
  Virendra J. Marathe, William N. Scherer III, Michael L. Scott 354

Optimistic Generic Broadcast
  Piotr Zieliński 369

Space and Step Complexity Efficient Adaptive Collect
  Yehuda Afek, Yaron De Levie 384

Observing Locally Self-stabilization in a Probabilistic Way
  Joffroy Beauquier, Laurence Pilard, Brigitte Rozoy 399

Asymptotically Optimal Solutions for Small World Graphs
  Michele Flammini, Luca Moscardelli, Alfredo Navarra,
  Stephane Perennes 414

Deciding Stability in Packet-Switched FIFO Networks Under the
Adversarial Queuing Model in Polynomial Time
  Maria J. Blesa 429

Compact Routing for Graphs Excluding a Fixed Minor
  Ittai Abraham, Cyril Gavoille, Dahlia Malkhi 442

General Compact Labeling Schemes for Dynamic Trees
  Amos Korman 457

The Dynamic And-Or Quorum System
  Uri Nadav, Moni Naor 472

Brief Announcements

Byzantine Clients Rendered Harmless
  Barbara Liskov, Rodrigo Rodrigues 487

Reliably Executing Tasks in the Presence of Malicious Processors
  Antonio Fernández, Chryssis Georgiou, Luis López,
  Agustín Santos 490

Obstruction-Free Step Complexity: Lock-Free DCAS as an Example
  Faith Ellen Fich, Victor Luchangco, Mark Moir, Nir Shavit 493

Communication-Efficient Implementation of Failure Detector Classes
$\Diamond Q$ and $\Diamond P$
  Mikel Larrea, Alberto Lafuente 495

Optimal Resilience for Erasure-Coded Byzantine Distributed Storage
  Christian Cachin, Stefano Tessaro 497

Agreement Among Unacquainted Byzantine Generals
  Michael Okun 499

Subscription Propagation and Content-Based Routing with Delivery
Guarantees
  Yuanyuan Zhao, Sumeer Bhola, Daniel Sturman 501

Asynchronous Verifiable Information Dispersal
  Christian Cachin, Stefano Tessaro 503

Towards a Theory of Self-organization
  Emmanuelle Anceaume, Xavier Defago, Maria Gradinariu,
  Matthieu Roy 505

Timing Games and Shared Memory
  Zvi Lotker, Boaz Patt-Shamir, Mark R. Tuttle 507

A Lightweight Group Mutual k-Exclusion Algorithm Using Bi-k-Arbiters
  Yu-Chen Kuo, Huang-Chen Lee 509

Could Any Graph Be Turned into a Small-World?
  Philippe Duchon, Nicolas Hanusse, Emmanuelle Lebhar,
  Nicolas Schabanel 511

Papillon: Greedy Routing in Rings
  Ittai Abraham, Dahlia Malkhi, Gurmeet Singh Manku 514

An Efficient Long-Lived Adaptive Collect Algorithm
  Burkhard Englert 516

Author Index 519

Digital Fountains and Their Application to Informed Content Delivery over Adaptive Overlay Networks
(Invited Talk)

Michael Mitzenmacher

Division of Engineering and Applied Sciences,
Harvard University,
USA

Abstract. We study how to optimize throughput of large transfers across richly connected, adaptive overlay networks, focusing on the potential of collaborative transfers between peers to supplement ongoing downloads. First, we make the case for an erasure-resilient encoding of the content, using the digital fountain paradigm. Such an approach affords reliability and a substantial degree of application-level flexibility, as it seamlessly accommodates connection migration and parallel transfers while providing resilience to packet loss. We explain the history of this paradigm, focusing on recent advances in coding that allow efficient implementations of digital fountains. We also describe our previous work showing the effectiveness of digital fountains for reliable multicast and parallel downloading.

In the setting of collaborative transfers on overlay networks, there is an additional consideration since sets of encoded symbols acquired by peers during downloads may overlap substantially. We describe a collection of useful algorithmic tools for efficient estimation, summarization, and approximate reconciliation of sets of symbols between pairs of collaborating peers, all of which keep messaging complexity and computation to a minimum. Through simulations and experiments on a prototype implementation, we demonstrate the performance benefits of our informed content delivery mechanisms.

P. Fraigniaud (Ed.): DISC 2005, LNCS 3724, p. 1, 2005.
© Springer-Verlag Berlin Heidelberg 2005

Securing the Net:
Challenges, Failures and Directions
(Invited Talk)

Amir Herzberg

Department of Computer Science,
Bar Ilan University,
Israel

Abstract. The Internet is infamously insecure (fraudulent and spoofed sites, phishing and spam e-mail, viruses and Trojans, Denial of Service attacks, etc.) in spite of extensive efforts, standards, tools, and research. We will discuss the problems and the pitfalls, and outline solutions and directions for future applied and analytical research.

P. Fraigniaud (Ed.): DISC 2005, LNCS 3724, p. 2, 2005.

Coterie Availability in Sites

Flavio Junqueira and Keith Marzullo

Department of Computer Science and Engineering,
University of California, San Diego
{flavio, marzullo}@cs.ucsd.edu

Abstract. In this paper, we explore new failure models for multi-site systems, which are systems characterized by a collection of sites spread across a wide area network, each site formed by a set of computing nodes running processes. In particular, we introduce two failure models that allow sites to fail, and we use them to derive coteries. We argue that these coteries have better availability than quorums formed by a majority of processes, which are known for having best availability when process failures are independent and identically distributed. To motivate introducing site failures explicitly into a failure model, we present availability data from a production multi-site system, showing that sites are frequently unavailable. We then discuss the implementability of our abstract models, showing possibilities for obtaining these models in practice. Finally, we present evaluation results from running an implementation of the Paxos algorithm on PlanetLab using different quorum constructions. The results show that our constructions have substantially better availability and response time compared to majority coteries.

1 Introduction

There has been a proliferation of large distributed systems that support a diverse set of applications such as sensor nets, data grids, and large simulations. Such systems consist of multiple sites connected by a wide area network, where a site is a collection of computing nodes running one or more processes. The sites are often managed by different organizations, and the systems are large enough that site and process failures are common facts of life rather than rare events.

Critical services in such systems can be made highly available using replication. In data grids, for example, data sets are the most important assets, and having them available under failures of sites is very desirable. To improve availability, the well-known *quorum update* technique can be used. This technique consists of implementing a mutual exclusion mechanism by reading and writing to sets of processes that intersect (*quorums*) [7]. As another example, the Paxos protocol [16] enables the implementation of fault-tolerant state machines for asynchronous systems. Paxos is a popular choice because of its ability to produce results when a majority of replicas survive, for its feature of not producing erroneous results when failures of more than a majority (indeed, up to a complete failure) occur, and its very weak assumptions about the environment. Underlying Paxos (and other similar protocols) is the same quorum update technique.

This paper considers quorum constructions for multi-site systems. The problem area of quorums for multi-site systems is large and not well studied. We address a set of

P. Fraigniaud (Ed.): DISC 2005, LNCS 3724, pp. 3–17, 2005.

problems from this area as an early foray. We first give a failure model for multi-site systems that is simple and has intuitive appeal, and then give a second failure model that has less intuitive appeal but theoretical and practical interest. Because sites can fail, the failures of processes are not independent, and so an IID (independent, identically distributed) model is not appropriate. We define a new metric for availability that is suitable to non-IID failures, and give optimal quorum constructions for both models. We discuss the implementability of the two failure models, and discuss an experiment of running Paxos on PlanetLab [21] that gives some validation of our results.

Related work. Quorum systems have been studied for over two decades. The first algorithms based on quorums use voting [8]. Garcia-Molina and Barbara generalized the notion of voting mechanisms, and proposed the use of minimal collections of intersecting sets, or *coteries* [7]. Most of the following work (such as [15,18,20]) has concentrated on how quorums can be constructed to give good availability, load and capacity assuming relatively simple system properties (such as identical processes and independent failures) [2,3,19]. Only recently the problem of choosing quorums according to properties of the system (such as location) has attracted some attention [9,14]. Of particular interest to our current work are the constructions of [15] and [6]. In [15], Kumar proposed, to the best of our knowledge, the first hierarchical quorum construction, and showed that by doing so one can have smaller quorums. The analysis in [15], however, assumes IID failures. The work by Busca *et al.* assumes a multi-site system similar to what we assume here, and their quorum construction [6] is very similar to our *Qsite* construction. Their focus, however, was on performance. If one considers the distribution of response times from a quorum system, performance is often measured using the average or median, while availability is a property of the tail of the distribution. Thus, high performance does not necessarily imply high availability. Availability in quorum systems has been studied before [2,3,19], but we argue here that the previous metrics are not suitable for multi-site systems. A notable exception is the work by Amir and Wool [1], which evaluates several existing quorum constructions in the context of a small, real network.

A *network partition* is a failure event that leads to one set of non-faulty processes being unable to communicate with another set of non-faulty processes (and, often, vice versa). Quorum systems are asynchronous, and so a network partition is treated identically to slow-to-respond processes. Long-lasting network partitions can make it impossible to obtain a quorum. A recent paper by Yu presents a probabilistic construction that does increase availability in the face of partitions, but it assumes a uniform distribution of servers across the network [24]. In comparison, our constructions are deterministic and make no assumption about distributions of sites.

2 System Model

We consider a system of a set P of processes. The processes are partitioned into *sites* $\mathcal{B} = \{B_1, B_2, \ldots, B_k\}$, and between each pair of processes there is a bidirectional communication channel. Processes can fail by crashing, and a crashed process can recover. Similarly, a site can fail and recover. A site failure represents the loss of a key resource used by the processes in the site (such as network, power, or a storage server) or some event that causes physical damage to the equipment on the site (such as loss of A/C); the processes in the site are all effectively crashed while the site is faulty.

Let $\mathcal{E}$ represent the executions of the system. Each execution $E \in \mathcal{E}$ is a sequence of system states. Each state $s \in E$ of an execution has an associated *failure pattern* $F(s, E) \subseteq P$, which is the set of processes that are faulty in s. If site B_i is faulty in s, then all of the processes in B_i are in $F(s, E)$. We use $NF(E, s) = P \setminus F(E, s)$ to denote the set of non-faulty processes in s. We say that a failure pattern f is valid iff $\exists E \in \mathcal{E} : \exists s \in E : f = F(E, s)$.

We use survivor sets to express valid failure patterns. Survivor sets were introduced in [11] to provide a more expressive model of process failures. Informally, a survivor set is a minimal subset of non-faulty processes. There are different ways to define survivor sets more formally: we have used probabilities [11] and have used the complement of maximal failure patterns [13]. We use the second one here. This definition does not rely on probabilities directly, although failure probabilities can be used to determine survivor sets; we discuss this point later in this paper. The definition is:

Definition 1. *Given a set of processes P, a set S is a survivor set if and only if:*[1]

$$\begin{aligned} &\bigwedge S \subseteq P \\ &\bigwedge \exists E \in \mathcal{E} : \exists s \in E : S = \mathrm{NF}(E, s) \\ &\bigwedge \forall p \in S : \forall E \in \mathcal{E} : \forall s \in E : S \setminus p \neq \mathrm{NF}(E, s) \end{aligned}$$

We use $\mathcal{S}_P$ to denote the set of survivor sets of P, and we call a pair $\langle P, \mathcal{S}_P \rangle$ a *system profile*.

We now repeat a few definitions that have appeared elsewhere and that we use in this paper. A coterie $\mathcal{Q}$ is a set of subsets of P that satisfies the following two properties [7]: 1) $\forall Q_i, Q_j \in \mathcal{Q} : Q_i \cap Q_j \neq \emptyset$; 2) $\forall Q_i, Q_j \in \mathcal{Q}, Q_i \neq Q_j : Q_i \not\subset Q_j \wedge Q_j \not\subset Q_i$. The first property is called 2-Intersection [13], and it says that quorums in a coterie pairwise intersect. This property guarantees mutual exclusion when executing operations on quorums, such as reads and writes, as every pair of quorums must have at least one process in common. The second property states that all quorums are minimal. A coterie $\mathcal{Q}$ is *dominated* if there is a coterie $\mathcal{Q}'$ such that: 1) $\mathcal{Q} \neq \mathcal{Q}'$; 2) $\forall Q \in \mathcal{Q} : \exists Q' \in \mathcal{Q}' : Q' \subseteq Q$. If no coterie dominates a coterie $\mathcal{Q}$, then we say that $\mathcal{Q}$ in *non-dominated*.

A *transversal* of a coterie is a subset of processes that intersects every quorum in the coterie. We use $\mathcal{T}(\mathcal{Q})$ to denote the set of transversals of the coterie $\mathcal{Q}$. Transversals are useful for defining the availability of a coterie: a coterie $\mathcal{Q}$ is available in a step s of some execution E if and only if $F(s, E) \notin \mathcal{T}(\mathcal{Q})$.

3   Computing Availability

The availability of coteries can be computed in various ways. One metric is *node vulnerability* which is the minimum number of nodes that, if removed, make it impossible

---

[1] We use the "bulleted conjunction" and the "bulleted disjunction" notation list invented in TLA$^+$ [17]. In Definition 1, the list corresponds to the conjunction of the statements to the right of the "$\bigwedge$" marks.

to obtain a quorum [3]. A similar metric, *edge vulnerability*, counts the minimum number of channels whose removal makes it impossible to obtain a quorum (no connected component contains a quorum). Both of these metrics are appropriate when failures are independent and identically distributed (IID) because they measure the minimum number of failures necessary to halt the system. They are not necessarily good metrics for multi-site systems. Consider the following three-site system in which a survivor set is the union of majorities of processes in a site for some majority of sites:[2]

$$P = \{a_1, a_2, a_3, b_1, b_2, b_3, c_1, c_2, c_3\}$$
$$\mathcal{B} = \{a_1a_2a_3, b_1b_2b_3, c_1c_2c_3\}$$
$$\mathcal{S}_P = \{a_ia_jb_lb_m : i, j, l, m \in \{1, 2, 3\} \wedge i \neq j \wedge l \neq m\}$$
$$\cup \{a_ia_jc_lc_m : i, j, l, m \in \{1, 2, 3\} \wedge i \neq j \wedge l \neq m\}$$
$$\cup \{b_ib_jc_lc_m : i, j, l, m \in \{1, 2, 3\} \wedge i \neq j \wedge l \neq m\}$$

From our system model, processes are pairwise connected. According to the results in [3], the best strategy for both node and edge vulnerability is then to use quorums formed of majorities, which for this system is any subset of five processes. By definition, for every $S \in \mathcal{S}_P$, there is some step s of some execution $E \in \mathcal{E}$ such that $S = F(s, E)$, where $\mathcal{E}$ is the set of executions of $\langle P, \mathcal{S}_P \rangle$. As P contains nine processes and every $S \in \mathcal{S}_P$ contains four processes, there are five faulty processes in such a step, and hence no majority quorum can be obtained. If one uses $\mathcal{S}_P$ as a coterie, however, then there is one quorum available in every step, by construction. $\mathcal{S}_P$ has therefore better availability than the majority construction.

An alternative to node and edge vulnerability is, given probabilities of failures, to directly compute the probability of the most likely failure patterns that make it impossible to obtain a quorum. Probability models, however, can become quite complex when failures are not IID. To avoid such complexity, we use a different counting metric: the number of survivor sets that allow a quorum to be obtained. More carefully,

Definition 2. *Let $\langle P, \mathcal{S}_P \rangle$ be a system profile and $\mathcal{Q}$ be a coterie over P. The availability of $\mathcal{Q}$ is given by:* $\mathcal{A}(\mathcal{Q}) = |\{S : S \in \mathcal{S}_P \wedge S \notin \mathcal{T}(\mathcal{Q})\}|$

A coterie $\mathcal{Q}$ *covers* a survivor set S if there is a quorum $Q \in \mathcal{Q}$ such that $Q \subseteq S$. By the definition, $\mathcal{A}(\mathcal{Q})$ is hence the number of survivor sets that $\mathcal{Q}$ covers.

This is a good metric because in every step s of an execution E, there is at least one survivor set in $\mathcal{S}_P$ that does not intersect $F(E, s)$. If a coterie allows a quorum to be obtained for more survivor sets, then this coterie is available during more steps. As node vulnerability and edge vulnerability, $\mathcal{A}()$ is a deterministic metric and as such has a similar limitation with respect to probabilities. If we assign probabilities of failure to subsets of processes, then our metric may lead to wrong conclusions, as there might be higher available coteries that include discarded survivor sets. For the constructions and examples we discuss in this paper, however, using this metric gives us coteries with optimal availability.

If a coterie $\mathcal{Q}$ is dominated, then by definition there is some other coterie $\mathcal{Q}'$ that dominates $\mathcal{Q}$. Under reasonable assumptions, the availability of $\mathcal{Q}'$ is at least as high as

---

[2] We use $x_1x_2 \ldots x_n$ as a short notation for the set $\{x_1, x_2, \ldots, x_n\}$.

the availability of Q. Thus, we use domination to break ties between coteries that cover the same number of survivor sets. We say that $Q \prec_a Q'$ iff:

$$\bigvee \mathcal{A}(Q') > \mathcal{A}(Q)$$
$$\bigvee (\mathcal{A}(Q') = \mathcal{A}(Q)) \wedge Q' \text{ dominates } Q$$

In Section 5, we give quorum constructions that are optimal with respect to this metric without the tiebreaker rule. We do not discuss how to construct non-dominated coteries from dominated ones; possible ways to do so are discussed in [4] and [7].

4   Failure Models

In this section, we present two failure models that we use to derive quorum constructions. Both models are specific to multi-site systems, and although they both model site failures, they model different system properties as we discuss in Section 6.

4.1   The Multi-site Hierarchical Model

The first model, which we call the *multi-site hierarchical model*, decouples site failures from process failures. The failure model has two components: $\mathcal{F}_s$, which characterizes the failures of sites, and $\mathcal{F}_p$, which characterizes failures within a site. More specifically, $\mathcal{F}_s$ is a set of maximal subsets of sites that can fail simultaneously, $|\mathcal{F}_s| > 0$. $\mathcal{F}_p$ is an array with one entry for each site, where $\mathcal{F}_p[i]$ is the set of maximal subsets of processes that can be simultaneously faulty in site B_i when B_i is not faulty, $|\mathcal{F}_p[i]| > 0$, $i \in \{1, \ldots, |\mathcal{B}|\}$. Given an instance of this model, a set $S_i \subseteq P$ is in S_P if and only if:

$$\exists FS \in \mathcal{F}_s : \bigwedge \forall B_j \in \mathcal{B} \setminus FS : \exists FP \in \mathcal{F}_p[j] : B_j \cap S_i = B_j \setminus FP$$
$$\bigwedge \forall B_j \in FS : S_i \cap B_j = \emptyset$$

The multi-site threshold model proposed in [14] is a threshold-based version of this model: f_s is the maximum number of sites that fail simultaneously, and $F_p[i]$ is the maximum number of processes that fail simultaneously in site B_i.

4.2   The Bimodal Model

The *bimodal model* is similar to the multi-site hierarchical model: it also has two components $\mathcal{F}_s$ and $\mathcal{F}_p$. In general, this model represents settings in which there are multiple sites ($|\mathcal{B}| > 1$), all sites can fail but one, and if only one site is not faulty, then all processes in it are correct. Thus, each site is a survivor set. If multiple sites are non-faulty, then the non-faulty sites can have faulty processes. We describe these process failures with $\mathcal{F}_s$ and $\mathcal{F}_p$. Finally, we assume that there exists at least one site B_i such that $B_i \notin FS$ for every $FS \in \mathcal{F}_s$. Although B_i is not in any element of $\mathcal{F}_s$, it can still fail in the case that there is one non-faulty site B_j with no faulty processes, and $j \neq i$. This assumption is necessary to derive an optimal construction, as we explain in Section 5.2.

The bimodal model contains the same failure patterns as the multi-site hierarchical model for the same components $\mathcal{F}_s$ and $\mathcal{F}_p$, but it contains $|\mathcal{B}|$ additional failure patterns, one for each site B_i. More specifically, a set $S_i \subseteq P$ is a survivor set for an instance of this model if and only if:

$$\bigvee \exists FS \in \mathcal{F}_s : \bigwedge \forall B_j \in \mathcal{B} \setminus FS : \exists FP \in \mathcal{F}_p[j] : B_j \cap S_i = B_j \setminus FP$$
$$\bigwedge \forall B_j \in FS : S_i \cap B_j = \emptyset$$
$$\bigvee \exists B_j \in \mathcal{B} : S_i = B_j$$

To construct a proper set of survivor sets, we need to impose the following constraint: $\forall FS \in \mathcal{F}_s : (|\mathcal{B} \setminus FS| > 1) \wedge (\forall B_i \in FS : \mathcal{F}_p[i] \neq \{\emptyset\})$. Without this constraint, the set of survivor sets might not be minimal, violating minimality.

The bimodal model does not have the intuitive appeal of the multi-site hierarchical model. Nonetheless, we argue in Section 6 that for at least two-site systems, it is practical. In addition, it has theoretical interest, which we describe in Section 5.

5 Quorum Constructions

In this section, we use the failure models described to derive quorum constructions that are optimal with respect to the metric $\mathcal{A}()$. The first construction covers all survivor sets in $\mathcal{S}_P$ by using $\mathcal{S}_P$ itself. We provide a necessary and sufficient condition for this to hold. The other construction is for systems in which it is not possible to cover all survivor sets. This is important when survivor sets do not pairwise intersect. This construction is also optimal with respect to the metric $\mathcal{A}()$ except that the resulting coterie may be dominated.

5.1 Achieving Optimal Availability

Let $\langle P, \mathcal{S}_P \rangle$ be a system profile, and suppose that we use the multi-site hierarchical model to determine $\mathcal{S}_P$. To cover all survivor sets in $\mathcal{S}_P$, it is necessary and sufficient that $\mathcal{F}_s$ and $\mathcal{F}_p$ satisfy the following property:

$$\forall FS, FS' \in \mathcal{F}_s : \exists B_i \in \mathcal{B} : \bigwedge B_i \notin FS$$
$$\bigwedge B_i \notin FS'$$
$$\bigwedge \forall FP, FP' \in \mathcal{F}_p[i] : \exists p \in B_i : p \notin FP \wedge p \notin FP'$$

In words, we require that there is at least one site shared between any two survivor sets, and within that site there is at least one process that is shared between the two survivor sets. To show that this property is necessary, suppose that this property is violated. That is, there are FS, FS' in $\mathcal{F}_s$ such that, for every $B_i \in \mathcal{B}$, at least one of the following holds: 1) $B_i \in FS$; 2) $B_i \in FS'$; 3) there are $FP, FP' \in \mathcal{F}_p[i]$ such that for every $p \in B_i$, either $p \in FP$ or $p \in FP'$. This implies that there are at least two disjoint survivor sets S and S' in $\mathcal{S}_P$. Now suppose by way of contradiction that there is a coterie $\mathcal{Q}$ that covers all survivor sets in $\mathcal{S}_P$, i.e., $\mathcal{A}(\mathcal{Q}) = |\mathcal{S}_P|$. We then have that there is a quorum $Q \in \mathcal{Q}$ such that $Q \subseteq S$. Similarly, there is a quorum $Q' \in \mathcal{Q}$ such that $Q' \subseteq S'$. Thus, if $S \cap S' = \emptyset$, then $Q \cap Q' = \emptyset$. We conclude that $\mathcal{Q}$ cannot be a coterie because it violates the 2–Intersection property.

To see that the property is sufficient is straightforward: by the definition of survivor sets, no survivor set is strictly contained in another, and the intersection property is guaranteed by assumption.

If we use $\mathcal{S}_P$ as a coterie, then we have achieved the best possible value for our availability metric because it covers all the survivor sets (i.e., $\mathcal{A}(\mathcal{S}_P)$ has the maximum value of $|\mathcal{S}_P|$). Using all the sites in the system, however, may be unnecessary. For example, if the system satisfies k–Intersection for some $k > 2$, then we may be able to construct a coterie over fewer sites. [3] We illustrate this point with a threshold version of the multi-site hierarchical model. Suppose that every set $FS \in \mathcal{F}_s$ has the same size $f_s \geq 0$, and that for every $B_i \in \mathcal{B}$ and every $FP \in \mathcal{F}_p[i]$, we have that $|FP| = t$ for some nonnegative integer t. Then, if $|\mathcal{B}| \geq 2f_s + 1$, we only need to select a subset $\mathcal{B}' \subseteq \mathcal{B}$ of $2f_s + 1$ sites. For each site $B_i \in \mathcal{B}'$, we select $2t + 1$ processes from B_i. A quorum is obtained by selecting a majority of processes from a majority of sites in $\mathcal{B}'$.

We call this construction *Qsite*. As an example, suppose that $|\mathcal{B}| = 4$, $f_s = 1$, and for each site B_i, we have that $|B_i| = 4$ and $t = 1$. We then use 3 sites, as $2f_s + 1 = 3$, and 3 processes from each site, as $2t + 1 = 3$. From the construction, a quorum in $\mathcal{Q}$ is hence composed of four processes, two from a site B_i and two from a site B_j, $i \neq j$. This system has nine processes, and so a majority would consist of five processes. For both majority and Qsite, the coterie is available as long as there are $f_s + 1 = 2$ non-faulty sites. Majority, however, not only requires that two sites are non-faulty, but also that at least one of the sites contains no faulty processes. A coterie generated by Qsite does not have this same constraint, and it is available as long as there are two non-faulty sites, each non-faulty site containing two non-faulty processes. This happens because majority uses larger quorums, and it tolerates fewer process failures.

It is not hard to see that Qsite requires fewer processes compared to majority coteries, and that the difference increases with the value of f_s (see [14] for details). Using fewer processes in each quorum reduces the load handled by any particular process, if quorums are uniformly selected, and increases the total capacity of the system [19].

5.2 The Bimodal Construction

It may be the case that the set of survivor sets do not satisfy 2–Intersection, and so can not be used as a coterie. For example, in the bimodal model, for each site B_i, B_i is a survivor set, and since sites are disjoint, $\mathcal{S}_P$ is not a coterie.

One can construct a coterie from any $\mathcal{S}_P$, though, by simply discarding survivor sets until remaining sets satisfy 2-Intersection. This procedure clearly will terminate with a coterie since a single set is a coterie of one quorum. To obtain a coterie that is optimal with respect to $\mathcal{A}()$, we need to determine the minimal set $\mathcal{S} \subset \mathcal{S}_P$ such that $\mathcal{S}_P \setminus \mathcal{S}$ is a coterie. The problem of computing the minimum number of survivor sets that have to be removed from $\mathcal{S}_P$ to obtain a coterie, however, is in general NP-Complete [12].

Under the bimodal model, it is simple to determine which survivor sets to discard. Consider the following intersection property that we call k-bimodal Intersection, $k > 1$:

$$\forall \text{ distinct } S_1, S_2, \ldots, S_{k+2} \in \mathcal{S}_P : \bigvee \exists i, j \in [1, k] : S_i \cap S_j \neq \emptyset$$
$$\bigvee S_{k+1} \cap S_{k+2} \neq \emptyset$$

Assume $\langle P, \mathcal{S}_P \rangle$ follows the bimodal failure model. According to the model, it contains $|\mathcal{B}|$ survivor sets that are disjoint, one for each site $B_i \in \mathcal{B}$. Also by the failure

---

[3] k–Intersection generalizes 2–Intersection, and states that all subsets of k quorums intersect.

model, there is a site B_i such that $B_i \notin FS$, for every $FS \in \mathcal{F}_s$. Let S_i be the survivor set consisting of the processes of B_i. If $\langle P, \mathcal{S}_P \rangle$ also satisfies k-bimodal Intersection, $k = |\mathcal{B}|$, then we know that any two survivor sets S_a, S_b in $\mathcal{S}_P \setminus \{S_1, S_2, \dots S_k\}$ intersect, and that $S_i \cap S_a \neq \emptyset$ and $S_i \cap S_b \neq \emptyset$. Since this is true for any S_a and S_b, the set $\mathcal{Q}_\ell = \{S_i\} \cup (\mathcal{S}_P \setminus \{S_1, S_2, \dots S_k\})$ is a coterie, and $\mathcal{A}(\mathcal{Q}_\ell) = |\mathcal{S}_P| - (k - 1)$. This is clearly optimal, since all of the remaining $k - 1$ survivor sets do not intersect S_i. Also, if $\langle P, \mathcal{S}_P \rangle$ does not satisfy k-bimodal Intersection, then there is no coterie that covers $|\mathcal{S}_P| - (k - 1)$ survivor sets, as there is no subset of $\mathcal{S}_P$ of size $|\mathcal{S}_P| - (k - 1)$ that pairwise intersect. We call this construction *Bsite*.

6 Failure Models in Practice

The failure models presented in Section 4 are abstract views of failures in a multi-site system. In this section, we present probabilistic models that we use to extract the parameters of our failure models. First, we use data from a real system to argue why we believe site failures are common in multi-site systems. In the remainder of the section, we discuss process failures for the two models we propose in this paper. For each model, we discuss a framework based on a Markov chain and illustrate with an example.

6.1 Site Failures

To understand how sites fail in a multi-site system, we studied the failure data of a particular system, the BIRN Grid [5,14]. We obtained monthly availability data for 15 BIRN sites from January 2004 through August 2004.[4] According to this data, a site becoming unavailable is surprisingly common. On average, each site did not have 100% availability during five of the eight months, and in any given month several sites had unplanned outages and became unavailable.

Figure 1 summarizes the availability of sites. For each month, we count the number of sites that had availability below some value α, for different values of α. We then compute the average across the eight months for each value. This average is what we plot in Figure 1. From the figure, on average over ten sites do not have 100% availability in a month.

In trying to determine what causes low monthly site availability, we identified a few reasons for a site to be unavailable, observed in BIRN sites, in TeraGrid sites [23], and in a local computer cluster. They are (in no par-

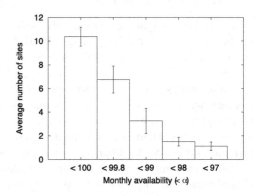

Fig. 1. Number of sites with availability below α. The error bars correspond to the standard error.

ticular order): Software problems; Power outages; Failure of shared resources (e.g. storage); Flooding resulting from broken pipes; Local campus network problems; Loss of air-conditioning. We are currently attempting to further quantify these failures.

---

[4] This data is consistently collected by the BIRN staff, and made available through their web page. Availability figures are based on active probing (via ping) and on notifications generated by the Storage Resource Broker (SRB) service.

6.2   Obtaining the Multi-site Hierarchical Model

The multi-site hierarchical model has two components: $\mathcal{F}_s$ that describes sites failures, and $\mathcal{F}_p$ that describes the failures of processes within a site. We can determine $\mathcal{F}_s$ using, for example, data such as described in Section 6.1. To determine $\mathcal{F}_p$, we need a model of failures within a site. Even when sites are not faulty, individual processes can fail due to, for example, hardware faults. In many multi-site systems, hardware and software platforms are the same across the computing nodes (where processes run) of a site because of the difficulty in managing a heterogeneous environment. We hence assume that the reliability of processes within a site is uniform and independent. Of course, this assumption may be violated by viruses and worms [10], but their effects are outside the scope of this work.

We can model failures in sites using a *Markov chain* [22]. Instead of modeling the whole system, we have chosen to model sites individually. We assume that sites operate independently, and that outside of expected message communication the operation of a process at a site has little or no influence on the operation of a process at another site. As a consequence, sites change their failure states concurrently.

As process failures are independent, states of the model correspond to the number of faulty processes in a site, and the probability of undergoing a transition from a state with f faulty processes to a state with $f + 1$ process is p. Repair transitions (from $f + 1$ to f), however, may have probabilities that change with the value of f. For example, resources to repair processes can be progressively allocated as more processes fail. As a result, the repair probability remains constant or even increases with the value of f.

Figure 2 depicts the chain we just described. Assuming that no transition probability is zero, we have that this chain is irreducible and ergodic. According to the model, processes fail independently, but the probability of repair (undergoing a transition from state $f + 1$ to f) may change with the value of f. In our model, we use r_f to denote the probability that the site undergoes a transition from state $f + 1$ to state f.

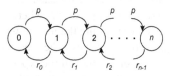

Fig. 2. Model for a single site with n process

Repairs in different sites happen independently, and hence the probability of a repair transition does not increase with failures in different sites. That is, if a process fails in site B_i and another in site B_j, $i \neq j$, they do not mutually affect their repair probabilities.

Using this model, we can easily compute a threshold on the number of failures for each site. First, we need to determine a target degree of reliability ρ, which is the probability that the number of simultaneous process failures in any site is higher than expected. Because our model is an irreducible ergodic Markov chain, we can compute the limiting probabilities of all states [22]. That is, the probability of being at a state j after a long time has elapsed, independent of the initial state i ($\pi_j = \lim_{n \to \infty} P_{ij}^n$). Using these limiting probabilities, we can determine a threshold for each site: the threshold for a site S_i is the number of failures associated to the first state that has a limiting probability smaller than ρ. This is implies that any state with failures above the threshold has probability lower than ρ.

To illustrate the process of obtaining a threshold for a site, we give an example. Let $\mathcal{B}$ be a collection of sites such that each site has three processes. Suppose that the probabilities of failure and repair are the same across all the sites. These probabilities are as follows: $p = 0.01$, $r_0 = 0.3$, $r_1 = 0.4$, and $r_2 = 0.5$. Computing the limiting probabilities, we have the following: $\pi_0 = 0.96695$, $\pi_1 = 0.03223$, $\pi_2 = 0.00080$, $\pi_3 = 0.00002$. If ρ is 0.001, for instance, we have that the threshold is one for every site, and $\mathcal{F}_p$ is as follows: $\mathcal{F}_p[i] = \{a_i : a_i \in B_i\}, \forall B_i \in \mathcal{B}$.

Note that the reverse order is also possible: choose a value for t and compute the corresponding probability of violating this threshold. Using one method or the other depends on design constraints.

6.3   Obtaining the Bimodal Model

From the description of the bimodal model in Section 4, when $k - 1$ sites fail, the remaining site has no faulty processes. This means that the processes of each site comprise a survivor set. At the same time, it is possible that all available sites have faulty processes. We model this with a framework based on a Markov chain. Due to the complexity of this model, our framework is only meant to give a more practical view rather than serve as a general framework.

As in the previous section, the basic idea consists in determining probabilities for the possible states of the system, and to use a degree of reliability (a value $\rho \in [0, 1]$) to determine the states that we consider as normal states. Compared to the chain from the previous section, a state corresponds to failures across all the sites. We then label states with counters, one for each site. That is, we have one state for each possible value of the string $f_1 \cdot f_2 \cdot \ldots \cdot f_k$, where $0 \leq f_i \leq |B_i|$ and $B_i \in \mathcal{B}$. Using a directed graph as a way of visualizing the model, we have that the states are represented by nodes, and the transitions by edges, where each edge has a weight that is the transition probability. In this model, we have three types of edges: site-failure edges, process-failure edges, and repair edges. A site-failure edge corresponds to the transition from a state in which a given site has one or more available processes to one in which all processes in this site are faulty. Using probability notation, let X_s be the random variable representing the state at step s. We then have that:

$$Pr\{X_{s+1} = f_1 \cdots |B_i| \cdot f_{i+1} \cdots f_k | X_s = f_1 \cdots f_i \cdot f_{i+1} \cdots f_k\} = p_s, f_i < |B_i| - 1$$
$$Pr\{X_{s+1} = f_1 \cdots |B_i| \cdot f_{i+1} \cdots f_k | X_s = f_1 \cdots |B_i| - 1 \cdot f_{i+1} \cdots f_k\} = p_f + p_s, f_i$$
$$= |B_i| - 1$$

where p_f is the probability of a process failure, and p_s is the probability of a site failure. As a simplifying assumption, we have that p_s and p_f are constant across the sites. A process-failure edge is a transition from a state in which some site B_i has f_i faulty processes to a state in which B_i has $f_i + 1$ faulty processes, $f_i < |B_i|$. Using probability notation, we have:

$$Pr\{X_{s+1} = f_1 \cdots f_i + 1 \cdots f_k | X_s = f_1 \cdots f_i \cdots f_k\} = p_f, f_i < |B_i|$$

Finally, we call a repair edge a transition from a state in which $f_i + 1$ processes of some site B_i are faulty to a state in which f_i processes of B_i are faulty. That is:

$$Pr\{X_{s+1} = f_1 \cdots f_i \cdots f_k | X_s = f_1 \cdots f_i + 1 \cdots f_k\} = p_r(f_1 \cdots f_i + 1 \cdots f_k), f_i \geq 0$$

where $p_r()$ is a repair probability mapping. Different from p_s and p_f, we assume that the repair probability may differ for different states. In fact, this control over repair probabilities is what we use to guarantee that the properties of the bimodal model hold. An additional assumption that completes the model is that all other possible transitions have zero probability.

Figure 3 illustrates a model for two identical sites B_1 and B_2 of n processes each. In the figure, we mark the undesirable states by including them in a gray region. These states are the ones that violate the Bsite construction, and therefore must have low probability. To determine the probability of a state, we use also limiting probabilities.

In this model, we assume that probabilities of failure are constant, and they cannot be changed as the system changes states. We assume, however, that we are able to have different repair probabilities for different states. As a physical explanation, repair probabilities change as the effort spent to repair the system

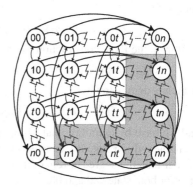

Fig. 3. Model for two sites

changes. Thus, we can increase the repair probability for an undesirable state, thereby decreasing the probability of being in this state. In practice, this means that the amount of physical resources used to repair processes must increase with the number of failures in the system. It is then necessary to be able to detect failures. A failure detector for this application, however, can be unreliable as the only side-effect is to have more resources used to repair processes unnecessarily. Having an unreliable failure detector implies that the repair probabilities have to take into account false positives. We therefore assume that it is possible to bound and estimate the frequency with which the failure detector makes mistakes.

As an example, suppose that $n = 3$, $p_s = 0.004$, $p_f = 0.001$, and $p_r(f_1 \cdot f_2) = 0.1$, if $f_1 \cdot f_4$ is outside the gray region, and $p_r(f_1 \cdot f_2) = 0.4$, if $f_1 \cdot f_2$ is inside the gray region. We have chosen these values using the following guidelines. First, as we observed in Section 6.1, site failures are common. We then assume that the probability of a site failure is higher than of a process failure, although we kept them in the same order of magnitude. Second, we assume that repair probabilities are much higher than the failure probabilities.

One still needs to choose a value for t, as repair probabilities depend upon this value. For such a small system, this choice is constrained to be either $t = 0$ or $t = 1$. If t is greater than 1, then the 2-bimodal intersection property cannot be satisfied, and we are not able to construct a coterie using the technique proposed in Section 5. We therefore assume that $t = 1$, and we have the following limiting probabilities:

$$M = \begin{bmatrix} 0.7815 & 0.0391 & 0.0332 & 0.0344 \\ 0.0391 & 0.0020 & 0.0004 & 0.0004 \\ 0.0332 & 0.0004 & 0.0003 & 0.0004 \\ 0.0344 & 0.0004 & 0.0004 & 0.0004 \end{bmatrix}$$

where $M[f_1 + 1, f_2 + 1]$ is the limiting probability of state $f_1 \cdot f_2$. More specifically, we have that $\pi_{f_1 \cdot f_2} = M[f_1 + 1, f_2 + 1]$.

Suppose now that a_1, a_2, a_3 are the processes on one site, b_1, b_2, b_3 are the processes on the other site, and $4 \times 10^{-4} < \rho < 2 \times 10^{-3}$. We have that: 1) $\mathcal{F}_s = \{\emptyset\}$; 2) $\mathcal{F}_p[1] = \{a_i : a_i \in B_1\}$; 3) $\mathcal{F}_p[2] = \{b_i : b_i \in B_2\}$. The set of survivor sets is as follows:

$$\mathcal{S}_P = \{a_1 a_2 a_3, b_1 b_2 b_3\} \cup \{a_i a_j b_l b_m : i, j, l, m \in \{1, 2, 3\} \wedge i \neq j \wedge l \neq m\}$$

and from the Bsite construction, we have, for example, the following coterie:

$$\mathcal{Q} = \{a_1 a_2 a_3\} \cup \{a_i a_j b_l b_m : i, j, l, m \in \{1, 2, 3\} \wedge i \neq j \wedge l \neq m\}$$

which is dominated by:

$$\mathcal{Q}' = \{a_1 a_2 a_3\} \cup \{a_i b_j b_l : i, j, l \in \{1, 2, 3\} \wedge j \neq l\}$$

and we have by definition that $\mathcal{Q} \prec_a \mathcal{Q}'$. From the matrix M, observe that $\mathcal{Q}'$ is unavailable only in state 30, considering only allowed states (states that have probability greater than the degree of reliability). This is optimal as there is no coterie that is available for both states 30 and 03.

Although the system of the example is a simple one, it illustrates well that the bimodal model is implementable. We believe that the results can be generalized for two-site systems with more processes, but it is an open question whether there is a practical implementation for systems with more than two sites.

7 Evaluating Coteries on PlanetLab

To evaluate the different choices for quorums in a multi-site system, we conducted an experiment on PlanetLab using an implementation of the Paxos algorithm [16]. In brief, Paxos assumes that processes have one or more of the three following roles: Proposer, Acceptor, and Learner. Proposers propose ballots that are accepted by Acceptors. To propose, a Proposer has to read from and write to a quorum of Acceptors. Once an Acceptor accepts a ballot, it notifies the set of Learners. A Learner decides upon a value once it receives notifications from a quorum of Acceptors.

In our experiment, we have three settings. In all settings, one single host (a UCSD host) has the roles of both a Proposer and a Learner, whereas the Acceptors are Planet-Lab hosts spread across three sites (UC Davis, UT Austin, Duke). The settings are:

3Sites: One host from each site. A quorum consists of any set of two hosts. This is the Qsite construction, for $f_s = 1$, and $t = 0$;

3SitesMaj: Three hosts from each site. A quorum consists of majorities of hosts from two sites, and it has size four. This is the Qsite construction for $f_s = 1$, and $t = 1$;

SimpleMaj: Three hosts from each site. A quorum consists of any simple majority of sites. That is, any subset of five Acceptors.

For each setting, we have the Proposer issuing a new ballot every 15 minutes, and we log the time it takes to decide upon a value on this ballot. To implement a reliable channel, we create a new thread for every message sent, and this thread tries to send the message through a TCP connection until it succeeds. As a consequence, we have that every message sent by one process to another is eventually received, as long as the receiving process eventually recovers if it fails.

To register failures, every time establishing a TCP connection to another host times out, we log it to a file. A failure in this case is the inability to reach the Acceptor, not necessarily implying that the host has crashed. That is, the unavailability of a host may be caused by a network partition.

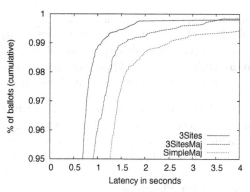

Fig. 4. Cumulative latency distribution

We had these three settings running in parallel for 27 days in April 2005. Figure 4 shows part of the cumulative distribution function for the latency of reaching agreement on each ballot. We also show in Table 1 the percentage of samples with value greater than $4s$.

It is not surprising that 3Sites has best response time for the average case, followed by 3SitesMaj and SimpleMaj, since quorums have fewer Acceptors in this exact order. However, the graph shows that there is a point (around $3.5s$) in which the curve for 3SitesMaj crosses 3Sites. This implies that there are fewer samples for 3SitesMaj with latency greater than $3.5s$ than for 3Sites. As the tail of the distribution for 3SitesMaj contains fewer samples, it has best availability among the three in this experiment.

To understand why this is the case, we need to understand what components are involved in deciding upon a ballot. The latency of a ballot has two main components: message latency and process failures. From the graph, the message latency component dominates until $3.5s$. After $3.5s$, the delay is mostly caused by the inability to reach enough Acceptors. Having more processes

	Latency $> 4s$ (%)
3Sites	0.0020
3SitesMaj	0.0016
SimpleMaj	0.0057

Table 1. Samples with value greater than 4 seconds

increases the latency for 3SitesMaj and SimpleMaj compared to 3Sites for values under $3.5s$, where the message latency component has more weight. On the other hand, 3Sites-Maj presents better response time for values greater than $3.5s$, when there are process failures. Thus, there is a tension between obtaining good response time on average and having a larger percentage of the samples within a bounded response time. This information is important, for example, when determining the time-out for a quorum-based service. Considering our three settings, if a time-out value greater than $3.5s$ is chosen, then 3SitesMaj is likely to time out less often than 3Sites and SimpleMaj. Finally, an interesting observation is that SimpleMaj not only had the worst average response time, but also had the largest percentage of samples with response time greater than $4s$. This indicates that using majority quorums is a poor choice for multi-site systems.

We also counted the number of ballots for which the Proposer could not initially contact enough Acceptors to obtain a quorum, and the decision on the ballot was therefore delayed until enough Acceptors were available. When this happens to a ballot, we say that this ballot is *postponed*. For each setting, we have the following:

3Sites: There were 3 postponed ballots;

3SitesMaj: There were 2 postponed ballots. Only for one of these ballots, there would be one quorum available in the simple majority scheme;

SimpleMaj: There were 4 postponed ballots. For all these ballots, using the majorities of two sites would give us an available quorum.

The data presented in this section is perhaps not conclusive because the number of failures observed was too small to be statistically valid. Moreover, PlanetLab is not a production system in the sense that sites are not designed to be highly available, and node repair is often leisurely. On the other hand, the results presented do not contradict any of our assumptions, thus indicating that our models may be suitable even for multi-systems such as PlanetLab.

8   Conclusions

This paper is a first step into the practical construction of coteries for multi-site systems. We base one coterie construction on a failure model that we motivate from failure measurements from a deployed multi-site system and from a Markov model. We also consider a weaker failure model that has some theoretical and practical interest. We define optimality by introducing a metric that is suitable to dependent failures, and we show that our quorum constructions are optimal with respect to this metric.

Being a first step, this paper leaves some questions unanswered. First, our multi-site hierarchical model is intuitive and is based on some failure data from a real system. How typical is this system? Is the model broadly applicable? Second, our bimodal model is based on the idea of having different repair probabilities for different states. This technique, which essentially integrates operating procedures with the failure model, appears to be a potentially powerful new direction for the design of novel and efficient protocols. Finally, we describe a method of building a coterie from survivor sets that do not satisfy 2-Intersection. The survivor sets are defined by some target availability, and the availability of the quorum system is reduced by discarding survivor sets. How does this strategy compare with one in which the initial target availability is increased until the survivor sets satisfy 2-Intersection?

Acknowledgments. We would like to express our gratitude to Geoff Voelker and the anonymous reviewers for valuable comments on this paper. Support for this work was provided by AFOSR MURI Contract F49620-02-1-0233.

References

1. Y. Amir and A. Wool. Evaluating quorum systems over the Internet. In *Proceedings of the 26th IEEE FTCS*, pages 26–37, Sendai, Japan, June 1996.
2. Y. Amir and A. Wool. Optimal availability quorum systems: Theory and practice. *Information Processing Letters*, 65(5):223–228, Mar. 1998.
3. D. Barbara and H. Garcia-Molina. The vulnerability of vote assignments. *ACM Transactions on Computer Systems*, 4(3):187–213, Aug. 1986.
4. J. Bioch and T. Ibaraki. Generating and approximating nondominated coteries. *IEEE Transactions on Parallel and Distributed Systems*, 6(9):905–914, Sept. 1995.
5. The Biomedical Informatics Research Network (BIRN). http://www.nbirn.net.
6. J.-M. Busca, M. Bertier, F. Belkouch, P. Sens, and L. Arantes. A performance evaluation of a quorum-based state-machine replication algorithm for computing grids. In *Proceedings of the 16th IEEE SBAC-PAD'04*, Foz do Iguaçú, PR, Brazil, Oct. 2004.
7. H. Garcia-Molina and D. Barbara. How to assign votes in a distributed system. *Journal of the ACM*, 32(4):841–860, Oct. 1985.
8. D. Gifford. Weighted voting for replicated data. In *Proceedings of ACM SOSP*, pages 150–162, Pacific Grove, CA, USA, Dec. 1979.
9. S. Gilbert and G. Malewicz. The Quorum Deployment Problem. In *Proceedings of OPODIS*, pages 218–228, Grenoble, France, Apr. 2004.
10. F. Junqueira, R. Bhagwan, A. Hevia, K. Marzullo, and G. M. Voelker. Surviving Internet catastrophes. In *Proceedings of USENIX Tech. Conference, General Track*, pages 45–60, Anaheim, CA, USA, Apr. 2005.
11. F. Junqueira and K. Marzullo. Synchronous consensus for dependent process failures. In *Proceedings of the 23rd IEEE ICDCS*, pages 274–283, Providence, RI, USA, May 2003.
12. F. Junqueira and K. Marzullo. Coterie availability in sites (extended version). Technical report, UC San Diego, La Jolla, CA, USA, June 2005.
13. F. Junqueira and K. Marzullo. Replication predicates for dependent-failure algorithms. In *Proceedings of the 11th Euro-Par Conference*, LNCS 3648, pages 617–632, Lisbon, Portugal, Aug. 2005.
14. F. Junqueira and K. Marzullo. The virtue of dependent failures in multi-site systems. In *Proceedings of the IEEE Workshop on Hot Topics in System Dependability*, Supplemental volume of DSN'05, pages 242–247, Yokohama, Japan, June 2005.
15. A. Kumar. Hierarchical Quorum Consensus: A new algorithm for managing replicated data. *IEEE Transactions on Computers*, 40(9):996–1004, Sept. 1991.
16. L. Lamport. The part-time parliament. *ACM Transactions on Computer Systems*, 16(2):133–169, May 1998.
17. L. Lamport. *Specifying systems: The TLA+ language and tools for hardware and software engineers*. Addison-Wesley, 2002.
18. M. Maekawa. A $\sqrt{n}$ algorithm for mutual exclusion in decentralized systems. *ACM Transactions on Computer Systems*, 3(2):145–159, May 1985.
19. M. Naor and A. Wool. The load, capacity, and availability of quorum systems. *SIAM Journal on Computing*, 27(2):423–447, Apr. 1998.
20. D. Peleg and A. Wool. Crumbling Walls: A class of practical and efficient quorum systems. In *Proceedings of ACM PODC*, pages 120–129, Ottawa, Ontario, Canada, Apr. 1995.
21. The Planetlab testbed. http://www.planet-lab.org/.
22. S. Ross. *Introduction to probability models*. Harcourt Academic Press, 2000.
23. The TeraGrid project. http://www.teragrid.org/.
24. H. Yu. Signed Quorum Systems. In *Proceedings of the 23rd ACM PODC*, pages 246–255, St. John's, Newfoundland, Canada, July 2004.

Keeping Denial-of-Service Attackers in the Dark

Gal Badishi[1], Amir Herzberg[2], and Idit Keidar[1]

[1] The Technion Department of Electrical Engineering
[2] Bar Ilan University, Department of Computer Science

Abstract. We consider the problem of overcoming (Distributed) Denial of Service (DoS) attacks by realistic adversaries that can eavesdrop on messages, or parts thereof, but with some delay. We show a protocol that mitigates DoS attacks by eavesdropping adversaries, using only available, efficient packet filtering mechanisms based mainly on (addresses and) port numbers. Our protocol avoids the use of fixed ports, and instead performs 'pseudo-random port hopping'. We model the underlying packet-filtering services and define measures for the capabilities of the adversary and for the success rate of the protocol. Using these, we analyze the proposed protocol, and show that it provides effective DoS prevention for realistic attack and deployment scenarios.

1 Introduction

Denial of service (DoS) attacks have proliferated in recent years, causing severe service disruptions [7]. The most devastating attacks stem from *distributed denial of service (DDoS)*, where an attacker utilizes multiple machines (often thousands) to generate excessive traffic [15]. Due to the acuteness of such attacks, various commercial solutions and off-the-shelf products addressing this problem have emerged.

The most common solution uses an existing firewall/router (or protocol stack) to perform *rate-limiting* of traffic, and to *filter* messages according to header fields like address and port number. Such mechanisms are cheap and readily available, and are therefore very appealing. Nevertheless, rate-limiting indiscriminately discards messages, and it is easy to spoof (fake) headers that match the filtering criteria: an attacker can often generate spoofed packets containing correct source and destination IP addresses, and arbitrarily chosen values for almost all fields used for filtering[1]. Therefore, the only hope in using such efficient filtering mechanisms to overcome DoS attacks lies in choosing values that are *unknown to the adversary*. E.g., TCP's use of a random initial sequence number is a simple version of this approach, but is inadequate if the attacker has some (even limited) eavesdropping capability.

More effective DoS solutions are provided by expensive commercial devices that perform stateful filtering [17,18,19]. These solutions specialize in protecting a handful of commonly-used stateful protocols, e.g., TCP; they are less effective for stateless traffic such as UDP [19]. Such expensive solutions are not suitable for all organizations.

---

[1] An exception is the TTL field of IP packets, which is automatically decremented by each router. This is used by some filtering mechanisms, e.g. BGP routers that receive only packets with maximal TTL value (255) to ensure the packets were sent by a neighboring router, and the Hop Counter Filtering proposal.

P. Fraigniaud (Ed.): DISC 2005, LNCS 3724, pp. 18–32, 2005.

Finally, the most effective way to filter out offending traffic is using secure source authentication with message authentication codes (MAC), as in, e.g., IP-Sec [3]. However, this requires computing a MAC for every packet, which can induce significant overhead, and thus, this approach may be even more vulnerable to DoS attacks.

Our goal is to address DoS attacks on end hosts, e.g., in corporate networks, assuming the network leading to the hosts is functional. (A complementary solution protecting the end network can be deployed at the ISP.) In this paper, we focus on fortifying the basic building block of two-party communication. Specifically, we develop a DoS-resistant datagram protocol, similar to UDP or raw IP. Our protocol has promising properties, especially in overcoming realistic attack scenarios where attackers can discover some of the control information included in protocol packets [1]. Nevertheless, additional work is required in order to devise a practical system based on our ideas.

Our solution uses a *dual-layer approach*: On the one hand, we exploit cheap, simple, and readily-available measures at the network layer. On the other hand, we leverage these network mechanisms at the application layer. The latter allows for more complex algorithms as it has to deal with significantly fewer packets than the network layer, and may have closer interaction with the application. The higher layer dynamically changes the filtering criteria used by the underlying layer, e.g., by closing certain ports and opening others for communication. It is important to note that the use of dynamically changing ports instead of a single well-known port does not increase the chance of a security breach, as a *single* application is listening on *all* open ports.

The main contribution of our work is in presenting a *formal framework* for understanding and analyzing the effects of proposed solutions to the DoS problem. The main challenges in attempting to formalize DoS-resistance for the first time are: coming up with appropriate models for the attacker and the environment, modeling the functionality that can be provided by underlying mechanisms such as firewalls, and defining meaningful metrics for evaluating suggested solutions. We capture the functionality of a simple network-level DoS-mitigation solution by introducing the abstraction of a *port-based rationing channel*. Our primary metric of an end-to-end communication protocol's resistance to DoS attacks is *success rate*, which is the worst-case expected portion of valid application messages that successfully reach their destination, under a defined adversary class.

Having defined our model and metrics, we proceed to give a generic analysis of the communication success rate over a port-based rationing channel in different attack scenarios. We distinguish between *directed* attacks, where the adversary knows the port used, and *blind* attacks, in which the adversary does not know the port. Not surprisingly, we show that directed attacks are extremely harmful: with as little as 100 machines (or a sending capacity 100 times that of the protocol) the success rate is virtually zero. On the other hand, the worst-case success rate that an attacker can cause in blind attacks in realistic scenarios is well over 90% even with 10,000 machines.

Our goal is therefore to "keep the attacker in the dark", so that it will have to resort to blind attacks. Our basic idea is to change the filtering criteria (i.e., ports) in a manner that cannot be predicted by the attacker. This *port-hopping* approach mimics the technique of frequency hopping spread spectrum in radio communication [20]. We assume that the communicating parties share a secret key unknown to the attacker; they apply a pseudo-random function [8] to this key in order to select the sequence of ports they will use. Note that such port-hopping has negligible effect on the communication overhead for realistic intervals between hops. The remaining challenge is synchronizing the processes, so that the recipient opens the port currently used by the sender. We present a protocol for doing so in a realistic partially synchronous model, where processes are equipped with bounded-drift bounded-skew clocks, and message latency is bounded.

1.1   Related Work

Our work continues the main line of research on prevention of Distributed Denial of Service attacks, which focuses on filtering mechanisms to block and discard the offending traffic. Our work is unique in providing rigorous model and analysis. Necessarily, we focus on what we consider as the most basic and common attack scenarios and on a simple network architecture, protecting the communication between two agents, both using our protocol. We hope that future work will extend our protocols, model and analysis to more complex attack scenarios and network architectures, as investigated in some of the related work.

Most closely related is the work presented in [1,12], which proposes realistic and efficient mechanisms that do not require global adoption, yet allow a server to provide services immune to DDoS attacks. These solutions, like ours, utilize efficient packet-filtering mechanisms between the server and predefined, trusted 'access point' hosts, and use an overlay network to allow clients to forward messages via the overlay network to the access points and then to the server. Our protocol is appropriate for use between the access points and the server, utilizing efficient packet filtering mechanisms (as available in current routers). The basic ideas of filtering based on ports or other simple identifiers ('keys'), and even of changing them, already appear in [1,12], but without analysis and details. On the other hand, [1] provides a discussion of attack types and limitations, justifying much of our model, including the assumption that the exposure of the identifier (port) number may be possible but not immediate.

There are other several proposed methods to filter offending DoS traffic. Some proposals, e.g., [10,13], filter according to the source IP address. This is convenient and efficient, allowing implementation in existing packet filtering routers. However, IP addresses are subject to spoofing; furthermore, using a white-list of source addresses of legitimate clients/peers is difficult, since many hosts may have dynamic IP addresses due to the use of NAT, DHCP and mobile-IP. Some proposals try to detect spoofed sender, using new routing mechanisms such as 'path markers' supported by some or all of the routers en route [21,22,2,14]; notice that global router modification is difficult to achieve. Few proposals try to detect spoofed senders using only existing mechanisms, such as the hop count (TTL) [9]. However, empirical evaluation of these approaches show rather disappointing results [6].

A different approach is to perform application-specific filtering for pre-defined protocols [11,16]. Such protection schemes are cumbersome, only work for a handful of well-known protocols, and are usually restricted to attackers that transmit invalid protocol packets.

In earlier work, we have presented Drum [5], a gossip-based multicast protocol resistant to DoS attacks at the application level. Drum does not make use of pseudo-random port-hopping, and it heavily relies on well-known ports that can be easily attacked. Therefore, Drum is far less resistant to DoS attacks than the protocol we present here. Finally, Drum focuses on multicast only, and as a gossip-based protocol, it relies on a high level of redundancy, whereas the protocol presented herein sends very little redundant information.

2 Model and Definitions

We consider a realistic *semi-synchronous* model, where processes have continuously-increasing local clocks with bounded drift Φ from real time. Each party may schedule events to occur when its local clock reaches a specific value (time). There is a bound Δ on the transmission delay, i.e., every packet sent either arrives within Δ time units, or is considered lost.

Our goal is to send messages from a sender A to a recipient B, in spite of attempts to disrupt this communication by an adversary. The basic technique available to the adversary is to clog the recipient by sending many packets. The standard defense deployed by most corporations is to rate-limit and filter packets, typically by a firewall. We capture this type of defense mechanism using a *port-based rationing channel* machine, which models the communication channel between A and B as well as the filtering mechanism. To send a message, A invokes a *ch_send(m)* event, a message is received by the channel in a *net_recv(m)* event, and B receives messages via *ch_recv(m)* events. We assume that the adversary cannot clog the communication to the channel, and that there is no message loss other than in the channel. The channel discards messages when it performs rate-limiting and filtering.

The channel machine is formally defined in [4]. We now provide an intuitive description of its functionality. Since we assume that the attacker can spoof packets with valid addresses, we cannot use these addresses for filtering. Instead, the channel filters packets using port numbers, allowing deployment using existing, efficient filtering mechanisms. Specifically, let the set of port numbers be $\{1, \ldots, \psi\}$. We are particularly interested in the case $\psi = 65536$, since this is the number of ports available for UDP recipients, and using them requires minimal changes on the sender side. The buffer space of the channel is a critical resource. The channel's interface includes the *alloc* action, which allows B to break the total buffer space of R messages into a separate allocation of R_i messages per port $i \in \{1, \ldots, \psi\}$, as long as $R \geq \sum_{i=1}^{\psi} R_i$. For simplicity, we assume that the buffers are read and cleared together in a single *deliver* event, which occurs exactly once on every integer time unit. If the number of packets sent to port i since the last *deliver* exceeds R_i, a uniformly distributed random subset of R_i of them is delivered.

We define several parameters that constrain the adversary's strength. The most important parameter is the *attack strength*, C, which is the maximal number of messages that the adversary may inject to the channel between two *deliver* events.

As shown in [1], attackers can utilize different techniques to try to learn the ports numbers expected by the filters (and used in packets sent by the sender). However, these techniques usually require considerable communication and time. To simplify, we allow the adversary to eavesdrop by exposing messages, but we assume that the adversary can expose packets no earlier than $\mathcal{E}$ time after they are sent, where $\mathcal{E}$ is the *exposure delay* parameter. The exposure delay reflects the time it takes an attacker to expose the relevant information, as well as to distribute it to the (many) attacking nodes, possibly using very limited bandwidth (e.g., if sending from a firewalled network). Our protocol works well with as little as $\mathcal{E} > 5\Delta$. Notice that while we assumed messages *always* arrive within Δ time, this is only a simplification, and our results are valid even if a few messages arrive later than that; therefore, Δ should really be thought of as the typical maximal round trip time, and not as an absolute bound on a message's lifetime (e.g., a second rather than 60 seconds).

Since the adversary may control some behavior of the parties, we take a conservative approach and let the adversary schedule the *app_send(m)* events in which the application (at A) asks to send m to B. To prevent the adversary from abusing these abilities by simply invoking too many *app_send* events before a *deliver* event, we define the *throughput*, $T \geq 1$, as the maximal number of *app_send* events in a single time unit. We further assume that $R \geq \Delta T$, i.e. that the capacity of the channel is sufficient to handle the maximal rate of *app_send* events.

Since we focus on connectionless communication such as UDP, our main metric for a system's resiliency to DoS attacks is its *success rate*, namely the probability that a message sent by A is received by B.

Definition 1 (Success rate μ). *Let E be any execution of a given two-party protocol operating over a given port-based rationing channel with parameters $\Psi, R, C, \Phi, \Delta, \mathcal{E}$ and T, with adversary ADV. Let $end(E)$ be the time of the last deliver event in E. Let $sent(E)$ (recv(E)) be the number of messages sent (resp., received) by the application, in app_send (resp., app_recv) events during E, prior to $end(E) - \Delta$ (resp, $end(E)$). The success rate μ of E is defined as $\mu(E) = \frac{recv(E)}{sent(E)}$. The success rate of adversary ADV is the average success rate over all executions of ADV. The success rate of the protocol, denoted $\mu(\Psi, R, C, \Phi, \Delta, \mathcal{E}, T)$, is the worst success rate over all adversaries ADV.*

Finally, a protocol can increase its success rate by sending redundant information, e.g., multiple copies or error-correcting codes. We therefore also consider a system's *message (bit) complexity*, which is the number of messages (resp. redundant bits) sent on the channel per each application message.

3   Analyzing the Channel's Success Rate in a Single Slot with a Single Port

This section provides generic analysis of the probability of successfully communicating over a port-based rationing channel under different attacks, when messages are sent to a single open port, p. This analysis is independent of the timing model and the particular protocol using the channel, and can therefore serve to analyze different protocols that use such channels, e.g., the one we present in the ensuing section. We focus on a single *deliver* event, and analyze the *channel's delivery probability*, which is the probability for a valid message in the channel's buffer to be delivered, in that event. Since every

$ch\_send(m)$ event eventually results in m being added to the channel's buffer, we can use the channel's delivery probability to analyze the success rates of higher level protocols.

Let R_p denote the ration allocated to port p in the last *alloc* event, and let $In(p)$ be the contents of the channel's buffer for port p (see [4] for more details). Consider a *deliver* event of a channel from A to B, when A sends messages only to port p. We introduce some notations:

$R_p = R$ is the value of the channel's R_p when *deliver* occurs.

$a_p = a$ is the number of messages whose source is A in the channel's $In(p)$ when *deliver* occurs. We assume $a \leq R$. If $a_p < R_p$ (i.e., $a < R$), we say that there is *over-provisioning* on port p.

c_p is the number of messages whose source is *not* A in $In(p)$ when *deliver* occurs.

Assume that $1 \leq a \leq R$. If $c_p < R - a + 1$ then B receives A's messages, and the attack does not affect the communication from A to B on port p. Let us now examine what happens when $c_p \geq R - a + 1$.

Lemma 1. *If* $c_p \geq R - a + 1$, *then the channel's delivery probability is* $\frac{R}{c_p+a}$.

Proof. The channel delivers $m \in In(p)$ if it is part of the R messages read uniformly at random from the $c_p + a$ available messages. Thus, the delivery probability is $\frac{R}{c_p+a}$.

If the attacker knows that B has opened port p, it can direct all of its power to that port, i.e., $c_p = C$, where we assume $C \geq R - a + 1$. We call this a *directed attack*.

Corollary 1. *In a directed attack at rate* C *on* B's *port* p, *the delivery probability on the attacked port is* $\frac{R}{C+a}$, *assuming* $1 \leq a \leq R$ *and* $C \geq R - a + 1$.

Lemma 2. *For fixed* R *and* c_p *such that* $1 \leq a \leq R$ *and* $c_p \geq R - a + 1$, *the probability of* B *receiving only invalid messages on port* p *decreases as* a *increases.*

The proof of this lemma is simple and is omitted due to space considerations.

3.1   Blind Attack

We define a *blind attack* as a scenario where A sends messages to a single open port, p, and the adversary cannot distinguish this port from a random one. We now analyze the worst-case delivery probability under a blind attack.

In general, an adversary's strategy is composed both of timing decisions and injected messages. The timing decisions affect a, the number of messages from A that are in the channel at a given delivery slot. Given that a is already decided, we define the set of all strategies of an attacker with sending rate C as:

$$S(C) \triangleq \left\{ \{c_i\}_{i \in \psi} \mid \forall i \in \psi : c_i \in \mathbb{N} \cup \{0\} \wedge \sum_{i=1}^{\psi} c_i = C \right\}$$

Each strategy $s \in S$ is composed of the number of messages the attacker sends to each port. Note that since the adversary wishes to minimize the delivery probability, we restrict the discussion to the set of attacks that fully utilize the attacker's capacity for sending messages. We denote by $\mu_B(a, C, R) : S(C) \to [0, 1]$ the channel's delivery probability under all possible blind attack strategies with the given a, C, and R. Since S is a finite set, μ_B has at least one minimum point, and we define the delivery probability to be that minimum:

$$\mu_B(a, C, R) \triangleq \min_{s \in S(C)} \mu_B(a, C, R, s)$$

We sometimes use μ_B instead of $\mu_B(a, C, R)$ when a, C, and R are clear from context. We want to find lower bounds on μ_B, depending on the attacker's strength. We say that port p_i is attacked in strategy s if $c_{p_i} > 0$. We partition $S(C)$ according to the number of ports being attacked, as follows:

$$S_k \triangleq \{s \in S(C) \mid \text{Exactly } k \text{ ports are being attacked in } s\}$$

In [4] we find a lower bound on μ_B as follows: We first derive a lower bound on $\{\mu_B(a, C, R, s_k) | s_k \in S_k\}$; this lower bound is given as a function of k. Incidently, the worst depredation occurs when the attacker divides its power equally among the attacked ports, i.e., when it sends $\frac{C}{k}$ messages to each attacked port. Then, we show lower bounds on $\mu_B(a, C, R)$ by finding the k that yields the minimum value. In [4], we prove the following lemma:

Lemma 3. $\mu_B(a, C, R)$ *is bounded from below by the following function* $f(a, C, R)$:

$$f(a, C, R) = \begin{cases} \frac{\psi a}{C + \psi a} & \text{if } R = a \text{ and } C \geq \psi \\ 1 - \frac{C}{\psi(1+a)} & \text{if } R = a \text{ and } C < \psi \\ \frac{\psi R}{C + \psi a} & \text{if } R > a \text{ and } C \geq \frac{\psi a}{\sqrt{\frac{R}{R-a}} - 1} \\ \frac{\psi a - C\left(\sqrt{\frac{R}{R-a}} - 1\right)}{\psi a} + \frac{R}{\psi} \cdot \frac{C\left(\sqrt{\frac{R}{R-a}} - 1\right)^2}{a^2 \sqrt{\frac{R}{R-a}}} & \text{if } R > a \text{ and } C < \frac{\psi a}{\sqrt{\frac{R}{R-a}} - 1} \\ 0 & \text{otherwise} \end{cases} \tag{1}$$

Lemma 3 provides us with some insights of the adversary's best strategy and of the expected degradation in delivery probability. If no over-provisioning is used (i.e., $R = a$), then the adversary's best strategy is to attack as many ports as possible. This is due to the fact that even a single bogus message to the correct port degrades the expected delivery probability. When the adversary has enough power to target all of the available ports with at least one message, it can attack with more messages per attacked port, and the delivery probability asymptotically degrades much like the function $\frac{1}{C}$. When not all ports are attacked, the adversary would like to use its remaining resources to attack more ports rather than target a strict subset of the ports with more than one bogus message per port. The degradation of the expected delivery probability is then linear as the attacker's strength increases.

When over-provisioning is used ($R > a$), it affects the attack and its result in two ways. First, the attacker's best strategy may not be to attack as many ports as it can, since a single bogus message per port does not do any harm now. Second, for an adversary with a given strength, the degradation in delivery probability is lower when over-provisioning is used than when it is not employed. We can see in Equation 1 that if the attacker has enough power to attack all the ports, the over-provisioning ratio $\frac{R}{a}$ is also the ratio by which the delivery probability is increased, compared to the case where $R = a$.

3.2 Actual Values

Figure 1 shows the expected worst-case delivery probabilities for various attack scenarios on a single port. For directed attacks, we show the actual delivery probability, and for blind attacks, the lower bound $f(a, C, R)$ is shown. We chose $\psi = 65536$, the number of ports in common Internet protocols, e.g., UDP. Figure 1(a) illustrates the major difference between a directed attack and a blind one: even for a relatively weak attacker ($C \leq 100$), the delivery probability under a directed attack approaches 0, whereas under a blind attack, it virtually remains 1.

Figure 1(b) examines blind attacks by much stronger adversaries (with C up to 10,000 for $R = 1$, and up to 20,000 for $R = 2$). We see that the delivery probability

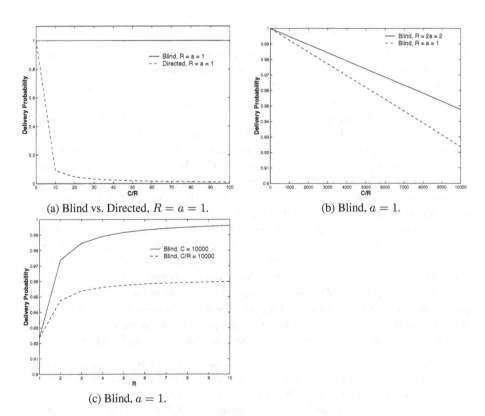

(a) Blind vs. Directed, $R = a = 1$.

(b) Blind, $a = 1$.

(c) Blind, $a = 1$.

Fig. 1. Delivery probability per slot in various attack scenarios on a single port, $\psi = 65536$

gradually degrades down to a low of 92.5% when $R = 1$. If we use an over-provisioned channel, i.e., have $a = 1$ (one message from A) when $R = 2$, the delivery probability improves to almost 95% for $C = 20,000$. (The ratio $\frac{C}{R}$ is the same for both curves). Figure 1(c) shows the effect of larger over-provisioning. We see that the cost-effectiveness of over-provisioning diminishes as $\frac{R}{a}$ increases.

4 DoS-Resistant Communication

We now describe a protocol that allows for DoS-resistant communication in a partially-synchronous environment. The protocol's main component is an ack-based protocol. B sends acknowledgments for messages it receives from A, and these acks allow the parties to hop through ports together. However, although the ack-based protocol works well as long as the adversary fails to attack the correct port, once the adversary gets a hold of the port used, it can perform a directed attack that renders the protocol useless. By attacking the found data port, or simultaneously attacking the found data and ack ports, the adversary can effectively drop the success rate to 0, and no port hopping will occur. To solve this matter, there is a time-based proactive reinitialization of the ports used for the ack-based protocol, independent of any messages passed in the system.

4.1 Ack-Based Port Hopping

We present a port-hopping communication protocol that has no indication of time. In the absence of a clock, A and B must rely on message-passing in order to synchronize their port-hopping. We present an *ack-based port-hopping* protocol, which uses two port-based rationing channels, from B to A (with ration R_{BA}) and vice versa (with ration R_{AB}). For simplicity we assume $R_{AB} = 2R_{BA} = 2R$. B always keeps two open ports for data reception from A, and A keeps one port open for acknowledgments (acks) from B. The protocol hops ports upon a successful round-trip on the most recent port used, using a *pseudo-random function*, PRF^*[2]. In order to avoid hopping upon adversary messages, all protocol messages carry authentication information, using a second pseudo-random function, PRF, on $\{0, 1\}^\kappa$. (We assume that PRF and PRF^* use different parts of A and B's shared secret key.)

The protocol's pseudocode appears in Figure 2. Both A and B hold a port counter P, initialized to some *seed* (e.g., 1). Each party uses its counter P in order to determine which ports should be open, and which ports to send messages to. B opens port p_{old} using the $(P - 1)^{th}$ element in the pseudo-random sequence, and p_{new}, using P. A sends data messages to the Pth port in the sequence, and opens the Pth port in a second pseudo-random sequence designated for acks. When B receives a valid data message from A on port p_{old}, it sends an ack to the old ack port. When it receives a valid message on port p_{new}, it sends an ack to the Pth ack port, and then increases P. When A receives

---

[2] Intuitively, we say that $f_{key}(data)$ is *pseudo-random function (PRF*)* if for inputs of sufficient length, it cannot be distinguished efficiently from a truly random function r over the same domain and range, by a PPT adversary which can receive $g(x)$ for any values of x, where $g = r$ with probability half and $g = f$ with probability half. For definition and construction, see [8].

a valid ack on port p_{ack}, it increases P. We note that several data messages may be in transit before a port hop takes place, since it takes at least one round-trip time for a port hop to take effect. The proof of the next theorem is given in [4].

PROTOCOL FOR RECIPIENT B:

On $ch\_recv(m, p_{new})$:
  if $m.auth = PRF_{S_{AB}}(P | \text{``data''})$ **then**
    $app\_recv(m.data)$
    $alloc(p_{old}, 0)$
    $p_{old} = p_{new}$
    $p_{new} = PRF^*_{S_{AB}}(P + 1 | \text{``data''})$
    $alloc(p_{new}, R_{AB}/2)$
    $ack = PRF_{S_{AB}}(P | \text{``ack''})$
    $ch\_send(ack, PRF^*_{S_{AB}}(P | \text{``ack''}))$
    $P = P + 1$

On $ack\_init(seed)$:
  $P = seed$
  $p_{old} = PRF^*_{S_{AB}}(P - 1 | \text{``data''})$
  $p_{new} = PRF^*_{S_{AB}}(P | \text{``data''})$
  $alloc(p_{old}, R_{AB}/2)$
  $alloc(p_{new}, R_{AB}/2)$

On $ch\_recv(m, p_{old})$:
  if $m.auth = PRF_{S_{AB}}(P - 1 | \text{``data''})$ **then**
    $app\_recv(m.data)$
    $ack = PRF_{S_{AB}}(P - 1 | \text{``ack''})$
    $ch\_send(ack, PRF^*_{S_{AB}}(P - 1 | \text{``ack''}))$

PROTOCOL FOR SENDER A:

On $ack\_init(seed)$:
  $P = seed$
  $p_{ack} = PRF^*_{S_{AB}}(P | \text{``ack''})$
  $alloc(p_{ack}, R_{BA})$

On $app\_send(data)$:
  $m = data | PRF_{S_{AB}}(P | \text{``data''})$
  $ch\_send(m, PRF^*_{S_{AB}}(P | \text{``data''}))$

On $ch\_recv(ack, p_{ack})$:
  if $ack.auth = PRF_{S_{AB}}(P | \text{``ack''})$ **then**
    $alloc(p_{ack}, 0)$
    $p_{ack} = PRF^*_{S_{AB}}(P + 1 | \text{``ack''})$
    $alloc(p_{ack}, R_{BA})$
    $P = P + 1$

Fig. 2. Two-party ack-based port-hopping

Theorem 1. *When using the ack-based protocol, the probability that a data message that A sends to port p arrives when p is open is 1 up to a polynomially-negligible factor[3].*

In order to compute the throughput that the protocol can support in the absence of a DoS attack (i.e., when $C = 0$), we need to take latency variations into consideration. Since messages sent up to Δ time apart can arrive in the same delivery slot, a throughput $T \leq R/\Delta$ ensures $a \leq R$. For the rest of this section, we assume $T \leq R/\Delta$.

We now analyze the protocol's success rate under DoS attacks. We say that the adversary is in *blind mode* if it does not know the ports used by the protocol. We first give a lower bound on the success rate in blind mode, and then give a lower bound on the probability to be in blind mode at a given time t. Finally, μ is bounded by the probability

---

[3] Namely, for every polynomial $g > 0$, there is some κ_g s.t. when $\kappa \geq \kappa_g$, then the success rate $\mu(t) \geq f(R, C, R) - g(\kappa)$.

to be in blind mode throughout the execution of the protocol, times the success rate in blind mode.

Suppose B opens port p with reception rate R_p, and that $a \leq R_p$ messages from A are waiting in its channel, along with c_p messages from the adversary ($c_p \geq 0$). By Lemma 1, the success rate monotonically non-increases with a. Since the adversary can control a by varying the network delays, it can set a as high as possible for a delivery slot. Therefore the worst case success rate occurs when $a = T\Delta$. Using Equation 1 in Section 3, we get that the success rate in blind mode is bounded from below by $f(T\Delta, C, R)$.

Note that the protocol begins in blind mode. We now analyze the probability that the protocol can keep the adversary in blind mode. The only way the adversary can learn of a port used by the protocol is using an *expose* event $\mathcal{E}$ time after a message is sent to this port. This information is only useful to the adversary if the port is still in use. Let us trace the periodic sequence of events that causes the data port to change (once the data port changes, the acks for the old port are useless). Assume that A continuously sends messages $m_1, m_2, \ldots$ to B starting at time 0, and consider an execution without an attack: (1) By time Δ, B receives a valid message from the channel and sends an ack to A; (2) By time 2Δ, A receives the ack and changes the sending port; (3) B gets the last message destined for the old port at most at time 3Δ.

If $\mathcal{E} \geq 3\Delta$, the adversary remains in blind mode. Now let us examine what happens under attack. In order to prevent the port from changing, the adversary must either prevent B from getting valid data messages or prevent A from receiving acks. By Lemma 2, the probability that all valid messages are dropped decreases when a increases. Thus, (as opposed to the previous analysis), in order to increase the probability that all valid messages are dropped, the adversary should set $a \leq 1$ whenever possible. Denote $\mu_B = f(1, C, R)$, the lower bound on the probability of a single message to be received on a single port given in Section 3.1.

Lemma 4. *If $\mathcal{E} = 2k\Delta$ for $k > 0$, and A sends messages to B at least every 2Δ time units, then the probability that the port changes while the attacker is still blind is at least $1 - (1 - \mu_B^2)^k$.*

Proof. The probability that the port does not change in a single round-trip is at most $1 - \mu_B^2$. Since A sends messages to B every 2Δ time units, at the conclusion of each maximal time round-trip, there is at least one new message on its own round-trip. In order for the port not to change while the adversary is still blind, every round-trip needs to fail. Since the attacker can react only after $2k\Delta$ time, there is time for k round-trips in which the attacker is blind, even if none of them succeed. The probability that all of them fail is less than $(1 - \mu_B^2)^k$. If one succeeds, the port changes. And so, the probability that the port changes is at least $1 - (1 - \mu_B^2)^k$.

The lower bound above is illustrated in Figure 3(a).

We now bound the probability to be in blind mode at time t, by assuming that once the attacker leaves the blind mode it never returns to it. The bound is computed using a Markov chain, where each state is the number of round-trips that have failed since the last port change. In the last state, all round-trips have failed before the exposure, and thus the attacker is no longer blind. The Markov chain for $\mathcal{E} = 4\Delta$ is shown in

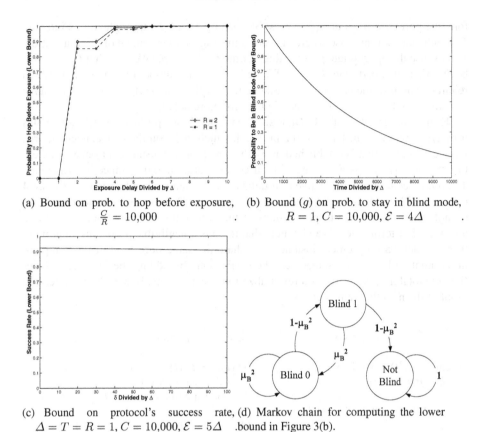

(a) Bound on prob. to hop before exposure, $\frac{C}{R} = 10,000$

(b) Bound (g) on prob. to stay in blind mode, $R = 1, C = 10,000, \mathcal{E} = 4\Delta$

(c) Bound on protocol's success rate, $\Delta = T = R = 1, C = 10,000, \mathcal{E} = 5\Delta$

(d) Markov chain for computing the lower bound in Figure 3(b).

Fig. 3. The effect of $\mathcal{E}$ on the ack-based protocol, $\psi = 65536$

Figure 3(d). We use the chain's transition matrix to compute the probability $g(t, \mathcal{E}, C, R)$ for remaining in blind mode at time t. Figure 3(b) shows values of g for $\mathcal{E} = 4\Delta$. We can see that the protocol works well only for a limited time.

Finally, we note that the protocol's message complexity is 2, since it sends an ack for each message, and its bit complexity is constant: $\log_2(\psi)$ bits for the port plus κ bits for the authentication code.

4.2   Adding Proactive Reinitializations

We now introduce a proactive reinitialization mechanism that allows choosing new seeds for the ack-based protocol depending on time and not on the messages passed in the system. We denote by $t_A(t)$ and $t_B(t)$ the local clocks of A and B, resp., where t is the real time. From Section 2 we get that $0 \leq |t_A(t) - t| \leq \Phi, 0 \leq |t_B(t) - t| \leq \Phi$. We also assume $t_A, t_B \geq 0$.

If A reinitializes the ack-based protocol and then sends a message to B at time $t_A(t_0)$, this message can reach B anywhere in the real time interval $(t_0, t_0 + \Delta]$. Therefore, the port used by A at $t_A(t_0)$ must be open by B at least throughout this interval. To handle the extreme case where A sends a message at the moment of reinitialization, B must use the appropriate port starting at time $t_B(t_0) - \Phi$. (We note that t_0 may also be Φ time units apart from $t_A(t_0)$.) We define δ as the number of time units between reinitializations of the protocol, and assume for simplicity and effectiveness of resource consumption that $\delta > 4\Phi + \Delta$ (see Figure 4 for more details).

Every δ time units, A feeds a new seed to the ack-based protocol, and B anticipates it by creating a new instance of the protocol, which waits on the new expected ports. Once communication is established using the new protocol instance, or once it is clear that the old instance is not going to be used anymore, the old instance is terminated. The pseudocode for the proactive reinitialization mechanism can be found in Figure 4 (where ABPI stands for *ack-based protocol instance*). Due to space considerations we do not detail the change in port rations at the recipient's side as protocol instances are created or terminated. We also note that there is a negligible probability that more than one ack-based protocol instance will share the same port. Even if this happens, differentiating between instances can be easily done by adding the instance number (i.e., the total number of times a reinitialization was performed) to each message. The proof of the next theorem is given in [4].

ADD-ON FOR SENDER A:

Whenever $t_A(t) \in \{0, \delta, 2\delta, \ldots\}$:
   $ack\_init(t_A(t)/\delta)$

ADD-ON FOR RECIPIENT B:

When $t_B(t) = 0$:
   Create 1st ABPI
   For that ABPI, $ack\_init(0)$

ADD-ON FOR RECIPIENT B (CONT'D):

Whenever $(t_B(t) + 2\Phi) \in \{\delta, 2\delta, 3\delta, \ldots\}$:
   Create a new ABPI
   For that ABPI, $ack\_init((t_B(t) + 2\Phi)/\delta)$

$4\Phi + \Delta$ time after creating a new ABPI
or Δ time after receiving 1st msg for that ABPI:
   Terminate all older ABPIs

Fig. 4. Proactive reinitialization of the ack-based protocol

Theorem 2. *When using the ack-based protocol with proactive reinitializations, the probability that a data message that A sends to port p arrives when p is open is 1 up to a polynomially-negligible factor.*

Proactive reinitialization every δ time units allows us to limit the expected degradation in success rate for a single ack-based protocol instance. Choosing δ is therefore an important part of the combined protocol. A small δ allows us to maintain high success rate in the ack-based protocol, but increases the average number of ports that are open in every time unit (due to running several protocol instances in parallel). When several ports are used the ration for each one of them is decreased, and so might the success rate. On the other hand, choosing a high δ entails lower success rate between reinitializations. We conclude the discussion above and the results presented in Section 4.1 with the following theorem:

Theorem 3. *The success rate of the proactively reinitialized ack-based protocol with throughput $T \leq R/\Delta$ and reinitialization periods of length δ is bounded from below by: $g(\delta + \Delta, \mathcal{E}, C, R) \cdot f(T\Delta, C, R)$ up to a polynomially-negligible factor.*

Figure 3(c) shows the value of $g(\delta + 1, \mathcal{E}, 10000, 1) \cdot f(1, 10000, 1, 1)$.

5 Conclusions and Directions for Future Work

We have presented a model for port-based rationing channels, and a protocol robust to DoS attacks, for communication over such channels. The protocol is simple, efficient and effective, as shown by our analysis. While this worst case analysis is valuable, it can be followed by simulations, experiments, and common case analysis. Moreover, the system aspects of deploying such a protocol in today's Internet are yet to be dealt with.

As the important field of application-level DoS mitigation is relatively new, there is much research space to explore. We now describe several future research directions. Clearly, many more directions can be sought.

Our model is realistic, as it only requires the underlying channel to provide port-based filtering; therefore, it can be efficiently implemented using existing mechanisms, typically at a firewall or router between the victim and the attacker. This raises an interesting question regarding the trade-off between the cost and the possible added value of implementing additional functionality by the channel (e.g., at the firewall).

This work has focused on two parties only. It would be interesting to extend it to multiparty scenarios, such as client-sever and multicast. These scenarios may require a somewhat different approach, and will obviously necessitate analyses of their own. Furthermore, we required the parties to share a secret key; we believe we can extend the solution to establish this key using additional parties, e.g., a key distribution center. Another approach is to use 'proof of work' (computational puzzles) techniques to establish the shared key, by sending an encrypted key together with a 'proof of work' that ensures that the sender worked much more than the recipient.

Our work has focused on resisting DoS attacks; however, it could impact the performance and reliability properties of the connection; in fact, it is interesting to explore combinations between our model and problem, and the classical problems of reliable communication over unreliable channels and networks. Furthermore, since our work requires a shared secret key, it may be desirable to merge it with protocols using shared secret key for confidentiality and authentication, such as SSL/TLS and IP-Sec.

One of the most important issues when designing a secure and robust protocol is to quantify its effectiveness under attack. This calls for a clear definition of a metric for that protocol. But even more importantly, such an analysis requires a clear definition of the adversary and the environment it operates in. The challenge in modeling the adversary and the environment rises because the model should reflect reality. Good models allow to test the protocol as if it deployed "in the wild", where real adversaries give it their best shot. Such models enable us to find the attacker's optimal strategy, or provide a bound thereof, thus permitting analytical analysis of the protocol. We hope that future work will take further strides towards defining realistic yet tractable models.

References

1. D. G. Andersen. Mayday: Distributed filtering for internet services. In *Proceedings of the 4th USENIX Symposium on Internet Technologies and Systems (USITS)*, 2003.
2. K. Argyraki and D. R. Cheriton. Active internet traffic filtering: Real-time response to denial-of-service attacks. In *Proceedings of the USENIX Annual Technical Conference*, April 2005.
3. R. Atkinson. Security architecture for the internet protocol. RFC 2401, IETF, 1998.
4. G. Badishi, A. Herzberg, and I. Keidar. Keeping denial-of-service attackers in the dark. TR CCIT 541, Department of Electrical Engineering, Technion, July 2005.
5. G. Badishi, I. Keidar, and A. Sasson. Exposing and eliminating vulnerabilities to denial of service attacks in secure gossip-based multicast. In *The International Conference on Dependable Systems and Networks (DSN)*, pages 223–232, June.July 2004.
6. M. Collins and M. K. Reiter. An empirical analysis of target-resident dos filters. In *Proceedings of the 2004 IEEE Symposium on Security and Privacy*, pages 103–114, May 2004.
7. CSI/FBI. Computer crime and security survey, 2003.
8. O. Goldreich, S. Goldwasser, and S. Micali. How to construct random functions. *Journal of the Association for Computing Machinery*, 33(4):792–807, 1986.
9. C. Jin, H. Wang, and K. G. Shin. Hop-count filtering: an effective defense against spoofed DDoS traffic. In V. Atluri and P. Liu, editors, *Proceedings of the 10th ACM Conference on Computer and Communication Security (CCS-03)*, pages 30–41, New York, Oct. 27–30 2003. ACM Press.
10. J. Jung, B. Krishnamurthy, and M. Rabinovich. Flash crowds and denial of service attacks: Characterization and implications for CDNs and web sites. In *Proceedings of the International World Wide Web Conference*, pages 252–262. IEEE, May 2002.
11. Juniper Networks. The need for pervasive application-level attack protection.
12. A. D. Keromytis, V. Misra, and D. Rubenstein. Sos: An architecture for mitigating ddos attacks. *Journal on Selected Areas in Communications*, 21(1):176–188, 2004.
13. B. Krishnamurthy and J. Wang. On network-aware clustering of Web clients. In *Proceedings of the SIGCOMM*, Aug. 2000.
14. P. Mahajan, S. M. Bellovin, S. Floyd, J. Ioannidis, V. Paxson, and S. Shenker. Controlling high bandwidth aggregates in the network. *Computer Communications Review*, 32(3):62–73, July 2002.
15. D. Moore, G. Voelker, and S. Savage. Inferring Internet denial-of-service activity. In *Proceedings of the 10th USENIX Security Symposium*, pages 9–22, August 2001.
16. NetContinuum. Web application firewall: How netcontinuum stops the 21 classes of web application threats.
17. P-Cube. DoS protection.
18. P-Cube. Minimizing the effects of DoS attacks.
19. Riverhead Networks. Defeating DDoS attacks.
20. S. M. Schwartz. Frequency hopping spread spectrum (fhss).
21. A. Yaar, A. Perrig, and D. Song. Pi: A path identification mechanism to defend against DDoS attacks. In *IEEE Symposium on Security and Privacy*, May 2003.
22. A. Yaar, A. Perrig, and D. Song. An endhost capability mechanism to mitigate DDoS flooding attacks. In *Proceedings of the IEEE Symposium on Security and Privacy*, May 2004.

On Conspiracies and Hyperfairness in Distributed Computing

Hagen Völzer

Institute for Theoretical Computer Science, University of Lübeck, Germany

Abstract. We study the phenomenon of *conspiracies*, a certain class of livelocks, in distributed computations. This elementary phenomenon occurs in systems with shared variables, shared actions as well as in message-passing systems. We propose a new and simple characterization via a new notion of *hyperfairness*, which postulates the absence of conspiracies. We argue that hyperfairness is a useful tool for understanding some impossibility results, in particular results involving crash-tolerance. As a main result, we show that a large subclass of hyperfairness can be implemented through partial synchrony and randomization.

1 Introduction

A *conspiracy* is a certain kind of livelock in a distributed computation. The phenomenon has been first described by Dijkstra [6] in his metaphor of the five philosophers. There, a philosopher b can starve when his two neighbors a and c *conspire* against him by eating alternately in such a way that b's forks are never available at the same time (Fig. 1.a, forks shown as bullets).

The metaphor of a conspiracy has also been used for an analogous phenomenon in systems with multiparty-interactions (e.g. [1,12]). A multiparty-interaction is a common action of two or more processes. A particular interaction may not occur because, although all participants are always eventually ready for the interaction, they are never, or at least not sufficiently often, ready at the same time, because they intermittently engage in conflicting interactions. For example (cf. Fig. 1.b), an interaction A of processes a and b may occur alternately with an interaction C of processes c and d such that b and c are always eventually ready for an interaction B but not together at the same time. Note that here interactions conspire (against a particular interaction) rather than processes.

Conspiracies have been described and studied in these two contexts, i.e., in systems where processes share either variables or actions. However, they can also occur in message passing systems: Fig. 2.a shows three processes in a directed ring with two tokens. A process that has exactly one token passes the token to its clockwise neighbor. A process with two tokens destroys both tokens. That system does not necessarily terminate. In a non-terminating run, each token is always eventually available to each process but they are never available at the same time. We could say here that the message-system (or the adversary) "conspires" against termination.

A similar "conspiracy" can occur in daily life when a pedestrian wants to cross a two-lane road and she cannot safely wait between the lanes. To cross, she needs two

P. Fraigniaud (Ed.): DISC 2005, LNCS 3724, pp. 33–47, 2005.

(a) Three philosophers   (b) Three interactions

Fig. 1. Conspiracy-prone systems

resources at the same time: A sufficiently wide free space on the first lane and one on the second lane. A "conspiracy" occurs when both resources are infinitely often available but never at the same time.

In the remainder of the paper, we motivate and propose a new characterization of these livelocks through a new notion of *hyperfairness*, which is based on the partial order of causality. Furthermore, we discuss some problems in distributed computing where these livelocks inherently arise, where we also point out a relationship between conspiracies and crash-tolerance. Finally, we show as a main result that a large subclass of hyperfairness can be implemented through partial synchrony and randomization. Missing proofs can be found in the full version of this paper [22].

2   Characterization

We assume that a distributed system is modelled as a directed graph, which is possibly infinite, where nodes represent global states and edges represent state transitions. State transitions are labelled with *action* names, which, for now, are just elements of some fixed alphabet $\mathcal{A}$. One node is distinguished as the *initial state* of the system. An action $\alpha \in \mathcal{A}$ is *enabled* in a global state if there is a state transition labelled with α that starts in that state. An *observation* of the system is a finite or infinite alternating sequence $\sigma = z_0, \alpha_1, z_1, \ldots$ of global states and actions that starts in the initial state such that (z_i, z_{i+1}) is an edge in the graph that is labeled with α_{i+1} for each position $i \geq 0$ of σ.

2.1   Previous Work

To our knowledge, Kwong [14] is the first to propose a partial characterization for conspiracies. Kwong defines that a sequential process p suffers from a "livelock of type 1" in an infinite observation σ if there is a position of σ such that no action of p is henceforth enabled but actions of p henceforth remain *reachable*, that is, for each state z_i of σ, there is a state z such that z is reachable from z_i (in the graph) and z enables some action of p. E. Best [3] generalizes that to the notion of ∞-*fairness* with respect to (w.r.t.) an action α of the system: An observation σ is not[1] ∞-*fair* w.r.t. α if α occurs at most finitely many times in σ and for each state z_i of σ there is a state z such that z is reachable from z_i and z enables α. Therefore, both notions do not rule out "conspiracies"

---

[1] We always define fairness implicitly, through the explicit definition of unfairness in this paper, i.e., we always state when a run is not fair.

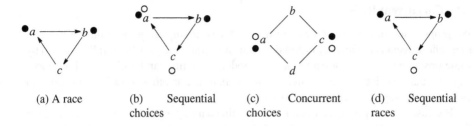

(a) A race   (b)   Sequential choices   (c)   Concurrent choices   (d)   Sequential races

Fig. 2. Systems exhibiting livelocks of different nature

that are specified in the system, for example: Philosophers a and c share a unique extra token (e.g. a napkin), which has to be taken to release the forks and which is released when forks are taken again, i.e., the algorithm enforces that a and c never *think* at the same time and hence b's forks cannot be available at the same time.

The notion of ∞-unfairness rules out all conspiracies described above (and below). However, there are different kinds of conspiracies which are not discriminated by ∞-fairness and therefore, ∞-fairness may be unnecessarily strong in many cases.

Consider the two systems illustrated in Figs. 2.a and b. The system in Fig. 2.a was already explained in Sect. 1. In Fig. 2.b, a process holding two tokens of different color sends one of them to its clockwise neighbor (through message-passing). It is free in deciding which one. A process holding two tokens of the same color destroys them, which forces termination. Both systems terminate under the assumption of ∞-fairness (w.r.t. the action "destroy"). While termination of the first example depends on the termination of a *race*—whether the one token will catch up to the other—the termination of the second example solely depends on the free choices of the processes, i.e., whether the white or the black token is sent. While races are exclusive to concurrent systems, choices also occur in sequential systems. The system in Fig. 2.b is in fact a sequential system. Fig. 2.c shows an example of a concurrent system that does not terminate due to uncoordinated free choices. There, a process holding two tokens sends one token to each of its neighbors with a free choice which neighbor receives which token. Again, a process holding two tokens of the same color destroys them.

An ∞-unfair run is in general a combination of "unfortunate" outcomes of races and choices. Conspiracies that are due to choices can be ruled out with high probability through randomization of the choices. Partial characterization can then be achieved by fairness notions that abstract from randomization, e.g., extreme fairness [19] and α-fairness [17]. We will deal only with conspiracies that are solely due to races in the rest of the paper.

Attie, Francez, and Grumberg [1] characterize with the notion of *hyperfairness* conspiracies that are solely due to races. However, their notion is relatively complex and strongly tied to their particular programming language. Moreover, whether a run is hyperfair or not depends in general on the entire behavior of the system. Lamport [16] generalizes Attie, Francez, and Grumberg's hyperfairness in a more general setting, which is similar to ours and independent of programming languages. However, Lamport's hyperfairness coincides with Best's ∞-fairness.

2.2   Concurrent Runs

We propose to characterize races and the livelocks arising from them on the basis of runs where events are partially ordered by causality (rather than being totally ordered by some observer). For the message-passing model, causality can be given by Lamport's happens-before relation [15], which we recall below. For other models, causality can usually be defined in a natural way as well.

For ease of exposition, we assume for now that a notion of causality is given, i.e., we first define hyperfairness independent of the computational model. We will later study hyperfairness in the concrete model of asynchronous message-passing. For now, let a *concurrent run* (or simply *run*) be a triple $\rho = (E, \prec, \ell)$ where

- E is a countable set of *events*,
- $\prec$ is a partial order on E, called the *causal order*, such that (1) the set $\mathrm{pred}(e) = \{e' \mid e' \leq e\}$ is finite for each event e and (2) for each infinite set $E' \subseteq E$, there exist $e, e' \in E'$ such that $e \prec e'$. Any finite union $C = \bigcup_{i=1,\dots,n} \mathrm{pred}(e_i)$ for $e_i \in E$ is called a *configuration* (also: cut, consistent cut) of ρ,
- ℓ is a labeling that maps each event to an action name and each configuration to a global state.

Two events e, e' are said to be *concurrent* if neither $e \prec e'$ nor $e' \prec e$. Condition (2) above rules out systems with infinitely many concurrent components. A configuration D is *reachable* from a configuration C if $C \subseteq D$. A *linearization* of a run $\rho = (E, \prec, \ell)$ is an alternating sequence $\sigma = C_0, e_1, C_1, \dots$ of configurations and events such that $C_0 = \quad$, $C_{i+1} = C_i \cup \{e_{i+1}\}$, $C_i \neq C_{i+1}$ for each position i of σ, and $\{e_i \mid i \text{ is a position of } \sigma\} = E$. If σ is a linearization of ρ, we call $\ell(\sigma) = \ell(C_0), \ell(e_1), \ell(C_1), \dots$ an *observation* of ρ. We associate with each system a set of concurrent runs ρ such that each observation of ρ is an observation of the system. Under weak technical assumptions, a concurrent run arises as an equivalence class of observations where two observations are equivalent if they only differ in the order of concurrent events.

An action is *enabled* in a configuration C if it is enabled in $\ell(C)$. An action α is *taken* in an event e if $\ell(e) = \alpha$.

2.3   Hyperfairness

Figs. 3.a and 3.b show runs of the five philosophers system where only three philosophers $a, b,$ and c take steps; $x.h$ represents philosopher x becoming hungry, $x.p$ represents x picking up both forks, $x.c$ stands for x becoming critical (i.e., eating), and $x.r$ represents x releasing both forks. Arrows represent direct causality, i.e., causality is the transitive closure of direct causality. Note that $a.c$ and $c.c$ are concurrent while $a.c$ and $b.c$ (as well as $b.c$ and $c.c$) are causally related.

Fig. 3.b shows a run ρ with a conspiracy that is due to a race condition. Whether action $b.p$ is enabled depends on the observation: ρ has an observation where $b.p$ is infinitely often enabled and ρ has an observation where $b.p$ is never enabled. We take that property, i.e., that the enabledness depends on the observation as the defining characteristic of a "race-conspiracy". We now define hyperfairness w.r.t. an *action label*, which is a subset $\lambda \subseteq \mathcal{A}$ of actions. Hyperfairness w.r.t. an action will be a special case of the definition.

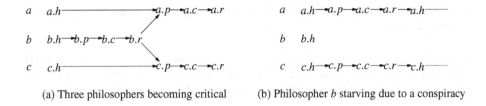

(a) Three philosophers becoming critical   (b) Philosopher b starving due to a conspiracy

Fig. 3. Two concurrent runs of the five philosophers system

Definition 1. *Let $\lambda \subseteq \mathcal{A}$. We say that λ is enabled in a state z if there is an action $\alpha \in \lambda$ that is enabled in z; λ is taken at a position i of an observation $\sigma = z_0, \alpha_1, z_1, \ldots$ if $\alpha_i \in \lambda$. A run ρ is not hyperfair w.r.t. λ if λ is taken at most finitely many times in ρ and there is an observation $\sigma = z_0, \alpha_1, z_1, \ldots$ of ρ in which λ is always eventually enabled, that is, for each position i of σ, there is a position $j \geq i$ such that z_j enables λ. A run ρ is not hyperfair w.r.t. an action α if it is not hyperfair w.r.t. the label $\{\alpha\}$.*

Hyperfairness as defined in Def. 1, ∞-fairness, and the notion of *strong fairness* are related as follows. Recall that an observation σ is *not strongly fair* w.r.t. a label λ if λ is taken at most finitely many times in σ and λ is always eventually enabled in σ. Strong fairness is weaker than hyperfairness which in turn is weaker than ∞-fairness. To state this formally, we need to define ∞-fairness and strong fairness on concurrent runs. The following definition is the natural way to do this.

Definition 2. *A concurrent run ρ is not strongly fair (not ∞-fair) w.r.t. a label λ if all observations of ρ are not strongly fair (not ∞-fair) w.r.t. λ.*

Strong fairness on concurrent runs coincides with the notion of the minimal equivalence completion of strong fairness in the literature [9,13]. Note that a run ρ is not hyperfair w.r.t. λ if and only if it has an observation that is not strongly fair w.r.t. λ.

Proposition 1. *If a run is ∞-fair w.r.t. λ, then it is also hyperfair w.r.t. λ; if it is hyperfair w.r.t. λ, then it is also strongly fair w.r.t. λ.*

The examples in Fig. 2 show that these implications are strict: The system in Fig. 2.a terminates under hyperfairness w.r.t. the action "two black tokens meet" but it does not terminate under strong fairness w.r.t. any label[2]. The systems in Figs. 2.b and c terminate under ∞-fairness but not under hyperfairness. "Conspiracies" are those runs which are strongly fair but not hyperfair w.r.t. an action or a label. A run that is strongly fair but not hyperfair w.r.t. a label λ has an observation that is strongly fair as well as one that is not strongly fair w.r.t. λ.

Note that, in general, one needs to require fairness for more than one action. Consider, for example, Fig. 2.d. Here, two meeting black tokens are turned into one white token and two meeting white tokens are destroyed. The system terminates if hyperfairness is assumed for both actions, "two black tokens meet" and "two white tokens meet".

---

[2] This and the following statements get a firm footing when we define concurrent runs in the message-passing model below.

Next we show that hyperfairness can be written in a way that is similar to the definition of strong fairness.

Proposition 2. *A run ρ is not hyperfair w.r.t. λ if and only if λ is taken at most finitely often and λ is always eventually enabled in ρ, that is, for each configuration C of ρ, there is a configuration D that is reachable from C and that enables λ.*

Our notion of hyperfairness has been defined as 0-transition fairness by Merceron [18] as a theoretical way to define fairness on concurrent runs, where, however, the relationship with conspiracies has not been pointed out. It also coincides with the minimal equivalence completion of strong fairness as defined by Francez, Back, and Kurki-Suonio [9] (cf. also [13]), which they have defined as a way to transform strong fairness into a fairness notion on observations that respects the equivalence described in Sect. 2.2.

2.4 Hyperfairness in Message-Passing Systems

For the sake of concreteness, we define now hyperfairness in a concrete system model, viz. in the asynchronous message-passing model. Consider a finite set P of sequential processes, which communicate by asynchronous reliable message passing, i.e., messages are not lost, duplicated, or corrupted during transit but may be received in a different order than in which they were sent. A process is modeled by an automaton over some countable set S of *local states*. A message is modeled as a pair (p, m), where p is a process denoting the receiver of the message and m, drawn from some countable set M, denotes the content. Let $\mathcal{M} = P \times M$ be the set of all messages. For convenience, we assume that each message is sent only once during a run[3].

The message system is modeled by associating with each process p an *output buffer* $p.\text{outp} \subseteq \mathcal{M}$ and an *input buffer* $p.\text{inp} \subseteq \mathcal{M}$. An *action* is either a *delivery action* $p.\text{del}(q, m)$ or a *computation action* $p.\text{comp}(s, X)$. A delivery action $p.\text{del}(q, m)$ is enabled if (q, m) is contained in $p.\text{outp}$. This action moves (q, m) from $p.\text{outp}$ to $q.\text{inp}$. A computation action $p.\text{comp}(s, X)$, where X is a set of messages, is enabled if process p is in state s and $X = p.\text{inp}$. This action empties p's input buffer and it computes a new local state and puts a finite set of messages into p's output buffer according to the specification of p's automaton.

Global states and the graph associated with such a system are defined in the usual and natural way. We now define concurrent runs through Lamport's happens-before relation [15]. Fix a system and let $\sigma = z_0, \alpha_1, z_1, \ldots$ be an observation of that system. Let $E = \{1, \ldots\}$ be the set of positions of σ and $\prec$ be the smallest transitive relation on E such that

1. $i \prec j$ if $i < j$, $\alpha_i = p.\text{comp}(s, X)$ and $\alpha_j = p.\text{comp}(s', X')$ and
2. $i \prec j \prec k$ if $\alpha_i = p.\text{comp}(s, X)$ is an action that puts (q, m) into $p.\text{outp}$, $\alpha_j = p.\text{del}(q, m)$, and $\alpha_k = q.\text{comp}(s', X')$ where $(q, m) \in X'$.

---

[3] That can be achieved by incorporating the identity of the sender and a sequence number in each message.

An observation (or run) is *admissible* if each message in each output buffer is eventually delivered and each process always eventually takes another action unless it crashes or it has eventually henceforth no more enabled action.

We are interested in synchronizations of messages and process states, e.g., whether a particular message is received in a particular local state of the process or whether particular messages are received together. We will therefore consider labels that describe such synchronizations.

Definition 3. *Let p be a process. A set λ of computation actions of p is called a synchronization label if p.comp$(s, X) \in \lambda$ and $X \subseteq Y$ implies p.comp$(s, Y) \in \lambda$.*

A synchronization label can be specified by a pair (p, Φ) where p is a process and $\Phi = \{(s_1, X_1), \ldots\}$ is a set of pairs where s_i is a state of p and X_i is a set of messages; (p, Φ) then denotes the set

$$\{p.\text{comp}(s, Y) \mid \exists (s, X) \in \Phi : X \subseteq Y\}.$$

Hyperfairness w.r.t. a synchronization label is defined through Def. 1. According to Prop. 2, a concurrent run ρ is not hyperfair w.r.t. λ if λ is taken at most finitely many times and there is always eventually a configuration and an $(s, X) \in \Phi$ such that p is in state s and all messages $m \in X$ are in transit to p.

Enabledness of an action p.comp(s, X) in a configuration C of a concurrent run intuitively means: In C, process p is in state s and if p waited there for some time, then it would receive all messages in X (and maybe more) together in one step. That means that "freezing" p at suitable times for a while could help to prevent a conspiracy. We will see in Sect. 4 under what circumstances this idea actually works.

When we write $\lambda = (p, Q, M_1, \ldots, M_k)$ we shall mean the synchronization label

$$\{p.\text{comp}(s, X) \mid s \in Q \text{ and } \forall i = 1, \ldots, k : M_i \cap X \neq \quad\},$$

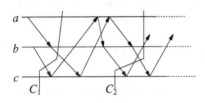

Fig. 4. A concurrent run that is not hyperfair

i.e., the set of computation actions where p being in a state in Q receives at least one message from each M_i.

Fig. 4 shows a run of the system in Fig. 2.a that is not hyperfair w.r.t. the synchronization labels (p, S, M_1, M_2) for $p \in \{a, b, c\}$ where S is the set of all local states and M_1 and M_2 denote the set of the messages containing the first and the second token respectively.

Configurations enabling (c, S, M_1, M_2) are represented by vertical dotted lines.

3   Problems with Inherent Conspiracies

We discuss three problems in this section where conspiracies inherently arise. First we discuss the committee coordination problem, then a crash-tolerant version of the dining philosophers problem, and finally the crash-tolerant consensus problem.

3.1 Committee Coordination

A classical problem where conspiracies arise is the committee coordination problem [5], which captures the problem of scheduling multiparty-interactions. Multiparty-interactions are a common construct in distributed programming and specification languages. Consider a finite set P of *professors* and a family $C \subseteq 2^P$ of nonempty *committees*. Each professor p is always either *quiet* or *ready* or *attending* a meeting of a committee C such that $p \in C$. Each professor is initially quiet. A quiet professor may remain quiet forever or it may become, at any time, *ready* to attend a meeting, i.e., it becomes ready to attend a meeting of any committee it is a member of. A meeting of a committee C can be seen as a common simultaneous action of all $p \in C$. This can be simulated in the message-passing model by each professor in C sending a message to each professor in C upon becoming attending and then waiting for receiving a message from each professor in C to leave that meeting. We say that a committee C is *ready* when all $p \in C$ are ready.

We now ask for an algorithm that *schedules* meetings, that is, based on the information which professors are ready, decides which ready committee shall meet next. The members of that committee are then informed by the algorithm, which triggers them to become attending. We assume that it takes some positive amount of time to inform a professor of a scheduling decision. Two committees can only meet concurrently if they are disjoint. Each committee meeting ends after a positive finite amount of time, and after a meeting of C, all professors $p \in C$ become quiet again.

The liveness requirement that was originally posed [5] is *deadlock freedom*: If a committee C is ready then it will eventually meet or a *conflicting* committee, i.e., a committee C' such that $C \cap C' \neq \quad$, will eventually meet. Deadlock-freedom does not rule out conspiracies w.r.t. a particular committee: Consider for example the three committees $A = \{p\}, B = \{p, q\}, C = \{q\}$. A conspiracy w.r.t. B arises when A and C alternately meet in such a way that p is quiet whenever q is ready and vice versa, i.e., the members of B are always eventually ready concurrently but not at the same time. Note that this may force the "starvation" of a particular professor: For example, if $C = \{A, B, C\}$ where $A = \{p\}, B = \{p, q, r\}, C = \{q\}$, then a conspiracy of A and C against B forces the starvation of r.

We consider the following two liveness requirements, where each admissible observation satisfies for each committee C:

 - If C is always eventually ready then C meets infinitely often. *(Starvation freedom)*
 - If each $p \in C$ is always eventually ready then C meets infinitely often. *(Recurrence)*

Clearly, recurrence implies starvation-freedom and starvation-freedom implies deadlock-freedom.

Theorem 1. *Define $c(p) = \{C \mid p \in C\}$ for each professor p. There is a committee coordination algorithm satisfying recurrence (or starvation-freedom) if and only if for all professors p, q, we have $c(p) \cap c(q) = \quad$ or $c(p) \subseteq c(q)$ or $c(q) \subseteq c(p)$.*

Proof. For the impossibility, fix p and q such that the above condition is violated. Then there exist $A \in c(p) \setminus c(q)$, $B \in c(p) \cap c(q)$, and $C \in c(q) \setminus c(p)$ (see Fig. 5). Suppose that a starvation-free algorithm exists.

1. Let all $p \in A$ and only those become ready, if necessary repeatedly, until A is scheduled but not yet meeting. (There may be subcommittees of A that are scheduled first by the algorithm. But if A is always eventually ready, A will eventually meet due to starvation-freedom.) B cannot meet because q is never ready. Now let all $r \in B \setminus A$ become ready. Since A is scheduled but not yet meeting, A is still ready and therefore, B is now ready as well. However B cannot meet because A is already scheduled. Let A now meet and become quiet again.

2. Repeat the previous step now with C in the role of A and p in the role of q.

3. Repeat the previous two steps infinitely often. In the obtained observation, B is infinitely often ready but never meets. The obtained observation therefore violates starvation-freedom contradicting our supposition.

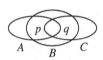

Fig. 5. Three committees

For the possibility, assume, without loss of generality, that each professor is a member of at least one committee. Let $P = \{p_1, \ldots, p_n\}$. Define $p_i \preceq p_j$ if $(c(p_i) \subset c(p_j))$ or $(c(p_i) = c(p_j)$ and $i < j)$. It is easy to verify that $\preceq$ is a partial order that represents a forest ($\preceq$ is irreflexive and transitive and we have: $p_i \preceq p_j$ and $p_i \preceq p_k$ implies $p_j \preceq p_k$ or $p_k \preceq p_j$). For each professor p, call the (w.r.t. $\preceq$) maximal professor q such that $p \preceq q$ the *root* of p. Committees are sets of professors that are pairwise comparable w.r.t. $\preceq$, hence a committee corresponds to a path from some professor p to its root. Therefore, all members of a committee have the same root and a root is a member of all the committees associated with its tree.

Upon becoming ready, a professor reports that to its root. Each root maintains a priority list over its committees. If a root becomes ready, it evaluates its incoming messages for ready committees. Among the ready committees, it schedules the one with the highest priority. All members of the winning committee are notified, all messages from professors that are not in the winning committee are buffered. The priority of the winning committee is set to least after notification. Committees are scheduled as long as a root knows of ready but unscheduled committees.

It is easy to see that the algorithm guarantees deadlock-freedom. We prove now recurrence. Suppose that each $p \in C$ is always eventually ready but C is eventually not scheduled anymore. Consider a time after which C is not scheduled anymore. Let $C = \{p^1, \ldots, p^k\}$ where $p^1 \preceq p^2 \preceq \ldots \preceq p^k$. Note that p^k is the root of C. It follows from the definition of $\preceq$ that if a professor p attends committees infinitely often and $p \preceq q$ so does q. We distinguish the following two cases:

1. No $p^i \in C$ is attending infinitely often. Since all p^i are always eventually ready, C is eventually ready forever. This contradicts deadlock-freedom.

2. There is an $i \in \{1, \ldots k\}$ such that $j < i$ implies p^j is eventually ready forever and $j \geq i$ implies p^j is infinitely often attending. There is a time after which the readiness of all p^j for $j < i$ is known to the root of C. Since p^i attends infinitely often, a committee $C' \in c(p^i)$ meets infinitely often. Because of $p^i \preceq p^j$ for $i < j$, we have $p^j \in C'$ for $i \leq j$. It follows that the root eventually sees the readiness of C whenever C' is scheduled. Due to the priority rule, C must be scheduled as well.

Thm. 1 extends a result of Joung [12] by considering distributed processes rather than processes that are scheduled by a centralized scheduler that has full knowledge of the history and that communicates synchronously with the professors. We also gave an alternative characterization of the impossibility and we extended the result from starvation-freedom to recurrence. Note that our solution is crash-tolerant to some extent: If we assume that professors may not crash in meetings or if we assume that professors can detect professors that have crashed in a meeting, then the crash of a professor only affects the committees it is a member of.

Theorem 2. *There is a committee coordination algorithm that satisfies recurrence (and therefore starvation-freedom) under hyperfairness.*

3.2 Dining Philosophers

We consider now the dining philosophers problem as defined by Chandy and Misra [5]. Consider a finite set P of *philosophers* and an irreflexive and symmetric relation $N \subseteq P \times P$. We call p and q *neighbors* if $(p, q) \in N$. A philosopher cycles through the states *quiet, hungry,* and *critical*. We assume that a critical philosopher always eventually becomes quiet while a quiet philosopher may remain quiet forever. We ask for an algorithm that solves the starvation-free mutual exclusion problem for each pair of neighbors simultaneously, i.e., we require

(S) Each two neighbors are never critical at the same time, and
(L) each hungry process eventually becomes critical (*starvation-freedom*).

Chandy and Misra have presented a solution to that problem [5]. We assume now that a philosopher may crash (permanently and unannounced) while it is enough to assume here that a critical philosopher may crash, i.e., may remain critical forever. As this may remain undetected in an asynchronous system, we weaken the starvation-freedom to

(L') Each hungry process eventually becomes critical unless itself or one of its neighbors crashes.

This still requires a hungry philosopher with at least distance 2 to a crashed philosopher to become critical. We show now that this problem has inherent conspiracies.

Theorem 3. *The crash-tolerant dining philosophers problem is solvable in asynchronous message-passing systems if and only if N is transitive.*

Proof. For the impossibility, consider $(p, q), (q, r) \in N$ and $(p, r) \notin N$. Let p become hungry and then critical, and let then q and r become hungry. If we now pretend p to be crashed then, by (L'), r eventually becomes critical. Now let p become quiet and then hungry again. We can now repeat the previous steps with p and r in swapped roles. Repeating infinitely, we obtain an observation where there is always either p or r critical and hence q must remain hungry violating (L'). It is easy to see that the run can be constructed in such a way that each message is eventually delivered.

For the possibility, observe that the reflexive closure of N is an equivalence. Provide a unique token for each equivalence class of philosophers, which is needed to become critical, which may be maintained by any philosopher in the equivalence class, and which is eventually given to each philosopher upon request.

Theorem 4. *The crash-tolerant dining philosophers problem can be solved under hyperfairness.*

Thm. 4 is proven by assuming a central coordinator that is distinct from the philosophers and that cannot crash. If N is acyclic, we can give a solution without a coordinator.

Theorem 5. *The crash-tolerant dining philosophers problem can be solved under hyperfairness without a coordinator if N is acyclic.*

The case without a coordinator where N is cyclic but not transitive is left open. Thms. 3 and 4 (as well as Thms. 1 and 2) imply that, in general, we cannot implement hyperfairness deterministically.

3.3 Consensus

We assume the reader to be familiar with the crash-tolerant consensus problem as defined by Fischer, Lynch, and Paterson [8]. Fischer, Lynch, and Paterson [8] exploit races between messages to show that the problem is not solvable as soon as one process may crash. We have elsewhere [20] explicitly constructed an inherent livelock that prevents processes from reaching consensus. That livelock is different[4] from those constructed in Thms. 1 and 3. Here, we show that consensus can indeed be solved under hyperfairness:

Theorem 6. *There is an algorithm that solves t-tolerant consensus for n processes under hyperfairness if and only if $n > 2t$.*

4 Implementation of Hyperfairness

In this section, we show that hyperfairness can be implemented to a large extent by help of partial synchrony and randomization. We first deal with hyperfairness with respect to only one synchronization label and generalize then to more than one label.

4.1 Bounded Hyperfairness

We will implement only *bounded hyperfairness*, a subclass of hyperfairness that often suffices. It will be clear from the sequel that a somewhat larger subclass can be implemented with the same techniques, however we conjecture that hyperfairness in general cannot be implemented even under strong synchrony assumptions and randomization.

Bounded hyperfairness rules out bounded conspiracies. Intuitively, a conspiracy is bounded if the effort that is needed to enable the action from an arbitrary configuration of the run is bounded.

Definition 4. *Let ρ be a run, C and D two configurations of ρ and $k \in$. We say that D is k-reachable from C if D is reachable from C and $|D \setminus C| \leq k$; ρ is not k-hyperfair w.r.t. a label λ if λ occurs at most finitely many times and for each configuration C of ρ there is a configuration that is k-reachable from C and that enables λ. A run is not bounded-hyperfair w.r.t. λ if there is a k such that it is not k-hyperfair w.r.t. λ.*

---

[4] In the livelock constructed in [20], the "conspiring" components are sets of processes that are not disjoint.

If a run is k-hyperfair w.r.t. λ, then it is also k'-hyperfair w.r.t. λ for $k' < k$. A run that is hyperfair w.r.t. λ is also bounded-hyperfair w.r.t. λ.

4.2 Partial Synchrony

Several forms of partial synchrony have been introduced in the literature, e.g., as a way to solve the crash-tolerant consensus problem [7]. In this paper, partial synchrony shall mean that the time each event of a given run consumes is bounded where, however, the bound is not known to the processes. To formalize this, we associate a value of a global clock with each event of a run. We assume that the clock progresses discretely and that each event takes at least one time unit.

Definition 5. *A timed run consists of a run $\rho = (E, <, \ell)$ and a mapping $\tau : E \to$ such that $e < e' \Rightarrow \tau(e) < \tau(e')$ for all events e, e'. The value $\tau(e)$ is called* completion time *of e. The value $\tau_0(e) = \max\{\tau(e') \mid e' < e\}$ is called* enabling time *of e; $\delta(e) = \tau(e) - \tau_0(e)$ is called* consumption time *of e. The* delivery time *of a message is the completion time of its delivery event.*

Definition 6. *Let $K \in$. A timed run ρ is* K-synchronous *if we have $\delta(e) \le K$ for all events e of ρ. It is* partially synchronous *if there is a K such that it is K-synchronous.*

4.3 Implementation with Respect to One Synchronization Label

Consider the three philosophers in Fig. 6.a. Each pair of neighbors shares a token by message-passing. Philosopher b can use an *adaptive timeout* to prevent a conspiracy against him, provided the system is partially synchronous: Whenever it has one token, it waits at least Δ time units for the second token. If the timeout occurs before the second token is received, it increases the timeout value Δ by some positive constant. Under partial synchrony, it will eventually have both tokens at the same time.

Consider a message-passing system that may have runs that are not bounded-hyperfair with respect to a synchronization label λ. We modify the system such that bounded-hyperfair runs (w.r.t. λ) are maintained and runs that are not bounded-hyperfair w.r.t. λ are ruled out by the assumption of partial synchrony.

We use the adaptive timeout mechanism: We assume that process p has a timer that can be set to a time $\Delta \in$, which guarantees that the timeout occurs not earlier than Δ time units after the timer has been set. Process p maintains a timeout value Δ and sets its timer whenever it goes to a state s such that there is a set X of messages such that $p.\mathrm{comp}(s, X) \in \lambda$, i.e., p's next computation step is delayed for at least Δ time units. If λ is not enabled after the timeout, then the timeout value Δ is increased by some positive constant.

Each timed run ρ' of the obtained system can be mapped to a timed run ρ of the original system by hiding the timer and its steps and adding the time that is used by a step of the timer to the consumption time of the previous computation step. We model a timer action as a single action that takes more than Δ time units (rather than as a sequence of Δ actions that take at least one time unit). Then ρ' is bounded-hyperfair w.r.t. λ if and only if ρ is. Furthermore, we will call ρ' K-synchronous if all events of ρ' except the steps of the timer consume not more than K time units.

(a) Three philosophers   (b) Four philosophers in a ring

Fig. 6. Two more systems of dining philosophers

Lemma 1. *If ρ is an admissible and partially synchronous timed run of the obtained system, then ρ is bounded-hyperfair w.r.t. λ.*

Proof. Let ρ be K-synchronous. Assume that for each configuration C of ρ, there is a configuration enabling λ that is k-reachable from C. It is easy to check that p takes infinitely many steps. It follows that p takes infinitely often a step where it sets its timer. If the timeout value is increased only finitely many times, then λ is taken infinitely many times and we are done. Hence assume the timeout value is increased infinitely often.

Consider a time where the timeout value is greater than $k \cdot K$. Fix a later time t at which the timer is set. It is easy to check that for each time $t \in$, the set $C_t := \{e \mid \tau(e) \le t\}$ is a configuration. Let D be a configuration that is k-reachable from C_t and that enables λ. Call s the state that p has in D. Let t' be the time that the computation step producing that state s in D is completed. Clearly $t \le t'$ and therefore $C_t \subseteq C_{t'} \subseteq D$. Due to the timer action, p leaves s not earlier than $t' + k \cdot K$. Consider a message m that is in transit to p in D. Since $D \setminus C_{t'}$ does not contain any step of p, all events in $D \setminus C_{t'}$ consume less than K time units. Furthermore, we have $|D \setminus C_{t'}| \le k$ and therefore, m is delivered not later than $t' + k \cdot K$. Hence all messages that are in transit in D are delivered in time for p's next computation step after D. Therefore λ is taken in that step of p. It follows that ρ is bounded-hyperfair w.r.t. λ.

4.4   Implementation with Respect to Multiple Labels

If we implement the mechanism from Sect. 4.3 at all processes simultaneously then we might delay the sending of a message for which the receiver already waits and has set a timer as well. Consider, for example, four philosophers in a ring (Fig. 6.b). If all philosophers hold their left fork simultaneously while using the adaptive time-out mechanism with the same timeout value, it can happen that all philosophers do the same at the same time and therefore no philosopher ever becomes critical.

Such a problem is a symmetry breaking problem, which can be solved through randomization as follows. We use the same construction as in Sect. 4.3, now for finitely many synchronization labels simultaneously, but now, each time when p goes to a state that is part of an action in λ, it flips a coin in order to decide whether to set the timer or not.

Theorem 7. *The property (ρ is partially synchronous $\Rightarrow$ ρ is bounded-hyperfair w.r.t. all labels) has probability 1 in the obtained system.*

Corollary 1. *The committee coordination problem can be solved such that recurrence is satisfied with probability 1 through partial synchrony and randomization. The crash-tolerant dining philosophers problem can be solved with probability 1 through partial synchrony and randomization.*

Joung [11] has proposed a different randomized algorithm that solves a generalization of the starvation-free committee coordination problem under partial synchrony. The used techniques are similar to ours. We have shown elsewhere [21] that adding randomization (but no synchrony assumption) is not enough to solve the crash-tolerant dining philosophers problem in general with high probability.

5   Conclusion

We have presented a new formalization of Attie, Francez, and Grumberg's concept of hyperfairness [1] in a language-independent way. It captures the intuitive notion of "conspiracies" that are due to race conditions. We have shown that these conspiracies also occur in message-passing systems and that they can be inherent to natural synchronization problems.

Our notion is strictly weaker than Best's ∞-fairness (resp. Lamport's hyperfairness) which means that an algorithm that is proven correct under hyperfairness is easier to implement than an algorithm that is proven correct under ∞-fairness. The relative weakness of hyperfairness w.r.t. ∞-fairness was important to give a generic implementation of bounded hyperfairness through partial synchrony and randomization.

That implementation is not efficient. However, our implementation shows what techniques can be used in an implementation. It also shows that hyperfairness can be seen as an abstraction from weak synchrony assumptions and randomization. As a fairness assumption on a semantic level, hyperfairness is a more abstract concept hiding synchrony assumptions than, for example, shared communication objects [10] or failure detectors [4], where the latter is only applicable in models where failures may occur. The more concrete abstractions of shared objects and failure detectors have the advantage that they can be defined on observations, i.e., no causality information is needed for them. The relationship of shared objects and failure detectors with hyperfairness will be subject of future work.

References

1. P. C. Attie, N. Francez, and O. Grumberg. Fairness and hyperfairness in multi-party interactions. *Distributed Computing*, 6:245–254, 1993.
2. M. Ben-Or. Another advantage of free choice: Completely asynchronous agreement protocols. In *Proc. 2nd PODC*, pp. 27–30. ACM, 1983.
3. E. Best. Fairness and conspiracies. *IPL*, 18:215–220, 1984. Erratum ibidem 19:162.
4. T. D. Chandra and S. Toueg. Unreliable failure detectors for reliable distributed systems. *Journal of the ACM*, 43(2):225–267, Mar. 1996.
5. K. M. Chandy and J. Misra. *Parallel Program Design: A Foundation*. Addison-Wesley, 1988.
6. E. W. Dijkstra. Hierarchical ordering of sequential processes. *Acta Inf.*, 1:115–138, 1971.

7. C. Dwork, N. Lynch, and L. Stockmeyer. Consensus in the presence of partial synchrony. *Journal of the ACM*, 35(2):288–323, Apr. 1988.
8. M. J. Fischer, N. A. Lynch, and M. S. Paterson. Impossibility of distributed consensus with one faulty process. *Journal of the ACM*, 32(2):374–382, Apr. 1985.
9. N. Francez, R.-J. J. Back, and R. Kurki-Suonio. On equivalence-completions of fairness assumptions. *Formal Aspects of Computing*, 4:582–591, 1992.
10. M. Herlihy. Wait-free synchronization. *ACM ToPLaS*, 11(1):124–149, Jan. 1991.
11. Y.-J. Joung. Two decentralized algorithms for strong interaction fairness for systems with unbounded speed variability. *Theor. Comput. Sci.*, 243(1-2):307–338, 2000.
12. Y.-J. Joung. On fairness notions in distributed systems, part I: A characterization of implementability. *Information and Computation*, 166:1–34, 2001.
13. Y.-J. Joung. On fairness notions in distributed systems, part II: Equivalence-completions and their hierarchies. *Information and Computation*, 166:35–60, 2001.
14. Y. Kwong. On the absence of livelocks in parallel programs. In *Semantics of Concurrent Computation, LNCS* 70, pp. 172–190. Springer, 1979.
15. L. Lamport. Time, clocks, and the ordering of events in a distributed system. *Communications of the ACM*, 21(7):558–565, July 1978.
16. L. Lamport. Fairness and hyperfairness. *Distributed Computing*, 13(4):239–245, 2000.
17. O. Lichtenstein, A. Pnueli, and L. Zuck. The glory of the past. In *Proc. Workshop on Logics of Programs, LNCS 193*, 1985.
18. A. Merceron. Fair processes. In *Advances in Petri Nets, LNCS* 266. Springer, 1987.
19. A. Pnueli. On the extremely fair treatment of probabilistic algorithms. In *Proc. 15th STOC*, pp. 278–290. ACM, 1983.
20. H. Völzer. A constructive proof for FLP. *IPL*, 92:83–87, 2004.
21. H. Völzer. On randomization versus synchronization in distributed systems. In *ICALP, LNCS* 3142, pp. 1214–1226. Springer, 2004.
22. H. Völzer. On conspiracies and hyperfairness in distributed computing. SIIM Technical Report SIIM-TR-A-05-20, Universität zu Lübeck, 2005.

On the Availability of Non-strict Quorum Systems[*]

Amitanand Aiyer[1], Lorenzo Alvizi[1], and Rida A. Bazzi[2]

[1] Department of Computer Sciences,
The University of Texas at Austin
{anand, lorenzo}@cs.utexas.edu
[2] Computer Science and Engineering Department,
Arizona State University,
bazzi@asu.edu

Abstract. Allowing read operations to return stale data with low probability has been proposed as a means to increase availability in quorums systems. Existing solutions that allow stale reads cannot tolerate an adversarial scheduler that can maliciously delay messages between servers and clients in the system and for such a scheduler existing solutions cannot enforce a bound on the staleness of data read. This paper considers the possibility of increasing system availability while at the same time tolerating a malicious scheduler and guaranteeing an upper bound on the staleness of data. We characterize the conditions under which this increase is possible and show that it depends on the ratio of the write frequency to the servers' failure frequency. For environments with a relatively large failure frequency compared to write frequency, we propose K-quorums that can provide higher availability than the strict quorum systems and also guarantee bounded staleness. We also propose a definition of k-atomicity and present a protocol to implement a k-atomic register using k-quorums.

1 Introduction

Quorum systems have been extensively studied in the literature. A traditional, or strict, quorum system is simply a collection of sets called quorums such that any two quorums have a non-empty intersection. Quorum systems have been used for mutual exclusion, coordination, and data replication in distributed systems.

In a particular protocol using quorum systems, quorums are accessed either to write a new value to a quorum or to read the values stored in a quorum. Important quality measures of quorum systems are *fault tolerance*, *availability*, *load*, and *quorum size*. In general, these quality measures are conflicting in strict quorum systems [13]. Systems with high availability tend to have large quorum sizes and high load. If the failure probability of individual nodes is less than 0.5, the system with the highest availability is the majority system in which a quorum

---

[*] This work was supported in part by NSF CyberTrust award 0430510, an Alfred P. Sloan Fellowhip and a grant from the Texas Advanced Technology Program.

P. Fraigniaud (Ed.): DISC 2005, LNCS 3724, pp. 48–62, 2005.

consists of a majority of the servers. Unfortunately, this system suffers from high load and large quorum size, which means that a large subset of servers need to be up in order for the system to be usable. However, in environments such as peer-to-peer networks, where the availability of individual nodes is not very high, the availability of the majority system is not high. If the failure probability of a node is more than 0.5, the best system in terms of availability is the singleton, but that system has a very high load [14].

In order to develop quorum systems with small quorum sizes and with availability higher than that of the majority system, probabilistic quorum systems have been proposed [11]. A probabilistic quorum system is a collection of sets together with an access strategy which specifies the probability that a quorum is chosen to be used in an access. In a probabilistic quorum system, two quorums chosen according to the access strategy have a non-empty intersection with probability $1 - \epsilon$, where ϵ is a system parameter. Using probabilistic quorum systems, a read access is guaranteed to get the value of the most up-to-date non-overlapping write access with probability $1 - \epsilon$.

More recently, Yu [20] proposed Signed Quorum systems which aim at overcoming problems with the definition of probabilistic quorum systems. Yu observed that probabilistic systems cannot be realized in a system in which the scheduler is an active adversary that delays responses from servers to prevent clients from following the probabilistic access strategy. He proposed a signed quorum system (SQS) in which the high probability of intersection depends on the assumptions that the probability that two clients observe conflicting (mismatch) states (up or down) of servers is low and that simultaneous mismatches of different servers are independent—the independent mismatch assumption. These assumptions are backed by trace results from a number of experiments [3,21]; further, Yu argues that in practice probabilistic quorum systems would require making explicit assumptions about the scheduler similar to the ones SQS makes. In SQS, a quorum consists of positive elements (servers that respond and are up) and negative elements (servers that do not respond and are assumed to be down). By allowing servers that are down to be part of a quorum, Yu's system can be used even if a small number of servers are up.

Both probabilistic systems and SQS make implicit or explicit assumptions about the scheduler [20]. Both systems would not perform as claimed if these assumptions do not hold. Both systems are unusable in the presence of an adversarial scheduler that controls the delay to various nodes in the system. In fact, in the presence of an adversarial scheduler, the returned values can be arbitrarily old. Also, due to their probabilistic nature, both probabilistic systems and signed quorum systems do not provide strict guarantees on the freshness of values returned by a quorum. With positive, albeit small, probability, a quorum might return a value that is old (even in the absence of an adversarial scheduler) and there is no way for a client to tell how old the value is.

This paper investigates the following question. "Is it possible to design a quorum system that: provides strict guarantees on the staleness of values returned, tolerates an adversarial scheduler, and, in the absence of an adversarial scheduler provides higher availability than the majority system?" It turns out that the answer to this question does not only depend on the nodes' failure probability, but it also depends on the rate at which write operations are executed, the mean time between failure ($mtbf$), and the mean time to recover ($mttr$) of individual nodes. We prove a lower bound on the possible increase in availability as a function of the staleness of values and the ratio of the frequency of writes to the frequency of failures ($1/mtbf$). We show that for some values of the ratio, the possible increase of availability is negligible. For the cases where the increase in availability is not negligible, we propose K-quorums, which can have higher availability (for the same system size) than that of the majority system when the system is well behaved (no adversarial scheduler) and that have bounded staleness in the presence of an adversarial scheduler. Our study of bounded-staleness also led us to revisit the properties of signed quorum systems. For signed quorum systems, we found that these systems are not guaranteed to behave as predicted in [20] if the times between writes is large compared to the times between failures.

In summary, we achieve the following in this paper.

- We prove a lower bound on the availability of systems that can tolerate an adversarial scheduler and provide guarantees on the staleness of returned values.
- We introduce K-quorum systems which, for some combination of system parameters, have lower load and higher availability than traditional quorums systems.
- We show how to use K-quorum systems for providing K-atomic implementations of a shared register.

The rest of the paper is organized as follows. Section 2 presents the probabilistic approaches to increasing the availability of quorum systems and discusses their limitations. Section 3 introduces K-consistency semantics, a formalization of relaxed access semantics with bounded staleness. Section 4 presents the system model and the definition of traditional quorum systems. Section 5 proves lower bounds on the availability of quorum system with worst-case guarantees on staleness. Section 6 introduces K-quorum systems and shows how they can be used to implement K-atomic registers. Section 7 gives an overview of related work.

2   Probabilistic Approaches

In strict quorum systems any read and write quorum sets have a non empty intersection. This allows for easy construction of registers with safe-semantics, where any read – that is not concurrent with any write – is guaranteed to return the value from the latest write.

Probabilistic approaches, such as PQS [11] and SQS [20], provide a high availability and low load at the cost of weakening consistency semantics. In these systems, the read and write quorums only intersect probabilistically. Hence, these systems can only provide safe-semantics probabilistically. Probabilistic guarantees can cause these systems to return arbitrarily old values. In synchronous systems, the probability that a read violates safe-semantics can be made arbitrarily small by using a large quorum size with an appropriate access strategy. However there can be no bound on this probability in an asynchronous system where an adversarial scheduler can affect the choice of quorums.

2.1 Probabilistic Quorum System

A probabilistic quorum system consists of read and write quorums similar to strict quorums, along with an access strategy for choosing quorums [11]. Any two quorums that are chosen according to the specified access strategy will intersect with a high probability.

In a simple construction of such a quorum system with n nodes, quorums are chosen to be sets of cardinality $l\sqrt{n}$ where l is a system parameter [11]. For large values of n, these systems provide a higher availability than the majority quorum system because they require only $l\sqrt{n}$ nodes to be accessible, as opposed to requiring $\frac{n+1}{2}$ in the majority quorum system. In a synchronous setting, using a uniform random access strategy guarantees that any two quorum sets of size $l\sqrt{n}$ intersect with probability at least $1 - e^{l^2}$. However, in an asynchronous system where the scheduler may be adversarial the probability of intersection can be much smaller – in fact it can be zero.

Examples. Consider a probabilistic quorum system over nodes $\{1, 2, \ldots, 100\}$, where any set of 30 nodes form a quorum. In the presence of an non-adversarial scheduler, if quorums are chosen uniformly at random, then the probability that two quorums do not intersect is less than 1.88×10^{-6}. However in an asynchronous system in which the scheduler arbitrarily delays read messages to $\{1, 2, \ldots, 50\}$ and also delay write messages to $\{51, 52, \ldots, 100\}$, read and write quorums will never intersect causing reads to always return arbitrarily old values.

2.2 Signed Quorum Systems

Signed quorum systems (SQS) [20], like PQS, provide a probabilistic guarantee of intersection. SQS utilizes the notion of a failure detector to form an estimate of nodes that may be inaccessible. Quorums in SQS consist of both positive and negative elements. Positive elements denoting the servers that have been contacted, and negative elements denoting servers that have been suspected to fail. Two quorums are said to intersect if and only if they intersect in a positive element. Like PQS, SQS also increases the availability by allowing non-intersecting quorums. However, SQS requires that no two non-intersecting quorums be accessible in the same configuration. In fact, SQS requires that the configurations in which two non-intersecting quorums are accessible differ in at least 2α node-states.

In a system with perfect failure-detectors, if the configuration of the nodes does not change (or less than 2α nodes change state), then SQS can always guarantee safe-semantics and behave like a strict quorum system. The probability of non-intersection is equal to the probability that more than 2α nodes used by a read and write access have different states and this probability is lower for larger values of α. In a asynchronous system, it is not possible to distinguish a failed node from a node whose messages are all delayed by the adversary (assuming that the only means to determine the state of a node is through message exchanges). In such a setting, an adversarial scheduler can present the reader and writer with totally different configurations so that the quorums used never intersect. A reader may then read an arbitrarily old value.

3   K-Consistency Semantics

The semantics of shared objects that are implemented with quorum systems can be classified as *safe, regular* or *atomic* [9]. For applications that can tolerate some staleness these notions of consistency are too strong. We propose the notion of *K-safe, K-regular* and *K-atomic* semantics, similar to those defined in [9], for formalizing consistency semantics in applications that can tolerate limited staleness.

1. *K*-**safe:** In a system that provides *K-safe* semantics, a read that does not overlap with a write is guaranteed to return the result of one of the latest *K* completed writes. The result of a read, that overlaps with a write is unspecified.
2. *K*-**regular:** A system that provides *K-regular* semantics, guarantees that any read, that does not overlap with a write, is guaranteed to return the result of one of the latest *K* completed writes. A read that overlaps with a write, returns either the result of one of the latest *K* completed writes, or the eventual result of one of the overlapping writes.
3. *K*-**atomic:** In a system with *K-atomic* semantics, there exists an order of the operations that is consistent with real time order and such that the values returned by a read operation is equal to one of the values written by the last *K* preceding writes in the order (assuming there are *K* initial writes with the same initial value).

4   Model and Definitions

4.1   Model

The system consists of n nodes, $\mathcal{P} = \{1, 2, \ldots, n\}$, each of which may be inaccessible with a probability p_f. Nodes are assumed to crash and recover independently, with a mean-time-to-failure of $mttf$ and a mean-time-to-recover of $mttr$. The mean-time-between-failures, is $mtbf = mttr + mttf$ and $p_f = \frac{mttr}{mtbf}$. If a node is up, then it is assumed to follow the specified protocol; i.e. we assume there are no malicious faults. Each node is assumed to have access to stable storage, such that the values written to the servers are persistent across crashes. The system is assumed to be asynchronous, with no bound on the relative speeds of the nodes. The links are modeled as *fair links*, i.e. if a message is sent infinitely often, it will eventually be delivered at the receiver.

In this paper, we assume that only servers fail. We assume that the duration of operations are small enough so that we can neglect the client failures during the operations. Our results, for the single writer multiple reader scenario, can however be easily extended to tolerate benign client-failures by incorporating a logging protocol at the client end.

4.2   Quorum Systems

Definition 1. *A* quorum system *over the set of nodes* $\mathcal{P}$ *is a tuple* $(\mathcal{R}, \mathcal{W})$; *where* $\mathcal{R} \subset 2^{\mathcal{P}}$ *is the set of read quorums and* $\mathcal{W} \subset 2^{\mathcal{P}}$ *is the set of write quorums.*

During a read (write) operation, the reader (writer) contacts a read quorum (write quorum) to perform a read (write) operation. The access strategy specifies which nodes need to be contacted to access a quorum set.

Definition 2. *An* access strategy *for a client specifies an algorithm for choosing a quorum set to access, possibly based on the previous local history at the client.*

For strict quorum systems, the access strategy allows the system to contact any of the quorums, as long as every write quorum intersects with a read quorum. In probabilistic quorum systems, the access strategy is probabilistic and the quorum is chosen at random, ignoring the local history at the client. In Section 6 we present protocols which provide stronger non-probabilistic consistency guarantees, using an access strategy that is dependent on the client's local history.

Definition 3. *A* configuration C *of a system specifies the state of each node in the system (either as accessible or inaccessible).*

For systems with independent failures, the probability of the system being in a configuration C, with K accessible nodes, is $P(C) = \binom{n}{k}(1 - p_f)^k p_f^{n-k}$.

An operation of a client is *successful* in a given configuration if the quorum set that should be accessed as specified by the access strategy (or one of the quorum sets, if the strategy specifies more than one valid set) consists of elements that are all available.

In what follows we define the availability for systems in which the scheduler is not adversarial. The availability of the system is only defined during periods in which the system is well behaved, i.e. periods where any message sent from a non-crashed node to another non-crashed node is guaranteed to be delivered within a fixed (may be unknown) time bound. If the network is asynchronous then an adversarial scheduler can delay all messages arbitrarily to stall any system from making progress, hence making the system unavailable and any definition of availability meaningless.

Definition 4. *The availability of the system for reads,* $a_r(C, t)$, *in a given configuration* C *over a time interval of duration* t, *is defined as the ratio of successful reads to the total number of reads in an interval of time of length* t *when the system is in the specified configuration* C.

Definition 5. *The availability of the system for reads, $a_r(C)$, in a given config-uration C is the probability that a read operation is successful when the system is in configuration C.* [1]

Let t be the random variable denoting the duration of a configuration C and whose probability distribution is determined by the failure behavior of the nodes. Let $t_1, t_2, \ldots$ denote the various realizations (time durations of configuration C) of t in an execution. If $succ_i$ denotes the number of successful reads, and tot_i denotes the number of attempted reads in the ith realization, then

$$a_r(C) = \lim_{m \to \infty} \frac{\sum_{i=1}^{m} succ_i}{\sum_{i=1}^{m} tot_i}$$

Definition 6. *The availability of the system for reads, a_r is defined as the ex-pected availability, $E[a_r(C)]$, over all the possible configurations.*

We define the availability of the system for writes, $a_w(C, t)$, $a_w(C)$, and a_w on lines similar to the availability definitions for reads.

Definition 7. *The availability of a Quorum System, is defined as the fraction of successful operations when the network is synchronous.*

Our definitions are a generalization of the definitions used previously in [11,14,20]. In the traditional quorum systems and probabilistic quorum systems, where the access strategy is independent of the local history, the availability $a_r(C, t)$ and $a_w(C, t)$ will be independent of t. However, this may not be the case if the access strategy is dependent on the local history.

5   Bounds on Increase in Availability

Consider a quorum system Q which provides a bounded staleness of K. For any configuration C, let $w_Q(C)$ be the write availability and $r_Q(C)$ be the read availability of the quorum system in the configuration C.

Let γ_r and γ_w be the rates of read and write operations in the system, and let $\tau(C)$ be the expected duration of a configuration C (we assume that the rates of read and writes are constants, but the results still apply by replacing the rates with expected rates).

Lemma 1. *If C is a configuration with l nodes that are up and $n - l$ nodes that are down, then the expected duration of the configuration, $\tau(C)$, is $\geq \frac{1}{\frac{l}{mttf} + \frac{n-l}{mttr}}$*

Proof. Consider a small duration of time dt. The probability of particular node, that is currently crashed, recovering during an interval of length dt is $\frac{dt}{mttr}$. Similarly, the probability of a node crashing is $\frac{dt}{mttf}$.

---

[1] This definition does not depend on the distribution of read operations if that distri-bution is independent from that of system configurations.

In configuration C, there are l nodes that are up and $n - l$ nodes that are down. Therefore the probability that the system, currently in configuration C, changes to some other configuration during an interval of time of length dt is $\leq \left(\frac{l}{mttf} + \frac{n-l}{mttr} \right) dt$. Hence, the expected duration for which a configuration lasts, $\tau(C)$, is $\geq \frac{1}{\frac{l}{mttf} + \frac{n-l}{mttr}}$.

For systems where nodes are available with a probability > 0.5, $mttf > mttr$ and

$$\tau(C) \geq \frac{1}{\frac{l}{mttf} + \frac{n-l}{mttr}} \geq \frac{1}{\frac{l}{mttr} + \frac{n-l}{mttr}} = \frac{mttr}{n} = \tau_{min}$$

The expected duration of any configuration is at least $\tau_{min} = \frac{mttr}{n}$. Let $AC(K)$ denote the set of all configurations C such that K writes can be executed successfully in C and a read can be executed successfully after K writes are executed in C.

Lemma 2. *For any configuration $C_i \in AC(K)$, there exist two sets $W(C_i)$ and $R(C_i)$ that are available during the configuration C_i and, $W(C_i) \cap R(C_i) \neq \emptyset$.*

Proof. If $C_i \in AC$, it follows that there can be K successful writes in the configuration C_i and a successful read after the kth write. Let R be the read quorum that was used for the successful read after the kth write. Let $W_1, W_2, \ldots, W_K$ be the set of servers contacted during the K successful writes. Since the system provides bounded staleness, it follows that

$$R \cap \bigcup_{j=1}^{j=k} W_j \neq \emptyset$$

Choose $W(C_i) = \bigcup_{j=1}^{j=k} W_j$ and $R(C_i) = R$. Since each W_j and R is available in C_i it follows that $W(C_i)$, and $R(C_i)$ are available in C_i.

Lemma 3. *For any two configurations, $C_i, C_j \in AC(K)$, $W(C_i) \cap R(C_j) \neq \emptyset$.*

Proof. Consider the configuration in which all nodes are accessible. Since the scheduler can be adversarial, it can arbitrarily delay messages from the writer to all nodes in $\mathcal{P} \setminus W(C_i)$, hence forcing the next K writes to be written to nodes in $W(C_i)$. Later, it can delay the messages from the reader to the nodes in $\mathcal{P} \setminus R(C_j)$, so that the reader is forced to choose $R(C_j)$ as the read quorum. Since the read is guaranteed to return one of the K latest written values, it follows that $W(C_i) \cap R(C_j) \neq \emptyset$

Lemma 4. *Let C be a configuration. If $C \notin AC(K)$, then $w_Q(C) + r_Q(C) \leq 1 + \epsilon$, where $\epsilon = \frac{k}{\gamma_w \tau_{min}}$.*

Proof. If $C \notin AC(K)$, there are two cases: either there are no more than K writes that can occur in C, or there is no read that can occur after the Kth write in C.

– If there are no more than K writes that can occur in C, then

$$w_Q(C) = \lim_{m \to \infty} \frac{\sum_{i=1}^{m} succ_i}{\sum_{i=1}^{m} tot_i} \leq \lim_{m \to \infty} \frac{mK}{\sum_{i=1}^{m} tot_i}$$

$$= \lim_{m \to \infty} \frac{mK}{m\gamma_w \tau(C)} = \frac{K}{\gamma_w \tau(C)} \leq \frac{K}{\gamma_w \tau_{min}}$$

$$w_Q(C) + r_Q(C) \leq \frac{K}{\gamma_w \tau_{min}} + 1 = 1 + \epsilon$$

– Let t be the time in the configuration by which the Kth write succeeded. If there are no successful reads after the Kth write, then all reads up to t can succeed but all later reads fail. Also there are at most K writes succeeding up to t, and writes after time t may succeed.

$$r_Q(C) \leq \frac{t}{\tau(C)}$$

$$w_Q(C) \leq \frac{K + \gamma_w(\tau(C) - t)}{\gamma_w \tau(C)}$$

$$w_Q(C) + r_Q(C) \leq \left(1 + \frac{K}{\gamma_w \tau(C)}\right) \leq \left(1 + \frac{K}{\gamma_w \tau_{min}}\right) = 1 + \epsilon$$

Consider the quorum system $Q'(\mathcal{W}', \mathcal{R}')$, where $\mathcal{W}' = \{W(C_i)|C_i \in AC(K)\}$, and $\mathcal{R}' = \{R(C_i)|C_i \in AC(K)\}$. Q' is a strict quorum system, that is available in all configurations $C \in AC(K)$.

Theorem 1. *The read and write availability of the strict quorum system, Q' is $\geq r_Q + w_Q - 1 - \frac{2\epsilon}{1-\epsilon}$*

Proof. The strict quorum system Q' is available, for both reads and writes, during any configuration $C \in AC(K)$. Let $P(C)$ denote the probability that the system is in configuration C, and let $P_{AC(K)} = \sum_{C \in AC(K)} P(C)$. The read availability of Q', $r_{Q'} \geq \sum_{C \in AC(K)} P(C) = P_{AC(K)}$. Similarly, $w_{Q'} \geq P_{AC(K)}$. For the bounded-staleness quorum system, Q,

$$w_Q = \sum P(C)w_Q(C) = \sum_{C \in AC(K)} P(C)w_Q(C) + \sum_{C \notin AC} P(C)w_Q(C)$$

$$\leq \sum_{C \in AC(K)} P(C) + \sum_{C \notin AC(K)} P(C)w_Q(C)$$

$$r_Q \leq \sum_{C \in AC} P(C) + \sum_{C \notin AC} P(C)r_Q(C)$$

$$w_Q + r_Q \leq 2 \sum_{C \in AC} P(C) + \sum_{C \notin AC} P(C)\big(r_Q(C) + w_Q(C)\big)$$

$$\leq 2 \sum_{C \in AC} P(C) + \sum_{C \notin AC} P(C)\big(1 + \epsilon\big)$$

$$\leq 2P_{AC} + (1 - P_{AC})(1 + \epsilon)$$

Therefore,

$$P_{AC} \geq \frac{w_Q + r_Q - 1 - \epsilon}{1 - \epsilon} > w_Q + r_Q - 1 - \frac{2\epsilon}{1 - \epsilon}$$

It follows that $w_{Q'}, r_{Q'} > w_Q + r_Q - 1 - \frac{2\epsilon}{1-\epsilon}$

Theorem 1 shows that the increase in availability due to relaxing the consistency guarantees to K-safe is dependent on the rate of write operations γ_w, and the expected duration τ_{min} of a configuration. τ_{min} increases *linearly* with the mean-time-between-failure for the nodes. Hence, for a large *mtbf*, the value of $\epsilon = \frac{K}{\gamma_w \tau_{min}}$ will be small. In such cases, if highly available K-safe quorum systems can be built, then a highly available strict quorum systems can also be built i.e. there is not much advantage gained by relaxing the consistency semantics to K-safe. However, for systems with a small *mtbf*, it may be possible to increase the availability and at the same time provide bounded staleness. We show a protocol to achieve this in section 6.

6 K-Quorums Protocols

We present K-quorum construction, for a single-writer-multiple-reader environment, which guarantees bounded staleness even in the presence of an adversarial scheduler. In Section 6.2, we prove that the proposed protocol achieves K-atomic semantics.

6.1   Construction and Protocols

A K-quorum system consists of a strict quorum system, $(\mathcal{R}, \mathcal{W})$, and a staleness parameter K that is the bound on the staleness allowed.

Read operations in K-quorums are similar to reads in strict quorum systems. At a high level, the reader contacts a quorum of servers $R \in \mathcal{R}$ and chooses the latest value. The writes are different. In K-quorums, a value is written to a subset of $\mathcal{P}$, such that the servers contacted during K consecutive writes form a write-quorum $W \in \mathcal{W}$. We henceforth call the set of servers contacted during a particular write a *partial-write-quorum*.

The single-writer-multiple-reader protocol for K-quorums, is shown in figure 1. For simplicity, the protocol presented assumes reliable channels. The protocol can be made to work with fair channels by using standard techniques, for building a reliable channels over fair channels, as described in [12].

Write operation. To perform a write operation the writer chooses a partial-write-quorum, and writes the value along with other meta-data to the partial-write-quorum. To ensure bounded staleness we require that any K partial-write-quorums, used for successive writes, collectively contain a write quorum. Formally, let W_i be the partial-write-quorum used in the ith write. We require that

$$\forall i : \exists W \in \mathcal{W} \ such \ that \ W \subseteq \bigcup_{j=i-K+1}^{i} W_j$$

```
// Writer Protocol
static k := 0; static ts := 0;
void Write( v )
begin
    ts := ts + 1; k := k + 1;
    find an available partial-write-quorum W_k such that ∃W ∈ W : W ⊆ ⋃_{i=k-K+1}^{i=k} W_i
    send (v, ts, PW) to servers in W_k, where PW = ⋃_{i=k-K+1}^{i=k-1} W_i
    wait for acknowledgments from servers in W_k
end
```

```
// Reader Protocol
int Read
begin
    find an available read quorum R
    send read requests to servers in R
    wait for replies from all servers
    calculate (v, ts, PW) := value with the largest time stamp
    write back the value (v, ts, PW) to a partial-write-quorum, W_r
        such that ∃W ∈ W : W ⊆ PW ∪ W_r
    wait for acknowledgments from servers in W_r
    return(v, ts, PW)
end
```

Fig. 1. K-quorum protocols

The protocol for write is shown in Figure 1. During the ith write, the writer writes the value v, the timestamp – ts, and the set PW of servers accessed in the previous $(K - 1)$ writes to each of the servers in W_i.

Read operation. Reads in K-quorums are similar to reads in strict quorum systems. The reader collects replies from a quorum of servers and chooses the reply (v, ts_{hst}, PW) with the largest time stamp. The reader then writes back the tuple (v, ts_{hst}, PW) to a set of servers W' such that $\exists W \in \mathcal{W} : W \subseteq PW \cup W'$. The protocol for a read is shown in Figure 1. Since a read quorum always intersects with one of the previous K partial-write-quorums, a read is guaranteed to return one of the K latest written values irrespective of the behavior of the scheduler.

6.2 K-Atomic Semantics

To prove that the protocols achieve $K - atomic$ semantics, we show the existence of an ordering that is consistent with real time order such that, each read returns the value written by one of the previous K writes. We define

Definition 8. *The* written-time *is the (global) time at which a value that is being written reaches (and is processed by) every server in partial-write-quorum.*

We will order the reads and writes such that :

- Writes are ordered according to their *written-time*.
- A read which returns a value (v, t, PW), which was written with timestamp t, can be scheduled any time between
  1. The written-time, τ_t of the value returned, (v, t, PW).
  2. and, before the written-time of the next K^{th} write, $(v', t + K, PW')$. i.e. before τ_{t+K}.

It is easy to see that, such an ordering satisfies the requirements of K-atomic semantics. We need to show that such a ordering can be done in a manner consistent with local history.

The scheduling of writes is trivial, because written-time of a write occurs between the time a write has begun and before the write ends.

We now show, by contradiction, that reads can also be scheduled. Assume, if possible, that the read interval does not overlap with the interval $[\tau_t, \tau_{t+K})$. There are two cases:

1. Read finishes before τ_t:
   This scenario is not possible, because a read completes only after performing a write-back on the value. Therefore a read can end only after the written-time of the value it returns.
2. Read begins after τ_{t+K}.
   Consider the union of the partial write quorums for K previous writes – $W = W_{t+1} \cup W_{t+2} \cup \ldots \cup W_{t+K}$. From the definition of a partial-write-quorum and the fact that any read quorum intersects with a (complete) write quorum, it follows that the reader would have received a value from at least one server in W. Since the reader chooses the highest time-stamp received, a read that starts after τ_{t+K} cannot return a value written before τ_K, which is a contradiction. $\Rightarrow\Leftarrow$

Theorem 2. *Protocols described in Figure 1 provide K-atomic semantics* $\square$

6.3 Availability

In environments with a relatively small $mtbf$, K-quorum systems can be used to achieve a higher availability than strict quorum systems. Consider a K-quorum system with staleness parameter K and where the read and write quorum sizes are rn and wn respectively. Let $r = rn/n$ and $w = wn/n$. Since the read and write (not partial write) quorums need to intersect, we require $r + w \geq \frac{n+1}{n}$.

For a read to be available, we need rn nodes out of n nodes. This can be made strictly smaller than the availability of majority if $r \leq 0.5$ and the goal is to simultaneously make the write availability be better than that of majority. For a system, where $mtbf$ is *relatively* small, the write availability is the probability of being able to access $\frac{wn}{K}$ nodes out of $\left(n - \frac{K-1}{K}wn\right)$ nodes (the availability of a given write is independent of that of previous writes). For a given n and p_f, with appropriate choice of r, w and K, even the write availability of the system can be increased. For example, consider a case where $n = 100$ and $p_f = 0.5$. The majority quorum system will be available with a probability 0.46. With K-quorums, using a read quorum of size 29, a write quorum of size 72 and a staleness bound of $K = 6$ can provide much better availability for both reads and writes. Reads are available with probability 0.99999 (29 out of 100 available), while writes are available with probability 0.997 (12 out of 40 available). Also, if the system is well behaved the probability that a read will get the value of the most recent write is 0.99.

For a given system size n, probability of failure p_f and staleness parameter K, choosing the optimal values for r and w presents similar trade-offs as in strict quorum system. For having a large read availability it is desirable to have a small value for r. Similarly, for having a large write availability, it is desirable to have a small value for w. However as we require that $r + w \geq \frac{n+1}{n}$, choosing a small value for r or w will require the other to be large, resulting in decreased write or read availability respectively. For optimal overall availability, this trade-off needs to be resolved based on the relative frequencies of reads and writes in the system, such that the overall availability is maximized.

Effect of $mtbf$ on Signed Quorum Systems. Realizing that the performance of K-quorum systems is highly dependent on the mean time between failure, we investigated their effect on the performance of systems such as signed quorum systems. We found that the performance of signed quorum systems deteriorates in environments in which the mean-time-between-failures is smaller than the mean time between a write and a read. One explanation for this is that if the system has a small mean time to failure, then nodes go up and down very quickly, so it is more likely that the reader and the writer see two different configurations of the system, thereby causing mismatches. For RON traces, where there are no node failures, the probability of mismatch due to network faults alone was found to be 0.05. However, in systems where $mtbf$ is small to the mean time between a write and a read, the probability of mismatch can be much higher even when ignoring network faults.

Lemma 5. *In a system with a small $mtbf$, if nodes are inaccessible with a probability p_f, then probability of mismatch ignoring any network faults is $2p_f(1-p_f)$.*

Proof. (sktech) For systems with a small $mtbf$, the expected duration of a configuration is small. So, the configuration of the system can change widely between the time a value is written to the system and the time when the value is read. For this setting the probability that a server if down during the read operation is independent of the probability of the server is down during the write operation. The probability that a node is accessible during a read, but not accessible during a write is $(1 - p_f)p_f$. Similarly the probability that a node is accessible during a write, but not accessible during a read is $p_f(1 - p_f)$. Therefore the probability of mismatch is at least $2p_f(1 - p_f)$, which can be as high as 0.5 depending on the value of p_f.

7 Related Work

There is a very large body of work on quorum systems and access semantics. In this section we concentrate on those works that are most closely related to the results of this paper.

Quorum systems are used for various distributed applications including replication, mutual exclusion, and consensus. The performance measures for quorum systems like load, availability and probe complexity, are mutually opposing – improving one tends to worsen the other. With large scale internet usage, researchers have been mainly focusing on improving the availability of the system [1,2,4,6,18,19]. Naor and Wool prove some basic bounds between the load and the availability of traditional quorum systems [13].

Lamport presents consistency semantics that have been widely used in the literature [9] . Traditional quorum systems, where any two quorum sets have a non-empty intersection, provide at least safe-semantics. However, these systems are not very highly available. Fox and Brewer [5] show bounds on availability in the presence of strong consistency guarantees.

Relaxing the consistency guarantees can allow systems to achieve better availability or performance. For database applications, a number of researchers ([8,16] for example) discuss weakened consistency semantics for increased concurrency. Epsilon consistency [16] attempts to increase availability by allowing query accesses to see some temporary inconsistencies in the data, however these inconsistencies are bounded and the system converges to a global serializability. Krishnamurthy et al present bounded ignorance [8], for increasing the concurrency in database applications, where the application may be unaware of at most N transactions. [7,15,17] implement file systems that provide various relaxed semantics. TACT is a toolkit that allows for dynamic changes in the consistency level of the system and can be used to specify various kinds of weakened semantics.

Probabilistic approaches to quorum systems [11,20] achieve a much higher availability than strict quorum systems by weakening the consistency. Lee and Welch [10] propose probabilistic relaxed semantics for use with probabilistic system. These systems provide a probabilistic bound on the violation of safe-semantics. However, as discussed in section 2, these systems are vulnerable to an adversarial scheduler and provide no bounds on the staleness of data.

References

1. D. S. Amr El Abbadi and F. Cristian. An efficient and fault-tolerant protocol for replicated data management. In *Proc. PODS*, 1985.
2. D. S. Amr El Abbadi and F. Cristian. Maintaining availability in partioned replicated databases. In *Proc. PODS*, 1986.
3. D. G. Andersen, H. Balakrishnan, M. F. Kaashoek, and R. Morris. Resilient overlay networks. In *Proc. 18th SOSP*, pages 131–145, 2001.
4. D. L. Eager and K. C. Sevcik. Achieving robustness in distributed database systems. *ACM Trans. Database Syst.*, 8(3):354–381, 1983.
5. A. Fox and E. A. Brewer. Harvest, yield and scalable tolerant systems. In *Wkshp on Hot Topics in Op Sys*, pages 174–178, 1999.

6. D. K. Gifford. Weighted voting for replicated data. In *Proc. 7th SOSP*, pages 150–162, New York, NY, USA, 1979. ACM Press.

7. R. G. Guy, J. S. Heidemann, W. Mak, T. W. Page, Jr., G. J. Popek, and D. Rothmeir. Implementation of the Ficus Replicated File System. In *Proceedings of the Summer 1990 USENIX Conference*, pages 63–71, June 1990.

8. N. Krishnakumar and A. J. Bernstein. Bounded ignorance in replicated systems. In *Proc. PODS*, pages 63–74, New York, NY, USA, 1991. ACM Press.

9. L. Lamport. On interprocess communication. part i: Basic formalism. *Distributed Computing*, 1(2):77–101, 1986.

10. H. Lee and J. L. Welch. Randomized registers and iterative algorithms. *Distributed Computing*, 17(3):209–221, 2005.

11. D. Malkhi, M. K. Reiter, A. Wool, and R. N. Wright. Probabilistic quorum systems. *Inf. Comput.*, 170(2):184–206, 2001.

12. J.-P. Martin, L. Alvisi, and M. Dahlin. Small Byzantine quorum systems. In *DSN*, pages 374–383, June 2002.

13. M. Naor and A. Wool. The load, capacity, and availability of quorum systems. *SIAM Journal on Computing*, 27(2):423–447, 1998.

14. D. Peleg and A. Wool. The availability of quorum systems. *Inf. Comput.*, 123(2):210–223, 1995.

15. K. Petersen, M. J. Spreitzer, D. B. Terry, M. M. Theimer, and A. J. Demers. Flexible update propagation for weakly consistent replication. In *Proc. 16th SOSP*, 1997.

16. C. Pu and A. Leff. Replica control in distributed systems: An asynchronous approach. In *SIGMOD Conference*, pages 377–386, 1991.

17. M. Satyanarayanan, J. J. Kistler, P. Kumar, M. E. Okasaki, E. H. Siegel, and D. C. Steere. Coda: A highly available file system for a distributed workstation environment. *IEEE Transactions on Computers*, 39(4):447–459, 1990.

18. D. Skeen and D. D. Wright. Increasing availability in partitioned database systems. In *Proc. PODS*, pages 290–299, New York, NY, USA, 1984. ACM Press.

19. H. G.-M. Susan Davidson and D. Skeen. Consistency in partioned network. *Computing Survey*, 17(3), 1985.

20. H. Yu. Signed quorum systems. In *Proc. 23rd PODC*, pages 246–255. ACM Press, 2004.

21. H. Yu and A. Vahdat. The costs and limits of availability for replicated services. In *Proc. 18th SOSP*, pages 29–42, 2001.

Musical Benches*

Eli Gafni and Sergio Rajsbaum

[1] Computer Science Department, UCLA, Los Angeles, CA 90024, USA
eli@cs.ucla.edu
[2] Math Institute, UNAM, Ciudad Universitaria, D.F. 04510, Mexico
rajsbaum@math.unam.mx

Abstract. We propose the *musical benches problem* to model a wait-free coordination difficulty that is orthogonal to previously studied ones such as agreement or symmetry breaking (leader election or renaming). A *bench* is the usual binary consensus problem for 2 processes. Assume $n+1$ processes want to sit in n benches as follows. Each one starts with a preference, consisting of a bench and one place (left or right) in the bench where it wants to sit. Each process should produce as output the place of the bench where it decides to sit. It is required that no two processes sit in different places of the same bench. Upon the observance of a conflict in one of the benches an undecided process can "abandon" its initial bench and place and try to sit in another bench at another place.

The musical benches problem is so called because processes jump from bench to bench trying to find one in which they may be alone or not in conflict with one another. If at most one process starts in each bench, the problem is trivially solvable– each process stays in its place. We show that if there is just one bench where two processes rather than one, start, the problem is wait-free unsolvable in read/write shared memory. This impossibility establishes a new connection between distributed computing and topology, via the Borsuk-Ulam theorem.

The musical benches problem seems like just a collection of consensus problems, where by the pigeon hole principle at least one of them will have to be solved by two processes. Consequently, one is tempted to try to find a bivalency impossibility proof of the FLP style. Our second result shows that there is no such proof: We present an algorithm to solve the musical benches problem using set agreement, a primitive stronger than read/write registers, but weaker than consensus. Thus, an FLP-style impossibility for musical benches will imply an FLP-style impossibility of set-consensus.

The musical benches problem can be generalized by considering benches other than consensus, such as set agreement or renaming, leading to a very interesting class of new problems.

1 Introduction

We consider an n processes asynchronous, single-writer/multi-reader shared memory system, where any number of processes may fail by crashing. A pro-

---

* This work has been supported by a grant from LAFMI (Franco-Mexican Lab in Computer Science), and from UNAM-PAPIIT

tocol in this model is *wait-free*: it guarantees that any process will terminate within a fixed number of steps, independent of the level of contention and the execution speeds of the other processes. Understanding the possibilities and limitations of this model is central to distributed computing for several reasons. Impossibility results in this model translate to impossibility results for a model where at most t processes can crash [9], sometimes with more powerful primitives [21], or translate into lower bounds on the round complexity of synchronous systems [14,17]. Indeed, some papers [25,27] have developed unified frameworks to study synchrony, asynchrony and even partial synchrony, where our wait-free model plays a central role. Furthermore, this model has been shown to have the same computational power as other models, such as message passing when $t < n/2$ [2].

The fundamental problem of wait-free computation is to characterize the circumstances under which synchronization problems have wait-free solutions, and to derive efficient solutions when they exist. This is a difficult problem because one must reason about complex algorithms that operate in the presence of uncertainty and partial information created by non-determinism, asynchrony, and failures. Powerful new tools have been developed based on algebraic topology for analyzing the semantics and complexity of distributed algorithms in a variety of models and architectures; see the surveys and tutorials [18,22,26] and references herein. We use such tools in this paper both to prove impossibility results and to derive algorithms.

Distributed computing theory development has been fostered by the identification of particular problems, that capture the essence of wait-free coordination difficulties. First, *consensus* [13] and *set agreement* [11] serve to model the difficulty of processes to converge on a small number of decisions. Other similar problems have been identified, like *approximate agreement* [12], or *loop agreement* [24]. The problems of *renaming* [3] and leader election [33] model the opposite difficulty: breaking symmetry.

This paper proposes a new schema to model a coordination difficulty that is orthogonal to the ones described above. It is inspired by the *musical chairs* game, where players march to music around a row of chairs numbering one less than the players and scramble for places when the music stops. The paper studies the *musical benches problem*. A *bench* is the usual binary consensus problem for 2 processes. Assume $n + 1$ processes want to sit in n benches as follows. Each one starts with a preference, consisting of a bench and one place (left or right) in the bench where it wants to sit. Each process should produce as output the place of the bench where it decides to sit. It is required that no two processes sit in different places of the same bench. Upon the observance of a conflict in one of the benches an undecided process can "abandon" its initial bench and place and try to sit in another bench at another place.

The musical benches problem is so called because processes jump from bench to bench trying to find one in which they may be alone or not in conflict with one another. If at most one process starts in each bench, the problem is trivially solvable– each process stays in its place. We show that if there is just one bench where two processes rather than one, start, the problem is wait-free unsolvable in read/write shared memory. This impossibility establishes a new connection between distributed computing and topology, via the Borsuk-Ulam theorem, a statement different in nature from previously used ones such as Sperner's lemma.

The musical benches problem can be generalized by considering benches other than consensus, such as set agreement or renaming, leading to an interesting class of new problems. The general idea is to consider a problem that is not solvable once the number of participants exceed some threshold, $k - 1$. We then replicate the problem as many times as we wish, calling each replica a bench, and wake up $k - 1$ processes in every bench but one, where we wake up k processes. Now we allow processes to jump from bench to bench each trying to acquire a valid seat in one of the benches, such that all those on the same bench comply with the bench seating requirement. For example, a $(2, 3)$-set agreement bench (3 processes need to agree on at most 2 different values) is wait-free solvable when there are at most 2 participants, but not when there are 3 or more; we would wake up 2 processes in every bench but one, where we wake up 3 processes. The *generalized musical benches conjecture* is that the schema always leads to an impossible problem.

In summary, our contributions are the following.

- The introduction of a schema that captures a new kind of distributed coordination difficulty, and the study of the binary consensus instantiation, the musical benches problem.
- An impossibility proof showing that the musical benches problem is wait-free unsolvable in read/write shared memory.
- This impossibility establishes a new connection between distributed computing and topology, via the Borsuk-Ulam theorem.
- An algorithm to solve the musical benches problem using set agreement, a primitive stronger than read/write registers, but weaker than consensus.

The musical benches problem seems like just a collection of consensus problems, and thus one is tempted to try to find a bivalency impossibility proof of the FLP style [13]. More precisely, by the pigeon hole principle at least one of the benches would have to be solved by two processes, since there are more processes than benches. Thus, two processes would have to solve consensus on that particular bench, contradicting FLP. The algorithm in the last item is significant because it shows that no bivalency argument of this style exists. Namely, it implies that if the musical benches problem is impossible then $(2, 3)$-set agreement is impossible. Thus, the existence of such a bivalency proof would imply the celebrated $(2, 3)$-set agreement impossibility [6,29,34]. But this impossibility requires Sperner's lemma, a higher dimensional statement for which no bivalency arguments are known.

The connection to a result as important as the Borsuk-Ulam theorem establishes one more significant bridge between distributed computing and topology. The theorem is "one of the most useful tools offered by elementary algebraic topology to the outside world" [31]. Recall that it implies Sperner's lemma (which is equivalent to Brouwer's fixed point theorem), but not the opposite.

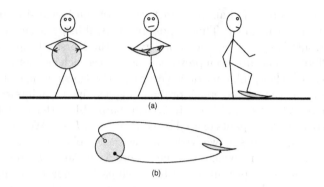

Fig. 1. Borsuk-Ulam Theorem in 2 dimensions

There are several equivalent versions of the Borsuk-Ulam theorem, the easiest to remember is illustrated in Figure 1 (from [31]), for the $n = 2$ dimensional case. It states that if you take a rubber ball, deflate and crumble it, and lay it flat, then there are two points on the surface of the ball that were diametrically opposite and now are lying on top of one another. More formally, we see in part (b) of the figure, that[1] for every continuous map $f : S^n \to \mathbb{R}^n$, there exist a point $x \in S^n$ such that $f(x) = f(-x)$.

The rest of this paper is organized as follows. In Section 2 we describe formally the musical benches problem. In Section 3 we show that it is impossible to solve wait-free in a read/write shared memory system. In Section 4 we present the algorithm that solves it using a $(2,3)$-set agreement object. Section 5 contains the conclusions. At the end there is an Appendix with some topology notions and additional details about our results.

2   The Musical Benches Problem

We consider the usual asynchronous shared memory model, composed of single-writer/multi-reader registers. In Section 4 we will extend the shared memory with $(2,3)$-set agreement objects. We now describe the binary-consensus musical benches problem, first intuitively and then more formally.

We can think of 2-process binary consensus as a bench with two places, designated 1 and -1. Processes p_1 and p_{-1}, wake up at places 1 and -1, respectively. In a solo execution a process must return the place it wakes up in. Otherwise, in an execution where both participate, they return the same place. This consensus task[2] is impossible to solve wait-free in the read-write shared-memory

---

[1] Where S^n is the n-dimensional unit sphere, and $\mathbb{R}^n$ the Euclidean space of dimension n.

[2] In the more usual description of consensus there is a set of possible inputs, and a process can wake up with any of these inputs. In our description a process has only one possible input, and different processes have different inputs. Both descriptions are equivalent, but the one we use is more comfortable for our purposes.

model [13,20], and trivially solvable if at most one process wakes up. We call an instance of this problem a *bench*. What will happen if we add a second bench, with places $2, -2$, and wake up either process p_2 at slot 2, or p_{-2} at slot -2, but not both? In executions with no conflict, i.e., either p_{-1} or p_1 wake up but not both, the participating processes return the places they wake up in. Only if both p_{-1} and p_1 wake up, then it is free-for-all and any participating process can go to any seat. Is the binary-consensus 2 benches problem read-write wait-free solvable? One feels a strong intuition (unlike in the set agreement impossibility) as to why it should not be solvable: if a process from bench 1 jumps to bench 2, it just creates the same problem in bench 2, since we have the freedom of who to wake up in bench 2 as to try to defeat consensus there. Indeed, the problem has no solution, but surprisingly, we later essentially prove that this intuition is not exactly right.

The musical benches problem is formalized in terms of the usual notion of *task*, a one-shot decision problem specified in terms of an input/output relation Δ. The processes start with private input values, and must eventually decide on output values, by writing to a write-once variable. The relation Δ specifies for each set of (ids, input values) pairs, what are the allowed output values for each id. In our case, each id is associated to a single input, so we may describe Δ as follows. The i-th *bench* is defined by the set of input vectors $\{(p_{-i}, p_i), (p_i), (p_{-i})\}$, and the relation:

$$\Delta(p_{-i}, p_i) = \{(-i, -i), (i, i)\},$$
$$\Delta(p_{-i}) = \{(-i)\},$$
$$\Delta(p_i) = \{(i)\}.$$

This is illustrated in Figure 2(a). It is sometimes convenient to consider only the output values, and disregard the processes ids, as depicted in Figure 2(b).

Consider an algorithm for processes p_{-i}, p_i where the first operation by a process is to write its id to shared memory, and that includes an operation to a write-once *decision variable*. A process *participates* in an execution if it executes its first operation. The *input vector* of an execution contains the ids of the participating processes. A process *decides* in an execution if it writes to the decision variable, and the value decided is the value written to the variable. The

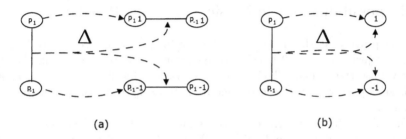

(a)   (b)

Fig. 2. The first consensus bench

output vector of an execution contains the values decided by the processes, or ⊥ if the process did not decide. The algorithm *solves* the i-th bench problem if in every execution with input vector I, the output vector O can be extended (by replacing ⊥ entries with other values) to a vector in $\Delta(I)$, and a process that does not fail decides.

The *musical benches problem* of size b is also a task specified in terms of a relation Δ. The input vectors are over $\{p_{-i}, p_i | 1 \leq i \leq b\}$, and the output vectors over $\{-i, i, \perp | 1 \leq i \leq b\}$. In this paper we study the case of $b = 2$, as illustrated in Figure 3, disregarding ids and omitting the dotted arrows of Δ for single vertices, to avoid cluttering the figure. Formally, Δ is:

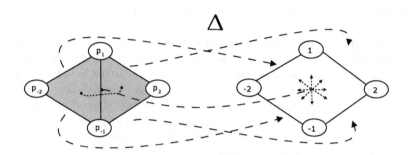

Fig. 3. Musical benches task

$$\Delta(p_{-1}, p_1, p_2) = \{(x_1, x_2, x_3) \, | \forall i, j, \; x_i \in \{1, -1, 2, -2\}, \; x_i + x_j \neq 0\}$$
$$\Delta(p_1, p_2) = \{(1, 2)\}$$
$$\Delta(p_{-1}, p_1) = \{(-1, -1), (1, 1), (-2, -2), (2, 2)\}$$
$$\Delta(p_{-1}) = \{(-1)\}$$
$$\Delta(p_1) = \{(1)\}$$

and so on for $\Delta(p_{-1}, p_1, p_{-2})$, $\Delta(p_1, p_{-2})$, $\Delta(p_{-1}, p_{-2})$, $\Delta(p_{-1}, p_2)$, $\Delta(p_{-2})$, and $\Delta(p_2)$. Notice it includes the first bench, and a restriction of the 2nd bench that disallows p_{-2} and p_2 participating together.

3   Impossibility of the Musical Benches Problem

Here we prove that the musical benches problem is wait-free unsolvable. For clarity we just prove the 2 benches case. Extension to any b is simple. For the proof we use the Borsuk-Ulam theorem, or rather, its discrete version, known as Tucker's lemma. We will need some basic topology notions, presented in the Appendix.

Tucker's lemma is described in [31] as follows. Let T be some (finite) triangulation of the n-dimensional ball B^n. We call T *antipodally symmetric on the boundary* if the set of simplices of T contained in $S^{n-1} = \partial B^n$ is a triangulation of S^{n-1} and it is antipodally symmetric; that is, if $\sigma \subset S^{n-1}$ is a simplex of T, then $-\sigma$ is also a simplex of T.

Theorem 1 (Tucker's lemma). *Let T be a triangulation of B^n that is antipodally symmetric on the boundary. Let*

$$\lambda : V(T) \longrightarrow \{1, -1, 2, -2, \ldots, n, -n\}$$

be a labeling of the vertices of T that satisfies $\lambda(-v) = -\lambda(v)$ for every vertex $v \in \partial B^n$ (that is, λ is antipodal on the boundary). Then there exists a 1-simplex (an edge) in T that is **complementary**; *i.e., its two vertices are labeled by opposite numbers.*

We will only need the 2-dimensional version, illustrated in Figure 4.

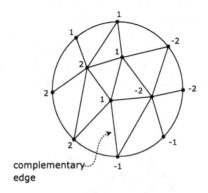

Fig. 4. Illustration of 2-dimensional Tucker's lemma

A task and an algorithm solving it can be represented geometrically using topology terminology, e.g. [23,29]. A task specification for $n + 1$ processes is given by an input complex $\mathcal{I}$, an output complex $\mathcal{O}$, and a relation Δ carrying each input simplex of $\mathcal{I}$ to a set of n-simplexes of $\mathcal{O}$. This definition has the following operational interpretation: $\Delta(S^m)$ is the set of legal final states in executions where only certain $m + 1$ processes corresponding to the vertices of S^m out of $n + 1$ processes participate (the rest fail without taking any steps). A protocol *solves* a task if when the processes run their programs, they start with mutually compatible input values, represented by a simplex S, communicate with one another, and eventually halt with some set of mutually compatible output values, representing a simplex in $\Delta(S)$. The musical benches problem of the previous section can be represented in this form by using simplices instead of vectors.

Any protocol that solves a task has an associated *protocol complex* $\mathcal{P}$, in which each vertex is labeled with a process id and that process's final state, called its *view*. Each simplex thus corresponds to an equivalence class of executions that "look the same" to the processes at its vertexes. For $0 \leq m \leq n$, we understand $\mathcal{P}(S^m)$ for a given S^m in the input complex to be the complex generated by all executions starting in S^m, in which only the processes in $ids(S^m)$ take part (the rest fail without taking any steps). If a simplex R is in $\mathcal{P}(S^m)$, we say that R is *reachable from* S^m.

Let $\mathcal{P}$ be the protocol complex for a protocol. If S is an input simplex, let $\mathcal{P}(S) \subset \mathcal{P}$ denote the complex of final states reachable from the initial state S. Expressed in the topology notation, we can see that a protocol solves a decision task $\langle \mathcal{I}^n, \mathcal{O}^n, \Delta \rangle$ if and only if there exists a color-preserving (i.e., process id-preserving) simplicial map $\delta : \mathcal{P} \rightarrow \mathcal{O}^n$, called a *decision map*, such that for every input simplex S, $\delta(\mathcal{P}(S)) \subset \Delta(S)$.

Our basic strategy is the following. We assume that we have a protocol with complex $\mathcal{P}$ that wait-free solves a task $\langle \mathcal{I}, \mathcal{O}, \Delta \rangle$. As in [8] without loss of generality we can assume that $\mathcal{P}$ is the result of some large enough number of iterated immediate snapshots. Let S^ℓ be an input simplex, $\mathcal{S}^\ell$ the complex of its faces, and $\mathcal{P}$ a protocol. For a wait-free model of computation, prior research (e.g. [5,6,34]) has shown that $\mathcal{P}(S^\ell)$ can be regarded as a subdivision of S^ℓ.

Assume there is an algorithm solving the musical benches problem with protocol complex $\mathcal{P}$. Let T be the input complex to the problem (illustrated in Figure 3). The next lemma shows that $\mathcal{P}(T)$ is a subdivision of T, as illustrated in the example of Figure 5.

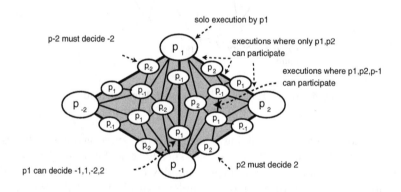

Fig. 5. A 1-round protocol subdividing the musical benches input complex

Lemma 1. *If T is the input complex to the musical benches problem then $\mathcal{P}(T)$ is a triangulation of B^2 that is antipodally symmetric on the boundary. Moreover, if λ is the labeling of the vertices of $\mathcal{P}(T)$ induced by the processes decisions, then λ is antipodal on the boundary.*

Sketch of Proof. First notice that $|T| \cong B^2$. Then, as mentioned above previous results imply that $\mathcal{P}(T)$ can be regarded as a subdivision of T, and hence as a triangulation of B^2. The boundary corresponds to executions with no conflict in bench 1, thus the problem specification implies that on a face (p_i, p_j) in the boundary processes return i and j, respectively. Since we take the same number of iterations on each face we can easily see that the triangulation is antipodally symmetric on the boundary of $\mathcal{P}(T)$. $\square$

Theorem 2. *There is no wait-free solution to the musical benches problem.*

Proof. It follows from Lemma 1 that we can apply Theorem 1 and conclude that there is an edge in $\mathcal{P}(T)$ that is complementary. Thus, its two vertices are labeled by opposite numbers, which means there is an execution where two processes decide opposite numbers, violating the musical benches problem consensus requirement.

4 Solving the Musical Benches Problem with More Powerful Primitives

We have seen that the binary-consensus musical benches problem is wait-free unsolvable in read/write shared memory. We show here that this impossibility implies the wait-free impossibility of solving $(2,3)$-set agreement in read/write shared memory [6,29,34]. We prove this by presenting an algorithm that solves the musical benches problem using a shared memory extended with $(2,3)$-set agreement objects. Our algorithm is described for the case of two benches (3 processes) since our main motivation is proving that no bivalency argument in the FLP style [13] exists for the musical benches. We know that the impossibility of $(2,3)$-set agreement cannot be proven without reference to the 2-connectivity of $\mathcal{P}$ for 3 processes [6,29,34].

A $(2,3)$-*set agreement object* can be accessed by 3 processes, and the object returns to a process one of the ids of a process that invoked it, such that at most 2 different ids are returned by the object. We assume w.l.o.g. that if a process p_i gets back from the object p_j, then p_j gets back itself, p_j [6].

The musical benches protocol appears in Figure 7. It accesses a single $(2,3)$-set agreement object. The main idea is to create a "hole" inside the immediate snapshots subdivision (of Figure 5), and we do this by doing participating set protocol [7] and sending all those stuck at level 3, to a $(2,3)$-set agreement object. A winner process that gets back its own id from the object stays at level 3. A loser, that gets back a different id, continues down to level 2 and proceeds with the participating set protocol. Since if all 3 are stuck at level 3, then at least one will lose, and we create the hole by preventing the formation of the all-see-all simplex in the center of the subdivision.

The code invokes a decision function f that takes as input a final *view* of a process and produces a decision value; it is specified in the Appendix. The corresponding protocol complex appears in Figure 6, together with the decision function f on each one of the final views. A process p_i computes its view, the pair $(S_i, view_i)$, by executing the protocol code, and it produces its decision value by applying f to its view (in the last line of the code).

The protocol works as follows. Local variables are subindexed by the process ids, and shared variables are not subindexed. The first part of the protocol is the

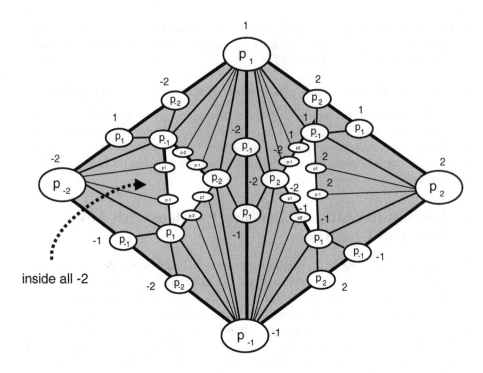

Fig. 6. The Musical Benches Protocol complex using $(2, 3)$-Set Agreement

Participating Set protocol of [7] for the case of 3 levels, except that it accesses a set agreement object. A process p_i computes in this part a set of ids S_i, such that

1. For all i, $i \in S_i$.
2. For all i, j, either $S_i \subseteq S_j$ or $S_j \subseteq S_i$.
3. For all i, j, if $i \in S_j$ then $S_i \subseteq S_j$.
4. There are at most two indices i, j such that $|S_i| = |S_j| = 3$.

The first three are the requirements of the participating set problem in [7]. Sets satisfying these properties correspond to the subdivided simplex in either side of Figure 5 (i.e., spanned by the corners p_{-1}, p_1, p_2 or p_{-1}, p_1, p_{-2}). The 4-th property is achieved through the set agreement object, invoked by p_i with the operation setAg(i). It has the effect of removing the simplex in the center of the subdivision (impossible that the three processes produce sets of size 3), and leaving just its boundary (at most two processes may produce sets of size 3). In the second part of the protocol only processes with sets of size 3 participate, and they compute the $view_i$ variables, which have the effect of subdividing this boundary. The following simple lemma implies that the complex of Figure 6 corresponds to the computed views $(S_i, view_i)$.

```
Initially:
    level[j] := 4 and id[j] := ⊥ for j ∈ {1, 2, 3}; OK_i := false; view_i = ∅;
    begin MB protocol(p_i)
        repeat
                    level[i] := level[i] − 1;
                    for j = 1 to 3 do level_i[j] := level[j] end for
                    S_i := {j : level_i[j] ≤ level[i], j ∈ {1, 2, 3}};
                    if |S_i| = 3 then       (* level[i] = 3 *)
                                        ans_i := setAg(i);
                                        if ans_i = i then OK_i := true
                                        end if
                    else                    (* level[i] < 3 or |S_i| < 3 *)
                                        OK_i := true
                    end if
        until |S_i| ≥ level[i] and OK_i;
        (* end of participating set section *)
        if |S_i| = 3 then
                    id[i] := i;
                    for j = 1 to 3 do id_i[j] := id[j] end for
                    view_i := {j : id_i[j] ≠ ⊥, j ∈ {1, 2, 3}};
        end if
        decide f(S_i, view_i)
    end protocol
```

Fig. 7. Musical Benches Protocol using $(2, 3)$-Set Agreement (for process p_i)

Lemma 2. *Let the views* $(S_i, view_i)$ *be the vertices of a complex* $\mathcal{C}$. *A simplex of* $\mathcal{C}$ *contains a set of vertices if they can be ordered such that both their* S_i's *and their* $view_i$'s *are ordered by containment. This complex* $\mathcal{C}$ *is well defined.*

The correctness of the MB protocol follows from this lemma, by proving that the decision function f does not produce a complementary edge, something that is easily verified in Figure 6 (and noting that on the boundary of $\mathcal{C}$ a process always decides its own id).

Theorem 3. *The MB protocol solves the musical benches problem.*

Notice that in Figure 6 there is a second subdivision, namely the one that subdivides the edges of the all-see-all simplex after the use of the set-agreement object. This subdivision is achieved through the use of read/write operations, and indeed it does not change the topological characteristics of the protocol complex (i.e., connectivity) [29]. It is nevertheless required to be able to associate output values to vertices without violating the problem specification e.g. [28].

5   Conclusions

We have introduced a scheme that models a new coordination difficulty, the *generalized musical benches problem*, that can be instantiated with any problem, which we call a *bench,* that is solvable for $k - 1$ participants, and is not solvable once the number of participants is at least k, for some threshold k. We have conjectured that the generalized musical benches problem is unsolvable for any such instantiation.

In this paper we studied the *musical benches problem,* which is the case obtained by using binary consensus benches. Recall that the consensus problem is impossible to wait-free solve in the read-write shared-memory model [13,20], but that it is solvable if we add a new possible output place, which is allowed to be returned in a non-solo execution (e.g. [30,32]). The "ambiguity of choosing" of [10] says that in a solution to the version with a new output place there exists an execution in which one process is "sitting" in one of two places, and like Heisenberg's uncertainty principle we cannot predict where it will appear, and hence the impossibility of solving the problem without the new place. We have seen the problem is unsolvable if we add an additional place. Namely, we have two new output places $-2, 2$ and wake up either process p_2 at slot 2, or p_{-2} at slot -2. The intuition behind this impossibility may seem more evident, than the impossibility of solving wait-free 3-processes 2-set agreement [6,29,34]. Processes p_1 and p_{-1} can resolve their differences only by at least one of them moving to the second bench. But then if (w.lo.g.) one of them moves to place 2, we wake up p_{-2}. Now we are almost at the mirror situation. To resolve the conflict at the second bench we would like to choose the place of a process in the first bench which might have stayed there, but this tantamount to 2-process consensus! It is then surprising that the musical benches impossibility problem is based on Borsuk-Ulam, a theorem more difficult to prove than Sperner's lemma, and not on a traditional bivalency argument.

In the "complement" to consensus benches, which we call 2-renaming benches (based on the renaming problem [3]), we have again two benches with places $1, -1, 2, -2$. Processes p_1 and p_{-1} both may wake at bench 1, while p_2 and p_{-2} wake up at the second bench, in place 2 or -2, respectively. We wake up either p_2 or p_{-2}, but not both. In executions in which not both p_1 and p_{-1} participate, processes return the place they woke up at. Else, all processes return distinct chairs. Again the intuition is evident. Processes p_1 and p_{-1} cannot resolve their differences in the first bench [5,23,29]. W.l.o.g at least one of them goes to the second bench, say place 2. We then wake up p_2, and have a mirror situation. We have a direct impossibility proof for this problem, similar to the one presented in this paper, as well as an impossibility proof by reduction from renaming. But nevertheless it is intriguing to find a single "meta-proof" that applies to both the renaming and the consensus instantiations of the generalized musical benches problem.

We showed that the impossibility of the musical benches problem implies the impossibility of 3-processes 2-set agreement, while the impossibility of renaming implies the impossibility of 2-renaming-benches. This puts the two problems somewhere between set agreement and renaming. Which is another step in understanding the R/W implementation relation between the set of R/W unsolvable tasks [15].

Acknowledgments. We are grateful to the anonymous referees for their comments.

References

1. Afek Y., Attiya H., Dolev D., Gafni E., Merritt M. and Shavit N., Atomic Snapshots of Shared Memory. *Journal of the ACM*, 40(4):873–890, 1993.
2. Attiya H., Bar-Noy A. and Dolev D., Sharing Memory Robustly in Message-Passing Systems. *Journal of the ACM*, 42(1): 124–142, 1995.
3. Attiya H., Bar-Noy A., Dolev D., Peleg D. and Reischuk R., Renaming In An Asynchronous Environment. *Journal of the ACM*, 37(3):524–548, 1990.
4. Attiya H. and Rachman O., Atomic Snapshots in $O(n \log n)$ Operations. *SIAM Journal of Computing*, 27(2):319-340, 1998.
5. Attiya H., Rajsbaum S., The Combinatorial Structure of Wait-Free Solvable Tasks. *SIAM J. Comput.* 31(4): 1286–1313, 2002.
6. Borowsky E. and Gafni E., Generalized FLP Impossibility Results for t-Resilient Asynchronous Computations. *Proc. 25th ACM Symposium on the Theory of Computing (STOC'93)*, ACM Press, pp. 91-100, June 1993.
7. Borowsky E. and Gafni E., Immediate Atomic Snapshots and Fast Renaming (Extended Abstract). *Proc. 12th ACM Symposium on Principles of Distributed Computing (PODC'93)*, ACM Press, pp. 41-51, August 1993.
8. Borowsky E. and Gafni E., A Simple Algorithmically Reasoned Characterization of Wait-Free Computations (Extended Abstract). *Proc. 16th ACM Symposium on Principles of Distributed Computing (PODC'97)*, ACM Press, pp. 189–198, August 1997.
9. Borowsky E., Gafni E., Lynch N. and Rajsbaum S., The BG Distributed Simulation Algorithm. *Distributed Computing,* 14(3):127–146, 2001.
10. Burns J. and Peterson G, The Ambiguity of Choosing. *Proc. 8th ACM Symposium on Principles of Distributed Computing (PODC)*, August 14–16, 1989, Edmonton, Alberta, Canada, pp. 145–157.
11. Chaudhuri S., More *Choices* Allow More *Faults:* Set Consensus Problems in Totally Asynchronous Systems. *Information and Computation,* 105:132-158, 1993.
12. Fekete A., Asymptotically Optimal Algorithms for Approximate Agreement. *Distributed Computing,* 4:9–29, 1990.
13. Fischer M.J., Lynch N.A. and Paterson M.S., Impossibility of Distributed Consensus with One Faulty Process. *Journal of the ACM*, 32(2):374-382, 1985.
14. Gafni, E. Round-by-Round Fault Detectors: Unifying Synchrony and Asynchrony (Extended Abstract). *Proc. 17th ACM Symposium on Principles of Distributed Computing (PODC)*, June 28–July 2, 1998, Puerto Vallarta, Mexico, pp. 143–152.
15. Gafni E. DISC/GODEL presentation: R/W Reductions. Oct. 4 2004. http://www.cs.ucla.edu/~ eli/eli/godel.ppt
16. Gafni E., Koutsoupias E., Three-Processor Tasks Are Undecidable. *SIAM J. Comput.* 28(3): 970–983, 1999.
17. Gafni E., Guerraoui R. and Pochon B., From a Static Impossibility to an Adaptive Lower Bound: The Complexity of Early Deciding Set Agreement. *Proc. 37th ACM Symposium on Theory of Computing (STOC'05)*, Baltimore (MD), May 2005.
18. Eric Goubault, *A historical note on "Geometry and Concurrency"*, http://www.di.ens.fr/~ goubault/index1.html
19. Havlicek J. Computable Obstructions to Wait-Free Computability. *Distributed Computing* 13(2): 59–83, 2000.

20. Herlihy M.P., Wait-Free Synchronization. *ACM Transactions on programming Languages and Systems*, 11(1):124-149, 1991.
21. Herlihy M., Rajsbaum S., The Decidability of Distributed Decision Tasks (Extended Abstract). *Proc. 29th ACM Symposium on the Theory of Computing (STOC'97)*, ACM Press, pp. 589-598, May 1997.
22. Herlihy M., Rajsbaum S., New Perspectives in Distributed Computing. *Proc. 24th International Symposium Mathematical Foundations of Computer Science (MFCS)*, in Miroslaw Kutylowski, Leszek Pacholski, Tomasz Wierzbicki (Eds.): Lecture Notes in Computer Science 1672, Springer, 170–186, 1999.
23. Herlihy H., Rajsbaum S., Algebraic spans. *Mathematical Structures in Computer Science* 10(4): 549–573, 2000.
24. Herlihy H., Rajsbaum S., A classification of wait-free loop agreement tasks. *Theor. Comput. Sci.* 291(1): 55–77, 2003.
25. Herlihy, M. Rajsbaum, S. and Tuttle, M. Unifying Synchronous and Asynchronous Message-Passing Models. *Proc. 17th ACM Symposium on Principles of Distributed Computing (PODC)*, June 28–July 2, 1998, Puerto Vallarta, Mexico, pp. 133–142.
26. Herlihy, M. Rajsbaum, S. and Tuttle, M. An Overview of Synchronous Message-Passing and Topology. *Electr. Notes Theor. Comput. Sci.* 39(2), 2001.
27. Herlihy, M. Rajsbaum, S. and Tuttle, M. An axiomatic approach to computing the connectivity of synchronous and asynchronous systems. *Proc. of the 6th workshop on Geometric and Topological Methods in Concurrency and Distributed Computing (GETCO)*, October 4, 2004.
28. Gunnar Hoest, Nir Shavit. Towards a Topological Characterization of Asynchronous Complexity (Preliminary Version). *Proc. 16th ACM Symposium on Principles of Distributed Computing (PODC)*, Santa Barbara, California, USA, August 21–24, pp. 199–208.
29. Herlihy M.P. and Shavit N., The Topological Structure of Asynchronous Computability. *Journal of the ACM*, 46(6):858-923, 1999.
30. Jayanti P., Chandra T. and Toueg S., Fault-tolerant wait-free shared objects. *Journal of the ACM*, 45(3):451-500, 1998.
31. Jiri Matousek, *Using the Borsuk-Ulam Theorem*, Lectures on Topological Methods in Combinatorics and Geometry, 2003, Springer.
32. Raynal, M., Real-time dependable decisions in timed asynchronous distributed systems. *Proc. 3rd Int. Workshop on Object-Oriented Real-Time Dependable Systems (WORDS 97)*. IEEE Computer Society Press, Newport Beach, 283–290, 1997.
33. Tel, G. *Introduction to Distributed Algorithms*, Cambridge University Press; 2 edition, February 15, 2001.
34. Saks M. and Zaharoglou F., Wait-Free k-Set Agreement is Impossible: The Topology of Public Knowledge. *SIAM Journal on Computing*, 29(5):1449-1483, 2000.

A   Appendix: Topology Notions

The unit ball $\{x \in I\!R^d : \| x \| \leq 1\}$ is denoted by B^d, while $S^{d-1} = \{x \in I\!R^d : \| x \| = 1\}$ is the $(d-1)$-dimensional unit sphere.

A *simplex* is a set of vertices, a *complex* is a set of simplexes closed under containment. The *dimension* d of a simplex σ is one less than its number of vertices, and is said to be a d-simplex, sometimes denoted σ^d. A subset of a simplex is called a *face*. It is sometimes convenient to assume a simplex σ is embedded in Euclidean space. For this its vertices are supposed to be affinely independent, and σ is the convex hull of its vertices. The union of all embedded simplices in a comlex $\mathcal{C}$, called the *polyhedron* of $\mathcal{C}$, is denoted $|\mathcal{C}|$, and can be regarded as the (point-set) union of the simplexes in $\mathcal{C}$. The *boundary* of an n-simplex is the subcomplex of σ^n obtained by deleting the single n-dimensional simplex and retaining all its faces.

A *triangulation* of a topological space X is a complex C such that $X \cong |X|$, namely with homeomorphic spaces. The simplest triangulation of the sphere S^{n-1} is the boundary of an n-simplex.

A *vertex map* carries vertices of one complex to vertices of another. A *simplicial map* is a vertex map that preserves simplexes, that is, it sends a set of vertices that form a simplex into a (possibly smaller) set of vertices that also form a simplex. In distributed computing we often consider *properly colored* complexes, where each vertex has associed a color, namely a process id, and no two vertices of the same simplex have the same id. For example, the complex in Figure 5 is colored. A simplicial map on properly colored complexes is *color preserving* if it associates vertexes of the same color. Notice that a color-preserving map preserves dimension.

A complex $\sigma(\mathcal{K})$ is a *subdivision* of a complex $\mathcal{K}$ if:

- each simplex in $\sigma(\mathcal{K})$ is contained in a simplex in $\mathcal{K}$, and
- each simplex of $\mathcal{K}$ is the union of finitely many simplexes in $\sigma(\mathcal{K})$.

Note that $|\mathcal{K}| = |\sigma(\mathcal{K})|$. If s is a point in $|\mathcal{K}|$, the *carrier* of s, denoted $carrier(s, \mathcal{K})$, is the unique smallest $T \in \mathcal{K}$ such that $s \in T$. As an example, the complex in Figure 5 is a subdivision of the complex in the left side of Figure 3.

B   Appendix: Decision Function of the Protocol

The MB protocol of Figure 7 uses a decision function f that is implicitly defined in Figure 6, by putting a number besides each vertex. Here we describe it explicitly by writing what is the view of the vertex, and what the value of f on that view $(S_i, view_i)$.

1. $f(S_i, view_i) = -2$ if $|S_i| = 2$ and $i = -1$.
2. $f(S_i, view_i) = -1$ if $|S_i| = 2$ and $i = 1$. **Otherwise:**
3. $f(S_i, view_i) = i$ if $|S_i| \leq 2$. **Otherwise:**
4. $f(S_i, view_i) = -2$ if $-2 \in S_i$. **Otherwise:**
5. $f(S_i, view_i) = 1$ if $view_i = \{-1\}$.
6. $f(S_i, view_i) = 2$ if $view_i = \{-1, 1\}$.
7. $f(S_i, view_i) = -1$ if $view_i = \{1\}$.
8. $f(S_i, view_i) = -1$ if $view_i = \{1, 2\}$ and $i = 1$.
9. $f(S_i, view_i) = -2$ if $view_i = \{1, 2\}$ and $i = 2$.
10. $f(S_i, view_i) = -2$ if $view_i = \{2\}$.
11. $f(S_i, view_i) = -2$ if $view_i = \{-1, 2\}$ and $i = -1$.
12. $f(S_i, view_i) = 1$ if $view_i = \{-1, 2\}$ and $i = 2$.

Obstruction-Free Algorithms Can Be Practically Wait-Free

Faith Ellen Fich[2], Victor Luchangco[1], Mark Moir[1], and Nir Shavit[1]

[1] Sun Microsystems Laboratories
[2] University of Toronto

Abstract. The obstruction-free progress condition is weaker than previous nonblocking progress conditions such as lock-freedom and wait-freedom, and as a result admits simpler implementations that are faster in the uncontended case. Pragmatic contention management techniques appear to be effective at facilitating progress in practice, but as far as we know, none *guarantees* progress.

We present a transformation that converts any obstruction-free algorithm into one that is wait-free when analyzed in the *unknown-bound* semisynchronous model. Because real-world systems satisfy the assumptions of the unknown-bound model, our result implies that, for all practical purposes, obstruction-free implementations can provide progress guarantees equivalent to wait-freedom. Our transformation does not diminish the practicality of the original obstruction-free algorithm and its original pragmatic contention manager.

1 Introduction

Researchers have invested substantial effort over the last decade in designing nonblocking shared data structure implementations, which aim to overcome the numerous problems associated with lock-based implementations. Despite this effort, designs satisfying traditional nonblocking progress conditions such as wait-freedom and—to a lesser extent—lock-freedom are usually complicated and expensive.

Significant progress in overcoming these problems has been achieved recently by designing implementations that satisfy the weaker *obstruction-free* nonblocking progress condition, which requires progress guarantees only in the (eventual) absence of interference from other operations. This weaker requirement allows simpler implementations that perform better in the common uncontended case. However, the lack of a progress guarantee under contention is not just a theoretical concern: such implementations are observed to suffer from livelock in practice. Therefore, obstruction-free implementations are combined with *contention management* techniques, which have proved effective in ensuring progress in practice. However, as far as we know none *guarantees* progress.

In this paper we show that the advantages of this pragmatic approach can be exploited *without* giving up strong progress guarantees. We do so by showing how to transform any obstruction-free implementation and its real-world contention

P. Fraigniaud (Ed.): DISC 2005, LNCS 3724, pp. 78–92, 2005.

manager so that it guarantees that every operation eventually completes, without diminishing the practicality of the original implementation.

By considering obstruction-free implementations, we significantly reduce the burden on the algorithm designer by eliminating the need to ensure progress under contention. Furthermore, because the underlying obstruction-free implementation behaves correctly in an asynchronous model of computation—that is, regardless of the relative execution speeds of different processes, whether some processes crash, etc.—designers of contention managers for obstruction-free implementations have a great deal of latitude. In particular, they can exploit timing information about the execution environment, for example to delay an operation to prevent it from interfering with another, without risk of jeopardising correctness. As a result, contention managers can be designed based on intuitively appealing heuristics, and several such contention managers developed recently appear to be effective in practice [13,15]. However, requiring contention managers to *guarantee* progress would impose a severe burden on their designers, and would thus largely eliminate the advantages gained by weakening the progress requirements of the underlying implementation. Our transformation shows that we can alleviate the burden on designers of *both* the underlying implementation *and* the contention manager, by transforming an obstruction-free algorithm and its practical contention manager into an equivalent implementation that guarantees progress.

The idea of combining an algorithm that is correct in an asynchronous model but does not guarantee progress with a mechanism that exploits timing information about the execution environment to ensure progress is not new. For example, failure detectors [1,2] can be used with asynchronous consensus algorithms to guarantee progress in the face of failures, and similarly the Disk Paxos algorithm [3] employs a leader election algorithm to ensure progress.

While these approaches share philosophy and advantages with the obstruction-free approach, there are significant differences both in motivation and in acceptable solution approaches. First, research on failure detectors primarily focuses on fault tolerance. Because it is known to be impossible to solve consensus in an asynchronous model in the presence of process crashes [4,5], it is *necessary* to exploit timing information of the execution environment in order to achieve acceptable solutions. In contrast, it has long been understood that we can implement any shared data structure so that it can tolerate process crashes, even in an asynchronous model [6], provided we use sufficiently strong synchronization primitives; such primitives are available in all modern shared memory multiprocessors. Even the weak obstruction-free progress condition guarantees that a crashed process cannot prevent progress by other processes. Thus, recent work on the obstruction-free approach to implementing nonblocking data structures is not motivated by fault tolerance, but by performance, simplicity of design, and separation of concerns: we achieve simpler implementations that perform better in the common uncontended case, and we allow the intuitive use of system-specific timing information in contention managers that attempt to facilitate progress, without allowing the implementation to behave incorrectly if timing assumptions are violated.

The Disk Paxos algorithm [3] uses a consensus algorithm to agree on transitions of a replicated state machine, but the consensus algorithm does not guarantee progress under contention. Therefore, the algorithm uses a leader election algorithm, and processes take steps of the consensus algorithm only when they believe themselves to be the leader. The leader election algorithm eventually ensures that exactly one process is the leader (provided some reasonable assumptions about system "stability" are eventually satisfied), and thereby ensures progress. This can be viewed as a form of contention management. However, such use of a leader election algorithm as a contention manager is not acceptable in the design of shared data structures, because it eliminates concurrency in the common case. This is natural in the case of Disk Paxos, because concurrent operations trying to reach consensus necessarily synchronize with each other, but operations on shared data structures should be able to proceed in parallel when they do not conflict. Therefore, we have taken care to design our transformation such that it uses its original contention manager as long as it is effective, and only attempts to serialize operations if this contention manager proves ineffective. This way, we guarantee that every operation eventually completes, while continuing to exploit the natural concurrency between nonconflicting operations.

Our transformation takes any obstruction-free shared data structure implementation and produces one in which every operation is guaranteed to eventually complete, provided the target system satisfies some weak timing assumptions— assumptions satisfied by all practical systems. The transformed implementation uses the original contention management mechanism of the implementation except when some process determines that it has executed an operation for too long without completing it. Unless this happens, the transformation introduces almost no overhead. Thus, in strengthening an implementation to provide progress guarantees, our transformation does not diminish the practicality of the original implementation.

The reasonable timing assumptions we consider for the target system are embodied by the *unknown-bound* semisynchronous model of computation [7,8]. Roughly speaking, this model assumes that some bound exists on the relative execution rates of any two processes in the system, but does not assume that the bound is known.

2   Background

Before presenting our transformation, we introduce background on nonblocking shared data structures, nonblocking progress conditions, and asynchronous and semisynchronous models of computation, and briefly describe some previous results that use semisynchronous models to analyze implementations.

2.1   Nonblocking Shared Data Structures

Today, almost all concurrent programs rely on blocking constructs such as mutual exclusion locks for synchronizing access to shared data structures. The use of locks introduces numerous problems, including deadlock, performance bottlenecks, and priority inversion [6]. Researchers have investigated nonblocking implementations in the hope of eliminating these problems.

An implementation of a shared data structure in a shared memory system provides a representation of the data structure using base objects in the system and provides algorithms for the processes of the system to perform *operations* on the data structure.

Most nonblocking algorithms are based on an *optimistic* approach to synchronization, in which an operation is attempted but may fail to take effect if another concurrent operation interferes. In this case, the operation is retried. A significant source of difficulty is guaranteeing that an operation is not retried repeatedly without ever completing. Generally, stronger nonblocking progress guarantees are more difficult to achieve, and require algorithms that are more complicated and more expensive.

2.2   Nonblocking Progress Conditions

A *wait-free* implementation [6] guarantees that when a process performs an operation, it completes the operation in a finite number of its own steps, regardless of how fast or slowly other processes execute, and even if they stop executing permanently. Such strong progress guarantees are attractive, but often very difficult to achieve. Most wait-free algorithms in the literature are too complicated and too expensive to be useful in practice.

A *lock-free* implementation guarantees that, starting from any state in which one or more processes are executing operations, *some* process will complete its operation within a finite number of steps. This weaker progress condition usually makes lock-free implementations easier to design than wait-free ones. Simple and practical lock-free implementations have been achieved for a small number of important data structures, such as stacks [9], queues [10], and worksteal-ing deques [11]. The weaker progress guarantee has generally been regarded as acceptable because well known contention management techniques such as *backoff* are effective at reducing contention when it arises, thereby achieving progress in practice, despite the lack of the strong theoretical guarantee of wait-freedom.

Herlihy et al. [12] recently proposed the obstruction-free approach to implementing nonblocking operations for shared data structures. An *obstruction-free* implementation simply guarantees that a process will complete its operation if it eventually executes enough steps without interference from other processes. Thus, if two or more processes repeatedly interfere with each other, it is possible that *none* of them completes its operation. The view is that, because contention management techniques such as backoff are required to achieve acceptable performance when contention arises anyway, it is unnecessary to make *any* progress guarantees in the case of contention between concurrent operations.

Several examples in the literature suggest that by providing only obstruction-free progress guarantees, significantly simpler implementations can be achieved that are faster in the uncontended case [12,13,14]. Furthermore, although an implementation that is obstruction-free but not lock-free will exhibit livelock if contention is ignored, experience shows that livelock can be effectively avoided by using simple contention management strategies, such as backoff [13].

2.3   Asynchronous and Semisynchronous Models of Computation

Concurrent algorithms are usually required to behave correctly regardless of how the steps of concurrent processes are interleaved, and (therefore) regardless of how fast or slowly any process executes. In other words, these algorithms should be proved correct in an *asynchronous* model of computation, in which the steps of processes are scheduled by an adversarial scheduler that can perform many steps of a process consecutively or perform them arbitrarily far apart. In such a model, it is impossible for a process to determine whether another process has crashed (i.e., stopped executing) or is just running very slowly.

Of course, in reality, there are limits to how fast or slowly processes can run. Some algorithms exploit assumptions about these limits to improve in various ways on algorithms designed for an asynchronous model. Such algorithms are proved correct and/or analyzed in synchronous or semisynchronous models of computation that embody timing assumptions made about the target execution environment.

In a *synchronous* model, all processes execute steps at the same rate (until they crash). This means that if a process does not perform a step when it should, other processes can detect that it has crashed. However, if the correctness of a particular algorithm depends on all (noncrashed) processes performing steps precisely at a given rate, then tiny variations in execution rate, for example due to one processor becoming warmer than another, can cause incorrect behavior. Consequently, such algorithms are not generally practical.

Semisynchronous models relax these timing requirements, allowing processes to execute steps at different rates, and even allowing the rate at which a particular process executes to vary over time. However, it is assumed that there is an upper bound on the relative execution rates of any pair of processes. To be more precise, let us define the *maximum step time* of an execution as the longest time from the point a process completes one step until the same process completes its next step, if any. We define *minimum step time* analogously. Semisynchronous models assume that there exists a finite R such that in all executions, the ratio of the maximum and minimum step times is at most R. The evaluation of algorithms in semisynchronous models has value for the practitioner because real-world systems satisfy the assumptions of such models, and has value to the theoretician in understanding the limitations of assumptions on timing.

In the *known-bound* model [8,16], R is known by all processes. This implies that a process can wait long enough to guarantee that every other process has taken another step, or has crashed. Some algorithms that depend on knowledge of R can behave incorrectly in systems that do not satisfy the assumed bound. Conservative estimates of the bound for a particular system generally translate into worse performance, so designers are faced with a dangerous tradeoff in using such algorithms. Thus, such algorithms are not easily portable and indeed may stop behaving correctly in a given system if the system stops satisfying the timing assumptions, for example due to increased temperature.

In the *unknown-bound* model [7,8], R is *not* known to processes. Thus, in contrast to the synchronous and known-bound models, it is not possible for a process to know how long to wait to ensure that every other process that has not crashed takes a step. Therefore, it is not possible for a process to detect that another process has crashed. Nonetheless, it is possible for algorithms to wait for increasingly longer periods, and to exploit the knowledge that *eventually* all noncrashed processes have taken a step during one of these periods.

It has been shown that an algorithm that is correct in this model does not violate any of its safety properties even in an asynchronous model, although progress properties proved in the unknown-bound model may not hold in an asynchronous model [8]. Thus, in principle, such algorithms are safe to use in any practical system for non-real-time applications.

Algorithms that are correct in an asynchronous model are nonetheless sometimes analyzed in a synchronous or semisynchronous model, thus allowing the analysis to depend on various timing assumptions. Because contention management techniques such as backoff fundamentally rely on operations waiting for some time before retrying, they cannot be meaningfully analyzed in an asynchronous model of computation, which has no notion of time whatsoever.

In this paper, we show how to transform any obstruction-free implementation into one that guarantees that every process performing an operation eventually completes the operation, when analyzed in the unknown-bound model. Thus, the resulting algorithm is safe to use in any non-real-time application, and guarantees that every operation eventually completes in any practical system.

2.4   Some Previous Work Using Semisynchronous Models

The study of algorithms in semisynchronous models has a long tradition in the distributed-computing community [7,17,18]. Semisynchronous algorithms have received considerable attention in the context of shared memory synchronization. For lack of space, we mention only a few of the results.

Fischer [17] was the first to propose a timing-based mutual exclusion algorithm. He showed that in a known-bound model, there is a simple and efficient algorithm that uses a single shared variable. This overcame the linear space lower bound of Burns and Lynch [19] for asynchronous systems. Unfortunately, that algorithm behaves incorrectly if the timing assumptions of the model are violated. Lynch and Shavit [16] improved on Fischer's algorithm: in the same model, they presented an algorithm that uses two variables and behaves correctly even if the timing assumptions are violated, although progress is not guaranteed in this case. Gafni and Mitzenmacher [20] analyzed this algorithm under various stochastic timing models. Alur, Attiya, and Taubenfeld [8] showed that timing-based mutual exclusion and consensus algorithms with constant time complexity in the uncontended case exist in the unknown-bound model.

Counting networks [21] have also been evaluated in semisynchronous models. For example, Lynch et al. showed that in the known-bound model, uniform counting networks are linearizable [22]. This result was generalized by Mavroni-colas et al. [23] to non-uniform networks under a variety of timing assumptions. In these results, the linearizability of the implementations depends on timing.

3   Our Transformation

We begin by explaining some simple ways of ensuring progress to each opera-tion under various different assumptions and models. These ideas motivate the techniques used in our algorithm, and explain why they are needed because of the weak assumptions of the unknown-bound model.

First, if we assume that processes never crash, then it is easy to ensure progress, even in an asynchronous model: order the operations using timestamps, and have each process wait until all earlier operations in this order have com-pleted before performing the steps of its own operation. This ensures that oper-ations do not encounter contention with concurrent operations while executing the original obstruction-free operation, so every operation eventually completes. However, if a process does crash while it has a pending operation, no operations that are later in the order can be executed.

In a synchronous model, if all processes know an upper bound B on the num-ber of consecutive steps that must be taken by a process running alone to ensure that its operation completes, then it is easy to guarantee that each operation completes, even if processes can crash. The idea is again to order operations, and to have processes refrain from executing their operations while operations earlier in the order are pending. However, unlike in the asynchronous model, a process can detect if another process crashed while executing its operation: if the operation is not completed within B steps, then the process executing it must have crashed. In this case, a process can execute its operation when every earlier operation in the order has either completed, or will not interfere further because the process executing it has crashed.

A similar approach works in the known-bound semisynchronous model. In this case, a process that is waiting for an earlier operation than its own to com-plete must conservatively assume that it is executing its steps at the maximum speed allowed by the model relative to the speed of the process executing the earlier operation. Thus, in this model, a process must wait for RB steps in order to be sure that another process has had time to execute B steps.

However, this technique does *not* work in the unknown-bound model because the bound R is not known to processes. In fact, it is impossible in this model for one process to determine that another has crashed. Nonetheless, ideas similar to those described above can be used to guarantee that each operation executed by a noncrashed process completes even in the unknown-bound model. The key idea is that, rather than delaying for an amount of time that is *known* to be long enough to allow another process to take B steps, a process can delay for increasingly long periods of time while an older operation has not completed. After each period of waiting, if the older operation has not been completed yet, then we *assume* that it has crashed, remove its timestamp from consideration in the order of operations, and proceed.

In case the process executing the older operation has in fact not crashed, it reinstates its operation into the order (using its original timestamp) and increments a counter, which serves the dual purposes of demonstrating that it has not crashed, and therefore must again be deferred to by operations later in the order, as well as increasing the number of steps for which later operations must defer. With this arrangement, if a process does crash while executing an operation, then it is removed from consideration and does not prevent progress by other operations. On the other hand, if an operation fails to complete because others did not wait long enough, then they will wait longer next time, so the bound provided by the model ensures that eventually they will wait long enough and the operation will complete.

It is important to note that the worst-case bound R for a particular system might be very high, because a process might occasionally take a very long time to take a single step. However, the algorithm has no knowledge of the bound, so the worst-case bound possible for the system does not impact the performance of the algorithm; only the particular execution behaviour does. Furthermore, even if an unlikely sequence of events causes progress to take a long time, this has no bearing on how the algorithm behaves in the future. Therefore, because in practice processes run at approximately the same speed most of the time, the *effective* bound will generally be small, even if in theory it is very large.

The description above captures the key idea of how we transform obstruction-free implementations to provide wait-free progress guarantees in the unknown-bound model. However, because the above-described strategy for ensuring progress essentially amounts to eliminating concurrency, it would not be practical if simply used as described above. Therefore, we have designed our transformation so this strategy does not take effect until the original algorithm and contention manager fail to complete an operation for too long.

The algorithm produced by applying our transformation to an obstruction-free algorithm *OFAlg* (which includes the original contention manager) is shown in Figure 1. We now describe the transformed algorithm in more detail.

3.1   Transformed Algorithm in Detail

The *PANIC* flag is used to preserve the practicality of the original obstruction-free algorithm and its original pragmatic contention manager until such time as some process determines that it has executed for too long without completing its operation. Observe that, having invoked an operation, a process checks to see that this flag is false (N1), and if so, executes its original operation for up to b steps (N2); b is a parameter of the transformation. If these steps are sufficient to complete its operation it simply returns (N3-N4). If every operation completes within b steps, then the *PANIC* flag remains false. Therefore, the transformed algorithm behaves exactly like the original one in this case, except that it must read one variable which is likely to be cached. Thus, an appropriate choice of b ensures that our transformation introduces almost no overhead provided the

```
invoke(op)
N1:  if ¬PANIC
N2:      execute up to b steps of OFAlg
N3:      if op is complete
N4:          return response
N5:      PANIC ← true                // panic mode
P1:  t ← fetch-and-increment(C)
P2:  A[i] ← 0
     repeat
P3:      T[i] ← t
P4:      A[i] ← A[i] + 1
P5:      m ← t                       // find minimum timestamp; reset all others
         k ← i
P6:      foreach j ≠ i
P7:          s ← T[j]
P8:          if s < m
P9:              T[k] ← ∞
P10:             m ← s
                 k ← j
             else
P11:             T[j] ← ∞
P12:     if k = i
P13:         while (op not completed and T[i] ≠ ∞)
P14:             execute up to b steps of OFAlg
P15:             if (op not completed) PANIC ← true
         else
             repeat
P16:             a ← A[k]
P17:             wait a steps
P18:         until a = A[k] or T[k] ≠ m
P19:         T[k] ← ∞
P20: until (op is complete)
P21: T[i] ← ∞
P22: PANIC ← false
P23: return response
```

Fig. 1. *OFAlg* transformed to guarantee progress in unknown-bound model

original contention manager is effective. However, when an operation fails to complete within b steps, it sets the *PANIC* flag to true. Thereafter, until the flag is reset, all new operations fail the test at N1, and therefore begin to participate in the strategy to ensure progress (P1-P23).

A process p_i participating in this strategy first acquires a timestamp (P1) and initializes its "active" counter $A[i]$ (P2), and then repeats the loop at lines P3 through P20 until its operation is complete. In each iteration of this loop, p_i announces its timestamp in $T[i]$ (P3), increments its active counter (P4), and then searches for the minimum timestamp announced by any process, resetting $T[j]$ to ∞ for all j other than the one with the minimum timestamp it observes

(P5-P11). If p_i determines that it has the minimum timestamp (P12), then it repeatedly takes up to b steps of the original algorithm (P14) and then—if it has not completed its operation—stores true to the *PANIC* flag (P15) in case it has been set to false by some other process completing (P22); this ensures that new operations continue to participate in the progress-ensuring strategy. Process p_i repeats these steps while its operation is not finished, and while no other process has reset $T[i]$ to ∞ (P13). Such resetting indicates that either another operation with a smaller timestamp has been detected (P11) or some other process thinks that p_i may have crashed (P19).

A process p_j that does not find its timestamp to be the minimum one enters the loop at lines P16 through P19. This loop repeatedly waits for a number of steps determined by reading the active counter of the process—call it p_k— that had the minimum timestamp (P16-P17). To ensure progress in this case, p_j breaks out of this loop if p_k does not increment its active counter in this time (and therefore may have crashed) or if p_k's timestamp changes, indicating either that another process detected an operation with a smaller timestamp or that p_k completed its operation.

We now explain how this strategy ensures that if p_i has the smallest timestamp among all noncrashed operations with uncompleted operations, it eventually completes its operation. Eventually, for every iteration of the loop at P3 through P20, p_i attempts to execute its operation for up to b steps (P14). Meanwhile, any other process determines that p_i's timestamp is the minimum, reads p_i's active counter (P16) and waits for a number of steps indicated by this counter. Because p_i repeatedly increments its active counter, if p_i does not complete its operation, then, eventually, the amount of time each process waits (P17) during an iteration of the loop at P16 through P18 increases.

After some point, all such processes will wait at line P17 long enough for p_i to complete an entire iteration of the outer loop and therefore reannounces its timestamp (P3) and increment its active counter (P4). Therefore, eventually none of these processes will leave the loop at P16 through P18 due to seeing p_i's active counter unchanged or due to seeing p_i's timestamp reset (because no process resets p_i's timestamp without first exiting the loop at P16 through P18).

Provided p_i continues taking steps, it does not encounter interference from other processes' operations, and because it executes some steps of the original obstruction-free algorithm during each iteration, it eventually completes its operation. On the other hand, if p_i crashes, then the other processes will no longer see $A[i]$ change, and will therefore stop waiting for p_i and reset its timestamp. Then the way is clear for the next operation in timestamp order (if any) to make progress. In the following section, we formalize this argument to show that every noncrashed process executing an operation eventually completes the operation.

An important feature of the transformed implementation is that if the original contention manager is occasionally ineffective, causing the *PANIC* flag to be set, the *PANIC* flag will be reset and normal execution will resume, provided the original contention manager does not *remain* ineffective. To see this, note that every operation either sees *PANIC* as false and does not set it (N1-N4), or sets it to false before returning (P22). Because every operation eventually completes, this implies that the $PANIC$ flag is true only if some operation has failed to complete having executed b steps of the original algorithm (and contention manager), and has still not completed. Thus, our mechanism is only invoked continually if the original contention manager continues to be ineffective.

4   Proof of Correctness

It is easy to see that the algorithm produced by applying our transformation to any obstruction-free algorithm retains the semantics of the original algorithm: the transformed algorithm performs the original algorithm on the original shared objects and does not apply any other steps to those objects. In this section, we prove that the resulting algorithm is wait-free (assuming that there is a bound on the ratio of the maximum and minimum times of process steps). This guarantees that every operation executed by a process that does not crash eventually completes, when analyzed in the unknown-bound model of computation.

We first prove the following lemma, which we use in the wait-freedom proof.

Lemma 1. *If processes p_i and p_j $(i \neq j)$ are both in the loop at lines P13–P15, then either $T[i] = \infty$ or $T[j] = \infty$.*

Proof. Before reaching line P13, each process must set its entry in T to the timestamp of its operation. Suppose, without loss of generality, that the last time p_i does so is before the last time p_j does so. Because p_j reached line P13, p_j must have set $T[i]$ to ∞ after it set $T[j]$, which was after the last time p_i set $T[i]$. Since no other process sets $T[i]$ to anything other than ∞, we have $T[i] = \infty$, as required.

Proof of Wait-Freedom

Suppose, for contradiction, there is an execution in which some process that has invoked an operation takes an infinite number of steps but does not complete its operation. The rest of the proof is in the context of this execution.

Any such process must have seen (or set) $PANIC = true$, and therefore, must have incremented C and gotten a unique timestamp for its last operation.[1] Let t^* be the minimum timestamp of such an operation, and p_{i*} be the process that invoked that operation. Thus, after some point in the execution, any process that gets a timestamp less than t^* for an operation it invokes either completes the operation or stops taking steps. Because p_{i*} takes infinitely many steps without completing its last operation, it must be in the loop at lines P3–P20 from some point on in the execution. Let X be the later of these two points.

Throughout the proof, we denote by v_i the local variable v of process p_i.

---

[1] The timestamp for each operation is unique because we use fetch-and-increment.

Claim. For any j, if at any point after X, $T[j] > t^*$, then it remains so thereafter.

Proof. Straightforward because after X, no process executes steps for an operation with timestamp less then t^*.

Claim. From any point after X, p_{i^*} reaches line P13 within a finite number of its steps.

Proof. The claim is obvious if p_{i^*} is in the loop at lines P13–P15.

If p_{i^*} is at lines P3–P5 or lines P19–P20, and $T[j] > t^*$ for all $j \neq i^*$, then within a finite number of steps, p_{i^*} reaches lines P5–P11, where it sets k_{i^*} to i^*, and thus, p_{i^*} reaches line P13 within a finite number of steps.

If p_{i^*} is at lines P3–P5 or lines P19–P20, and $T[j^*] < t^*$ for some $j^* \neq i^*$, then within a finite number of steps, p_{i^*} reaches lines P5–P11, where it sets k_{i^*} to k, where $T[k]$ has the minimum timestamp that it saw, and it also sets $T[j]$ to ∞ for all $j \neq k$. Thus, after this point, $T[j] > t^*$ for all $j \notin \{i^*, k\}$. If $k = i^*$ (some other process may have set $T[j^*]$ to ∞ before p_{i^*} read it), which is the previous case. Otherwise, p_{i^*} goes to line P16, waits for $A[k]$ steps (note that $A[k]$ does not change because p_k does not take any more steps), and then exits the loop and sets $T[k]$ to ∞. Thus, at this point, $T[j] > t$ for all $j \neq i$, so this case is reduced to the previous case.

If p_{i^*} is at lines P16–P18, then $m_{i^*} < t^*$, so either $T[k_{i^*}] \neq m_{i^*}$ or $p_{k_{i^*}}$ has stopped taking steps, and so $A[k_{i^*}]$ stops changing. In either case, p_{i^*} exits the loop in a finite number of steps, reaching line P19, thus reducing this case to one of the previous two cases.

Finally, if p_{i^*} is at lines P6–P12, then in a finite number of its steps, p_{i^*} reaches either line P13 or line P16, which either directly proves the claim, or reduces it to the previous case.

Claim. There exists some point after X after which either $T[j] > t^*$ for all $j \neq i^*$ or p_{i^*} is always at lines P13-P15.

Proof. This claim follows from the proof of the previous claim. Notice that if p_{i^*} is at lines P3–P5 or lines P16–P20, then the proof of the previous claim shows that eventually, $T[j] > t^*$ for all $j \neq i^*$, and that if p_{i^*} is at lines P6–P12, then p_{i^*} reaches either line P13 or line P16. In the latter case, we again have $T[j] > t^*$ for all $j \neq i^*$ eventually. If p_{i^*} is at lines P13–P15, then either it remains in that loop forever, or it reaches line P20, in which case, eventually, $T[j] > t^*$ for all $j \neq i^*$.

Claim. There is no point after which p_{i^*} is at lines P13–P15 forever.

Proof. If there were such a point, there would also be such a point after X; call this later point Y. Then from Y on, $T[i^*] = t^*$ (because otherwise, p_{i^*} would exit that loop after at most b steps). Thus, any process that reaches line P3 after Y never completes its operation: to do so, it must set $T[i^*]$ to ∞ either when finding the minimum timestamp (if it finds one smaller than t^*) or after it exits the loop at lines P16–P18. Indeed, any such process must stop taking steps without returning to line P3 again. Therefore, entries in the A array can be incremented and *PANIC* can be set to *false* at most as many times as there are processes at lines P3–P23 at Y, which is at most n. Since p_{i*} takes an infinite number of steps, and each iteration of lines P13–P15 has a finite number of steps, p_{i*} sets *PANIC* to *true* an infinite number of times.

Let Z be a point at which p_{i*} sets *PANIC* to *true* after the last time *PANIC* is set to *false* and the last time any entry in A is incremented; after Z, *PANIC* = *true* forever and the A array never changes. Thus, any process that invokes an operation after Z must reach line P3 (unless it stops before getting there). By the reasoning above, it must stop taking steps in any case. Also, any process in the loop at lines P16–P18 after Z must stop taking steps because otherwise, since A does not change, the process must exit the loop and reach line P3. Any process p_j other than p_{i*} in the loop at lines P13–P15 must also stop taking steps; otherwise, it would exit the loop and reach line P3 because $T[j] = \infty$ by Lemma 1 (since $T[i^*] = t^* \neq \infty$). Finally, any process earlier in the loop must stop taking steps or reach one of the inner loops in a finite number of steps, and by the reasoning above, stop taking steps anyway.

Thus, at some point, all processes other than p_{i*} stop taking steps. However, in this case, p_{i*} runs alone, and it keeps running steps of *OFAlg*, so because *OFAlg* is obstruction-free, it must complete its operation in a finite number of steps, contradicting the definition of p_{i*}.

Claim. There exists some point Z after X after which $T[j] > t^*$ for all $j \neq i^*$.

Proof. Immediate from the two previous claims.

Claim. $A[i^*]$ increases without bound.

Proof. Note that p_{i*} is at lines P3–P20 forever after X. If p_{i*} reaches line P3 at any point after Z, then because p_{i*} takes an infinite number of steps and $t^* < T[j]$ for any $j \neq i^*$, p_{i*} increments $A[i^*]$ and then enter the loop at lines P13–P15. Because p_{i*} never stays forever in that loop, it again reaches line P3, incrementing $A[i^*]$. Thus, if p_{i*} ever reaches line P3 after Z, the claim holds.

If after Z, p_{i*} is in the loop at lines P16–P18, then $m_{i*} < t^* < T[j]$ for all $j \neq i^*$, and $k_{i*} \neq i$, so after waiting a_{i*} steps, p_{i*} exits the loop at lines P16–P18and reaches line P3.

If after Z, p_{i*} is in the loop at lines P13–P15, then it does not stay in this loop forever, and after it exits the loop, it reaches line P3.

Otherwise, after a finite number of steps, p_{i*} must reach either line P13 or line P16, and in either case, it exits the loop and reaches line P3.

We now show that p_{i*} must complete its operation, which contradicts its definition, and thus, the initial supposition that the algorithm is not wait-free.

Because *OFAlg* is obstruction-free, there is a (possibly unknown) upper bound on how many steps are required for any process running alone to complete its operation. Because there is a (possibly unknown) upper bound on the ratio of the maximum time for p_{i*} to take a step and the minimum time for any other process to take a step, and because $A[i^*]$ increases without bound, $A[i^*]$ eventually becomes large enough that any process reaching line P17 will wait there long enough for p_{i*} to complete any finite number of steps.

Because p_{i*} sets $T[i^*]$ to t^* before each time it increments $A[i^*]$, every other noncrashed process executing an operation eventually sees $T[i^*] = t^*$, which (after Z) is less than the the timestamp of its operation and any other timestamp in the T array; therefore, that process reaches line P17. Thus, for any finite number, p_{i*} eventually runs without interference for that number of steps. However, this implies that p_{i*} must complete, which contradicts its definition.

5   Concluding Remarks

We have shown that any obstruction-free algorithm and its real-world contention manager can be transformed into a new algorithm that is wait-free when analyzed in the unknown-bound semisynchronous model of computation. Because real-world systems satisfy the assumptions of this model, our result shows that obstruction-free algorithms and ad hoc contention managers can be used in practice without sacrificing the strong progress guarantees of wait-freedom.

Our result can easily be made stronger from both theoretical and practical points of view. First, as presented, our transformation introduces the need to know of the maximum number of processes that use the implementation. However, this disadvantage can easily be eliminated using results of Herlihy et al. [24]. From a theoretical point of view, our use of the fetch-and-increment can be eliminated by using standard timestamping techniques based on an array of single-writer-multiple-reader registers.

References

1. Chandra, T.D., Toueg, S.: Unreliable failure detectors for reliable distributed systems. J. ACM **43** (1996) 225–267
2. Lo, W.K., Hadzilacos, V.: Using failure detectors to solve consensus in asynchronous sharde-memory systems (extended abstract). In: WDAG '94: Proceedings of the 8th International Workshop on Distributed Algorithms, London, UK, Springer-Verlag (1994) 280–295
3. Gafni, E., Lamport, L.: Disk paxos. In: DISC '00: Proceedings of the 14th International Conference on Distributed Computing, London, UK, Springer-Verlag (2000) 330–344
4. Fischer, M., Lynch, N., Paterson, M.: Impossibility of distributed consensus with one faulty process. Journal of the ACM (1985) 374–382
5. Loui, M.C., Abu-Amara, H.H.: Memory requirements for agreement among unreliable asynchronous processes. In Preparata, F.P., ed.: Advances in Computing Research. Volume 4. JAI Press, Greenwich, CT (1987) 163–183
6. Herlihy, M.: Wait-free synchronization. ACM Transactions on Programming Languages and Systems **13** (1991) 124–149
7. Dwork, C., Lynch, N., Stockmeyer, L.: Consensus in the presence of partial synchrony. J. ACM **35** (1988) 288–323

8. Alur, R., Attiya, H., Taubenfeld, G.: Time-adaptive algorithms for synchronization. SIAM J. Comput. **26** (1997) 539–556
9. Treiber, R.K.: Systems programming: Coping with parallelism. Technical Report RJ 5118, IBM Almaden Research Center (1986)
10. Michael, M., Scott, M.: Nonblocking algorithms and preemption-safe locking on multiprogrammed shared - memory multiprocessors. Journal of Parallel and Distributed Computing **51** (1998) 1–26
11. Arora, N.S., Blumofe, R.D., Plaxton, C.G.: Thread scheduling for multiprogrammed multiprocessors. Theory of Computing Systems **34** (2001) 115–144
12. Herlihy, M., Luchangco, V., Moir, M.: Obstruction-free synchronization: Double-ended queues as an example. In: Proc. 23rd International Conference on Distributed Computing Systems. (2003)
13. Herlihy, M., Luchangco, V., Moir, M., Scherer III, W.N.: Software transactional memory for supporting dynamic-sized data structures. In: Proc. 22th Annual ACM Symposium on Principles of Distributed Computing. (2003) 92–101
14. Luchangco, V., Moir, M., Shavit, N.: Nonblocking k-compare-single-swap. In: SPAA '03: Proceedings of the fifteenth annual ACM symposium on Parallel algorithms and architectures, ACM Press (2003) 314–323
15. Scherer III, W.N., Scott, M.L.: Contention management in dynamic software transactional memory. In Moir, Shavit, eds.: In Proceedings of Workshop on Concurrency and Sycnhronization in Java Programs. (2004)
16. Lynch, N.A., Shavit, N.: Timing-based mutual exclusion. In: IEEE Real-Time Systems Symposium, IEEE Press (1992) 2–11
17. Fischer, M.: Personal communication with Leslie Lamport. (1985)
18. Attiya, H., Mavronicolas, M.: Efficiency of semisynchronous versus asynchronous networks. Math. Syst. Theory **27** (1994) 547–571
19. Burns, J.E., Lynch, N.A.: Bounds on shared memory for mutual exclusion. Information and Computation **107** (1993) 171–184
20. Gafni, E., Mitzenmacher, M.: Analysis of timing-based mutual exclusion with random times. In: PODC '99: Proceedings of the eighteenth annual ACM symposium on Principles of distributed computing, ACM Press (1999) 13–21
21. Aspnes, J., Herlihy, M., Shavit, N.: Counting networks. Journal of the ACM **41** (1994) 1020–1048
22. Lynch, N., Shavit, N., Shvartsman, A., Touitou, D.: Timing conditions for linearizability in uniform counting networks. Theor. Comput. Sci. **220** (1999) 67–91
23. Mavronicolas, M., Papatriantafilou, M., Tsigas, P.: The impact of timing on linearizability in counting networks. In: IPPS '97: Proceedings of the 11th International Symposium on Parallel Processing, IEEE Computer Society (1997) 684–688
24. Herlihy, M., Luchangco, V., Moir, M.: Space- and time-adaptive nonblocking algorithms. In: Proceedings of Computing: The Australasian Theory Symposium (CATS). (2003)

Efficient Reduction for Wait-Free Termination Detection in a Crash-Prone Distributed System

Neeraj Mittal[1],*, Felix C. Freiling[2],
S. Venkatesan[1], and Lucia Draque Penso[2],**

[1] Department of Computer Science, The University of Texas at Dallas,
Richardson, TX 75083, USA
{neerajm, venky}@utdallas.edu
[2] Department of Computer Science, RWTH Aachen University,
D-52056 Aachen, Germany
freiling@informatik.rwth-aachen.de
lucia@i4.informatik.rwth-aachen.de

Abstract. We investigate the problem of detecting termination of a distributed computation in systems where processes can fail by crashing. Specifically, when the communication topology is fully connected, we describe a way to transform *any* termination detection algorithm $\mathcal{A}$ that has been designed for a failure-free environment into a termination detection algorithm $\mathcal{B}$ that can tolerate process crashes. Our transformation assumes the existence of a *perfect failure detector*. We show that a perfect failure detector is in fact necessary to solve the termination detection problem in a crash-prone distributed system even if *at most one* process can crash.

Let $\mu(n, M)$ and $\delta(n, M)$ denote the message complexity and detection latency, respectively, of $\mathcal{A}$ when the system has n processes and the underlying computation exchanges M application messages. The message complexity of $\mathcal{B}$ is at most $O(n + \mu(n, 0))$ messages per failure more than the message complexity of $\mathcal{A}$. Also, its detection latency is at most $O(\delta(n, 0))$ per failure more than that of $\mathcal{A}$. Furthermore, the overhead (that is, the amount of control data piggybacked) on an application message increases by only $O(\log n)$ bits per failure.

The fault-tolerant termination detection algorithm resulting from the transformation satisfies two desirable properties. First, it can tolerate failure of up to $n - 1$ processes, that is, it is *wait-free*. Second, it does not impose any overhead on the fault-sensitive termination detection algorithm until one or more processes crash, that is, it is *fault-reactive*. Our transformation can be extended to arbitrary communication topologies provided process crashes do not partition the system.

Keywords: distributed system, termination detection, faulty processes, wait-free algorithm, failure detector, algorithm transformation.

* Work by Neeraj Mittal was performed in part while visiting RWTH Aachen University and supported by Deutsche Forschungsgemeinschaft (DFG) within the Graduiertenkolleg "Software for Mobile Communication Systems".
** Lucia Draque Penso was supported by Deutsche Forschungsgemeinschaft (DFG) as part of the Graduiertenkolleg "Software for Mobile Communication Systems" at RWTH Aachen University.

P. Fraigniaud (Ed.): DISC 2005, LNCS 3724, pp. 93–107, 2005.

1   Introduction

One of the fundamental problems in distributed systems is to detect termination of an ongoing distributed computation. The termination detection problem was independently proposed by Dijkstra and Scholten [1] and Francez [2] more than two decades ago. Since then, many researchers have studied this problem and, as a result, a large number of efficient algorithms have been developed for detecting termination (*e.g.*, [3,4,5,6,7,8,9,10,11,12,13,14]). Most of the termination detection algorithms in the literature have been developed assuming that both processes and channels stay operational throughout an execution. Real-world systems, however, are often prone to failures. For example, processes may fail by crashing and channels may be lossy. In this paper, we investigate the termination detection problem when processes can fail by crashing. We assume that process crashes do not result in restarting of the primary computation.

One of the earliest fault-tolerant algorithm for termination detection was proposed by Venkatesan [15], which was derived from the fault-sensitive (that is, fault-*in*tolerant) termination detection algorithm by Chandrasekaran and Venkatesan [9]. Venkatesan's algorithm achieves fault-tolerance by *replicating* state information at multiple processes. However, it assumes a *prespecified* bound k on the maximum number of processes that can fail by crashing. Its message complexity is $O(kM + c)$, where M is the number of application messages exchanged by the underlying computation and c is the number of channels in the communication topology. As a result, the overhead incurred by the algorithm depends on the *maximum* number of processes that can fail during an execution rather than the *actual* number of processes that fail during an execution. Moreover, the algorithm assumes that it is possible to send up to $k + 1$ (possibly different) messages to different processes in an *atomic* manner. Unlike other fault-tolerant termination detection algorithms, however, Venkatesan's algorithm does not assume that the communication topology is fully connected and works as long the topology is $(k + 1)$-connected [15].

Lai and Wu [16] and Tseng [17] modify fault-sensitive termination detection algorithms by Dijkstra and Scholten [1] and Huang [8], respectively, to derive two different fault-tolerant termination detection algorithms. Both algorithms assume that the communication topology is fully connected. However, unlike Venkatesan's algorithm, both have low message complexity of $O(M + fn + n)$, where n is the initial number of processes in the system f is the actual number of processes that fail during an execution. The algorithm by Lai and Wu [16] has high detection latency of $O(n)$ whereas the algorithm by Tseng [17] has high application and control message overheads of $O(M)$ and $O(f \log n + nM)$, respectively.

Shah and Toueg give a fault-tolerant algorithm for taking a consistent snapshot of a distributed system in [18]. Their algorithm is derived from the fault-sensitive consistent snapshot algorithm by Chandy and Lamport [19]. As a result, each invocation of their snapshot algorithm may generate up to $O(c)$ control messages. It is easy to verify that, when their algorithm is used for termination detection, the message complexity of the resulting algorithm is $O(cM)$ in the worst-case. Similarly, Gärtner and Pleisch [20] give an algorithm for detecting an arbitrary stable predicate in a crash-prone distributed system. (Note that termination is a stable property.) In their algorithm, every relevant local event is *reliably and causally broadcast* to a set of monitors, thereby increasing the message complexity significantly.

In this paper, when the communication topology is fully connected, we describe a way to transform any fault-sensitive termination detection algorithm $\mathcal{A}$ into a fault-tolerant termination detection algorithm $\mathcal{B}$. Our transformation assumes the existence of a perfect failure detector, which we show is necessary to solve the problem. Let $\mu(n, M)$ and $\delta(n, M)$ denote the message complexity and detection latency, respectively, of $\mathcal{A}$ when the system has n processes and the underlying computation exchanges M application messages. The message-complexity of $\mathcal{B}$ is $O(f(n + \mu(n, 0)))$ messages more than the message complexity of $\mathcal{A}$. Also, the detection latency of $\mathcal{B}$ is $O(f\delta(n, 0))$ more than the detection latency of $\mathcal{A}$. For most termination detection algorithms, when the topology is fully connected, $\mu(n, 0)$ is either $O(n)$ or $O(c)$, and $\delta(n, 0)$ is $O(1)$. (For example, for the Dijkstra and Scholten's algorithm [1], $\mu(n, 0) = O(n)$ and $\delta(n, 0) = O(1)$ when their algorithm is adopted for a non-diffusing computation.) Further, the application and control message overheads of $\mathcal{B}$ are at most $O(f \log n)$ and $O(f \log n + n \log M)$ more than those for $\mathcal{A}$. (Message overhead refers to the amount of control information piggybacked on a message.) The overhead of $O(n \log M)$ applies only to those control messages that are exchanged whenever a crash is detected. The fault-tolerant termination detection algorithm resulting from the transformation satisfies two desirable properties. First, the it can tolerate failure of up to $n-1$ processes, that is, it is *wait-free*. Second, it does not impose any overhead on the fault-sensitive termination detection algorithm if no process actually crashes during an execution, that is, it is *fault-reactive*.

Typically, generalized transformations tend to be inefficient compared to customized/specialized transformations. However, when our transformation is applied to fault-sensitive termination detection algorithms by Dijkstra and Scholten [1] and Huang [8], the resulting fault-tolerant algorithms compare very favorably with those by Lai and Wu [16] and Tseng [17]. Specifically, when our transformation is applied to Dijkstra and Scholten's algorithm [1], the resulting algorithm has the same message-complexity and detection latency as the algorithm by Lai and Wu [16]. However, the message overhead—application as well as control—is higher for our algorithm. On the other hand, when our transformation is applied to Huang's weight throwing algorithm [8] (which is similar to Mattern's credit distribution and recovery algorithm [7]), the resulting algorithm has the same message-complexity and detection latency as that of the algorithm by Tseng [17] but has slightly higher application message overhead ($O(\log M + f \log n)$ versus $O(\log M)$). Surprisingly, the overhead of control messages exchanged due to process crashes by our algorithm, which is given by $O(f \log n + n \log M)$, is *much lower* than that of Tseng's algorithm [17], which is given by $O(f \log n + nM)$. For comparison between various fault-tolerant termination detection algorithms, please refer to Table 1. The results of applying our transformation to some important termination detection algorithms are given in [21].

The main idea behind our approach is to *restart* the fault-sensitive termination detection algorithm whenever a *new* failure is detected. A separate mechanism is used to account for those application messages that are in-transit when the termination detection algorithm is restarted. Arora and Gouda [22] also

Table 1. Comparison of various fault-tolerant termination detection algorithms

	Venkatesan [15]	Lai and Wu [16]	Tseng [17]	Our Approach [this paper]
Message Complexity	$O(kM + c)$	$O(M + fn + n)$	$O(M + fn + n)$	$\mu(n, M) +$ $O(f (n + \mu(n, 0)))$
Detection Latency	$O(M)$	$O(n)$	$O(f + 1)$	$\delta(n, M) +$ $O(f \delta(n, 0))$
Application Message Overhead	k-way duplication	$O(f \log n + \log M)$	$O(\log M)^*$	$\alpha(n, M) +$ $O(f \log n)$
Control Message Overhead — Termination Detection	$O(\log n + \log M)$	$O(f \log n + \log M)$	$O(\log M)^*$	$\beta(n, M) +$ $O(f \log n)$
Control Message Overhead — Failure Recovery	-	$O(f \log n + \log M)$	$O(f \log n + nM)$	$O(f \log n) +$ $O(n \log M)$
Assumptions	FIFO channels + atomic multicast	fully connected topology	fully connected topology	fully connected topology

*Assuming an efficient implementation of weight throwing scheme such as the one described in [7]
n: initial number of processes in the system
c: number of channels in the communication topology
f: actual number of processes that crash during an execution
k: maximum number of processes that can crash during an execution
M: number of application messages exchanged
$\mu(n, M)$: message complexity of the fault-sensitive termination detection algorithm with n processes and M application messages
$\delta(n, M)$: detection latency of the fault-sensitive termination detection algorithm with n processes and M application messages
$\alpha(n, M)$: application message overhead of the fault-sensitive termination detection algorithm with n processes and M application messages
$\beta(n, M)$: control message overhead of the fault-sensitive termination detection algorithm with n processes and M application messages

provide a mechanism to reset a distributed system. Their approach is different from our approach in many ways. First, the semantics of their reset operation is different from the semantics of our restart operation. Specifically, if their reset mechanism is applied to our system, then it will not only reset the termination detection algorithm but will also reset the underlying distributed computation (whose termination is to be detected). Further, application messages exchanged by the underlying computation before it is reset will be discarded. If a failure occurs near the completion of the underlying computation, the entire work needs to be redone if the distributed reset procedure is used. In contrast, in our case, the distributed computation continues to execute without interruption. (When there are process crashes, we assume that the primary computation may be able to cope with process failures without the need to restart itself.) Therefore, in our case, application messages exchanged before the termination detection algorithm is restarted, especially those exchanged between correct processes, cannot be ignored. Arora and Gouda's approach is more suitable for applications that can be reset on occurrence of a failure whereas our approach is more suitable for applications that continue to execute despite failures. Second, in their approach, the system may be reset more than once for the same failure. This may happen, for example, when multiple processes detect the failure of the same process at different times. Third, their reset operation, which is self-stabilizing in nature, is designed to tolerate much broader and more severe kinds of faults such as restarts, message losses and arbitrary state perturbations than just crash failures. Not surprisingly, their reset operation has higher message and time complexities than our restart operation. Fourth, their approach is *non-masking fault-tolerant*, which implies that the safety specification of the application may be *violated temporarily*, even if there is a single crash fault. When translated to our problem, this means that the termination detection algorithm may falsely announce termination, a case which our approach avoids.

We build upon the work by Wu *et al* [23]. We do this in the context of the failure detector hierarchy proposed by Chandra and Toueg [24], a way to compare problems based on the level of *synchrony* required for solving them. We show that termination detection needs the synchrony assumptions of a perfect failure detector to be solvable even if at most one process can crash. This result can be used to further understand the relationship between termination detection and other problems in fault-tolerant distributed computing, such as consensus and atomic broadcast.

Our transformation can also be extended to an arbitrary communication topology provided process crashes do not partition the system. (In case partitioning occurs, termination is detected separately in each partition.) For an arbitrary topology, however, the increase in message-complexity and detection latency per failure is higher than that for fully connected topology. Due to lack of space, we only focus on the transformation for fully connected topology in this paper. Details of the transformation for arbitrary topology can be found elsewhere [21].

This paper is organized as follows. In Sect. 2, we present our model of a crash-prone distributed system and describe what it means to detect termination in such a system. We discuss our transformation in Sect. 3. In Sect. 4 we determine the type of failure detector which is necessary for solving termination detection. Finally, we present our conclusions and outline directions for future research in Sect. 5.

2   Model and Problem Definition

2.1   System Model

We assume an asynchronous distributed system consisting of multiple processes, which communicate with each other by exchanging messages over a set of communication channels. There is no global clock or shared memory.

Processes are not reliable and may fail by crashing. Once a process crashes, it halts all its operations and never recovers. We use the terms "non-crashed process", "live process" and "operational process" interchangeably. A process that crashes is called *faulty*. A process that is not faulty is called *correct*. Note that there is a difference between the terms "live process" and "correct process". A live process has not crashed yet but may crash in the future. Let $P = \{p_1, p_n, \ldots, p_n\}$ denote the initial set of processes in the system. We assume that there is at least one correct process in the system at all times.

We assume that all channels are bidirectional but may not be FIFO (first-in-first-out). Channels are reliable in the sense that if a process never crashes, then every message destined for it is eventually delivered. A message may, however, take an arbitrary amount of time to reach its destination. Unless otherwise stated, we assume that the communication topology is fully connected, that is, every pair of operational processes can directly communicate with each other.

We assume the existence of a *perfect failure detector* [24], a device which gives processes reliable information about the operational state of other processes. Upon querying the local failure detector, a process receives a list of *currently suspected* processes. A perfect failure detector satisfies two properties [24]: *strong accuracy* (no correct process is ever suspected) and *strong completeness* (a crashed process is eventually permanently suspected by every correct process). By varying definitions of completeness and accuracy, different types of failure detectors can be defined. For example, the eventually perfect failure detector satisfies *eventually strong accuracy* (eventually no correct process is ever suspected) and strong completeness.

2.2   Termination Detection in a Crash-Prone System

Informally, the termination detection problem involves determining when a distributed computation has ceased all its activity. The distributed computation satisfies the following four properties or rules. First, a process is either *active* or *passive*. Second, a process can send a message only if it is active. Third, an active process may become passive at any time. Fourth, a passive process may become active only on receiving a message. Intuitively, an active process is involved in some local activity, whereas a passive process is idle. In case both processes and channels are reliable, a distributed computation terminates once all processes become passive and stay passive thereafter. In other words, a distributed computation is said to be *classically-terminated* once all processes become passive and all channels become empty.

In a crash-prone distributed system, once a process crashes, it ceases all its activities. Moreover, any message in-transit towards a crashed process can be ignored because the message cannot initiate any new activity. Therefore, a crash-prone distributed system is said to be *strictly-terminated* if all live processes are passive and no channel contains a message in-transit towards a live process. Wu *et al* [23] establish that, for the strict-termination detection problem to be solvable in a crash-prone distributed system, it must be possible to *flush* the channel from a crashed process to a live process. A channel can be flushed using either *return-flush* [15] or *fail-flush* [16] primitive. Both primitives allow a live process to ascertain that its incoming channel from the crashed process has become empty.

In case neither return-flush nor fail-flush primitive is available, Tseng suggested *freezing* the channel from a crashed process to a live process [17]. When a live process freezes its channel with a crashed process, any message that arrives after the channel has been frozen is ignored. (A process can freeze a channel only after detecting that the process at the other end of the channel has crashed.) We say that a message is *deliverable* if it is destined for a live process along a channel that has not been frozen yet; otherwise it is *undeliverable*. We say that the system is *effectively-terminated* if all live processes are passive and there is no deliverable message in-transit towards a live process. Trivially, strict-termination implies effective-termination but not vice versa. Deciding which of the two termination conditions is to be detected depends on the application semantics. We believe that detecting effective-termination is sufficient in most cases.

Wu *et al* [23] also show that in order for strict-termination detection to be solvable, process faults must be *detectable*. Translated into the terminology of Chandra and Toueg [24], the failure detector used should satisfy strong completeness. We fulfill this requirement by assuming the existence of a perfect failure detector, which additionally satisfies strong accuracy. We justify this assumption later by proving that we need at least a perfect failure detector to solve even effective-termination detection in a crash-prone distributed system. Further, we assume that it is possible to freeze the channel from a crashed process to a live process (that is, application allows messages from crashed processes to be discarded). Hereafter, we focus on effective-termination detection. The transformation results in Section 3, however, remain valid even for strict-termination detection assuming that channels can be flushed instead of frozen.

For convenience, we refer to messages exchanged by the underlying distributed computation as *application messages* and to messages exchanged by the termination detection algorithm as *control messages*. The performance of a termination detection algorithm is measured in terms of three metrics: message complexity, detection latency and message overhead. Message complexity refers to the number of control messages exchanged by the termination detection algorithm in order to detect termination. Detection latency measures the time elapsed between when the underlying computation terminates and when the termination detection algorithm actually announces termination. Finally, message overhead refers to the amount of control data piggybacked on a message by the termination detection algorithm.

We call a termination detection algorithm *fault-tolerant* if it works correctly even in the presence of faults; otherwise it is called *fault-sensitive* or *fault-intolerant*. In this paper, we use the terms "crash", "fault" and "failure" interchangeably.

3   From Fault-Sensitive Algorithm to Fault-Tolerant Algorithm

We assume that the given fault-sensitive termination detection algorithm is able to detect termination of a non-diffusing computation, when any subset of processes can be initially active. This is not a restrictive assumption as it is proved in [25] that any termination detection algorithm for a diffusing computation, when at most one process is initially active, can be efficiently transformed into a termination detection algorithm for a non-diffusing computation. The transformation increases the message complexity of the underlying termination detection algorithm by only $O(n)$ messages and moreover, does not increase its detection latency. We also assume that, as soon as a process learns about the failure of its neighbouring process, it freezes its incoming channel with the process.

Due to lack of space, we only describe the main idea behind our transformation. Further, we only state the main lemmas and theorems that are used to prove its correctness and analyze its performance. The formal description of the algorithm and omitted proofs can be found in [21].

3.1   The Main Idea

The main idea behind our transformation is to *restart* the fault-sensitive termination detection algorithm algorithm on the set of *currently operational processes* whenever a new failure is detected. We refer to the fault-sensitive termination detection algorithm—an input to our transformation—by $\mathcal{A}$, and to the fault-tolerant termination detection algorithm—the output of our transformation—by $\mathcal{B}$. Before restarting $\mathcal{A}$, we ensure that all operational processes agree on the set of processes that have failed. This is useful as explained further.

Consider a subset of processes Q. We say that a distributed computation has *terminated with respect to Q* (classically or strictly or effectively) if the respective termination condition holds when evaluated only on processes and channels in the subsystem induced by Q. Also, we say that Q has become *safe* if (1) all processes in $P \setminus Q$ have failed, and (2) every process in Q has learned about the failure of all processes in $P \setminus Q$. We have,

Theorem 1. *Consider a safe subset of processes Q. Assume that all processes in Q stay operational. Then a distributed computation has effectively-terminated with respect to P if and only if it has classically-terminated with respect to Q.*

The above theorem implies that if all alive processes agree on the set of failed processes and there are no further crashes, then it is sufficient to ascertain that the underlying computation has classically-terminated with respect to the set of operational processes. An advantage of detecting classical termination is that we can use $\mathcal{A}$, a fault-sensitive termination detection algorithm, to detect termination. We next show that even if one or more processes crash, $\mathcal{A}$ does not announce false termination.

Theorem 2. *When a fault-sensitive termination detection algorithm is executed on a distributed system prone to process crashes then the algorithm still satisfies the safety property, that is, it never announces false termination.*

Now, when $\mathcal{A}$ is restarted, a mechanism is needed to deal with application messages that were sent before $\mathcal{A}$ is restarted but are received after $\mathcal{A}$ has been restarted. Such application messages are referred to as stale or *old application messages*. Clearly, the current instance of $\mathcal{A}$ may not be able to handle an old application message correctly. One simple approach is to "hide" an old application message from the current instance of $\mathcal{A}$ and deliver it directly to the underlying distributed computation. However, on receiving an old application message, if the destination process changes its state from passive to active, then, to the current instance of $\mathcal{A}$, it would appear as if the process became active spontaneously. This violates one of the four rules of the distributed computation. Clearly, the current instance of $\mathcal{A}$ may not work correctly in the presence of old application messages and therefore *cannot be directly* used to detect termination of the underlying computation.

We use the following approach to deal with old application messages. We *superimpose* another computation on top of the underlying computation. We refer to the superimposed computation as the *secondary computation* and to the underlying computation as the *primary computation*. As far as live processes are concerned, the secondary computation is almost identical to the primary computation except possibly in the beginning. Whenever a process crashes and all live processes agree on the set of failed processes, we *simulate a new instance of the secondary computation* in the subsystem induced by the set of operational processes. The processes in the subsystem are referred to as the *base set* of the simulated secondary computation. We then use a *new instance of the fault-sensitive termination detection algorithm* to detect termination of the secondary computation. The older instances of the secondary computation and the fault-sensitive termination detection algorithm are simply aborted. We maintain the following invariants. First, if the secondary computation has classically terminated then the primary computation has classically terminated as well. Second, if the primary computation has classically terminated, then the secondary computation classically terminates eventually. Note that the new instances of both the secondary computation and the fault-sensitive termination detection algorithm start at the same time on the same set of processes.

We now describe the behavior of a process with respect to the secondary computation. Intuitively, a process stays active with respect to the secondary computation at least until it knows that it cannot receive any old application message in the future. Consider a safe subset of processes Q. Suppose an instance of the secondary computation is initiated in the subsystem induced by Q. A process $p_i \in Q$ is passive with respect to the current instance of the secondary computation if one of the following conditions hold:

1. it is passive with respect to the primary computation, and
2. it knows that there is no old application message in transit towards it from any process in Q

An old application message is delivered directly to the primary computation and is hidden from the current instance of the secondary computation as well as the current instance of the fault-sensitive termination detection algorithm. Specifically, only those application messages that are sent by the current instance of the secondary computation are tracked by the corresponding instance of the fault-sensitive termination detection algorithm. (In other words, all application messages are exchanged *through the current instance* of the termination detection algorithm except for old application messages.) It can be verified that the secondary computation is "legal" in the sense that it satisfies all the four rules of the distributed computation. Therefore the fault-sensitive termination detection algorithm $\mathcal{A}$ can be safely used to detect (classical) termination of the secondary computation even in the presence of old application messages. First, we show that, to detect termination of the primary computation, it is safe to detect termination of the secondary computation.

Theorem 3. *Consider a secondary computation initiated in the subsystem induced by processes in Q. Then, if the secondary computation has classically terminated with respect to Q, then the primary computation has classically terminated with respect to Q.*

Next, we prove that, to detect termination of the primary computation, it is sufficient to detect the termination of the secondary computation under certain conditions.

Theorem 4. *Consider a secondary computation initiated in the subsystem induced by processes in Q. Assume that the primary computation has classically terminated with respect to Q and each process in Q eventually learns that there are there are no old application messages in transit towards it sent by other processes in Q. If all processes in Q stay operational, then the secondary computation eventually classically terminates with respect to Q.*

We next describe how to ensure that all operational processes agree on the set of failed processes before restarting the secondary computation the fault-sensitive termination detection algorithm. Later, we describe how to ascertain that there are no relevant old application messages in transit. We assume that both application and control messages are piggybacked with the complement of the base set of the current instance of the secondary computation in progress, which can be used to identify the specific instance of the secondary computation.

Achieving Agreement on the Set of Failed Processes: Whenever a process crashes, one of the live processes is chosen to act as the *coordinator*. Specifically, the process with the smallest identifier among all live processes acts as the coordinator. Every process, on detecting a new failure, sends a NOTIFY message to the coordinator containing the set of all processes that it knows have failed. The coordinator maintains, for each operational process p_i, processes that have failed according to p_i. On determining that all operational processes agree on the set of failed processes, the coordinator sends a RESTART message to each operational process. A RESTART message instructs a process to initiate a new instance of the secondary computation on the appropriate set of processes, and, also, start a new instance of the fault-sensitive termination detection algorithm to detect its termination.

It is possible that, before receiving a RESTART message for a new instance, a process receives an application message that is sent by a more recent instance of the secondary computation than that of the secondary computation currently in progress at that process. In that case, before processing the application message, it behaves as if it has also received a RESTART message and acts accordingly.

Tracking Old Application Messages: A process stays active with respect to the current instance of the secondary computation at least until it knows that it cannot receive any old application message from one of the processes in the relevant subsystem. To that end, each process maintains a count of the number of application messages it has sent to each process so far and, also, a count of the number of application messages it has received from each process so far.

A process, on starting a new instance of the secondary computation, sends an OUTSTATE message to the coordinator; the message contains the number of application messages it sent to each process before restarting the secondary computation. The coordinator, on receiving an OUTSTATE message from every operational process, sends an INSTATE message to all live processes. An INSTATE message sent to process p_i contains the number of application messages that each process has sent to p_i before starting the current instance of the secondary computation. This information can be easily computed by the coordinator after it has received an OUTSTATE message from all live processes.

Clearly, once a process has received an INSTATE message from the coordinator, it can determine how many old application messages are in transit towards it and at least wait until it has received all those messages before becoming passive for the first time with respect to the current instance of the secondary computation.

3.2   Proof of Correctness

We now prove that our transformation produces an algorithm $\mathcal{B}$ that solves the effective-termination detection problem given that $\mathcal{A}$ is a correct fault-sensitive algorithm for solving the classical termination detection problem. The following proposition can be easily verified:

Proposition 1. *Whenever an instance of $\mathcal{A}$ is initiated on a process set Q, all processes in $P \setminus Q$ have in fact crashed and all channels from processes in $P \setminus Q$ to Q have been frozen.*

First, we prove the safety property.

Theorem 5 (safety property). *If $\mathcal{B}$ announces termination, then the underlying computation has effectively terminated.*

Next, we show that $\mathcal{B}$ is live. That is,

Theorem 6 (liveness property). *Once the underlying computation effectively terminates, $\mathcal{B}$ eventually announces termination.*

3.3   Performance Analysis

Let $\mu(n, M)$ and $O\delta(n, M)$ denote the message complexity and detection latency, respectively, of $\mathcal{A}$ when the system has n processes and the underlying computation exchanges M application messages. We now analyze the message complexity and detection latency of the fault-tolerant termination detection algorithm $\mathcal{B}$. Let f denote the actual number of processes that fail during an execution of $\mathcal{B}$.

Lemma 1. *The number of times $\mathcal{A}$ is restarted is bounded by f.*

To compute the message complexity of $\mathcal{B}$, we assume that $\mu(n, M)$ satisfies the following constraint for $k \geq 1$:

$$\sum_{i=1}^{k} \mu(n, M_i) \leq \mu(n, \sum_{i=1}^{k} M_i) + (k-1)\,\mu(n, 0) \tag{6.1}$$

For all existing termination detection algorithms that we are aware of, $\mu(n, M)$ is linear in M. It can be verified that if $\mu(n, M)$ is a linear function in M, then the inequality (6.1) indeed holds.

Theorem 7 (message complexity). *The message complexity of $\mathcal{B}$ is given by* $\mu(n, M) + O(f\,(n + \mu(n, 0)))$.

We now bound the detection latency of $\mathcal{B}$. To compute detection latency in an asynchronous distributed system, it is typically assumed that message delay is at most one time unit. Moreover, we assume that the failure detection latency is bounded by one time unit as well.

Theorem 8 (detection latency). *The detection latency of $\mathcal{B}$ is given by* $\delta(n, M) + O(f\delta(n, 0))$.

We next bound the message overhead of $\mathcal{B}$. Let $\alpha(n, M)$ and $\beta(n, M)$ denote the application and control message overhead, respectively, of $\mathcal{A}$ when the system has n processes and the underlying computation exchanges M application messages.

Theorem 9 (application message overhead). *The application message overhead of $\mathcal{B}$ is $\alpha(n, M) + O(f \log n)$.*

Finally, we bound the control message overhead of $\mathcal{B}$. Note that control messages can be categorized into two groups. The first group consists of control messages exchanged by different instances of $\mathcal{A}$. The second group consists of control messages exchanged as a result of process crash, namely NOTIFY, RESTART, OUTSTATE and INSTATE. We refer to the messages in the first group as termination detection messages and to the messages in the second group as failure recovery messages.

Theorem 10 (control message overhead). *The control message overhead of $\mathcal{B}$ for termination detection messages is given by $\beta(n, M) + O(f \log n)$ and for failure recovery messages is given by $O(f \log n + n \log M)$.*

4   The Weakest Failure Detector for Termination Detection

Failure detectors are not only an abstraction to yield information about the operational state of processes, they can also be regarded as *synchrony abstractions* since they are usually implemented using heartbeat messages and timeouts [26]. For example, an eventually perfect failure detector is strictly weaker than a perfect failure detector, and, therefore, can be implemented with weaker synchrony assumptions (namely those of *partial synchrony* [27] instead of full synchrony). Proving that a certain type of failure detector is *necessary* for solving a problem gives an indication about the minimal amount of synchrony needed to solve that problem. In this section, unless otherwise stated, "termination" refers to "effective-termination".

We now show that a perfect failure detector is necessary for solving termination detection in a crash-prone distributed system. To that end, we transform an instance of a fault-tolerant termination detection algorithm into a perfect failure detector at one process q, that is, q is able to reliably detect process crashes. A perfect failure detector can then be implemented by using n parallel instances of the transformation algorithm, one per process.

Assume that we are given an algorithm $\mathcal{A}$ that can detect termination of an arbitrary computation among n processes even in the presence of process crashes. We now set up n independent computations C_i, one for each process p_i. The computation C_i is such that process p_i is initially active and all processes apart from p_i are passive. In the computation no messages are sent and received and p_i never becomes passive. Now consider some process $q \neq p_i$ and the corresponding computation C_i. Process q starts an instance of the termination detection algorithm $\mathcal{A}$ with respect to the computation C_i. Whenever $\mathcal{A}$ announces the termination of C_i, q henceforth permanently suspects p_i. The same actions are performed for every other process in the system, that is, q invokes n parallel instances of $\mathcal{A}$, one for each computation C_i.

We now show that this algorithm implements a perfect failure detector if $\mathcal{A}$ correctly solves the effective-termination detection problem. First consider strong accuracy (a process is never suspected before it crashes) and assume that q suspects p_i. It follows from our transformation that $\mathcal{A}$ has announced termination of the computation C_i. This means that all processes in C_i are either crashed or passive. Since C_i is such that p_i is always passive, it implies that p_i has crashed.

Now consider strong completeness (eventually every crashed process is suspected by every correct process) and assume that p_i has crashed and q is correct. Once p_i crashes, clearly the termination condition holds for the computation C_i. Since $\mathcal{A}$ is a correct termination detection algorithm, $\mathcal{A}$ eventually announces termination of C_i at q. Upon announcing termination, q starts suspecting p_i, concluding the proof.

Overall, this shows that if we can solve termination detection in a crash-prone distributed system, then we can also implement a perfect failure detector in such a system. Hence, it is impossible to solve termination detection when one or more processes can crash assuming only a failure detector that is strictly weaker than a perfect failure detector. In other words, a perfect failure detector is *necessary* for solving the effective-termination detection problem.

The *weakest failure detector* for a problem is a failure detector that is necessary and sufficient to solve that problem. We show above that a perfect failure detector is necessary. Our transformation in Sect. 3 shows that a perfect failure detector is also sufficient. Combining the two, we can conclude that a perfect failure detector is the weakest failure detector for solving the effective-termination detection problem. The result holds as long as at least one process can crash and assuming that channels can be frozen. Therefore, it generalizes the result of Wu *et al* [23], which shows that a failure detector must be complete. Our result also further clarifies the relationship between the termination detection problem and the *consensus problem*: Wu *et al* [23] show that consensus is at least as hard to solve as termination detection. By relating termination detection to the failure detector hierarchy of Chandra and Toueg [24], our result has two interesting corollaries. First, termination detection is strictly harder than consensus in environments where a majority of processes remains correct. This follows from the result that in such cases the weakest failure detector for consensus is strictly weaker than a perfect failure detector [24]. Second, when any number of processes can crash, termination detection is actually equivalent to consensus [28].

5   Conclusions and Future Work

In this paper, we presented a transformation using a perfect failure detector that can be used to convert any termination detection algorithm for a fully connected communication topology that has been designed for a failure-free environment into a termination detection algorithm that can tolerate process crashes. Our transformation does not impose any additional overhead on the system (besides that imposed by the underlying termination detection algorithm) if no process actually crashes during an execution. Moreover, when applied to fault-sensitive termination detection algorithms by Dijkstra and Scholten [1] and Huang [8], the resulting fault-tolerant termination detection algorithms compare very favorably with those by Lai and Wu [16] and Tseng [17]. Our transformation can be generalized to an arbitrary communication topology provided process crashes do not partition the system. We also proved that a perfect failure detector is the weakest failure detector for solving the termination detection problem in a crash-prone distributed system. This holds even if at most one process can crash.

As part of future work, we plan to investigate the termination detection problem when crashed processes may recover and channels may be lossy. We also plan to apply ideas proposed in this paper to transform other fault-sensitive algorithms—such as for detecting other stable properties—into fault-tolerant algorithms.

References

1. Dijkstra, E.W., Scholten, C.S.: Termination Detection for Diffusing Computations. Information Processing Letters (IPL) **11** (1980) 1–4
2. Francez, N.: Distributed Termination. ACM Transactions on Programming Languages and Systems (TOPLAS) **2** (1980) 42–55
3. Rana, S.P.: A Distributed Solution of the Distributed Termination Problem. Information Processing Letters (IPL) **17** (1983) 43–46
4. Shavit, N., Francez, N.: A New Approach to Detection of Locally Indicative Stability. In: Proceedings of the International Colloquium on Automata, Languages and Systems (ICALP), Rennes, France (1986) 344–358
5. Mattern, F.: Algorithms for Distributed Termination Detection. Distributed Computing (DC) **2** (1987) 161–175
6. Dijkstra, E.W.: Shmuel Safra's Version of Termination Detection. EWD Manuscript 998. Available at http://www.cs.utexas.edu/users/EWD (1987)
7. Mattern, F.: Global Quiescence Detection based on Credit Distribution and Recovery. Information Processing Letters (IPL) **30** (1989) 195–200
8. Huang, S.T.: Detecting Termination of Distributed Computations by External Agents. In: Proceedings of the IEEE International Conference on Distributed Computing Systems (ICDCS). (1989) 79–84
9. Chandrasekaran, S., Venkatesan, S.: A Message-Optimal Algorithm for Distributed Termination Detection. Journal of Parallel and Distributed Computing (JPDC) **8** (1990) 245–252

10. Tel, G., Mattern, F.: The Derivation of Distributed Termination Detection Algorithms from Garbage Collection Schemes. ACM Transactions on Programming Languages and Systems (TOPLAS) **15** (1993) 1–35
11. Khokhar, A.A., Hambrusch, S.E., Kocalar, E.: Termination Detection in Data-Driven Parallel Computations/Applications. Journal of Parallel and Distributed Computing (JPDC) **63** (2003) 312–326
12. Mahapatra, N.R., Dutt, S.: An Efficient Delay-Optimal Distributed Termination Detection Algorithm. To Appear in Journal of Parallel and Distributed Computing (JPDC) (2004)
13. Wang, X., Mayo, J.: A General Model for Detecting Termination in Dynamic Systems. In: Proceedings of the 18th International Parallel and Distributed Processing Symposium (IPDPS), Santa Fe, New Mexico (2004)
14. Mittal, N., Venkatesan, S., Peri, S.: Message-Optimal and Latency-Optimal Termination Detection Algorithms for Arbitrary Topologies. In: Proceedings of the Symposium on Distributed Computing (DISC), The Netherlands (2004) 290–304
15. Venkatesan, S.: Reliable Protocols for Distributed Termination Detection. IEEE Transactions on Reliability **38** (1989) 103–110
16. Lai, T.H., Wu, L.F.: An $(N-1)$-Resilient Algorithm for Distributed Termination Detection. IEEE Transactions on Parallel and Distributed Systems (TPDS) **6** (1995) 63–78
17. Tseng, Y.C.: Detecting Termination by Weight-Throwing in a Faulty Distributed System. Journal of Parallel and Distributed Computing (JPDC) **25** (1995) 7–15
18. Shah, A., Toueg, S.: Distributed Snapshots in spite of Failures. Technical Report TR84-624, Department of Computer Science, Cornell University, Ithaca, NY (1984) (Revised February 1985).
19. Chandy, K.M., Lamport, L.: Distributed Snapshots: Determining Global States of Distributed Systems. ACM Transactions on Computer Systems **3** (1985) 63–75
20. Gärtner, F.C., Pleisch, S.: (Im)Possibilities of Predicate Detection in Crash-Affected Systems. In: Proceedings of the 5th Workshop on Self-Stabilizing Systems (WSS), Lisbon, Portugal, Springer-Verlag (2001) 98–113
21. Mittal, N., Freiling, F.C., Venkatesan, S., Penso, L.D.: Efficient Reductions for Wait-Free Termination Detection in Crash-Prone Systems. Technical Report AIB-2005-12, Department of Computer Science, Rheinisch-Westfälische Technische Hochschule (RWTH), Aachen, Germany (2005)
22. Arora, A., Gouda, M.G.: Distributed Reset. IEEE Transactions on Computers **43** (1994) 1026–1038
23. Wu, L.F., Lai, T.H., Tseng, Y.C.: Consensus and Termination Detection in the Presence of Faulty Processes. In: Proceedings of the International Conference on Parallel and Distributed Systems (ICPADS), Hsinchu, Taiwan (1992) 267–274
24. Chandra, T.D., Toueg, S.: Unreliable Failure Detectors for Reliable Distributed Systems. Journal of the ACM **43** (1996) 225–267
25. Peri, S., Mittal, N.: On Termination Detection in an Asynchronous Distributed System. In: Proceedings of the ISCA International Conference on Parallel and Distributed Computing Systems (PDCS), California (2004) 209–215
26. Larrea, M., Fernández, A., Arévalo, S.: On the Implementation of Unreliable Failure Detectors in Partially Synchronous Systems. IEEE Transactions on Computers **53** (2004) 815–828
27. Dwork, C., Lynch, N., Stockmeyer, L.: Consensus in the Presence of Partial Synchrony. Journal of the ACM **35** (1988) 288–323
28. Delporte-Gallet, C., Fauconnier, H., Guerraoui, R., Hadzilacos, V., Kouznetsov, P., Toueg, S.: The Weakest Failure Detector to Solve Certain Fundamental Problems in Distributed Computing. In: Proceedings of the ACM Symposium on Principles of Distributed Computing (PODC), St. Johns, Newfoundland, Canada (2004)

Non-blocking Hashtables with Open Addressing

Chris Purcell[1] and Tim Harris[2]

[1] Computer Laboratory, University of Cambridge, 15 JJ Thomson Avenue,
Cambridge CB3 0FD, UK
`Chris.Purcell@cl.cam.ac.uk`
[2] Microsoft Research Ltd., Roger Needham Building, 7 JJ Thomson Avenue,
Cambridge CB3 0FB, UK
`tharris@microsoft.com`

Abstract. We present the first non-blocking hashtable based on open
addressing that provides the following benefits: it combines good cache
locality, accessing a single cacheline if there are no collisions, with short
straight-line code; it needs no storage overhead for pointers and memory
allocator schemes, having instead an overhead of two words per bucket;
it does not need to periodically reorganise or replicate the table; and it
does not need garbage collection, even with arbitrary-sized keys. Open
problems include resizing the table and replacing, rather than erasing,
entries. The result is a highly-concurrent set algorithm that approaches
or outperforms the best externally-chained implementations we tested,
with fixed memory costs and no need to select or fine-tune a garbage
collector or locking strategy.

1 Introduction

This paper presents a new design for non-blocking hashtables in which collisions
are resolved by open addressing, i.e. probing through the other buckets of the
table, rather than external chaining through linked lists.

The key idea is that rather than leaving tombstones to mark where deletions
occur, we store per-bucket upper bounds on the number of other buckets that
need to be consulted. This means that unlike the earlier designs we discuss in
Section 2.2, ours supports a mixed workload of insertions and deletions without
the need to periodically replicate the table's contents to clean out tombstones.
Consequently, the table can operate without the need for dynamic storage management so long as its load factor remains acceptable.

Our design is split into three parts. Section 3.1 deals with maintaining the
shared bounds associated with each bucket. The key difficulty here is ensuring
that a bound remains correct when several entries are being inserted and removed
at once. Section 3.2 builds on this to provide a hashtable. The main problem in
doing so is guaranteeing non-blocking progress while ensuring that at most one
instance of any key can be present in the table. In Section 3.3, we present a more
complicated design allowing larger keys and a better progress guarantee, and in
Section 3.4 we discuss open problems with the algorithm.

P. Fraigniaud (Ed.): DISC 2005, LNCS 3724, pp. 108–121, 2005.
© Springer-Verlag Berlin Heidelberg 2005

Section 4 evaluates the performance of our algorithm, compared to state-of-the-art designs based on external chaining. As with these, we rely only on the single-word atomic operations found on all modern processor families. Additionally, our algorithm has many properties that machines rely on for optimal performance: operations run independently, updating disjoint memory locations (*disjoint access parallel*) and not modifying shared memory during logically read-only operations (*read parallel*), and hence typically run in parallel on multiprocessor machines. Finally, a low *operation footprint* (shared memory touched per operation) gives greater throughput under stress by easing pressure on the memory subsystem.

Our results reflect this, demonstrating performance comparable with the best existing designs in all tested cases. On highly-parallel workloads with many updates, our algorithm ran 35% faster; while a single-threaded run with mostly read-only operations was the worst case, running 40% slower than the best existing design.

Proof of correctness and progress properties can be found in [11].

2   Background

2.1   Non-blocking Progress Guarantees

Data structures are easiest to implement when accessed in isolation, but general schemes for enforcing that isolation — for instance, using mutual exclusion locks — typically result in poor scalability and robustness in the face of contention and failure. Concurrent algorithms that avoid mutual exclusion are generally *non-blocking*: suspension of any subset of threads will not prevent forward progress by the rest of the system.

The weakest non-blocking guarantee is *obstruction-freedom*: if at any time a thread runs in isolation, it will complete its operation within a bounded number of steps. This precludes mutual exclusion, as suspension of a lock-holding thread will prevent others waiting on that lock from making progress. *Lock-freedom* combines this with guaranteed throughput: any active thread taking a bounded number of steps ensures global progress. Unfortunately, creating *practical* non-blocking forms of even simple data structures is notoriously difficult.

2.2   Related Work

Externally-chained hashtables store each bucket's collisions[1] in a list. Michael introduced the first practical lock-free hashtables based on external chaining with linked lists [8]. Shalev and Shavit described *split-ordered lists* that allow the number of buckets to vary dynamically [9]. Fraser detailed lock-free skip-lists and binary search trees [2]. Recently, Lea has contributed a high-performance, scalable, *lock-based*, externally-chained hashtable design to the latest version

---

[1] We refer to a key stored outside its primary bucket as a *collision*.

of Java (5.0), which avoids locking on most read-operations, preserving read-parallelism.

All of the above designs rely on an out-of-band garbage collector. Michael reported that reference counting was unacceptably slow for this purpose as it did not preserve read-parallelism; he proposed using safe memory reclamation [7] to get a strictly bounded memory overhead. Fraser used a simple low-overhead garbage collection scheme, *epoch-based reclamation*, where all threads maintain a current epoch, and memory is reclaimed only after all epochs change; this has a potentially unbounded memory footprint, and a large one in practice.

Tombstones are the traditional means of handling deletion in an open addressed hashtable [3], but cause degenerate search times in the face of a random workload with frequent deleting. Martin and Davis [5] proposed using periodic table replication to limit tombstone growth, relying on garbage collection to reclaim old tables. More recently, Gao *et al.* [1] presented a design with in-built garbage collection.

Both designs limit tombstone reuse to reinsertions of the old key, to achieve linearizability, and do not address the issue of storing multi-word keys directly in the table. The rest of our paper presents solutions to these problems, which we believe are compatible with the replication algorithms already proposed.

3   Memory-Management-Free Open Addressing

Each bucket in our hashtable stores a bound on its collisions' indices in the probe sequence (Figure 1). When running in isolation, a reader follows the probe sequence this number of steps before terminating; an insert that collides raises the bound if necessary; and an erase that empties the last bucket in this truncated probe sequence searches back for the previous collision and decreases the bound accordingly.

We make this safe for concurrent use in two steps, first maintaining each bucket's bound in Section 3.1, then ensuring keys are not duplicated in Section 3.2.

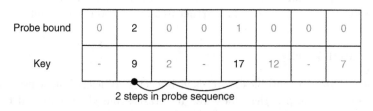

Fig. 1. Bounds on collision indices for a hash table holding keys $\{3, 7, 9, 12, 17\}$. Hash function is (key mod 8), probe sequence is quadratic $[\frac{1}{2}(i^2 + i)]$. Key 17 is stored two steps along the probe sequence for bucket 1, so the probe bound is 2.

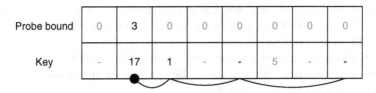

After a collision is removed, a thread scans for the previous collision.

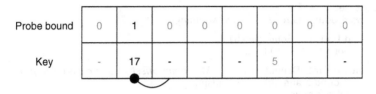

If a concurrent erasure is missed, the bound may be left too large.

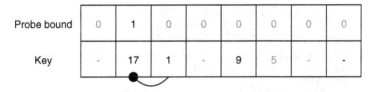

Worse, if a concurrent insertion is missed, the bound may be made too small.

Fig. 2. Problems maintaining a shared bound after a collision is removed from the end of the probe sequence

3.1   Bounding Searches

Maintaining the probe bounds concurrently is complicated by the need to lower them: simply scanning the probe sequence for the previous collision and swapping it into the bound field may result in the bound being too large if the collision is removed, slowing searches, or too small if another collision is inserted, violating correctness (Figure 2).

In order to keep the bounds correct during erasures, we use a *scanning phase* during which the thread erasing the last collision in the probe sequence searches through the previous buckets to compute the new bound (lines 18–22). A thread announces that it is in this phase by setting a *scanning bit* to true (line 18); this bit is held in the same word as the bound itself, so both fields are updated atomically.

Dealing with insertions is now easy: they atomically clear the scanning bit and raise the bound if necessary (lines 9–12). Deletions also clear the scanning bit (line 16), but are complicated by the scanning phase. We rely on the fact that at most one thread can be in the process of erasing a given collision, and that threads only start scanning when erasing the last collision in the probe sequence. The collision's index value thus identifies the scanning thread and, if it is still present as the bound when scanning completes, and if the scanning bit is still set, we know there have been no concurrent updates (line 22). Otherwise, we retry the scanning phase.

Given a lock-free atomic compare-and-swap (CAS) function, the pseudocode in Figure 3 is lock-free. We represent the packing of an int and a bit into a machine word with the $\langle .,. \rangle$ operator.

```
1   class Set {
        word bounds[size] // ⟨bound,scanning⟩

3       void InitProbeBound(int h):
            bounds[h] := ⟨0,false⟩

5       int GetProbeBound(int h): // Maximum offset of any collision in probe seq.
            ⟨bound,scanning⟩ := bounds[h]
7           return bound

        void ConditionallyRaiseBound(int h, int index): // Ensure maximum ≥ index
9       do
            ⟨old_bound,scanning⟩ := bounds[h]
11          new_bound := max(old_bound,index)
        while ¬CAS(&bounds[h],⟨old_bound,scanning⟩,⟨new_bound,false⟩)

13      void ConditionallyLowerBound(int h, int index): // Allow maximum < index
            ⟨bound,scanning⟩ := bounds[h]
15      if scanning = true
            CAS(&bounds[h],⟨bound,true⟩,⟨bound,false⟩)
17      if index > 0 // If maximum = index > 0, set maximum < index
            while CAS(&bounds[h],⟨index,false⟩,⟨index,true⟩)
19          i := index-1 // Scanning phase: scan cells for new maximum
            while i > 0 ∧ ¬DoesBucketContainCollision(h, i)
21          i--
            CAS(&bounds[h],⟨index,true⟩,⟨i,false⟩)
```

Fig. 3. Per-bucket probe bounds (continued below)

3.2 Inserting and Removing Keys

Inserting and removing keys concurrently is complicated by the lack of a pre-determined bucket for any given key. Inserting into the first empty bucket is not sufficient because, as Figure 4 shows, a concurrent erasure may alter which bucket is 'first', and a key may be duplicated. If duplicate keys are allowed in the table, concurrent key erasure becomes impractical.

To ensure uniqueness, we split insertions into three stages (Figure 5). First, a thread reserves an empty bucket and publishes its attempt by storing the key it is inserting, along with an 'inserting' flag. Next, the thread checks the other positions in the probe sequence for that key, looking for other threads with 'inserting' entries, or for a completed insertion of the same key. If it finds another insertion in progress in a bucket then it changes that bucket's state to 'busy', stalling the other insertion at that point in time. If it finds another completed insertion of the same key, then its own insertion has failed: it empties its bucket and returns 'false'. In the final stage, it attempts to finish its own

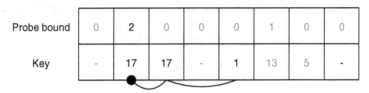

Probe bound	0	2	0	0	0	1	0	0
Key	-	9	-	-	1	13	5	-

One thread determines that the first empty bucket is at offset 1, and prepares to insert key 17 there.

Probe bound	0	2	0	0	0	1	0	0
Key	-	-	-	-	1	13	5	-

Another thread removes key 9, and prepares to insert key 17. The first empty bucket is now at offset 0.

Probe bound	0	2	0	0	0	1	0	0
Key	-	17	17	-	1	13	5	-

The two threads now insert, creating a duplicate of the key.

Fig. 4. Problems concurrently inserting keys

insert, changing the 'inserting' flag in its bucket to 'member'. It must do this with a CAS instruction so that it fails if stalled by another thread; if stalled, the thread republishes its attempt and restarts the second stage.

The pseudocode in Figure 6 is obstruction-free. Each bucket contains a four-valued state, one of *empty, busy, inserting* or *member*, and, for the latter two states, a key. The key and state must be modified atomically; we use the $\langle ., . \rangle$ operator to represent packing them into a single word. A key k is considered inserted if some bucket in the table contains $\langle k, member \rangle$. The *Hash* function selects a bucket for a given key. The three insertion stages can be found in lines 42–50, 51–60 and 61, respectively.

Unlike Martin and Davis' approach [5], deleted buckets are immediately free for arbitrary reuse, so table replication is not needed to clear out tombstones. The algorithm preserves read parallelism and, assuming disjoint keys hash to separate memory locations, disjoint access parallelism. In the expected case where the bucket contains no collisions, the operation footprint is two words — a single cache line if buckets and bounds are interleaved.

Probe bound	0	2	0	0	1	0	0	0
State	empty	member	member	empty	member	inserting	empty	member
Key	-	9	1	-	17	12	-	7

Initial state

Probe bound	0	2	0	0	1	1	0	0
State	empty	member	member	empty	member	inserting	inserting	member
Key	-	9	1	-	17	12	12	7

Publish the attempted insertion in the second cell in the probe sequence, and raise the probe bound to cover it.

Collision offset bound	0	2	0	0	1	1	0	0
State	empty	member	member	empty	member	busy	inserting	member
Key	-	9	1	-	17	-	12	7

Stall all concurrent insertion attempts.

Probe bound	0	2	0	0	1	1	0	0
State	empty	member	member	empty	member	busy	member	member
Key	-	9	1	-	17	-	12	7

Move bucket into 'member' state.

Fig. 5. Inserting key 12

3.3 Extensions: Lock-Freedom and Multi-word Keys

We now turn to two flaws in the above algorithm. The first is that concurrent insertions may live-lock, each repeatedly stalling the other. One solution is to use an out-of-line contention manager: Scherer and Scott have described many suitable for use in any obstruction-free algorithm [10], which are easy to adopt. Another solution, which we cover in more detail as it is a non-trivial problem, is to make the algorithm lock-free.

The standard method of achieving lock-freedom is to allow operations to assist as well as obstruct each other. As given, however, the hash table cannot support concurrent assistance, as Figure 7 demonstrates: a cell's contents can change arbitrarily before returning to a previous state, allowing a CAS to succeed incorrectly. This is known as the ABA problem, and we return to it in a moment.

The second problem is storing keys larger than a machine word: in the algorithm as given, this requires a multi-word CAS, which is not generally available. However, we note that a cell's key is only ever modified by a single writer, when the cell is in busy state. This means we only need to deal with concurrent single-writer multiple-reader access to the cell, rather than provide a general multi-word atomic update. We can therefore use Lamport's version counters [4] (Figure 8).

If a cell's state is stored in the same word as its version count, the ABA problem is circumvented, allowing threads to assist concurrent operations. This

```
23      word buckets[size] // ⟨key,state⟩

        word* Bucket(int h, int index): // Size must be a power of 2
25          return &buckets[(h + index*(index+1)/2) % size] // Quadratic probing

        bool DoesBucketContainCollision(int h, int index):
27          ⟨k,state⟩ := *Bucket(h,index)
            return (k ≠ - ∧ Hash(k) = h)

29  public:
        void Init():
31          for i := 0 .. size-1
                InitProbeBound(i)
33              buckets[i] := ⟨-,empty⟩

        bool Lookup(Key k): // Determine whether k is a member of the set
35          h := Hash(k)
            max := GetProbeBound(h)
37          for i := 0 .. max
                if *Bucket(h,i) = ⟨k,member⟩
39                  return true
            return false

41      bool Insert(Key k): // Insert k into the set if it is not a member
            h := Hash(k)
43          i := 0 // Reserve a cell
            while ¬CAS(Bucket(h,i), ⟨-,empty⟩, ⟨-,busy⟩)
45              i++
                if i ≥ size
47                  throw "Table full"
            do // Attempt to insert a unique copy of k
49              *Bucket(h,i) := ⟨k,inserting⟩
                ConditionallyRaiseBound(h,i)
51              max := GetProbeBound(h) // Scan through the probe sequence
                for j := 0 .. max
53                  if j ≠ i
                        if *Bucket(h,j) = ⟨k, inserting⟩ // Stall concurrent inserts
55                          CAS(Bucket(h,j), ⟨k,inserting⟩, ⟨-,busy⟩)
                        if *Bucket(h,j) = ⟨k,member⟩ // Abort if k already a member
57                          *Bucket(h,i) := ⟨-,busy⟩
                            ConditionallyLowerBound(h,i)
59                          *Bucket(h,i) := ⟨-,empty⟩
                            return false
61          while ¬CAS(Bucket(h,i), ⟨k,inserting⟩, ⟨k,member⟩)
            return true

63      bool Erase(Key k): // Remove k from the set if it is a member
            h := Hash(k)
65          max := GetProbeBound(h) // Scan through the probe sequence
            for i := 0 .. max
67              if *Bucket(h,i) = ⟨k,member⟩ // Remove a copy of ⟨k, member⟩
                    if CAS(Bucket(h,i), ⟨k,member⟩, ⟨-,busy⟩)
69                      ConditionallyLowerBound(h,i)
                        *Bucket(h,i) := ⟨-,empty⟩
71                      return true
            return false
73  }
```

Fig. 6. Obstruction-free set (continued from Figure 3)

State	empty	inserting
Key	-	12

A single thread is about to complete its insertion of key 12. The next step is to atomically move the cell from inserting to member state.

State	empty	member
Key	-	12

The thread is suspended, and its insertion assisted to completion by another thread.

State	member	inserting
Key	12	12

The key is now removed, and two other threads are concurrently attempting to reinsert key 12. One has just succeeded, and the other is about to remove itself. If the first thread wakes up at this point, it will still atomically move the cell from inserting to member state, duplicating key 12.

Fig. 7. Problems assisting concurrent operations

lets us create a lock-free insertion algorithm (diagram in Figure 9, pseudo-code in Figure 10).

Each bucket contains: a version count; a state field, one of *empty, busy, collided, visible, inserting* or *member*; and a key field, publically readable during the latter three stages. The version count and state are maintained so that no state (except busy) will recur with the same version.

As before, a thread finds an empty bucket and moves it into 'inserting' state (lines 65–76), and checks the probe sequence for other threads with 'inserting' entries, or a completed insertion of the same key (lines 86–106). However, if multiple 'inserting' entries are found, the earliest in the probe sequence is left unaltered, and the others moved into 'collided' state. When the whole probe sequence has been scanned and all contenders removed, the earliest entry is moved into 'member' state (line 105) and the insertion concludes (lines 78–83).

This version of the hashtable is lock-free.

3.4   Open Problems: Dynamic Growth and Key Replacement

If the set population approaches the number of buckets, we must replicate into a larger table. The Gao *et al.* [1] replication algorithm may be adaptable for this purpose. No aggregate time or memory cost is incurred on operations, as if the population stabilises, no further replications are required. Assuming each new table doubles in size, discarding the old table after growth is a memory overhead no greater than the final size of the table.

Even if a garbage collector is running, the bounded memory footprint provides several advantages. Many collectors are only activated when memory becomes scarce, so will benefit from less memory usage. Lacking pointers, no costly read or write barriers are needed to ensure memory is not leaked. Finally, the small number of memory allocations needed helps avoid any synchronization the allocator code may contain. The performance and latency benefits of these will depend on the memory management algorithms used.

As given, the algorithm cannot implement a dictionary, storing a value with each key, as there is no way to replace keys.

We hope to report these modifications in future work.

```
23    struct BucketT {
        word vs // ⟨version,state⟩
25      Key key
      } buckets[size]
27    word buckets[size] // ⟨key,state⟩

      BucketT* Bucket(int h, int index): // Size must be a power of 2
29      return &buckets[(h + index*(index+1)/2) % size] // Quadratic probing

      bool DoesBucketContainCollision(int h, int index):
31      ⟨version1,state1⟩ := Bucket(h,index)→vs
        if state1 = visible ∨ state1 = inserting ∨ state1 = member
33        if Hash(Bucket(h,index)→key) = h
            ⟨version2,state2⟩ := Bucket(h,index)→vs
35          if state2 = visible ∨ state2 = inserting ∨ state2 = member
              if version1 = version2
37              return true
        return false

39  public:
      void Init():
41      for i := 0 .. size-1
          InitProbeBound(i)
43        buckets[i].vs := ⟨0,empty⟩

      bool Lookup(Key k): // Determine whether k is a member of the set
45      h := Hash(k)
        max := GetProbeBound(h)
47      for i := 0 .. max
          ⟨version,state⟩ := Bucket(h,index)→vs // Read cell atomically
49        if state = member ∧ Bucket(h,index)→key = k
            if Bucket(h,index)→vs = ⟨version,member⟩
51            return true
        return false

53      bool Erase(Key k): // Remove k from the set if it is a member
        h := Hash(k)
55      max := GetProbeBound(h)
        for i := 0 .. max
57        ⟨version,state⟩ := Bucket(h,index)→vs // Atomically read/update cell
          if state = member ∧ Bucket(h,index)→key = k
59          if CAS(Bucket(h,i)→vs, ⟨version,member⟩, ⟨version,busy⟩)
              ConditionallyLowerBound(h,i)
61            Bucket(h,i)→vs := ⟨version+1,empty⟩
              return true
63      return false
```

Fig. 8. Version-counted derivative of Figure 6 (continued in Figure 10)

Probe bound	0	2	0	0	1	0	0	0
Version	18	2	3	6	4	3	24	7
State	empty	member	member	empty	member	inserting	empty	member
Key		9	1		17	12		7

Initial state

Probe bound	0	2	0	0	1	1	0	0
Version	18	2	3	6	4	3	24	7
State	empty	member	member	empty	member	inserting	inserting	member
Key		9	1		17	12	12	7

Write key and raise probe sequence bound

Probe bound	0	2	0	0	1	1	0	0
Version	18	2	3	6	4	3	24	7
State	empty	member	member	empty	member	inserting	collided	member
Key		9	1		17	12	12	7

Earlier 'inserting' entry found; move bucket into 'collided' state.

Probe bound	0	2	0	0	1	1	0	0
Version	18	2	3	6	4	3	24	7
State	empty	member	member	empty	member	member	collided	member
Key		9	1		17	12	12	7

Assist completion of earlier entry

Probe bound	0	2	0	0	1	0	0	0
Version	18	2	3	6	4	3	25	7
State	empty	member	member	empty	member	member	empty	member
Key		9	1		17	12		7

Empty bucket, lower probe sequence bound and return `false`.

Fig. 9. Inserting key 12 (lock-free algorithm)

4   Results

In order to assess the performance of our new obstruction-free hashtable, we implemented a range of designs from the literature: Michael's 'dynamic lock-free hashtable', which uses external chains to manage collisions and safe-memory-reclamation (MM-SMR) to manage storage, a variant of Michael's design using epoch-based garbage collection (MM-Epoch), a further variant of Michael's design using reference counting (MM-RC), and Shalev and Shavit's 'split-ordered lists' using epoch-based garbage collection (SS-Epoch). We also tested Lea's lock-based hashtable design, again using epoch-based collection. Since performance depends on the locking algorithm and the level of granularity (number of locks), we used a basic spinlock and the MCS lock [6] at different granularities.

```
        bool Insert(Key k): // Insert k into the set if it is not a member
65         h := Hash(k)
           i := -1 // Reserve a cell
67         do
              if ++i ≥ size
69               throw "Table full"
              ⟨version,state⟩ := Bucket(h,i)→vs
71         while ¬CAS(&Bucket(h,i)→vs, ⟨version,empty⟩, ⟨version,busy⟩)
           Bucket(h,i)→key := k
73         while true // Attempt to insert a unique copy of k
              *Bucket(h,i)→vs := ⟨version,visible⟩
75            ConditionallyRaiseBound(h,i)
              *Bucket(h,i)→vs := ⟨version,inserting⟩
77            r := Assist(k,h,i,version)
              if Bucket(h,i)→vs ≠ ⟨version,collided⟩
79               return true
              if ¬r
81               ConditionallyLowerBound(h,i)
                 Bucket(h,i)→vs := ⟨version+1,empty⟩
83               return false
              version++

85   private:
        bool Assist(Key k,int h,int i,int ver_i): // Attempt to insert k at i
87         // Return true if no other cell seen in member state
           max := GetProbeBound(h) // Scan through probe sequence
89         for j := 0 .. max
              if i ≠ j
91               ⟨ver_j,state_j⟩ := Bucket(h,j)→vs
                 if state_j = inserting ∧ Bucket(h,j)→key = k
93                  if j < i // Assist any insert found earlier in the probe sequence
                       if Bucket(h,j)→vs = ⟨ver_j,inserting⟩
95                        CAS(&Bucket(h,i)→vs, ⟨ver_i,inserting⟩, ⟨ver_i,collided⟩)
                          return Assist(k,h,j,ver_j)
97                  else // Fail any insert found later in the probe sequence
                       if Bucket(h,i)→vs = ⟨ver_i,inserting⟩
99                        CAS(&Bucket(h,j)→vs, ⟨ver_j,inserting⟩, ⟨ver_j,collided⟩)
                 ⟨ver_j,state_j⟩ := Bucket(h,j)→vs // Abort if k already a member
101              if state_j = member ∧ Bucket(h,j)→key = k
                    if Bucket(h,j)→vs = ⟨ver_j,member⟩
103                    CAS(&Bucket(h,i)→vs,⟨ver_i,inserting⟩,⟨ver_i,collided⟩)
                       return false
105        CAS(&Bucket(h,i), ⟨ver_i,inserting⟩, ⟨ver_i,member⟩)
           return true
107  }
```

Fig. 10. Lock-free insertion algorithm (continued from Figure 8)

We compared these against our new design, as presented in Figures 3, 8 and 10 (PH).

Our benchmark is parameterized by the number of concurrent threads and by the range of key values used. We present results for 1–12 threads (running on a Sun Fire V880 with eight 900MHz UltraSPARC-III CPUs) and with 2^{15} keys chosen from $[0, 2^{15}M)$, M = 2 or 10. Each update step consists of removing a key then inserting another; finding keys and empty slots is done by trial-and-repetition, choosing candidates uniformly at random, giving $\frac{M^2}{M-1}$ searches on average for each update step. This was designed to avoid hashtable resizing,

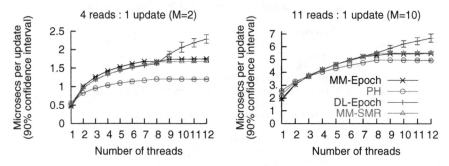

Fig. 11. Performance on 8-way SPARC machine

which simplifies our algorithm, as well as allowing a fine locking granularity and greater read-parallelism in Lea's, but which unfortunately negates the benefit of split-ordered lists.

Each trial lasted ten seconds, after a three second warm-up period to fill caches, and trials were repeated 20 times, interleaved to avoid short-lived anomalies, to obtain a 90% confidence interval. Our results are shown in Figure 11.

MM-Epoch and MM-SMR consistently outperform MM-RC and SS-Epoch (which, for clarity, are not shown in the results), thanks to low overhead and read-parallelism. Below 8 threads, DL-Epoch performs best with low-overhead spinlocking, avoiding the high cost of spinning with a fine locking granularity.

Searching for a key that is not in the table requires two memory accesses for the PH algorithm, but only one for all others tested. In the absence of contention, this is clearly visible in the results. Applications with a higher lookup hit rate would lower this cost. However, in all test with at least four threads, PH outperforms the other designs; this can largely be attributed to touching fewer cachelines (one rather than two) in the common-case code path for update operations — inter-processor cacheline exchange dominates runtime in massively parallel workloads. Applications with much larger, multi-cacheline keys would lose most of this advantage, and may favour an externally-chained scheme to lower the memory footprint of empty buckets.

5   Conclusions

We have presented a lock-free, disjoint-access and read parallel set algorithm based on open addressing, with no need for garbage collection, and touched upon removing population constraints. It has high straight-line speeds and a low operation footprint leading to excellent performance, matching and besting state-of-the-art external-chaining implementations in the tests we performed.

We wish to thank Sun Microsystems, Inc. for donating the SPARC v880 server on which this work was evaluated, and the University of Rochester, New York, for hosting it.

References

1. GAO, H., GROOTE, J. AND HESSELINK, W. Almost Wait-Free Resizable Hashtables In *Proceedings of the 18th International Parallel and Distributed Processing Symposium*, April 2004, p.50a.
2. FRASER, K. Practical Lock-Freedom. *University of Cambridge Computer Laboratory, Technical Report number 579*, February 2004.
3. KNUTH, D. The Art of Computer Programming. Part 3, Sorting and Searching. Addison-Wesley, 1973.
4. LAMPORT, L. Concurrent Reading and Writing. In *Communications of the ACM*, 1977, pp.806-811.
5. MARTIN, D. AND DAVIS, R. A Scalable Non-Blocking Concurrent Hash Table Implementation with Incremental Rehashing. Unpublished manuscript, 1997.
6. MELLOR-CRUMMEY, J. AND SCOTT, M. Algorithms for Scalable Synchronization on Shared-Memory Multiprocessors. In *ACM Transactions on Computer Systems*, Volume 9, Issue 1, February 1991, pp. 21–65.
7. MICHAEL, M. Safe Memory Reclamation for Dynamic Lock-Free Objects using Atomic Reads and Writes. In *Proceedings of the 21st Annual Symposium on Principles of Distributed Computing*, July 2002, pp.21-30.
8. MICHAEL, M. High performance dynamic lock-free hash tables and list-based sets In *Proceedings of the 14th Annual Symposium on Parallel Algorithms and Architectures*, August 2002, pp.73-82.
9. SHALEV, O. AND SHAVIT, N. Split-Ordered Lists: Lock-free Extensible Hash Tables. In *Proceedings of the 22nd Annual Symposium on Principles of Distributed Computing*, July 2003, pp.102-111.
10. SCHERER, W. AND SCOTT, M. Contention Management in Dynamic Software Transactional Memory. In *PODC Workshop on Concurrency and Synchronization in Java Programs*, July 2004, pp.70–79.
11. PURCELL, C. AND HARRIS, T. Non-blocking Hashtables with Open Addressing. *University of Cambridge Computer Laboratory, Technical Report number 639*, September 2005.

Computing with Reads and Writes
in the Absence of Step Contention
(Extended Abstract)

Hagit Attiya[1], Rachid Guerraoui[2], and Petr Kouznetsov[2]

[1] Department of Computer Science, Technion
[2] School of Computer and Communication Sciences, EPFL

Abstract. This paper studies implementations of concurrent objects that exploit the absence of *step contention*. These implementations use only reads and writes when a process is running solo. The other processes might be busy with other objects, swapped-out, failed, or simply delayed by a contention manager. We study in this paper two classes of such implementations, according to how they handle the case of step contention. The first kind, called *obstruction-free* implementations, are not required to terminate in that case. The second kind, called *solo-fast* implementations, terminate using powerful operations (e.g., C&S).

We present a generic obstruction-free object implementation that has a linear contention-free step complexity (number of reads and writes taken by a process running solo) and uses a linear number of read/write objects. We show that these complexities are asymptotically optimal, and hence generic obstruction-free implementations are inherently slow. We also prove that obstruction-free implementations cannot be *gracefully degrading*, namely, be nonblocking when the contention manager operates correctly, and remain (at least) obstruction-free when the contention manager misbehaves.

Finally, we show that any object has a *solo-fast* implementation, based on a solo-fast implementation of consensus. The implementation has linear contention-free step complexity, and we conjecture solo-fast implementations must have non-constant step complexity, i.e., they are also inherently slow.

1 Introduction

At the heart of many distributed systems are *shared objects*—data structures that are concurrently accessed by many processes. Often, these objects are *implemented* in software, out of more elementary *base objects*. Lock-free implementations of such objects do not rely on mutual exclusion or locking, and thereby allow processes to overcome adverse operating systems affects. This includes both *wait-free* algorithms, in which *every* process completes its operations in a finite number of steps, and *nonblocking* algorithms, where *some* process completes an operation in every sufficiently long execution [15]. The safety property typically required from both nonblocking and wait-free implementations is *linearizability* [15,18]; roughly, every operation on the object should appear instantaneous.

P. Fraigniaud (Ed.): DISC 2005, LNCS 3724, pp. 122–136, 2005.

Although they provide very attractive guarantees, lock-free implementations were claimed to have limited usability. This is because nonblocking implementations of many objects are often impossible, e.g., when only read/write objects are available [12,10,23]. Even when the implementations are possible, which can be achieved under specific timing assumptions (e.g., encapsulated within failure detector abstractions), or using strong synchronization operations (like C&S), these implementations are typically complex and expensive [9, 20, 7]. The complexity and computability price paid by lock-free algorithms often originates in situations in which there is *step contention*, i.e., steps of concurrent processes are interleaved.

In this paper, we study implementations that exploit the fact that in practice, step contention is rare, or at least can be made so through operating system support. That is, only one process is typically performing visible (non local) steps within any object operation, whereas the rest of the processes are busy with other objects, swapped-out or failed. The absence of step contention does not preclude common scenarios where other processes have pending operations on the same implemented object but are not accessing the base objects. This is fundamentally different from alternative contention metrics: *point* contention [5] and *interval* contention [2]; both count also failed or swapped-out processes. (See the scenario presented in Figure 1.)

We first study *obstruction-free* implementations that guarantee termination only in the absence of step contention. This is formalized by the *solo termination* property [11]: a process that takes sufficiently many steps on its own returns a value. Clearly, obstruction-free implementations cannot rely on mutual exclusion or locks, and hence, they are lock-free. On the other hand, implementations that would guarantee termination only in the absence of interval (or point) contention can be obtained using locks. Whereas all nonblocking implementations are obstruction-free, the converse is not necessarily true, however, since obstruction-free implementations may incur scenarios (when there is step contention) in which no process is able to complete its operation in a finite number of steps.

An obstruction-free implementation has to provide a *legal* response if it returns at all, but termination is required only under very restricted conditions.

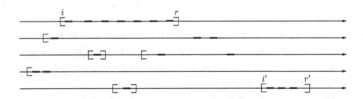

Fig. 1. An example illustrating types of contention: Operation $[i, r]$ has interval contention 5, point contention 4, and step contention 3; operation $[i', r']$ has interval and point contention 4, and step contention 1 ($[i', r']$ is step contention-free). (Square brackets denote invocations and responses, while solid intervals denote steps on base objects.)

One contribution of this paper is to disambiguate the behavior of an obstruction-free implementation when an operation cannot return a legal response. In the presence of step contention, an operation may return control to a higher-level entity, which we call the *client*. Ideally, the obstruction-free implementation should only be allowed to return a *fail* indication to the client, enabling it to choose whether to re-invoke the same operation, or to invoke another operation. We show however that there is inherent uncertainty as to whether the operation could have had an effect on the object or not, by reduction to wait-free consensus. This implies that the implementation must sometimes return a special *pause* value, indicating that the client should re-invoke the same operation. We extend the notion of linearizability so as to accommodate failed operations and re-invocations of paused operations.

An obstruction-free implementation of any object is presented (Section 3.2), which exemplifies how pause and fail values are returned when a legal response is not possible. A natural way to evaluate obstruction-free implementations is by considering the *contention-free step complexity*, namely, the number of steps taken by a process running alone, until it returns a value. Our implementations have linear contention-free step complexity and use a linear number of read/write base objects. By reduction to the lower bound of Jayanti, Tan and Toueg [19], we show that obstruction-free implementations of many long-lived objects from historyless base objects must have $\Omega(n)$ contention-free step complexity and must use $\Omega(n)$ historyless objects.

In practice, the burden of providing termination of obstruction-free implementations is shifted to a system-supported *contention manager* that relies on low-level mechanisms such as timers, identifiers and interrupts [25,17]. The contention manager instructs the clients if and when to invoke operations, trying to ensure that only a single process eventually accesses the concurrent object. To explore inherent characteristics of obstruction-free implementations, we consider a specific contention manager that can turn any obstruction-free implementation into a nonblocking one (none of those of [25,26,14,17] can do so). The contention manager indicates the client whether to continue or not (a binary indication), and should eventually indicate only to a single client to continue [8]. [1]

We show (Section 3.5) that there are no *gracefully degrading* consensus implementations, which are nonblocking when the contention manager operates correctly, but remain (at least) obstruction-free when the contention manager is unsuccessful.

We finally explore *solo-fast* implementations. These are wait-free linearizable object implementations that use only read/write base objects when there is no step contention, but may fall back on more powerful objects like compare&swap, when contention occurs. Luchangco, Moir and Shavit [24] presented a generic object implementation that uses only reads and writes when an operation runs in

---

[1] This specification style is inspired by the way *failure detectors* [9, 8] abstract away (partial) synchrony assumptions. It highlights the intriguing connection between obstruction-free implementations and Paxos-style algorithms for consensus and state-machine replication [21].

the absence of contention. However, in their implementation this also means lack of pending operations, namely, lack of *point* contention; moreover, a transient increase in point contention will cause a subsequent operation (that has no point contention) to invoke costly C&S operations. In light of this, it is challenging to design truly solo-fast implementations that do not invoke C&S operations in the more common case of no *step* contention.

Surprisingly, we show in this paper that any object has a solo-fast implementation by describing a solo-fast consensus implementation, and employing it within Herlihy's universal construction [15] (Section 4). The implementation has linear contention-free step complexity. We conjecture that solo-fast ones are inherently slow: they must have (at least) non-constant step complexity.

2 Model

A system contains a set Π of $n > 1$ *processes* $p_1, \ldots, p_n$ that communicate through shared *objects*.

Every object has a *type* that is defined by a triple (O, R, Δ), where O is a set of *invocations*, R is a set of *responses*, and Δ is a set of sequences of invocation-response pairs. The set Δ, known as the *sequential specification* of the type, contains all the sequences of invocations and responses allowed by the object.

For example, the *compare&swap* (C&S) object is accessed by a $CS(r_1, r_2, m)$ operation; the operation compares that value in memory location m with the content of local variable r_1, and if equal, writes the value of r_2 to m. The operation returns the *old* value of m. The sequential specification of the *compare&swap* type includes all sequences of CS operations that obey this rule.

Another important example is the *consensus* object, on which processes perform a *propose* operation with an argument in some set V. The sequential specification of consensus includes all sequences of *propose* operations that return the argument of the first operation in every sequence.

To implement a (high-level) object from a collection of *base* objects, processes follow an *algorithm* A, which is a collection of state machines $A_1, \ldots A_n$, one for each process.

When receiving an *invocation* (to the high-level object), process p_i takes steps according to A_i. In each step, p_i can either (a) invoke an operation on a base object, or (b) receive the response of its previous base operation, or (c) perform some local computation. After each step, p_i changes its local state according to A_i, and possibly returns a response on the pending high-level operation.

We investigate implementations that work when process speeds are highly-variable, and at the extreme case, a process may stop taking steps.

An *execution* e of an algorithm A is a sequence of interleaved *events*. Every execution induces a *history* that includes only the invocations and responses of the high-level operations. Each invocation or response is associated with a single process and a single object. A *local history* of process p_j in H, $H|j$, is the subsequence of H containing only events of p_j. Similarly, $H|x$ is the subsequence of H of operations on an object x.

A response *matches* an invocation if they are associated with the same process and the same object. A local history is *well-formed* if it is a sequence of matching invocation-response pairs, except perhaps for the last invocation in a finite local history. A history H is *well-formed* if every local history in H is well-formed.

A matching invocation-response pair $[i, r]$ is called a *complete operation*, and we say that i *returns* r. An invocation i without a matching response is called a *pending operation*; a *completion* of a pending operation, that is, an invocation, is the invocation together with an appropriate response. The fragment of H (or e, its corresponding execution) between the invocation i and its matching response r (if it exists) is the operation's *interval*.

In an infinite execution, a process is *correct* if it takes an infinite number of steps or it has no pending operation; otherwise, it is *faulty*.

A history H is *sequential* if every invocation is immediately followed by its matching response. A sequential history H is *legal* if for every object x, $H|x$ is in the sequential specification of x.

Two different invocations i and i' on the same object x are *concurrent* in a history H, if i and i' are both pending in some finite prefix of H. This implies that their intervals overlap. We say that two operations $[i, r]$ and $[i', r']$ (or i' if i' is pending) are *non-concurrent* if their intervals are non-overlapping: Either r appears before i' in H, in which case we say that $[i, r]$ *precedes* $[i', r']$, or r' appears before i in H, in which case we say that $[i, r]$ *follows* $[i', r']$.

A well-formed history H satisfies *extended linearizability* [15] (see also [6, Chapter 10]) if there is a permutation H' containing all the complete operations and completions of a subset of the pending operations in H, such that (1) H' is legal, and (2) H' respects the order of non-concurrent operations in H.

This paper explores the benefits induced by the scenarios in which contention is rare. Formally, we define the *step contention* of a fragment in execution e to be the number of processes that take steps in this fragment. An operation is *step contention-free in e* if step contention of its interval in e is 1. An operation is *eventually step contention-free in e* if its interval in e has a suffix with step contention 1.

Alternative ways to measure contention during an operation's interval were previously defined [5, 2]: The *interval contention* during is the number of processes whose operations are concurrent with an operation op in e. The *point contention* of op is the maximum number of operations *simultaneously* concurrent with op in e. Note that interval contention is always equal to or higher than step contention, but point contention is incomparable to step contention. Note also when no operation overlaps op, then both the point contention and the interval contention are 1.

3   Obstruction-Free Implementations

This section considers obstruction-free implementations [17, 16], which guarantee progress only in the absence of step contention.

3.1   Definitions

Originally [17,16], an implementation is called obstruction-free *"if it guarantees progress for every thread that eventually executes in isolation. Even though other threads may be in the midst of executing operations, ... "* [17, Page 522]. For deterministic implementations, this requirement is equivalent to *solo termination* [11], and it echoes the liveness correctness conditions stated for Paxos-style algorithms for state-machine replication [21].

Using our terminology, an implementation is *obstruction-free* if every operation that is eventually step contention-free eventually returns.

Obstruction-freedom is a very weak liveness condition, and it requires the operation to return only under very restricted conditions. In all other circumstances, we only require that an operation's response is legal, *if it returns a response at all.*

If an operation cannot return a legal response, it is useful to return control to a higher-level entity, which we call the *client*. The client may consult a system-specific mechanism called a *contention manager*, in order to expedite termination.

There are two ways in which an obstruction-free implementation returns control to the client, depending on whether the implementation is certain that the operation did not have any effect on the object or not. If the implementation is certain that the operation did not have an effect, a special *fail* value is returned, indicating that the operation was not applied, and the client is free to invoke any operation it wishes. Otherwise, a special *pause* value $\perp$ is returned, and the client must re-invoke the same operation until a non-$\perp$ response is received. (We discuss the need for the two indications below.)

We add to R, the set of responses of an object, a special *pause* value $\perp \notin R$ and a special *fail* value $\emptyset \notin R$. The definition of a *well-formed* local history is extended to require that if an invocation i is followed by the response $\perp$, then the subsequent event, if exists, is i.

The definition of extended linearizability is further extended so that invocations returning *fail* are removed from the linearized history, while a sequence of invocations returning *pause* are considered as one pending operation.

Formally, let H be any history, and $\bar{H}$ be any well-formed local history of H. Let i be an invocation in $\bar{H}$ on an object x. A fragment of the form i, r in $\bar{H}$, where $r \in R$, is called an *occurrence of i* (returning r). Since an invocation occurrence might return $\perp$ and be re-invoked later, there might be a number of occurrences of i in a history. Consider the longest fragment of the form i or $i, \perp, i, \ldots, \perp, i$ in $\bar{H}$. If the fragment is followed by a matching response $r \notin \{\perp, \emptyset\}$, we call i, r or, resp., $i, \perp, i \ldots, \perp, i, r$ a *complete operation*. If the fragment is followed by a fail response $\emptyset$, we call $i, \emptyset$ or, resp., $i, \perp, i \ldots, \perp, i, \emptyset$ a *failed operation*. If the fragment is followed by no event or by $\perp$, we call i or $i, \perp$ or, resp., $i, \perp, i, \ldots, \perp, i$ or $i, \perp, i \ldots, \perp, i, \perp$ a *pending operation*. Since $\bar{H}$ is well-formed, a pending operation is a suffix of $\bar{H}$ ($\perp$ cannot be followed by an invocation other than i). The operation's interval is the shortest fragment of

Shared variables: *register* X, initially $\perp$, and *"only-fail" OF consensus object* C

Code for process p_0:	Code for process p_1:

```
Code for process p₀:              Code for process p₁:
  upon propose(v₀) do               upon propose(v₁) do
    d₀ ← C.propose(v₀)                X ← v₁
    if d₀ = ∅ then                    repeat
      d₀ ← X                            d₁ ← C.propose(v₁)
    return d₀                         until d₁ ≠ ∅
                                      return d₁
```

Fig. 2. Wait-free consensus from "only-fail" obstruction-free consensus

H that includes all events of that operation. If the fragment $i, \perp, i, \ldots, \perp, i$ is followed by no event in $\bar{H}$ then the operation's *interval* is infinite.

As defined before, a well-formed history H is *linearizable* if there is a permutation H' containing all the complete operations in H and completions of a subset of the pending operations in H, such that H' is legal and it respects the order of non-concurrent operations in H. When taken in the context of the extended notions of complete and pending operations, this definition means that we order all non-failed operations, with the interval of a paused operation "spanned" across its re-invocations.

An implementation is *live* if every invocation occurrence return in a finite number of its own steps (although a value in $\{\perp, \emptyset\}$ can be returned). An implementation is *valid* if (1) an invocation occurrence returns $\perp$ (that is, *pause*) only when it is not step contention-free, and (2) an invocation occurrence i returns $\emptyset$ (that is, *fail*) only when the corresponding *operation* (the longest fragment of the form $i, \emptyset$ or $i, \perp, i, \ldots, \perp, i, \emptyset$ in the local history) is not step contention-free. It is immediate that any live and valid implementation is obstruction-free.

Ideally, an obstruction-free implementation should only be allowed to return valid responses and, in the case of step contention, *fail* indications to the client, enabling the client to either re-invoke the operation, or to invoke another operation. However, below we show that no obstruction-free consensus implementation from registers can enjoy this property. Thus, it is sometimes unavoidable to return $\perp$ in obstruction-free implementations.

Theorem 1. *There is no obstruction-free consensus implementation from registers that never returns* $\perp$.

Proof. By contradiction, consider an implementation of obstruction-free consensus that is allowed to return only $\emptyset$ in the case of step contention. Then it is possible to implement wait-free consensus for two processes p_0 and p_1 using one such consensus object, denoted C, and one register X, contradicting [10,23]. The algorithm is presented in Figure 2.

Validity of the algorithm follows from the fact that $\emptyset$ is returned only in case of step contention. If C returns $\emptyset$ at p_0, then p_1 can only decide its own value. Thus, Agreement is satisfied. Since p_1 eventually runs in the absence of contention, it eventually decides. Thus, Termination is also satisfied. $\square$

3.2   Obstruction-Free Generic Object Implementation

This section gives an algorithm that obstruction-free implements any object of type T, using only registers. Like previous universal implementations, it is built from consensus objects. (A simple obstruction-free consensus algorithm, derived from Paxos-style consensus algorithms, appears in the full version of the paper.)

The universal obstruction-free implementation relies on a sequential implementation of the object type T; it is live, valid and linearizable. Herlihy's universal nonblocking implementation [15] cannot be applied "off-the-shelf" since it does not handle re-invocations and failing. Instead, the algorithm builds on similar ideas, while making sure that *pause* or *fail* are returned only in the absence of step contention.

An object of type T is represented as a linked list; an element of the list represents an operation applied to the object. The list of operations clearly determines the list of corresponding responses. A process makes an invocation by appending a new element to the end of the list. The algorithm assumes a function *response(invs, inv)* that returns the response matching the invocation *inv* in a sequential execution of invocations from list *invs* (under the condition that $inv \in invs$).

The algorithm (Figure 3) uses the following shared variables:

- n atomic single-writer, multi-reader registers $L_1, \ldots, L_n$. Process p_i stores in L_i its last view of the object state in the form of a linked list of operations that p_i witnessed to be applied on the object.
- $C[\,]$ is an unbounded array of obstruction-free consensus objects. The array is used to agree on the order in which invocations are put into the linked list of operations.

Roughly, the algorithm works as follows. When a process p_i executes an invocation *inv*, it identifies the longest list L_j (let $k = |L_j|$). If *inv* is already in L_j, the response associated with *inv* in L_i is returned (line 5). This ensures that an operation takes effect at most once, even if repeated several times. If it is not the first instance of *inv*, and $k > |L_i|$ (i.e., *inv* was not decided in any OF Consensus to which it was proposed), p_i returns $\emptyset$ (line 9). Otherwise, p_i proposes *inv* to $C[k+1]$ (line 10). If $C[k+1]$ returns $\perp$ (step contention is detected), then p_i returns $\perp$ (line 13). If the propose operation fails, or returns a non-*inv* response while it is not the first instance of *inv*, then p_i returns $\emptyset$ (line 16). If $C[k+1]$ returns *inv*, then p_i returns the response associated with *inv* (line 20). Otherwise, the procedure is repeated, now at position $k+2$. Now if $C[k+2]$ returns a non-$\{inv, \perp\}$ response, then p_i returns $\emptyset$ (line 29). The second consensus operation ensures *validity* of the implementation, namely, that $\emptyset$ is never returned in line 29 if the corresponding operation is step contention-free.

This algorithm implies the next theorem (the correctness proof appears in the full version of the paper).

Theorem 2. *Every sequential type T has an obstruction-free linearizable implementation from registers.*

Shared variables:
      Register $L_1, \ldots, L_n \leftarrow \emptyset, \ldots, \emptyset$
      OF-Consensus $C[\,]$

```
 1: upon Invoking inv do
 2:     invs ← longest({L₁, ..., Lₙ})                  { Select the longest invocation list }
 3:     if  inv ∈ invs then
 4:         check ← false
 5:         return response(invs, inv)                 { Return if inv is already completed }
 6:     k ← |invs|
 7:     if  (k > |Lᵢ|) and check then
 8:         check ← false
 9:         return ∅                                   { Fail the operation }
10:     dec ← C[k + 1].propose(inv)                    { The 1st consensus operation }
11:     if  dec = ⊥ then
12:         check ← true
13:         return ⊥
14:     if  (dec = ∅) or (dec ≠ inv and check)  then
15:         check ← false
16:         return ∅                                   { Fail the operation }
17:     invs ← invs · dec; Lᵢ ← invs                   { Update Lᵢ }
18:     if dec = inv then
19:         check ← false
20:         return response(invs, inv)                 { Return if inv is decided }
21:     dec ← C[k + 2].propose(inv)                    { The 2nd consensus operation }
22:     if  dec = ⊥ then
23:         check ← true
24:         return ⊥
25:     if dec ≠ ∅ then invs ← invs · dec; Lᵢ ← invs
26:     if dec = inv then
27:         check ← false
28:         return response(invs, inv)                 { Return if inv is decided }
29:     return ∅                                       { Fail if inv is ignored twice }
```

Fig. 3. An obstruction-free implementation of T: code for process p_i

Remark. Our algorithm satisfies one additional property. In any execution, every operation takes effect (if it does) before it stops taking steps in that execution. In other words, the implementation stays linearizable even if we restrict an operation's interval to the shortest fragment of the execution which contains all steps of that operation. As a result, an operation invoked by a faulty process takes effect (if it does) before the process fails, which makes our implementations *strictly linearizable* [3].

A simpler proof of Theorem 2 can be obtained by presenting an algorithm that returns only $\perp$ indications in the case of step contention. However, our algorithm is better in the sense that it carefully detects the scenarios in which an applied operation did not take effect, and thus $\emptyset$ can be returned, which makes our algorithm more convenient to use.

3.3   Obstruction-Free Implementations Are Slow

The universal construction presented in Figure 3 is not very efficient: finding the longest list of invocations requires to collect information from all processes.

The next theorem shows that this is inherent in obstruction-free universal implementations from read/write base objects, by proving a lower bound of $\Omega(n)$ on the number of steps and on the number of registers for implementing a compare&swap object.

Theorem 3. *Let A be any obstruction-free implementation of n-valued compare&swap from registers, then A has an execution in which a step contention-free operation takes $n-1$ or more steps and accesses $n-1$ or more different objects.*

Proof. Follows directly from the result of Jayanti, Tan and Toueg [19]. They show that any implementation of n-valued compare&swap that satisfies the solo termination property has an execution in which a solo operation (i.e., an operation that does not observe step contention) takes $n-1$ or more steps and accesses at $n-1$ or more different objects. Since any obstruction-free implementation ensures the solo termination property, we immediately have the theorem.   □

3.4 Leveraging Obstruction-Free Objects

The next two subsections discuss how obstruction-free implementations can be turned into nonblocking or wait-free ones using a contention manager. The contention manager we consider provides the client with a binary indication whether to continue or not. The contention manager works well when it indicates only to a single client to continue. Formally, in response to the client's query, the contention manager returns either 0 or 1, telling the client to abort or to continue (respectively); in the latter case, we say that the client is a *leader*. The *eventual* contention manager, denoted Ω, guarantees that eventually exactly one correct client with a pending operation (if such a client exists) is a leader; it is deliberately similar to the "sloppy leader" failure detector and can be implemented using partial synchrony assumptions [8].

A single obstruction-free consensus object and Ω can implement *nonblocking* consensus using the following simple algorithm: A process queries the contention manager and, if it is a leader, the process makes a *propose* invocation on the underlying obstruction-free consensus object. If the response is neither $\perp$ nor $\emptyset$, it is returned; otherwise, the process repeats. This implies the following result:

Theorem 4. *Consensus has a nonblocking implementation from (only) obstruction-free consensus and Ω.*

3.5 Graceful Degradation of Obstruction-Free Implementations

Obstruction-free consensus can be implemented from registers only [4]. On the other hand, *wait-free* consensus can be implemented from registers using Ω [22]. However, these two liveness properties cannot be combined in the same implementation, namely, there is no wait-free consensus implementation using registers and Ω which becomes (at least) obstruction-free when the contention manager fails to eventually elect a single correct leader. In fact, we prove the claim even for *nonblocking* consensus implementations.

Theorem 5. *There is no nonblocking consensus implementation using registers and Ω that ensures obstruction-freedom when the contention manager fails to eventually elect a single correct leader.*

Proof. Suppose, by contradiction, that an algorithm A provides such an implementation. We show that it is then possible to devise an algorithm A' that implements nonblocking consensus for two processes, p_1 and p_2 with registers only — a contradiction with [10, 23].

In A', processes take steps like in A, except that, instead of using Ω, processes assume that Ω always indicates p_1 as the only leader. In doing so, processes cyclically invoke *propose* operations until a non-$\{\bot, \emptyset\}$ value is returned. Note that A' cannot violate safety properties of consensus, since every finite execution of A' is also an execution of A. To establish a contradiction, it is thus sufficient to show that at least one correct process eventually terminates in A', i.e., obtains a non-$\{\bot, \emptyset\}$ value from the underlying algorithm A.

Every execution of A' belongs to one of the following classes:
(1) Executions in which p_1 is correct, i.e., the assumed output of the contention manager complies with the specification of Ω. Such an execution is indistinguishable to p_1 and p_2 from executions of A in which processes $p_3, \ldots, p_n$ are initially faulty, and p_1 is the only correct leader. Since A implements a nonblocking consensus using Ω, some correct process (p_1 or p_2) eventually obtains a non-$\{\bot, \emptyset\}$ value from A and decides.
(2) Executions in which p_1 is faulty, i.e., the assumed output of the contention manager does not comply with the specification of Ω. Assume that p_2 is correct in such an execution (if both p_1 and p_2 are faulty, consensus is trivially solved). Any finite prefix of our execution is indistinguishable to p_2 from an execution of A in which processes $p_3, \ldots, p_n$ are initially faulty, and the contention manager malfunctions. Since p_2 is eventually running in the absence of step contention, and A ensures obstruction-freedom even when the contention manager is incorrect, p_2 eventually obtains a non-$\{\bot, \emptyset\}$ value from A and decides.

In other words, A' guarantees that whenever there is at least one correct process, some correct process eventually decides — a contradiction. $\square$

4   Solo-Fast Implementations

We say that a wait-free linearizable implementation of a sequential type T from registers and other objects (e.g., compare&swap) is *solo-fast* if only read and write operations are invoked by any step contention-free operation on it.

4.1   Solo-Fast Generic Object Implementation

Figure 4 presents a solo-fast consensus implementation. The algorithm proceeds in rounds (lines 13–25). Starting the algorithm, every process first computes in line 3 the smallest round k in which a value can be *fixed*, i.e., returned in line 19 (we say that p_i *joins* in round k). The algorithm guarantees that if any process

---

Shared variables:
    Registers $\{A_j\}, \{B_j\}, j \in \{1, 2, \ldots, n\}$, initially $\perp$
    C&S $C_1, \ldots C_{n-1}$, initially $\perp$

```
1:  upon propose(input_i) do
2:    V ← collect A                                    { ⊥'s are ignored in each collect }
3:    k_i ← min{k ≥ 1 |∀(k', v') ∈ V : k' ≤ k ∧ ∀(k, v'), (k, v'') ∈ V : v' = v''}
4:    if ∃(k, v) ∈ V then
5:      v_i ← v
6:    else
7:      V' ← collect B
8:      if V' ≠ ∅ then
9:        v_i ← the highest timestamped value in V'
10:     else
11:       v_i ← input_i
12:   while (true) do
13:     A_i ← (k_i, v_i)
14:     V ← collect A
15:     if ∀(k', v') ∈ V : k' < k_i ∨ (k' = k_i ∧ v' = v_i) then
16:       B_i ← (k_i, v_i)
17:       V ← collect A
18:       if ∀(k', v') ∈ V : k' < k_i ∨ (k' = k_i ∧ v' = v_i) then
19:         return v_i
20:     V' ← collect B
21:     if V' ≠ ∅ then
22:       v_i ← the highest timestamped value in V'
23:     v' ← C_{k_i}.CS(⊥, v_i)
24:     if v' ≠ ⊥ then v_i ← v'
25:     k_i ← k_i + 1
```

Fig. 4. An n-process solo-fast consensus: code for process p_i

fixes a value, then no process can ever fix a different value. In every round, starting from round k, p_i tries to fix its current estimate. It is ensured that if no other process tries to fix concurrently a different value in the current or higher round, then the estimate must be fixed. If p_i is not able to fix the estimate in the current round (we say that p_i *aborts* in that round), which can only happen when there is step contention, it updates the estimate using a C&S operation and goes to the next round. The algorithm guarantees that whenever process p_i aborts in round k, and no process joins in round $k + 1$, then p_i fixes its estimate in round $k + 1$ (C&S ensures that no two processes that abort in round k try to fix different values in round $k + 1$). We show that no process can join in round n or later, and thus p_i fixes its estimate in round $k \leq n$. The algorithm is solo-fast, since no process can abort in a round (and thus use a C&S operation) in the absence of step contention.

This algorithm implies the next theorem (the correctness proof appears in the full version of the paper).

Theorem 6. *There is a solo-fast consensus implementation from registers and C&S objects, that takes $O(n)$ steps in the solo path.*

From Theorem 6 and Herlihy's universal construction [15], we immediately obtain:

Corollary 1. *Every sequential type T has a solo-fast implementation from registers and C&S objects.*

4.2 Lower Bounds and Reductions

Our implementation has linear space and contention-free step complexity. Proving that it is asymptotically optimal is not straightforward. Unlike obstruction-free implementations (see the proof of Theorem 3), the lower bound of [19] cannot be applied to solo-fast implementations, since processes *can* access non-historyless objects such as C&S, which is not allowed in [19]. Nevertheless, if we assume that the C&S objects are *non-readable*, then a simple variation of [19] implies that the step and space complexity for solo-fast is at least linear. (This matches the complexity of our implementation.)

The apparent similarity between obstruction-free and solo-fast implementations tempts to think that a linear lower bound on space and step complexity of a solo-fast implementation can be obtained by a reduction from an obstruction-free one (applying Theorem 3). However, despite of the similarity, such a reduction seems difficult to achieve. For instance, a seemingly straightforward transformation from a solo-fast implementation to an obstruction-free one in which hardware C&S objects are recursively substituted with their solo-fast implementations does not guarantee solo termination if the underlying C&S objects are readable. Indeed, even on a solo path, any read operation on a C&S object would recursively call a solo-fast version of it, and so on.

5 Discussion

This paper studies the notion of step contention, which inherently does not charge for processes stalled, e.g., due to failures or swap-outs, and is, in this sense, fundamentally different from point or interval contention. We show that registers are powerful enough to ensure liveness in the absence of step contention (which leads to a wider set of executions than when looking at other forms of contention). However, we suggest that building such implementations using only registers in the absence of step contention is inherently expensive and of limited benefit.

There are several interesting avenues for further research:

Complexity of obstruction-free consensus. We have shown tight bounds on the cost of *generic* obstruction-free implementations. However, there might be more efficient obstruction-free solutions for specific problems. For obstruction-free consensus, for example, an $\Omega(\sqrt{n})$ lower bound on the number of registers (or historyless objects) can be derived from the lower bound of Fich, Herlihy and Shavit [11]. This bound is not tight (the upper bound is $O(n)$) and moreover, it does not bound the *contention-free* step complexity of obstruction-free consensus.

Complexity of solo-fast implementations. Our solo-fast implementation performs $O(n)$ read and write steps, even in the absence of step contention; by employing adaptive collect [1,5], the step complexity can be made to depend only on the point contention; by employing adaptive collect for unbounded concurrency [13], it can be made independent of the number of processes.

We conjecture that a non-constant lower bound on the contention-free step complexity of any generic solo-fast implementation holds even if underlying compare&swap objects are readable, making solo-fast implementations rather inefficient. On the other hand, it is possible that the step and space complexities of solo-fast consensus can be made constant if objects *slightly* more powerful than read/write registers, e.g., counters or queues, are used on a solo path.

Contention management. The contention manager we considered is fundamentally different from those considered in [25,26,14,17]. It is easy to see that none of those can transform any obstruction-free implementation into a nonblocking one. Those contention managers do not provide any worst case nonblocking deterministic guarantees (with the exception of [14] in the absence of failures), and were actually rather designed to provide a high throughput in the average case. Devising a contention manager that would provide deterministic worst case guarantees with acceptable average case throughput is an interesting research direction.

Acknowledgments. We would like to thank Partha Dutta, Danny Hendler, Ron Levy, and Eric Ruppert for important discussions on the topic of this paper, and the anonymous reviewers for helpful comments.

References

1. Y. Afek, G. Stupp, and D. Touitou. Long-lived adaptive collect with applications. In *Proceedings of the 40th Annual Symposium on Foundations of Computer Science (FOCS)*, pages 262–272, 1999.
2. Y. Afek, G. Stupp, and D. Touitou. Long-lived adaptive splitter and applications. *Distributed Computing*, 15(2):67–86, 2002.
3. M. K. Aguilera and S. Frølund. Strict linearizability and the power of aborting. Technical report, HP Laboratories Palo Alto, 2003.
4. J. Aspnes and M. Herlihy. Fast randomized consensus using shared memory. *J. Algorithms*, 11(3):441–461, 1990.
5. H. Attiya and A. Fouren. Algorithms adapting to point contention. *J. ACM*, 50(4):444–468, 2003.
6. H. Attiya and J. L. Welch. *Distributed Computing: Fundamentals, Simulations and Advanced Topics (2nd edition)*. Wiley, 2004.
7. B. N. Bershad. Practical considerations for non-blocking concurrent objects. In *Proceedings of the 14th IEEE International Conference on Distributed Computing Systems (ICDCS'93)*, pages 264–273, 1993.
8. T. D. Chandra, V. Hadzilacos, and S. Toueg. The weakest failure detector for solving consensus. *Journal of the ACM*, 43(4):685–722, July 1996.
9. T. D. Chandra and S. Toueg. Unreliable failure detectors for reliable distributed systems. *Journal of the ACM*, 43(2):225–267, March 1996.

10. D. Dolev, C. Dwork, and L. J. Stockmeyer. On the minimal synchronism needed for distributed consensus. *Journal of the ACM*, 34(1):77–97, January 1987.

11. F. Fich, M. Herlihy, and N. Shavit. On the space complexity of randomized synchronization. *J. ACM*, 45(5):843–862, 1998.

12. M. J. Fischer, N. A. Lynch, and M. S. Paterson. Impossibility of distributed consensus with one faulty process. *Journal of the ACM*, 32(3):374–382, April 1985.

13. E. Gafni, M. Merritt, and G. Taubenfeld. The concurrency hierarchy, and algorithms for unbounded concurrency. In *Proceedings of the 20th Annual ACM Symposium on Principles of Distributed Computing (PODC)*, pages 161–169, 2001.

14. R. Guerraoui, M. Herlihy, and B. Pochon. Toward a theory of transactional contention managers. In *Proceedings of the 24th Annual ACM Symposium on Principles of Distributed Computing (PODC)*, 2005.

15. M. Herlihy. Wait-free synchronization. *ACM Transactions on Programming Languages and Systems*, 13(1):124–149, January 1991.

16. M. Herlihy, V. Luchangco, M. Moir, and W. N. Scherer III. Software transactional memory for dynamic-sized data structures. In *Proceedings of the 22nd Annual ACM Symposium on Principles of Distributed Computing (PODC)*, pages 92–101, 2003.

17. M. Herlihy, V. Luchango, and M. Moir. Obstruction-free synchronization: Double-ended queues as an example. In *Proceedings of the 23rd IEEE International Conference on Distributed Computing Systems (ICDCS'03)*, pages 522–529, 2003.

18. M. Herlihy and J. M. Wing. Linearizability: a correctness condition for concurrent objects. *ACM Transactions on Programming Languages and Systems*, 12(3):463–492, June 1990.

19. P. Jayanti, K. Tan, and S. Toueg. Time and space lower bounds for nonblocking implementations. *SIAM Journal on Computing*, 30(2):438–456, 2000.

20. A. LaMarca. A performance evaluation of lock-free synchronization protocols. In *Proceedings of the 13th Annual ACM Symposium on Principles of Distributed Computing (PODC)*, pages 130–140, 1994.

21. L. Lamport. The part-time parliament. *ACM Transactions on Computer Systems*, 16(2):133–169, May 1998.

22. W.-K. Lo and V. Hadzilacos. Using failure detectors to solve consensus in asynchronous shared-memory systems. In *Proceedings of the 8th International Workshop on Distributed Algorithms (WDAG'94)*, volume 857 of *LNCS*, pages 280–295. Springer Verlag, 1994.

23. M. C. Loui and H. H. Abu-Amara. Memory requirements for agreement among unreliable asynchronous processes. *Advances in Computing Research*, pages 163–183, 1987.

24. V. Luchango, M. Moir, and N. Shavit. On the uncontended complexity of consensus. In *Proceedings of the 17th International Symposium on Distributed Computing (DISC'03)*, pages 45–59, 2003.

25. M. L. Scott and W. N. Scherer III. Contention management in dynamic software transactional memory. In *PODC Workshop on Concurrency and Synchronization in Java Programs*, July 2004.

26. M. L. Scott and W. N. Scherer III. Advanced contention management for dynamic software transactional memory. In *Proceedings of the 24th Annual ACM Symposium on Principles of Distributed Computing (PODC)*, 2005.

Restricted Stack Implementations

Matei David, Alex Brodsky, and Faith Ellen Fich

Department of Computer Science, University of Toronto,
10 King's College Road,
Toronto, Canada
{matei, abrodsky, fich}@cs.toronto.edu

Abstract. We introduce a new object, BH, and prove that a system with one BH object and single-writer Registers has the same computational power as a system with countably many commutative and overwriting objects. This provides a simple characterization of the class of objects that can be implemented from commutative and overwriting objects, and creates a potential tool for proving impossibility results.

It has been conjectured that Stacks and Queues shared by three or more processes *are not* in this class. In this paper, we use a BH object to show that two different restricted versions of Stacks *are* in this class. Specifically, we give an implementation of a Stack that supports any number of poppers, but at most two pushers. We also implement a Stack (or Queue) shared by any number of processes, but, in which, all stored elements are the same.

1   Introduction

Stacks and Queues are important and well studied data structures. However, they are not usually available in the hardware and, to use them, one has to implement them from the basic types available in the system. If the distributed system provides Registers and objects with consensus number ∞ (such as Compare&Swap or LL/SC), wait-free Stack and Queue implementations exist, regardless of the number of processes in the system.

Since Stacks and Queues have consensus number 2, they can be implemented in a wait-free manner from Registers and any type of objects of consensus number 2 in a system with at most two processes [Her91]. No such implementations are known when the number of processes is at least three. In fact, it is conjectured that they do not exist [Li01, Dav04b]. Proving this negative result would also solve Herlihy's long-standing open question regarding the ability of Fetch&Add objects to implement every other consensus number 2 object in systems with more than two processes.

In this paper, we consider the problem of implementing wait-free Stacks and Queues in systems where only commutative and overwriting objects (such as Test&Set objects, Fetch&Add objects, Swap objects, and Registers) are available. Two operations *commute* if the order in which they are applied does not change the resulting state of the object. One operation *overwrites* another if applying this operation results in the same object state whether or not the other operation is applied immediately before it. *Commutative and overwriting objects* are objects such that every pair of operations performed by different processes either commute or one overwrites the other. All of them have

P. Fraigniaud (Ed.): DISC 2005, LNCS 3724, pp. 137–151, 2005.

consensus number at most 2 [Her91]. The class of all commutative and overwriting read-modify-write objects with consensus number 2 is called Common2. Many objects in this class are provided in real systems.

Afek, Weisberger, Weisman [AWW93] prove that any Common2 object shared by any number of processes can be implemented from Registers and any type of objects of consensus number 2. Hence, if a Queue or Stack can be implemented from Registers and Common2 objects, it can be implemented from Registers and any type of objects of consensus number 2. Proving that such an implementation is impossible would imply that characterizing an object to be of consensus number 2 is insufficient to describe its computational power in systems of more than 2 processes.

Attempts to prove the impossibility of such an implementation for Queues have resulted in the development of a number of restricted implementations of Queues from Registers and Common2 objects. Specifically, there are wait-free implementations of Queues shared by one or two dequeuers and any number of enqueuers [HW90, Li01], and wait-free implementations of Queues shared by one enqueuer and any number of dequeuers [Dav04a].

Another natural restriction is to consider Stacks and Queues with domain size 1, i.e., where all the elements stored in the Stack or Queue are the same. Note that single-valued Stacks and Queues behave identically. Push and Enqueue increase the number of stored elements by one. Pop and Dequeue decrease the number of stored elements by one, if there was at least one, and return whether or not this was the case. We prove that a single-valued Stack shared by any number of pushers and poppers can be implemented from Registers and Common2 objects. This means that the difficulty of implementing a general Stack is not simply coordinating pushers and poppers so that they can all complete their operations, but must involve poppers determining the order in which the steps of different pushers are linearized.

We obtain our implementation by first constructing an implementation of a Stack with arbitrary domain shared by one pusher and any number of poppers. Then we show how to transform it to obtain an implementation of a single-valued Stack shared by any number of pushers and poppers. We also show how to extend the number of pushers from one to two when the domain is arbitrary. In contrast, it is not known how to implement a Queue shared by two or more enqueuers and any number of dequeuers from commutative and overwriting objects.

The implementations in this paper do not directly use Common2 objects. Instead, we introduce a new object, BH, with a single operation, Sign, and we show that, for any number of processes, a BH object can be implemented from a single Fetch&Add object. Then we implement our Stacks from a single BH object and one single-writer Register per pusher. The form of our implementations is very simple: To perform a Push, a process appends information to its single-writer Register, and performs one or two Sign operations (depending on the implementation). To perform a Pop, a process appends information to its single-writer Register, performs two Sign operations, and then collects the single-writer Registers of all pushers.

We also show that any countably infinite collection of Fetch&Add objects and single-writer Registers can be simulated using one BH object and one single-writer Register per process. In this case, a process can perform any operation by appending the operation and its arguments to its single-writer Register, applying one Sign operation to the BH object, and then reading the single-writer Registers of all other processes. Thus, a system with one BH object and one single-writer Register per process, and a system with Common2 objects and Registers are *equally powerful*. In particular, to show that an object cannot be implemented from Registers and objects in Common2, it suffices to prove that it has no implementation from one BH object and one single-writer Register per process. Moreover, it suffices to prove the lower bound for a restricted class of implementations in which each operation is simulated by an algorithm with a fixed, very simple form. This restriction enables us to better understand the flow of information between processes and to analyze the interaction between them.

In Section 2, we discuss the BH object and its properties. Section 3 contains our stack implementations. Throughout the paper, we assume that all objects are deterministic and linearizable and we consider only wait-free implementations.

2   The BH Object

In this section, we define the BH object, show how to implement it using a single Fetch&Add object, and show how it can be used to implement any collection of Common2 objects. Our goal is to show the existence of such implementations. We do not address their efficiency.

2.1   Definition of BH

Consider an object with only one operation, in which a process appends its own ID to a shared log. We refer to an occurrence of a process ID in the log as a *signature*. We assume process IDs are positive integers, so a list of signatures is a finite sequence of positive integers. The object keeps, by means of its internal state, a complete ordered list of signatures. As a process signs the log, that process receives, in response, the entire list of signatures, including the one being applied by its current operation. This object has consensus number ∞, because processes can decide on the input value of the process whose ID is the first signature in the log. Hence, this does not capture the limited power of a system with Registers and Common2 objects.

Informally, a BH object, short for *Blurred History*, works much like the object described above, but it is restricted so that it can be implemented from Registers and Common2 objects. As before, the object has one operation, Sign, and the state of the BH object is the complete list of signatures applied so far. However, the response a process P_a gets from Sign is not the exact state σ of the BH object, but instead, a set of sequences *indistinguishable* (in the sense defined below) to P_a from σ.

Two sequences of integers σ, σ' are *a-indistinguishable* if there exist $b \neq c$, both different from a, such that $\sigma = \sigma_1 \cdot bc \cdot \sigma_2$, $\sigma' = \sigma_1 \cdot cb \cdot \sigma_2$ and neither b nor c appears in σ_2. In other words, σ' is exactly the same as σ, except for the last consecutive occurrences of two different elements other than a, which are swapped. Two sequences σ, σ' are also a-indistinguishable if there is a sequence σ'' which is a-indistinguishable from both. Thus, a-indistinguishability is transitively closed. We use the terms a-indistinguishable and indistinguishable to P_a to refer to the same relation.

To provide further intuition, we also give a direct, yet equivalent, definition for the notion of indistinguishability. We can view a state σ as providing two types of information:

- the number of signatures by each process, and
- for each signature, which signatures precede it (and, hence, which signatures follow it).

Let σ be the state of a BH object immediately after P_a performs Sign. In response to its operation, P_a will receive the following information from σ:

- the number of signatures in σ by each process, and
- the relative order of each pair of signatures in σ, provided that at least one of the signatures in the pair is by P_a or is followed by another signature by the same process.

Hence, P_a won't be able to tell the *relative order* of the last signatures by other processes, when those signatures are consecutive. For example, if the BH object is in state 123 and P_1 applies Sign, the response will be $\{1231, 1321\}$, which we can write as $1\{23\}1$. As a more elaborate example, if the BH object is in the state 1324451671718 and P_9 applies Sign, P_9 will get the response $1\{23\}4\{45\}1671\{178\}9$. Notice that, in this example, P_9 can derive the exact location of the last (and only) signature by P_6 because it knows the location of the two surrounding signatures (the second by P_1 and the first by P_7).

When two sequences σ, σ' are a-indistinguishable, one is a permutation of the other, and the set of locations of last signatures by processes other than P_a is the same in both. From the response to a Sign operation, P_a can compute the response of any previous Sign operation by some other process P_b, except for possibly the last operation by P_b. To see this, note that P_a knows the location of any signature of P_b except possibly the last signature of P_b, and furthermore, later steps (by P_b and by other processes) can only add information about the exact state at the end of P_b's operation. For example, if P_1 receives the response $124\{24\}353151$ to a Sign operation, it can see that the response P_5 got from its first Sign operation is $124\{234\}5$. In this example, P_1 knows the location of the first signature by P_3, but it can see that P_5 couldn't have had that information from the response to its first Sign.

2.2 Implementing a BH Object

In this section, we informally explain how to implement a BH object using a Fetch&Add object. A more formal description of this implementation appears in [Dav04b]. The initial state of the BH object is an empty sequence, and the initial value of the Fetch&Add object in our implementation is 0.

We can view the value V stored in the Fetch&Add object as an infinite sequence of bits, $\{b_i \mid i = 0, 1, \ldots\}$. Let N denote the number of processes in the system and, for $i = 1, \ldots, N$, let V_a denote the infinite subsequence of bits $\{b_j \mid (j \bmod N) + 1 = a\}$. Then $V_1, \ldots, V_N$ are mutually disjoint. At any point in time, V_a encodes a finite sequence of non-negative integers as the concatenation of the unary representations of these integers, each integer separated from the next by 10, and followed by an infinite sequence of 0's. For example, u_1, u_2, u_3 is encoded as $1^{u_1+1}01^{u_2+1}01^{u_3+1}00\cdots$. Then any positive integer can be appended to the end of the sequence by only changing certain bits of V_a from 0 to 1.

We implement every Sign operation by P_a using one Fetch&Add operation on V that appends a number to the sequence encoded in V_a. Since P_a is the only process changing V_a, it can keep the value of V_a in a local register v_a. Whenever P_a needs to append a number to the sequence encoded in V_a, it can inspect v_a to decide which bits of V_a have to be changed from 0 to 1. P_a can then set those bits using a Fetch&Add operation on V with an appropriate argument. For example, if V_a stores $2, 0, 3$, encoded as $111010111100\cdots$, and P_a needs to append the value 1 to this sequence, it has to change the 12-th and 13-th bits of V_a from 0 to 1. P_a can accomplish this by performing a Fetch&Add operation on V with argument $2^{a-1+11N} + 2^{a-1+12N}$.

In our BH implementation, every process P_a has, in addition to v_a, a second local register w_a. This register has initial value 0. It is used to store the last value received by P_a from a Fetch&Add operation on V. A Sign operation by P_a is implemented as follows:

- using v_a and w_a, process P_a computes a value x such that performing a Fetch&Add operation on V with argument x has the effect of appending w_a to the sequence encoded in V_a;
- P_a appends w_a to v_a;
- P_a performs Fetch&Add on V with argument x;
- P_a stores the response from this Fetch&Add operation in w_a;
- using w_a, process P_a computes the response from Sign.

The computation of x was described above. Thus, it remains to explain how to compute the response from the Sign operation.

From the response to its Fetch&Add operation, P_a can compute the number of previous signatures by some other process P_b as the number of runs of 1's in the sequence V_b. It can also compute $u_{b,i}$, the i-th non-negative integer in the sequence encoded by V_b. Note that $u_{b,i}$ is the response P_b received from the Fetch&Add operation it performed during its $(i-1)$-st Sign operation. Hence, P_a can compute which signatures precede the $(i-1)$-st signature by P_b. The only information about the signature log that P_a cannot compute is the relative order of the last signatures by other processes, when those signatures are consecutive. This is precisely the information needed to construct the class of states indistinguishable to P_a from the signature log.

2.3 Implementations Using a BH Object

In this section, we show that a system with one single-writer Register per process and one BH object can be used to simulate a system with infinitely many Common2 objects and Registers. To do that, we implement a countably infinite collection of Fetch&Add objects and single-writer Registers using one single-writer Register per process and one BH object. Our claim follows from the fact that any Register can be implemented from single-writer Registers [VA86], and that any Common2 object can be implemented from Fetch&Add objects and Registers [AWW93].

Consider a system of countably infinitely many Fetch&Add objects and single-writer Registers. Assume the objects in this system are indexed by positive integers. A process may perform three types of high-level operations: Fetch&Add(k, x), if k is the index of a Fetch&Add object, Read(k), if k is the index of a Register, and Write(k, x), if k is the index of one of the Registers to which it may Write. In a system with one single-writer Register per process and one BH object, we implement each of the three types of operations as follows:

- P_a appends the current high-level operation to its Register;
- P_a Signs the BH object;
- P_a Reads the Registers of all processes;
- P_a locally computes the result of the implemented operation.

Throughout the implementation, the value held in P_a's Register is an ordered list of all the high-level operations that P_a has started. We linearize a high-level operation at the moment the process executing it Signs the BH object. Thus, given the responses P_a gets from its Sign and Read operations, P_a can compute which high-level operations have occurred so far. It can also compute the linearization of these operations, except for what is blurred in the response it gets from the BH object. This information is enough for P_a to compute the result of its high-level operation:

- If the high-level operation is a Write, its response is simply OK.
- If the high-level operation is Read(k), we know that only one process P_b writes to the single-writer Register with index k. In this case, P_a returns the argument of the last Write operation by P_b to this Register that is linearized before this Read. If there is no such Write operation, then the initial value of the Register is returned.
- If the high-level operation is Fetch&Add(k, x), P_a needs to compute the sum of the arguments of all the Fetch&Add operations on this object that are linearized before the current operation. Note that P_a does not need to know the order in which these operations are linearized, since addition is commutative.

Something stronger can be said about a system with one single-writer Register per process and one BH object.

Theorem 1. *Let S_1 be a system with countably infinitely many Common2 objects and Registers. Let S_2 be a system with one single-writer Register per process and one BH object. If there exists an implementation of some object O in S_1, then there exists an implementation of O in S_2. Furthermore, to perform a high-level operation on O, process P_a begins by appending this operation to its single-writer Register and then alternately performs Sign and Reads of all Registers.*

In the construction, a process uses its single-writer Register to record which operation it performs, on which object it performs this operation, and any parameters of this operation. Thus, when implementing a single object that supports a single operation that takes no parameters, the single-writer Registers are not needed.

3   Stack Implementations from a BH Object

3.1   A Single-Pusher Stack Implementation

In this section, we give a single-pusher many-popper Stack implementation from one BH object B and an unbounded array V of single-writer Registers, each capable of holding one Stack element and each of which can only be written by the single pusher P_1. Alternatively, V can be a single-writer register capable of holding any sequence of Stack elements. The initial state of B is the empty sequence. Let process P_a be a popper, for $a > 1$. The implementation is presented in Figure 1.

The pusher P_1 holds a local variable *last*, initialized to 0, which is used to store the index of the last slot of V to which P_1 wrote. To push an element x onto the Stack, P_1 increments *last* and writes x into $V[last]$. P_1 then signs B. A signature of P_1 in B is called a *push step*. Recall that this is an occurrence of 1 in the state of B.

To pop an element off the Stack, P_a first performs two Sign operations on B. From the result of its second operation, which is an equivalence class of a-indistinguishable sequences, P_a selects any representative σ. Then P_a locally computes a function f of σ (see Figure 1). The value of this function is either 0, in which case P_a returns ϵ, indicating an empty Stack, or a positive integer, which P_a uses to index V. In the second case, the value stored in that location of V is the result of P_a's Pop. The signatures of poppers in B are called *pop steps*. The signature produced by the first Sign occurring in a Pop operation is called a *first pop step*, and the signature produced by the second Sign is called *a second pop step*.

The heart of this implementation is the function f. It takes a BH state σ as input, and decides which value the process computing it should pop from the Stack. Inside the function, we consider each Push operation ϕ, starting with the latest, and try to match it with the earliest completed Pop operation α that starts after the push step of ϕ. If no such α exists, we erase ϕ from σ and continue. On the other hand, if α exists, we erase both α and ϕ from σ and continue. If α turns out to be the Pop operation that invoked f on σ, which is the case if the second pop step of α is the last signature in σ, we decide that α should return the value pushed on the Stack by ϕ.

For the purposes of proving the correctness of this implementation, it will be convenient to assume that P_1 is pushing the values $1, 2, 3, \ldots$, thus identifying the value stored in a cell of V with the index of that cell.

A crucial fact in proving the correctness of this algorithm is given in Lemma 5, where we show that the choice of σ made in line 6 does not affect the output of a Pop operation. Specifically, the result of applying f to two indistinguishable states is the same. In order to establish this result, we prove several Lemmas saying that, under certain conditions, swapping two consecutive steps of σ does not change the result of f. The last pop step in σ, which is the second pop step of the Pop operation that invoked f, is never moved.

Let $\sigma = \tau_1, a, b, \tau_2$ and $\sigma' = \tau_1, b, a, \tau_2$, where $a \neq b$ and τ_2 is not empty. Lemmas 1, 2 and 3 describe situations in which $f(\sigma) = f(\sigma')$.

Lemma 1. *Swapping two consecutive pop steps by different processes, of which at least one is a first pop step, does not affect the result of f. Formally, if a is a first pop step and b is a pop step, then $f(\sigma) = f(\sigma')$.*

```
Procedure P₁:Push(x)

1.  increment( last )
2.  Write( V[last], x )
3.  Sign( B, 1 )


Procedure Pᵈ:Pop, for d > 1

4.  Sign( B, d )
5.  C ⟵ Sign( B, d )
6.  σ ⟵ any sequence in C
7.  l ⟵ f(σ)
8.  if l = 0
9.          return ε
    else
10.         return Read( V[l] )
    endif


Function f(σ)

11. while there exist push steps in σ
12.        i ⟵ location of last push step in σ
13.        A ⟵ { ( j, j' ) : j and j' are the locations of the first
                  and second steps of a pop operation and i < j }
14.        if A is not empty
15.              ( k, k' ) ⟵ pair with minimum j' in A
16.              if k' is the last location in σ
17.                    return number of push steps in σ
                 endif
18.              delete signatures at i, k and k' from σ
           else
19.              delete signature at i from σ
           endif
    endwhile
20. return 0
```

Fig. 1. A Single-Pusher Implementation

Proof. During every iteration of the while loop, membership in A is determined in line 13 by the order between push steps and first pop steps, and the selection of a pop operation in line 15 is determined by the order between second pop steps. Hence, the computations of f on σ and σ' take exactly the same decision during every iteration of the while loop.

The same argument can be used to show:

Lemma 2. *Swapping a consecutive push step and second pop step does not affect the result of f. Formally, if a is a push step and b is a second pop step, $f(\sigma) = f(\sigma')$.*

Lemma 3. *Swapping two consecutive second pop steps does not affect the result of f. Formally, if both a and b are second pop steps, $f(\sigma) = f(\sigma')$.*

Proof. We use induction on the number of executions of the while loop to show that $f(\sigma) = f(\sigma')$.

The only difference in the computations of f on σ and σ' can arise in an iteration in which both pop operations involved in the swap are in the set A, one of them is selected in $f(\sigma)$ and the other is selected in $f(\sigma')$. Let τ and τ' be the respective sequences at the beginning of that iteration. Without loss of generality, we must have

$$\tau = \tau_1, 1, \tau_2, a_1, \tau_3, b_1, \tau_4, a_2, b_2, \tau_5 \text{ and}$$
$$\tau' = \tau_1, 1, \tau_2, a_1, \tau_3, b_1, \tau_4, b_2, a_2, \tau_5,$$

where the 1 following τ_1 is the last step by the pusher P_1. Hence $\tau_2, \tau_3, \tau_4, \tau_5$ contain no 1's. The steps a_1 and a_2 are the first and second steps of a pop operation by P_a, and b_1 and b_2 are the first and second steps of a pop operation by P_b. Notice that in this case τ_3 cannot contain pop steps by P_a because P_a has a pending operation.

In this scenario, $1, a_1, a_2$ are deleted in $f(\sigma)$ and $1, b_1, b_2$ are deleted in $f(\sigma')$. Let

$$\overline{\tau} = \tau_1, \tau_2, \tau_3, b_1, \tau_4, b_2, \tau_5 \text{ and}$$
$$\overline{\tau}' = \tau_1, \tau_2, a_1, \tau_3, \tau_4, a_2, \tau_5.$$

Then $f(\sigma) = f(\tau) = f(\overline{\tau})$ and $f(\sigma') = f(\tau') = f(\overline{\tau}')$. The computation of f is not affected by what popper is performing a particular Pop operation. It is only affected by the locations of pop steps in the sequence. Hence, $f(\overline{\tau}) = f(\overline{\tau}'')$, where

$$\overline{\tau}'' = \tau_1, \tau_2, \tau_3, a_1, \tau_4, a_2, \tau_5.$$

Since τ_3 contains no pop steps by P_a and no push steps, $\overline{\tau}'$ can be transformed into $\overline{\tau}''$ by repeatedly swapping the first pop step a_1 with pop steps that immediately precede it. By Lemma 1, $f(\overline{\tau}') = f(\overline{\tau}'')$.

Lemma 4. *Removing the first step of an incomplete Pop does not affect the result of f.*

Proof. The first step of an incomplete pop operation is never considered when building the set A, nor when selecting a pop operation from A, so removing it will cause no change in the computation of f.

Lemma 5. *Let σ be the BH state at the end of a pop operation by some process P_d. Let σ' be a sequence indistinguishable to P_d from σ. Then $f(\sigma) = f(\sigma')$.*

Proof. By properties of the BH object, there is a sequence of states $\sigma^{(0)}, \sigma^{(1)}, \ldots, \sigma^{(m)}$ with $\sigma = \sigma^{(0)}$ and $\sigma^{(m)} = \sigma'$ such that any two consecutive states $\sigma^{(e)}, \sigma^{(e+1)}$ can be obtained from one another by swapping two consecutive last steps by some processes other than P_d. We have three possibilities:

- One of these steps is a first pop step. Since it is the last step by that process, it must be part of an incomplete pop operation. By Lemma 4, removing it will not affect the result of f. But removing it erases the difference between $\sigma^{(e)}$ and $\sigma^{(e+1)}$, so $f(\sigma^{(e)}) = f(\sigma^{(e+1)})$.
- Both steps are second pop steps. By Lemma 3, $f(\sigma^{(e)}) = f(\sigma^{(e+1)})$.
- One is a push step, the other is a second pop step. By Lemma 2, $f(\sigma^{(e)}) = f(\sigma^{(e+1)})$.

Inductively, $f(\sigma) = f(\sigma')$.

Next, we assign linearization points for Push operations and for completed Pop operations. We do not linearize any incomplete Pop operations (which only apply one Sign). A Push operation is linearized at its push step. Let α be a complete Pop operation and let σ_α be the BH state when α is completed. We define the linearization point of α as follows:

- If there are no Push operations deleted unmatched (i.e. on line 19) during the computation of f on σ_α, then α is linearized at its second pop step.
- Otherwise, α is linearized immediately before the Push operation ϕ deleted on line 19 whose push step occurs earliest in σ_α. If multiple Pop operations are linearized at the same place, they are put in the same order that their second pop steps appear in σ_α.

Note that, in the second case, the push step of ϕ occurs between the two pop steps of α: Since ϕ occurs in σ_α, the second pop step cannot occur before the push step. If the first pop step occurs after the push step, then A is not empty at the end of the first iteration of the computation of f on σ_α and ϕ is deleted on line 18, rather than line 19.

Furthermore, if $\tau_0, d_1, \tau_1, 1, \tau_2, d_2$ is the BH state when the Pop operation α completes, d_1 and d_2 are the two pop steps of α, and τ_2 does not contain any push step or both pop steps of any Pop operation, then α is not linearized at its second pop step. This follows from the fact that A is empty during the first iteration of f on $\tau_0, d_1, \tau_1, 1, \tau_2, d_2$ and, hence, the last Push operation is deleted unmatched.

Given σ, we define $h(\sigma)$ to be the Stack history associated with σ. It contains the sequence of operations in the order they are linearized, together with their return values. For example, $h(11216264241266)$ is the sequence

(Push, OK), (Push, OK), (Pop by P_2, 2), (Push, OK), (Pop by P_6, 3),
(Pop by P_4, 1), (Pop by P_2, ϵ), (Push, OK), (Pop by P_6, 4).

Theorem 2. *For every state σ, the Stack history $h(\sigma)$ is legal.*

Proof. We use induction on the number of push steps in σ.

First, let σ be a history with no push steps. Any Pop operation which is completed during σ will output ϵ, hence $h(\sigma)$ is legal.

Now let $k \geq 0$ and assume that, for all sequences σ' with at most k push steps, $h(\sigma')$ is legal. Let σ be a history with $k + 1$ push steps. Let ϕ denote the last Push operation.

First, consider the case where σ contains no completed Pop operations that start after its last push step ℓ. Then $\sigma = \pi, \ell, \rho$, where ρ contains no push steps. Let $\sigma' = \pi, \rho$.

All Push operations in σ' return the same result, OK, as in σ and each is linearized in the same place in $h(\sigma')$ and $h(\sigma)$.

Any Pop operation α whose second pop step occurs before ℓ in σ is linearized before ϕ in $h(\sigma)$ Moreover, since $\sigma_\alpha = \sigma'_\alpha$, it follows that α has the same result in σ and σ' and is linearized in the same place in $h(\sigma)$ and $h(\sigma')$.

Now let α be a Pop operation whose second pop step occurs after ℓ in σ. Since there are no completed Pop operations that start after ℓ, the first pop step of α occurs in π. Then $\sigma = \tau_0, d_1, \tau_1, \ell, \tau_2, d_2, \tau_3$, where d_1 and d_2 are the pop steps of α and τ_2, τ_3 does not contain any push step or both pop steps of any Pop operation. By the observation following the definition of the linearization points, α is not linearized at its second pop step and ϕ is deleted unmatched during the computation of f on σ_α. It follows that α has the same result in both σ and σ'.

If α is not linearized immediately before ℓ, then it is linearized immediately before a push step that occurs in π and whose Push operation is also deleted during the computation of f on σ_α. Hence, α is linearized in the same place in $h(\sigma)$ and $h(\sigma')$.

Each Pop operation that is linearized immediately before ℓ in $h(\sigma)$ is linearized at its second pop step in $h(\sigma')$. These operations are linearized after the last Push operation in $h(\sigma')$ and are linearized in the same relative order as they are in $h(\sigma)$.

Thus $h(\sigma) = h(\sigma')$, (Push, OK). By the induction hypothesis, $h(\sigma')$ is legal. Thus, so is $h(\sigma)$.

Now consider the case where σ contains at least one completed Pop operation that starts after the last push step ℓ. Then $\sigma = \tau_0, \ell, \tau_1, d_1, \tau_2, d_2, \tau_3$, where d_1 and d_2 are the two steps of the first completed Pop operation α that starts after ℓ. Then τ_1, τ_2, τ_3 contains no push steps and τ_1, τ_2 does not contain both steps of any Pop operation.

Since ϕ ends before α begins, it is linearized before α. Any other (Pop) operation β that is linearized between ϕ and α must be linearized at β's second pop step, c_2. Since this occurs before d_2, the definition of α implies that β's first pop step, c_1, must occur before ℓ. Thus $\sigma_\beta = \rho_0, c_1, \rho_1, \ell, \rho_2, c_2$, where ρ_2 does not contain any push step or the both pop steps of any Pop operation. But then the observation following the definition of the linearization points says that β is not linearized at c_2, which is a contradiction. Thus, there are no operations linearized between ϕ and α in $h(\sigma)$.

During the first iteration of the computation of f on $\sigma_\alpha = \tau_0, \ell, \tau_1, d_1, \tau_2, d_2$, variable i contains the location of ℓ and, by the choice of α, variables k and k' contain the locations of α's first and second pop steps. Thus f returns the number of push steps in σ_α, which is the index of the location in V to which ϕ writes. By Lemma 5, the sequence that is chosen on line 6 during α gives the value for f as σ_α. Hence α returns the value pushed by ϕ.

Now we argue that removing both ϕ and α does not change the relative order of the linearization points of the the remaining operations nor the results of these operations. Let $\sigma' = \tau_0, \tau_1, \tau_2, \tau_3$. Note that the linearization points of each Push operation (except ϕ) is the same in σ' as in σ. We consider a number of different cases for completed Pop operations.

A Pop operation whose second pop step is in τ_0 has $\sigma_\alpha = \sigma'_\alpha$. Thus it is linearized at the same point and returns the same value in σ and σ'.

If a Pop operation β has its second pop step in τ_3, then, during the first iteration of the computation of f on σ_β, ϕ and α are matched and deleted on line 18, leaving σ'. Thus β has the same linearization point in σ as it does in σ' and returns the same value.

Finally, consider a Pop operation β whose second pop step is either in τ_1 or τ_2. Since ϕ is matched with α during the computation of f on σ_α and σ_β is a proper prefix of σ_α, ϕ is deleted unmatched during the first iteration of the computation of f on σ_β. The only difference between the resulting sequence and σ'_β is the first pop step d_1 of α, which, by Lemma 4 does not affect the result of f. Hence, β returns the same value in $h(\sigma)$ and $h(\sigma')$.

By definition of α, β's first pop step is in τ_0. Since no operations are linearized between ϕ, which is linearized at ℓ, and α, which is linearized at d_2, β is not linearized at its second pop step in σ. Hence it is linearized immediately before some push step. If that push step is not ℓ, then β has the same linearization point in σ', since the same Push operations are deleted unmatched in the computations of f on σ_β and σ'_β.

The only other Pop operations are those whose second pop steps are in τ_1, τ_2 and which are linearized immediately before ℓ in σ. They are linearized in order of their second pop steps. Since the last Push operation, ϕ, is the earliest unmatched Push operation in the computation of f on σ_β, it must be the only unmatched Push operation. Thus, in σ'_β, there are no unmatched Push operations, so in σ', these operations are linearized at their second pop steps. Hence, they have the same relative order in σ and σ'. Since the linearization point of all other operations are in τ_0 or in τ_3, all operations in $h(\sigma')$ occur in the same order in $h(\sigma)$.

Since we show that each operation in $h(\sigma')$ returns the same result as it does in $h(\sigma)$. It follows that $h(\sigma)$ is exactly equal to $h(\sigma')$ with an inserted pair of consecutive operations, the Push ϕ and the matching Pop α. By the induction hypothesis, $h(\sigma')$ is legal, so, from the specifications of a Stack object, $h(\sigma)$ is also legal.

3.2   A Single-Valued Stack Implementation

The single-popper Stack implementation is based on the observation that the number of times each pusher signs the BH object prior to a Pop is precisely the number of elements that were pushed on the Stack prior to that Pop. If there is only one pusher, there is no ambiguity about the order in which the Push operations occurred. Unfortunately, this is not the case when there are many pushers. For example, suppose processes P_1 and P_2 each pushed a value on the Stack by signing the BH object and then process P_3 popped a value by signing the BH object twice. The resulting state 1233 of the BH object is indistinguishable to P_3 from 2133, the state that results when P_1 and P_2 perform their operations in the opposite order. Consequently, it is not clear if the value pushed by P_1 or P_2 is the one which should be popped. While we can overcome this problem for the special case of exactly two pushers (see following section), the general solution remains elusive. However, if all the values pushed on the Stack are the same, then the problem of choosing which value to match with which Pop is obviated.

A process performing a Pop on a single-valued Stack only needs to determine whether or not its Pop operation has some matching Push. It does not matter which pusher performed the Push. This is essentially the problem that is solved by the single-pusher Stack implementation (in the previous section).

To perform a Push, a process appends 1 to its single-writer Register and signs the BH object once. To perform a Pop, a process appends 2 to its single-writer Register, signs the BH object twice, and then reads the Registers of all other processes. Let C denote the equivalence class of BH states returned as a result of the second Sign operation in a Pop. As in line 6, we select any representative σ from C. However, before we compute f on σ, we replace every push step in σ with a push step by a virtual process, P_0. A step by some process P_a is a push step if the corresponding value in P_a's Register is a 1. If f returns 0 on the modified sequence, the Pop returns ϵ; otherwise the Pop returns the single value in the domain.

The proof of correctness is essentially the same as the the proof for the single-pusher Stack, except for the addition of the following lemma, which handles two Push operations whose order cannot be distinguished.

Lemma 6. *Swapping two consecutive push steps does not affect the result of f.*

3.3 A Two-Pusher Stack implementation

We will now extend the algorithm given in Section 3.1 to allow two pushers instead of just one. The basic idea is similar to the "helping" mechanism that appears in Herlihy's universal construction [Her91]: the completion of a Push operation by one pusher might "help" linearize a pending Push operation by the other pusher.

Let P_1 and P_2 be the two pushers, and let P_d be a popper, for $d > 2$. We assume that, in addition to a BH object B, we have two unbounded arrays V_1, V_2 of single-writer Registers, where V_a is written by pusher P_a. To push the value x, P_a first writes x in the next available location in V_a. P_a then applies *two* Sign operations on B. Recall that in the single-pusher implementation, a Push operation consisted of only one Sign.

A Pop operation by P_d begins by applying two Sign operations on the BH object. The return value of the second operation is an equivalence class of states indistinguishable to P_d from the real state of B. We then select any representative σ, as in line 6. However, before we can apply function f on σ, we need to transform σ from a two-pusher history into a single-pusher history. This transformation is performed by a new function, g, described below.

The function g takes as arguments a two-pusher history σ, and the arrays V_1, V_2. It constructs a single-pusher history τ and an array V. The two histories, σ and τ, contain exactly the same pop steps. The push steps by P_1 and P_2 in σ are replaced in τ with push steps by a virtual process, P_0. The idea is that a Push operation ϕ is linearized either at its second step, or at the second step of the first push operation ϕ' by the other pusher which was started and completed after the first step of ϕ. The function g can be computed as follows.

- Find the earliest second push step in σ; call that push operation ϕ'.
- If there is a push operation ϕ which has a first step that occurs before the first push step of ϕ', delete both ϕ and ϕ', and insert two steps by P_0 in τ at the location of the second push step of ϕ'.
- If no such ϕ exists, delete ϕ' and insert a step by P_0 in τ at the location of the second push step of ϕ'.

- Whenever we delete the i-th Push operation by P_a, write $V_a[i]$ into the first empty location in V. In the first case, when we delete ϕ and ϕ', append the value corresponding to ϕ before the one corresponding to ϕ'.
- Repeat until no push operation in σ has two steps.
- At the end, delete any remaining first push steps.

For the purposes of proving correctness, we may assume that the i-th value pushed by P_a and written in $V_a[i]$ is the pair (a, i). For example, if $\sigma = 1112332611241$ 3322431426 (where second push steps and second pop steps are underlined), we have $g(\sigma, V_1, V_2) = (\tau, V)$ where $\tau = 0330064033043406$ and $V = (1,1), (1,2), (2,1), (1,3),$ $(2,2), (2,3)$.

After computing $g(\sigma) = (\tau, V)$, a Pop operation computes $f(\tau)$. If the latter evaluates to 0, the Pop returns ϵ; otherwise the Pop returns the element in location $f(\tau)$ of V, the array computed in g. For example, for σ, τ, V from the previous example, $f(\tau) = 2$ and $V[f(\tau)] = (1, 2)$.

The following two Lemmas are needed to prove the correctness of this extension.

Lemma 7. *Let σ be the state at the end of a Pop operation by P_d and let σ' be a state indistinguishable to P_d from σ. Let $g(\sigma) = (\tau, V)$ and $g(\sigma') = (\tau', V')$. Then $V = V'$ and $f(\tau) = f(\tau')$.*

Lemma 8. *Let σ be a BH state. Let σ' be any prefix of σ. Let $g(\sigma) = (\tau, V)$ and let $g(\sigma') = (\tau', V')$. Then τ' is a prefix of τ and V' is a prefix of V.*

Finally, we argue that our algorithm is linearizable. Given a two-pusher history σ, let $g(\sigma) = (\tau, V)$. We define the linearization points for Push operations in σ to be the corresponding steps where they appear in τ. We define linearization points for Pop operations in σ the same way they are defined in the single-pusher history τ. By Lemma 8, all Pop operations completed in σ have returned the exact same values as if they had occurred in τ. Since the single-pusher history τ is linearizable, so is σ.

4   Conclusions

In this paper, we have showed that it is possible to construct wait-free implementations of certain restricted Stacks using only Registers and Common2 objects. Specifically, it is possible to implement single-valued Stacks (and Queues) shared by any number of process, and general (multi-valued) Stacks shared by one or two pushers and any number of poppers.

Queue implementations exist for any number of enqueuers and at most two dequeuers [Li01], and for one enqueuer and any number of dequeuers [Dav04a]. In a Stack implementation, only the poppers output relevant values. If there are only two poppers, they might be able to agree on the sequence of values to output. This suggests that Stack implementations for any number of pushers and at most two poppers might exist. However, we conjecture that implementing a Stack with domain size 2, shared by three pushers and three poppers, is impossible to implement from Registers and Common2 objects.

Since modern distributed systems do provide more powerful types, our results are mainly of theoretical interest. The BH object is not an object one would want to implement in hardware or use in an efficient implementation. Moreover, the implementations we present use an unbounded size BH object and an unbounded number of single-writer Registers (or single-writer Registers of unbounded size).

However, we believe the BH object is a very useful tool for studying the computational power of Registers and objects in Common2. It provides a simple characterization of the information a process can obtain from such objects during the course of a computation. This makes it much easier to show the existence of algorithms for this model and has the potential of leading to the development of interesting impossibility results dealing with questions at the foundations of our understanding of shared memory distributed computing.

Acknowledgments

This research was supported by an Ontario Graduate Scholarship, the Natural Sciences and Engineering Research Council of Canada, and the Scalable Synchronization Research Group of Sun Microsystems.

References

[AWW93]   Yehuda Afek, Eytan Weisberger, and Hanan Weisman. A completeness theorem for a class of synchronization objects. In *Proceedings of the 12th ACM Symposium on Principles of Distributed Computing*, pages 159–170, 1993.

[Dav04a]   Matei David. A single-enqueuer wait-free queue implementation. In *Proceedings of DISC 2004*, pages 132–143, 2004.

[Dav04b]   Matei David. Wait-free linearizable queue implementations. Master's thesis, Univ. of Toronto, 2004.

[Her91]   Maurice Herlihy. Wait-free synchronization. *ACM Transactions on Programming Languages and Systems*, 13(1):124–149, January 1991.

[HW90]   Maurice Herlihy and Jeanette Wing. Linearizability: A correctness condition for concurrent objects. *ACM Transactions on Programming Languages and Systems*, 12(3):495–504, January 1990.

[Li01]   Zongpeng Li. Non-blocking implementation of queues in asynchronous distributed shared-memory systems. Master's thesis, Univ. of Toronto, 2001.

[VA86]   Paul Vitanyi and Baruch Awerbuch. Atomic shared register access by asynchronous hardware. In *Proceedings of the 27th IEEE Symposium on Foundations of Computer Science*, pages 233–243, 1986.

Proving Atomicity: An Assertional Approach

Gregory Chockler[1], Nancy Lynch[1], Sayan Mitra[1], and Joshua Tauber[1]

MIT CSAIL, The Stata Center, Bldg.32, 32 Vassar Street,
Cambridge MA 02139, USA
{grishac, lynch, mitras, josh}@csail.mit.edu

Abstract. Atomicity (or *linearizability*) is a commonly used consistency criterion for distributed services and objects. Although atomic object implementations are abundant, proving that algorithms achieve atomicity has turned out to be a challenging problem. In this paper, we initiate the study of systematic ways of verifying distributed implementations of atomic objects, beginning with read/write objects (registers). Our general approach is to replace the existing operational reasoning about events and partial orders with assertional reasoning about invariants and simulation relations. To this end, we define an abstract state machine that captures the atomicity property and prove correctness of the object implementations by establishing a simulation mapping between the implementation and the specification automata. We demonstrate the generality of our specification by showing that it is implemented by three different read/write register constructions: the message-passing register emulation of Attiya, Bar-Noy and Dolev, its optimized version based on real time, and the shared memory register construction of Vitanyi and Awerbuch. In addition, we show that a simplified version of our specification is implemented by a general atomic object construction based on the Lamport's replicated state machine algorithm.

1 Introduction

Many distributed and network-based services can be modeled as shared objects accessible to (possibly remote) clients through well-defined interfaces. Atomicity [16,21] (also known as *linearizability* [10]) is a desirable property for such objects as it allows clients using the objects to perceive the operations that occur in each run as occurring atomically, in some sequential order. This perception makes it easier to understand the behavior of a system using distributed services, and so, simplifies the task of system design.

Atomic services could be implemented simply on single server machines. However, to achieve high availability in a distributed system and to tolerate failures, atomic services are typically implemented by distributed algorithms.

* This work is supported by MURI–AFOSR SA2796PO 1-0000243658, USAF–AFRL #FA9550-04-1-0121, NSF Grant CCR-0121277, NSF-Texas Engineering Experiment Station Grant 64961-CS, and DARPA F33615-01-C-1896.

P. Fraigniaud (Ed.): DISC 2005, LNCS 3724, pp. 152–168, 2005.

Many distributed algorithms have been proposed for implementing atomic objects; see, for example, [17,15,36,27,33,32,10,35,14,19,18,22,23,8]. These use a range of techniques to achieve the appearance of total ordering, for example, assigning timestamps and processing operations in timestamp order, or using quorum configurations.

Although atomic object implementations are abundant, proving that algorithms achieve atomicity has turned out to be a challenging problem. Most existing proofs for such algorithms are long, subtle, and difficult to understand and check. As evidence of the difficulty, we note that several published proofs for implementations of atomic shared read/write memory objects have later been shown to be incorrect. We believe that a fundamental reason for the difficulty of these proofs is their style: they are based on detailed, not-very-systematic, reasoning about events and their ordering. Useful structure in such proofs is often provided by lemmas about partial orders of operations on objects, for example, Proposition 3 of [16] (for single-writer read/write objects) and Lemma 13.16 of [21] (for multi-writer read/write objects). These lemmas provide sufficient conditions for correctness of atomic read/write object implementations, based on a list of properties that a partial ordering of operations must satisfy. However, showing that these properties hold still requires detailed, ad hoc reasoning about events (see, e.g., [22,23]).

In this paper, we study systematic ways of verifying distributed implementations of atomic objects, beginning with read/write objects (registers). Our general approach is to replace operational reasoning about events and partial orders with assertional reasoning about invariants and simulation relations. The assertional methods differ from the traditional operational arguments in two important ways. First, the system properties are stated precisely in terms of predicates over the system state components. Second, assertional proofs can be checked by examining individual state transitions of the algorithm without reasoning about entire executions. As such they lend themselves to mechanization, i.e., the process of checking a proof can be carried out using interactive tools, such as theorem provers.

Our approach to carrying out assertional atomicity proofs is first to define an abstract state machine that captures the atomicity property and then, prove correctness of the object implementations by establishing a simulation mapping between the implementation and the specification automata. The challenge is to find a specification automaton that is general enough to apply to many existing implementations, and at the same time sufficiently close to the actual implementations to simplify the task of finding the mapping. One example of an atomicity specification that turned out to be too abstract for carrying out simulation proofs is the canonical atomic object automaton of Section 13.1.2 of [21]. The canonical object automaton maintains a buffer used to store incoming client requests. Buffered requests can later be applied to the object state, and the generated responses are returned to their originators. Unfortunately, this specification, though simple, does not provide sufficient detail to allow for easy match with concrete implementations.

We therefore, give more detailed specifications. Namely, we define an abstract state machine, which we call the *Partial-Order Machine (PO-Machine)*, which records information about operations and their orders in its state. The PO-Machine expresses the common behavior of many existing atomic register implementations, in which client operation requests are gradually ordered relative to other operation requests until all the necessary ordering constraints are achieved. The ordering constructed is, in the limit, guaranteed to be a partial order of the requested operations that satisfies sufficient conditions for showing atomicity.

We use the PO-Machine as a formal specification for distributed algorithms that implement atomic memory. We show that it is implemented by three different read/write register constructions: the message-passing emulation of Attiya, Bar-Noy, and Dolev (ABD) [3] (extended to handle multiple writers as in [23]), an optimized version of ABD that takes advantage of synchronized clocks at writers [8], and the unbounded version of the shared memory construction of a multi-writer/multi-reader register from single-writer/single-reader registers of [36]. We also show that a slight modification of the PO-Machine, called the *TO-Machine*, can be used to prove atomicity of a general (i.e., not necessarily read/write) object implementation based on the replicated state machine protocol of Lamport [15].

We specify the PO-Machine and the algorithms formally using the I/O Automata (IOA)[20] and Timed IOA [12,11] models, in fact, using formal specification languages that have been defined for these models. The IOA/TIOA specification languages lead to very stylized assertional proofs for invariants and simulation relations that can be partially automated using theorem provers. Moreover, the same IOA specifications can be used by the IOA compiler [31,30] to produce executable Java code.

Other related work: Our use of a partial order automaton as an abstract specification was inspired by prior work of Fekete et al. on specifying the behavior of an Eventually Serializable Data Service [9]. Their specification used a (different) partial-order machine, which expresses weaker consistency requirements than atomicity. The algorithm studied in [9], based on an earlier algorithm of Liskov et al. [13], was shown to achieve this weaker form of consistency.

The only other published simulation-based atomicity proofs we are aware of are those of Bogdanov [5] (replicated state machine), and Doherty et al. (lock-free queue) [7]. The proofs in both these papers are complicated: They involve multiple levels of asbtraction as well as both forward and backward simulations. In contrast, every construction considered in this paper is shown to be atomic by exhibiting a single forward simulation directly from the implementation automaton to a specification automaton.

Another example of using assertional reasoning for proving atomicity is the work by Wang and Stoller [37], which uses static analysis combined with model checking to verify atomicity of code blocks involving lock-free synchronization primitives. A more general discussion of assertional proof techniques can be found in [28].

The rest of the paper is organized as follows: In Section 2, we introduce preliminary definitions and notation used throughout the paper. The sufficient condition for proving atomicity is specified in Section 3. The PO-Machine is described in Section 4. The ABD algorithm is presented and proved correct in Section 5. A time-based version of ABD is discussed in Section 6. Section 7 briefly discusses the proofs of the Vitanyi-Awerbuch's register construction, and of the Lamport's replicated state machine. Section 8 discusses future directions. For lack of space, we only outline intuition and highlight basic ideas underlying the correctness proofs. The detailed proofs can be found in the full version of the paper [6].

2   Preliminary Definitions

We use the I/O Automata (IOA)[20] model to formally specify services, describe algorithms and carry out proofs. An I/O automaton is a non-determenistic state machine whose state can change atomically through a discrete transition labeled by a discrete *action*. The set of the automaton's actions is called the *action signature* of the automaton. The actions can be either *external* or *internal*. The external actions, which can be either *input* or *output*, model interaction with the automaton's environment; and the internal actions model local computation steps. In Section 6, we also use the Timed I/O Automata (TIOA) model [12,11], which, in addition to discrete transitions, also allows the automata state to evolve by *trajectories*, which describe evolution of the state over time.

We use *forward simulations* to carry out atomicity proofs. Informally, a forward simulation is a relationship between the states of two automata requiring that the transitions of one system can in some sense be mimicked by the other. A precise definition of the simulation formalism can be found in [21].

The read/write service: A read/write object (a *register*) type consists of the following components: (1) an arbitrary set of values V with an initial value v_0, (2) the set of operations of the form $write(v)$, $v \in V$, and $read$, (3) the set of responses are ack and $v \in V$, and (4) the sequential specification f such that $f(w, write(v)) = (v, ack)$ and $f(w, read) = (w, w)$.

A read/write service implements a shared read/write register. To access the service, a client issues an *operation descriptor* consisting of a location identifier loc, and an operation identifier id. In addition, the write operation descriptor also contains a value val. We often refer to an operations descriptor x simply as *operation* x, and denote its various components by $x.loc$, $x.id$, and $x.val$. We denote by $\mathcal{O}_w$ and $\mathcal{O}_r$ the sets of the write and the read operations respectively, and by $\mathcal{O} = \mathcal{O}_w \cup \mathcal{O}_r$ the set of all operations. For a set $X \subseteq \mathcal{O}$, we denote by $X.id = \{x.id : x \in X\}$ the set of identifiers of operations in X.

Clients use the actions of the form request(x), $x \in \mathcal{O}$, and response(x, v), $x \in \mathcal{O}$, $v \in V \cup \{ack\}$, to issue operation requests and receive responses respectively. Given a sequence β of the request and response actions, an requested operation x is said to be complete in β if β contains response(x, v) for some $v \in V \cup \{ack\}$ which we call the *return* value of x.

We say that β is *well-formed* if there exists a function *cause* mapping each response event to a preceding request event in β so that the following is satisfied: (1) For each response event $e = \mathsf{response}(x, *)$, $cause(e) = \mathsf{request}(x)$ (i.e., responses are not spuriously generated); and (2) *cause* is one-to-one (i.e., responses are not duplicated)[1].

The following definition will be used throughout the paper: Let Π be a set of read and write operations, and R be a binary relation over Π. For an operation $\pi \in \Pi$ we define $last\text{-}prec\text{-}writes(\pi, R) = \{\omega \in \mathcal{O}_w : (\omega, \pi) \in R \wedge \nexists \omega' \in \mathcal{O}_w : (\omega, \omega') \in R \wedge (\omega', \pi) \in R\}$.

3   Atomicity

Atomicity (or linearizability) is specified as a property satisfied by the object implementation traces. It is typically defined in terms of the existence of *serialization points* for operations so that shrinking the operations to occur at their serialization points results in a valid sequential execution of the read/write register (see, e.g., Chapter 13 of [21], Chapter 9 of [4], or [10]). For our purposes in this paper, it is enough to give a sufficient condition for proving atomicity; this condition is equivalent to the one in Lemma 13.16 of [21].

Let β be a well-formed sequence of the actions of the read/write service interface that contains no incomplete operations, and Π be the set of operations requested in β. We say that β satisfies *Partial Order* property (henceforth, referred to as *PO*) if there exists an irreflexive partial ordering $\prec$ of all the operations in Π, satisfying the following:

Property 1 (PO Constraints)

1. *If the response event for π precedes the request event for ϕ in β, then $\phi \nprec \pi$.*
2. *For any two write operations π and ϕ in Π, either $\pi \prec \phi$ or $\phi \prec \pi$.*
3. *If π is a write operation in Π and ϕ is a read operation in Π whose request event follows the response event for π, then $\pi \prec \phi$.*
4. *If π is a read operation in Π and ϕ is a read operation whose request event follows the response event for π, then for each $\omega \in last\text{-}prec\text{-}writes(\pi, \prec)$, $\omega \prec \phi$.*
5. *Let π be a read operation in Π, and v be the value returned by π. If $last\text{-}prec\text{-}writes(\pi, \prec) \neq \emptyset$, then $v = \omega.val$ for some $\omega \in last\text{-}prec\text{-}writes(\pi, \prec)$. Otherwise, $v = v_0$.*

The following lemma is proved in [6]:

Lemma 1. *β satisfies PO iff there exists an irreflexive partial ordering of all the operations in Π, satisfying the (more restrictive) constraints of Lemma 13.16 of [21].*

---

[1] Note that our notion of well formedness is weaker than that usually found in the literature as it allows requests from the same location to be issued concurrently.

From the above result and Lemma 13.16 of [21], we obtain:

Lemma 2. *If β is well-formed and satisfies PO, then β satisfies atomicity.*

4 The PO-Machine

In this section we define the Partial-Order Machine. First, we formally specify the environment assumptions of the read/write service. This environment is represented by a single automaton, called *Users*, whose code could be found in [6]. The *Users* automaton contains a single variable *requested* to keep track of the ids of requested operations, in order to avoid repeats. An implementation of the environment would not have such a variable, but would use some other mechanism to ensure unique operation ids (e.g., client id and a counter).

Lemma 3. *For $x, y \in requested$, $x = y \Leftrightarrow x.id = y.id$.*

The PO-Machine signature and state variables appear in Figure 1, and its transitions appear in Figure 2. This automaton maintains a partial order in its state, represented by variables *vertices* and *edges*. Vertices correspond to requested operations, and edges to ordering relationships that have been determined for these operations. When a request arrives, it is put into *vertices*; later, it becomes classified as *ordered*, then *completed*, and finally, *responded*. Edges may be added at any time from ordered write operations to unordered ones (see action add-edge).

An unordered operation π may become ordered at any time after it has acquired incoming edges from all write operations that completed before π began (i.e., all writes in $prec(\pi)$). This ensures that constraints 1 and 3 of Property 1 hold among all writes, and between writes and reads. Constraint 1 is also trivially preserved among reads as edges originating at read requests are disallowed by the PO signature (see Figure 1). When a write operation π becomes ordered, new edges are inserted to ensure that π is ordered with respect to all previously-ordered write operations (see action order) so that constraint 2 of Property 1 is satisfied.

An ordered operation may become completed at any time; when a read operation ϕ completes, it also forces each write operation π immediately preceding ϕ in the partial order to complete. This ensures that every read operation invoked after ϕ completes will find π in its *prec* set, and will therefore, become ordered only after it has an incoming edge from π. This guarantees that constraint 4 of Property 1 is satisfied, and also captures the essence of the "helping" mechanism found in many atomic register implementations.

A completed operation is allowed to return a response. The response returned by a read operation is the value written by the last preceding (in the partial order) write operation, or the initial value if no such write exists (see action response). Thus, constraint 5 of Property 1 is satisfied.

In [6], we prove that the limit of the transitive closure of *(vertices, edges)*, maintained in the derived variable *dag*, satisfies Property 1. Since every trace of PO-Machine is obviously well-formed, by Lemma 2, PO-Machine implements an atomic register:

Theorem 1. *Each trace of the PO-Machine satisfies atomicity.*

Signature:

Input:
   request(x), $x \in \mathcal{O}$

Output:
   response(x, v), $x \in \mathcal{O}$,
      $v \in V \cup \{ack\}$

Internal:
   add-edge(x, y), $x \in \mathcal{O}_w$, $y \in \mathcal{O}_w \cup \mathcal{O}_r$
   order(x), $x \in \mathcal{O}$
   complete(x), $x \in \mathcal{O}$

State:

vertices $\subseteq \mathcal{O}$, initially empty
ordered $\subseteq \mathcal{O}$, initially empty
completed $\subseteq \mathcal{O}$, initially empty

responded $\subseteq \mathcal{O}$, initially empty
edges $\subseteq \mathcal{O} \times \mathcal{O}$, initially empty
prec is a partial function from $\mathcal{O}$ to subsets of $\mathcal{O}$,
   initially empty

Derived vars:

dag, the transitive closure of (*vertices*, *edges*)

For $x \in \mathcal{O}_r$, *last-writes*$(x) = $ *last-prec-writes*(x, dag)

Fig. 1. PO-Machine signature and states

Input request(x)
Effect:
   vertices := *vertices* $\cup \{x\}$
   prec(x) := *completed* $\cap \mathcal{O}_w$

Internal add-edge(x, y)
Precondition:
   $y \in$ *vertices* $-$ *ordered*
   $x \in$ *ordered*
Effect:
   edges := *edges* $\cup \{(x, y)\}$

Internal order(x), $x \in \mathcal{O}_w$
Precondition:
   $x \in$ *vertices* $-$ *ordered*
   $\forall y \in$ *prec*(x) : $(y, x) \in dag$
Effect:
   edges := *edges* $\cup \{(x, y)$: $y \in$ *ordered* $\cap \mathcal{O}_w \wedge$
                $(y, x) \notin dag\}$
   ordered := *ordered* $\cup \{x\}$

Internal order(x), $x \in \mathcal{O}_r$
Precondition:
   $x \in$ *vertices* $-$ *ordered*
   $\forall y \in$ *prec*(x) : $(y, x) \in dag$
Effect:
   ordered := *ordered* $\cup \{x\}$

Internal complete(x)
Precondition:
   $x \in$ *ordered* $-$ *completed*
Effect:
   completed := *completed* $\cup \{x\}$
   if $x \in \mathcal{O}_r$ then
      $\forall y \in$ *last-writes*(x) do
         completed := *completed* $\cup \{y\}$

Output response(x, ack), $x \in \mathcal{O}_w$
Precondition:
   $x \in$ *completed* $-$ *responded*
Effect:
   responded := *responded* $\cup \{x\}$

Output response(x, v_0), $x \in \mathcal{O}_r$
Precondition:
   $x \in$ *completed* $-$ *responded*
   last-writes(x) $= \emptyset$
Effect:
   responded := *responded* $\cup \{x\}$

Output response(x, v), $x \in \mathcal{O}_r$
Precondition:
   $x \in$ *completed* $-$ *responded*
   last-writes(x) $\neq \emptyset$
   $v = w.val$: $w \in$ *last-writes*(x)
Effect:
   responded := *responded* $\cup \{x\}$

Fig. 2. PO-Machine transitions

5   The Attiya, Bar-Noy, and Dolev Algorithm

In this section, we present a distributed wait-free implementation of an atomic multi-writer/multi-reader register based on the well-known message-passing algorithm of Attiya, Bar-Noy, and Dolev [3] (which we call ABD). We prove correctness of ABD by showing that ABD implements PO-Machine, which by Theorem 1, implies that ABD implements an atomic register.

The original ABD protocol implements a wait-free atomic read/write register using a collection of n processes communicating among themselves through reliable point-to-point channels. The implementation is resilient to up to $n/2$ process crashes. Each process in ABD is responsible for both: handling the client operation requests, and storing and updating the local copy of the register value.

Here, we present a generalized version of ABD where we let the two roles in the ABD protocol be performed by two classes of agents: *clients* and *replicas*. This design allows for flexibility in assigning roles to actual network locations thus simplifying the algorithm deployment in real systems. We also use a separate client to handle each user request so that the actual clients can handle any number of requests and in whatever order (for example, requests can be partitioned among several threads, or executed sequentially). Our implementation also supports multiple writers using the technique of [23].

We now describe the ABD implementation (the ABD automaton) in more detail. Let P be a finite set of replicas. We define a *quorum system* $\mathcal{Q}$ on P to be the union of a set of *write quorums* $\mathcal{Q}_w$ and the set of *read quorums* $\mathcal{Q}_r$. $\mathcal{Q}_w$ and $\mathcal{Q}_r$ are sets of subsets of P such that for each $Q_w \in \mathcal{Q}_w$ and $Q_r \in \mathcal{Q}_r$, $Q_w \cap Q_r \neq \emptyset$. The ABD automaton is the composition of the Users automaton of Section 4, the client automata C_x, $x \in \mathcal{O}$, the replica automata R_p, $p \in P$, and the reliable point-to-point channel automata connecting each client C_x with replica R_p and vice versa. The client's interface and state variables appear in Figure 3. The code of the reader client, the writer client and the replica appear in Figures 4, 5, and 6 respectively. We do not present the specification for the channel automata as their functionality is obvious.

The value stored at each replica is associated with a *tag*. Tags are two-field records consisting of a sequence number sn, which is a non-negative integer, and a request identifier id. Tags are ordered lexicographically with the precedence to the sequence number field.

Clients access read (resp. write) quorums by first sending a message to all the replicas, and then awaiting responses from a write (resp. a read) quorum. The request handling at clients involves two rounds of quorum accesses, called the *read* phase and the *write* phase respectively, such that a read quorum is contacted during the read phase, and a write quorum is contacted during the write phase. A client keeps track of the request progress through the phases using the variable *status*. The operation's status is initially *idle*. It is changed to *pending* (p) at the beginning of the read phase. It becomes *sending* (s) at the beginning of the write phase. It is changed to *committed* (c) upon completion of the write phase, and finally to *responded* (r) after a response is returned.

Specifically, to handle a write request x, the client C_x (see Figure 5) performs a read phase to determine the highest tag t associated with the values stored at some read quorum. It then performs a write phase to store the value v associated with tag $(t.sn, x.id)$ at a write quorum. It then responds with ack. To handle a read request y, client C_y (see Figure 4) first performs a read phase to determine the value v associated with the highest tag t among those associated with the values stored at some read quorum. It then performs a write phase to guarantee that the pair (t, v) is stored at a write quorum. It then responds with v.

The replica's algorithm (see Figure 6) is simple: In response to a read phase message, a replica p either responds with its current tag (for write requests), or the current tag and the value (for read requests). In response to a write phase message carrying a tag which is bigger than p's current tag, p overwrites its current tag and the value with those in the message. Otherwise, the p's state is left unchanged. In both cases, p responds with *ack*.

Types:

$Tag = \mathcal{N}^{\geq 0} \times \mathcal{O}.id$, with selectors sn and id, ordered lexicographically

$Phase = \{\text{idle}, \text{p}, \text{s}, \text{c}, \text{r}\}$, ordered so that $\text{idle} < \text{p} < \text{s} < \text{c} < \text{r}$

Signature:
Input:
  request(x)
  receive(m)$_{p,x}$, $p \in P$, $m \in \{ack\} \cup$
                $\mathcal{N}^{\geq 0} \cup (Tag \times V)$

Internal:

  rq-collected(q)$_x$, $q \in \mathcal{Q}_r$

  wq-collected(q)$_x$, $q \in \mathcal{Q}_w$

Output:
  response(x, v), $v \in V \cup \{ack\}$
  send(m)$_{x,p}$, $p \in P$, $m \in \{r, w\} \cup$
                $(Tag \times V)$

State:
$status \in Phase$, initially idle
$val \in V$, initially undefined
$tag \in Tag$, initially $(0, i_0)$

$read\text{-}resp \in P$, initially empty
$write\text{-}resp \in P$, initilly empty
for each $p \in P$: $req\text{-}buffer_p \in seqof(\{r, w\} \cup$
                $(Tag \times V))$, initially λ

Fig. 3. The state and signature of client automata C_x, $x \in \mathcal{O}$ for ABD

Input request(x)
Effect:
    $status := \text{p}$
    for each $p \in P$:
      append $\langle r \rangle$ to $req\text{-}buffer_p$

Input receive(v, t)$_{p,x}$
Effect:
    $read\text{-}resp := read\text{-}resp \cup \{p\}$
    if $status = \text{p} \wedge t > tag$ then
        $val := v$
        $tag := t$

Internal rq-collected(q)$_x$
Precondition:
    $status = \text{p}$
    $read\text{-}resp \supseteq q$
Effect:
    $status := \text{s}$
    for each $p \in P$:
      append $\langle tag, val \rangle$ to $req\text{-}buffer_p$

Input receive(ack)$_{p,x}$
Effect:
    $write\text{-}resp := write\text{-}resp \cup \{p\}$

Internal wq-collected(q)$_x$
Precondition:
    $status = \text{s}$
    $write\text{-}resp \supseteq q$
Effect:
    $status := \text{c}$

Output response(x, v)
Precondition:
    $status = \text{c}$
    $val = v$
Effect:
    $status := \text{r}$

Output send(m)$_{x,p}$
Precondition:
    $req\text{-}buffer_p \neq \lambda$
    $m = head(req\text{-}buffer_p)$
Effect:
    delete head of $req\text{-}buffer_p$

Fig. 4. Transitions of reader C_x, $x \in \mathcal{O}_r$ for ABD

Input request(x)
Effect:
    $status := \mathsf{p}$
    for each $p \in P$:
        append $\langle w \rangle$ to $req\text{-}buffer_p$

Input receive$(sn)_{p,x}$, $sn \in \mathcal{N}^{\geq 0}$
Effect:
    $read\text{-}resp := read\text{-}resp \cup \{p\}$
    if $status = \mathsf{p} \wedge sn > tag.sn$ then
        $tag.sn := sn$

Internal rq-collected$(q)_x$
Precondition:
    $status = \mathsf{p}$
    $read\text{-}resp \supseteq q$
Effect:
    $status := \mathsf{s}$
    $tag.sn := tag.sn + 1$
    for each $p \in P$:
        append $\langle tag, x.val \rangle$ to $req\text{-}buffer_p$

Input receive$(ack)_{p,x}$
Effect:
    $write\text{-}resp := write\text{-}resp \cup \{p\}$

Internal wq-collected$(q)_x$
Precondition:
    $status = \mathsf{s}$
    $write\text{-}resp \supseteq q$
Effect:
    $status := \mathsf{c}$

Output response(x, ack)
Precondition:
    $status = \mathsf{c}$

Effect:
    $status := \mathsf{r}$

Output send$(m)_{x,p}$
Precondition:
    $m = head(req\text{-}buffer_p)$
Effect:
    delete head of $req\text{-}buffer_p$

Fig. 5. Transitions of writer C_x, $x \in \mathcal{O}_w$ for ABD

Signature:
Input: Output:
    receive$(m)_{x,p}$, $x \in \mathcal{O}$, $m \in \{r, w\} \cup (Tag \times V)$ send$(m)_{p,x}$, $x \in \mathcal{O}$, $p \in R$, $m \in \{ack\} \cup (Tag \times V)$

State:

$val \in V$, initially v_0

$tag \in Tag$, initially $(0, i_0)$

For each $x \in \mathcal{O}$: $resp\text{-}buffer_x \in seqof(\{ack\} \cup \mathcal{N}^{\geq 0} \cup (Tag \times V))$, initially λ

Transitions:

Input receive$(r)_{x,p}$
Effect:
    append $\langle val, tag \rangle$ to $resp\text{-}buffer_x$

Input receive$(w)_{x,p}$
Effect:
    append $\langle tag.sn \rangle$ to $resp\text{-}buffer_i$

Input receive$(t, v)_{x,p}$
Effect:
    if $t > tag$ then
        $tag := t$
        $val := v$
    append $\langle ack \rangle$ to $resp\text{-}buffer_x$

Output send$(m)_{p,x}$
Precondition:
    $resp\text{-}buffer_x \neq \lambda$
    $m = head(resp\text{-}buffer_x)$
Effect:
    delete head of $resp\text{-}buffer_x$

Fig. 6. Replica automaton R_p, $p \in P$ for ABD

Correctness of ABD: We now prove that ABD implements an atomic register. Our strategy will be to show that ABD implements PO-Machine by exhibiting a forward simulation from ABD to PO-Machine. In the following, for each $x \in \mathcal{O}$, we will use subscript x to refer to the state variables of C_x. It is convenient for the ABD correctness proof to define several derived variables for the ABD automaton. These are summarized in Figure 7.

Among these variables, the most interesting one is *min-tag* which is used to keep track of the lowest possible tag that could ever be determined by a client at the end of the read phase. At the beginning and before any replica has responded, *min-tag* is the smallest tag among the maximum tags carried by replicas in every read quorum. As the client is progressing through the read phase it might get a response from a replica whose tag is bigger than the current value of *min-tag*.

- $pending = \{x \in \mathcal{O} : status_x \geq p\}$
- $ordered = \{x \in \mathcal{O} : status_x \geq s\}$
- $completed = \{x \in \mathcal{O} : status_x \geq c\}$
- $responded = \{x \in \mathcal{O} : status_x \geq r\}$
- For $r \in \mathcal{O}_r$: $last\text{-}writes(r) = \{w \in \mathcal{O}_w \cap ordered : s.tag_w = s.tag_r\}$
- For $x \in \mathcal{O}$, $p \in P$:

$$new\text{-}tag(x, p) = \begin{cases} t, & \text{if } \exists v \in V : \langle v, t \rangle \in resp\text{-}buffer_{p,x} \cup channel_{p,x} \\ (sn, x.id), & \text{if } \langle sn \rangle \in resp\text{-}buffer_{p,x} \cup channel_{p,x} \\ tag_p, & \text{otherwise} \end{cases}$$

- For $x \in \mathcal{O}$:

$$min\text{-}tag(x) = \begin{cases} \max[tag_x, \min_{Q \in \mathcal{Q}_r} \max\{new\text{-}tag(x, p) : p \in Q \setminus read\text{-}resp_x\}], \\ \qquad \text{if } \forall Q \in \mathcal{Q}_r, \; read\text{-}resp \not\supseteq Q \\ tag_x, \text{otherwise} \end{cases}$$

Fig. 7. Derived variables for the ABD automaton

In this case, the definition of *min-tag* ensures that *min-tag* is assigned to that higher value. Finally, upon completion of the read phase, the value of *min-tag* is fixed to be the maximum tag received during the phase. The simulation proof relies on the following key property of *min-tag*:

Lemma 4. *For each $x \in \mathcal{O}$, min-tag(x) is non-decreasing.*

The simulation mapping from the states of ABD to the states of the PO-Machine appears in Figure 8. The first four components of the mapping are straightforward: All the operations that have ever been requested (indicated by status > idle) are mapped to *vertices*; the operations that have completed the read phase and acquired final tags (indicated by status > p) are mapped to *ordered*; and the operations that have responded (indicated by status > c) are mapped to *responded*.

The set of edges consists only of edges among operations that have completed their read phases (8.7). The edges among these operations are determined by their tag order and type. Specifically, any two writes x and y, such that $tag_x < tag_y$, are connected by edge (x, y) (8.8); and each read x and write y such that $tag_x = tag_y$, are connected through edge (y, x) (8.9). To maintain the mapping for *edges*, each rq-collected(x) for $x \in \mathcal{O}_w$ is simulated by a sequence of add-edge(y, x) for each ordered write operation y such that $tag_y \leq tag_x$, followed by order(x); and each rq-collected(x) for $x \in \mathcal{O}_w$ is simulated by a sequence of add-edge(y, x) for each ordered operation y such that $tag_y = tag_x$. No actions involving unordered operations (i.e., the operations with status < s) result in adding new edges.

The most interesting part of the proof is to show that order(x) becomes enabled once all the (y, x) edges have been added. For that we need to show that the tag acquired by x at the end of the read phase is at least as big as the tag of every operation that had completed before x began. Since at the end of the read phase, $tag_x = min\text{-}tag(x)$, the necessary enabling condition is provided by part 8.6 of the mapping that requires that for each $y \in prec(x)$, $tag_y \leq min\text{-}tag(x)$.

f is the relation over $states(PO - Machine) \times states(ABD)$ such that each $(s, u) \in f$ iff:

1. $u.requested = s.requested$
2. $u.vertices = s.pending$
3. $u.ordered = s.ordered$
4. $u.completed = s.completed \cup \bigcup_{r \in \mathcal{O}_r \cap s.completed} s.last\text{-}writes(r)$
5. $u.responded = s.responded$
6. For all $x \in u.vertices$, if $y \in u.prec(x)$, then $s.tag_y \leq s.min\text{-}tag(x)$
7. $u.dag \subseteq s.ordered \times s.ordered$
8. For all $x, y \in \mathcal{O}_w \cap u.ordered$, if $(x, y) \in u.dag$, then $s.tag_x < s.tag_y$
9. For all $x \in \mathcal{O}_w \cap u.ordered$ and $y \in \mathcal{O}_r \cap u.ordered$, $(x, y) \in u.edges$ iff $s.tag_x = s.tag_y$

Fig. 8. Forward simulation from ABD to PO-Machine

To show that 8.6 is maintained throughout the read phase of x, request(x) is simulated by the request(x) action of the PO-Machine; and each receive is simulated by the empty sequence. Since at the time x is invoked, the tag of every $y \in prec(x)$ has been stored at a write quorum of replicas, and because every pair of write and read quorums intersects, $\min_{Q \in \mathcal{Q}_r} \max_{p \in Q} \{tag_p\} \geq tag_y$. Hence, 8.6 is preserved by request(x). Finally, since $min\text{-}tag(x)$ is non-decreasing (Lemma 4) and $prec(x)$ is not affected by any action except request, 8.6 is preserved by receive. Hence, by the end of the read phase of x, for each $y \in prec(x)$, $tag_y \leq min\text{-}tag(x)$ as required.

We argued informally that the mapping in Figure 8 is a forward simulation from ABD to the PO-Machine. A detailed proof appears in [6].

Lemma 5. *The mapping in Figure 8 is a forward simulation from ABD to the PO-Machine.*

Since by Theorem 1, each trace of the PO-Machine satisfies atomicity, the same is true for every trace of ABD:

Theorem 2. *Each trace of ABD satisfies atomicity.*

Automated Tools Support: We have used the TIOA to PVS translator and TAME library [2] to generate descriptions of the PO-Machine and the ABD algorithm in the language of the Prototype Verification System (PVS) [26]. We used PVS to substantially increase the level of detail and assurance of some of our previous hand proofs. In fact, we discovered several gaps and bugs in our hand proofs. Automatic translation enabled us to easily tweak the simulation relations and rerun the proof scripts. We also used the IOA code generator tool [31,30] to compile the verified ABD automaton into an executable Java code. This way, a single formal representation of the ABD algorithm was used for specification, verification, and execution.

6   Timed ABD

In this section, we present an optimized version of the ABD protocol, called *Timed-ABD*, that takes advantage of perfectly synchronized clocks at the writers to eliminate the read phase of the write implementation (see [8]).

The Timed-ABD is the composition of the following timed automata: the replica and reader client automata in Figures 6 and 4 respectively augmented with arbitrary trajectories that keep their state unchanged; and the writer client automata whose code appears in Figure 9. To model synchronized clocks, each writer maintains a local variable *clock* whose trajectory is $d(clock) = 1$ (i.e., the clock value grows continuously, at the same rate as the real time).

The writer algorithm is as follows: To write a value, the writer first takes its current clock reading, and then delays its execution until its clock exceeds the initial reading. The second clock reading is used as the tag with which the client performs the write phase.

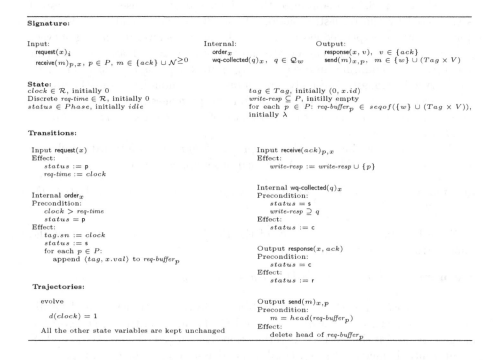

Fig. 9. Writer client C_x, $x \in \mathcal{O}_w$ for Timed-ABD

The simulation mapping from the states of Timed-ABD to the states of Timed-PO (i.e., the PO-Machine augmented with arbitrary trajectories that do not change its state) appears in Figure 10. To see that the mapping is preserved, we observe that a write operation becomes ordered once it is verified that a non-zero amount of time has elapsed since it was requested. We therefore, simulate each Timed-ABD trajectory corresponding to a non-zero time interval by a trajectory of Timed-PO of the same length, followed by a sequence of **add-edge** actions, followed by **order**. The rest of the simulation proof is straightforward (see [6] for details).

f is the relation over $states(Timed\text{-}ABD) \times states(Timed\text{-}PO)$ such that $(s, u) \in f$ iff:

1-5:   Identical to 1-5 in Figure 8
   6:   For all $x \in u.vertices \cap \mathcal{O}_r$, if $y \in u.prec(x)$, then $s.tag_y \leq s.min\text{-}tag(x)$
7-8:   Identical to 7-8 in Figure 8
   9:   For all $x \in u.vertices \cap \mathcal{O}_w$, if $y \in u.prec(x)$, then $s.tag_y.sn \leq s.req\text{-}time_x$
  10:   For all $x \in (u.vertices - u.ordered) \cap \mathcal{O}_w$, $y \in u.ordered \cap \mathcal{O}_w$, if $s.tag_y.sn < s.clock_x$, then $(y, x) \in u.edges$.

Fig. 10. Forward simulation from Timed-ABD to Timed-PO

7   Other Algorithms

We discuss briefly how to prove atomicity of the unbounded multi-writer/multi-reader register construction of Vitanyi and Awerbuch [36] (referred to henceforth as VA), and of a general atomic object implementation based on the replicated state machine algorithm of Lamport [15] (referred to henceforth as RSM).

First, we observe that VA can be recast as a special case of ABD with the write quorums being the rows and the read quorums being the collumns of the matrix. Therefore, the simulation proof of VA is almost identical to that of ABD. In particular, it is easy to see that the simulation from ABD to PO-Machine in Figure 8 is also a forward simulation from VA to PO-Machine.

To prove atomicity of RSM, we use a simplified version of the PO-Machine, called *TO-Machine*. The TO-Machine constructs a single total order of all the requested operations. In particular, every operation becomes ordered only after it is ordered relative to all the other ordered operations. The TO-Machine is parameterized by the emulated object sequential specification and initial state which are used to compute responses. The simulation proof is based on the observation that in RSM, an operation x becomes ordered once the *local* timestamp at each replica becomes greater than that of x. The full proof appears in [6].

8   Conclusions and Future Work

Our work with four algorithms so far suggests to us that our PO-Machine (or small variants) may be general enough to capture many of the existing atomic register algorithms. We plan to use these methods to study a wider variety of algorithms, such as bounded-timestamp-based constructions (see e.g., [34]), whose proofs have been notoriously difficult and bug-prone. An interesting challenge will be to extend our framework to capture implementations that are not explicitly based on timestamps, for example, the construction that creates atomic bits from safe bits [32]. Another interesting direction deals with adapting the PO-Machine to capture weaker register semantics, such as safe registers, regular registers (including the multi-writer regular registers of Welch [29]), and sequentially consistent registers. There is an increased recent interest in these semantics as they capture the guarantees provided by many Byzantine-resilient storage systems [24,25,1] based on Byzantine quorums [24].

Yet another interesting application domain for our techniques is the verification of multi-threaded programs based on lock-free synchronization primitives (such as CAS, LL/SC, etc.). This area has recently been receiving an increased attention due to the growing popularity of multi-processor computing platforms, and the introduction of lock-free synchronization primitives into the Java concurrency package.

Finally, we are interested in identifying common patterns behind many diverse implementations of atomic objects. This will make it easier to understand and compare different algorithms. We expect that such patterns should be expressible in terms of common specification automata (e.g., a unified version of the PO- and TO-Machines).

References

1. Ittai Abraham, Gregory Chockler, Idit Keidar, and Dahlia Malkhi. Byzantine disk paxos: Optimal resilience with byzantine shared memory. In *Proceedings of the 23st ACM Symposium on Principles of Distributed Computing (PODC'04)*, pages 226–235, St John's Newfoundland, Canada, July 2004.
2. Myla Archer. TAME: PVS Strategies for special purpose theorem proving. *Annals of Mathematics and Artificial Intelligence*, 29(1/4), February 2001.
3. Hagit Attiya, Amotz Bar-Noy, and Danny Dolev. Sharing memory robustly in message-passing systems. *Journal of the ACM*, 42(1):124–142, January 1995.
4. Hagit Attiya and Jennifer Welch. *Distributed Computing: Fundamentals, Simulations, and Advanced Topics*. McGraw-Hill Publishing Company, UK, 1998.
5. Andrej Bogdanov. Formal verification of simulations between i/o automata. Master's thesis, Massachusetts Institute of Technology, July 2001.
6. G. Chockler, N. Lynch, S. Mitra, and J. Tauber. Proving atomicity: An assertional approach. Technical Report MIT/LCS/TR-XXX, MIT Laboratory for Computer Science, 2005.
7. Simon Doherty, Lindsay Groves, Victor Luchangco, and Mark Moir. Formal verification of a practical lock-free queue algorithm. In *FORTE*, pages 97–114, 2004.
8. Shlomi Dolev, Seth Gilbert, Nancy A. Lynch, Alex A. Shvartsman, and Jennifer L. Welch. GeoQuorums: Implementing atomic memory in ad hoc networks.
9. Alan Fekete, David Gupta, Victor Luchangco, Nancy Lynch, and Alex Shvartsman. Eventually-serializable data services. In *Proceedings of the Fifteenth Annual ACM Symposium on Principles of Distributed Computing*, pages 300–309, Philadelphia, PA, May 1996.
10. Maurice P. Herlihy and Jeannette M. Wing. Linearizability: A correctness condition for concurrent objects. *ACM Transactions on Programming Languages and Systems*, 12(3):463–492, July 1990.
11. D. Kaynar, N. Lynch, R. Segala, and F. Vaandrager. The theory of timed I/O automata. Technical Report MIT/LCS/TR-917a, MIT Laboratory for Computer Science, 2004. Available at http://theory.lcs.mit.edu/tds/reflist.html.
12. Dilsun K. Kaynar, Nancy Lynch, Roberto Segala, and Frits Vaandrager. Timed I/O automata: A mathematical framework for modeling and analyzing real-time system. In *RTSS 2003: The 24th IEEE International Real-Time Systems Symposium*, Cancun,Mexico, December 2003.
13. Rivka Ladin, Barbara Liskov, Liuba Shrira, and Sanjay Ghemawat. Providing high availability using lazy replication. *ACM Transactions on Computer Science*, 10(4):360–391, 1992.

14. L. Lamport. The part-time parliament. *ACM Transactions on Computer Systems*, 16(2):133–169, May 1998. Earlier version in Research Report 49, Digital Equipment Corporation Systems Research Center, Palo Alto, CA, September 1989.

15. Leslie Lamport. Time, clocks, and the ordering of events in a distributed system. *Communications of the ACM*, 21(7):558–565, July 1978.

16. Leslie Lamport. On interprocess communication: Part I and II. *Dist. Comput.*, 1:77–101, 1986.

17. Leslie Lamport. On interprocess communication, Part II: Algorithms. *Distributed Computing*, 1(2):86–101, April 1986.

18. Leslie Lamport. Paxos made simple. *ACM SIGACT News (Distributed Computing Column)*, 32(4):18–25, December 2001.

19. Butler Lampson. The ABCD's of paxos. In *Proceedings of the Twentieth Annual ACM symposium on Principles of Distributed Computing*, Newport, RI, August 2001.

20. N. A. Lynch and M.R. Tuttle. An introduction to Input/Output Automata. *CWI Quarterly*, 2(3):219–246, 1989.

21. Nancy Lynch. *Distributed Algorithms*. Morgan Kaufmann Publishers, Inc., San Mateo, CA, March 1996.

22. Nancy Lynch and Alex Shvartsman. Robust emulation of shared memory using dynamic quorum-acknowledged broadcasts. In *Twenty-Seventh Annual International Symposium on Fault-Tolerant Computing (FTCS'97)*, pages 272–281, Seattle, Washington, USA, June 1997. IEEE.

23. Nancy Lynch and Alex Shvartsman. RAMBO: A reconfigurable atomic memory service for dynamic networks. In D. Malkhi, editor, *Distributed Computing (Proceedings of the 16th International Symposium on DIStributed Computing (DISC), Toulouse, France, October 2002)*, volume 2508 of *Lecture Notes in Computer Science*, pages 173–190. Springer-Verlag, 2002. Also, Technical Report MIT-LCS-TR-856.

24. Dahlia Malkhi and Michael Reiter. Byzantine quorum systems. *Journal of Distributed Computing*, 11(4):203–213, 1998.

25. J. P. Martin, L. Alvisi, and M. Dahlin. Minimal Byzantine storage. In *16th International Symposium on Distributed Computing (DISC'02), Toulouse, France*, Lecture Notes in Computer Science, pages 311–325. Springer-Verlag, 2002.

26. S. Owre, S. Rajan, J.M. Rushby, N. Shankar, and M.K. Srivas. PVS: Combining specification, proof checking, and model checking. In Rajeev Alur and Thomas A. Henzinger, editors, *Computer-Aided Verification, CAV '96*, number 1102 in Lecture Notes in Computer Science, pages 411–414, New Brunswick, NJ, July/August 1996. Springer-Verlag.

27. Gary L. Peterson and James E. Burns. Concurrent reading while writing II: The multi-writer case. In *28th Annual Symposium on Foundations of Computer Science*, pages 383–392, Los Angeles, California, October 1987. IEEE.

28. A. Udaya Shankar. An introduction to assertional reasoning for concurrent systems. *ACM Comput. Surv.*, 25(3):225–262, 1993.

29. Cheng Shao, Evelyn Pierce, and Jennifer L. Welch. Multi-writer consistency conditions for shared memory objects. In *Proceedings of the 17th International Conference on Distributed Computing (DISC)*, pages 106–120, October 2003.

30. Joshua A. Tauber. *Verifiable Compilation of I/O Automata without Global Synchronization*. PhD thesis, Massachusetts Institute of Technology, Cambridge,MA, September 2004.

31. Joshua A. Tauber, Nancy A. Lynch, and Michael J. Tsai. Compiling IOA without global synchronization. In *Proceedings of the The 3rd IEEE International Symposium on Network Computing and Applications, (IEEE NCA04)*, pages 121–130, September 2004.

32. John Tromp. How to construct an atomic variable. In *LNCS 392, Proc. 3rd International Workshop On Distributed Algorithms*, pages 292–302. Springer-Verlag, 1989.

33. K. Vidyasankar. Concurrent reading while writing revisited. *Distributed Computing*, 4:81–85, 1990.

34. Paul Vitanyi. Simple wait-free multireader registers. In *Proceedings of the 16th International Symposium on Distributed Computing (DISC'02)*, volume 2508 of *Lecture Notes in Computer Science*, pages 118–132. Springer-Verlag, Berlin, 2002.

35. Paul M. B. Vitányi. Distributed elections in an Archimedean ring of processors. In *Proceedings of the Sixteenth Annual ACM Symposium on Theory of Computing*, pages 542–547, Washington, D.C., April/May 1984.

36. P.M.B. Vitanyi and B. Awerbuch. Atomic shared register access by asynchronous hardware. In *27th IEEE Annual Symposium on Foundations of Computer Science*, pages 233–243, 1986.

37. Liqiang Wang and Scott D. Stoller. Static analysis for programs with non-blocking synchronization. In *Proc. ACM SIGPLAN 2005 Symposium on Principles and Practice of Parallel Programming (PPoPP)*. ACM Press, June 2005.

Time and Space Lower Bounds
for Implementations Using k-CAS
(Extended Abstract)

Hagit Attiya[1] and Danny Hendler[2]

[1] Department of Computer Science, Technion
[2] Department of Computer Science, University of Toronto

Abstract. This paper presents lower bounds on the time- and space-complexity of implementations that use the k compare-and-swap (k-CAS) synchronization primitives. We prove that the use of k-CAS primitives cannot improve neither the time- nor the space-complexity of implementations of widely-used concurrent objects, such as counter, stack, queue, and collect. Surprisingly, the use of k-CAS may even *increase* the space complexity required by such implementations.

We prove that the worst-case *average* number of steps performed by processes for any n-process implementation of a counter, stack or queue object is $\Omega(\log_{k+1} n)$, even if the implementation can use j-CAS for $j \leq k$. This bound holds even if a k-CAS operation is allowed to *read* the k values of the objects it accesses and return these values to the calling process. This bound is tight.

We also consider more realistic *non-reading* k-CAS primitives. An operation of a non-reading k-CAS primitive is only allowed to return a success/failure indication. For implementations of the *collect* object that use such primitives, we prove that the worst-case average number of steps performed by processes is $\Omega(\log_2 n)$, regardless of the value of k. This implies a *round complexity* lower bound of $\Omega(\log_2 n)$ for such implementations. As there is an $O(\log_2 n)$ round complexity implementation of collect that uses only reads and writes, these results establish that non-reading k-CAS is no stronger than read and write for collect implementation round complexity.

We also prove that k-CAS does not improve the space complexity of implementing many objects (including counter, stack, queue, and single-writer snapshot). An implementation has to use at least n base objects even if k-CAS is allowed, and if all operations (other than read) swap exactly k base objects, then the space complexity must be at least $k \cdot n$.

1 Introduction

Lock-free implementations of concurrent objects require processes to coordinate without relying on mutual exclusion, thus avoiding the inherent problems of *locking*, e.g., deadlock, convoying, and priority-inversion. *Synchronization primitives* are often evaluated according to their power to implement other objects in a

P. Fraigniaud (Ed.): DISC 2005, LNCS 3724, pp. 169–183, 2005.

lock-free manner. A *conditional* synchronization primitive may modify the value of the object to which it is applied only if the object has a specific value. The *compare-and-swap* synchronization primitive (abbreviated CAS) is an example of a conditional primitive: $CAS(O, old, new)$ changes the value of an object O to *new* only if its value just before CAS is applied is *old*; otherwise, CAS does not change the value of O.

CAS can be used, together with read and write, to implement any object in a deterministic wait-free manner [20]. It has consequently became a synchronization primitive of choice, and hardware support for it is provided in many multiprocessor architectures [22,27,29].

In recent years, the question of supporting multi-object conditionals in hardware has been deliberated in both industrial and academic circles [12,16,17,19]. The design of concurrent data structures seems to be easier if conditional primitives can be applied to multiple objects [17]. On the other hand, almost all of the current architectures support conditional primitives only on a single object.

To help resolve this debate, it is natural to ask whether multi-object conditionals admit more efficient implementations. Of concrete interest are k-CAS synchronization primitives that atomically check and possibly modify several objects; when $k = 2$, this is the familiar *double compare&swap* (DCAS) primitive.

In this paper, we prove lower bounds on the time- and space-complexity of implementations of widely-used objects that use multi-object conditional primitives such as k-CAS. We show that the use of such primitives does not improve neither the time- nor the space-complexity of implementing these objects.

We start by proving that the worst-case *average* number of steps performed by processes in *solo-terminating* implementations of counters, stacks and queues is $\Omega(\log_{k+1} n)$, assuming the implementation uses only j-word conditionals for $j \leq k$, read and write. This extends a *worst-case* lower bound of $\Omega(\log_2 n)$ on the number of steps needed for implementing these objects using unary conditionals [23]. Both lower bounds hold even when implementations can use *reading* conditional primitives, which read and return the values of all the objects they access. As an example, a reading DCAS operation returns the values of the two objects it accesses just before it is applied. Solo termination [13,25] requires a process running alone to complete its operation within a finite number of its steps. (This property is provided by *obstruction-free* implementations [21].)

At this point, it is natural to question the validity of charging only a single unit for a reading k-CAS operation, that compares, possibly swaps, and returns k values. For the purpose of proving lower bounds, it is easier to state what *cannot* be done in one step, rather than to stipulate the correct price tag for a reading k-CAS operation. It is clearly overly optimistic to assume that k values can be read in one step, and thus, we investigate *non-reading* k-CAS primitives that only return a boolean success indication.

For the weaker wake-up problem [15], even a non-reading k-CAS primitive is more powerful than 1-CAS. The algorithm of Afek et al. [1] can be adapted to yield an $O(\log_{k+1} n)$ worst-case step implementation, whereas [23] proves a worst-case lower bound of $\Omega(\log_2 n)$ steps on implementations of wake-up that can use unary conditional primitives.

Interestingly, there exist widely-used objects such as *collect*, for which non-reading k-CAS is no stronger than read and write. We prove that the worst-case average time complexity of solo-terminating implementations of collect is $\Omega(\log_2 n)$, even if k-CAS primitives can be used, for any k. The proof hinges on the fact that a non-reading k-CAS operation only tells us whether the values of the k objects to which it is applied equal a *particular* vector of values or not. Thus, such an operation provides only a single bit of information about the objects it accesses. This intuition is captured, in a precise sense, by adapting a technique of Beame [10], originally applied in the synchronous CRCW PRAM model. This implies that the *round complexity* [11] of such implementations is $\Omega(\log_2 n)$, matching an $O(\log_2 n)$ round complexity implementation of collect using read and write, given by Attiya, Lynch, and Shavit [8].

Finally, we turn to study the space complexity of implementations that use multi-object conditional primitives. We extend a result of Fich, Hendler and Shavit [14], who show a linear space lower bound on implementations that use read, write, and unary conditional primitives. They prove this bound for wait-free implementations of many widely-used concurrent objects, such as stack, queue, counter, and single-writer snapshot. We show that an implementation cannot escape this lower bound by using multi-object conditional primitives. Moreover, if all operations (other than read) swap exactly k locations, then the space complexity is at least $k \cdot n$.

Our results indicate that supporting multi-object conditional primitives in hardware may not yield performance gains: under reasonable cost metrics, they do not improve the efficiency of implementing many widely-used object.

Several shared object implementations use k-CAS, most often DCAS, to simplify design (e.g. [5,18]). Doherty et al. [12] argue that in certain cases, e.g., for implementing double-ended queues, even DCAS does not suffice and that simple and easy-to-prove implementations should rely on 3-CAS. There is a variety of algorithms for simulating multi-object k-CAS (and other objects) from single-object CAS, load-linked and store-conditional (e.g. [3,6,7,9,28]). A few papers investigate the consensus number of multi-object operations [2,24]. Attiya and Dagan [7] prove that any implementation of two-object conditional primitives from unary conditional primitives requires $\Omega(\log \log^* n)$ steps. The *k-compare-single-swap* synchronization primitive of [26] is a weaker variant of non-reading k-CAS, and our lower bounds hold for it.

2   The Shared Memory System Model

We consider a standard model of an asynchronous shared memory system, in which processes communicate by applying operations to shared objects. An *object* is an instance of an abstract data type. It is characterized by a domain of possible values and by a set of *operations* that provide the only means to manipulate it. No bound is assumed on the size of an object (i.e., the number of different possible values the object can have). An *implementation* of an object shared by a set $\mathbf{P}=\{p_1,\cdots,p_n\}$ of n processes provides a specific data-representation for the object from a set $\mathbf{B}$ of shared *base objects*, each of which is assigned an initial value, and algorithms for each process in $\mathbf{P}$ to apply each operation to the object being implemented. To avoid confusion, we call operations on the base objects *primitives* and reserve the term *operations* for the objects being implemented.

A *wait-free* implementation of a concurrent object guarantees that any process can complete an operation in a finite number of its own steps. A *solo-terminating* implementation guarantees only that if a process eventually runs by itself while executing an operation then it completes that operation within a finite number of its own steps. Each *step* consists of some local computation and one shared memory *event*, which is a primitive applied to a vector of objects in $\mathbf{B}$. We say that the event *accesses* these base objects and that it *applies* the primitive to them. In this extended abstract we consider only *deterministic implementations*, in which the next step taken by a process depends only on its state and the response it receives from the event it applies.

An *execution fragment* is a (finite or infinite) sequence of events. We denote the empty execution fragment by ϵ. An *execution* is an execution fragment that starts from an *initial configuration*. This is a configuration in which all base objects in $\mathbf{B}$ have their initial values and all processes are in their initial states. If $o \in \mathbf{B}$ is a base object and E is a finite execution, then $value(E,o)$ denotes the value of o at the end of E. If no event in E changes the value of o, then $value(E,o)$ is the initial value of o. In other words, in the configuration resulting from executing E, each base object $o \in \mathbf{B}$ has value $value(E,o)$. For any finite execution fragment E and any execution fragment E', the execution fragment EE' denotes the concatenation of E and E'.

An *operation instance*, $\Phi = (O, Op, p, args)$, is an application by process p of operation Op with arguments $args$ to object O. In an execution, processes apply their operation instances to the implemented object. To apply an operation instance Φ, a process *issues* a sequence of one or more events that access the base objects used by the implementation of O. If the last event of an operation instance Φ has been issued in an execution E, we say that Φ *completes in E*. The events of an operation instance issued by a process can be interleaved with events issued by other processes.

If a process has not completed its operation instance, it has exactly one *enabled* event, which is the next event it will perform, as specified by the algorithm it is using to apply its operation instance to the implemented object. We say that a process p is *active* after E if p has not completed its operation instance in E. If p is not active after E, we say that p is *idle* after E. We say that an execution E is *quiescent* if every instance that starts in E completes in E.

Processes communicate with one another by issuing events that apply *read-modify-write* (RMW) primitives to vectors of base objects. We assume that a primitive is always applied to vectors of the same size. This size is called the *arity* of the primitive. RMW primitives with arity 1 are called *single-object RMW primitives*. RMW primitives with arity larger than 1 are called *multi-object*

RMW primitives. For presentation simplicity we assume that all the base objects to which a primitive is applied are over the same domain. A RMW primitive, applied to a vector of k base objects over some domain D, is characterized by a pair of functions, $\langle g, h \rangle$, where g is the primitive's *update function* and h is the primitive's *response function*. The update function $g : D^k \times W \rightarrow D^k$, for some input-values domain W, determines how the primitive updates the values of the base objects to which it is applied. Let e be an event, issued by process p after execution E, that applies the primitive $\langle g, h \rangle$ to a vector of base objects $\langle o_1, \ldots, o_k \rangle$. Then e atomically does the following: it updates the values of objects $o_1, \ldots, o_k$ to the values of the components of the vector $g(\langle v_1, \ldots, v_k \rangle, w)$, respectively, where $\overrightarrow{v} = \langle v_1, \ldots, v_k \rangle$ is the vector of values of the base objects after E, and $w \in W$ is an input parameter to the primitive. We call $\overrightarrow{v}$ the *object-values vector* of e after E. The RMW primitive returns a response value, $h(\overrightarrow{v}, w)$, to process p. If W is empty, we say that the primitive *takes no input*.

A *k-compare-and-swap* (k-CAS), for some integer $k \geq 1$, is an example of a RMW primitive. It receives an input vector, $\langle old_1, \ldots, old_k, new_1, \ldots, new_k \rangle$, from D^{2k}. Its update function, $g(\overrightarrow{v}, \langle old_1, \ldots, old_k, new_1, \ldots, new_k \rangle)$, changes the values of base objects $o_1, \ldots, o_k$ to values $new_1, \ldots, new_k$, respectively, if and only if $v_i = old_i$ for all $i \in \{1, \ldots, k\}$. If this condition is met, we say that the k-CAS event was *successful*, otherwise we say that the k-CAS event was *unsuccessful*. The response function of a *non-reading* k-CAS primitive returns *true* if the k-CAS event was successful or *false* otherwise. The response function of a *reading* k-CAS primitive returns $\overrightarrow{v}$.

Read is a single-object RMW primitive. It takes no input, its update function is $g(\langle v \rangle) = \langle v \rangle$ and its response function is $h(\langle v \rangle) = v$. Write is another example of a single-object RMW primitive. Its update function is $g(\langle v \rangle, w) = \langle w \rangle$, and its response function is $h(\langle v \rangle, w) = ack$. A RMW primitive is *nontrivial* if it may change the values of some of the base object to which it is applied, e.g., read; it is *trivial*, otherwise. *Fetch&add* is another example of a single-object RMW primitive. Its update function is $g(\langle v \rangle, w) = \langle v + w \rangle$, for v, w integers, and its response function simply returns the previous value of the base object to which it is applied.

Next, we define the concept of conditional synchronization primitives.

Definition 1. *A RMW primitive $\langle g, h \rangle$ is* conditional *if, for every possible input w, $\left| \left\{ \overrightarrow{v} \mid g(\overrightarrow{v}, w) \neq \overrightarrow{v} \right\} \right| \leq 1$. Let e be an event that applies the primitive $\langle g, h \rangle$ with input w. A vector c_w such that $g(c_w, w) \neq c_w$ is called the* change point *of e. Any vector $v \neq c_w$ is called a* fixed point *of e.*

In other words, a RMW primitive is a conditional primitive if, for every input w, there is at most one vector c_w such that $g(c_w, w) \neq c_w$. k-CAS is a conditional primitive for any integer $k \geq 1$. The single change point of a k-CAS event with input $\langle old_1, \ldots, old_k, new_1, \ldots, new_k \rangle$ is the vector $\langle old_1, \ldots, old_k \rangle$. Read is also a conditional primitive.

Next we define the notion of invisible events. This is a generalization of the definition provided in [14] that can be applied to multi-object primitives.

Informally, an invisible event is an event by some process that cannot be observed by other processes.

Definition 2. *Let e be a RMW event applied by process p to a vector of objects $\langle o_1, \ldots, o_k \rangle$ in an execution E, where $E = E_1 e E_2$. We say that e is* invisible *in E on o_i, for $i \in \{1, \ldots, k\}$, if either the value of o_i is not changed by e or if $E_2 = E'e'E''$, e' is a write event to o_i, E' is p-free, and no event in E' is applied to o_i. We say that e is* invisible *in E if e is invisible in E on all objects o_i, for $i \in \{1, \ldots, k\}$.*

All read events are invisible. A write event is invisible if the value of the object to which it is applied equals the value it writes. A RMW event is invisible if its object-values vector is a fixed point of the event when it is issued. A RMW event (and specifically a write event) e that is applied by process p to an objects vector is invisible if, before p applies another event, a write event is applied to each object o_i that is changed by e before another RMW event is applied to o.

If a RMW event e is not invisible in an execution E on some object o, we say that e *is visible in E on o*. If e is not invisible in E, we say that e is a *visible* event in E.

3   Step Lower Bounds for Counters and Related Objects

In this section we prove a lower bound on the average step complexity of solo-terminating implementations of a counter that use only read, write and conditional primitives. We then prove the same result for stacks and queues by using a simple reduction to counters. For the lower bounds obtained in this paper, we only consider executions in which every process performs at most a single operation instance. This can only strengthen our lower bounds.

A *counter* is an object whose domain is $\mathcal{N}$. It supports a single operation, *fetch&increment*. A counter implementation A is correct if the following holds for any non-empty *quiescent* execution E of A: the responses of the *fetch&increment* instances that complete in E constitute a contiguous range of integers starting from 0.

In order to prove the lower bound we argue about the extent to which processes must be aware of the participation of other processes in any execution of a counter implementation. Intuitively, a process p is aware of the participation of another process q in an execution if information flow from q to p is possible in that execution. The following definitions formalize this notion.

Definition 3. *Let E be an execution and p, q be two distinct processes. Let e_q be an event in E, by process q, that applies a non-trivial primitive to a vector v of base objects. We say that p is* aware *of e_q in E through event f if v contains a base object o such that at least one of the following holds:*

- *There is a prefix E' of E such that e_q is visible on o in E' and there is a RMW event f that applies a primitive other than write to o, issued by p, that follows e_q in E',*

- *there is a process $r \notin \{p, q\}$ that is aware of e_q in E through an event g and p is aware of g in E through f.*

If p is aware of an event e in E through one or more (other) events, we say that p is aware *of e in E. If p is aware of an event e of q in E, then p is also aware of all of q's previous events in E.*

If p is aware of any event by q in E, then p may be aware of q's participation in the execution. The key intuition behind our step lower bound proof is that in any n-process execution of a counter implementation, 'many' processes need to be aware of the participation of 'many' other processes in the execution. The following definition provides a quantification of the extent to which a process is aware of the participation of other processes in an execution.

Definition 4. *Let E be an execution and let p and q be processes. We say that p is* aware of q *after E if either $p = q$ or if p is aware of some event of q in E. We denote by $F(E, p)$ the set of processes that p is aware of after E. We call this set the* awareness set of p *after E. If p is aware of q after E and $p \neq q$, we denote the last event of q in E that p is aware of in E by* lastAware(E,p,q).

Information about processes that participate in the execution flows through base objects. The following definition provides a quantification to the number of other processes a process can become aware of when it reads from a base object.

Definition 5. *Let E be an execution, o be a base object and q be a process. We say that o has record of q after E if there exists an event e in E such that all of the following hold. (1) $E = E_1 e E_2$, (2) e is an application of a non-trivial primitive to an objects-vector that contains o by some process r such that $q \in F(E_1 e, r)$, and (3) e is visible in E on o. We define the* familiarity set of o *after E as the set of all processes that o has record of after E, and denote it by $F(E, o)$.*

Definition 5 only provides an upper bound (not necessarily tight) on the number of other processes that a process may become aware of when it accesses a base object. This can only strengthen our lower bound. We also note that requirement (2) of Definition 5 makes sure that a RMW event e that modifies an object o extends o's familiarity set with the familiarity sets of all other objects accessed by e.

The following lemma proves an intuitively-clear relation between the value returned by a *fetch&increment* operation instance of a process in some execution and the size of that process' awareness set after that execution.

Lemma 1. *Let E be an execution of a counter implementation. If the* fetch&increment *instance by p returns i in E then $|F(E, p)| > i$.*

The following corollary is an immediate consequence of Lemma 1.

Corollary 1. *Let E be a quiescent n-process execution of a solo-terminating counter implementation, then the following holds:*
$$\sum_{p \in P} F(E, p) \geq (n + 1) \cdot (n + 2)/2.$$

We need the following technical definition and lemma.

Definition 6. *Let* $S = \{e_1, \cdots, e_k\}$ *be a set of events by different processes that are enabled after some execution* E, *all about to apply write and/or conditional RMW primitives. We say that an ordering of the events of* S *is a weakly-visible-schedule of* S *after* E, *denoted by* $\sigma(E, S)$, *if the following holds. Let* $E_1 = E\sigma(E, S)$, *then*

1. *at most a single event of* S *is visible on any one object in* E_1. *If* $e_j \in S$ *is visible on a base object in* E_1, *then* e_j *is issued by a process that is not aware of any event of* S *in* E_1,
2. *any process is aware of at most a single event of* S *in* E_1, *and*
3. *All the read events of* S *are scheduled in* $\sigma(E, S)$ *before any event of* $\sigma(E, S)$ *changes a base object.*

Lemma 2. *Let* $S = \{e_1, \cdots, e_k\}$ *be a set of events by different processes that are enabled after some execution* E, *all about to apply write and/or conditional RMW primitives. Then there is a weakly-visible-schedule of* S *after* E.

Lemma 2 is proved by a careful ordering of the events of S that is done in an iterative manner. Our step complexity lower bounds follow.

Theorem 1. *Let* A *be an* n-process *solo-terminating implementation of a counter from base objects that support only read, write and either reading or non-reading conditional primitives with arity* k *or less. Then* A *has an execution* E *that contains* $\Omega(n \log_{k+1} n)$ *events, in which every process performs a single* fetch&increment *instance.*

Proof. We construct an n-process execution, E, of length $\Omega(n \log_{k+1} n)$ in which every process performs a single *fetch&increment* instance. The construction proceeds in rounds, indexed by the integers $1, 2, \cdots, r$ for some $r \in \Omega(\log_{k+1} n)$. We prove that the construction maintains the following invariant: before round i starts, the awareness set of any process and the familiarity set of any base object has size at most $(2k + 1)^{i-1}$.

Before execution starts, objects have no record of processes and processes are only aware of themselves, thus the induction claim holds. If a process p has not completed its *fetch&increment* instance before round i starts, we say that p is *active in round* i. All processes are active in round 1. All the processes that are active in round i have an enabled event in the beginning of round i. We denote the set of these events by S_i. We denote the execution that consists of all the events issued in rounds $1, \ldots, i$ by E_i.

From Lemma 2, there is a weakly-visible-schedule, $\sigma(E_{i-1}, S_i)$, of the events of S_i after E_{i-1}. E_i is constructed by extending E_{i-1} with $\sigma(E_{i-1}, S_i)$.

Assume the induction hypothesis holds before round i starts. Let o be some base object. From Definition 6, at most one event of S_i is visible on o in E_i. If there is no such event, then $F(E_i, o) = F(E_{i-1}, o)$. Otherwise there is a single such event, e, issued by some process p. Let $o_1, \ldots, o_j$, for some $j, 1 \leq j \leq k-1$ be the base objects accessed by e in addition to o, if any. From Definition 6, p is not aware of any event from S_i in E_i. Thus $F(E_i, o) \subset F(E_{i-1}, o) \cup F(E_{i-1}, p) \cup_{l=1}^{j} F(E_{i-1}, o_l)$ hence, from the induction hypothesis, $|F(E_i, o)| \leq (k+1)(2k+1)^{i-1}$. Therefore the induction hypothesis for round $i+1$ holds for all base objects.

Let us now consider the maximal size of the awareness set of any process right after round i terminates. Clearly, $F(E_i, p) = F(E_{i-1}, p)$ for any process p that is not active in round i. From Definition 3, the same holds for all the processes that issue a write event in round i. Let p be a process that issues a read event in round i that accesses some base object o. As reads are scheduled before any event changes a base object in round i, we have $F(E_i, p) \subset F(E_{i-1}, p) \cup F(E_{i-1}, o)$ hence $|F(E_i, p)| \leq 2(2k+1)^{i-1}$.

Consider a conditional RMW event e by process p that is issued in round i and accesses base objects $o_1, \ldots, o_j$ for some $j \leq k$. From Definition 6, if e is visible in E_i, then p is aware of no event of S_i in E_i. Hence $F(E_i, p) \subset F(E_{i-1}, p) \cup_{l=1}^{j} F(E_{i-1}, o_l)$. Otherwise e is invisible in E_i and, again from Definition 6, p is aware of at most a single event e' from S_i in E_i. Let q be the process that issues e', then q is not aware of any event of S_i in E_i. Let $o'_1, \ldots, o'_{j_1}$, for some $1 \leq j_1 \leq k-1$, be the base objects accessed by e' in addition to o, if any.

Thus we have $F(E_i, p) \subset F(E_{i-1}, p) \cup F(E_{i-1}, q) \cup_{l=1}^{j} F(E_{i-1}, o_l) \cup_{l=1}^{j_1} F(E_{i-1}, o'_l)$. Consequently, we have $|F(E_i, p)| \leq (2k+1)^i$ regardless of whether e is visible in E_i or not. Thus the induction hypothesis holds for all processes before round $i+1$ starts.

From Corollary 1, there are at least $n/3$ processes the awareness set of each of which contains at least $n/4$ other processes after E. Consequently each of these processes is active in at least the first $\log_{2k+1}(n/4 - 1)$ rounds, hence each of these processes performs at least $\log_{2k+1}(n/4 - 1)$ events in E.   ∎

The full version contains a similar result for stacks and queues.

Theorem 2. *Let A be an n-process solo-terminating implementation of a stack or a queue from base objects that support only read, write and either reading or non-reading conditional primitives with arity k or less. Then A has an execution E that contains $\Omega(n \log_{k+1} n)$ events, in which every process performs a single fetch&increment instance.*

By using techniques from [23], Theorems 1 and 2 can be extended to hold also if base objects support the *validate*, *swap* and *move* primitives.

4   Step and Round Lower Bounds for Collect

In this section we consider a variation on collect that we call the *input collection problem* (ICP). The input to ICP is an n-bit vector that is given in an array of n base objects, each of which stores one bit. An ICP object supports a single operation called *collect*, which every process performs at most once. The response of the *collect* operation is an n-bit number whose i'th bit equals the i'th input bit. We prove step- and round complexity lower bounds on implementations of ICP. It can easily be seen that these bounds hold also for the ordinary collect object (defined in, e.g., [4]) by considering executions of collect in which every process performs a *store* instance immediately followed by a *collect* instance.

Round complexity is defined as follows. Let E be an execution. A *round* of E is a consecutive sequence of events in E, in which every process that is active just before the sequence begins issues at least one event. A *minimal round* is a round such that no proper prefix of it is a round. Every execution can be uniquely partitioned into minimal rounds. The round complexity of E is the number of rounds in this partition. Let A be an implementation. A's round complexity is the supremum over the round complexity of all its executions. Round complexity is a meaningful measure of time for fail-free executions in which processes operate at approximately the same speed.

Attiya et al. [8] present an $O(\log_2 n)$ round complexity implementation of ICP from read and write. They prove a matching lower bound for such implementations. In this section we prove an $\Omega(\log_2 n)$ round complexity lower bound for ICP implementations that can use non-reading k-CAS primitives for any k, in addition to read and write. Thus we show that non-reading k-CAS is no stronger than read and write in terms of ICP implementation round complexity.

Beame [10] proves a lower bound of $\Omega(\log_2 n)$ for a problem similar to ICP in the concurrent-read concurrent-write (CRCW) PRAM model. We use a variation on his technique to prove a similar lower bound for solo-terminating implementations of ICP even when non-reading conditional primitives *of any arity* may be used. Clearly a fan-in argument would not work in this case.

Fix an implementation A of ICP. For notational simplicity we assume in this section that all base objects are indexed, where o_j denotes the base object indexed by j. The base objects of the input array are $o_1, \ldots, o_n$.

The proofs presented in this section consider only the subset of synchronous executions of A, denoted $\mathcal{E}(A)$, in which the participating processes issue their events in lock-step. Clearly $\mathcal{E}(A)$ is a proper subset of all the possible executions of A; proving our lower bound for this subset can only strengthen it.

In detail, an execution E in $\mathcal{E}(A)$ proceeds in *rounds*. In the beginning of each round, each of the participating processes whose instance of *collect* has not yet been completed has an enabled event. All processes have an enabled event in the beginning of round 1. In each round these enabled events are scheduled in a *specific* order, which we will shorty describe. As we consider deterministic implementations, this implies the following: the states of all processes and the values of all base objects right after each round of E terminates depend solely on the input vector. Thus, we denote the single execution of $\mathcal{E}$ that results when the input vector is I by E_I. An execution $E_I \in \mathcal{E}(A)$ terminates after the *collect* instances of all the processes complete.

Let E_I be the execution of $\mathcal{E}(A)$ for some input vector I. We denote by $E_{I,t}$ the prefix of E_I that contains all the events issued in rounds $1, \ldots, t$ of E_I. We denote by $S(E_{I,t})$ the set of the events that are enabled just before round t of E_I starts. Then in round t we extend $E_{I,t-1}$ with a weakly-visible-schedule of $S(E_{I,t})$ after $E_{I,t-1}$ to obtain $E_{I,t}$. Lemma 2 guarantees that this can be done.

The following definition formalizes the notion of partitions, which is the key concept of the technique of Beame [10] that we apply.

Definition 7. *We let $PV(i,t)$ (respectively $CV(j,t)$) denote the set of all possible states of process p_i (respectively the possible values of object o_j) right after round t of an execution $E \in \mathcal{E}(A)$ terminates. The sets $PV(i,t)$ and $CV(j,t)$ induce a partitioning of the input vectors to equivalence classes. The process partition $P(i,t)$ is the partition of the input vectors to equivalence classes that is induced by the set $PV(i,t)$. Two input vectors I_1, I_2 are in the same class of $P(i,t)$ if and only if there is a state $s \in PV(i,t)$ so that p_i is in state s after round t of both executions E_{I_1} and E_{I_2}. We define an object partition, $C(j,t)$, similarly.*

From Definition 7, we have $|PV(i,t)|, |CV(j,t)| \leq |\mathcal{E}(A)| = 2^n$, $|PV(i,t)| = |P(i,t)|$ and $|CV(j,t)| = |C(j,t)|$, for any process p_i, object o_j and round t.

In the following we consider a *full-information model*, i.e., we assume that the state of any process reflects the entire history of the events it issued (and their corresponding responses) and that objects are large enough to store any such state. This assumption can obviously only strengthen our lower bound.

Theorem 3. *Let A be a solo-terminating implementation of ICP from base objects that support only read, write and non-reading conditional primitives of any arity. Then there is an execution of $\mathcal{E}(A)$ in which some process issues $\Omega(\log_2 n)$ events as it performs its instance of* collect.

Proof. Assume there is a process p_i whose instance of *collect* completes in round m or an earlier round in every execution of $\mathcal{E}(A)$. We show that $m \in \Omega(\log_2 n)$. The *collect* instance of p_i returns different responses for different input vectors. As the response of the *collect* instance performed by p_i depends only on p_i's state before the response is returned, we have: $|P(i,m)| = 2^n$. Let $r_t = \max_i |P(i,t)|$ and $c_t = \max_j |C(j,t)|$ respectively denote the maximum size of all process and object partitions right after round t. Let r_0 and c_0 respectively denote the maximum size of any process partition and object partition just before execution starts. We prove that the sequences r_t, c_t satisfy the recurrences: (1) $r_{t+1} \leq r_t \cdot c_t$, and (2) $c_{t+1} \leq n \cdot r_t + c_t$ with initial conditions: (3) $r_0 = 1$, and (4) $c_0 \leq 2$.

Before any execution starts, we have $\forall j \in \{1,\ldots,n\} : |C(j,1)| = 2$, as the single bit in every input base object partitions the set of input vectors to 2. We also have $\forall j > n : |C(j,1)| = 1$, as other base objects have the same initial value regardless of the input. Additionally we have $\forall i : |P(i,1)| = 1$, as the initial state of a process does not depend on the input vector. Thus initial conditions (3) and (4) hold.

Assume the claim holds for rounds $1, \cdots, t$ and consider round $t+1$. Let us consider $|P(i,t+1)|$, the partition size of process p_i right after round $t+1$ terminates. p_i's partition size can grow in round $t+1$ only because of executions in which p_i applies a read or a non-reading conditional primitive in round $t+1$. The primitive applied by p_i in round $t+1$ and the base objects to which it is applied are only a function of p_i's state before round $t+1$ begins. Thus the number of different events applied by p_i in round $t + 1$ of all the executions of $\mathcal{E}(A)$ is at most $P(i,t) \leq r_t$.

We consider the following two possibilities. If p_i applies a non-reading conditional primitive in round $t + 1$ of an execution, then it receives a single bit response. In this case every state of p_i before round $t + 1$ starts can change to one of at most two states. If p_i applies a read to some object o_j in round $t + 1$ of an execution, then, from Definition 6, the read is applied before o_j is changed in round $t + 1$. Thus, from induction hypothesis, the event can read at most $|CV(i,t)| \leq c_t$ different values. Hence p_i's state in each such execution can change to one of at most c_t different states. In either case we get: $|P(i,t+1)| \leq r_t \cdot c_t$, which proves recurrence (1).

Let o_j be some base object. We now consider the set of values, $CV(j,t+1)$, that object o_j may assume right after round $t+1$ terminates in all the executions of $\mathcal{E}(A)$. There may be executions in which no process writes to o_j during round $t + 1$, thus we may have:

$$CV(j,t) \subseteq CV(j,t+1). \tag{1}$$

Let $n(j,t+1)$ denote the number of distinct values that o_j may assume right after round t+1 in all of the executions in which its value is modified during that round. Let E_I be such an execution. From Definition 6, at most a single event of $S(E_{I,t+1})$ may be visible on o_j after $E_{I,t+1}$. If there is such an event, then it is issued by a process that is not aware of any event of $S(E_{I,t+1})$. Thus the number of distinct values written to o_j by any process p_i in round $t + 1$ of all executions is at most $|P(i,t)| \leq r_t$. As any process may write to o_j in round $t + 1$ we get:

$$n(j,t+1) \leq \sum_{k=1}^{n} |P(k,t)| \leq n \cdot r_t. \tag{2}$$

Combining Equations 1 and 2 proves recurrence (2). As shown in [10], solving the recurrences for the sequences r_i, c_j yields $m \geq \log_2 n + 1 - \log(1 + \log_2 2n)$. Thus, there is an execution in which some process performs $\Omega(\log_2 n)$ events. ■

The following lower bound on the *average* step complexity of ICP also follows from the proof of Theorem 3.

Theorem 4. *Let A be a solo-terminating implementation of ICP from base objects that support only read, write and non-reading conditional primitives of any arity. Then A has an execution that contains $\Omega(n \log_2 n)$ events.*

5   Space Complexity

Fich et al. [14] consider wait-free implementations of a class of *visible* objects. Intuitively, a visible object supports some operation Op such that any instance of Op must issue a visible event before it completes. This class contains widely-used objects such as counter, stack, queue, and single-writer snapshot. They show that any wait-free implementation of a visible object from base objects that support only *unary* conditional primitives, read and write must use $\Omega(n)$ such objects. In this section we generalize this result and show that it holds also for implementations that may use conditional primitives of any arity. The results of this section apply to both reading and non-reading conditional primitives.

Let A be a wait-free implementation of a visible object. Lemma 3.2 in [14] proves that A can be brought to a state where all processes have pending indexed events whose visibility depends on their index: an event with index i cannot be made invisible by events with indices larger than i. Such a state is called an n-levelled state. This is being formalized by the following definition.

Definition 8. *The state resulting from a finite execution E is n-levelled if there is a sequence $e_1, e_2, \ldots, e_n$ of events by different processes, all about to apply non-trivial primitives, such that, for every nonempty execution fragment E' consisting of some subset of these events (in any order), e_j is visible in EE', where $j = \min\{i | e_i \in E'\}$. We call $e_1, e_2, \ldots, e_n$ an n-levelled sequence and say that event e_j is at level j.*

An object that only supports read and write primitives is called a *register*. An object that can only be accessed by conditional primitives (of any arity) is called a *multi-conditional* object. An object that only supports read, write and may be accessed by conditional primitives (of any arity) is called a *read-write-multi-conditional* object.

Let e be a write or a conditional event. The *change set of e*, denoted $\mathcal{C}(e)$, is the set of base objects whose values may be changed by e; its size is called the *change multiplicity* of e and denoted $c(e)$. If e is a write event, then $\mathcal{C}$ contains the single object accessed by e. If e is a conditional event, then $\mathcal{C}(e)$ is the set of objects whose values are changed by e if e is issued when its object-values vector is a change-point of e.

In what follows we consider an implementation, A, that uses base objects that only support read, write and conditional primitives of any arity. We let $SPACE(A)$ denote the number of base objects used by A. We prove that if A can be brought to an n-levelled state, then $SPACE(A) = \Omega(n)$. In fact, multi-object conditionals may *worsen* the implementation's space complexity: the lower bound on space complexity that we obtain is proportional to the sum of the change multiplicities of the issued events.

Lemma 3. *Assume that after execution E, A is in an n-levelled state. Let $S = \{e_1, \ldots, e_n\}$ be a corresponding n-levelled sequence. Let S_w and S_c respectively denote the subset of write events of S and the subset of conditional events of S.*

1. *If A uses only registers and multi-conditional objects, then*
   $SPACE(A) \geq \sum_{i=1}^{n} c(e_i)$.
2. *If A uses only read-write-multi-conditional objects, then*
   $$SPACE(A) \geq max\left((\sum_{i=1}^{n} c(e_i)) - |S_w|, \lceil n/2 \rceil\right).$$

Proof. Let e_i, e_j be two events of S, $i < j$. Assume first that both e_i and e_j are conditional events. We now show that $\mathcal{C}(e_i) \cap \mathcal{C}(e_j) = \phi$. Assume otherwise to obtain a contradiction, then there is some object $o \in \mathcal{C}(e_i) \cap \mathcal{C}(e_j)$. From Definition 8, e_i is visible in Ee_i and e_j is visible in Ee_j. Thus the object-values vector of e_i (respectively e_j) after E is a change-point of e_i (respectively e_j). As $i < j$, again from Definition 8, e_i is visible in Ce_je_i. However, as o is in the change set of e_j, its value is changed by e_j. Consequently the object-values vector of e_i after Ee_j is a fixed-point of e_i. This is a contradiction to the assumption that e_i is visible in Ee_j. It is easily seen that $\mathcal{C}(e_i) \cap \mathcal{C}(e_j) = \phi$ also when e_i, e_j are both write events. This proves *(1)*.

Assume that A uses only read-write-multi-conditional objects. As at most one write event and one conditional event may change any one object, we have $SPACE(A) \geq \lceil n/2 \rceil$. If $\mathcal{C}(e_i) \cap \mathcal{C}(e_j) \neq \phi$ then it must be that e_i is a write event and e_j a conditional event, thus $|\mathcal{C}(e_i) \cap \mathcal{C}(e_j)| = 1$. This proves *(2)*. ∎

The above lemma and Lemma 3.2 of [14] immediately imply the following:

Theorem 5. *Let A be an n-process wait-free implementation of a visible object.*

- *If A uses only registers or multi-conditional objects, then $SPACE(A) \geq n$.*
- *If A uses only multi-conditional objects and $\mathcal{C}(e) \geq k$ for any conditional event e issued in an execution of A, then $SPACE(A) \geq k \cdot n$.*
- *If A uses only read-write-multi-conditionals objects, then $SPACE(P) \geq \lceil n/2 \rceil$.*

Acknowledgements. The authors thank Maged Michael who triggered this research by asking whether the results of [14] hold with k-CAS primitives. We would also like to thank Faith Ellen Fich for referring us to Paul Beame's technique, and Nir Shavit for helpful discussions on the topics of this paper. Danny Hendler was supported by Sun Microsystems.

References

1. Y. Afek, D. Dauber, and D. Touitou. Wait-free made fast. In STOC, pages 538547, 1995.
2. Y. Afek, M. Merritt, and G. Taubenfeld. The power of multi-objects. Information and Computation, 153(1):117138, 1999.
3. Y. Afek, M. Merritt, G. Taubenfeld, and D. Touitou. Disentangling multi-object operations. In PODC, pages 111120, 1997.
4. Y. Afek, G. Stupp, and D. Touitou. Long-lived adaptive collect with applications. In FOCS, page 262, 1999.
5. O. Agesen, D. Detlefs, C. H. Flood, A. T. Garthwaite, P. A. Martin, M. Moir, N. Shavit, and G. L. S. Jr. Dcas-based concurrent deques. Theory Comput. Syst., 35(3):349386, 2002.
6. J. H. Anderson and M. Moir. Universal constructions for multi-object operations. In PODC 95: Proceedings of the fourteenth annual ACM symposium on Principles of distributed computing, pages 184193, New York, NY, USA, 1995. ACM Press.
7. H. Attiya and E. Dagan. Improved implementations of binary universal operations. Journal of the ACM, 48(5):10131037, 2001.

8. H. Attiya, N. Lynch, and N. Shavit. Are wait-free algorithms fast? Journal of the ACM, 41(4):725763, July 1994.

9. G. Barnes. A method for implementing lock-free shared data structures. In SPAA, pages 261270, 1993.

10. P. Beame. Limits on the power of concurrent-write parallel machines. Information and Computation, 76(1):1328, 1988.

11. R. Cole and O. Zajicek. The apram: incorporating asynchrony into the pram model. In SPAA, pages 169178, 1989.

12. S. Doherty, D. Detlefs, L. Groves, C. H. Flood, V. Luchangco, P. A. Martin, M. Moir, N. Shavit, and G. L. S. Jr. DCAS is not a silver bullet for nonblocking algorithm design. In SPAA, pages 216224, 2004.

13. F. Fich, M. Herlihy, and N. Shavit. On the space complexity of randomized synchronization. Journal of the ACM, 45(5):843862, Sept. 1998.

14. F. E. Fich, D. Hendler, and N. Shavit. On the inherent weakness of conditional synchronization primitives. In PODC, pages 8087, 2004.

15. M. J. Fischer, S. Moran, S. Rudich, and G. Taubenfeld. The wakeup problem. SIAM Journal on Computing, 25(6):13321357, Dec. 1996.

16. K. Fraser. Practical Lock-Freedom. PhD thesis, Kings College University of Cambridge, Sept. 2003.

17. M. Greenwald. Non-Blocking Synchronization and System Design. PhD thesis, Stanford University Technical Report STAN-CS-TR-99-1624, Palo Alto, CA, Aug. 1999.

18. M. B. Greenwald and D. R. Cheriton. The synergy between non-blocking synchronization and operating system structure. In OSDI, pages 123136, 1996.

19. P. H. Ha and P. Tsigas. Reactive multi-word synchronization. In 12th International Conference on Parallel Architectures and Compilation Techniques, pages 184193, 2003.

20. M. Herlihy. Wait-free synchronization. ACM Transactions On Programming Languages and Systems, 13(1):123149, Jan. 1991.

21. M. Herlihy, V. Luchango, and M. Moir. Obstruction-free synchronization: Doubleended queues as an example. In ICDCS, pages 522529, 2003.

22. Intel Corporation. Intel itanium processor-specific application binary interface, 2001.

23. P. Jayanti. A time complexity lower bound for randomized implementations of some shared objects. In PODC, pages 201210, 1998.

24. P. Jayanti and S. Khanna. On the power of multi-objects. In WDAG, pages 320332, 1997.

25. P. Jayanti, K. Tan, and S. Toueg. Time and space lower bounds for non-blocking implementations. Siam J. Comput., 30(2):438456, 2000.

26. V. Luchangco, M. Moir, and N. Shavit. Nonblocking k-compare-single-swap. In SPAA, pages 314323, 2003.

27. Motorola. MC68020 32-Bit Microprocessor Users Manual. Prentice-Hall, 2nd edition, 1986.

28. N. Shavit and D. Touitou. Software transactional memory. Distributed Computing, 10(2):99116, February 1997.

29. SPARC International, Inc., Mountain View, CA. The SPARC Architecture Manual Version 9, 1/e. Prentice Hall, 1994.

(Almost) All Objects Are Universal
in Message Passing Systems
(Extended Abstract)

Carole Delporte-Gallet[1], Hugues Fauconnier[2], and Rachid Guerraoui[3]

[1] ESIEE-IGM Marne-La-Vallee, France
[2] LIAFA Univ Paris VII, France
[3] EPFL Lausanne, Switzerland

Abstract. This paper shows that all shared atomic object types that can solve consensus among $k > 1$ processes have the same weakest failure detector in a message passing system with process crash failures. In such a system, object types such as test-and-set, fetch-and-add, and queue, known to have weak synchronization power in a shared memory system are thus, in a precise sense, equivalent to universal types like compare-and-swap, known to have the strongest synchronization power. In the particular case of a message passing system of two processes, we show that, interestingly, even a register is in that sense universal.

1 Introduction

1.1 Atomic Objects

A shared atomic object is a data structure exporting a set of operations that can be invoked concurrently by the processes of the system. *Atomicity* means that any object operation appears to execute at some individual instant between its invocation and reply time events [14,11]. Thanks to atomicity, the type of an object can solely be defined according to its *sequential specification*: the set of all possible sequential executions of the object operations [11].

Many distributed algorithms are designed assuming, as underlying synchronization primitives, atomic objects, sometimes provided as hardware devices of a multiprocessor, and sometimes emulated in software. These include objects of types register, test-and-set, fetch-and-add, queue, and compare-and-swap.

Some of these atomic object types have been shown to have more *synchronization power* than others in the sense that they can solve the seminal *consensus* problem [9] among more processes [12]. What is meant here by a *type solving consensus* is that instances of that type can be used in a deterministic algorithm that solves the consensus problem; we consider here the *uniform* variant of consensus where no two processes can decide differently: the problem can be casted as an atomic object type also called consensus.

The ability for a type to solve consensus among a certain number k of processes is important as it implies the ability to emulate any other type in a system of k processes, irrespective of how many of these processes may crash.

P. Fraigniaud (Ed.): DISC 2005, LNCS 3724, pp. 184–198, 2005.

The type register is in this sense weak as it can only solve consensus for exactly one process [16]. Test-and-set, fetch-and-add, or queue can solve consensus among exactly 2 processes. Interestingly, for any number k, there is a type that can solve consensus among exactly k processes [12]. This leads to a hierarchy of types, called the *consensus hierarchy*, classifying types according to their *consensus number (k)*. Types such as compare-and-swap can solve consensus among any number of processes, and are said to be *universal* [12]: their consensus number is ∞ and they are at the top of the hierarchy.

1.2   Atomic Object Implementations in Message Passing Systems

This paper studies necessary and sufficient conditions for implementing atomic object types in a distributed system where processes communicate by exchanging messages: no physical shared memory is assumed. The processes are assumed to communicate through reliable channels but can fail by crashing. Through such implementations, algorithms based on shared atomic objects can be automatically ported into a message passing system prone to crash failures. We focus on *robust* [2] implementations where any process that invokes an object operation and does not crash eventually gets a reply.

Two fundamental results are known about such implementations in an asynchronous message passing system (with no synchrony assumptions). The type register can only be implemented if we assume that a majority of the processes do not crash [2], and most of the types cannot be implemented, including test-and-set, fetch-and-add, queue, and compare-and-swap, if at least one process may crash [9].

In most distributed systems however, certain synchrony assumptions can be made, and these can even be precisely expressed through axiomatic properties of a *failure detector* abstraction [5]: a distributed oracle that provides processes with hints about crashes, and which can itself be implemented based on synchrony assumptions, e.g., timeouts.

Two related results, of particular interest in this paper, have been recently established. First, the *weakest* failure detector to implement the basic type register in a message passing system (with any number of crashes) has been shown to be an oracle, denoted by Σ, and which outputs, at any time and at every process, a set of processes such that (1) any two sets always intersect and (2) eventually every set contains only correct processes [6,8]. This result means that (a) there is a distributed algorithm that implements the type register using Σ, and (b) for every failure detector $\mathcal{D}$ such that some algorithm implements the type register using $\mathcal{D}$, there is an algorithm that implements Σ using $\mathcal{D}$. Failure detector $\mathcal{D}$ encapsulates information about failures that are at least as strong as those encapsulated by Σ.

Second, the weakest failure detector to solve consensus (with any number of crashes) has been shown to be an oracle, denoted by $\Sigma * \Omega$, and which outputs, at any time and at every process, both outputs of failure detector Σ and failure detector Ω. Failure detector Ω outputs, at any time and at every process, a single (leader) process, such that, eventually this process is the same at all processes and is correct [4,6,8]. The fact that $\Sigma * \Omega$ was established as the weakest failure detector to solve consensus directly implies that it is also the weakest to implement compare-and-swap, and more generally, any other universal type.

1.3   Contributions

Naturally, this raises the following question. What about all other types like queue, test-and-set, or fetch-and-add? More generally, what about all types that can solve consensus among $k > 1$ processes but not $k + 1$. This paper shows that the weakest failure detectors to implement these types do all boil down to the same one: $\Sigma * \Omega$.

In other words, we show that the weakest failure detector to implement any type that solves consensus among at least 2 processes is $\Sigma * \Omega$.

Our result conveys the interesting fact that, in a message passing system (unlike in a shared memory system), all these types are, in a precise sense, equivalent and universal. Hence, if we exclude types that cannot solve consensus among two processes such as register, the consensus hierarchy is thus *flat* in a message passing system. From a practical perspective, and given that many synchronization problems can be casted through atomic object types, our result suggests that, as far as failure detection is concerned, adopting an ad hoc approach focusing on each problem individually is not more economic than a generic approach where the failure detector $\Sigma * \Omega$ would be implemented in a message passing system as a common service underlying all problems, i.e., all type implementations.

Stating and proving our result goes through defining a general model of distributed computation encompassing different kinds of abstractions: atomic objects, message passing and failure detectors. Such a model is interesting by itself. To our knowledge, besides the model we introduce in this paper, the only model that captured these different abstractions in a unified framework has recently been defined (using I/O automata) by considering a restricted form of failure detectors [1]. In this paper, we establish the weakest failure detector to implement atomic object types among *all* failure detectors. Our model, and in particular our notion of implementation, is a slight generalization of both the notions of shared memory object implementations of [12] as well as failure detector reductions of [5].

To prove our result, we first consider the problem of solving consensus among a subset of processes S in the system. We observe that failure detector $\Sigma_S * \Omega_S$, obtained by restricting Σ and Ω to S, is the weakest to solve consensus in S. Then we show that the weakest failure detector to solve consensus among any subset of $k > 1$ processes is the same as the weakest to solve consensus among any subset of $k + 1$ processes. The crucial technical step to establish this result is to show that the composition of Ω_S over all pairs S of processes in the system is Ω. (The analogous result for Σ_S is also needed but more easily obtained).

An interesting particular case is when the system simply consists of two processes. We show that, in this case, $\Sigma * \Omega$ is equivalent to Σ. This equivalence also has a surprising ramification: whereas no algorithm can solve consensus using a register in a system of two processes where at least one can crash [16], any failure detector that can be used to implement a register in a message passing system of two processes, where at least one can crash, can also be used to solve consensus.

1.4   Roadmap

To summarize, this paper shows that all atomic object types that can solve consensus among $k > 1$ processes have the same weakest failure detector in a message passing system with process crash failures. In the particular interesting case of a message passing system of two processes, this failure detector is also the weakest to implement a register.

The rest of the paper is organized as follows. Section 2 defines our model. Section 3 introduces failure detectors Σ_S and Ω_S and establishes some preliminary results. Section 4 determines the weakest failure detector to implement consensus among any subset of $k > 1$ processes in the system. Section 5 derives our main results on the weakest failure detector to implement atomic types. Section 6 relates our results with weakest failure detector results in the shared memory model. For space limitations, several proofs are omitted from this extended abstract and given in a companion technical report [7].

2   System Model

We consider a distributed system composed of a finite set of n processes $\Pi = \{p_1, p_2, \ldots, p_n\}$; $|\Pi| = n \geq 3$. (Sometimes, processes are denoted by p and q.) A discrete global clock is assumed, and Φ, the range of the clock's ticks, is the set of natural numbers. The global clock is not accessible to the processes.

2.1   Failure Patterns and Failure Detectors

Processes can fail by crashing. A process p is said to crash at time τ if p does not perform any action after time τ (the notion of action is defined below). Otherwise the process is said to be alive at time τ. Failures are permanent, i.e., no process recovers after a crash. A correct process is a process that does never crash (otherwise it is faulty). A failure pattern is a function F from Φ to 2^Π, where $F(\tau)$ denotes the set of processes that have crashed by time τ. The set of correct processes in a failure pattern F is noted $correct(F)$. As in [5], we assume that every failure pattern has at least one correct process. An environment is a set of failure patterns. Unless explicitly stated otherwise, our results are stated for all environments and hence we do not mention any specific environment.

Roughly speaking, a failure detector $\mathcal{D}$ is a distributed oracle which gives hints about failure patterns of a given environment $\mathcal{E}$. Each process p has a local failure detector module of $\mathcal{D}$, denoted by $\mathcal{D}_p$. Associated with each failure detector $\mathcal{D}$ is a range $R_\mathcal{D}$ (when the context is clear we omit the subscript) of values output by the failure detector. A failure detector history H with range R is a function H from $\Pi \times \Phi$ to R. For every process $p \in \Pi$, for every time

$\tau \in \Phi$, $H(p, \tau)$ denotes the value of the failure detector module of process p at time τ, i.e., $H(p, \tau)$ denotes the value output by $\mathcal{D}_p$ at time τ. A failure detector $\mathcal{D}$ is more precisely a function that maps each failure pattern F of $\mathcal{E}$ to a set of failure detector histories with range $R_{\mathcal{D}}$: $\mathcal{D}(F)$ denotes the set of all possible failure detector histories permitted for the failure pattern F. Let $\mathcal{D}$ and $\mathcal{D}'$ be any two failure detectors, $\mathcal{D} * \mathcal{D}'$ denotes the failure detector, with range $R_{\mathcal{D}} * R_{\mathcal{D}'}$, which associates to every failure pattern F, the set of histories $\mathcal{D} * \mathcal{D}'(\mathcal{F}) = \{(\mathcal{H}, \mathcal{H}') \mid \mathcal{H} \in \mathcal{H}(\mathcal{D}), \mathcal{H}' \in \mathcal{H}'(\mathcal{D}')\}$. This notation is naturally extended to a finite set of failure detectors K: $*\{\mathcal{D} \mid \mathcal{D} \in K\}$.

2.2   Actions, Runs and Schedules

To access its local state or shared services, a process p executes (deterministic) actions from a (possibly infinite) alphabet $\mathcal{A}_p$. Each action is associated with exactly one process and the set of all actions $\mathcal{A}$ is a disjoint union of the $\mathcal{A}_{p_i}$ ($1 \leq i \leq n$). The state of a process after it executes action a in state s, is denoted $a(s)$. A configuration C is a function mapping each process to its local state. When applied to a configuration C, action a of $\mathcal{A}_{p_i}$ gives a new unique configuration denoted $a(C)$: for all $j \neq i$ $(a(C))(p_j) = C(p_j)$ and $(a(C))(p_i) = a(C(p_i))$.

An infinite sequence of actions is called a schedule. In the following, $Sc[i]$ denotes the i-th action of schedule Sc. Given $seq = a_1 \ldots a_i a_{i+1}$ a prefix of a schedule and C a configuration, the new configuration $seq(C)$ resulting from the execution seq on some C is defined by induction as $a_{i+1}((a_1 \ldots a_i)(C))$. To each schedule $Sc = a_1 \ldots a_i a_{i+1} \ldots$ and configuration C_0 correspond a unique sequence of configurations $C_0 C_1 \ldots C_i C_{i+1} \ldots$ such that $C_{i+1} = a_{i+1}(C_i)$.

A run is a tuple $R = < F, C, Sc, T >$, where F is a failure pattern, C a configuration, Sc a schedule, and T a time assignment represented by an infinite sequence of increasing values such that: (1) for all k, if $Sc[k]$ is an action of process p then p is alive at time $T[k]$ ($p \notin F(T[k])$) and (2) if p is correct then p executes an infinite number of actions. An event e is the occurrence of an action in Sc, and if e is the k-th action in Sc, then $T[k]$ is the time at which event e is executed.

Consider an alphabet of actions $\mathcal{A}$ and any subset $\mathcal{B}$ of $\mathcal{A}$. Let $Sc|\mathcal{B}$ be the subsequence of Sc consisting only of the actions of $\mathcal{B}$, and $T|\mathcal{B}$ be the subsequence of T corresponding to actions of $\mathcal{B}$ in $R = < F, C, Sc, T >$. We call $< F, C, Sc|\mathcal{B}, T|\mathcal{B} >$ the history corresponding to $\mathcal{B}$, and we simply denote it by $R|\mathcal{B}$. In particular, when $\mathcal{B} = \mathcal{A}_{p_i}$, $R|\mathcal{A}_{p_i}$ is called the history of process p_i in R.

2.3   Services

A service is defined by a pair $(Prim, Spec)$. Each element of $Prim$, denoted by $prim$, is a tuple $< s, p, arg, ret >$ representing an action of process p identified by a sort s, an input argument arg from some (possibly infinite) range In and an output argument (or return value) ret from some (possibly infinite) range Out. An empty argument is denoted by λ. The specification $Spec$ of a service X is defined by a set of runs. In this paper, we consider three kinds of services: *message passing*, *atomic objects* and *failure detectors*.

Message passing. The classical notion of point-to-point message passing channel, represented here by a service and denoted MP, is defined through primitive *send(m) to q* of process p and primitive *receive() from q* of process p.[1] Primitive *receive() from q* returns either some message m or the null message λ; in the first case we say that p received m. Each non null message is uniquely identified and has a unique sender as well as a unique potential receiver. The specification *Spec* of MP stipulates that: (1) the receiver of m receives it at most once and only if the sender of m has sent m; (2) if process p is correct and if process q executes an infinite number of *receive from p* primitives, then all messages sent by p to q are received by q.

Failure detector. The only primitive defined for a failure detector service is a query without argument that returns one value in the failure detector range. A run $R = <F, C, Sc, T>$ satisfies the specification of a failure detector $\mathcal{D}$ if there is a failure detector history $H \in \mathcal{D}(F)$ such that for all k, if $Sc[k]$ is a query of $\mathcal{D}$ by process p that outputs v, then $H(p, T[k]) = v$. Any such history is said to be associated with run R.

Atomic object. Atomic objects are services defined by a sequential specification, and which can be accessed through invocation and reply primitives associated with each operation of the object. It is common to call a pair of invocation and subsequent reply primitives the occurrence of the operation and identify an invocation and the associated operation. The sequential specification of an atomic object is defined by its type and an initial state. A type $\mathcal{T}$ is a tuple $<Q, Op, I, L>$: where Q is the set of states of the type, Op is a set of operations, I is a set of replies, and L is a relation that carries each state $st \in Q$ and operation op to a set of state and reply pairs, which are said to be legal, and denoted by $L(st, op)$. When L is a function, the type is said to be deterministic. An invocation returns λ, and a reply has λ as argument and returns a value in I. An invocation inv and a reply rep are said to be matching if they are actions of the same process p and if there exist states st and st' such that (st', rep) belongs to $L(st, inv)$. A (finite or infinite) sequence $\sigma = (o_0 r_0)(o_1 r_1) \ldots (o_j r_j) \ldots$ where, for all l, o_l and r_l are respectively operations and replies, is legal from state s if there is a corresponding sequence of states $s = s_0, s_1, \ldots s_j, \ldots$ such that, for each l $(s_{l+1}, r_{l+1}) \in L(s_l, o_l)$. Such a sequence is called a sequential history of object O from initial state s. [2]

Only well-formed schedules are considered. Consider a schedule Sc, and its restriction to a process $Sc|p$, we say that some occurrence of invocation is pending if there is no matching reply. We say that a schedule Sc is well-formed if (i) no prefix of $Sc|p$ has more than one occurrence of a pending invocation and (ii) $(Sc|p)|Prim$ begins with an invocation and has alternating matching invocations and replies. By extension, a run $R = <F, C, Sc, T>$ is well-formed if its schedule

---

[1] More formally, these primitives are respectively a tuple $< send\_to\_q, p, m, \lambda >$ with $m \in M$ where M is a set of messages and a tuple $< receive\_from\_q, p, \lambda, x >$ with $x \in M \cup \{\lambda\}$.

[2] The definition of the *Spec* part of an atomic object O is the same as in [12].

Sc is well-formed and there is no pending invocation for correct processes in F. When reasoning about the atomicity of an object, we consider only operations that terminate, i.e., both invocation inv and a matching reply have taken place. If a process p performs an invocation inv and then p crashes before getting any reply, we assume that either the state of the object appears as if inv has not taken place, or inv has indeed terminated. An operation is said to precede another if the first terminates before the second start and two operations are concurrent if none precedes the other.

Let $R = < F, C, Sc, T >$ be any well-formed run, and $R|Prim$ be the history corresponding to object $O = < Prim, Spec >$ of type T, a linearization of $R|Prim$ with respect to T and state s is a pair (H, T') such that: (1) H a sequential history of O from state s; (2) H includes all non pending invocations of operation in S; (3) If some invocation inv is pending in S, then either H does not include this pending invocation or includes a matching reply; (4) H includes no action other than the ones mentioned in (2) and (3); (5) T' is an infinite sequence such that $Sc[k]$ is an invocation and $Sc[k']$ the matching reply, corresponding respectively to $H[l]$ and $H[l+1]$ then $T'[l] = T'[l+1]$ belongs to the interval $(T[k], T[k'])$ A run R is linearizable for type T and state s if R has a linearization with respect to T and state s. The specification $Spec$ associated to an object O of type T and initial state s is the set of runs well-formed for O that are linearizable with respect to T and state s [11].

2.4   Algorithms and Implementations

An algorithm $A = < A_1, \cdots, A_n, Serv >$, using a set of services $Serv$, is a collection of n deterministic automata A_i (one per process p_i) with transitions labeled by actions in $\mathcal{A}_i$ such that all operations defined for services in $Serv$ are included in $\mathcal{A}$. Every transition of A_i is a tuple (s, a, s') where s and s' are local states of p_i and a is a action of p_i such that $a(s) = s'$. Computation proceeds in steps of the algorithm: in each step of an algorithm A, a process p atomically executes an action in $\mathcal{A}$. If a is an action of p_i and C is a configuration, a is said to be applicable to C if there is a transition (s, a, s') in A_i such that $s = C(p_i)$. By extension, a schedule $Sc = Sc[1]Sc[2]\ldots Sc[k]\ldots$ is applicable to a configuration C if for each $k > 1$, $Sc[k]$ is applicable to configuration $(Sc[1]\ldots Sc[k-1])(C)$. A run of algorithm A is a run $R = < F, C, Sc, T >$ such that Sc is a schedule applicable to configuration C, such that R satisfies the specifications of services in $Serv$.

Roughly speaking, implementing a service X using a set of services $Serv$ means providing the code of a set of subtasks associated with every process: one subtask for each primitive sort of X as well as a set of additional subtasks. The subtasks associated to the primitives are assumed to be sequential in the following sense: if a process p executes a primitive $prim$ (of the service to be implemented), the process launches the associated subtask and waits for it to terminate and return a reply before executing another primitive. All subtasks use services in $Serv$ to implement service X, in the sense that the only primitives used in these subtasks are primitives defined in $Serv$. More precisely, an implementation of a service $X = < Prim, Spec >$ with primitives of sorts $ps_1, \ldots, ps_m$, using a set of services $Serv$, among n processes, is defined by $I(X, n, Serv) = < (X_1, (ps_1^1, \ldots, ps_m^1)), \ldots, (X_n, (ps_1^1, \ldots, ps_m^n)) >$ where, for each i, X_i is the implementation subtask of p_i and ps_j^i is the primitive implementation subtask associated to process p_i and the primitive of sort ps_j of X such that the only primitives occurring in these subtasks are primitives defined in $Serv$.

An implementation $I(X, n, Serv)$ for environment $\mathcal{E}$ ensures that: for each algorithm $A = < A_1, \cdots, A_n, Serv' \cup \{X\} >$, the corresponding algorithm $A' = < A_1', \cdots, A_n', Serv \cup Serv' >$ in which X is implemented by $I(X, n, Serv)$ where, for each i, A_i' is the automaton corresponding to the subtasks $A_i, X_i, ps_1^i, \ldots, ps_j^i$ is such that all runs R of A', restricted to actions of $A_1, \cdots, A_n$, are runs of A.

Note that, we implicitly consider robust [2] implementations of services: every correct process that executes a primitive of an implemented service should eventually get a reply from that invocation. We will sometimes focus on implementations of $S-$services: the primitives of such a service can only be invoked by processes of a subset S of the system. In such implementation, the only restriction is the fact that only the processes in S contain each one subtask per primitive sort of the S-service (but all processes contain implementation tasks). If we do not specify the subset S, we implicitly assume the set of all processes.

2.5   Weakest Failure Detector

The notion of failure detector $\mathcal{D}2$ being reducible to $\mathcal{D}1$ in a given environment $\mathcal{E}$ ($\mathcal{D}1$ is said to be stronger than $\mathcal{D}2$ in $\mathcal{E}$ and written $\mathcal{D}2 \preceq_{\mathcal{E}} \mathcal{D}1$) of [5], means in our context that there is an algorithm that implements $\mathcal{D}2$ using $\mathcal{D}1$ and MP in $\mathcal{E}$. All the implementation subtasks use only MP and $\mathcal{D}$. For every run $R = < F, C, Sc, T >$, and failure detector history $H \in \mathcal{D}1(F)$ such that F is in $\mathcal{E}$, the output of the algorithm in R is a history of $\mathcal{D}2(F)$. We say that $\mathcal{D}1$ is equivalent to $\mathcal{D}2$ in $\mathcal{E}$ ($\mathcal{D}1 \equiv_{\mathcal{E}} \mathcal{D}2$), if $\mathcal{D}2 \preceq_{\mathcal{E}} \mathcal{D}1$ and $\mathcal{D}1 \preceq_{\mathcal{E}} \mathcal{D}2$ in $\mathcal{E}$.

We say that a failure detector $\mathcal{D}_1$ is the weakest to implement a given service in environment $\mathcal{E}$ if and only if the two following conditions are satisfied: (1) there is an algorithm that implements the service using $\mathcal{D}_1$ in $\mathcal{E}$, and (2) if there is an algorithm that implements the service using some failure detector $\mathcal{D}_2$ in $\mathcal{E}$, then $\mathcal{D}_2$ is stronger than $\mathcal{D}_1$ in $\mathcal{E}$. As pointed out earlier, given that most of our results hold for all environments, we will generally not mention (and implicitly assume) any environment when stating and proving results.

3   The Quorum and Leader Failure Detectors

We introduce here two failure detectors: the *Quorum* and the *Leader*. Both are defined relatively to a subset S of processes in the system. The first one, denoted by Σ_S, is a generalization of Σ [6,8]. The second one, denoted by Ω_S, generalizes Ω [4].

3.1 Failure Detector Σ_S

Given any subset S of processes in Π, failure detector Σ_S outputs, at each process in S, and at any time, a list of processes, called *trusted* processes, such that every list intersects with every other list, and eventually, all lists contain only correct processes. For presentation simplicity, we consider that, at any process of S that has crashed, the list that is output is simply Π. More generally, the lists that are output satisfy the two following properties:

- *Intersection.* Every two lists of trusted processes intersect: $\forall F \in \mathcal{E}, \forall H \in \Sigma_S(F), \forall p, q \in S, \forall \tau, \tau' \in \Phi : H(p, \tau) \cap H(q, \tau') \neq \emptyset$
- *Completeness.* Eventually, every list of processes trusted by every correct process contains only correct processes: $\forall F \in \mathcal{E}, \forall H \in \Sigma_S(F), \forall p \in S \cap correct(F), \exists \tau \in \Phi, \forall \tau' > \tau \in \Phi : H(p, \tau') \subseteq correct(F)$

Failure detector Σ introduced in [6,8] is simply Σ_Π.

In the following, we state a result on a register shared by the processes of a subset S, and denoted by $S-$register: the *read()* and *write()* operations can only be invoked by the processes in S. (The sequential specification of a register stipulates that the *read()* returns the last value *written*.) The proof of this proposition is in [7].

Proposition 1. Σ_S is the weakest failure detector to implement a $S-$register.

3.2 Failure Detector Ω_S

Given any subset S of processes in Π, failure detector Ω_S outputs at any time and at any process, one process called the *leader*, such that the following property is satisfied:

- *Unique eventual leader:* $\forall F \in \mathcal{E}, \forall H \in \Omega_S(F), \exists l \in correct(F), \exists \tau \in \Phi, \forall \tau' > \tau, \forall x \in correct(F) \cap S, H(x, \tau') = \{l\}$

Intuitively, the guarantee here is that all processes inside S eventually get the same correct leader. Processes outside S might never get the same leader. However, the leader process that is output does not need to be in S: it can be any process in Π. Failure detector Ω corresponds to Ω_Π.

We state now a result on the consensus type (an abstraction of the consensus problem) shared by the processes of a subset S, denoted by $S-$consensus: the *propose()* operation can only be invoked by the processes of S. (The sequential specification of consensus stipulates that all *propose()* operations return the first value proposed.) The proof of this proposition is in [7].

Proposition 2. $\Sigma_S * \Omega_S$ is the weakest failure detector to implement $S-$consensus.

4   From k-consensus to $(k+1)$-consensus

To prove our main result on the weakest failure detector to implement types with a given consensus number k, we address the question of the weakest failure detector to implement k-process consensus (we simply write k-consensus). In short, an algorithm implements k-consensus if it implements S-consensus for any subset S of size k. We show that, for any k s.t. $1 < k < n$, the weakest failure detector to implement k-consensus is also the weakest to implement $(k+1)$-consensus.

To prove this, we go through intermediate results about the composition, over a family of subsets S, of all Σ_S and of all Ω_S.

The following proposition is a direct consequence of the definitions:

Proposition 3. *Let S be any subset of Π and let $\mathcal{L}$ be any family of subsets of S such that, for all $p, q \in S$, there exists some set $L \in \mathcal{L}$ such that p and q belong to L. We have: $\Sigma_S \equiv *\{\Sigma_X | X \in \mathcal{L}\}$.*

An interesting particular case is where subsets X are pairs, i.e., for any $S \subseteq \Pi$, $\Sigma_S \equiv *\{\Sigma_{\{p,q\}} | p, q \in S\}$. The composition of all Σ_S, over all subsets S of size 2, is in this case Σ:

Corollary 1. *For all $S \subseteq \Pi$, $\Sigma_S \equiv *\{\Sigma_{\{p,q\}} | p, q \in S\}$.*

Concerning Ω_S, we get the following:

Proposition 4. *Let $\mathcal{L}$ be any family of subsets of Π such that, for all $p, q \in \Pi$, there exists some $L \in \mathcal{L}$ such that $p \in L$ and $q \in L$. $\Omega \equiv *\{\Omega_L | L \in \mathcal{L}\}$.*

Proof. As Ω is also Ω_L for every $L \subseteq \Pi$, we directly get: $*\{\Omega_L | L \in \mathcal{L}\} \preceq \Omega$.

The opposite inequality is more involved.

Consider a run R with a failure pattern F, and let τ_0 be a time such that (1) after time τ_0 no more process crashes and (2) the output of failure detectors Ω_L, $L \in \mathcal{L}$, does not change after τ_0.

In the following, we show how to implement failure detector $\Diamond S$, which is equivalent to Ω [4]. Failure detector $\Diamond S$ outputs subsets of *suspected* processes and ensures: (1) completeness, i.e. eventually every faulty process is permanently suspected by every correct process; and (2) accuracy, i.e. eventually, some correct process is never suspected.

Consider the digraph $G =< V, E >$ for which $V = correct(F)$, and $(p, q) \in E$ if and only if q is leader for p for some Ω_L such that $p \in L$.

Now consider $G' =< V', E' >$ the digraph of the strongly connected component of G: V' is the set of strongly connected components of G and $(C, C') \in E'$ if and only if there is at least one $p \in C$ and one $q \in C'$ such that $(p, q) \in E$. We say that $C \in V'$ is a *sink* if there is no edge going out of C: note that this means that (a) if p belongs to some sink S, and $(p, q) \in E$ then $q \in S$.

First, there exists at least one sink in G'. Indeed, assume the contrary and let C_0 be any vertex in G'; by induction, we construct a sequence (C_u) $(u > 0)$ of vertices such that (i) $(C_{u-1}, C_u) \in E'$ and (ii) $C_{u-1} \neq C_u$. As we assume that there is no sink, this sequence is infinite. Moreover this sequence is cycle free: if $C_u = C_m$ for some $m < u$, then a direct induction proves that all C_k ($m \leq k \leq u$) are the same strongly connected component contradicting (ii). This implies an infinite number of different C_i contradicting the fact that G is finite.

Consider process p in some C, and process q in some sink S. By definition of $\mathcal{L}$, there is at least one L of $\mathcal{L}$ such that p and q both belong to L. By (a), l, the common leader for p and q, belongs to S. Proving that (b) for every p and every sink S, there exists a process $l \in S$ such that $(p, l) \in E$.

Moreover, let S and S' be two sinks, by (b) there is an edge from S to S' and an edge from S' to S in G', proving that S and S' are in the same strongly connected component and then $S = S'$. Hence, there is only one sink in G'. In the following S will denote this unique sink of G'.

In order to implement $\Diamond\mathcal{S}$, each process p proceeds as follows.

Process p maintains (1) a set $Leader_p^p$ of all its leaders, (2) for each q, a set $Leader_p^q$ of the known leaders of q and, (3) a digraph $G_p = <V_p, E_p>$ for which $V_p = \Pi$, and $(k, q) \in E_p$ if and only if $q \in Leader_p^k$ and, (4) $Trust_p$, the output of the emulated failure detector: this output will be the set of processes q such that there is a path from p to q in G_p.

Process p updates its variables as follows:

- $Leader_p^p$ is always the set of processes output as leader from Ω_L for all L on $\mathcal{L}$ such that $p \in L$. p broadcasts forever $Leader_p^p$.
- If p receives from some q a set X of processes, then p replaces $Leader_p^q$ by X.
- $G_p = <V_p, E_p>$ for which $V_p = \Pi$, and $(k, q) \in E_p$ if and only if $q \in Leader_p^k$. Variable $Trust_p$ holds the set of processes q such that there is a path from p to q in G_p. If $Leader_p^p$ or $Leader_p^q$ change, then p computes again G_p and $Trust_p$.

As (1) any change in $Trust$ variables comes from changes in the output of Ω_L's, and (2) no message is lost, there is a time $\tau_1 \geq \tau_0$ after which no variable $Trust_p$ changes.

Consider a correct process p. Observe that if (q, r) is an edge of G_p then r is a leader for q, and hence if q is a correct process then r is correct too. Then by an easy induction, after time τ_1, every process on a path from p in G_p is a correct process and $Trust_p$ contains only correct processes. This proves the *completeness* property of required for $\Diamond\mathcal{S}$.

Observe also that, after time τ_1, for every correct process p, the set of processes q such that there is a path from p to q in G is equal to $Trust_p$. Moreover, if $(x, y) \in E$ then $Trust_y \subseteq Trust_x$ and, by an easy induction, (c) if there is a path from x to y in G then $Trust_y \subseteq Trust_x$. This proves that, if x and y are in the same strongly connected component of G, then $Trust_x = Trust_y$. In particular, for all q in the sink S of G', $Trust_q = S$. By (b) and (c), for every correct process p, $Trust_q \subseteq Trust_p$ for at least one process q in S, therefore $S \subseteq Trust_p$. This proves the *accuracy* property of $\Diamond\mathcal{S}$. Hence we get $\Omega \preceq *\{\Omega_L | L \in \mathcal{L}\}$ and then $\Omega \equiv *\{\Omega_L | L \in \mathcal{L}\}$.

In particular, for the family of subsets of two elements:

Corollary 2. $\Omega \equiv *\{\Omega_{\{p,q\}} | p, q \in \Pi\}$.

It is important to notice a difference here between Proposition 3 and Proposition 4, and this conveys a fundamental difference between Σ and Ω. Consider a strict subset S of Π. If we can implement a $\{p, q\}$-register within every pair $\{p, q\}$ of S, then we can implement a S-register in S. This is not true with $\{p, q\}$-consensus and this follows from the fact that some leaders output by $\Omega_{\{p,q\}}$ might not belong to the set S. We prove the following in [7]:

Proposition 5. *There exists a system of n processes, a non-empty subset of Π, S, an environment $\mathcal{E}$ and a set of failure detectors $\Omega_{\{p,q\}}$, for all p, q in S, such that $\Omega_S \not\equiv_{\mathcal{E}} *\{\Omega_{\{p,q\}} \mid p, q \in S\}$.*

If we restrict ourselves however to the overall set of processes Π, the difference (i.e., the proposition above) does not hold. That is, to implement consensus (resp. a register), it is necessary and sufficient to implement consensus (resp. register) among all subsets of at least two processes.

Corollary 3. *For any $n \geq k \geq 2$, $\Omega \equiv *\{\Omega_S || S| = k\}$ and $\Sigma \equiv *\{\Sigma_S || S| = k\}$.*

Proof. We apply Proposition 3 and Proposition 4 to the family of all subsets of k $(n \geq k \geq 2)$ processes.

We directly get from the previous Corollary and Proposition 2 the following:

Corollary 4. *For every k such that $2 \leq k \leq n$, for any failure detector $\mathcal{D}$, $\mathcal{D}$ implements consensus if and only if $\mathcal{D}$ implements S-consensus for all S such that $|S| = k$.*

It is important to notice again that the previous corollary holds only for consensus, and not for S-consensus if $S \neq \Pi$.

5 Implementing Atomic Object Types

In the following, we will say that types $T_1, \cdots, T_n$ emulate k-consensus if there is an algorithm that uses only instances of types $T_1, \cdots, T_n$ to implements k-consensus.

Proposition 6. *If a type T emulates 2-consensus, then (1) the weakest failure detector to implement T is $\Sigma * \Omega$ and (2) any failure detector that implements T implements any type.*

Proof. Let T be any type emulating 2-consensus. This means that there is an algorithm using T and message passing that implements 2-consensus. Clearly, this algorithm with any failure detector $\mathcal{D}$ implementing T implements 2-consensus too and by Corollary 4 it implements consensus. Then, by Proposition 2 we get: (a) $\Sigma * \Omega \preceq \mathcal{D}$.

Remark that $\Sigma * \Omega$ implements any number of instances of consensus. Hence, using the universality result of consensus [12], we derive that $\Sigma * \Omega$ implements any type. Then by (a) any failure detector that implements T implements any type proving (2). Moreover, as $\Sigma * \Omega$ implements any type, it implements in particular T. Together with (a), this proves (1).

An interesting application of Proposition 6 concerns the environment where $n-1$ process might fail (which we call the wait-free environment) and the notion of consensus number, which we recall now.

In fact, several definitions of the notion of consensus number of a type T (sometimes also called consensus power) have been be considered [13]. All are based on the maximum number k of processes for which there is an algorithm that, using T, emulates k-consensus. The definitions differ on whether or not the implementation can use several instances of T, and whether the type register can also be used. Hierarchy h_1 means one instance and no register, h_1^r means one instance and registers, h_m means many instances, no register, and h_m^r means many instances and many registers.[3]

From Proposition 6, the weakest failure detector to implement type T such that $h_1(T) = 2$ or $h_m(T) = 2$ is $\Sigma * \Omega$. If T is deterministic, we can derive from [3] that $h_m(T) = h_m^r(T)$. Hence we get the following:

Proposition 7. *In the wait-free environment, for every k such that $2 \le k \le n$, $\Sigma * \Omega$ is the weakest failure detector to implement (1) any type T such that $k = h_1(T)$, (1') any type T such that $k = h_m(T)$, (2) any deterministic type T such that $k = h_1^r(T)$, and (2') any deterministic type T such that $k = h_m^r(T)$.*

We finally consider the special case where $n = 2$. In this case, implementing a register is in some sense equivalent to implementing consensus. More precisely, we prove the following:

Proposition 8. *For $n = 2$, $\Sigma \equiv \Sigma * \Omega$.*

Proof. We actually prove a stronger result. We show that for $n = 2$, Σ is equivalent to $\mathcal{S}$ which is a failure detector introduced in [5], and which outputs subsets of *suspected* processes and ensures: (1) completeness, i.e. eventually every faulty process is permanently suspected by every correct process and (2) accuracy, i.e. some correct process is never suspected. As $\mathcal{S}$ implements consensus [5], from proposition 2, we get: $\Sigma \preceq \Sigma * \Omega \preceq \mathcal{S}$. Denote by p_1 and p_2 the two processes of the system. Consider a failure pattern F. If no process crashes in F, then by the *intersection* property of Σ, one correct process is trusted forever by p_1 and p_2. If some process, say p_1, crashes, then by the *completeness* property of Σ, after some time τ, p_2 is the only process trusted by p_2. By the *intersection* property of Σ, p_2 has been trusted forever by p_2. Therefore, in all cases, at least one correct process is never suspected. This proves the *accuracy* property of $\mathcal{S}$. Hence $\mathcal{S} \preceq \Sigma$.

As a direct consequence, we get: for $n = 2$, $\Sigma \equiv \Sigma * \Omega \equiv \mathcal{S}$.

---

[3] We implicitly assume here n-ported types, i.e., every instance of a type has n ports in our system of n processes [13].

6   Concluding Remarks

The question we address in this paper is that of the weakest failure detector to implement atomic object types (of certain consensus numbers) in a message passing system. This question is complementary to the question of the weakest failure detector to solve consensus in a system of n processes, given object types of consensus number $k < n$ [15,17,10]. In this paper, the goal was to actually implement the types themselves.

It would be interesting to determine, for any $k > 1$, the weakest failure detector to implement any type with consensus number k, given any type of consensus number $j < k$. We conjecture that our proof technique could help show that Ω is the weakest failure detector to implement, with register objects (instead of message passing channels), any object type with a consensus number higher than 2. Going from any type with consensus number $k > 2$ to any type with consensus number $j < k < n$ would probably need a combination of our proof technique with that of [10].

Acknowledgments

Comments from Partha Dutta, Petr Kouznetsov, Bastian Pochon, and Michel Raynal helped improve the presentation of this paper.

References

1. P. Attie, R. Guerraoui, P. Kouznetsov, N. Lynch, and S. Rajsbaum. The impossibility of boosting distributed service resilience. In *Proceedings of the 25th International Conference on Distributed Computing Systems*. IEEE Computer Society Press, June 2005.
2. H. Attiya, A. Bar-Noy, and D. Dolev. Sharing memory robustly in message passing systems. *J. ACM*, 42(2):124–142, Jan. 1995.
3. R. A. Bazzi, G. Neiger, and G. L. Peterson. On the use of registers in achieving wait-free consensus. *Distributed Computing*, 10(3):117–127, 1997.
4. T. D. Chandra, V. Hadzilacos, and S. Toueg. The weakest failure detector for solving consensus. *J. ACM*, 43(4):685–722, July 1996.
5. T. D. Chandra and S. Toueg. Unreliable failure detectors for reliable distributed systems. *J. ACM*, 43(2):225–267, Mar. 1996.
6. C. Delporte-Gallet, H. Fauconnier, and R. Guerraoui. Shared memory vs message passing. Technical Report 200377, EPFL Lausanne, 2003.
7. C. Delporte-Gallet, H. Fauconnier, and R. Guerraoui. Implementing atomic objects in a message passing system. Technical report, EPFL Lausanne, 2005.
8. C. Delporte-Gallet, H. Fauconnier, R. Guerraoui, V. Hadzilacos, P. Koutnetzov, and S. Toueg. The weakest failure detectors to solve certain fundamental problems in distributed computing. In *23th ACM Symposium on Principles of Distributed Computing*, July 2004.
9. M. J. Fischer, N. A. Lynch, and M. S. Paterson. Impossibility of distributed consensus with one faulty process. *J. ACM*, 32(2):374–382, Apr. 1985.

10. R. Guerraoui and P. Kouznetsov. On failure detectors and type boosters. In *Proceedings of the 17th International Symposium on Distributed Computing*, LNCS 2848, pages 292–305. Springer-Verlag, 2003.

11. M. Herlihy and J. M. Wing. Linearizability: A correctness condition for concurrent objects. *ACM Trans. Program. Lang. Syst.*, 12(3):463–492, 1990.

12. M. P. Herlihy. Wait-free synchronization. *ACM Trans. Prog. Lang. Syst.*, 13(1):123–149, Jan. 1991.

13. P. Jayanti. On the robustness of herlihy's hierarchy. In *12th ACM Symposium on Principles of Distributed Computing*, pages 145–157, 1993.

14. L. Lamport. On interprocess communication; part I and II. *Distributed Computing*, 1(2):77–101, 1986.

15. W.-K. Lo and V. Hadzilacos. Using failure detectors to solve consensus in asynchronous shared memory systems. In *Proceedings of the 8th International Workshop on Distributed Algorithms*, LNCS 857, pages 280–295, Sept. 1994.

16. M. Loui and H. Abu-Amara. Memory requirements for agreement among unreliable asynchronous processes. *Advances in Computing Research*, 4:163–183, 1987.

17. G. Neiger. Failure detectors and the wait-free hierarchy. In *14th ACM Symposium on Principles of Distributed Computing*, 1995.

Ω Meets Paxos:
Leader Election and Stability Without Eventual Timely Links

Dahlia Malkhi[1], Florin Oprea[2,*], and Lidong Zhou[3]

[1] Microsoft Research Silicon Valley and the Hebrew University of Jerusalem
[2] Department of Electrical and Computer Engineering, Carnegie Mellon University
[3] Microsoft Research Silicon Valley

Abstract. This paper provides a realization of distributed leader election without having any eventual timely links. Progress is guaranteed in the following weak setting: Eventually one process can send messages such that every message obtains f timely responses, where f is a resilience bound. A crucial facet of this property is that the f responders need **not** be fixed, and may change from one message to another. In particular, this means that no specific link needs to remain timely. In the (common) case where $f = 1$, this implies that the FLP impossibility result on consensus is circumvented if one process can at any time communicate in a timely manner with one other process in the system.

The protocol also bears significant practical importance to well-known coordination schemes such as Paxos, because our setting more precisely captures the conditions on the elected leader for reaching timely consensus. Additionally, an extension of our protocol provides leader *stability*, which guarantees against arbitrary demotion of a qualified leader and avoids performance penalties associated with leader changes in schemes such as Paxos.

1   Introduction

A fundamental design guideline pioneered in the Paxos protocol [1] and later employed in numerous coordination protocols is to separate *safety* properties from *liveness* properties. Safety must be preserved at all times, and hence, its implementation must not rely on synchrony assumptions. Liveness, on the other hand, may be hampered during periods of instability, but eventually, when the system resumes normal behavior, progress should be guaranteed. In various coordination protocols such as Paxos, liveness hinges on a separate leader election algorithm, with the problem of finding a good leader election algorithm left open.

It is well known in the theory of distributed computing that liveness of consensus cannot be guaranteed in a purely asynchronous system with no timing assumptions [2]. Ω is known to be the weakest failure detector [3,4] that is sufficient for consensus, hence provides the liveness properties of consensus. Ω

---

* Work done during a summer internship at Microsoft Research Silicon Valley.

P. Fraigniaud (Ed.): DISC 2005, LNCS 3724, pp. 199–213, 2005.

essentially implements an eventual leader election, where all non-faulty processes eventually trust the same non-faulty process as the leader.

While Ω captures the abstract properties needed to provide liveness, it does not say under which pragmatic system conditions is progress guaranteed. It leaves open the interesting questions of what synchrony conditions should be assumed when implementing Ω and what additional properties would yield an ideal leader election algorithm for practical coordination schemes such as Paxos.

A revisit of Paxos. In this paper, rather than cooking up arbitrary synchrony assumptions and additional properties, we derive the desired features of our protocols from Paxos, a cornerstone coordination scheme employed in various reliable storage systems such as Petal [5], Frangipani [6], Chain Replication [7], and Boxwood [8].

At a high level, Paxos is a protocol for a set of processes to reach consensus on a series of proposals. With a leader election algorithm, a process p that is elected leader first carries out the **prepare** phase of the protocol. In this phase, p sends a **prepare** message to all processes to declare the *ballot number* it uses for its proposals, learns about all the existing proposals, and requests promises that no smaller ballot numbers be accepted afterwards. The **prepare** phase is completed once p receives acknowledgments from $n - f$ processes. Once the **prepare** phase is completed, to have a proposal committed, leader p initiates the **accept** phase by sending an **accept** message to all processes with the proposal and the ballot number it declares in the **prepare** phase. The proposal is *committed* when p receives acknowledgments from $f + 1$ processes. Whenever a higher ballot number is encountered in the **prepare** phase or the **accept** phase, the leader has to initiate a new **prepare** phase with an even higher ballot number. This could happen if there are other processes acting as leaders, unavoidable in an asynchronous system.

To implement a replicated state machine, Paxos streamlines a series of consensus decisions. A new leader p carries out the **prepare** phase once for all its proposals. After the completion of the **prepare** phase, p carries out only the **accept** phase for each proposal until a new leader emerges by initiating a new **prepare** phase.

Our goal is to distill the conditions under which Paxos can have new proposals committed in a timely fashion and to provide a leader election protocol exactly under those conditions. Therefore, we make the following observations:

- After an initial **prepare** phase, in order for a leader p to make timely progress, it suffices for p to obtain timely responses for its **accept** message from any set of $f + 1$ processes (or f processes besides itself). The set could change for different **accept** messages.
- Any leader change incurs the cost of an extra round of communication for the **prepare** phase.

Contribution. Complying with the conditions under which we wish to enable progress in Paxos, our leader algorithm features the following two desired properties[1]:

---

[1] Formal definitions of these properties are provided in the body of the paper.

First, the algorithm guarantees to elect a leader without having any eventual timely links. Progress is guaranteed in the following surprisingly weak setting: Eventually one process can send messages such that every message obtains f timely responses, where f is a resilience bound. We name such a process $\Diamond f$-*accessible*. A crucial facet of this property is that the f responders need *not* be fixed, and may change from one message to another. We emphasize that this condition stems from the workings of Paxos, whose safety does not necessitate that the f processes with which a leader interacts be fixed.

Our solution bears the following ramification on the foundations of distributed computing. It implies that the FLP [2] impossibility result on consensus with one failure ($f = 1$) is circumvented if one process can at any time interact in a timely manner with one other process in the system.

No previous leader election protocol provides any guarantee in these settings. In fact, the approach taken in most previous protocols is fundamentally incompatible with this condition, because previous protocols gossip about *suspicions* until the system converges. This does not allow for a leader to communicate at different times with different subsets of the system, as the leader will constantly be under suspicion of some part of the system. Thus, no easy "engineering" of previous protocols can provide progress under the $\Diamond f$-accessibility condition.

The second contribution provided by our algorithm is leader *stability*. This is based on the observation that a leader change necessitates an execution of a **prepare** phase by the new leader, an often costly operation. We therefore embrace the notion of stability that a *qualified* leader not be demoted, where a leader is considered qualified if it remains capable of having proposals committed in a timely fashion. For Paxos, when $n = 2f + 1$ holds, a leader is qualified if it is non-faulty and maintains timely communication with a set of f other processes at all times, with the set possibly changing over time.

An important practical measure for a leader election protocol is its communication complexity [9]. It is desirable that under a *steady state*, where a qualified leader operates without being suspected by any other process, only the leader incurs periodic communication with the rest of the system (hence achieving $O(n)$ steady-state link-utilization communication complexity.) In Section 6, we sketch an extension of our protocol that achieves this ideal. This extension works only with the basic version of our protocol for Ω, which does not uphold stability. It is left as an open question whether a stable leader election algorithm with $O(n)$ steady-state message complexity exists under the condition of $\Diamond f$ accessibility.

2   Related Work

Our review of previous work concentrates on the two properties of interest to us: synchrony conditions and leader stability.

On synchrony conditions. A simple solution for the leader election problem is as follows [1,10]. Periodically send alive messages from all to all, and let each process collect data on all the processes it heard from within the last broadcast period. Each process elects as leader the process with the lowest process *id* from its view. This implementation requires that eventually all n^2 communication links become timely with a known communication bound.

A number of papers [11,9] relax this by assuming an *unknown* communication bound. The reduction to the known bound model involves gradually increasing timeout periods until no false alarms incur on the current leader. This "trick" may be used in almost all leader-election protocols, as is done, e.g., in [11,9,12,13,14,15]. Nevertheless, all communication links are required to be eventually synchronous.

Aguilera et al. further relaxes the model to one that has a process maintaining eventually timely links with the rest of system [12] and to one that has a process whose outgoing links to the rest of the system are eventually timely [13]. In [13], a single correct process called ◇-source is assumed to have outgoing non-lossy and timely links eventually . Their protocol works by processes sending accusation messages to one another when they timeout. Intuitively, every process converges on the suspicions of the ◇-source process, since its accusations are guaranteed to arrive timely at their destinations.

More recently, and most relevant to our work, there are several pieces of work that require surprisingly weak synchrony conditions for implementing Ω and consensus. This line of work limits the scope of timely links from the correct pivot process to only a subset of the system. There are two main flavors, one deals with failure-detection abstractions without explicit mentioning of synchrony conditions, and the second builds directly over partial synchrony conditions. We start with the first approach, which historically precedes the second.

The work of [16,17] introduces the notion of *limited scope failure detectors*, where the scope of the accuracy property of an unreliable failure detector is defined with respect to a parameter (x) as the minimum number of processes that must not erroneously suspect a correct process to have crashed. This yields failure detector classes S_x (respectively, $\Diamond S_x$), whose accuracy properties are required to hold only on a subset of the processes whose size is x. The usual failure detectors S (respectively, $\Diamond S$) implicitly consider a scope equal to the total number of processes. A limited-scope detector in the classes S_k or $\Diamond S_k$ is straight-forward to implement using periodic alive messages and timeouts, given a system in which one correct process (eventually) has x outgoing timely links. Therefore, under these conditions, a possible construction of Ω is to as follows: first implement $\Diamond S_x$; then transform $\Diamond S_x$ to $\Diamond S$ [14]; finally transform $\Diamond S$ to Ω [18].

Aguilera et al. [15] adopts a more direct approach. Define a process p to be a $\Diamond f$-source if eventually it has f outgoing links that are timely. Any of the f recipient endpoints of these links may be faulty. Assuming a bound f on the number of crashed processes, Aguilera et al. [15] presents an Ω construction with the existence of one correct $\Diamond f$-source. The protocol counts suspicions of processes about all other processes and exchanges vectors of suspicion-counters. Each process elects as leader the process with the lowest suspicion counter, breaking ties by process *ids*. Intuitively, the suspicion counters of crashed processes grow indefinitely, whereas the $\Diamond f$-source has a guaranteed bounded suspicion-counter. This guarantees that eventually a correct process is elected as leader (among all the ones whose counters are bounded), and furthermore, it remains so permanently because all counters are non-decreasing.

Both the S_f condition and the $\Diamond f$-source condition are neither weaker nor stronger than ours: Let p denote, respectively, the pivot correct process that upholds any of these models. The $\Diamond f$-source assumption and the $\Diamond S_f$ accuracy assumption require timeliness only on f *outgoing* links from p, and no correctness of the f recipients. Our $\Diamond f$-accessible assumption requires f bi-directional timely links from p, as well as correctness from the f recipients, which are stronger assumptions. However, in $\Diamond f$-source, the set of f links is *fixed* throughout the execution, as is the limited-scope subset of $\Diamond S_f$, whereas $\Diamond f$-accessible allows the f links to vary in time, which is a weaker assumption.

Although formally these models are incomparable, we note that our assumptions are strongly motivated by practical needs, particularly those of the Paxos protocol. In Paxos, if there is a single leader, the leader can carry out the **accept** phase and make progress so long as it is able to communicate with f processes. This is exactly the condition under which our Ω implementation is guaranteed to operate. In particular, the leader may in realistic settings have a "moving set" of f timely links. But so long as at any moment, some set of f links are timely, our protocol can guarantee progress. Under these conditions, the $\Diamond f$-source assumption does not hold, nor does $\Diamond S_f$, and the protocols of [14,15] may fail.

Leader stability. The only previous work we are aware of that considers some form of leader stability is the protocol of Aguilera et al. [12]. Their notion of stability relates to a leader that is recognized by all non-faulty processes as leader. For practical consensus protocols such as Paxos, this condition might have limited value, because no process inside the system can know when a leader is known to all others. In Paxos, a process must know whether it is a leader in order to decide whether to initiate the **prepare** phase. Therefore, our stability condition uses the leader's own perspective as the determining time to when its leadership stabilizes. This is what Paxos needs to avoid having leaders being arbitrarily de-crowned due to unnecessary **prepare** messages.

3   Informal Model

The system consists of a set P of n processes, each pair of which can directly communicate by sending and receiving messages over a bi-directional link. Each process is equipped with a drift-free local clock. Clocks of different processes need not be synchronized. When we reason about the system, we often use a global wall-clock t, which is not known or used by the processes within the system.

Each process executes a sequence of steps triggered either by message reception or timer expiration. In a step, a process may perform any number of local computations, send messages, and set timers. For simplicity, we denote the time it takes to perform a step as zero.

Process and Communication Faults. Processes may fail by crashing permanently, and otherwise are non-faulty. A failure pattern F_p is a function from wall clock time to sets of processes that have crashed by that time. We say that p is non-faulty at time t if $p \notin F_p(t)$. We say that p is non-faulty if it is always non-faulty. There is a known resilience bound $f \leq \lfloor \frac{n-1}{2} \rfloor$ on the number of crashed processes.[2]

Communication links are reliable, in the sense that no message from a non-faulty process can be dropped, duplicated, or changed, and no messages are generated by the links.

Communication Synchrony. The conditions regarding timeliness of links are at the heart of our investigation. There is a known upper bound δ on the round-trip delay of messages, but it does not hold on all pairs of processes at all times. What is known is that eventually there is one process that is able to exchange messages within the δ delay with f other processes. We will now make this notion precise.

Definition 1. *Let $\overline{(p, q)}$ denote the communication link between p and q. We say that $\overline{(p, q)}$ is timely at time t if any message sent by p to q at time t receives a response within δ time. Note that if q becomes faulty before handling p's message, or q is slow to respond, then by definition the link is not timely.*

Definition 2. *A process $p \in P$ is said to be f-accessible at time t if there exist f other processes q such that the links $\overline{(p, q)}$ are timely at t.*

Our synchrony requirement is the following.

Definition 3. *($\Diamond f$-accessibility) There is a time t and a process p such that for all $t' \geq t$, p is f-accessible at t'.*

Note that the definition of f-accessibility allows a process p to be considered f-accessible even if the sets of f processes accessed by p at different times change. This property is fundamentally more practical than fixing a subset with which p must interact forever. This definition is derived from the way consensus protocols like Paxos [1] and revolving-coordinator consensus [3] operate.

We also note that there are several known ways to weaken our model with variations that bear practical importance. First, it is easy to extend the model to account for a non-zero bound on local processing time and clock drifts, but this would just be a syntactic burden. Second, it is possible to relax the assumption that the communication round-trip bound δ is a priori known. The trick for overcoming this uncertainty is to start with an aggressively-low guess of δ and gradually increase it when premature expirations are encountered. Most of the

---

[2] It is easy to generalize the discussion to use *quorum systems* instead of counting processes. A *read/write quorum system* for P, denoted $\mathcal{R}(P), \mathcal{W}(P) \subseteq 2^P$, is a pair of sets of subsets of P, such that every pair $Q_1 \in \mathcal{W}(P), Q_2 \in \mathcal{W}(P) \cup \mathcal{R}(P)$ has a non-empty intersection, $Q_1 \cap Q_2 \neq \emptyset$. Each subset is called a *quorum*. Quorums generalize thresholds as follows. Operations on $(f+1)$-subsets are replaced with operations on write quorums; operations on $(n - f)$-subsets are replaced with operations on read quorums.

claims in this paper can be adapted to reflect this technique of learning δ. For simplicity, we omit this from the discussion. Finally, our non-timely reliable links may be easily replaced with fair lossy-links as in [15], which are links that deliver infinitely many times any message-type that has been sent infinitely often. This requires repeatedly sending messages until acknowledged, and once again, is omitted from the discussion.

Problem statement. Our goal is to construct in our model a weak leader Ω, defined as follows [3]: Ω provides every process q at any time t with a local hint $\Omega_q(t)$, such that the following holds:

Definition 4 (Ω). *There exist a time t and a non-faulty process p, such that for any $t' \geq t$, every process q that is not faulty at time t' has $\Omega_q(t') = p$.*

4 Ω with $\Diamond f$-Accessibility

Our first protocol implements Ω under the $\Diamond f$-accessibility condition. The protocol for process p appears in Figure 1. It works as follows.

Each process maintains for itself a non-decreasing *epoch number*, as well as an *epoch freshness counter*. Epochs are implemented using the following data types and variables. An epoch number is a pair that consists of an integer field named *serialNum* and another field named *processId*, which stores either a process *id* or null. We assume a total ordering on process *ids* with null smaller than any process *id*. Epoch numbers are ordered lexicographically, first by *serialNum* and then by *processId*.

We define a state to be a pair consisting of an epoch-number field named *epochNum* and an integer field named *freshness*. States are ordered lexicographically, first by *epochNum* and then by *freshness*.

A process refreshes its epoch number in fixed periodicity of length Δ, by incrementing the epoch freshness counter and writing it to its *registry*, which is replicated on all processes in the system. If the refresh fails to complete updating the registry at $f+1$ processes within the known δ round-trip bound, the process increases its own epoch number. The vector *registry*[] records locally at each process the latest state it received from others: *registry*[q] is updated upon receipt of a refresh message from q.

Process p records the states it reads of all other processes in a vector named *views*[]. A process updates its view by periodically reading the entire registry vector from $n - f$ processes. Each entry *views*[q] has two fields. One is a *state* field, and the other is a bit called *expired* indicating whether q's state has been continuously refreshed or not. Initially, all *serialNum* and *freshness* fields are zeroed, and *expired* field set to true.

The idea is to select as a leader the process with the lowest non-expired epoch number (breaking ties using process *ids*). To assess whether an epoch number has expired or not, every process reads the registry of all processes from $n - f$ processes periodically. The exact period between the completion of a previous read and the start of the next must be at least $\Delta + \delta$ to guarantee that every process has had a chance to refresh its registry at least once between reads. If a process p detects no change in another process q's counter, p expires q's epoch number and no longer considers q a contender for leadership until a new epoch is detected for q.

The intuition behind the success of the protocol is as follows. First, unless a process always manages to write its registry to f other processes within δ time units after some point, its epoch number will increase indefinitely or will be considered expired (e.g., when it fails).

Second, consider a process p that after a certain time t always manages to write its registry to f other processes within δ. It follows that eventually p stops increasing its epoch number. Note that this is true for any $\Diamond f$-accessible process. Let p be the process whose epoch number stops increasing at the lowest value in the system. Denote that lowest epoch number as e_p. The timely refreshing of e_p makes it eventually known as p's epoch by all non-faulty processes. Observe that e_p never expires at any other process, because p succeeds in refreshing e_p's freshness counter every Δ time period. Furthermore, eventually all higher epoch numbers either become known to all non-faulty processes, or belong to processes whose (lower) epoch numbers expire. Hence, eventually all other processes will consider p leader.

The protocol also makes use of monotonically increasing counters, such as *refreshNum* and *readNum*, to associate responses with requests. These counters are initialized to 0. Variables *epochStartTime* and *lastCompletedReadStartTime* are introduced for later use, when the protocol is extended for stability in Section 5.

Process p also has a variable *leader* : $P \cup$ null, that captures p's view of the current leader. *leader* is initially set to null. $\Omega_p(t)$ is thus defined to be the value of *leader*$_p$ on process p at time t. The correctness proof showing that the protocol in Figure 1 implements Ω appears in the full version of this paper [19].

5   Stability

Driven by our need to employ Ω within repeated consensus instances of the Paxos protocol, we now introduce a crucial addition to Ω.

The definition of Ω mandates that eventually a single leader stabilizes and is never replaced. However, it allows many leaders to be replaced many times until that time arrives. This is undesirable in many respects. In Paxos, replacing a leader is a costly operation. The new leader needs to perform an extra round of communication in order to collect information about the latest actions of the previous leader. In many other settings, electing a new leader involves heavy re-configuration procedures, which should be avoided if possible.

We therefore would like to require that a qualified leader (e.g., a $\Diamond f$-accessible leader) never be demoted. To this end, we first need to define precisely what it means for a process to be a leader. Our definition is simple and is grounded in practice: A process p is a leader at time t if it considers itself a leader at time t. More precisely, we have the following simple definition:

Start `refreshTimer` with Δ time units; Start `readTimer` with $\Delta + \delta$ time units;

REFRESH:
    Upon `refreshTimer` timeout: /* time to refresh the registry */
        start `refreshTimer` with Δ time units;
        $ackMsgCount := 0$; $refreshNum$ ++;
        send $\langle$refresh$, p, registry[p], refreshNum \rangle$ to every $q \in P$;
        start `roundTripTimer` with δ time units;

    Upon receiving $\langle$refresh$, q, rg, rn \rangle$:
        if $(registry[q] < rg)$ $registry[q] := rg$; send to q $\langle$ack$, p, q, rn \rangle$; **end if**

    Upon receiving $\langle$ack$, q, p, rn = refreshNum \rangle$:
        if $(++ackMsgCount \geq f + 1)$
            stop `roundTripTimer`; $registry[p].freshness$ ++;
        end if

ADVANCE EPOCH:
    Upon `roundTripTimer` timeout: /* no timely links to a quorum */
        $views[p].expired :=$ **true**; $registry[p].epochNum.serialNum$ ++;
        $epochStartTime :=$ **currentTime**;

COLLECT:
    Upon `readTimer` timeout: /* time to read the registries */
        $lastReadStartTime :=$ **currentTime**; $readNum$ ++;
        $statusMsgCount := 0$; $oldViews := views$; /* store for comparison */
        send $\langle$collect$, p, readNum \rangle$ to every $q \in P$;

    Upon receiving $\langle$collect$, q, rn \rangle$: send to q $\langle$status$, p, q, rn, registry \rangle$;

    Upon receiving $\langle$status$, q, p, rn = readNum, qReg \rangle$:
        for each $r \in P$ $views[r].state := \mathtt{max}(qReg[r], views[r].state)$; **end for**
        if $(++statusMsgCount \geq n - f)$ /* responses from a quorum collected */
            $lastCompletedReadStartTime := lastReadStartTime$;
            for every $r \in P$ /* check if r has refreshed its epoch number */
                if $(views[r].state \leq oldViews[r].state)$ $views[r].expired :=$ **true**; **end if**
                if $(views[r].state.epochNum > oldViews[r].state.epochNum)$
                    $views[r].expired :=$ **false**;
                end if
            end for
            $leaderEpoch := \mathtt{min}(\{views[q].state.epochNum \mid views[q].expired = \mathtt{false}\}$
            $\cup \{\langle 0, \mathtt{null} \rangle\})$;
            $leader := leaderEpoch.processId$; start `readTimer` with $\Delta + \delta$ time units;
        end if

Fig. 1. Ω with $\diamond f$-accessibility

Definition 5. *Process p is a leader at time t iff $\Omega_p(t) = p$.*

Intuitively, this definition is desirable because, once p considers itself a leader, it takes actions as leader and may incur any cost mentioned earlier associated with leadership. Leader stability is then defined simply as follows:

Definition 6 (Leader Stability:). *Let p be a leader at time t, and assume that p is f-accessible during the period $[t - \delta, t + \tau]$. We say that a protocol implementing Ω satisfies leader stability at time $t+\tau$ if p is still a leader at time $t + \tau$, and no other process $q \neq p$ is a leader at time $t + \tau$.*

Ω with Stability

In this section, we introduce changes to the above protocol in order to provide for leader stability. In order for these changes to work, however, we require $n = 2f + 1$.[3]

In the protocol of Figure 1, p considers itself a leader immediately when p sets $leader_p$ to p; that is, when p's current epoch number is the lowest non-expired epoch number in p's view. This is insufficient; the scenario that disrupts stability is as follows. Suppose a process p becomes a leader at time t because its current epoch number e_p is the lowest non-expired epoch number in its view at t. In the meantime, another process q times out on an epoch number $e_q < e_p - 1$ and advances to a new epoch number $e_q + 1 < e_p$. If q now becomes f-accessible, $e_q + 1$ will eventually become the lowest epoch number, demoting leader p even if p has been f-accessible; leader stability is thus violated.

To achieve stability, for a process p to become a leader, we not only require that p's epoch number be the lowest non-expired epoch number in p's view, but further require that p declare itself a leader only after making sure that no non-expired lower epoch number will cause other processes to claim leadership. This can be achieved by the following two extensions to the first protocol:

1. Whenever a process initiates a new epoch number, rather than incrementing the epoch number by 1, it learns the highest existing epoch number through a timely communication (with bound δ) with $n - f$ processes and then picks an epoch number that is higher than any existing epoch number.
2. Process p not only checks whether its current epoch number is the lowest in its current view, but also waits for sufficiently long to ensure that all non-expiring epoch numbers that can be lower than e_p must have been reflected in p's view.

   To be precise, let t be the time when the current epoch number e_p is chosen, a process p has to wait until the completion of a collect/status round that starts at least $2\Delta + 3\delta$ time units after time t. This is because a non-faulty and f-accessible p will start its first refresh for e_p at $t + \Delta$ and receive $f + 1$ responses before $t + \Delta + \delta$. In order for another process q to pick an epoch

---

[3] Alternatively, we could require that an accessible process have timely links to $n - f$ processes, rather than $f + 1$ processes.

Start `refreshTimer` with Δ time units; Start `readTimer` with $\Delta + \delta$ time units;

REFRESH: same as in Figure 1

ADVANCE EPOCH:

    Upon initialization or `roundTripTimer` timeout:
        /* no timely links to a quorum, retrieving existing epoch numbers */
        stop `refreshTimer`;
        $refreshNum$ ++; $isLeader :=$ `false`; $views[p].expired :=$ `true`;
        $epochCount := 0$;
        $globalMaxEn := registry[p].epochNum$;
        $seqNum$ ++;
        send $\langle$getEpochNum$, p, seqNum\rangle$ to each process $q \in P$;
        start `getEpochTimer` with δ time units;

    Upon `getEpochTimer` timeout: /* no timely links to a quorum, retry */
        $seqNum$ ++;
        $epochCount := 0$;
        $globalMaxEn := registry[p].epochNum$;
        send $\langle$getEpochNum$, p, seqNum\rangle$ to each process $q \in P$;
        start `getEpochTimer` with δ time units;

    Upon receiving $\langle$getEpochNum$, q, sn\rangle$:
        $localMaxEn :=$max$\{registry[r].epochNum \mid r \in P\}$;
        send to q $\langle$retEpochNum$, p, q, sn, localMaxEn\rangle$;

    Upon receiving $\langle$retEpochNum$, q, p, sn = seqNum, en\rangle$:
        if $(en > globalMaxEn)$ $globalMaxEn := en$; **end if**
        if $(++epochCount \geq n - f)$ /* epoch numbers from a quorum collected */
        $registry[p].serialNum := globalMaxEn.serialNum + 1$;
        $epochStartTime :=$ `currentTime`;
        start `refreshTimer` with Δ time units;
        end if

COLLECT: same as in Figure 1

BECOME LEADER:

    Upon change to $lastCompletedReadStartTime$
        if $(leaderEpoch = registry[p].epochNum \wedge$
        $lastCompletedReadStartTime - epochStartTime \geq 2\Delta + 3\delta)$
        $isLeader :=$ `true`;
        end if

Fig. 2. Stable Leader Election Protocol with $\Diamond f$-accessibility

number e_q lower than e_p, q must have started the (timely) communication to learn existing epoch numbers before $t + \Delta + \delta$ and then started epoch e_q at $t + \Delta + 2\delta$; otherwise, due to $n - f + f + 1 > n$, one of the $n - f$ processes reporting existing epoch numbers will be among the $t + 1$ that know e_p and will report an epoch number that is e_p or higher. If q never expires e_q, then it will complete its refresh for e_q at $t + 2\Delta + 3\delta$. Any collect/status round after $t + 2\Delta + 3\delta$ will reflect e_q; therefore, e_p is not the lowest non-expired epoch and p will not become a leader.

To capture the condition under which a process considers itself a leader, we introduce, in addition to variable $leader_p$, a boolean local variable $isLeader_p$ for each process p and define Ω_p as follows:

$$\Omega_p := \begin{cases} p & isLeader_p = \texttt{true} \\ leader_p & leader_p \neq p \wedge leader_p \neq \texttt{null} \\ \texttt{null} & \text{otherwise} \end{cases}$$

The full protocol is given in Figure 2. The correctness proofs appear in the full version of this paper [19].

6   Reducing Message Complexity

As suggested in [9], a crucial measure of communication complexity is the number of links that are utilized infinitely often in the protocol. Our protocols use all-to-all communication infinitely often to keep leader information up to date, hence employ $O(n^2)$ infinite-utilization links.

For the protocol in Figure 1, the steady-state communication complexity can be reduced to $O(n)$, where in a steady state there exists a unique f-accessible leader that is never suspected by any non-faulty process. We briefly sketch the required changes here. The full paper [19] contains a precise protocol description and its correctness proof.

The first change is related to the refreshing of epoch numbers. A process p that is not currently the leader need not refresh its own epoch number; it can simply let it become *inactive*, since it is not contending for the leadership. Therefore, we disable the periodic refresh at p when it is not a leader. A process increments its epoch number only when it experiences a roundTripTimer timeout, as in the original protocol, and may "revive" an inactive epoch number when becoming a leader.

The second change is related to the monitoring of epoch numbers in the system. In a steady state, there is no reason for a process p to monitor the states of all other processes. Therefore, we disable periodic collect altogether.

A process p that does not obtain any refresh message carrying the current presumed leader's epoch number for some timeout period suspects that the current leader has failed. Likewise, a process p that hears a refresh message carrying a lower epoch number than the current presumed leader's epoch number assumes that it does not have up-to-date information about the current leader .

In these two cases (only), a process activates the collect procedure twice, where the second one is activated at least $\Delta + \delta$ time units after the first one completes, as in the original protocol. Process p then determines the lowest active epoch number and compares it with its current epoch number. If p's current epoch number is no higher than the lowest active epoch number, p becomes a leader and activates refresh periodically as in the original protocol. Otherwise, p will consider the process owning the lowest epoch number as the leader and expect to receive refresh messages from that process periodically.

The intuition behind the success of the modified protocol is somewhat similar to our original protocol, but with crucial differences. As before, consider a process p that, after a certain time t, always manages to write its registry to f other processes within δ. It follows that eventually p stops increasing its epoch number. Note that this is true for any $\Diamond f$-accessible process.

Now, consider a non-crashed process q with the lowest current epoch number in the system. If q is not the leader yet, then q believes that there exists a lower active epoch number than its own. Because such an epoch number no longer exists, eventually q times out on that epoch number and performs two collects. Because its epoch number is the lowest among the non-crashed processes, it will learn that its epoch number is no higher than the lowest active epoch number in the system and become a leader. If q is not $\Diamond f$-accessible, eventually it will fail updating its own freshness counter and will increase its epoch number.

Together, we have that, on the one hand, the $\Diamond f$-accessible processes stop increasing their epoch numbers. On the other hand, any non $\Diamond f$-accessible process either crashes or increases its own epoch number to be higher than the lowest epoch number in the system. As before, the process p whose epoch stops increasing at the lowest value in the system becomes a permanent leader.

In terms of message complexity, once an f-accessible leader is elected and all processes receive its refresh messages without suspecting the leader, eventually all non-leader processes stop refreshing their epochs and stop reading, hence the communication complexity drops to $O(n)$.

7   Discussion

The condition we introduced to uphold stability in this paper, namely $n = 2f+1$, is stronger than what is required in practice. It is worth noting that, for both Paxos and our stable leader election protocol, it suffices for a leader p to interact in a timely fashion *once* with $n - f$ processes. Subsequently, p can maintain its leadership and proceed with consensus decisions, provided that it can interact at any time with $f + 1$ processes.

Stability also appears to be in conflict with the ability to reduce the steady-state message complexity to $O(n)$. Intuitively, the reduced message complexity forces a process to decide whether to become a leader based on less accurate information, thereby creating opportunities for unnecessary demotion. For example, in our protocol, to ensure stability, a process becomes a leader only when it is certain that no process can have a lower active epoch number. This is hard because epoch numbers can remain inactive (and unknown to other processes) before they are revived. It is left as an open question whether a stable leader protocol exists under $\Diamond f$-accessibility with $O(n)$ steady-state message complexity.

8   Conclusion

It is our firm belief that leader election algorithms that implement Ω should be studied in the context of practical coordination schemes that realize consensus. This paper makes two contributions toward this goal.

First, it contributes to the study of weak synchrony conditions that enable leader election. $\Diamond f$-accessibility, the synchrony condition we require, is new and surprisingly weak, in that it requires no eventual timely links. It is incomparable to (but also not stronger than) previously known conditions for leader election. The condition is derived by our observations on Paxos, leading to an implementation of Ω under f-accessibility.

Second, it provides practical and stable leader election protocol that eliminates unnecessary and potentially expensive leader changes. The paper therefore provides Paxos with a "good" leader election protocol; this was left as an open problem in Lamport's original Paxos paper [1].

References

1. Lamport, L.: The part-time parliament. ACM Transactions on Computer Systems **16** (1998) 133–169
2. Fischer, M.J., Lynch, N.A., Paterson, M.S.: Impossibility of distributed consensus with one faulty process. Journal of the ACM **32** (1985) 374–382
3. Chandra, T.D., Toueg, S.: Unreliable failure detectors for reliable distributed systems. Journal of the ACM **43** (1996) 225–267
4. Chandra, T.D., Hadzilacos, V., Toueg, S.: The weakest failure detector for solving consensus. Journal of the ACM **43** (1996) 685–722
5. Lee, E.K., Thekkath, C.: Petal: Distributed virtual disks. In: Proceedings of the 7th International Conference on Architectural Support for Programming Languages and Operating Systems (ASPLOS 1996). (1996) 84–92
6. Thekkath, C., Mann, T., Lee, E.K.: Frangipani: A scalable distributed file system. In: proceedings of the 16th ACM Symposium on Operating Systems Principles (SOSP 1997). (1997) 224–237
7. van Renesse, R., Schneider, F.B.: Chain replication for supporting high throughput and availability. In: Proceedings of the 6th Usenix Symposium on Operating System Design and Implementation (OSDI 2004). (2004) 91–104
8. MacCormick, J., Murphy, N., Najork, M., Thekkath, C.A., Zhou, L.: Boxwood: Abstractions as the foundation for storage infrastructure. In: Proceedings of the 6th Usenix Symposium on Operating System Design and Implementation (OSDI 2004). (2004) 105–120

9. Larrea, M., Fernndez, A., Arvalo, S.: Optimal implementation of the weakest failure detector for solving consensus. In: Proceedings of the 19th IEEE Symposium on Reliable Distributed Systems (SRDS 2000). (2000) 52–59

10. Prisco, R.D., Lampson, B., Lynch, N.: Revisiting the Paxos algorithm. In: Proceedings of the 11th Workshop on Distributed Algorithms(WDAG). (1997) 11–125

11. Larrea, M., Arvalo, S., Fernndez, A.: Efficient algorithms to implement unreliable failure detectors in partially synchronous systems. In: Proceedings of the 13th International Symposium on Distributed Computing (DISC 1999). (1999) 34–48

12. Aguilera, M., Delporte-Gallet, C., Fauconnier, H., Toueg, S.: Stable leader election. In: Proceedings of the 15th International Symposium on Distributed Computing (DISC 2001). (2001)

13. Aguilera, M.K., Delporte-Gallet, C., Fauconnier, H., Toueg, S.: On implementing Omega with weak reliability and synchrony assumptions. In: Proceedings of the Twenty-Second Annual ACM Symposium on Principles of Distributed Computing (PODC 2003), ACM Press (2003) 306–314

14. Anceaume, E., Fernndez, A., Mostefaoui, A., Neiger, G., Raynal, M.: A necessary and sufficient condition for transforming limited accuracy failure detectors. J. Comput. Syst. Sci. **68** (2004) 123–133

15. Aguilera, M.K., Delporte-Gallet, C., Fauconnier, H., Toueg, S.: Communication-efficient leader election and consensus with limited link synchrony. In: Proceedings of the 23rd Annual ACM Symposium on Principles of Distributed Computing (PODC 2004), ACM Press (2004) 328–337

16. Yang, J., Neiger, G., Gafni, E.: Structured derivations of consensus algorithms for failure detectors. In: Proceedings of the 17th Annual ACM Symposium on Principles of Distributed Computing (PODC 1998). (1998) 297–308

17. Mostefaoui, A., Raynal, M.: Unreliable failure detectors with limited scope accuracy and an application to consensus. In: Proceedings of the 19th International Conference on Foundations of Software Technology and Theoretical Computer Science (FST&TCS99), Springer-Verlag LNCS #1738 (1999) 329–340

18. Chu, F.: Reducing Ω to $\Diamond W$. Information Processing Letters **67** (1998) 298–293

19. Malkhi, D., Oprea, F., Zhou, L.: Omega meets Paxos: Leader election and stability without eventual timely links. Technical Report MSR-TR-2005-93, Microsoft Research, Redmond, WA (2005)

Plausible Clocks with Bounded Inaccuracy

Brad T. Moore and Paolo A.G. Sivilotti

The Ohio State University, Columbus OH 43210, USA
{mooreb, paolo}@cse.ohio-state.edu

Abstract. In a distributed system with N processes, time stamps of size N (such as vector clocks) are necessary to accurately track potential causality between events. Plausible clocks are a family of time-stamping schemes that use smaller time stamps at the expense of some accuracy. To date, all plausible clocks have been designed to use fixed-sized time stamps, and the inaccuracy of these schemes varies from run to run. In this paper, we define a new metric, imprecision, that formally characterizes the fidelity of a plausible clock. We present a new plausible clock system that guarantees an arbitrary constant bound on imprecision. This bound is achieved by allowing time stamps to grow and shrink over the course of the computation. We verify the correctness of our algorithm, present results of a simulation study, and evaluate its performance.

1 Introduction

The events of a distributed system can be ordered by potential causality: whether one event might have affected another. Determining this ordering between events is of fundamental importance to a variety of distributed algorithms. For example, a global snapshot consists of a set of events such that no pair is causally related [1,2,3]. Cache-coherence protocols can maintain consistency by ordering updates to a shared object by potential causality [4,5,6] Resource allocation algorithms can use this relation to resolve contention for a shared resource [7,8].

Many logical time-stamping schemes exist to track potential causality between events. Lamport clocks [9], for example, time stamp each message and event with an integer, while vector clocks [10,11] time stamp each message and event with an array of integers. Although Lamport clocks require less overhead, they carry limited information: Lamport clocks order *all* events that are causally related but may also order events that are not causally related. On the other hand, the larger time stamps of vector clocks permit them to be completely accurate: Vector clocks order *all* and *only* events that are causally related.

This trade-off between space and accuracy is inherent to the problem. For a system with N processes, time stamps of size N are both sufficient and necessary for complete accuracy [12]. This result means that no time-stamping scheme can simultaneously guarantee small time stamps and perfect accuracy.

A *plausible clock* is a time-stamping system that satisfies the requirement that all events that are causally related be ordered, but not necessarily the additional requirement that *only* events that are causally related be ordered [13]. Because

P. Fraigniaud (Ed.): DISC 2005, LNCS 3724, pp. 214–228, 2005.

plausible clocks do not guarantee perfect accuracy, they can be implemented with small time stamps. Several plausible clock schemes have been developed [13,14] that use constant-sized time stamps. The accuracy achieved by these schemes varies from run to run and even over the course of a single execution. Their performance, therefore, is quantified in terms of their expected-case inaccuracy and is generally assessed through simulation.

In this paper, we introduce a new performance measure: *imprecision*. Informally, the imprecision of a time stamp is the maximum number of incorrect orderings permitted by such a stamp. Thus, imprecision reflects an upper bound on the inaccuracy of a time-stamping system. Existing plausible clock algorithms are parameterized by the size of time stamps used. For any chosen size less than N, however, the imprecision of such an algorithm can be quite high. In contrast, we describe a new algorithm that is parameterized by the amount of imprecision. This algorithm allows time stamps to grow and shrink over the course of the computation as necessary to maintain the desired level of precision. To our knowledge, this is the first guaranteed precision plausible clock algorithm.

We quantify the performance of our algorithm in two ways. Firstly, we study the expected-case time-stamp size through simulation. That is, we determine the average time-stamp size needed to maintain a given level of precision, under a variety of circumstances. Secondly, we examine the expected-case accuracy achieved by our algorithm through simulation. That is, we determine how close the actual inaccuracy comes to the upper bound reflected in the selected level of imprecision. We compare the performance of our algorithm with that of two existing plausible clock algorithms.

2   Background and Definitions

2.1   The Model

A distributed system consists of N processes. Processes communicate by message-passing, which is asynchronous, point-to-point, and fault-free. The execution of a process p_i is a finite sequence of events denoted H_i. Each event is either a *local*, *send*, or *receive* event. There is a one-to-one correspondence between send events and their matching receive events. The execution of the system is the set of all events from the individual histories, $H = (\cup i : 1 \leq i \leq N : H_i)$.[1]

The *happens before* ($\rightarrow$) relation [9] orders the events in H by their potential causal relationship. For two events $a \in H_i$ and $b \in H_j$, $a \rightarrow b$ if and only if:

1. $i = j$ and a occurs before b on p_i,
2. a is a send event and b is the corresponding receive event, or
3. there exists an event $c \in H$ such that $a \rightarrow c$ and $c \rightarrow b$.

---

[1] The notation we use for quantification throughout this paper is (*op vars* : *ranges* : *exp*), where *op* is an associative and commutative operator with an identity element, *vars* is the set of bound variables, *ranges* is a predicate restricting the ranges of the bound variables, and *exp* is the expression to be quantified.

Two events are *concurrent* when neither happens before the other:

$$a \parallel b \equiv \neg(a \to b) \wedge \neg(b \to a) \ .$$

2.2   Logical Clocks

A *time-stamping system* X [13] is a tuple $(\langle S, \overset{X}{\to} \rangle, G, X.\textbf{stamp}, X.\textbf{tag})$, where:

S is a set of logical time values used locally (*time stamps*),
$\overset{X}{\to}$ is an irreflexive transitive relation on time stamps,
G is a set of logical time values appended to messages (*time tags*),
$X.\textbf{stamp}$ is the time stamping function mapping events to stamps, and
$X.\textbf{tag}$ is the tagging function mapping event time stamps to message time tags.

The relation $\overset{X}{\to}$ is irreflexive and transitive, therefore $\langle S, \overset{X}{\to} \rangle$ is a strict partial order. This strict partial order induces further relations: for $r, s \in S$,

$$r \overset{X}{=} s \ \equiv \ r = s$$
$$r \overset{X}{\parallel} s \ \equiv \ \neg(r \overset{X}{\to} s) \wedge \neg(s \overset{X}{\to} r) \wedge \neg(r \overset{X}{=} s) \ .$$

For convenience, we will overload the definitions of these relations to allow them to directly compare events of H. For instance, given two events $a, b \in H$,

$$a \overset{X}{\to} b \ \equiv \ X.\textbf{stamp}(a) \overset{X}{\to} X.\textbf{stamp}(b) \ .$$

In practice, the function $X.\textbf{stamp}$ is guaranteed to be locally computable by defining it inductively. First, time stamps are defined for all initial events. Then, a function on $S \times G$ is given that determines the time stamp of an event based upon the most recent local time stamp and the most recently received message time tag. When the time-stamping system is clear from context, we will omit the name and write simply **stamp** and **tag**.

2.3   Example: Vector Clocks

The vector clock is a logical clock that *characterizes* the happens before relation (i.e., $a \to b \ \equiv \ a \overset{\text{Vector}}{\to} b$). A time stamp $s \in S$ is a vector of N integers ($S = \mathbb{Z}^N$). The **stamp** function is defined inductively. The time stamp of an initial (local) event on p_i is all 0's except for the ith entry, which is 1. A subsequent local or send event on p_i has the same stamp as its immediate predecessor on p_i, except the ith entry is incremented. Finally, the time stamp of a receive event is the element-wise max of the current stamp (with the ith entry incremented) and the incoming tag.

Time tags are identical to time stamps ($G = S$). The **tag** function is the identify function: The time tag appended to a message is the time stamp of the corresponding send event. The $\overset{\text{Vector}}{\to}$ relation is defined to be[2]

---

[2] The bound variables i and j will be understand to range from 1 to N and so the range can be omitted.

$$r \overset{\text{Vector}}{\rightarrow} s \equiv (\forall i :: r[i] \le s[i]) \wedge (\exists j :: r[j] < s[j]) \,.$$

A vector clock maintains the two important properties. First, events on a given process are mapped to a strictly increasing sequence of integers. That is, for two time stamps $r = \mathbf{stamp}(a)$ and $s = \mathbf{stamp}(b)$ on process p_i, $a \rightarrow b \equiv r[i] < s[i]$. Second, a stamp records the *most recent* happens before event from each process. For instance, consider a time stamp $r = \mathbf{stamp}(a)$ on process p_i. For each entry $r[j]$ where $j \neq i$, there exists a time stamp $s = \mathbf{stamp}(b)$ on p_j such that $s[j] = r[j]$. This event b is the most recent event on p_j that happens before a. More formally, $b \rightarrow a \wedge \neg (\exists c \in H_j :: b \rightarrow c \wedge c \rightarrow a)$.

2.4   Plausible Clocks

A time-stamping system P is *plausible* if and only if it satisfies, for all $a, b \in H$,

$$a \rightarrow b \Rightarrow a \overset{P}{\rightarrow} b \tag{1}$$

$$a = b \equiv a \overset{P}{=} b \,. \tag{2}$$

Equation (1) requires that a plausible clock's ordering relation on time stamps be *consistent* with the happens before relation between events: Every pair of causally-related events is correctly ordered by the plausible clock, although some unrelated (i.e., concurrent) events may *also* be ordered. Equation (2) requires that a plausible clock's time stamps can be used to distinguish different events.

2.5   Inaccuracy

The *inaccuracy* of a plausible clock is the ratio of the number of incorrectly ordered event pairs to the number of concurrent event pairs in the system [14]. Formally, we define C as the set of concurrent pairs in the system, and M as the set of incorrectly ordered pairs. The inaccuracy of a plausible clock P on a history H, $\rho(P, H)$, is therefore defined by

$$C = \{(a, b) \in H \times H : a \parallel b : (a, b)\}$$

$$M = \{(a, b) \in H \times H : a \parallel b \wedge \neg(a \overset{P}{\parallel} b) : (a, b)\}$$

$$\rho(P, H) = \frac{|M|}{|C|} \,.$$

Accuracy can then be defined as $1 - \rho(P, H)$. Note that $\parallel$ and $\overset{P}{\parallel}$ are both symmetric, so a single pair of events is counted twice in both C and M.

2.6   Imprecision

Our goal is to create a plausible clock that can guarantee an arbitrary bound on inaccuracy. To be practical, there should be no presumption of global information nor should the clock modify the underlying computation (e.g., by sending extra messages). Our approach is to bound the inaccuracy by controlling the maximum possible error permitted by individual time stamps. To this end, we redefine inaccuracy in terms of this error.

First, we define the *local error* of a plausible clock to be the number of mistakes it makes with respect to a given event. More precisely, it is the number of (concurrent) events that are mistakenly ordered *before* the event in question. Formally, we define the local error of P with respect to an event b by

$$\delta(P,H,b) = |\{\, a \in H \;:\; a \parallel b \wedge a \xrightarrow{P} b \;:\; a \,\}| \;.$$

We can now define the total number of mistakes in terms of the local error for each event (note, we do not double-count pairs in the definition of local error):

$$|M| = 2 * \left(\sum b \in H \;::\; \delta(P,H,b) \right) \;.$$

Therefore, inaccuracy can be written as

$$\rho(P,H) = 2 * \frac{\left(\sum b \in H \;::\; \delta(P,H,b) \right)}{|C|} \;.$$

Our definition of $\rho(P,H)$ is still problematic. We would like to define inaccuracy in terms of the local error per event; however, it is currently the ratio between the sum of local error and the total number of concurrent event pairs. To this end, we define $\epsilon(H)$ as the ratio between the total number of concurrent pairs and the total number of events:

$$\epsilon(H) = 1/2 * \frac{|C|}{|H|} \;.$$

For computations that exhibit regular communication patterns and whose processes are not partitioned, the value of $\epsilon(H)$ remains constant as H is extended with new events. If the processes were partitioned (say one process ceases to communicate), this ratio would increase without bound as H is extended with new events. For the remainder of the paper, we will assume fault-free executions where all processes actively communicate within the system. Rewriting the total number of concurrent pairs in terms of this concurrency ratio, we have

$$\rho(P,H) = 1/\epsilon(H) * \frac{\left(\sum b \in H \;::\; \delta(P,H,b) \right)}{|H|} \;.$$

Since we assume that $\epsilon(H)$ is a constant, we need only to bound the mean value of δ in order to bound the inaccuracy. Unfortunately, we cannot use δ directly in our algorithm; the **stamp** function is defined inductively over time stamps and not histories. Therefore, we define a new metric that is based on time stamps and hence can be used directly by a plausible clock to reason about fidelity. We call this metric *imprecision*. The imprecision of a time stamp generated by a plausible clock is an upper bound on the number of ordering mistakes made for an event with that time stamp. More formally, let $\mathcal{H}(P, s)$ be the set of histories for which the plausible clock P generates the time stamp s:

$$\mathcal{H}(P, s) = \{\, H \;:\; (\,\exists a \in H \;::\; P.\mathbf{stamp}(a) = s\,) \;:\; H \,\} \; .$$

Imprecision, $\psi(P, s)$, then is defined by

$$\psi(P, s) = (\,\mathbf{Max}\, H \in \mathcal{H}(P, s),\; a \in H \;:\; P.\mathbf{stamp}(a) = s \;:\; \delta(P, H, a)\,) \; .$$

Intuitively, imprecision is the worst-case value of δ for an event with a given time stamp. Note that imprecision is independent of history and therefore is a function of the information contained within a time stamp. If we guarantee that all time stamps generated during a computation have an imprecision below some arbitrary bound, K, then the mean value of δ is also below that bound. The resulting bound on inaccuracy is given by

$$\rho(P, H) \leq 1/\epsilon(H) * \frac{(\sum b \in H \;::\; \psi(P, P.\mathbf{stamp}(b))\,)}{|H|} \leq K/\epsilon(H) \; .$$

3   A Guaranteed Precision Plausible Clock

3.1   Logical Time Intervals

With vector clocks, the time stamps of events on process p_i all differ in their i^{th} entry. This one entry orders these events and distinguishes between them. The other entries serve a different purpose: Each one uniquely identifies the most recent happens-before event on the corresponding remote process. Our approach is conceptually similar. Time stamps are vectors where the ith entry orders and distinguishes between events on p_i, while the other entries indicate the most recent happens-before events on remote processes. The difference is that a *range* of values, rather than a single one, is used as an entry in the array and hence the most recent happens-before events are not uniquely identified.

At the core of our algorithm is the concept of a time *interval*. A time interval is a tuple $\langle beg, end \rangle$ where beg and end are integers and $beg \leq end$. Unlike the integer entry of vector clocks which corresponds to a single event, a time interval corresponds to a set of events. The event of interest is within this range. Thus, when comparing two time intervals, we can conclude something about the ordering of the respective events of interest only when the ranges do not overlap. The ordering between two intervals m and n is given by

$$m \overset{int}{<} n \;\equiv\; m.end < n.beg$$

$$m \overset{int}{\approx} n \;\equiv\; \neg(m \overset{int}{<} n) \wedge \neg(n \overset{int}{<} m)$$

$$m \overset{int}{\lesssim} n \;\equiv\; (m \overset{int}{<} n) \vee (m \overset{int}{\approx} n) \; .$$

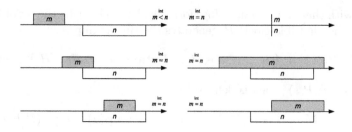

Fig. 1. Examples of time interval comparison

We define a *precise* interval to be one in which the begin and end points are equal. In the case of precise intervals, an overlap reflects exact equality:

$$\textbf{precise}(m) \equiv m.beg = m.end$$

$$m \overset{int}{=} n \equiv \textbf{precise}(m) \wedge \textbf{precise}(n) \wedge m = n \ .$$

3.2   Definition of S and G

A time stamp $s \in S$ is a vector of N time intervals. Let $\textbf{min\_beg}(s)$ ($\textbf{min\_end}(s)$) be the minimum begin (end) point in s. Like vector clocks, our time stamps map the events of a given process to an increasing sequence. That is, for two time stamps $r = \textbf{stamp}(a)$ and $s = \textbf{stamp}(b)$ on process p_i ,

$$\textbf{precise}(r[i]) \wedge \textbf{precise}(s[i]) \tag{3}$$

$$a \rightarrow b \equiv r[i] \overset{int}{<} s[i] \ . \tag{4}$$

A time stamp s also satisfies several additional properties. First, all imprecise intervals of s share the same end value. Second, all precise intervals of s are greater than the imprecise intervals. Both properties are captured by:

$$(\forall i : \neg\textbf{precise}(s[i]) : s[i].end = \textbf{min\_end}(s) \ ) \ . \tag{5}$$

Like time stamps, a time tag t is also a vector of N time intervals. It satisfies all the properties of time stamps and, in addition, the property that imprecise intervals have the same begin point:

$$(\forall i : \neg\textbf{precise}(s[i]) : s[i].beg = \textbf{min\_beg}(s) \ ) \ . \tag{6}$$

Thus, $G \subset S$. See Fig. 2 for an illustration of a time stamp and a time tag.

Ordering. The comparison of time stamps in our algorithm is similar to that of vector clocks. The $\overset{P}{\rightarrow}$ relation is formally defined by:

$$r \overset{P}{\rightarrow} s \equiv (\forall i :: r[i] \overset{int}{\gtrapprox} s[i] \ ) \wedge (\exists j :: r[j] \overset{int}{<} s[j] \ ) \ .$$

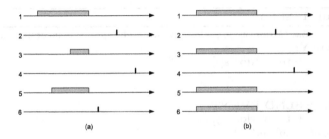

Fig. 2. A time stamp (a) and a time tag (b) in a system with 6 processes. Imprecise entries in a time tag share a common interval.

Space Complexity. Since precise intervals can be encoded with a single integer and all imprecise intervals share the same end point, time stamps can be encoded with $N + 1$ integers (i.e., N begin values and one common end value).

For a time tag with R precise intervals, $R \log N$ bits are required to encode the mapping between precise intervals and their respective processes. Since all imprecise intervals are the same, a time tag requires $R(L + \log N) + 2L$ bits, where L bits are used to encode a single integer.

Imprecision. The size of the intervals determines the imprecision of a time stamp. In any given history, the local error possible for a stamp s with respect to some process p_i is the size of the ith interval of s. Hence, the imprecision is the sum of these interval lengths:

$$\psi(s) = \left(\sum i :: s[i].end - s[i].beg \right) .$$

3.3   Definition of Stamp

The **stamp** function is defined inductively for process p_i as follows. Initially, all time stamp entries are precise intervals equal to $\langle 0, 0 \rangle$ except for the ith entry which is set to $\langle 1, 1 \rangle$. During a local/send event, the ith entry is incremented. Thus, if r is the old stamp on p_i, the new stamp s is defined by

$$\textbf{precise}(s[i]) \wedge s[i].end = r[i].end + 1$$
$$(\forall j : j \neq i : s[j] = r[j]) .$$

Upon receiving a time tag, the max of the *beg* and *end* points of each entry is taken and the ith entry is incremented. Thus, if r is the old stamp on p_i and t is the time tag of the incoming message, the new stamp s is defined by

$$\textbf{precise}(s[i]) \wedge s[i].end = max(r[i].end, t[i].end) + 1$$
$$(\forall j : j \neq i : s[j] = \langle max(r[j].beg, t[j].beg), max(r[j].end, t[j].end) \rangle) .$$

Algorithm 1: stamp

Data: r is old stamp on p_i, s is new stamp on p_i, t is incoming tag
INITIALLY:
    for $j := 1$ to N do $s[j] := \langle 0, 0 \rangle$
    $s[i] := \langle 1, 1 \rangle$

LOCAL or SEND EVENT:
    for $j := 1$ to N do $s[j] := r[j]$
    $s[i].end := s[i].end + 1$
    $s[i].beg := s[i].end$

RECEIVE EVENT:
    for $j := 1$ to N do
        $s[j].end := \max(r[j].end, t[j].end)$
        $s[j].beg := \max(r[j].beg, t[j].beg)$
    end
    $s[i].end := s[i].end + 1$
    $s[i].beg := s[i].beg$

3.4 Definition of Tag

The goal of the **tag** algorithm is to construct the smallest possible time tag while not exceeding its bound on imprecision. Informally, the time tag is constructed by iteratively adding the greatest precise intervals until the error of the time tag is below the imprecision bound, K. The common imprecise interval of the time tag is formed by taking the max end value and the min beg value of the remaining intervals not in the time tag. The pseudo-code for **tag** is Algorithm 2. The function **ith_max**(i, s) returns the index of the ith largest precise interval in time stamp s.

3.5 Example

Figure 3 depicts two examples of a process executing three events: a local event, a receive event, and a send event. In these example, the process is p_3, there are a total of 6 processes, and the bound on imprecision is 30. Observe that the time stamps satisfy property (5), while the time tags satisfy (5) and (6). Also note that the imprecision of each stamp (and tag) is less than the bound.

When a message is received, the new stamp is calculated as the element-wise max of the old stamp and the incoming message. The result of this operation is a valid time stamp (i.e., it satisfies (5)). In Fig. 3(a) the imprecision of the local stamp increases as the result of an incoming message (from 6 to 15), while in Fig. 3(b) it decreases (from 6 to 3).

Message tags are constructed from time stamps using the largest possible common interval such that the imprecision of the tag is less than the bound. In

Algorithm 2: tag

Data: r is the time stamp of the send event, t is the outgoing tag

```
for j := 1 to N do   t[j] := ⟨0,0⟩
minbeg := ( Min j : 1 ≤ j ≤ N : r[j].beg )
i := 1
k := ith_max(i, r)
while (N − i + 1) ∗ (r[k].end − minbeg) > K do
    t[k] := r[k]
    i := i + 1
    k := ith_max(i, r)
end
for j := 1 to N do
    if t[j] = ⟨0,0⟩ then
        t[j].end = r[k].end
        t[j].beg = minbeg
    end
end
```

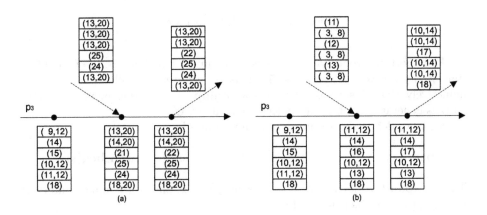

Fig. 3. Sample executions illustrating **stamp** and **tag**

Fig. 3(b), for example, entries 1,2,4, and 5 are part of the common interval, giving an imprecision of $4 * (14 − 10) = 16$. The next largest common interval would include entry 3 and so would be $\langle 10, 17 \rangle$. The resulting imprecision, however, would be $5 * (17 − 10) = 35$ which exceeds the bound.

4   Proofs of Correctness

In this section, we sketch the proof of correctness for our time-stamping scheme. Only the main theorems and lemmas are given, while details are available in [15].

We first define two operators on time stamps, then use these operators to show plausibility and boundedness of imprecision.

4.1   The Join ($\bowtie$) and Expand Operators

We define the *join* ($r \bowtie s$) of two time stamps by

$$(\forall i :: \quad (r \bowtie s)[i].beg = \mathbf{max}(r[i].beg, s[i].beg)$$
$$\land (r \bowtie s)[i].end = \mathbf{max}(r[i].end, s[i].end)) .$$

The **stamp** function for receive events can be redefined in terms of join. Figure 4 is a graphical representation of this operator.

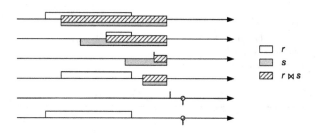

Fig. 4. The join ($\bowtie$) operator

An important property is that S is closed under join. That is, the join of two time stamps, r and s, satisfies (5). This closure property allows us to prove, inductively, that all stamps generated by **stamp** are indeed elements of S and all tags generated by **tag** are indeed elements of G.

Next, we define the **expand** of a time stamp by

$$\mathbf{expand}(s) = (\sum i : \neg \mathbf{precise}(s[i]) : \mathbf{min\_end}(s) - \mathbf{min\_beg}(s)) .$$

Thus, **expand**(s) is the size of the *smallest* (i.e., shortest common interval) time tag that can be generated from s.

We can show that the join operation does not increase the worst-case error of the system. That is, the **expand** of the join of two time stamps is less than or equal to the max of their respective **expand**'s:

$$\mathbf{expand}(r \bowtie s) \leq \mathbf{max}(\mathbf{expand}(r), \mathbf{expand}(s)) .$$

This property allows us to prove inductively that the **expand** of all stamps generated by **stamp** and all tags generated by **tag** is below a specified bound.

4.2   Proof of Plausibility

In order to prove that P is plausible, we begin by showing that the $\xrightarrow{P}$ relation holds between pairs of events on the same process as well as send-receive pairs.

Theorem 1. *If a and b both occur on a process p_i, $a \to b \Leftrightarrow a \xrightarrow{P} b$.*

Theorem 2. *If a is a send event and b is the corresponding receive, $a \xrightarrow{P} b$.*

Another property of P is that the ith (precise) interval can be used to order events on p_i with other events.

Theorem 3. *If a and b occur on processes p_i and p_j respectively, $a \neq b \wedge$ $\textbf{stamp}(a)[i] \stackrel{int}{=} \textbf{stamp}(b)[i] \Rightarrow a \to b$, and $\textbf{stamp}(a)[i] \stackrel{int}{<} \textbf{stamp}(b)[i] \Rightarrow a \to b$.*

Theorem 4. *P is plausible.*

Proof. There are two proof obligations: properties (1) and (2) of plausible clocks.

Property (1): $a \to b \Rightarrow a \xrightarrow{P} b$. Assume $a \to b$. Therefore, there exists a chain of events $c_0, c_1, ..., c_n$ where $c_0 = a$ and $c_n = b$ and $(\forall k : 0 \leq k < n : c_k \to c_{k+1})$ such that adjacent pairs in this chain are either on the same process or matching send/receive events. From Theorems 1 and 2, we have $(\forall k : 0 \leq k < n : c_k \xrightarrow{P} c_{k+1})$. Furthermore, since end intervals are non-decreasing along this chain, $\xrightarrow{P}$ is transitive along this chain. Therefore, $a \xrightarrow{P} b$.

Property (2): $a = b \equiv a \stackrel{P}{=} b$. The forward direction follows immediately from the definition of $\stackrel{P}{=}$. For the reverse direction, assume $a \stackrel{P}{=} b$. Let p_i (p_j) be the process on which a (b) occurs and let r (s) be $\textbf{stamp}(a)$ ($\textbf{stamp}(b)$). Since $r \stackrel{P}{=} s$, $r[i] \stackrel{int}{=} s[i]$ and $r[j] \stackrel{int}{=} s[j]$. From (3), both $r[i]$ and $s[j]$ are precise. From Theorem 3, neither $r[j]$ nor $s[i]$ are precise. Since precise intervals are greater than imprecise intervals, these two intervals cannot be simultaneously equivalent unless $a = b$. $\qquad\square$

4.3   Proof That Imprecision is Bounded

Theorem 5. *$\psi(\textbf{stamp}(a)) = (\sum i :: \textbf{stamp}(a)[i].end - \textbf{stamp}(a)[i].beg)$*

Proof. Consider an event b that occurs on process p_j. From Theorem 3, a and b are correctly ordered when the jth intervals of their stamps are ordered by $\stackrel{int}{=}$ or $\stackrel{int}{<}$. Hence, ordering mistakes can only occur when the jth intervals are related by $\stackrel{int}{\approx}$. From (3) and (4), at most $\textbf{stamp}(a)[j].end - \textbf{stamp}(a)[j].beg$ such events exist. Thus, $(\sum i :: \textbf{stamp}(a)[i].end - \textbf{stamp}(a)[i].beg)$ is an upper bound on the number of incorrectly related events ($\xrightarrow{P}$ but not $\to$). This bound is tight since, for any time stamp s a history can be constructed in which there is an event whose stamp is s and for which $(\sum i :: \textbf{stamp}(a)[i].end - \textbf{stamp}(a)[i].beg)$ ordering mistakes are made. $\qquad\square$

5   Experimental Evaluation

We consider a client-server system with 2 clients and 98 servers. A client performs local events and sends messages to a random server. While waiting for a response, a client performs only local events. Servers reply to messages in FIFO order, and only perform local events if there are no outstanding requests from clients. Event arrivals follow a negative exponential distribution.

For our analysis, we consider only events from the *middle* of the computation (i.e., events that have are causally related to some event from each process which, in turn, is also causally related to some event from each process). We exclude events at the beginning and end since plausible clocks (including our own) perform better during the startup of a computation than in steady-state.

The two primary characteristics we evaluate are: the relationship between message size and inaccuracy; and the difference between the (worst-case) inaccuracy bound determined by imprecision and the actual (expected-case) inaccuracy achieved. The former allows a comparison between our algorithm and other plausible clock algorithms in terms of trading off accuracy for message overhead. The latter is unique to our algorithm, where imprecision can be controlled.

Figure 5 depicts the relationship between message size and resulting inaccuracy. The plausible clocks considered are R-Entries Vector (REV) and Comb (a combination of REV and k-Lamport) [13]. We fix the k-Lamport component of Comb to 5 entries while varying the size of its REV component. The results show that, on average, our algorithm (labeled "Common Interval" in the figure) yields better accuracy than either of the other two.

Although this figure compares these plausible clocks directly, it is worth remembering that these clocks differ in a fundamental way: Our algorithm does not guarantee a constant message overhead, while other plausible clock algorithms do not guarantee any level of accuracy.[3] Therefore, while it is useful to compare their performance in trading off accuracy for message overhead, the choice of which algorithm to use will likely be driven by the primary performance property being optimized.

Figure 6 depicts the relationship between the inaccuracy bound (derived from imprecision) and the observed inaccuracy. We see that the resulting inaccuracy is significantly less than the inaccuracy bound. Imprecision measures the worst-case error per time stamp. Actual runs, however, may not generate events that result in error equal to each time stamp's imprecision. Thus, while our algorithm provides a guarantee on the worst case behavior, it does not do this at the expense of degrading the expected case inaccuracy.

6   Related Work

Several algorithms have been proposed as scalable solutions to vector clocks. For instance, in [16] Baldoni and Melideo proposed k-dependency vectors. Their al-

---

[3] Notice that the data points for our algorithm have error bars in the horizontal axis since time tag size varies.

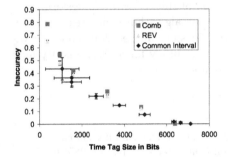
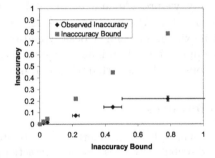

Fig. 5. Performance comparison with other plausible clocks

Fig. 6. Actual observed inaccuracy compared to upper bound

gorithm affixes a constant-size vector of integers to application messages. The trade-off for this approach is that extra computation may be required to detect the causal relationship between events. The algorithm requires a dedicated checker process to determine the causal order of events.

The definition of plausible clocks was formalized in [13], where it was also shown that such clocks could be combined to improve accuracy. Two plausible clock algorithms were presented: REV and k-Lamport, along with their combination, Comb. In [13,17], the performance of Comb was analyzed through simulation. The results of those studies showed good performance of Comb and also the dependency of that performance on several factors (e.g., local history size, communication pattern, system size). However, formal analysis of the expected behavior of a plausible clock algorithm was left for future work.

NUREV clocks were proposed in [14]. This plausible clock uses a fixed vector size and a dynamic mapping of processor ids to vector entries. Several mappings were proposed to minimize the ordering errors produced by this clock, and hence maximize the expected accuracy. This work did not consider the cost of encoding the dynamic map in the time tag.

Unlike these other approaches, our notion of imprecision–since it reflects a worst-case bound–permits the evaluation of plausible clock performance independent of a particular history or set of histories.

7 Conclusion

The contribution of this work is threefold. Firstly, we have defined a new metric, *imprecision*, which quantifies the worst-case accuracy of a plausible clock time-stamping system. This metric characterizes the system itself, independent of any particular history. Existing plausible clocks are parameterized by message time tag size and (even those with good average-case accuracy) have unbounded imprecision. Our second contribution is a new plausible clock algorithm which is parameterized by imprecision. This algorithm guarantees a maximum, bounded imprecision by varying the size of time tags as needed during a computation.

Finally, we provide an experimental evaluation of this algorithm's performance. We find that the expected message size for our algorithm compares favorably with existing plausible clocks. We also note that since imprecision is a conservative upper bound on inaccuracy, the actual inaccuracy for a given history may be considerably less than this guaranteed bound.

References

1. Chandy, K.M., Lamport, L.: Distributed snapshots: Determining global states of distributed systems. ACM Transactions on Computer Systems **3** (1985) 63–75
2. Netzer, R., Xu, J.: Necessary and sufficient conditions for consistent global snapshots. IEEE Transactions on Parallel and Distributed Systems **6** (1995) 165–169
3. Elnozahy, M., Alvisi, L., Wang, Y.M., Johnson, D.B.: A survey of rollback-recovery protocols in message passing systems. Technical Report CMU-CS-96-181, School of Computer Science, Carnegie Mellon University, Pittsburgh, PA, USA (1996)
4. Ahamad, M., Neiger, G., Burns, J.E., Kohli, P., Hutto, P.W.: Causal memory: Definitions, implementation, and programming. Distributed Computing **9** (1995) 37–49
5. Prakash, R., Raynal, M., Singhal, M.: An adaptive causal ordering algorithm suited to mobile computing environments. Journal of Parallel and Distributed Computing **41** (1997) 190–204
6. Fernández, A., Jiménez, E., Cholvi, V.: On the interconnection of causal memory systems. In: Proceedings of the Nineteenth Annual ACM Symposium on Principles of Distributed Computing. (2000) 163–170
7. Ricart, G., Agrawala, A.K.: An optimal algorithm for mutual exclusion in computer networks. Communications of the ACM **24** (1981) 9–17
8. Maekawa, M.: A $\sqrt{N}$ algorithm for mutual exclusion in decentralized systems. ACM Transactions on Computer Systems **3** (1985) 145–159
9. Lamport, L.: Time, clocks, and the ordering of events in a distributed system. Communications of the ACM **21** (1978) 558–565
10. Fidge, C.J.: Timestamps in message-passing systems that preserve the partial ordering. In: Proc. of the 11th Australian Computer Science Conf. (1988) 55–66
11. Mattern, F.: Virtual time and global states of distributed systems. In: Proceedings of the International Workshop on Parallel & Distributed Algorithms. Elsevier Science Publishers B. V. (1989) 215–226
12. Charron-Bost, B.: Concerning the size of logical clocks in distributed systems. Information Processing Letters **39** (1991) 11–16
13. Torres-Rojas, F.J., Ahamad, M.: Plausible clocks: constant size logical clocks for distributed systems. Distributed Computing **12** (1999) 179–196
14. Gidenstam, A., Papatriantafilou, M.: Adaptive plausible clocks. In: Proceedings of the 24th International Conference on Distributed Computing Systems (ICDCS'04), IEEE Computer Society (2004) 86–93
15. Moore, B.T.: Plausible clocks with bounded inaccuracy. Master's thesis, The Ohio State University (2005) available as technical report OSU-CISRC-7/05-TR52.
16. Baldoni, R., Melideo, G.: k-dependency vectors: A scalable causality-tracking protocol. In: Proceedings of the 11th Euromicro Conference on Parallel, Distributed and Network-Based Processing. (2003)
17. Torres-Rojas, F.J.: Performance evaluation of plausible clocks. In: Proceedings of the 7th Euro-Par Conference. (2001) 476–481

Causing Communication Closure: Safe Program Composition with Non-FIFO Channels[*]

Kai Engelhardt[1] and Yoram Moses[2,**]

[1] School of Computer Science and Engineering,
The University of New South Wales, and NICTA[***]
Sydney, NSW 2052, Australia
kaie@cse.unsw.edu.au
[2] Department of Electrical Engineering, Technion,
Haifa, 32000 Israel
moses@ee.technion.ac.il

Abstract. A semantic framework for analyzing safe composition of distributed programs is presented. Its applicability is illustrated by a study of program composition when communication is reliable but not necessarily FIFO. In this model, special care must be taken to ensure that messages do not accidentally overtake one another in the composed program. We show that barriers do not exist in this model. Indeed, no program that sends or receives messages can automatically be composed with arbitrary programs without jeopardizing their intended behavior. Safety of composition becomes context-sensitive and new tools are needed for ensuring it. A notion of *sealing* is defined, where if a program P is immediately followed by a program Q that seals P then P will be communication-closed—it will execute as if it runs in isolation. The investigation of sealing in this model reveals a novel connection between Lamport causality and safe composition. A characterization of sealable programs is given, as well as efficient algorithms for testing if Q seals P and for constructing a seal for a significant class of programs. It is shown that every sealable program that is open to interference on $O(n^2)$ channels can be sealed using $O(n)$ messages.

1 Introduction

Much of the distributed algorithms literature is devoted to solutions for individual tasks. Implicitly it may appear that these solutions can be readily combined to create larger applications. Composing such solutions is not, however, automatically guaranteed to maintain their correctness and their intended behavior. For example, algorithms are typically designed under the assumption that they begin executing in a well-defined initial global state in which all channels are empty. In most cases, the algorithms are not guaranteed to terminate in such a state. Another inherent feature of distributed systems

[*] Work was partially supported by ARC Discovery Grant RM02036.
[**] Work on this paper happened during a sabbatical visit to the School of Computer Science and Engineering, The University of New South Wales, Sydney, NSW 2052, Australia.
[***] National ICT Australia is funded through the Australian Government's *Backing Australia's Ability* initiative, in part through the Australian Research Council.

P. Fraigniaud (Ed.): DISC 2005, LNCS 3724, pp. 229–243, 2005.

is that, even though they are often designed in clearly separated phases, these phases typically execute concurrently. For instance, Lynch writes in [12, p. 523]:

> "An MST algorithm can be used to solve the leader-election problem [...]. Namely, after establishing an MST, the processes participate in the *STtoLeader* protocol to select the leader. Note that the processes do not need to know when the MST algorithm has completed its execution throughout the network; it is enough for each process i to wait until it is finished locally, [...]."

In general, when two phases, such as implementations of an MST algorithm and of the *STtoLeader* algorithm, are developed independently and then executed in sequence, one phase may confuse messages originating from the other with its own messages. Perhaps the first formal treatment of this issue was via the notion of *communication-closed layers* introduced by Elrad and Francez in [2]. Consider a program $P = P_1 \parallel \ldots \parallel P_n$ consisting of n concurrent processes $P_i = Q_i; L_i; Q'_i$, the execution of which is, intuitively, divided into three phases, Q_i, L_i, and Q'_i. Elrad and Francez define $L = L_1 \parallel \ldots \parallel L_n$ to be a *communication-closed layer (CCL) in P* if under no execution of P does a command in some L_i communicate with a command in any Q_j or Q'_j [2]. If a program P can be decomposed into a sequence of CCLs then every execution of P can be viewed as a concatenation of executions of P's layers in order. Hence, reasoning about P can be reduced to reasoning about its layers in isolation. This approach has been investigated further and applied to a variety of problems by Janssen, Poel, and Zwiers [9,7,8,13]. Stomp and de Roever considered related notions in the context of synchronous communication [14]. Gerth and Shrira considered the issue of using distributed programs as off-the-shelf components to serve as layers in larger distributed programs [6]. They observe that the above definition of CCL is made with respect to the whole program P as context, and hence is unsuitable for off-the-shelf components. They solve the problem by defining L to be a *General Tail Communication Closed (GTCC)* layer if, roughly speaking, for *all* layers $T_1 \parallel \ldots \parallel T_n$ we have that L is a CCL in $L_1; T_1 \parallel \ldots \parallel L_n; T_n$. Since this definition does not refer to the surrounding program context of a layer, it asserts a certain quality of composability. Sequentially composing GTCC layers guarantees that each one of them is a CCL.

We develop a framework for defining and reasoning about various notions central to the design of CCLs in different models of communication. The communication model used in most of the literature concerning CCLs is that of reliable FIFO channels. In practice, channels often fail to satisfy this assumption. Three main sources of imperfection are loss, reordering, and duplication of messages by a channel. This paper studies the impact of message reordering on the design of CCLs. Our communication model, which we call REL, will therefore assume that channels neither lose nor duplicate messages but message delivery is not necessarily FIFO. As we shall see, in REL, the CCL property depends in an essential way on Lamport causality [11]. Indeed, to ensure CCL, causality is *all* that is needed in REL, whereas either duplication or loss already mandate the need for headers in messages [5,4].

Consider for instance the task of transmitting a message m from process i to process j where it is stored in variable x. The task is accomplished by i performing $\text{SND}_m^{i \to j}$ to send the message and j performing $\text{RCV}_x^{j \leftarrow i}$ to receive it into variable x. This implementation denoted $\text{MT}_{m \to x}^{i \to j}$ (for *Message-Transmit*) works fine in isolation. Composing two copies[1] of $\text{MT}^{i \to j}$, however, does not guarantee the same behavior as executing the first to completion and then executing the second. Since communication is not FIFO, the second message sent by i could be the first one received by j. On the other hand, if $\text{MT}^{i \to j}$ is followed by $\text{MT}^{j \to i}$ no such interference occurs. Moreover, no later program can ever interfere with the first $\text{MT}^{i \to j}$ in this pair. Of course the second program, $\text{MT}^{j \to i}$, is still susceptible to interference, e.g., by another $\text{MT}^{j \to i}$. In fact, non-trivial programs are never safe from interference in REL. As we shall show, for any terminating program P transmitting a message from i to j there is a program Q potentially interfering with communication in P. One consequence is that no terminating program that sends messages can be a GTCC layer.

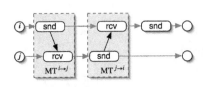

Fig. 1. $\text{MT}^{i \to j}$ seals $\text{MT}^{j \to i}$

The above discussion suggests that it is necessary to inspect the next layer in order to determine whether a given layer is a CCL. In fact, we shall define a notion of a program Q *sealing* its predecessor P, which will ensure that P is a CCL in P immediately followed by Q. For example, $\text{MT}^{j \to i}$ seals $\text{MT}^{i \to j}$ and vice versa. Intuitively, Q seals P if Q guarantees that no message sent after P can be received in P. Let us consider why $\text{MT}_{\text{ACK}}^{j \to i}$ seals $\text{MT}^{i \to j}$. Suppose that a later message is sent on the channel from i to j as in Fig. 1. This send is performed only after the message sent in the opposite direction has been received by i, which in turn must have been sent after the first message has been received by j. Consequently, j's receive event must precede i's sending of the later message. Therefore, the later message cannot compete with the earlier one. A message transmitted in the opposite direction is often called an *acknowledgment*. More interesting examples of sealing presented in Figures 2(a) and 3. For a decomposition of a program P into a sequence of ℓ layers $L^{(1)}, \ldots, L^{(\ell)}$, it follows that if $L^{(k+1)}$ seals $L^{(k)}$ for all $1 \le k < \ell$ then each layer $L^{(k)}$ is a CCL in P.

In [11] Lamport defined causality among events of asynchronous message passing systems. Causality implies temporal precedence. As discussed above, transmitting an acknowledgment guarantees that the receive of the first message causally precedes any later sends on the same channel. Observe that the same effect could be obtained by other means ensuring the intended precedence. For instance, a causal chain consisting of a sequence of messages starting at j, going through a number of intermediate processes, and ending at i could be used just as well. While this *transitive* form of acknowledgment appears to be inefficient, a given message can play a role in a number of transitive acknowledgments. Fig. 2(a) illustrates a program consisting of the transmission of three messages over three different channels. It is sealed using transitive acknowledgments by the program displayed in Fig. 2(b), which sends only two messages.

Indeed, we shall later show how $O(n)$ messages can usefully substitute for $\Omega(n^2)$ acknowledgments. Not all programs can be sealed. We shall later prove that program X shown in Fig. 3(a) is unsealable. The same program executed in the presence of a third process as in Fig. 3(b) is, however, sealable. Any seal of this program will necessarily

---

[1] We omitted the subscript in $\text{MT}^{i \to j}$. Whenever a parameter is irrelevant to the point being made, we tend to omit it.

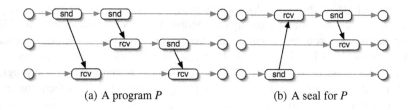

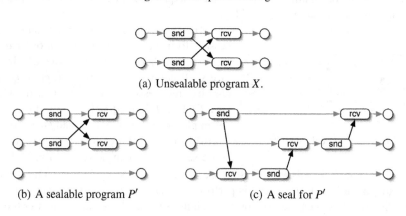

Fig. 2. An example of sealing

Fig. 3. An example of a program for two processes that is unsealable unless a third process is added

use transitive acknowledgments as discussed above. See Fig. 3(c) for an illustration of one way this program can be sealed.

Contributions. The first main contribution of this paper is in the presentation of a framework studying safe composition of layers of distributed programs in different models of communication. Within the framework we define notions including CCL and barriers. Moreover, it is possible to define new notions such as sealing that play an important role in ensuring safe composition. In this paper the power of the framework is illustrated by a comprehensive study of safe composition in REL. In a companion paper [3] the framework is used to define additional notions that are used to study safe composition in FIFO-models with duplicating and/or lossy channels.

Our second main contribution is in identifying the notion of sealing and demonstrating its central role in the design of CCLs in REL. We study the theory of sealing in REL and present the following results.

- Sealable straight-line programs are completely characterized.
- A definition of the sealing *signature* of straight-line programs is given, which characterizes the sealing behavior of a program concisely, for both purposes, sealing and being sealed. The size of the signature is $O(n^2)$.
- An algorithm for deciding whether Q seals P based only on their signatures is presented.

- An algorithm for constructing seals for sealable straight-line programs is presented. It produces seals that perform less than $3n$ message transmissions even though $\Omega(n^2)$ channels may need to be sealed.

The restriction to straight-line programs is motivated by the undecidability of the corresponding problems for general programs. Specifically,the halting problem can be reduced to each of these problems for general programs. As far as communication closure is concerned, straight-line programs already display most of the interesting aspects relevant to the subject of sealing.

2   A Model of Distributed Programs with Layering

In this section we define a simple language for writing message-passing concurrent programs. Its composition operator "$*$" is called *layering*. Layering subsumes the two more traditional operators "$;$" and "$\|$" (as discussed by Janssen in [7]). The meaning of $P * Q$ is that each process i first executes its share of P and then proceeds directly to execute its share of Q. In particular, layering does not impose any barrier synchronization between P and Q. In other words, in $P * Q$ process i need not wait for any other processes to finish their shares of P before moving on to Q. Consequently, programs execute between *cuts* rather than global states. We shall define a notion $r[c,d] \Vdash P$ of a program P *occurring* over an *interval* $r[c,d]$ between the cuts c and d of a run r.

Our later analysis will be concerned with CCLs P. Thus we need to ensure that no message crosses any initial or final cut of an interval over which P occurs. A concise way of capturing this formally is via a new language construct, the *phase operator*, τ. Writing τP specifies that all communication involving P is internal to P, that is, P is a CCL. If P is a CCL in a given larger program L then every execution of P in L is also an execution of τP. In other words, P can be substituted for τP in L. We adopt a standard notion of *refinement* to indicate substitutability of programs. Program P *refines* program Q if every execution of P over an interval $r[c,d]$ is also one of Q, regardless of what happens before c and after d. The notions of "$*$", "τ", and refinement provide a unified language for defining notions of safe composition. The programming language and its semantics are formally defined as follows.

2.1   Syntax

Let $n \in \mathbb{N}$ and $\mathbb{P} = \{1,\ldots,n\}$ be a set of processes. Throughout the paper n will be reserved for denoting the number of processes. Let $(Var_i)_{i \in \mathbb{P}}$ be mutually disjoint sets ofs *program variables (of process i)* not containing the name h_i which is reserved for i's *communication history*. Let $Expr_i$ be the set of arithmetic expressions over Var_i. Let $\mathcal{L}$ be propositional logic over atoms formed from expressions with equality "$=$" and less-than "$<$". We define a syntactic category Prg of *programs*:

$$Prg \ni P \ ::= \ \varepsilon \mid x := e \mid \text{SND}_e^{i \to j} \mid \text{RCV}_x^{j \leftarrow i} \mid [\phi] \mid \tau P \mid P * P \mid P + P \mid P^\omega$$

where $x \in Var_i$, $e \in Expr_i$, $i, j \in \mathbb{P}$, and $\phi \in \mathcal{L}$.

The intuitive meaning of these constructs is as follows. The symbol ε denotes the *empty program*. It takes no time to execute. *Assignment statement* $x := e$ evaluates expression e and assigns its value to variable x. The $\text{SND}_e^{i \to j}$ statement sends a message containing the value of e on the channel from i to j. Communication is asynchronous, and sending is non-blocking. The $\text{RCV}_x^{j \leftarrow i}$ statement, however, blocks until a message arrives on the channel from i to j. It takes a message off the channel and assigns its content to x. The *guard* $[\phi]$ expresses a constraint on the execution of the program: in a run of the program, ϕ must hold at this location. Guards take no time to execute. The program τP behaves the same as P, with the additional restriction that it does not communicate with statements outside P. The operation "$*$" represents *layered composition* following Janssen et al. [8]. Layering statements of distinct processes is essentially the same as parallel composition whereas layering of statements of the same process corresponds to sequential composition. We tend to omit "$*$" when no confusion will arise. The symbol "$+$" denotes nondeterministic choice. By P^ω we denote zero or more (possibly infinitely many) repetitions of program P.[2]

2.2 Semantics

A *send record (for i)* is a triple $(i \to j, v)$, which records sending a message with contents v from i to the receiver j. Similarly, $(j \leftarrow i, v)$ is a *receive record (for j)*. A *local state (for process i)* is a mapping from Var_i to values and from h_i to a sequence of send and receive records for i. A *local run (for process i)* is an infinite sequence of local states. We identify an *event (of i)* with the transition from one local state in a local run of i to the next. An event is either a *send*, a *receive*, or an *internal* event. A *(global) run* is a tuple $r = ((r_i)_{i \in \mathbb{P}}, \delta_r)$ of local runs — one for each process — plus an injective *matching function* δ_r associating a send event with each receive event in r. The mapping δ_r is restricted such that:[3]

1. If $\delta_r(e) = e'$ and e is a receive event of process j resulting in the appending of $(j \leftarrow i, v)$ to j's message history then e' is a send event of process i appending the corresponding send record $(i \to j, v)$ to i's message history.
2. Lamport's causality relation $\xrightarrow{\text{L}}$ induced by δ_r on the events of r, as defined below, is an irreflexive partial order, hence acyclic.

The first condition captures the property that messages are not corrupted in transit. The fact that the function δ_r is total precludes the reception of spurious messages, whereas injectivity ensures that messages are not duplicated in transit. Further restrictions on δ_r can be made to capture additional properties of the communication medium such as reliability, FIFO, fairness, etc.

---

[2] Using guards, choices, and repetition it is possible to define **if** ϕ **then** P **else** Q **fi** as an abbreviation for $[\phi]P + [\neg\phi]Q$ and **while** ϕ **do** P **od** for $([\phi]P)^\omega[\neg\phi]$. The results in this paper also hold for a language based on **if** and **while** instead of $[.]$, $+$, and $^\omega$.

[3] Our choice of execution model is closely related to the more standard one of infinite sequences of global states, representing an *interleaving* of moves by processes. Our conditions on δ_r guarantee the existence of such an interleaving. In general, each of our runs represents an equivalence class of interleavings.

In [11] Lamport defined a "happened before" relation $\overset{L}{\to}$ on the set of events occurring in a run r of a distributed system. The relation $\overset{L}{\to}$ is defined as the smallest transitive relation subsuming (1) the total orders on the events of process i given by the r_i, and (2) the relation $\{\,(e_1, e_2) \mid \delta_r(e_2) = e_1\,\}$ between send and receive events induced by the matching function δ_r.

Cuts and Channels. Write $\mathbb{N}_+$ for $\mathbb{N} \cup \{\infty\}$. A *cut* is a pair (r, c) consisting of a run r and a $\mathbb{P}$-indexed family $c = (c_i)_{i \in \mathbb{P}}$ of $\mathbb{N}_+$-elements. We write "$\leq$" for the componentwise extension of the natural ordering on $\mathbb{N}_+$ to cuts within the same run. A cut is *finite* if all its components are.

Say that an event e performed by process i is *in* a cut (r, c) if e occurs in r_i at an index no larger than c_i. A cut (r, c) corresponds to the, possibly implausible, situation in which the events in the cut have occurred for each process $i \in \mathbb{P}$. A cut (r, c) is *consistent* if every $\overset{L}{\to}$ predecessor of an event in the cut is also in the cut. We define the *channel* $\mathrm{chan}_{i \to j}$ at a cut (r, c) to be the set of i's send events to j and j's receive events from i in (r, c) that are not matched by δ_r to any event also in (r, c). Finally, a formula $\phi \in \mathcal{L}$ *holds at* (r, c), and we write $(r, c) \models \phi$, if ϕ holds in standard propositional logic when, for each $i \in \mathbb{P}$, program variables in Var_i are evaluated in the local states $r_i(c_i)$ if c_i is finite, and are considered unspecified otherwise.[4]

Semantics of Programs. We define the meaning of programs by stating when a program occurs over an interval. An *interval* consists of two cuts (r, c) and (r, d) over the same run with $c \leq d$, which we denote for simplicity by $r[c, d]$. An event is *in* $r[c, d]$ if it is in (r, d) but not in (r, c). We define the occurrence relation $\Vdash$ between intervals and programs by induction on the structure of programs. The interesting cases are those of $*$ and τ. Formally, program $P \in Prg$ *occurs* over interval $r[c, d]$, denoted $r[c, d] \Vdash P$, iff:[5]

$r[c, d] \Vdash \varepsilon$ if $c = d$.

$r[c, d] \Vdash x := e$ if $d = c[i \mapsto c_i + 1]$ and $r_i(d_i) = r_i(c_i)[x \mapsto v]$, where v is the value of e in $r_i(c_i)$.

$r[c, d] \Vdash \mathrm{SND}_e^{i \to j}$ if $d = c[i \mapsto c_i + 1]$ and $r_i(d_i) = r_i(c_i)[h_i \mapsto r_i(c_i)(h_i) \cdot \langle (i \to j, v) \rangle]$, where v is the value of e in $r_i(c_i)$.

$r[c, d] \Vdash \mathrm{RCV}_x^{i \leftarrow j}$ if $d = c[i \mapsto c_i + 1]$ and $r_i(d_i) = r_i(c_i)[h_i \mapsto r_i(c_i)(h_i) \cdot \langle (i \leftarrow j, v) \rangle, x \mapsto v]$.

$r[c, d] \Vdash [\phi]$ if $c = d$ and $(r, c) \models \phi$.

$r[c, d] \Vdash \tau P$ if $r[c, d] \Vdash P$ and no communication event in $r[c, d]$ is matched by δ_r with an event outside $r[c, d]$.

$r[c, d] \Vdash P * Q$ if there exists c' satisfying $c \leq c' \leq d$ such that $r[c, c'] \Vdash P$ and $r[c', d] \Vdash Q$.

$r[c, d] \Vdash P + Q$ if $r[c, d] \Vdash P$ or $r[c, d] \Vdash Q$.

$r[c, d] \Vdash P^\omega$ if, intuitively, an infinite or finite number (possibly zero) of iterations of P occur over $r[c, d]$. More formally, $r[c, d] \Vdash P^\omega$ if there exists a finite or infinite sequence $(c^{(k)})_{k \in I}$ such that I is a non-void prefix of $\mathbb{N}_+$, $c^{(0)} = c$, $c^{(k)} \leq c^{(k')}$ for all $k < k' \in I$, $\bigsqcup_{k \in I} c^{(k)} = d$, and $r[c^{(k)}, c^{(k+1)}] \Vdash P$ for all $k, k+1 \in I$.

---

[4] Recall that local states assign values to local variables.

[5] We shall denote by $f[a \mapsto b]$ the function that agrees with f on everything but a, and maps a to b.

The program semantics is insensitive to deadlocks because deadlocking executions are not represented by runs. We deliberately chose to ignore deadlocks to simplify the presentation and focus on the main aspects of composition. Whether a program deadlocks can be analyzed using standard techniques [12, p. 635f].

General assumption. From now onward, we shall only consider programs that are deadlock-free.

Refinement. We shall capture various assumptions about properties of systems by specifying sets of runs. For instance, REL is the class of runs with reliable communication, and RELFI is its subclass in which channels are also FIFO.

   Given a set Γ of runs, we say that P *refines* Q in Γ, denoted $P \leq_\Gamma Q$, iff $r[c,d] \Vdash P$ implies $r[c,d] \Vdash Q$, for all $r \in \Gamma$ and $c,d \in (\mathbb{N}_+)^\mathbb{P}$. In other words, every execution of P (in a Γ run) is also one of Q, regardless of what happens before and after. Therefore, we may replace Q by P in any larger program context. This definition of refinement is thus appropriate for stepwise top-down development of programs from specifications. The refinement relation on programs is transitive (in fact a pre-order) and all programming constructs are monotone w.r.t. the refinement order.

3   Capturing Safe Composition

The phase operator τ allows us to delineate the interactions that a layer can have with other parts of the program. When combined with refinement it is useful for defining various notions central to the study of safe composition, as we now illustrate.

CCL. We can express that the program L is a CCL in the program $P * L * Q$ w.r.t. Γ by:

$$\tau(P * L * Q) \quad \leq_\Gamma \quad P * \tau L * Q .$$

In words, any isolated execution of $P * L * Q$ will have the property that all communication in L is internal and hence L executes as in isolation. This definition is context-sensitive.

Barriers. More modular would be a notion that guarantees safe composition regardless of the program context. One technique to ensure that two consecutive layers do not interfere with each other is to place a barrier B between them. Formally, program B is a *barrier* in Γ if

$$\tau(P * B * Q) \quad \leq_\Gamma \quad \tau P * \tau B * \tau Q , \text{ for all programs } P \text{ and } Q.$$

TCC. Some programs can be safely composed without the need for any barrier [2,10]. Depending on the model Γ, there may be programs P that safely compose with all following layers. We say that P *is tail communication closed (TCC)* in Γ if,

$$\tau(P * Q) \quad \leq_\Gamma \quad \tau P * \tau Q , \text{ for all programs } Q.$$

Thus, if P is TCC then any execution of P starting in empty channels will also end with all channels empty. Therefore TCC programs can be readily composed.[6] It is straight-

---

[6] TCC follows and is closely related to the notion of GTCC introduced by Gerth and Shrira [6]. The main difference is that their notion is defined w.r.t. a set of initial states.

forward to check that the programs ε, $[\phi]$, $x := e$, and τP are TCC in any Γ. Moreover, if P and Q are TCC in Γ then so are $P + Q$, $P * Q$, and P^{ω}. Observe that every barrier B in Γ is in particular TCC in Γ.

Seals. In many models of interest, only trivial programs are TCC. This is the case, for example, in REL, as shown in Section 4 below. In such models, an alternative methodology is required for determining when it is safe to compose given programs. Next we define a notion of *sealing* that formalizes the concept of program S serving as an impermeable layer between P and later phases such that no later communication will interact with P. We say that S *seals* P *in* Γ if, for all programs Q,

$$\tau(P * S * Q) \quad \leq_{\Gamma} \quad \tau P * \tau(S * Q) \ .$$

Thus, if S seals P in Γ then neither S nor any later program can interfere with communication in P. If S seals P and Q seals S, then S will behave in $\tau(P * S * Q)$ as it does in isolation. Sealing allows incremental program development while maintaining CCL-style composition.

Lemma 1.   *1. If both P and P' are sealed by S in Γ then so is $P + P'$.*
 2. If both S and S' seal P in Γ then $S + S'$ (properly) seals P in Γ.
 3. If S seals P in Γ then $S * Q$ seals P in Γ.
 4. If both S seals P and S' seals S in Γ, then S' seals $P * S$ in Γ.
 5. If P seals itself in Γ then P seals P^{ω} in Γ.
 6. TCC subsumes sealing: P is TCC in Γ iff all programs seal P in Γ.

It follows from this lemma that, if program P can be decomposed into a sequence of ℓ layers $L^{(1)}, \ldots, L^{(\ell)}$, it follows that if $L^{(k+1)}$ seals $L^{(k)}$ for all $1 \leq k < \ell$ then each layer $L^{(k)}$ is a CCL in P.

For example, as discussed in the introduction, any program of the form $\mathrm{MT}^{j \to i}$ seals any program of the form $\mathrm{MT}^{i \to j}$ in REL. Consequently, a program of the form $\mathrm{MT}^{i \to j} * \mathrm{MT}^{j \to i}$ seals itself in REL. On the other hand, the shorter program $\mathrm{MT}^{i \to j}$ does not seal itself in REL—in an execution of $\mathrm{MT}^{i \to j} * \mathrm{MT}^{i \to j}$ the two messages sent by i could be received in the reverse order of sending.

Proper Seals. Suppose that $\mathbb{P} = \{1,2\}$ and $x_i \in Var_i$ for $i \in \mathbb{P}$. Then the program $Q = \textbf{while } true \textbf{ do } (x_1 := 5 * x_2 := 17) \textbf{ od}$ is TCC in RELFI, a CCL in REL, and seals any program in REL. For it necessarily *diverges*, that is, it occurs only over intervals $r[c,d]$ with non-finite d. This implies that no layer following Q has any impact on the semantics of the whole program. It follows trivially that no communication of a later layer can interfere with anything before. Programs such as Q are not particularly useful as seals, in contrast to ones that seal without diverging. This motivates the following definition. We say that S is a *proper seal* of P in Γ if S seals P and S never diverges after P. That is, for all $r \in \Gamma$ and c, d, d', whenever $r[c,d] \Vdash \tau P$, and $r[d,d'] \Vdash S$ and d is finite then so is d'.

For instance, since $\mathrm{MT}^{i \to j}$ is a terminating program that seals $\mathrm{MT}^{j \to i}$ in REL, it is in particular a proper seal.

4   Case Study: Safe Composition in REL

We now consider safe composition in the model REL. Communication events can cause a program *not* to be TCC in REL. For example, reconsider the program $\text{MT}^{i \to j}_{e \to x} = \text{SND}^{i \to j}_e * \text{RCV}^{j \leftarrow i}_x$. It is TCC in RELFI but not TCC in REL. That $\text{MT}^{i \to j}$ is not TCC in REL is no coincidence. Next we show that no terminating program performing any communication whatsoever is TCC in REL.

Theorem 2. *If $r[c,d] \Vdash P$ for some $r \in$ REL and finite c,d such that all channels are empty in (r,c) and there is at least one send or receive event in $r[c,d]$, then P is not TCC in REL.*

Since a barrier is necessarily TCC we immediately obtain

Corollary 3. *No program can serve as a barrier in REL.*

Having shown that TCC and thus barriers are not generally useful notions in REL, we turn our attention to (proper) sealing. It is instructive that not all terminating programs can be properly sealed in REL:

Lemma 4. *If $\mathbb{P} = \{1,2\}$ then the program $X = \text{SND}^{1 \to 2}_{x+1} * \text{SND}^{2 \to 1}_{y+1} * \text{RCV}^{1 \leftarrow 2}_x * \text{RCV}^{2 \leftarrow 1}_y$ illustrated in Fig. 3(a) cannot be sealed properly in REL.*

Our programming language *Prg* is Turing-complete. Since the halting problem for *Prg* can be reduced to sealability in REL we obtain

Theorem 5. *Sealability in REL is undecidable.*

Given this theorem we shall restrict our attention to more tractable subclasses of programs. Program P is *balanced (in REL)* if, whenever $r[c,d] \Vdash P$ and all channels are empty at (r,c), then every channel contains the same number of sends and receives at (r,d). Note that balanced programs are TCC in RELFI. The following theorem shows that in REL balance is a necessary prerequisite for being properly sealable.

Theorem 6. *In REL, every non-divergent program that is properly sealable is also balanced.*

Program P is said to *closes* $\text{chan}_{i \to j}$ *(in REL)* if $\text{chan}_{i \to j}$ is empty after P in any execution of P starting at a cut with empty channels. More formally this is expressed as follows. For all $r \in$ REL and programs Q, if $r[c,d'] \Vdash \tau(P * Q)$ and $r[c,d] \Vdash P$ then $\text{chan}_{i \to j}$ is empty in (r,d). A channel that is not closed is *open*. The state of a program's channels is the essential element in determining sealability.

Program P is *straight-line* if it contains neither nondeterministic choices nor loops nor guards. In other words, P is built from sends, receives, and assignments using layering only. Our focus in this section is on balanced straight-line programs, or *BSL* for short.

The *program graph* of a BSL P is a graph (V,E) that has a node for every send and receive event in P plus an initial dummy node FST_i and a final dummy node LST_i for each process i. The edge set E consists of the successor relation over events in the same process extended to the dummy nodes plus an edge between the k'th send and the k'th receive on channel $\mathsf{chan}_{i \to j}$, for all k, i, and j. All the graphs in Figures 2 and 3 are program graphs. The size of a BSL P's program graph is of the order of the size of the program.

Next we investigate the connection between program graphs and Lamport causality. We use E^+ to refer to the irreflexive transitive closure of E and call edges not containing dummy nodes *normal*. The subset of normal edges is denoted by N_E. In RELFI, the normal edges induce the full causality relation on the events of the program. As we shall show, in REL the normal edges of a program graph are also $\xrightarrow{\text{L}}$ edges.

Lemma 7. *Let $r \in$ REL, let P be a BSL with program graph (V,E), and let Q be a program. If $r[c,d] \Vdash \tau(P * Q)$ then $N_E \subseteq \xrightarrow{\text{L}}$.*

Lemma 7 implies that all edges in $(N_E)^+$ will be $\xrightarrow{\text{L}}$ edges in every run $r \in$ REL of $\tau(P * Q)$. We note that $(N_E)^+$ is the largest set of edges with this property, because $(N_E)^+ = (\xrightarrow{\text{L}} \cap V^2)$ if $r \in$ RELFI.

A more concise representation than the program graph is called the *signature of P* and denoted by $\text{SIG}(P)$. It has size $O(n^2)$ while preserving the information necessary to decide what channels are left open, respectively closed, by P. Given the program graph (V,E) of a BSL P we can obtain $\text{SIG}(P)$ as follows. After calculating E^+, we remove all nodes except for the dummy nodes and the first send and last receive on each channel. The graph is further reduced by removing the node $\text{SND}^{i \to j}$ whenever $(\text{FST}_j, \text{SND}^{i \to j}) \in E^+$. Similarly, $\text{RCV}^{j \gets i}$ is removed whenever $(\text{RCV}^{j \gets i}, \text{LST}_i) \in E^+$. The sends and receives remaining in the signature are precisely the ones that could interfere with receives in a preceding layer or with sends in a succeeding layer.

The complexity of computing $\text{SIG}(P)$ is in $O(\|P\|^3)$ since it requires the causality relation obtained as the transitive closure of the edge relation of P's program graph. We remark that for BSLs P and Q, $\text{SIG}(P * Q)$ can be obtained from their respective signatures at a cost of $O(n^2)$.

Let P be a BSL and let $G = (V,E)$ be $\text{SIG}(P)$. Then P leaves channel $\mathsf{chan}_{i \to j}$ open iff $\text{RCV}^{j \gets i} \in V$. For instance, the program $\text{MT}^{i \to j}$ leaves $\mathsf{chan}_{i \to j}$ open — there is a node $\text{RCV}^{j \gets i}$ in $\text{SIG}(\text{MT}^{i \to j})$, which is depicted in Fig. 4(a). As we have shown earlier, $\text{MT}^{j \to i}$ seals $\text{MT}^{i \to j}$ in REL, which implies that $\text{MT}^{j \to i}$ closes $\mathsf{chan}_{i \to j}$ once. Since $\text{MT}^{j \to i}$ does not re-open the channel, the $\text{RCV}^{j \gets i}$ node found in $\text{SIG}(\text{MT}^{i \to j})$ is not present in the $\text{SIG}(\text{MT}^{i \to j} * \text{MT}^{j \to i})$ shown in Fig. 4(b).

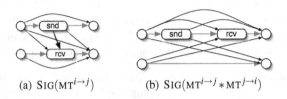

(a) $\text{SIG}(\text{MT}^{i \to j})$ (b) $\text{SIG}(\text{MT}^{i \to j} * \text{MT}^{j \to i})$

Fig. 4. Examples of signatures. Thin arrows denote transitive causality edges.

4.1 Deciding Sealing

Whether one BSL seals another can be decided on the basis of their signatures. Suppose BSL P leaves $\text{chan}_{i \to j}$ open and Q seals P. Then, if Q sends on that channel, then P's last receive $\text{RCV}^{j \leftarrow i}$ on the channel must causally precede Q's first send $\text{SND}^{i \to j}$ on it. Otherwise, Q must ensure that any later send on $\text{chan}_{i \to j}$ is causally preceded by P's last receive. This is guaranteed exactly if P's signature contains an edge $(\text{RCV}^{j \leftarrow i}, \text{LST}_k)$ and Q's signature contains an edge $(\text{FST}_k, \text{LST}_i)$, for some $k \in \mathbb{P}$. (See Fig. 5.)

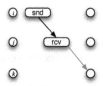
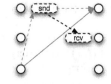

(a) Channel $\text{chan}_{i \to j}$ left open by P and a causality edge to LST_k.

(b) Sealing the channel by causality. The dashed part accounts for Q sending on $\text{chan}_{i \to j}$.

Fig. 5. Excerpts of the signatures of BSLs P and Q

Based on the above observation the following theorem characterizes sealing among BSLs.

Theorem 8. *Let P and Q be BSLs and let $(V_P, E_P) = \text{SIG}(P)$ and $(V_Q, E_Q) = \text{SIG}(Q)$. Then Q properly seals P iff, for all $\text{RCV}^{j \leftarrow i} \in V_P$, there exists $k \in \mathbb{P}$ such that $(\text{RCV}^{j \leftarrow i}, Ld_k) \in E_P$, $(\text{FST}_k, \text{LST}_i) \in E_Q$, and, if $\text{SND}^{i \to j} \in V_Q$ then $(\text{FST}_k, \text{SND}^{i \to j}) \in E_Q$.*

Given the theorem above, the complexity of deciding whether Q seals P, given their signatures, is obviously determined by the size of P's signature, which we recall is $O(n^2)$.

4.2 A Characterization of Sealability

Observe that the set of channels closed by a BSL P when executed from a cut with empty channels is uniquely determined by P and can be derived from its signature. We can thus associate a *closed-channel graph* with each BSL . Formally, the closed-channel graph $C_P = (\mathbb{P}, E_P)$ of a BSL P is given by $(i, j) \in E_P$ iff $i \neq j$ and $\text{chan}_{i \to j}$ is closed by P in REL. In the following we denote the undirected version of a graph G by G^u.

Theorem 9 (Sealability). *Let P be a BSL. Then P can be sealed properly in REL iff C_P^u is connected. Moreover, if P is properly sealable in REL then it can be sealed by a BSL that transmits less than $3n$ messages.*

Sketch of proof. We now sketch the "if"-direction of the claim. Let $T \subseteq E_P$ such that $(\mathbb{P}, T)^u$ is a spanning tree of C_P^u and let v be its root. We construct a seal S for P in three phases. In the first phase we establish that for every edge $(i, j) \in T$ the channel on this edge directed towards v is closed. This is achieved by sending an acknowledgment should this channel not be closed already by P. The second phase consists of a convergecast from all leaves of T towards the root v. Finally, the third phase is a broadcast from v to the leaves. It follows that S closes every channel at least once and is therefore a seal for P. Moreover, each of the three phases transmits at most $n - 1$ messages.   □

Example 10. Consider a phase $L = *_{i \in \mathbb{P}} L_i$. In L each process $i \neq 1$ sends a message to every other process $k \notin \{1, i\}$ before receiving the $n - 2$ messages sent to it in this phase. Finally, process i transmits a message to process 1. We can define process i's program L_i more formally by

$$L_i \;=\; \left(*_{k \notin \{1,i\}} \mathrm{SND}^{i \to k} \right) * \left(*_{k \notin \{1,i\}} \mathrm{RCV}^{i \leftarrow k} \right) * \mathrm{SND}^{i \to 1} \;.$$

Process 1 in turn receives those messages sent last in the L_i, that is:

$$L_1 \;=\; *_{i \neq 1} \mathrm{RCV}^{1 \leftarrow i}$$

Executing L beginning with empty channels leaves $n^2 - 3n + 3$ channels open. Nevertheless, L can be sealed efficiently by the program

$$S \;=\; *_{i \neq 1} (\mathrm{SND}^{1 \to i} * \mathrm{RCV}^{i \leftarrow 1}) \;,$$

which transmits $n - 1$ messages. (See Fig. 6 for the program graph of S.)

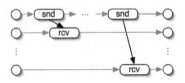

Fig. 6. $O(n)$ transmissions close $\Omega(n^2)$ open channels

5   Conclusion and Future Work

A subtle yet crucial issue in developing distributed applications is the safe composition of smaller programs into larger ones. The notion of CCL captures when a program works as if it were executed in isolation in the context of a given larger program. The literature on CCLs focused mostly on reliable FIFO communication. In that setting programs can be designed that are inherently CCLs in any program context.

Observe that neither termination detection nor barrier-style techniques can be applied in REL without careful inspection of the surrounding program context. Any such mechanism will form a layer in the resulting program which in turn must be shown to safely compose with the other layers. A popular approach to running distributed applications on non-RELFI systems is to construct an intermediate data-link layer providing RELFI communication to the application. This typically involves sealing every single message transmission from interference by previous and later layers. Popular algorithms for data-link achieve this by adding message headers and/or acknowledging every single message, thereby incurring a significant overhead [1,15]. As we show for REL, it is often possible to do better than that. Our analysis of sealing can be used to add the minimal amount of glue between consecutive layers to ensure that they compose safely, without changing the layers at all.

We have introduced a framework for studying safe program composition. It facilitates the formal definition of standard notions such as CCL, barriers, and TCC. Gerth and Shrira showed that—as a context-sensitive notion—CCL is unsuitable for compositional development of larger systems from off-the-shelf components. As we have shown, neither barriers nor TCC layers are useful for such development in REL, that is, when communication is reliable but not FIFO. In another paper [3], we use essentially the same framework to investigate safe composition in models with message duplication or loss. Barriers and TCC layers are also absent in those models. The framework introduced here is used to define two more notions, namely fitting after and separating, that are more readily applicable in those models.[7] We illustrate our approach by applying it to the case of REL. Notably, the approach allows for seamless composition of programs without need for translation or headers.

The central notion introduced and explored in this paper is that of one program *sealing* another. Larger programs can be composed from smaller ones provided each smaller program seals its predecessor. For instance, recall that $\text{MT}^{i\to j} * \text{MT}^{j\to i}$ seals itself in REL. Lemma 1.5 can be used to show that a program of the form **while** *true* **do** $\text{MT}^{i\to j} *$ $\text{MT}^{j\to i}$ **od** can serve to transmit a sequence of values from i to j in REL. Indeed, if the return messages from j to i are not merely acknowledgments, it can perform sequence exchange. The notion of sealing in REL is shown to be intimately related to Lamport causality. Based on this connection, we devise efficient algorithms for deciding and constructing seals for the class of straight-line programs.

Acknowledgment. We would like to thank Manuel Chakravarty, Yael Moses, and Ron van der Meyden for helpful comments on preliminary versions of this paper.

References

1. Y. Afek, H. Attiya, A. Fekete, M. Fischer, N. Lynch, Y. Mansour, D.-W. Wang, and L. Zuck. Reliable communication over unreliable channels. *Journal of the ACM*, 41(6):1267–1297, 1994.
2. T. Elrad and N. Francez. Decomposition of distributed programs into communication-closed layers. *Science of Computer Programming*, 2(3):155–173, Dec. 1982.
3. K. Engelhardt and Y. Moses. Safe composition of distributed programs communicating over order-preserving imperfect channels. Submitted; see ftp://ftp.cse.unsw.edu.au/pub/users/kaie/EM2005b.pdf, June 2005.
4. K. Engelhardt and Y. Moses. Single-bit messages are insufficient in the presence of duplication. In preparation; see ftp://ftp.cse.unsw.edu.au/pub/users/kaie/EM2005c.pdf, June 2005.

---

[7] We say that P *fits after* Q if $\tau(P * Q) \leq_\Gamma \tau P * \tau Q$. Program S *separates* P *from* Q if $\tau(P * S * Q) \leq_\Gamma \tau P * \tau S * \tau Q$.

5. A. Fekete and N. Lynch. The need for headers: An impossibility result for communication over unreliable channels. In *CONCUR '90: Proceedings on Theories of Concurrency: Unification and Extension*, pages 199–215. Springer-Verlag, 1990.

6. R. Gerth and L. Shrira. On proving communication closedness of distributed layers. In K. V. Nori, editor, *Foundations of Software Technology and Theoretical Computer Science, Sixth Conference*, volume 241 of *LNCS*, pages 330–343, New Delhi, India, 18–20 Dec. 1986. Springer-Verlag.

7. W. Janssen. *Layered Design of Parallel Systems*. PhD thesis, University of Twente, 1994.

8. W. Janssen. Layers as knowledge transitions in the design of distributed systems. In U. H. Engberg, K. G. Larsen, and A. Skou, editors, *Proceedings of the Workshop on Tools and Algorithms for the Construction and Analysis of Systems, TACAS* (Aarhus, Denmark, 19–20 May, 1995), number NS-95-2 in Notes Series, pages 304–318, Department of Computer Science, University of Aarhus, May 1995. BRICS.

9. W. Janssen, M. Poel, and J. Zwiers. Action systems and action refinement in the development of parallel systems. In J. C. M. Baeten and J. F. Groote, editors, *Proceedings of CONCUR '91, 2nd International Conference on Concurrency Theory, Amsterdam, The Netherlands*, volume 527 of *LNCS*, pages 298–316, 1991.

10. W. Janssen and J. Zwiers. From sequential layers to distributed processes, deriving a minimum weight spanning tree algorithm, (extended abstract). In *Proceedings 11th ACM Symposium on Principles of Distributed Computing*, pages 215–227. ACM, 1992.

11. L. Lamport. Time, clocks, and the ordering of events in a distributed system. *Communications of the ACM*, 7:558–565, 1978.

12. N. A. Lynch. *Distributed Algorithms*. Morgan Kaufmann, 1996.

13. M. Poel and J. Zwiers. Layering techniques for development of parallel systems. In G. von Bochmann and D. K. Probst, editors, *Computer Aided Verification, Fourth International Workshop, CAV '92*, volume 663 of *LNCS*, pages 16–29, Montreal, Canada, June 29 – July 1 1992. Springer-Verlag.

14. F. A. Stomp and W.-P. de Roever. A principle for sequential reasoning about distributed algorithms. *Formal Aspects of Computing*, 6(6):716–737, 1994.

15. D.-W. Wang and L. D. Zuck. Tight bounds for the sequence transmission problem. In *PODC '89: Proceedings of the eighth annual ACM Symposium on Principles of Distributed Computing*, pages 73–83. ACM Press, 1989.

What Can Be Implemented Anonymously?

Rachid Guerraoui[1] and Eric Ruppert[2]

[1] EPFL, Lausanne, Switzerland
[2] York University, Toronto, Canada

Abstract. The vast majority of papers on distributed computing assume that processes are assigned unique identifiers before computation begins. But is this assumption necessary? What if processes do not have unique identifiers or do not wish to divulge them for reasons of privacy? We consider asynchronous shared-memory systems that are anonymous. The shared memory contains only the most common type of shared objects, read/write registers. We investigate, for the first time, what can be implemented deterministically in this model when processes can fail. We give anonymous algorithms for some fundamental problems: timestamping, snapshots and consensus. Our solutions to the first two are wait-free and the third is obstruction-free. We also show that a shared object has an obstruction-free implementation if and only if it satisfies a simple property called idempotence. To prove the sufficiency of this condition, we give a universal construction that implements any idempotent object.

1 Introduction

Distributed computing typically studies what can be computed by a system of n processes that can fail independently. Variations on the capacities of the processes (e.g., in terms of memory or time), their means of communication (e.g., shared memory or message passing), and their failure modes (e.g., crash failures or malicious failures) have led to an abundant literature. In particular, a prolific research trend has explored the capabilities of a system of crash-prone asynchronous processes communicating through basic read-write objects (registers).

Several properties have been defined to describe the progress made by an algorithm regardless of process crashes or asynchrony. The strongest is *wait-freedom* [18], which requires *every* non-faulty process to complete its algorithm in a finite number of its own steps. However, wait-free algorithms are often provably impossible or too inefficient to be practical. In many settings, a weaker progress guarantee is sufficient. The *non-blocking* property (sometimes called lock-freedom) is one such guarantee, ensuring that, eventually, *some* process will complete its algorithm. It is weaker than wait-freedom because it permits individual processes to starve. A third condition that is weaker still is *obstruction-freedom* [19], which can be very useful when low contention is expected to be the common case, or if contention-management is used. Obstruction-freedom guarantees that a process will complete its algorithm whenever it has an opportunity to take enough steps without interruption by other processes.

P. Fraigniaud (Ed.): DISC 2005, LNCS 3724, pp. 244–259, 2005.

Virtually all of the literature on those topics assumes that processes have distinct identities. Besides intellectual curiosity, it is practically appealing to revisit this fundamental assumption. Indeed, certain systems, like sensor networks, consist of mass-produced tiny agents that might not even have identifiers [4]. Others, like web servers [29] and peer-to-peer file sharing systems [11], sometimes mandate preserving the anonymity of the users and forbid the use of any form of identity for the sake of privacy [10]. Instead of revealing its identity to a server that houses a shared-memory object, a process might use a trusted third party that can itself be approximated by a decentralized mechanism [16]. This party forwards the process's invocations to the server (stripped of the process's id) and then forwards the server's responses back to the process. But what can actually be done in an *anonymous* system? In such a system, processes are programmed identically [5,7,8,12,23,28]. In particular, processes do not have identifiers. There has been work on anonymous message-passing systems, starting with Angluin [3]. The very small amount of research that has looked at anonymous shared-memory systems assumed failure-free systems or the existence of a random oracle to build randomized algorithms. (See Sect. 2.)

We explore in this paper, for the first time, the types of shared objects that can be implemented *deterministically* in an anonymous, asynchronous shared-memory system. We assume that any number of unpredictable crash failures may occur. The shared memory is composed of registers that are (multi-reader and) multi-writer, so that every process is permitted to write to every register. In contrast, usage of single-writer registers would violate total anonymity by giving processes at least some rudimentary sense of identity: processes would know that values written into the same register at different times were produced by the same process. Some problems, such as leader election, are clearly impossible in this model because symmetry cannot be broken; if processes run in lockstep, they will perform exactly the same sequence of operations. However, we show that some interesting problems *can* be solved without breaking symmetry.

We first consider *timestamps*, which are frequently used to help processes agree on the order of various events. Objects such as fetch&increment and counters, which are traditionally used for creating timestamps, cannot be implemented in our model, so we introduce a weaker object called a *weak counter* which provides sufficiently good timestamps for our applications. We construct, in Sect. 4, an efficient, wait-free implementation of a weak counter.

In non-anonymous systems, the *snapshot* object [1,2,6] is probably the most important example of an object that has a wait-free implementation from registers. It is an abstraction of the problem of obtaining a consistent view of many registers while they are being updated by other processes. There are many known implementations of snapshot objects but, to our knowledge, all do make essential use of process identities. Wait-free algorithms generally rely on helping mechanisms, in which fast processes help the slow ones complete their operations. One of the challenges of anonymity is the difficulty of helping other processes when it is not easy to determine who needs help. In Sect. 5, we show that a wait-free snapshot implementation does exist and has fairly efficient time complexity. The timestamps provided by the weak counter are essential in this construction. We also give a non-blocking implementation with better space complexity.

In non-anonymous systems, most objects have no wait-free (or even non-blocking) implementation [18]. However, it is possible to build an obstruction-free implementation of any object by using a subroutine for *consensus*, which is a cornerstone of distributed computing that does itself have an obstruction-free implementation [19]. Consensus also arises in a wide variety of process-coordination tasks. There is no (deterministic) wait-free implementation of consensus using registers, even if processes do have identifiers [18,26]. In Sect. 6, we note that an obstruction-free anonymous consensus algorithm can be obtained by simply derandomizing the randomized anonymous algorithm of Chandra [13]. The resulting algorithm uses unbounded space. We then give a new algorithm that uses a bounded number of registers, with the help of our snapshots.

Theorem	Implemented Object	Using	Space	Progress	Uses
1	weak counter	registers	$O(k)$	wait-free	
3	weak counter	binary registers	$O(k)$	non-blocking	
4	m-component snapshot	registers	m	non-blocking	
5	m-component snapshot	registers	$O(m+k)$	wait-free	1
6	binary consensus	binary registers	unbounded	obs-free	
7	binary consensus	registers	$O(n)$	obs-free	4
9	consensus	binary registers	unbounded	obs-free	6, 8
9	consensus	registers	$O(n \log d)$	obs-free	7, 8
10	idempotent object	binary registers	unbounded	obs-free	3, 9
12	idempotent object	registers	object-dependent	obs-free	3, 7

Fig. 1. Summary of implementations, where n is the number of processes, k is the number of operations invoked, and d is the number of possible inputs to consensus

Finally, we give a complete characterization of the types of objects that have obstruction-free implementations in our model in Sect. 7. An object can be implemented if and only if it is idempotent: *i.e.* applying any permitted operation twice in a row (with the same arguments) has the same effect as applying it once. We use a symmetry argument to show this condition is necessary. To prove sufficiency, we give a "universal" construction that implements any idempotent object, using our weak counter object and our consensus algorithm.

To summarize, we show that the anonymous asynchronous shared-memory model has some, perhaps surprising, similarities to the non-anonymous model, but there are also some important differences. We construct a wait-free algorithm for snapshots and an obstruction-free algorithm for consensus that uses bounded space. Not every type of object has an obstruction-free anonymous implementation, however. We give a characterization of the types that do. Table 1 summarizes all anonymous implementations given in this paper, indicating which implementations are used as subroutines for others.

2   Related Work

Some research has studied anonymous shared-memory systems when no failures can occur. Johnson and Schneider [23] gave leader election algorithms using versions of single-writer snapshots and test&set objects. Attiya, Gorbach and Moran [8] gave a characterization of the tasks that are solvable without failures using registers if n is not known. The characterization is the same if n is known [14]. Consensus is solvable in these models, but it is not solvable if the registers cannot be initialized by the programmer [22]. Aspnes, Fich and Ruppert [5] looked at failure-free models with other types of objects, such as counters. They also characterized which shared-memory models can be implemented if communication is through anonymous broadcasts, showing the broadcast model is equivalent to having shared counters and strictly stronger than shared registers.

There has also been some research on randomized algorithms for anonymous shared-memory systems with no failures. For the naming problem, processes must choose unique names for themselves. Processes can randomly choose names, which will be unique with high probability. Registers can be used to detect when the names chosen are indeed unique, thus guaranteeing correctness whenever the algorithm terminates, which happens with high probability [25,30]. Two papers gave randomized renaming algorithms that have finite expected running time, and hence terminate with probability 1 [15,24].

Randomized algorithms for systems with crash failures have also been studied. Panconesi *et al.* [28] gave a randomized wait-free algorithm that solves the naming problem using single-writer registers, which give the system some ability to distinguish between different processes' actions. Several impossibility results have been shown for randomized naming using only multi-writer registers [12,15,24]. Interestingly, Buhrman *et al.* [12] gave a randomized wait-free anonymous algorithm for consensus in this model that is based on Chandra's randomized consensus algorithm [13]. Thus, producing unique identifiers is strictly harder than consensus in the randomized setting. Aspnes, Shah and Shah [7] extended the algorithm of Buhrman *et al.* to a setting with infinitely many processes.

Solving a decision task can be viewed as a special case of implementing objects: each process accesses the object, providing its input as an argument, and later the object responds with the output the process should choose. Herlihy and Shavit [20] gave a characterization of the decision tasks that have wait-free solutions in non-anonymous systems using ideas borrowed from algebraic topology. They also describe how the characterization can be extended to systems with a kind of anonymity: processes have identifiers but are only allowed to use them in very limited ways. Herlihy gave a *universal construction* which describes how to create a wait-free implementation of any object type using consensus objects [18]. Processes use consensus to agree on the exact order in which the operations are applied to the implemented object. Although this construction requires identifiers, it was the inspiration for our obstruction-free construction in Sect. 7. Recently, Bazzi and Ding [9] introduced, in the context of Byzantine systems, non-skipping timestamps, a stronger abstraction than what we call a weak counter. (Our weak counter does not preclude skipping values.)

3   Model

We consider an *anonymous* system, where a collection of n processes execute identical algorithms. In particular, the processes do not have identifiers. The system is *asynchronous*, which means that processes run at arbitrarily varying speeds. It is useful to think of processes being allocated steps by an adversarial scheduler. Algorithms must work correctly in all possible schedules. Processes are subject to *crash failures*: they may stop taking steps without any warning. The algorithms we consider are *deterministic*.

Processes communicate with one another by accessing shared data structures, called *objects*. The *type* of an object specifies what states it can have and what operations may be performed on it. The programmer chooses the initial state of the objects used. Except for our weak counter object in Sect. 4, all objects are linearizable (atomic) [21]: although operations on an object take some interval of time to complete, each appears to happen at some instant between its invocation and response. An operation atomically changes the state of an object and returns a response to the invoking process. (The weak counter object can be viewed as a set-linearizable object [27].) We consider *oblivious* objects: all processes are permitted to perform the same set of operations on it and its response to an operation does not depend on the identity of the invoking process. (Non-oblivious objects are somewhat inconsistent with the notion of totally anonymous systems, since processes must identify themselves when they invoke an operation.)

Some types of objects are provided by the system and all other types needed must be implemented from them. An *implementation* specifies the code that must be executed to perform each operation on the implemented object. Since we are considering anonymous systems, all processes execute identical code to perform a particular operation. (We refer to such an implementation as an anonymous implementation.) The implementation must also specify how to initialize the base objects to represent any possible starting state of the implemented object.

We assume the shared memory contains the most basic kind of objects: *registers*, which provide two types of operations. A *read* operation returns the state of the object without changing it. A *write(v)* changes the state to v and returns *ack*. Every process can access every register. If the set of possible values that can be stored is finite, the register is *bounded*; otherwise it is *unbounded*. A *binary* register has only two possible states. When describing our algorithms in pseudocode, names of shared objects begin with upper-case letters, and names of the process's private variables begin with lower-case letters.

4   Weak Counters

A *weak counter* provides a single operation, GETTIMESTAMP, which returns an integer. It has the property that if one operation precedes another, the value returned by the later operation must be larger than the value returned by the earlier one. (Two concurrent GETTIMESTAMP operations may return the same value.) Furthermore, the value returned to any operation should not exceed the number of invocations that have occurred so far. This object will be used as a building block for our implementation of snapshots in Sect. 5 and our characterization of implementable types in Sect. 7. It is used in those algorithms to provide timestamps to different operations. The weak counter is essentially a weakened form of a fetch&increment object: a fetch&increment object has the additional requirement that all values returned should be distinct. It is known that a fetch&increment object has no wait-free implementation from registers, even if processes have identifiers [18]. By considering our weaker version, we have an object that is implementable, and still strong enough for our purposes.

We give an anonymous, wait-free implementation of a weak counter from unbounded registers. A similar but simpler construction, which provides an implementation that satisfies the weaker non-blocking progress property, but uses only binary registers, is then described briefly. Processes must know n, the number of processes in the system, (or at least an upper bound on n) for the wait-free implementation, but this knowledge is not needed for the non-blocking case.

Our wait-free implementation uses an array $A[1, 2, \ldots]$ of binary registers, each initialized to $\bot$. To obtain a counter value, a process locates the first entry of the array that is $\bot$, changes it to $\top$, and returns the index of this entry. (See Fig. 2.) The key property for correctness is the following invariant: if $A[k] = \top$, then all entries in $A[1..k]$ are $\top$. To locate the first $\bot$ in A efficiently, the algorithm uses a binary search. Starting from the location a returned by the process's previous GETTIMESTAMP operation, the algorithm probes locations $a + 1, a + 3, a + 7, \ldots, a + 2^i - 1, \ldots$ until it finds a $\bot$ in location b. (For the first operation by the process, we initialize a to 1.) We call this portion of the algorithm, corresponding to the first loop in the pseudocode, phase 1. The process then executes a binary search of $A[a..b]$ in the second loop, which constitutes phase 2.

To ensure processes cannot enter an infinite loop in phase 1 (while other processes write more and more $\top$'s into the array), we incorporate a helping mechanism. Whenever a process writes a $\top$ into an entry of A, it also writes the index of the entry into a shared register L (initialized to 0). A process may terminate early if it sees that n writes to L have occurred since its invocation. In this case, it returns the largest value it has seen in L. The local variables j and t keep track of the number of times the process has seen L change, and the largest value the process has seen in L, respectively.

Theorem 1. *Fig. 2 gives a wait-free, anonymous implementation of a weak counter from registers.*

Proof. We first give three simple invariants.
Invariant 1: For each process's value of a, if $a > 1$, then $A[a - 1] = \top$.
Once $\top$ is written into an entry of A, that entry's value will never change again. It follows that line 14 maintains Invariant 1. Line 6 does too, since the preceding iteration of line 3 found that $A[b] = \top$.
Invariant 2: If $A[k] = \top$, then $A[k'] = \top$ for all $k' \leq k$.
This follows from Invariant 1: whenever line 17 is executed, we have $a = b$, so $A[b - 1]$ is already $\top$.

GETTIMESTAMP
```
 1  b ← a + 1
 2  ℓ ← L; t ← ℓ; j ← 0
 3  loop until A[b] = ⊥
 4          if L ≠ ℓ
 5              then ℓ ← L; t ← max(t, ℓ); j ← j + 1
 6                      if j ≥ n then a ← b + 1; return t and halt
 7                      end if
 8          end if
 9          b ← 2b − a + 1
10  end loop
11  loop until a = b
12          mid ← (a+b−1)/2      ▷ This is an integer, since b − a + 1 is a power of 2
13          if A[mid] = ⊥ then b ← mid
14          else a ← mid + 1
15          end if
16  end loop
17  write ⊤ to A[b]
18  L ← b
19  return b
```

Fig. 2. Wait-free implementation of a weak counter from registers

Invariant 3: Whenever a process P executes line 11 during a GETTIMESTAMP operation op, P's value of b has the property that $A[b]$ was equal to $\bot$ at some earlier time during op.

This is easy to prove by induction on the number of iterations of the second loop.

Wait-freedom: To derive a contradiction, assume there is an execution where some operation by a process P runs forever without terminating. This can only happen if there is an infinite loop in Phase 1, so an infinite number of ⊤'s are written into A during this execution. This means that an infinite number of writes to L will occur. Suppose some process Q writes a value x into L. Before doing so, it must write ⊤ into $A[x]$. Thus, any subsequent invocation of GETTIMESTAMP by Q will never see $A[x] = \bot$. It follows from Invariant 3 that Q can never again write x into L. Thus, P's operation will eventually see n different values in L and terminate, contrary to the assumption.

Correctness: Suppose one GETTIMESTAMP operation op_1 completes before another one, op_2, begins. Let r_1 and r_2 be the values returned by op_1 and op_2, respectively. We must show that $r_2 > r_1$. If op_1 terminates in line 6, then, at some earlier time, some process wrote r_1 into L and also wrote ⊤ into $A[r_1]$. If op_1 terminates in line 19, it is also clear that $A[r_1] = \top$ when op_1 terminates.

If op_2 terminates in line 19, then $A[r_2]$ was $\bot$ at some time during op_2, by Invariant 3. Thus, by Invariant 2, $r_2 > r_1$. If op_2 terminates in line 6, op_2 has seen the value in L change n times during its run, so at least two of the changes were made by the same process. Thus, at least one of those changes was made by an operation op_3 that started after op_2 began (and hence after op_1 terminated). Since op_3 terminated in line 19, we have already proved that the value r_3 that

op_3 returns (and writes into L) must be greater than r_1. But op_2 returns the largest value it sees in L, so $r_2 \geq r_3 > r_1$. ∎

In any finite execution in which k GETTIMESTAMP operations are invoked, at most $O(k)$ of the registers are ever accessed, and the worst-case time for any operation is $O(\log k)$. An amortized analysis can be used to prove the stronger bound of $O(\log n)$ on the *average* time per operation in any finite execution. Intuitively, if some process P must perform a phase 1 that is excessively long, we can charge its cost to the many operations that must have written into A since P did its previous operation. (See [17] for a detailed proof of the following.)

Proposition 2. *If n processes perform a total of k invocations of the* GET-TIMESTAMP *algorithm in Fig. 2, the total number of steps by all processes is $O(k \log n)$ and $O(k)$ registers are accessed.*

If we do not require the weak counter implementation to be wait-free, we do not need the helping mechanism. Thus, we can omit lines 2, 4–8 and 18, which allow a process to terminate early if it ever sees that n changes to the shared register L occur. This yields a non-blocking implementation that uses only *binary* registers. The proof of correctness is a simplified version of the proof of Theorem 1, and the analysis is identical to the proof of Proposition 2.

Theorem 3. *There is a non-blocking, anonymous implementation of a weak counter from binary registers. In any execution with k invocations of* GETTIMES-TAMP *in a system of n processes, the total number of steps is $O(k \log n)$ and $O(k)$ registers are accessed.*

5   Snapshot Objects

The snapshot object [1,2,6] is an extremely useful abstraction of the problem of getting a consistent view of several registers when they can be concurrently updated by other processes. It has wait-free (non-anonymous) implementations from registers, and has been widely used as a basic building block for other algorithms. A snapshot object consists of a collection of $m > 1$ components and supports two kinds of operations: a process can update the value stored in a component and atomically scan the object to obtain the values of all the components. Since we are interested in anonymous systems, we consider the multi-writer version, where any process can update any component. Many algorithms exist to implement snapshots, but all use process identifiers. The following proposition can be proved using a simple modification of the standard non-blocking snapshot algorithm for non-anonymous systems [1]. A proof appears in [17].

Proposition 4. *There is a non-blocking, anonymous implementation of an m-component snapshot object from m registers.*

More surprisingly, we show that a standard algorithm for (non-anonymous) wait-free snapshots [1] can also be modified to work in an anonymous system.

SCAN

UPDATE(i, x)

1 $t \leftarrow$ GETTIMESTAMP
2 $v \leftarrow$ SCAN
3 write (x, v, t) in R_i

```
SCAN
1   t ← GETTIMESTAMP
2   loop
3        read R_1, R_2, …, R_m
4        if a register contained (∗, v, t′) with t′ ≥ t
5            then return v
6        elseif n + 1 sets of reads gave same results
7            then return the first field of each value
8        end if
9   end loop
```

Fig. 3. Wait-free implementation of a snapshot object from registers.

The original algorithm could create a unique timestamp for each UPDATE operation. We use our weak counter to generate timestamps that are not necessarily distinct, but are sufficient for implementing the snapshot object. The non-uniqueness of the identifiers imposes a need for more iterations of the loop than in the non-anonymous algorithm. Our algorithm uses m (large) registers, $R_1, \ldots, R_m$, and one weak counter, which can be implemented from registers, by Theorem 1. Each register R_i will contain a value of the component, a view of the entire snapshot object and a timestamp. See Fig. 3.

Theorem 5. *The algorithm in Fig. 3 is an anonymous, wait-free implementation of a snapshot object from registers. The average number of steps per operation in any finite execution is $O(mn^2)$.*

Proof. (Sketch) See [17] for a detailed proof. It can be shown that the registers either keep changing continually, eventually including timestamps that will satisfy the first termination condition, or stop changing so that the second termination condition will eventually be satisfied. UPDATES are linearized when the write occurs. If a SCAN sees $n + 1$ identical sets of reads, it can be shown that these values were all in the register at one instant in time, which is used as the linearization point. If a SCAN uses the vector recorded from another SCAN as its output, the two SCANS are linearized at the same time. The timestamp mechanism is sufficient to guarantee that the linearization point so chosen is between the invocation and response of the SCAN.   ∎

6   Consensus

In the consensus problem, processes each start with a private input value and must all choose the same output value. The common output must be the input value of some process. These two conditions are called *agreement* and *validity*, respectively. Herlihy, Luchangco and Moir [19] observed that a randomized wait-free consensus algorithm can be "derandomized" to obtain an obstruction-free consensus algorithm. If we derandomize the *anonymous* consensus algorithm of Chandra [13], we obtain the following theorem. (A proof appears in [17].)

Theorem 6. *There is an anonymous, obstruction-free binary consensus algorithm using binary registers.*

The construction that proves Theorem 6 uses an unbounded number of binary registers. In this section, we give a more interesting construction of an obstruction-free, anonymous algorithm for consensus that uses a bounded number of (multivalued) registers. First, we focus on *binary consensus*, where all inputs are either 0 or 1, and give an algorithm using $O(n)$ registers.

In the unbounded-space algorithm, each process maintains a preference that is either 0 or 1. Initially, a process's preference is its own input value. Intuitively, the processes are grouped into two teams according to their preference and the teams execute a race along a course of unbounded length that has one track for each preference. Processes mark their progress along the track (which is represented by an unbounded array of binary registers) by changing register values from $\bot$ to $\top$ along the way. Whenever a process P sees that the opposing team is ahead of P's position, P switches its preference to join the other team. As soon as a process observes that it is sufficiently far ahead of all processes on the opposing team, it stops and outputs its own preference. Two processes with opposite preferences could continue to race forever in lockstep but a process running by itself will eventually out-distance all competitors, ensuring obstruction-freedom.

Our bounded-space algorithm uses a two-track race course that is circular, with circumference $4n + 1$, instead of an unbounded straight one. The course is represented by one array for each track, denoted $R_0[1, 2, \ldots, 4n + 1]$ and $R_1[1, 2, \ldots, 4n + 1]$. We treat these two arrays as a single snapshot object R, which we can implement from registers. Each component stores an integer, initially 0. As a process runs around the race course, it keeps track of which lap it is running. This is incremented each time a process moves from position $4n + 1$ to position 1. The progress of processes in the race is recorded by having each process write its lap into the components of R as it passes.

Several complications are introduced by using a circular track. After a fast process records its progress in R, a slow teammate who has a smaller lap number could overwrite those values. Although this difficulty cannot be eliminated, we circumvent it with the following strategy. If a process P ever observes that another process is already working on its kth lap while P is working on a lower lap, P jumps ahead to the start of lap k and continues racing from there. This will ensure that P can only overwrite one location with a lower lap number, once sufficiently many k's have been written. There is a second complication: because some numbers recorded in R may be artificially low due to the overwrites by slow processes, processes may get an incorrect impression of which team is in the lead. To handle this, we make processes less fickle: they switch teams only when they have lots of evidence that the other team is in the lead. Also, we require a process to have evidence that it is leading by a very wide margin before it decides. The algorithm is given in Fig. 4, where we use $\bar{v}$ to denote $1 - v$.

Theorem 7. *The algorithm in Fig. 4 is an anonymous, obstruction-free binary consensus algorithm that uses $8n + 2$ registers.*

PROPOSE(*input*)

```
 1   v ← input; j ← 0; lap ← 1
 2   loop
 3         S ← SCAN of R
 4         if S_v[i] < S_v̄[i] for a majority of values of i ∈ {1, .., 4n + 1}
 5              then v ← v̄
 6         end if
 7         if   min   S_v[i] >   max   S_v̄[i]
            1≤i≤4n+1        1≤i≤4n+1
 8              then return v
 9         elseif some element of S is greater than lap
10              then lap ← maximum element of S; j ← 1
11         else    j ← j + 1
12              if j = 4n + 2 then lap ← lap + 1; j ← 1
13              end if
14         end if
15         UPDATE the value of R_v[j] to lap
16   end loop
```

Fig. 4. Obstruction-free consensus using $O(n)$ registers

Proof. We use $8n + 2$ registers to get a non-blocking implementation of the snapshot object R using Proposition 4.

Obstruction-freedom: Consider any configuration C. Let m be the maximum value that appears in any component of R in C. Suppose some process P runs by itself forever without halting, starting from C. It is easy to check that P's local variable lap increases at least once every $4n + 1$ iterations of the loop until P decides. Eventually P will have $lap \geq m+1$ and $j = 1$. Let v_0 be P's local value of v when P next executes line 7. At this point, no entries in R are larger than m. Furthermore, $R_{v_0}[i] \geq R_{v̄_0}[i]$ for a majority of the values i. (Otherwise P would have changed its value of v in the previous step.) From this point onward, P will never change its local value v, since it will write only values bigger than m to R_{v_0}, and $R_{v̄_0}$ contains no elements larger than m, so none of P's future writes will ever make the condition in line 4 true. During the next $4n + 1$ iterations of the loop, P will write its value of lap into each of the entries of R_{v_0}, and then the termination condition will be satisfied, contrary to the assumption that P runs forever. (This termination occurs within $O(n)$ iterations of the loop, once P has started to run on its own, so termination is guaranteed as soon as any process takes $O(n^4)$ steps by itself, since the SCAN algorithm of Proposition 4 terminates if a process takes $O(n^3)$ steps by itself.)

Validity: If all processes start with the same input value v, they will never switch to preference $v̄$ nor write into any component of $R_{v̄}$.

Agreement: For each process that decides, consider the moment when it last scans R. Let T be the first such moment in the execution. Let S^* be the SCAN taken at time T. Without loss of generality, assume the value decided by the process that did this SCAN is 0. We shall show that every other process that terminates also decides 0. Let m be the minimum value that appears in S_0^*. Note that all values in S_1^* are less than m.

We first show that, after T, at most n UPDATES write a value smaller than m into R. If not, consider the first $n+1$ such UPDATES after T. At least two of them are done by the same process, say P. Process P must do a SCAN in between the two UPDATES. That SCAN would still see one of the values in R_0 that is at least m, since $4n+1 > n$. Immediately after this SCAN, P would change its local variable lap to be at least m and the value of lap is non-decreasing, so P could never perform the second UPDATE with a value smaller than m.

We use a similar proof to show that, after T, at most n UPDATE operations write a value into R_1. If this is not the case, consider the first $n+1$ such UPDATES after T. At least two of them are performed by the same process, say P. Process P must do a SCAN between the two UPDATES. Consider the last SCAN that P does between these two UPDATES. That SCAN will see at most n values in R_1 that are greater than or equal to m, since all such values were written into R_1 after T. It will also see at most n values in R_0 that are less than m (by the argument in the previous paragraph). Thus, there will be at least $2n+1$ values of i for which $R_0[i] \geq m > R_1[i]$ when the SCAN occurs. Thus, immediately after the SCAN, P will change its local value of v to 0 in line 5, contradicting the fact that it writes into R_1 later in that iteration.

It follows from the preceding two paragraphs that, at all times after T, $\min_{1\leq i\leq 4n+1} R_1[i] < m \leq \max_{1\leq i\leq 4n+1} R_0[i]$. Any process that takes its final SCAN after T cannot decide 1. ∎

Just as a randomized, wait-free consensus algorithm can be "derandomized" to yield an obstruction-free algorithm, the algorithm of Theorem 4 could be used as the basis of a randomized wait-free anonymous algorithm that solves binary consensus using bounded space.

Theorems 6 and 7 can be extended to non-binary consensus using the following proposition, which is proved using a fairly standard technique of agreeing on the output bit-by-bit (see [17]).

Proposition 8. *If there is an anonymous, obstruction-free algorithm for binary consensus using a set of objects S, then there is an anonymous, obstruction-free algorithm for consensus with inputs from the countable set D that uses $|D|$ binary registers and $\log|D|$ copies of S. Such an algorithm can also be implemented using $2\log|D|$ registers and $\log|D|$ copies of S if $|D|$ is finite.*

Corollary 9. *There is an anonymous, obstruction-free algorithm for consensus, with arbitrary inputs, using binary registers. There is an anonymous, obstruction-free algorithm for consensus with inputs from a finite set D that uses $(8n+4)\log|D|$ registers.*

7   Obstruction-Free Implementations

We now give a complete characterization of the (deterministic) object types that have anonymous, obstruction-free implementations from registers. We say that an object is idempotent if, starting from any state, two successive invocations of the same operation (with the same arguments) return the same response and leave the object in a state that is indistinguishable from the state a single application would leave it in. (This is a slightly more general definition of idempotence than the one used in [5].) This definition of idempotence is made more precise using the formalism of Aspnes and Herlihy [6]. A *sequential history* is a sequence of steps, each step being a pair consisting of an operation invocation and its response. Such a history is called *legal* (for a given initial state) if it is consistent with the specification of the object's type. Two sequential histories H and H' are *equivalent* if, for all sequential histories G, $H \cdot G$ is legal if and only if $H' \cdot G$ is legal. A step p is *idempotent* if, for all sequential histories H, if $H \cdot p$ is legal then $H \cdot p \cdot p$ is legal and equivalent to $H \cdot p$. An object is called idempotent if all of its operations are idempotent. Examples of idempotent objects include registers, sticky bits, snapshot objects and resettable consensus objects.

Theorem 10. *A deterministic object type T has an anonymous, obstruction-free implementation from binary registers if and only if T is idempotent.*

Proof. ($\Rightarrow$) We assume $n > 2$. The special case $n = 2$ is deferred to the full paper. Assume there is such an implementation of T. Let P, Q and R be distinct processes. Let H be any legal history and let $p = (op, res)$ be any step such that $H \cdot p$ is legal. Let α be the execution of the implementation where some process P executes the code for the sequence of operations in H, and then Q executes op. Since the object is deterministic, Q must receive the result res for operation op. Let β be the execution where P executes the code for the sequence of operations in H, and then processes Q and R execute the code for op, taking alternate steps. Since Q and R access only registers, they will take exactly the same sequence of steps, and both will terminate and return res. Thus, $H \cdot p \cdot p$ must be legal also.

The internal state of P is the same at the end of α and β. The value stored in each register is also the same at the end of these two runs. Thus any sequence of operations performed by P after α will generate exactly the same sequence of responses as they would if P executed them after β. It follows that, for any history G, $H \cdot p \cdot G$ is legal if and only if $H \cdot p \cdot p \cdot G$ is legal, so T is idempotent.

($\Leftarrow$) Let T be any idempotent type. We give an anonymous, obstruction-free algorithm that implements T from binary registers. The algorithm uses an unbounded number of consensus objects $Con[1, 2, \ldots]$, which have an obstruction-free implementation from binary registers, by Corollary 9. The algorithm also uses the GETTIMESTAMP operation that accesses a weak counter, which can also be implemented from binary registers, according to Theorem 3. These will be used to agree on the sequence of operations performed on the simulated object. All other variables are local. The *history* variable is initialized to an empty sequence, and i is initialized to 1. The code in Fig. 5 describes how a process simulates an operation op.

Obstruction-freedom: If, after some point of time, only one process takes steps, all of its subroutine calls will terminate, and it will eventually increase i

Do(op)

```
 1  loop
 2          t ← GETTIMESTAMP
 3          (op', t') ← PROPOSE(op, t) to Con[i]
 4          res ← result returned to op' if it is done after history
 5          history ← history ·(op, res)
 6          i ← i + 1
 7          if (op', t') = (op, t)
 8              then return res
 9          end if
10  end loop
```

Fig. 5. Obstruction-free implementation of an idempotent object from binary registers

until it accesses a consensus object that no other process has accessed. When that happens, the loop is guaranteed to terminate.

Correctness: We must describe how to linearize all of the simulated operations. Any simulated operation that receives a result in line 3 that is equal to the value it proposed to the consensus object is linearized at the moment that consensus object was first accessed. All (identical) operations linearized at the moment $Con[i]$ is first accessed are said to belong to group i.

The following invariant follows easily from the code (and the fact that the object is idempotent): At the beginning of any iteration of the loop by any process P, $history_P$ is equivalent to the history that would result from the the first $i_P - 1$ groups of simulated operations taking place (in order), where i_P and $history_P$ are P's local values of the variables i and $history$. Thus, the results returned to all simulated operations are consistent with the linearization.

We must still show that the linearization point chosen for a simulated operation is between its invocation and response. Let D be an execution of Do(op) in group i. The linearization point T of D is the first access in the execution to $Con[i]$. Clearly, this cannot be after D completes, since D itself accesses $Con[i]$. Let D' be the execution of Do(op') that first accesses $Con[i]$. (It is possible that $D = D'$.) Since D is linearized in group i, it must be the case that $op = op'$, and also that the timestamps used in the proposals by D and D' to $Con[i]$ are equal. Let t be the value of this common timestamp. Note that T occurs after D' has completed the GETTIMESTAMP operation that returned t. If T were before D is invoked, then the GETTIMESTAMP operation that D calls would have to return a timestamp larger than t. Thus, T is after the invocation of D, as required. ∎

The algorithm used in the above proof does not require processes to have knowledge of the number of processes, n, so the characterization of Theorem 10 applies whether or not processes know n. Since unbounded registers are idempotent, it follows from the theorem that they have an obstruction-free implementation from binary registers, and we get the following corollary.

Corollary 11. *An object type T has an anonymous, obstruction-free implementation from unbounded registers if and only if T is idempotent.*

In the more often-studied context of non-anonymous wait-free computing, counters (with separate increment and read operations) can be implemented from registers [6], while consensus objects cannot be [18,26]. The reverse is true for anonymous, obstruction-free implementations (since consensus is idempotent, but counters are not). Thus, the traditional classification of object types according to their consensus numbers [18] will not tell us very much about anonymous, obstruction-free implementations since, for example, consensus objects cannot implement counters, which have consensus number 1.

If large registers are available (instead of just binary registers), the algorithm in Fig. 5 could use, as a consensus subroutine, the algorithm of Theorem 7 instead of the algorithm of Theorem 6. If the number of different operations that are permitted on the idempotent object type is d and k invocations occur, then the number of registers needed to implement each consensus object is $O(n \log(dk))$, by Proposition 8, and at most k consensus objects are needed. This yields the following proposition.

Proposition 12. *An idempotent object with a operation set of size d has an implementation that uses $O(kn \log(dk))$ registers in any execution with k invocations on the object.*

Acknowledgements. We thank Petr Kouznetsov for helpful conversations. This research was supported by the Swiss National Science Foundation (NCCR MICS project) and the Natural Sciences and Engineering Research Council of Canada.

References

1. Y. Afek, H. Attiya, D. Dolev, E. Gafni, M. Merritt, and N. Shavit. Atomic snapshots of shared memory. *J. ACM*, 40(4):873–890, 1993.
2. J. H. Anderson. Composite registers. *Distributed Computing*, 6(3):141–154, 1993.
3. D. Angluin. Local and global properties in networks of processors. In *12th ACM Symp. on Theory of Computing*, pages 82–93, 1980.
4. D. Angluin, J. Aspnes, Z. Diamadi, M. J. Fischer, and R. Peralta. Computation in networks of passively mobile finite-state sensors. In *23rd ACM Symp. on PODC*, pages 290–299, 2004.
5. J. Aspnes, F. Fich, and E. Ruppert. Relationships between broadcast and shared memory in reliable anonymous distributed systems. In *Distributed Computing, 18th Intl Symp.*, pages 260–274, 2004.
6. J. Aspnes and M. Herlihy. Wait-free data structures in the asynchronous PRAM model. In *2nd ACM SPAA*, pages 340–349, 1990.
7. J. Aspnes, G. Shah, and J. Shah. Wait-free consensus with infinite arrivals. In *34th ACM Symp. on Theory of Computing*, pages 524–533, 2002.
8. H. Attiya, A. Gorbach, and S. Moran. Computing in totally anonymous asynchronous shared memory systems. *Inf. and Computation*, 173(2):162–183, 2002.
9. R. A. Bazzi and Y. Ding. Non-skipping timestamps for byzantine data storage systems. In *Distributed Computing, 18th Intl Conf.*, pages 405–419, 2004.

10. O. Berthold, H. Federrath, and M. Köhntopp. Project "anonymity and unobservability in the internet". In *10th Conf. on Computers, Freedom and Privacy*, pages 57–65, 2000.

11. S. C. Bono, C. A. Soghoian, and F. Monrose. Mantis: A lightweight, server-anonymity preserving, searchable P2P network. Technical Report TR-2004-01-B-ISI-JHU, Information Security Institute, Johns Hopkins University, 2004.

12. H. Buhrman, A. Panconesi, R. Silvestri, and P. Vitanyi. On the importance of having an identity or, is consensus really universal? In *Distributed Computing, 14th Intl Conf.*, volume 1914 of *LNCS*, pages 134–148, 2000.

13. T. D. Chandra. Polylog randomized wait-free consensus. In *15th ACM Symp. on PODC*, pages 166–175, 1996.

14. C. Drulă. The totally anonymous shared memory model in which the number of proces ses is known. Personal communication.

15. O. Eğecioğlu and A. K. Singh. Naming symmetric processes using shared variables. *Distributed Computing*, 8(1):19–38, 1994.

16. D. Goldschlag, M. Reed, and P. Syverson. Onion routing. *Commun. ACM*, 42(2):39–41, 1999.

17. R. Guerraoui and E. Ruppert. What can be implmented anonymously? Technical Report 200496, School of Computer and Communications Sciences, EPFL, 2004.

18. M. Herlihy. Wait-free synchronization. *ACM TOPLAS*, 13(1):124–149, 1991.

19. M. Herlihy, V. Luchangco, and M. Moir. Obstruction-free synchronization: Double-ended queues as an example. In *23rd IEEE Intl Conf. on Distributed Computing Systems*, pages 522–529, 2003.

20. M. Herlihy and N. Shavit. The topological structure of asynchronous computability. *J. ACM*, 46(6):858–923, 1999.

21. M. P. Herlihy and J. M. Wing. Linearizability: A correctness condition for concurrent objects. *ACM TOPLAS*, 12(3):463–492, 1990.

22. P. Jayanti and S. Toueg. Wakeup under read/write atomicity. In *Distributed Algorithms, 4th Intl Workshop*, volume 486 of *LNCS*, pages 277–288, 1990.

23. R. E. Johnson and F. B. Schneider. Symmetry and similarity in distributed systems. In *4th ACM Symp. on PODC*, pages 13–22, 1985.

24. S. Kutten, R. Ostrovsky, and B. Patt-Shamir. The Las-Vegas processor identity problem (How and when to be unique). *J. Algs*, 37(2):468–494, 2000.

25. R. J. Lipton and A. Park. The processor identity problem. *Inf. Process. Lett.*, 36(2):91–94, 1990.

26. M. C. Loui and H. H. Abu-Amara. Memory requirements for agreement among unreliable asynchronous processes. In F. P. Preparata, editor, *Advances in Computing Research*, volume 4, pages 163–183. JAI Press, Greenwich, Connecticut, 1987.

27. G. Neiger. Set-linearizability. In *13th ACM Symp. on PODC*, page 396, 1994.

28. A. Panconesi, M. Papatriantafilou, P. Tsigas, and P. Vitányi. Randomized naming using wait-free shared variables. *Distributed Computing*, 11(3):113–124, 1998.

29. M. K. Reiter and A. D. Rubin. Crowds: Anonymity for web transactions. *ACM Trans. on Inf. and System Security*, 1(1):66–92, 1998.

30. S.-H. Teng. Space efficient processor identity protocol. *Inf. Process. Lett.*, 34(3):147–154, 1990.

Waking Up Anonymous Ad Hoc Radio Networks*

Andrzej Pelc[1]

Département d'informatique, Université du Québec en Outaouais,
Gatineau, Québec J8X 3X7, Canada
pelc@uqo.ca

Abstract. We consider the task of waking up an anonymous ad hoc radio network from a single source, by a deterministic algorithm. In the beginning only the source is awake and has to wake up other nodes by disseminating messages throughout the network. Nodes of the network do not know its topology and they do not have distinct labels. In such networks some nodes are impossible to reach. A node in a network is *accessible* if it can be woken up by some (possibly network-dependent) deterministic algorithm. A deterministic wakeup algorithm for ad hoc networks is *universal* if it wakes up all accessible nodes in all networks. We study the question of the existence of such a universal wakeup algorithm. For synchronous communication we design a universal wakeup algorithm, and for asynchronous communication we show that no such algorithm exists.

1 Introduction

A radio network is a collection of stations, which can act as *transmitters* or as *receivers*. Stations will be referred to as *nodes* of the network. The network is modeled as an undirected connected graph on the set of these nodes. An edge e between two nodes means that transmissions of one end of e can reach the other end. Time is divided into equal *steps* (time slots). In every step every node acts either as a transmitter or as a receiver. A node acting as a transmitter sends a message which can potentially reach all of its neighbors. An important distinction at the receiving end is between a message being *delivered* and being *heard*, i.e., received successfully by a node. In the synchronous scenario, a message sent by a node in a given step t is delivered to all neighbors in the same step. In the asynchronous scenario, it is delivered to each neighbor in some step $t' \geq t$, and this choice is made by an adversary, for each neighbor.

A node acting as a receiver in a given step *hears* a message, if and only if, a message from exactly one of its neighbors is delivered in this step. The message heard in this case is the one that was delivered from the unique neighbor. If messages from at least two neighbors v and v' of u are delivered simultaneously in a given step, none of the messages is heard by u in this step. In this case we

---

* Research partially supported by NSERC discovery grant and by the Research Chair in Distributed Computing at the Université du Québec en Outaouais.

P. Fraigniaud (Ed.): DISC 2005, LNCS 3724, pp. 260–272, 2005.

say that a *collision* occurred at u. It is assumed that the effect at node u of a collision is the same as that of no message being delivered in this step, i.e., a node cannot distinguish a collision from silence.

A standard assumption made when considering deterministic radio communication is that nodes have distinct labels which can be parameters for a communication algorithm. However, in practice, nodes of unknown identities may join the network over time in a distributed fashion, and thus it is important to design communication algorithms that do not depend on node identities. Therefore in this paper we drop the assumption of distinct node identities and consider *anonymous ad hoc radio networks*. In ad hoc networks (cf. [7,20]) nodes do not know the topology of the network. In our present scenario, knowledge of nodes is even more restricted: they know neither the topology of the network nor their labels. We assume that there is one distinguished node called the *source*, which has a *wakeup message* to be disseminated in the network. All other nodes are identical. Nodes know only their status source/non-source but they do not have any other a priori information (global or local) concerning the network: they know neither the topology of the network nor its size, nor even their own degree.

Waking up a radio network from a single source is the following basic task. In the beginning, one distinguished node, called the *source*, is *awake* and all other nodes are *dormant*. The source starts the wakeup process by sending a message, which is then relayed by awake nodes. Every node that hears a message becomes awake and can send further messages. Dormant nodes do not send any messages, i.e. they act as receivers until being woken up. All nodes have individual clocks that tick at the same rate, measuring time steps. The clock of a node starts in the step when the node is woken up. Waking up is closely related to *broadcasting*, which is one of the fundamental primitives in network communication. Its goal is to transmit a message from the source of the network, to all other nodes. Remote nodes get the source message via intermediate nodes, along paths in the network. The difference between waking up from a single source and broadcasting is that, in waking up, dormant nodes do not send any messages, and in broadcasting, such spontaneous transmissions, containing some control messages and sent before the source message reaches a given node, may be allowed.

We consider only deterministic wakeup algorithms. In our anonymous scenario it is clear that, for some networks, not all nodes can be woken up. For example, in the 4-cycle, the node at distance 2 from the source cannot be woken up by any algorithm, due to the impossibility of breaking symmetry. Hence we say that a node in a network is *accessible* if it can be woken up by some (possibly network-dependent) algorithm. Broadcasting (whose aim is to reach *all* nodes) may be impossible in anonymous networks, for the same reason as above. Therefore, waking up anonymous networks is rather related to *multicasting* whose goal is to transmit source information to all accessible nodes. Since our context is that of ad hoc networks, we are interested in network-independent wakeup algorithms. A wakeup algorithm for ad hoc networks is *universal* if it wakes up all accessible nodes in all networks.

1.1   Our Results

We study the fundamental question of the existence of a deterministic universal wakeup algorithm. Such an algorithm, if it exists, is very general, in that – without knowing the network – it is still capable of disseminating source information in every possible network to all nodes that can be reached by some deterministic communication algorithm (even specifically designed for this particular network). We focus attention on feasibility of universal wakeup. It turns out that the existence of a universal wakeup algorithm depends on the synchrony of communication. For synchronous communication we design a universal wakeup algorithm, and for asynchronous communication we show that no such algorithm exists.

1.2   Open Problems

Since we show a universal wakeup algorithm in the synchronous setting and refute its existence in the asynchronous setting, it is natural to ask if a universal wakeup algorithm exists in the partially synchronous setting, in which there is an upper bound t on the delay between sending and delivery of a message, and t can be used as an input to the algorithm. On the other hand, in this paper we focus attention on feasibility of universal wakeup and not on its efficiency. It remains open if there exists a universal wakeup algorithm (in the synchronous or partially synchronous setting), which wakes up all accessible nodes in all networks in time polynomial in the size of the network.

1.3   Related Work

Models used in the literature about algorithmic aspects of radio communication differ mostly in the amount of information about the network that is assumed available to nodes. However, all previous results concerning deterministic algorithms for radio communication assume that nodes have distinct identities, and each node knows its identity.

Deterministic centralized broadcasting assuming complete knowledge of the network was considered, e.g., in [6], where a $\mathcal{O}(D \log^2 n)$-time broadcasting algorithm was given for all n-node networks of radius D. This was improved to $\mathcal{O}(D \log n + \log^2 n)$ in [21]. In [16], $\mathcal{O}(D + \log^5 n)$-time broadcasting was proposed. This was improved to $\mathcal{O}(D + \log^4 n)$ in [15]. On the other hand, in [1] the authors proved the existence of a family of n-node networks of radius 2, for which any broadcast requires time $\Omega(\log^2 n)$.

One of the first papers to study deterministic distributed broadcasting in radio networks whose nodes have only limited knowledge of the topology, was [3]. The authors assumed that nodes know only their own label and labels of their neighbors. Many authors [5,7,8,12,13] studied deterministic distributed broadcasting in radio networks under the assumption that nodes know only their own label (but not labels of their neighbors). In [7] the authors gave a broadcasting algorithm working in time $\mathcal{O}(n)$ for arbitrary n-node networks, assuming that nodes can transmit spontaneously, before getting the source message. For this model, a matching lower bound $\Omega(n)$ on deterministic broadcasting time was proved in [19] even for the class of networks of constant diameter. On the other hand, in [5] a lower bound $\Omega(D \log n)$ was proved for n-node networks of radius D, if spontaneous transmissions are not allowed.

In [7,8,12,14] the model of directed graphs was used. Increasingly faster broadcasting algorithms working on arbitrary (directed) radio networks were constructed, the currently fastest being the $\mathcal{O}(n \log^2 D)$-time algorithm from [14]. On the other hand, in [13] a lower bound $\Omega(n \log D)$ on broadcasting time was proved for directed n-node networks of radius D.

Randomized broadcasting algorithms in radio networks were studied, e.g., in [3,23]. For these algorithms, no topological knowledge of the network was assumed, and no distinct identities of nodes were supposed. In [3] the authors showed a randomized broadcasting algorithm running in expected time $\mathcal{O}(D \log n + \log^2 n)$. In [23] it was shown that for any randomized broadcasting algorithm and parameters $D \leq n$, there exists an n-node network of radius D requiring expected time $\Omega(D \log(n/D))$ to execute this algorithm. It should be noted that the lower bound $\Omega(\log^2 n)$ from [1], for some networks of radius 2, holds for randomized algorithms as well. A randomized algorithm working in expected time $\mathcal{O}(D \log(n/D) + \log^2 n)$, and thus matching the above lower bounds, was presented in [20] (cf. also [14]).

The wakeup problem in radio networks was first studied in [17] for single-hop networks (modeled by complete graphs), and then in [11,9] for arbitrary networks. In [18] the authors studied randomized wakeup algorithms for radio networks. In all these papers it was assumed that a subset of all nodes wake up spontaneously and have to wake up other (dormant) nodes.

In all the above papers communication was carried out in the synchronous model, in which a message is delivered to a neighbor in the time step in which it is sent. Asynchronous radio communication was first considered in [10], where the authors studied an efficiency measure of an asynchronous broadcasting algorithm called the work (the total number of messages sent). They used various adversaries to model asynchrony of radio communication. The model of asynchrony used in the present paper was called edge adversary in [10].

To the best of our knowledge, the present paper is the first to study deterministic communication algorithms for anonymous ad hoc radio networks. Various computational tasks in anonymous networks of different nature were studied, e.g., in [2,4,22].

2   Preliminaries

2.1   Algorithms and Histories

Since in our setting networks are anonymous and nodes are not aware of the topology, the decision made by a node in a given step, whether it should transmit or not, can be based solely on the messages previously heard by this node. Hence a (deterministic) wakeup algorithm can be viewed as a function that takes the communication history of a node before the given step and returns a message to be sent in a given step or the decision to send no message. From the point of view of node accessibility we can restrict attention to algorithms that instruct nodes to send a particular type of messages: when, according to its history, a node is supposed to send a message in a given step, the message is the entire history of the node before this step. Since the history is the only information based on which decisions are made, any wakeup algorithm can be simulated by an algorithm sending entire histories, and hence, if a node in a network is accessible by any algorithm, it is accessible by an algorithm whose messages are entire histories.

In what follows we formally define the notions of history and of a wakeup algorithm that correspond to the above intuitions. The *history* of a node v in step i, denoted by $H(i, v)$, is a finite sequence of symbols $1, [,]$. It corresponds to what the node heard until step i and is inductively defined as follows. $H(0, v)$ is the sequence $[1]$ (where 1 is the one-bit wakeup message of the source), if v is the source, and it is the sequence $[\,]$ otherwise. The latter sequence is denoted by ϵ and is called the *empty* history. Suppose that $H(j, w)$ is defined for all $j < i$ and all nodes w. Consider a node v and step $i > 0$.

- If node v heard a message m in step i then $H(i, v)$ is the concatenation of $H(i-1, v)$ and of the sequence $[m]$.
- If node v did not hear any message in step i and v is awake then $H(i, v)$ is the concatenation of $H(i-1, v)$ and of the sequence $[\,]$.
- If node v is dormant (i.e., it is not the source and did not hear any message in any step $j \leq i$) then $H(i, v)$ is the sequence $[\,]$.

In particular, this definition formalizes the intuition that nodes other than the source start counting steps from the time of their waking up by the first message they hear, and the source starts counting steps from the beginning. Histories of dormant nodes are all the same in all steps and equal to ϵ.

Let $\mathcal{H}$ denote the set of all histories. A *wakeup algorithm* is any function $\mathcal{A} : \mathcal{H} \longrightarrow \{0, 1\}$, such that $\mathcal{A}(\epsilon) = 0$. Intuitively $\mathcal{A}(H) = 1$ means that algorithm $\mathcal{A}$ instructs a node with history H to act as a transmitter in a given step and send a message containing H, while $\mathcal{A}(H) = 0$ means that algorithm $\mathcal{A}$ instructs a node with history H to act as a receiver and thus not send any message.

In the above definitions, histories of nodes depend on messages *heard*, and algorithms give instructions about *sending*. The notion of an *execution* of a wakeup algorithm in a given communication environment gives the relation between the above. Fix a wakeup algorithm $\mathcal{A}$ and a network G with source s. In the case of asynchronous communication also fix an adversary A, which, for every step i, every node v, such that v sends a message in step i, and for every neighbor w of v, determines the step $j \geq i$ in which the message is *delivered* to w (not necessarily *heard* by w). Similarly as in [10] we do not allow amalgamating messages sent in different steps by a node, i.e., if two messages were sent by a node v in distinct steps, they must be delivered at each neighbor of v in distinct steps as well. In the case of synchronous communication we assume that the adversary always determines step $j = i$, i.e., it delivers a message in the step in which it is sent. The execution of algorithm $\mathcal{A}$ in (G, s), under adversary A, defines the message *heard* in any step i by any node. It is the notion of execution that captures both the role of collisions, and the role of the adversary in successful receiving of messages. Fix a node v and a step i, in which v acts as a receiver, according to $\mathcal{A}$. If a message m from exactly one neighbor w of v is delivered at v in step i then v hears m in step i. Otherwise v hears nothing. It follows from the above that if a node v hears a message in step i then this message must be $H(j, w)$, for some $j < i$ and some neighbor w of v, and in the case of synchronous communication it must be $H(i - 1, w)$. A node other than the source is *awake* when it already heard some message.

Suppose that a network G with source s and an adversary are fixed. For any wakeup algorithm $\mathcal{A}$, any time step i and any node v of this network, the execution of $\mathcal{A}$ defines a history of the algorithm $\mathcal{A}$ in node v at time i. This history is denoted by $H(i, v, \mathcal{A})$.

2.2 Node Accessibility

A node of a network G with source s, for adversary A, is *accessible* if there exists a wakeup algorithm $\mathcal{A}$ such that the execution of $\mathcal{A}$ in this network, under adversary A, causes node v to hear a message in some step. Note that this algorithm may be tailored specifically to wake up this particular node, and thus may depend on the network and even on the specific node v.

As mentioned in the introduction, some nodes in some networks are not accessible, as witnessed by the example of the 4-cycle. Below we give a simple sufficient condition for inaccessibility of a node, exploiting the symmetry of the network. Consider a network $G = (V, E)$ with source s. Nodes w and w' are called *similar* if there exists a graph automorhism f of the graph G (i.e., a bijection $f : V \longrightarrow V$ such that u is adjacent to v iff $f(u)$ is adjacent to $f(v)$) for which $f(s) = s$ and $f(w) = w'$. A node v is called *blocked* if v is not the source and if, for every u adjacent to v, there exists a node $u' \neq u$ adjacent to v and similar to u.

Proposition 1. *In synchronous communication, every blocked node is inaccessible.*

Proof. We first prove by induction on step i that similar nodes have identical histories in all steps i in the synchronous execution of any wakeup algorithm. Fix a wakeup algorithm $\mathcal{A}$. For $i = 0$ this property is obvious. Suppose that it holds for $i \geq 0$ and let u and u' be similar nodes. Let $f : V \longrightarrow V$ be an automorphism of G, for which $f(s) = s$ and $f(u) = u'$. We want to prove $H(i+1, u, \mathcal{A}) = H(i+1, u', \mathcal{A})$. By the inductive hypothesis we have $H(i, u, \mathcal{A}) = H(i, u', \mathcal{A})$. If none of the nodes u, u' hears any message in step $i + 1$, we are done. Hence we may assume, without loss of generality, that u hears a message in step $i + 1$. Let v be the neighbor of u from which u heard this message. The node $f(v)$ is a neighbor of u', similar to v. By the inductive hypothesis we have $H(i, v, \mathcal{A}) = H(i, f(v), \mathcal{A})$. Hence algorithm $\mathcal{A}$ causes $f(v)$ to transmit the same message as v in step $i + 1$. If u' hears this message, we are done. Hence assume that u' does not hear any message in step $i + 1$. This means that either

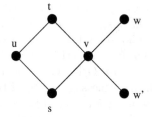

Fig. 1. A network with a non-blocked inaccessible node

u' itself or some neighbor $w \neq f(v)$ of u' transmits in this step. In the first case u also transmits in this step because $H(i, u, \mathcal{A}) = H(i, u', \mathcal{A})$, which contradicts the assumption that u hears a message in step $i + 1$. In the second case, the neighbor $f^{-1}(w)$ of node u is similar to w and, by the inductive hypothesis, we have $H(i, w, \mathcal{A}) = H(i, f^{-1}(w), \mathcal{A})$. Consequently, $f^{-1}(w)$ transmits in step $i + 1$, since w does. However, node $f^{-1}(w)$ is a neighbor of u different from v, which contradicts the fact that u hears the mesage from v in step $i + 1$. Thus we got contradiction in both cases and the property is proved by induction.

Now suppose that a blocked node $v \neq s$ is accessible, and let $\mathcal{A}$ be a wakeup algorithm whose synchronous execution causes v to hear a message for the first time in step j. Suppose that this message comes from neighbor u of v. Since v is blocked, there exists a neighbor $u' \neq u$ that is similar to u. Hence histories of u' and u are identical up to step $j - 1$. Consequently, if u sends a message in step j, so does u'. This prevents v from hearing any message in step j. Contradiction. □

The sufficient condition for node inaccessibility from Proposition 1 permits to establish this feature of nodes in many cases. For example, consider a square grid of odd size with the source in the center of the grid. Symmetries with respect to each of the diagonals are clearly automorphisms of the grid that fix the source. It follows that every node of the diagonal is blocked, and consequently it is inaccessible, for the synchronous adversary. However, the condition from Proposition 1 is not necessary for inaccessibility. Consider the network from Fig. 1. It is easy to see that nodes u and v are not similar, and hence node t is not blocked. However, it is inaccessible for the following reason. Nodes w and w' have identical histories in all steps in the synchronous execution of any wakeup algorithm. Consequently they cannot inform node v of their existence and hence the symmetry between nodes u and v cannot be broken. These nodes have identical histories in all steps in the synchronous execution of any wakeup algorithm, hence no algorithm can wake up node t.

3   A Universal Synchronous Wakeup Algorithm

In this section we consider the synchronous setting, in which every message is delivered to neighbors of a sending node in the same step in which it is sent. In this setting we can define the notion of *time* of any nonempty history H, denoted by $T(H)$. This is the number of the time step (counted from the start of the wakeup process), in which the history is taken. $T(H)$ can be easily computed, given H. It is clear how to do it for time step 1. Suppose that it is computed for histories in time steps $j < i$, and consider a history H in step i. Consider the subsequence H' of H corresponding to the first message forming H. The sequence H' is some history at a time $j < i$, hence by induction $T(H')$ can be computed. Every step after j is reflected in the sequence H either by a subsequence [ ] if no message was heard in this step, or by a subsequence $[m]$, where m is the message heard in this step. The number x of these subsequences (easy to identify by pairing parantheses [and]), added to $T(H')$, gives $T(H)$.

Example 1. Consider the history $H = ([\ ][H'][H_1][\ ][\ ][H_2][\ ][H_3])$. The first segment [ ] codes the fact that the node is not the source. The next segment $[H']$ means that the first heard message was H'. Suppose that $T(H')$, computed recursively, is 5. The end segment $[H_1][\ ][\ ][H_2][\ ][H_3]$ of the sequence H means that the node heard message H_1 in step 6, no message in steps 7 and 8, message H_2 in step 9, no message in step 10, and message H_3 in step 11. Thus $T(H) = 11$.

Consider any wakeup algorithm $\mathcal{A}$ and any time step i. The *truncation* of $\mathcal{A}$ to i, denoted $\mathcal{A}|i$, is the restriction of the function $\mathcal{A}$ to the set of those histories H for which $T(H) \leq i$. Let Σ_i be the set of all truncations to i. For each integer i, Σ_i is a finite set. Enumerate all elements of all sets Σ_i by distinct positive integers (since truncations are functions from a set of sequences to $\{0, 1\}$, a canonical enumeration could be, e.g., the lexicographic ordering of these functions). For any truncation $\mathcal{A}|i$, let $\Phi(\mathcal{A}|i)$ denote the positive integer associated to $\mathcal{A}|i$ in this enumeration. Call it the *code* of truncation $\mathcal{A}|i$. By definition, distinct truncations have distinct codes.

We are now ready to define the algorithm $\mathcal{U}$ that will be proved universal. The idea of the algorithm is the following. Let p_j denote the jth prime number. For any truncation $\mathcal{A}|i$ with code j, algorithm $\mathcal{U}$ simulates decisions of algorithm $\mathcal{A}$ made in steps $k \leq i$ by making identical decisions in steps p_j^k. This idea is formalized as follows.

Let H be a history and j a positive integer. We define the jth *projection* of H, denoted $\Pi_j(H)$, by induction on $T(H)$. We have $\Pi_j([\ ]) = ([\ ])$ and $\Pi_j([1]) = ([1])$. Suppose that $\Pi_j(H')$ is defined for all histories with $T(H') < T(H)$. Let H^* be the subsequence of H corresponding to time steps that are powers of p_j. Let $H^* = ([H_1][H_2] \dots [H_r])$, where H_t are either histories or empty sequences. Now $\Pi_j(H)$ is defined as $([\Pi_j(H_1)][\Pi_j(H_2)] \dots [\Pi_j(H_r)])$. Intuitively, $\Pi_j(H)$ extracts from H the part that happened in time steps which are powers of p_j.

Now the algorithm $\mathcal{U}$ is defined as follows. Let H be a nonempty history. If $T(H)$ is not $p_j^k - 1$, for any j and k, then $\mathcal{U}(H) = 0$, i.e., nodes do not transmit in time steps that are not powers of primes. If $T(H) = p_j^k - 1$, for some j and k, then let $\mathcal{A}|i$ be a truncation with code j. If $k \leq i$ then $\mathcal{U}(H) = \mathcal{A}(\Pi_j(H))$, i.e., $\mathcal{U}$ simulates the decision of (the truncation of) $\mathcal{A}$. If $k > i$ then $\mathcal{U}(H) = 0$ (the simulation of the truncation $\mathcal{A}|i$ is finished).

This concludes the definition of the wakeup algorithm $\mathcal{U}$. It remains to prove its main property.

Theorem 1. *The wakeup algorithm $\mathcal{U}$ is universal.*

Proof. Consider an accessible node v in a network G with source s. Let $u_1, u_2, \ldots,$ u_m be neighbors of v. Denote $v = u_0$. Suppose that a wakeup algorithm $\mathcal{A}$ wakes up node v in step i. Hence v hears the message from some neighbor u_q in step i. Let j be the code of truncation $\mathcal{A}|i$. Consider the step $t = p_j^i$. Let H_r, for $r = 0, 1, \ldots, m$, be the history of node u_r in time step $t - 1$, under algorithm $\mathcal{U}$, i.e., $H_r = H(t-1, u_r, \mathcal{U})$, and let $\hat{H}_r$ be the history of node u_r in time step $i-1$, under algorithm $\mathcal{A}$, i.e., $\hat{H}_r = H(i-1, u_r, \mathcal{A})$. Hence $\hat{H}_r = \Pi_j(H_r)$. Since v was woken up by u_q in algorithm $\mathcal{A}$, we have $\mathcal{A}(\hat{H}_q) = 1$ and $\mathcal{A}(\hat{H}_r) = 0$, for all $r \neq q$. By the definition of algorithm $\mathcal{U}$ we have $\mathcal{U}(H_r) = \mathcal{A}(\Pi_j(H_r)) = \mathcal{A}(\hat{H}_r)$. Hence $\mathcal{U}(H_q) = 1$ and $\mathcal{U}(H_r) = 0$, for all $r \neq q$. Consequently, v hears the message from u_q in time step t. It follows that all accessible nodes are woken up by algorithm $\mathcal{U}$, and hence this algorithm is universal. $\qquad\square$

4   Impossibility of Universal Asynchronous Wakeup

In this section we prove that a universal wakeup algorithm does not exist if communication is asynchronous. We will show this impossibility result even for a restricted adversary that cannot amalgamate messages: messages sent by a neighbor w of v in different steps have to be delivered at v in different steps.

In order to carry out our impossibility argument, we first define the following class $\mathcal{N}$ of networks. Networks of this class are indexed by finite nondecreasing sequences. Let $r = (r_1, \ldots, r_k)$ be such a sequence, where $r_1 \leq \cdots \leq r_k$. The network N_r is defined as follows. The source s has neighbors $u_1, \ldots, u_k$, which have another common neighbor t, at distance 2 from s. Moreover, to each node u_m a path of length r_m is attached, and all paths are pairwise disjoint and do

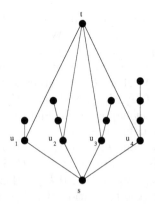

Fig. 2. The network $N_{(1,2,2,3)}$

not contain s or t (see Fig. 2). A network N_r is called *leading*, if the largest term of the sequence r is unique (i.e., if $r_k > r_{k-1}$). Thus the network $N_{(1,2,2,3)}$ is leading and the network $N_{(1,2,3,3)}$ is not.

We first prove the following fact.

Lemma 1. *In every leading network every node is accessible.*

Proof. Let N_r be a leading network, and let r_k be the unique largest term of r. The following algorithm (called Algorithm Dedicated because it is specially tailored for the network N_r and depends on $r = (r_1, \ldots, r_k)$) wakes up all nodes of N_r. We describe the algorithm informally but it can be easily translated to correspond to our definition from Section 2.

Algorithm Dedicated

- The source sends a message with counter -1;
- a node that was woken up by a message with counter x in some step, sends a message with counter $x + 1$ in the next step;
- a node that heard a message with counter r_k in some step, sends the message *elected* in the next step;
- a node that heard the message *elected* for the first time in some step, sends the message *elected* $k - 1$ times, in the $k - 1$ following steps.

It is easy to see that all nodes of N_r, other than node t, are woken up by messages with counters. The message *elected* is generated only in the unique longest path, and consequently only one neighbor of the source, namely node u_k corresponding to this longest path, sends k messages: one message with counter 0 and $k - 1$ messages *elected*. Every other neighbor of the source sends only one message (with counter 0). There are at most $k - 1$ different steps in which messages from nodes $u_1, \ldots, u_{k-1}$ are delivered. Hence at least one of the k messages from node u_k is delivered to t in a step in which it is the only message delivered to t. Consequently, node t is woken up as well. $\qquad\square$

In order to prove the impossibility of universal asynchronous wakeup, it is now sufficient to show the following result.

Lemma 2. *For every wakeup algorithm $\mathcal{A}$ there exists a leading network and an adversary, for which node t is not woken up by $\mathcal{A}$.*

Proof. Consider any wakeup algorithm $\mathcal{A}$, a network N_r and a neighbor u_m of the source. Fix the following partial behavior of the adversary: all messages sent by the source and all messages sent along edges of the path of length r_m attached to u_m are delivered in the time step in which they are sent (i.e., on this part of the network the adversary is synchronous). Any message sent by any neighbor u_k of the source in step i is delivered at s and at t in the same step $j \geq i$ (j is to be specified later). Consider the part of the execution of $\mathcal{A}$ before node t is woken up. The only messages u_m can hear during this part are either from its neighbor on the path of length r_m attached to u_m, or from the source. Since during this part the source does not hear any message (otherwise node t would also hear a message in the same step), its history (possibly heard by u_m) is of the form $([1][\ ][\ ]\dots[\ ])$. Hence messages heard by u_m during this part of the execution of $\mathcal{A}$ (for the above partially described behavior of the adversary) depend only on r_m (and not on the entire topology of N_r). Consequently, the histories of u_m also depend only on r_m during this part.

In view of this property, the following function $f : N \longrightarrow N \cup \{\infty\}$ is well defined. Take any positive integer x and consider a neighbor u_m of the source s in a network N_r. Suppose that $x = r_m$ is the length of the path attached to u_m.

First suppose that, by some time step i, node t of network N_r is not woken up and that by this time step node u_m sends y messages. Suppose that u_m does not send any more messages before node t is woken up. Then we define $f(x) = y$. It remains to specify when we set $f(x) = \infty$. This is the case if the following property is satisfied. For any positive integer k there exists an integer i such that if node t is not woken up by step i then node u_m sends at least k messages by step i. This concludes the definition of function f. Consider two cases.

Case 1. $f(x) = \infty$, for some x.

Consider the network $N_{(x,x,x+1)}$. This is a leading network. Suppose that all messages sent by neighbors u_1 and u_2 of the source are delivered at t and at s in the step in which they are sent (hence the adversary is synchronous for these nodes). Let these be steps $i_1, i_2, \dots$, until t is woken up. Let the jth message be sent by u_3 in step z_j, until t is woken up. We complete the description of the behavior of the adversary by imposing the step d_j in which this jth message of u_3 is delivered at t and at s: d_j is the smallest step i_k larger than all $d_{j'}$, for $j' < j$ and larger than z_j. Hence none of the messages sent by u_1, u_2, u_3 is heard by t, due to collisions. Consequently, t can never be woken up.

Case 2. $f(x)$ is a positive integer, for all x.

Subcase 2.1. $f(x) \leq f(1)$, for all positive integers x.

In this case, there exist two positive integers $x_1 < x_2$, such that $c = f(x_1) = f(x_2)$. Consider the network $N_{(x_1,x_2)}$. This is a leading network. Let i be a time step by which neighbors u_1 and u_2 of the source send their first c messages. Now we complete the description of the behavior of the adversary by imposing steps when messages sent by u_1 and u_2 are delivered at t and at s: in both cases they are delivered in steps $i+1, i+2, \dots, i+c$. Hence none of these messages is heard by t, due to collisions. Consequently, t is not woken up by any of these messages. However, u_1 and u_2 will not send any more messages, and hence t can never be woken up.

Subcase 2.2. $f(x) > f(1)$, for some positive integer x.

In this case denote $f(1) = a$ and $f(x) = b$. Let $c = \lceil b/a \rceil$. Consider the network N_r, where $r = (r_1, \dots, r_{c+1})$, with $r_1 = \dots = r_c = 1$ and $r_{c+1} = x$. Let i be a time step by which neighbors $u_1, \dots, u_c$ of the source send their first a messages and neighbor u_{c+1} of the source sends its first b messages. We complete the description of the behavior of the adversary by imposing steps when messages sent by nodes u_m, for $m \leq c + 1$, are delivered at t and at s. The b messages sent by node u_{c+1} are delivered in steps $i + 1, i + 2, \ldots, i + b$. The a messages sent by node u_m, for $m < c$, are delivered in steps $i + (m - 1)a + 1, i + (m - 1)a + 2, \ldots, i + ma$. Finally, the a messages sent by node u_c are delivered in steps $i + b - a + 1, i + b - a + 2, \ldots, i + b$. Hence none of these messages is heard by t, due to collisions. Consequently, t is not woken up by any of these messages. However, none of the nodes u_m will send any more messages, and hence t can never be woken up. □

Lemmas 1 and 2 imply the main result of this section:

Theorem 2. *There does not exist a universal asynchronous wakeup algorithm.*

References

1. Alon, N., Bar-Noy, A., Linial, N., Peleg, D.: A lower bound for radio broadcast. Journal of Computer and System Sciences **43** (1991) 290–298.
2. Attiya, H., Snir, M., Warmuth, M., Computing on an Anonymous Ring, Journal of the ACM **35**, (1988), 845–875.
3. Bar-Yehuda, R., Goldreich, O., Itai, A.: On the time complexity of broadcast in radio networks: an exponential gap between determinism and randomization. Journal of Computer and System Sciences **45** (1992) 104–126.
4. Boldi, P., Vigna, S., Computing anonymously with arbitrary knowledge, Proc. 18th ACM Symp. on Principles of Distributed Computing , (PODC 1999).
5. Bruschi, D., Del Pinto, M.: Lower bounds for the broadcast problem in mobile radio networks. Distributed Computing **10** (1997) 129–135.
6. Chlamtac, I., Weinstein, O.: The wave expansion approach to broadcasting in multihop radio networks. IEEE Transactions on Communications **39** (1991) 426–433.
7. Chlebus, B., Gąsieniec, L., Gibbons, A., Pelc, A., Rytter, W.: Deterministic broadcasting in ad hoc radio networks. Distributed Computing **15** (2002) 27–38.
8. Chlebus, B., Gąsieniec, L., Östlin, A., Robson, J.M.: Deterministic radio broadcasting. Proc. 27th International Colloquium on Automata, Languages and Programming (ICALP'2000), LNCS 1853, 717–728.
9. Chlebus, B., Kowalski, D.: A better wake-up in radio networks, Proc. 23rd Annual Symp. on Principles of Distributed Computing (PODC 2004).
10. Chlebus, B., Rokicki, M.: Asynchronous broadcast in radio networks, Proc. 11th Int. Coll. on Structural Information and Communication Complexity, (SIROCCO'2004), LNCS 3104, 57–68.
11. Chrobak, M., Gąsieniec, L., Kowalski, D.: The wake-up problem in multi-hop radio networks, Proc. 15th ACM-SIAM Symposium on Discrete Algorithms (SODA 2004), 985 – 993.
12. Chrobak, M., Gąsieniec, L., Rytter, W.: Fast broadcasting and gossiping in radio networks. Proc. 41st Symposium on Foundations of Computer Science (FOCS'2000) 575–581.
13. Clementi, A.E.F., Monti, A., Silvestri, R. , Selective families, superimposed codes, and broadcasting on unknown radio networks, Proc. 12th Ann. ACM-SIAM Symposium on Discrete Algorithms (SODA'2001), 709–718.
14. Czumaj, A., Rytter, W.: Broadcasting algorithms in radio networks with unknown topology. Proc. 44th Symposium on Foundations of Computer Science (FOCS'2003) 492–501.

15. Elkin, M., Kortsarz, G.: Improved broadcast schedule for radio networks. Proc. 16th ACM-SIAM Symposium on Discrete Algorithms (SODA 2005).

16. Gaber, I., Mansour, Y.: Centralized broadcast in multihop radio networks. Journal of Algorithms **46** (1) (2003) 1–20.

17. Gąsieniec, L., Pelc, A., Peleg, D.: The wakeup problem in synchronous broadcast systems, SIAM Journal on Discrete Mathematics **14** (2001), 207-222.

18. Jurdzinski, T., Stachowiak, G.:, Probabilistic algorithms for the wakeup problem in single-hop radio networks, Proc. 13th International Symposium on Algorithms and Computation (ISAAC 2002), LNCS 2518, 535 – 549.

19. Kowalski, D., Pelc, A.: Time complexity of radio broadcasting: adaptiveness vs. obliviousness and randomization vs. determinism, Theoretical Computer Science **333** (2005), 355-371.

20. Kowalski, D., Pelc, A.: Broadcasting in undirected ad hoc radio networks. Proc. 22nd ACM Symposium on Principles of Distributed Computing (PODC'2003) 73–82.

21. Kowalski, D., Pelc, A.: Centralized deterministic broadcasting in undirected multi-hop radio networks, Proc. 7th International Workshop on Approximation Algorithms for Combinatorial Optimization Problems (APPROX'2004), LNCS 3122, 171-182.

22. Kranakis, E., Krizanc, D., van der Berg, J., Computing Boolean Functions on Anonymous Networks, Information and Computation **114**, (1994), 214–236.

23. Kushilevitz, E., Mansour, Y.: An $\Omega(D\log(N/D))$ lower bound for broadcast in radio networks. SIAM Journal on Computing **27** (1998) 702–712.

Fast Deterministic Distributed Maximal Independent Set Computation on Growth-Bounded Graphs

Fabian Kuhn[1], Thomas Moscibroda[1], Tim Nieberg[2,*], and Roger Wattenhofer[1]

[1] Computer Engineering and Networks Laboratory,
ETH Zurich,
8092 Zurich, Switzerland
{kuhn, moscitho, wattenhofer}@tik.ee.ethz.ch
[2] Department of Applied Mathematics,
University of Twente,
Postbus 217, 7500 AE Enschede, The Netherlands
t.nieberg@utwente.nl

Abstract. The distributed complexity of computing a maximal independent set in a graph is of both practical and theoretical importance. While there exists an elegant $O(\log n)$ time randomized algorithm for general graphs [20], no deterministic polylogarithmic algorithm is known. In this paper, we study the problem in graphs with bounded growth, an important family of graphs which includes the well-known unit disk graph and many variants thereof. Particularly, we propose a deterministic algorithm that computes a maximal independent set in time $O(\log \Delta \cdot \log^* n)$ in graphs with bounded growth, where n and Δ denote the number of nodes and the maximal degree in G, respectively.

1 Introduction

The distributed complexity of computing a maximal independent set (MIS) in a graph has been one of the tantalizing problems in distributed computing. While there are well-known and elegant randomized algorithms that compute a MIS in expected time $O(\log n)$ [20], the open problem formulated by Linial [19], whether there exists a *deterministic* distributed algorithm that finds a MIS in a graph in *polylogarithmic* time, is open.

If every node has a unique identifier, there is a trivial distributed MIS algorithm which works as follows. Every node joins the MIS if it has the smallest ID among its neighbors and if none of its neighbors has already joined the MIS. Unfortunately, this algorithm can result in an entirely sequential execution and linear running time because there may be only a single point of activity at any time. While there exist algorithms that greatly outperform the trivial sequential

---

* This work is partially supported by the European research project Embedded WiSeNts (FP6-004400) and by the Dutch project Smart Surroundings (BSIK-03060).

P. Fraigniaud (Ed.): DISC 2005, LNCS 3724, pp. 273–287, 2005.

algorithm, e.g., [22], the quest for a polylogarithmic algorithm has so far been in vain.

The particular interest in the MIS problem stems on the one hand from its practical importance in various application settings. Specifically, in a network graph consisting of nodes representing processors, a MIS defines a set of processors which can operate in parallel without interference. On the other hand, the maximal independent set problem is also of outstanding theoretical interest, because it prototypically captures the notion of *symmetry breaking*, one of the central aspects in distributed computing, in a simple, well-defined way. While it is easily conceivable that the symmetry between nodes can be broken using randomization, doing so deterministically appears to be intrinsically difficult.

Recently, maximal independent sets have been granted particular attention by the wireless networking community. In wireless ad hoc and sensor networks, clustering is one of the foremost network organization techniques to enable efficient routing and to cope with failures and mobility. The clustering induced by a MIS has been shown to exhibit particularly desirable properties [2]. Yet, in spite of the multiplicity of papers written in the wireless networking literature, not much is known about the fundamental principles governing the computation of maximal independent sets in the kind of network graphs that have typically been used to model wireless networks.

In wireless networking, the usually studied graphs are unit disk graphs (UDG) in which all nodes are assumed to be located in the Euclidean plane and there exists a communication edge between two nodes u and v iff the Euclidean distance $d(u, v)$ is at most 1. In this paper, we study the distributed complexity of computing a MIS in unit disk graphs. Specifically, we show that for unit disk graphs, Linial's question can be answered in the affirmative. In particular, we present a novel deterministic distributed algorithm that computes a MIS in unit disk graphs in time $O(\log \Delta \cdot \log^* n)$, where Δ denotes the maximal degree in the network graph.

Obtaining a MIS deterministically is easy if each node knows it exact location, and the location of its neighbors. Moreover, if nodes can sense the distance to their neighbors, a MIS can be computed deterministically in time $O(\log^* n)$ as shown in [16]. Hence, it is an important aspect about our result that the nodes do not require *any position or distance* information. That is, the only information available at a node is the *connectivity information* to its neighbors. In graph theoretical terms, this corresponds to a problem definition in which the geometric representation of the graph is not given. Notice that even in the case of centralized algorithms, the absence of a geometric representation of a given unit disk graph renders many problems much harder. Particularly, given a unit-disk graph, it is NP-hard to find its graphical representation or even an approximation thereof [6,14].

The absence of position or distance information implies that our algorithm works for arbitrary graphs, even though it achieves the claimed $O(\log \Delta \cdot \log^* n)$ running time only in graphs with bounded growth, such as the unit disk graph. However, we establish our result not only for unit disk graphs, but for the more general notion of *growth-bounded graphs*. This more general family of graphs captures the intuitive notion that if many nodes are located close from each other, many of them must be within mutual transmission range. In graph theoretical terms, a graph is growth-bounded if the number of independent nodes in a node's r-neighborhood is bounded.

As we show in this paper, the notion of growth-bounded graphs is closely related to *unit ball graphs* (UBG) introduced in [16]. As opposed to the two-dimensional Euclidean metric in UDGs, we assume the points to be located in an arbitrary metric space. Two nodes can communicate with one another if their mutual distance is at most 1. Our deterministic algorithm works for any metric space, but its running time depends on the *doubling dimension* of the underlying metric. A metric's doubling dimension is the smallest ρ such that every ball can be covered by at most 2^ρ balls of half the radius. Specifically, our algorithm terminates in time $O(\log \Delta \cdot \log^* n)$ if the underlying metric is *doubling*, that is, its doubling dimension ρ is constant. In this case, the resulting unit ball graph is polynomially growth-bounded.

Clearly, our claim for unit disk graphs then follows directly as a special case of this more general result, because a UDG is growth-bounded and a UBG with constant doubling dimension. Intriguingly, this result shows that in graphs with bounded growth, our deterministic algorithm outperforms Luby's randomized algorithm which requires $O(\log n)$ expected time.

Besides being of theoretical interest of its own, the reason for studying more general growth-bounded graphs instead of merely unit disk graphs are twofold. First, it is well known that unit disk graphs, while generally being respected as a first modelling step, do in many ways not capture the reality experienced in wireless networks closely. Secondly, it has been argued that the distance metric induced by Internet latencies is growth-bounded and incudes a doubling metric.

The remainder of the paper is organized as follows. We give an overview over related work in Section 2. Section 3 formally introduces our model of computation and necessary notation. The algorithm is then presented and analyzed in Section 4. Finally, Section 5 concludes the paper.

2   Related Work

The distributed (randomized and deterministic) complexity of computing a MIS has been of fundamental interest to the distributed computing community for various reasons [20,7,4,18]. A major breakthrough in the understanding of the distributed computational complexity of MIS was the elegant randomized algorithm by Luby [20] that has a running time of $O(\log n)$ (see also [1,11]). The distributed computation of maximal independent sets have also been studied in the context of backbone construction in wireless networks [2,8] and in radio network models [21]. However, all these algorithms either have linear running time [2] or are probabilistic [8,21].

The fastest known *deterministic* distributed algorithms are based on the notion of network decompositions introduced in [4]. A $(d(n), c(n))$-*network de-*

composition of a graph $G = (V, E)$ is a partition of V into disjoint *clusters*, such that the subgraph induced by each cluster is connected, the diameter of each cluster is in $d(n)$, and the chromatic number of the resulting cluster graph is in $c(n)$, where the cluster graph is obtained by contracting each cluster into a single node. Given a $(d(n), c(n))$-decomposition a MIS can easily be computed in time $d(n) \cdot c(n)$. First all clusters of the first color compute a MIS in parallel in time $d(n)$. Subsequently, clusters of the next colors iteratively add their contributions to the MIS. In [4] authors present a deterministic $O(f(n)^c)$ time algorithm for computing an $(f(n)^c, f(n)^c)$-decomposition, where c is a constant, and $f(n) = n^{\sqrt{\log \log n / \log n}}$, yielding a deterministic $O(f(n)^c)$ MIS algorithm. The fastest currently known deterministic MIS algorithm was given in [22]. Based on a $(g(n)^d, g(n))$-decomposition in time $O(g(n)^d)$, where $g(n) = n^{\sqrt{1/\log n}}$ and d is a constant, the authors obtain a deterministic $O(g(n)^d)$ MIS algorithm.

On the other hand, the first lower bound given for the distributed computation of maximal independent sets has been given by Linial in [18]. This lower bound says that even on a ring topology, at least time $\Omega(\log^* n)$ is required to compute a maximal independent set. Subsequently, it was shown in [15] that in general graphs, every (possibly randomized) algorithm requires at least $\Omega(\sqrt{\log n / \log \log n})$ or $\Omega(\log \Delta / \log \log \Delta)$ communication rounds for computing a MIS.

While all of the above results hold for general graphs, much less is known about the complexity in unit disk graphs or growth-bounded graphs. In fact, if distances are unknown, the fastest deterministic algorithm to compute a MIS in unit disk graphs is the algorithm given in [22] for general graphs.

Bounded growth metrics in general and doubling metrics in particular have found quite a lot of attention recently [10,12,13,24,25]. It is proposed that latencies of many real networks such as peer-to-peer networks or the Internet are doubling. The network-related problems which are solved include metric embeddings [10,12], distance labeling and compact routing [25], and nearest neighbor search [13]. The doubling dimension has been introduced in [10], however, a similar notion has already been used in [3].

The notion of a unit ball graph (UBG) has been introduced in [16] in which the authors prove that if the underlying metric space exhibits constant doubling dimension, it is possible to construct a $(O(1), O(1))$-network decomposition in $O(\log^* n)$ communication rounds, which is asymptotically optimal. As shown above, this implies a $O(\log^* n)$ time algorithm for computing a MIS in UBGs. However, in contrast to our paper, [16] assumes that nodes can sense the *distances* to their neighboring nodes. That is, nodes know about the underlying metric space, whereas in this paper, nodes must base their decision merely on the connectivity information induced by the UBG.

3   Model and Definitions

For our algorithms, we use the standard message passing model. The network is modelled as an undirected graph $G = (V, E)$. Two nodes $u, v \in V$ of the network are connected by an edge $(u, v) \in E$ whenever there is a direct bidirectional communication channel connecting u and v. For simplicity, we assume a synchronous communication model where time is divided in rounds. In each round, every node can send a message of size $O(\log n)$ to each of its neighbors in G. The time complexity of an algorithm is the number of rounds it needs to complete. Note that at the cost of higher message complexity, every synchronous message passing algorithm can turned into an asynchronous algorithm with the same time complexity.

As discussed, finding a fast deterministic algorithm for computing a MIS on a general network graph is a hard problem. We therefore restrict our attention to an important class of graphs which we call *growth-bounded* graphs and which are defined as follows.

Definition 1. *(Growth-Bounded Graph) We call a graph G f-growth-bounded if there is a function $f(r)$ such that every r-neighborhood in G contains at most $f(r)$ independent nodes.*

Note that $f(r)$ does not depend on the number of nodes n or any other property of G. Hence, for constant r, the number of independent nodes in an r-neighborhood is constant.

The class of growth-bounded graphs seems to cover the class of graphs which can occur in wireless networks quite well. In wireless networks, nodes have some geographic position. Nearby nodes tend to hear each other, far-away nodes cannot communicate because with the available power, radio signals can only be transmitted up to some distance. In particular the class of growth-bounded graphs covers the widely used unit disk graphs as well as UDG variants (e.g. [5,17]). In [16], the unit disk graph model has been extended to general metric spaces resulting in so-called unit ball graphs (UBG). The nodes of a UBG are the points of a metric space; two nodes are connected if and only if their distance is at most 1. The following lemma shows that if the underlying metric space of a UBG G has constant doubling dimension, G is polynomially growth-bounded

Lemma 1. *Let G be a unit ball graph and let ρ be the doubling dimension of the underlying metric space. Every r-neighborhood of G contains at most $(2r)^\rho$ independent nodes.*

Proof. By the definition of a UBG, the r-neighborhood of node v in G is completely covered by the ball $B_r(v)$ with radius r around v. By the definition of the doubling dimenstion ρ, $B_r(v)$ can be covered by at most $2^{\rho(1+\log_2 r)}$ balls of radius $1/2$. By the triangle inequality, two nodes inside a ball of radius $1/2$ have distance at most 1, that is, the nodes inside a ball of radius $1/2$ form a clique in G. The number of independent nodes in the r-neighborhood of v, therefore is at most $2^{\rho(1+\log_2 r)} = 2^\rho r^\rho$.

For the description and analysis of our MIS algorithm, we need a formal notion for the density of an independent set. To do so, we use the following definition from [23]. Let $S \subseteq V$ be a subset of the nodes of a graph $G = (V, E)$.

S is called r-*ruling* if for each node $u \in V \setminus S$, the distance to the closest node in S is at most r.

If the set S in the above definition is an independent set, we speak of an r-ruling independent set. Note that a MIS is a 1-ruling independent set.

Throughout the paper, we will make use of node neighborhoods of particular radii. By $\Gamma_r(v)$ we denote the set of nodes $u \neq v$ which have distance at most r from v. We further define

$$\Gamma_r^+(v) := \Gamma_r(v) \cup \{v\} \text{ and } \Gamma(v) := \Gamma_1(v).$$

4   Distibuted MIS Construction

In this section, we describe and analyze our distributed deterministic MIS construction for growth-bounded graphs. The algorithm consists of three phases. In the first phase, in time $O(\log \Delta \cdot \log^* n)$, an $O(\log \Delta)$-ruling independent set S of the network graph G is computed. The second phase transforms the sparse set S in to a dense independent set S' such that each node v of G has a node $u \in S'$ at distance at most 3, that is, S' is 3-ruling. For growth-bounded graphs, such a dense independent set induces an $(O(1), O(1))$-decomposition which can be used to finally extend S' to a maximal independent set in the third phase.

4.1   Constructing a Sparse Independent Set

The first phase of our MIS construction is a distributed algorithm which locally computes an $O(\log \Delta)$-ruling independent set S for a given undirected growth-bounded graph $G = (V, E)$ in time $O(\log \Delta \log^* n)$. A detailed description of the first phase is given by Algorithm 1. Before analyzing the algorithm, we give an informal description of the code.

At the beginning, S is empty and all nodes are active (denoted by the variables $b(v)$ for $v \in V$). Nodes are active as long as they have not decided whether to join the independent set S. As soon as a node becomes passive, it has either joined S in line 20 or it has decided not to join S. From a general perspective, Algorithm 1 tries to eliminate active vertices from the network until single, locally independent nodes are left. It does so with the help of edge-induced subgraphs of bounded degree. In each iteration of the while loop, a constant-degree graph $\overline{G}$ consisting of active nodes and edges of G is computed. On $\overline{G}$, we can construct a MIS in time $O(\log^* n)$ [7,9,18]. Only the nodes of the MIS of $\overline{G}$ stay active after the iteration of the while loop. This way, the number of active nodes is reduced by at least a constant factor in every while loop iteration. As soon as an active node v has no active neighbors, v joins the independent set S (line 20). The graph $\overline{G}$ is constructed as follows. First, each active node v chooses an active neighbor $d(v)$. Then, each active node u which has been chosen by at least one neighbor v, selects a neighbor $p(u)$ for which $d(p(u)) = u$. The edge set of $\overline{V}$ consists of all edges of the form $(u, p(u))$. Because a node u can only be connected to $d(u)$ and $p(u)$, $\overline{G}$ has at most degree 2. Now, consider a single execution of the while loop (lines 3–22, Figure 1).

Algorithm 1 Computing an IS (code for vertex v)

1: $S := \emptyset$;
2: $b(v) := act$;
3: **while** $b(v) = act$ **do**
4:     **if** $\exists u \in \Gamma(v) \mid b(u) = act$ **then**
5:       $d(v) := \min\{u \in \Gamma(v) \mid b(u) = act\}$;
6:       inform neighbor $d(v)$;
7:       $A_v := \{u \in \Gamma(v) \mid d(u) = v\}$;
8:       **if** $A_v \neq \emptyset$ **then**
9:         $p(v) := \min A_v$;
10:         inform neighbor $p(v)$
11:     **fi**;
12:     $B_v := \{u \in \Gamma(v) \mid p(u) = v\}$;
13:     **if** $(A_v = \emptyset) \wedge (B_v = \emptyset)$ **then**
14:       $b(v) := pass$
15:     **else**
16:       construct MIS I on graph $\overline{G} = (\overline{V}, \overline{E})$ with $\overline{V} := \{u \in V \mid b(u) = act\}$ and $\overline{E} := \{(u, p(u)) \mid u \in \overline{V} \wedge A_u \neq \emptyset\}$;
17:       **if** $v \notin I$ **then** $b(v) := pass$ **fi**
18:     **fi**
19:   **else**
20:     $S := S \cup \{v\}$; $b(v) := pass$
21:   **fi**
22: **od**

Lemma 2. *In the graph $\overline{G} = (\overline{V}, \overline{E})$, every vertex has degree at most 2.*

Proof. Consider $v \in \overline{V}$, then there are at most two vertices adjacent to v by an edge in $\overline{E}$, namely $d(v)$ if $p(d(v)) = v$, and $p(v)$.

Note that due to this lemma, line 16 of the algorithm, that is, the local construction of a MIS I on $\overline{G}$, can be completed in $O(\log^* n)$ rounds using methods described in [7,9,18].

Lemma 3. *Let V_A denote the set of active nodes. After k iterations of the while loop, $S \cup V_A$ is a $2k$-ruling set of G.*

Proof. We prove the lemma by induction over the number k of while loop iterations. Initially all nodes are active, thus the lemma is satisfied for $k = 0$. For the induction step, we show that if a node v becomes passive in an iteration of the while loop, either v joins S or there is an active node at distance at most 2 from v which remains active for until the next while loop iteration. Node v can become passive in lines 14, 17, or 20. If v becomes passive in line 20, it joins S and therefore the condition of the lemma is satisfied. In line 17, v is a node of $\overline{G}$ and has a neighbor u of v which is in the MIS I of $\overline{G}$. Thus, node u remains active.

The last remaining case is that v decides to become passive in line 14. By the condition in line 4, we can assume that v has at least one active neighbor at the

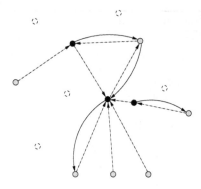

Fig. 1. One iteration of Algorithm 1. The dashed nodes are passive at the outset of the iteration. The dashed arrows between active nodes denote the links $d(v)$. The graph $\overline{G}$ is induced by the links $p(v)$ which are denoted by the solid, bended arrows. Finally, the algorithm computes a MIS on $\overline{G}$, leaving only the black nodes active for the next iteration.

beginning of the while loop iteration. Therefore, v can choose a node $u = d(v)$ in line 5. Since $A_u \neq \emptyset$, u chooses a node $p(u)$ and therefore u is a node of $\overline{G}$. Because all nodes of the MIS I of $\overline{G}$ remain active, either u or a neighbor w of u is still active after completing the while loop iteration. Since $\mathrm{dist}_G(v, w) = 2$, this completes the proof.

The following two lemmas are used to give bounds on the number of rounds needed by Algorithm 1 to complete, and to explain the resulting structure in G for general graphs and for growth-bounded graphs, respectively.

Lemma 4. *After $O(\log n)$ consecutive executions of the while loop, Algorithm 1 terminates with a $O(\log n)$-ruling independent set S on any graph G.*

Proof. Let n_{act} be the number of active nodes at the beginning of an iteration of the while loop. We prove that in one while loop iteration, at least $n_{\mathrm{act}}/3$ nodes become passive. The claim then follows by Lemma 3.

Let $\overline{n} \leq n_{\mathrm{act}}$ be the number of nodes of $\overline{G}$ of some particular iteration of the while loop. All nodes which are not part of $\overline{G}$ become passive in lines 14 or 20. It therefore suffices to prove that at least one third of the nodes of $\overline{G}$ become passive. However, $\overline{G}$ is constructed such that it does not contain isolated nodes, that is, all nodes of $\overline{G}$ have at least degree 1. Note that $\overline{G}$ is an edge-induced subgraph of G. Because the maximum degree of a node in $\overline{G}$ is 2 (Lemma 2), the MIS I consists of at most $2\overline{n}/3$ nodes. Hence, at least $\overline{n}/3$ nodes become passive in line 17.

The following lemma shows that for growth bounded graphs, the run time can even be reduced to $O(\log \Delta)$ executions of the while loop where Δ denotes the maximum degree of the network graph G.

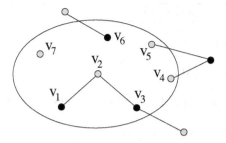

Fig. 2. The cluster with the edges in $\overline{G}$. Black nodes will remain active in the next iteration. The nodes v_1, v_2, and v_3 are in C_i. Nodes v_4, v_5, and v_6 are connected only to nodes outside of the cluster and hence, are in set C_o. Finally, $v_6 \in C_p$.

Lemma 5. *If the network graph G is growth-bounded, after $O(\log \Delta)$ consecutive execution of the while loop, Algorithm 1 terminates with an $O(\log \Delta)$-ruling independent set S.*

Proof. Let M be a maximal independent set of G. The set M defines a clustering of G as follows. We associate a cluster $\mathcal{C}_u$ with each node $u \in M$. Each node $v \notin M$ is assigned to the cluster of an adjacent node $u \in M$. Note that each cluster contains at most $\Delta + 1$ nodes. Let us define the cluster graph $\mathcal{G}_\mathcal{C}$ as follows. The nodes of $\mathcal{G}_\mathcal{C}$ are the clusters $\mathcal{C}_u$. Two nodes $\mathcal{C}_u$ and $\mathcal{C}_v$ are connected if there is an edge connecting the respective clusters. Because we assume that G is growth bounded, there is a function f such that there are at most $f(3) = O(1)$ independent nodes at distance at most 3 from a node u. Therefore, the maximum degree of $\mathcal{G}_\mathcal{C}$ is bounded by $d := f(3)$.

In the following, we show that the maximum number of active nodes per cluster is reduced by a factor 2 in a constant number of while loop iterations. For convenience, we define a unit of time to be one iteration of the while loop. Let α be the maximum number of active nodes per cluster at some time t. We will show that there is a constant k such that at time $t + k$ each cluster contains at most $\alpha/2$ active nodes. Note that this implies the lemma because we have $\alpha \leq \Delta + 1$ at time $t = 0$. Let $\mathcal{C}_u$ be a cluster with $c > \alpha/2$ active nodes. Let us look at a single iteration of the while loop of Algorithm 1. We partition the c active nodes of $\mathcal{C}_u$ into three groups according to their neighbors in $\overline{G}$ (Figure 2). We denote the set of nodes v which become passive in line 6 because there is no node w for which $d(w) = u$ by C_p. The set of nodes which have a neighbor inside $\mathcal{C}_u$ and which are only connected to nodes outside $\mathcal{C}_u$ are called C_i and C_o, respectively. Clearly, we have $|C_p| + |C_i| + |C_o| = c$. Because the maximum degree of $\overline{G}$ is 2, during the construction of the MIS in line 10 at least one third of the nodes in C_i become passive. The nodes in C_o can be divided into the nodes C_o^p which become passive and the nodes C_o^a which stay active. Each node outside $\mathcal{C}_u$ is connected to at most 2 nodes in C_o^a. Therefore, at least $|C_o^a|/2$ nodes outside $\mathcal{C}_u$ become passive. Let $c_i := |C_p| + |C_i| + |C_o^p|$ and $c_o := |C_o^a|$. We have $c_i + c_o = c$. In each iteration of the while loop at least $c_i/3$ nodes in

---
Algorithm 2 Computes a dense IS

Input: t-ruling independent set S
Output: 3-ruling independent set S
1: $S' := S$;
2: **while** S' is not 3-ruling **do**
3:    **for each** $u \in S'$ **do**
4:        compute $\hat{S}_u \subset \Gamma_4^+(u)$ such that $S' \cup \hat{S}_u$ is an IS and $\forall v \in \Gamma_3^+(u), \exists w \in S' \cup \hat{S}_u : \{v, w\} \in E$;
5:        $\mathcal{G}$ is the graph induced by $\bigcup_{u \in S'} \hat{S}_u$;
6:        $S' := S' \cup \text{MIS}(\mathcal{G})$;
7:    **od**;
8: **od**

$\mathcal{C}_u$ and at least $c_o/2$ nodes of clusters which are adjacent to $\mathcal{C}_u$ become passive. Assume that after k iterations of the while loop, there are still $\alpha/2$ active nodes in $\mathcal{C}_u$. Let $c^{(j)}$, $c_i^{(j)}$, and $c_o^{(j)}$ be the values of c, c_i, and c_o of the jth iteration, respectively. Because there are at most α nodes at the beginning, we have

$$\frac{1}{3} \cdot \sum_{j=1}^{k} c_i^{(j)} \leq \frac{\alpha}{2} \tag{1}$$

because otherwise at least $\alpha/2$ nodes of $\mathcal{C}_u$ would have become passive. Therefore, the number of nodes in the neighbor clusters of $\mathcal{C}_u$ which have become passive is at least

$$\frac{1}{2} \cdot \sum_{j=1}^{k} c_o^{(j)} = \frac{1}{2} \cdot \sum_{j=1}^{k} c^{(j)} - c_i^{(j)} \geq \frac{k\alpha}{4} - \frac{1}{2} \cdot \sum_{j=1}^{k} c_i^{(j)}.$$

Because of Equation (1), this is at least $(k-3)\alpha/4$. Because there are at most $d\alpha$ active nodes in neighbor clusters of $\mathcal{C}_u$ at the beginning, after $O(d) = O(1)$ iterations of the while loop there are no active nodes in the neighborhood of $\mathcal{C}_u$ left. From then on, at least one third of the nodes in $\mathcal{C}_u$ becomes passive in every further iteration.

Summarizing the Lemmas 2–5, we obtain the following theorem.

Theorem 1. *Algorithm 1 is a local, distributed algorithm which computes an $O(\log \Delta)$-ruling independent set in $O(\log \Delta \cdot \log^* n)$ rounds for any growth-bounded graph $G = (V, E)$.*

For general graphs, the Algorithm terminates in $O(\log n \cdot \log^* n)$ rounds producing an $O(\log n)$-ruling independent set. All messages are of size $O(\log n)$.

4.2   Making the Independent Set Dense

In the following, we show how the relatively sparse independent set which we constructed so far can be made dense enough to obtain an $(O(1), O(1))$-decomposition for growth-bounded graphs. Specifically, we show how on growth-bounded graphs, a t-ruling independent set can be transformed into a 3-ruling independent set in $O(t \log^* n)$ rounds using messages of size $O(\log n)$. Algorithm 2 describes the basic method to achieve this. The idea is to enlarge the independent set in small steps such that it gets denser in each step. Before coming to a detailed analysis, we give a rough overview. In line 3, each node of the independent set adds new nodes to the independent set such that each neighbor in distance at most 3 has a neighbor in the extended set. Because every independent set node adds new nodes, it is not guaranteed that the additional nodes generated by different independent set nodes are independent. Therefore, in lines 4 and 5, the independence of the extended independent set is restored by computing a MIS on the new nodes (see Lemma 7). The following lemma shows that in each iteration of the while loop, the maximum distance of any node to the next node of S' decreases by at least 1.

Lemma 6. *Let S' be a t-ruling independent set for $t > 3$. After one iteration of the while loop of Algorithm 2, S' is a $(t-1)$-ruling independent set.*

Proof. We first prove that S' remains an independent set throughout the algorithm. The sets $\hat{S}_u$ are constructed such that nodes in S' and nodes in $\hat{S}_u$ are independent. We therefore only have to prove that all the new nodes form an independent set. However, this is clearly guaranteed because in line 6, a maximal independent set of the graph induced by all the new nodes is computed.

To prove that the maximum distance from a node to the next independent set node decreases, we consider a node $v \in V$ for which the distance to the nearest node $u \in S'$ is $t > 3$. We prove that after an iteration of the while loop, the distance between v and the closest node in S' is at most $t - 1$. The set $\hat{S}_u$ is constructed such that every node w in the 3-neighborhood $\Gamma_3^+(u)$ has a neighbor in $S' \cup \hat{S}_u$. On a shortest path (of length t) connecting u and v, let x be the node which is at distance exactly 3 from u. There must be a neighbor y of x for which $y \in \hat{S}_u$. After computing the MIS in line 6, either y or a neighbor z of y join the independent set S'. The distance between v and y is $t - 1$ and the distance between v and z is $t - 1$ which concludes the proof.

It remains to show that Algorithm 2 can indeed be implemented by an efficient distributed algorithm. Lemma 7 gives exact bounds on the distributed complexity of the Algorithm 2.

Lemma 7. *Let G be a growth bounded graph. On G, Algorithm 2 can be executed by a distributed algorithm with time complexity $O(t \log^* n)$ using messages of size $O(\log n)$.*

Proof. By Lemma 6, Algorithm 2 terminates after at most t iterations of the while loop. We therefore have to prove that each while loop iteration can be exectuted in time $O(\log^* n)$ using messages of size $O(\log n)$. Let us first look at the construction of $\hat{S}_u$ for some node $u \in S'$. A node $v \in \Gamma_4^+(u)$ can potentially join $\hat{S}_u$ if it has neighbor in $S' \cup \hat{S}_u$ and if it has an uncovered neighbor $w \in \Gamma_3^+(u)$, that is, w has no neighbor in $S' \cup \hat{S}_u$. We call such a node v candidate. We add a candidate v to $\hat{S}_u$ if it has a lower ID than all adjacent candidates. Finding out whether a node is a candidate and whether it has the lowest ID among its neighbor candidates can be done in 3 rounds. First, all nodes of $S' \cup \hat{S}_u$ inform their neighbors that they are in the independent set. Then, all covered nodes in $\Gamma_3^+(u)$ inform their neighbors which can now decide whether they are candidates. Finally, the candidates exchange their IDs. We call those 3 rounds a step. In each step, at least the candidate with the highest ID joins $\hat{S}_u$. Because we assume that G is a growth bounded graph, there can be at most $f(4) = O(1)$ independent nodes in $\Gamma_u^+(u)$ for some function f. Hence, the number of nodes in $\hat{S}_u$ and therefore the number of steps needed to construct $\hat{S}_u$ is constant. Note that if there was no restriction on the message size, u could collect the complete 4-neighborhood, locally compute $\hat{S}_u$, and inform the nodes in $\hat{S}_u$ in 8 rounds.

It now remains to prove that the construction of the MIS in line 6 of Algorithm 2 can be computed in $O(\log^* n)$ rounds. Let us therefore have a look at the structure of the graph $\mathcal{G}$ which is induced by the union of the sets $\hat{S}_u$ for all $u \in S'$. Consider a node v of $\mathcal{G}$, that is, $v \in \hat{S}_u$ for some $u \in S'$. Further, let w be a neighbor of v in $\mathcal{G}$. The node w is in $\hat{S}_{u'}$ for some node $u' \in S' \setminus \{u\}$. Because $\hat{S}_{u'}$ consists of nodes of $\Gamma_4^+(u')$, the distance between v and u' is at most 5. Since G is a growth bounded graph, there exists a function f such that there are at most $f(5)$ independent nodes at distance at most 5 from v. Thus, there are at most $f(5)$ possible nodes $u' \in S'$ which can cause neighbors w for v. Because all nodes in $\hat{S}_{u'}$ are independent, the number of neighbors of w in $\hat{S}_{u'}$ is at most $f(1)$. Therefore, the maximum degree of the graph $\mathcal{G}$ can be upper bounded by $f(5) \cdot f(1) = O(1)$. It is well-known that on a constant-degree graph, a MIS can be constructed in $O(\log^* n)$ rounds using messages of size $O(\log n)$ [7,9,18].

Combining Lemmas 6 and 7 we obtain the next theorem.

Theorem 2. *On a growth-bounded graph, a t-ruling independent set can be transformed into a 3-ruling independent set in $O(t \log^* n)$ rounds using messages of size $O(\log n)$.*

4.3　Computing the MIS

We will now describe the last phase of our algorithm, turning the 3-ruling independent set S' from Algorithm 2 into a MIS. Set S' induces a natural clustering of the nodes of G. For each node $u \in S'$, we define the cluster $\mathcal{C}_u$ to be the set of all nodes $v \in V$ for which u is the nearest node of S', ties are broken arbitrarily. The cluster graph $\mathcal{G}_{S'}$ induced by S' is then defined as follows. The node set of $\mathcal{G}_{S'}$ is the set of clusters $\{\mathcal{C}_u | u \in S'\}$. The clusters $\mathcal{C}_u$ and $\mathcal{C}_v$ are connected by an edge in $\mathcal{G}_{S'}$ if and only if there are nodes $u' \in \mathcal{C}_u$ and $v' \in \mathcal{C}_v$ which are neighbors in the network graph G. Because S' is a 3-ruling set, the distance between the centers u and v of two neighboring clusters $\mathcal{C}_u$ and $\mathcal{C}_v$ can be at most 7. The degree of $\mathcal{G}_{S'}$ is therefore bounded by $f(7) = O(1)$ if G is f-growth-bounded. The first step of the third phase of our MIS algorithm is to compute $\mathcal{G}_{S'}$ and to color $\mathcal{G}_{S'}$ with $f(7) + 1$ colors, resulting in a $(O(1), O(1))$-decomposition of G. Applying algorithms from [7,9,18], this can be achieved in $O(\log^* n)$ rounds using messages of size $O(\log n)$.

Having computed this decomposition, we can now compute a MIS M of G by sequentially computing the contributions from each color of the coloring of $\mathcal{G}_{S'}$. For each node v, let x_v be the color of v's cluster. Using the cluster colors and the node identifiers, we define a lexicographic order $\prec$ on the set V such that for $u, v \in V$, $u \prec v$ if and only if $x_u < x_v$ or if $x_u = x_v \wedge \mathrm{ID}(u) < \mathrm{ID}(v)$. Each node now proceeds as follows. Initially, we set $M = S'$. All nodes v of S' inform their neighbors about the joining of M by sending a JOIN(v) message. If a node u receives a JOIN(v) message from a neighbor v, it cannot join the MIS any more and therefore sends a COVERED(u) message to all neighbors. If a node v has not received a JOIN(u) message but has received a COVERED(u) from all $u \in \Gamma(v)$ for which $u \prec v$, it can safely join M. Note that all neigbors $w \in \Gamma(v)$ with $w \succ v$, would need to receive a COVERED(v) message from v before joining M. If a node v joins M, it informs its neighbors by sending a JOIN(v) message. As shown by the next lemma, the described algorithm computes a MIS M in time $O(1)$.

Lemma 8. *On f-growth-bounded graphs the above algorithm computes a MIS M in time $2f(7)f(3)$.*

Proof. We first show that M indeed is an independent set of G. For the sake of contradiction, assume that there are two adjacent nodes u and v which both join M. W.l.o.g., we assume that $u \prec v$. Assuming that v joins M means that v must have received a COVERED(u) message from u. However, this is a contradition to the assumption that u joins M. To see that M is a MIS, observe that as long as M is not maximal, there is a smallest node u (with respect to $\prec$) which is not covered.

It remains to prove the time complexity of the above algorithm. First note that because the radius of each cluster is at most 3, there can be at most $f(3)$ MIS nodes per cluster. Let us now look at a single cluster $\mathcal{C}_u$ of the smallest color 1. Because with respect to the order $\prec$, the nodes of $\mathcal{C}_u$ are smaller than all nodes of neighboring clusters, the smallest uncovered node of $\mathcal{C}_u$ is always free to join M. When a node v joins M, it takes two rounds until the neighbors of v have forwarded the information that they have been covered. Because there are at most $f(3)$ nodes of $\mathcal{C}_u$ which join M, it takes at most $2f(3)$ rounds until all nodes of color 1 are covered or have joined M. As soon as there is no uncovered node of a color i, the above argument holds for color $i + 1$. Therefore, after at most $f(7) \cdot 2f(3)$ rounds, all nodes are either covered or have joined M.

Combining Theorems 1, and 2 and Lemma 8, we obtain the main theorem of this paper.

Theorem 3. *Let G be a growth-bounded network graph. There is a deterministic distributed algorithm which constructs a maximal independent set on G in time $O(\log \Delta \cdot \log^* n)$.*

5   Conclusions

In this paper, we have given a deterministic distributed algorithm which computes a maximal independent set in time $O(\log \Delta \cdot \log^* n)$ in unit ball graphs if the underlying metric has constant doubling dimension. This includes the practically important special case of unit disk graphs. Our algorithms does not rely on any representation of the underlying metric space, i.e., nodes do not need to know about the distances to their neighbors.

The MIS problem being of fundamental nature, our result sheds new light into the intriguing question of the possibilities and limitations of different models in distributed computing. It is therefore interesting to compare our solution with MIS algorithms in other models. In the radio network model, where collisions between neighboring senders may occur, the fastest known algorithm for unit disk graph runs in time $O(\log^2 n)$ and requires randomization [21]. In the message passing model, the fastest known algorithm for general graphs is randomized and runs in time $O(\log n)$ [20]. Finally, [16] showed that if nodes know the distances to their neighbors, there exists a deterministic $O(\log^* n)$ time algorithm in graphs with bounded growth. The last comparison particularly highlights the importance of *distance information*, which appears to render the MIS problem much simpler.

References

1. N. Alon, L. Babai, and A. Itai. A fast and simple randomized parallel algorithm for the maximal independent set problem. *J. Algorithms*, 7(4):567–583, 1986.
2. K. Alzoubi, P.-J. Wan, and O. Frieder. Message-Optimal Connected Dominating Sets in Mobile Ad Hoc Networks. In *Proceedings of the 3rd ACM Int. Symposium on Mobile Ad Hoc Networking and Computing (MOBIHOC)*, pages 157–164, EPFL Lausanne, Switzerland, 2002.
3. P. Assouad. Plongements lipschitziens dans $\mathbf{R}^n$. *Bull. Soc. Math. France*, 111(4):429–448, 1983.
4. B. Awerbuch, A. V. Goldberg, M. Luby, and S. A. Plotkin. Network decomposition and locality in distributed computation. In *Proc. of the 30th Symp. on Foundations of Computer Science (FOCS)*, pages 364–369, 1989.
5. L. Barrière, P. Fraigniaud, and L. Narayanan. Robust Position-Based Routing in Wireless Ad Hoc Networks with Unstable Transmission Ranges. In *Proc. of the 5th International Workshop on Discrete Algorithms and Methods for Mobile Computing and Communications (DIAL-M)*, pages 19–27. ACM Press, 2001.
6. H. Breu and D. G. Kirkpatrick. Unit Disk Graph Recognition is NP-hard. *Computational Geometry. Theory and Applications*, 9(1-2):3–24, 1998.
7. R. Cole and U. Vishkin. Deterministic Coin Tossing with Applications to Optimal Parallel List Ranking. *Information and Control*, 70(1):32–53, 1986.
8. R. Gandhi and S. Parthasarathy. Distributed Algorithms for Coloring and Connected Domination in Wireless Ad Hoc Networks. In *Foundations of Software Technology and Theoretical Computer Science (FSTTCS)*, 2004.
9. A. Goldberg, S. Plotkin, and G. Shannon. Parallel Symmetry-Breaking in Sparse Graphs. *SIAM Journal on Discrete Mathematics (SIDMA)*, 1(4):434–446, 1988.

10. A. Gupta, R. Krauthgamer, and J. Lee. Bounded Geometries, Fractals, and Low-Distortion Embeddings. In *Proc. of 44th IEEE Symp. on Foundations of Computer Science (FOCS)*, 2003.

11. A. Israeli and A. Itai. A Fast and Simple Randomized Parallel Algorithm for Maximal Matching. *Information Processing Letters*, 22:77–80, 1986.

12. J. Kleinberg, A. Slivkins, and T. Wexler. Triangulation and Embedding using Small Sets of Beacons. In *Proc. of 45th IEEE Symp. on Foundations of Computer Science (FOCS)*, 2004.

13. R. Krauthgamer and J. Lee. Navigating Nets: Simple Algorithms for Proximity Search. In *Proc. of 15th ACM-SIAM Symp. on Discrete Algorithms (SODA)*, 2004.

14. F. Kuhn, T. Moscibroda, and R. Wattenhofer. Unit Disk Graph Approximation. In *Proceedings of the 2004 Joint Workshop on Foundations of Mobile Computing (DIALM)*, pages 17–23, New York, NY, USA, 2004. ACM Press.

15. F. Kuhn, T. Moscibroda, and R. Wattenhofer. What Cannot Be Computed Locally! In *Proc. of the 23rd ACM Symp. on Principles of Distributed Computing (PODC)*, pages 300–309, 2004.

16. F. Kuhn, T. Moscibroda, and R. Wattenhofer. The Locality of Bounded Growth. In *Proc. of the 24th ACM Symp. on Principles of Distributed Computing (PODC)*, 2005.

17. F. Kuhn, R. Wattenhofer, and A. Zollinger. Ad-Hoc Networks Beyond Unit Disk Graphs. In *Proceedings of 1st Joint Workshop on Foundations of Mobile Computing (DIALM-POMC)*, pages 69–78. ACM Press, 2003.

18. N. Linial. Locality in Distributed Graph Algorithms. *SIAM Journal on Computing*, 21(1):193–201, February 1992.

19. N. Linial. Local-Global Phenomena in Graphs. *Combinatorics Probability and Computing*, 2:491–503, 1993.

20. M. Luby. A Simple Parallel Algorithm for the Maximal Independent Set Problem. *SIAM Journal on Computing*, 15:1036–1053, 1986.

21. T. Moscibroda and R. Wattenhofer. Maximal Independent Sets in Radio Networks. In *Proc. of the 23rd ACM Symp. on Principles of Distributed Computing (PODC)*, 2005.

22. A. Panconesi and A. Srinivasan. Improved distributed algorithms for coloring and network decomposition problems. In *Proc. of the 24th annual ACM symposium on Theory of computing (STOC)*, pages 581–592. ACM Press, 1992.

23. D. Peleg. *Distributed Computing: A Locality-Sensitive Approach*. SIAM, 2000.

24. C. G. Plaxton, R. Rajaraman, and A. W. Richa. Accessing Nearby Copies of Replicated Objects in a Distributed Environment. In *Proceedings of the 9th Annual ACM Symposium on Parallel Algorithms and Architectures (SPAA)*, pages 311–320, 1997.

25. K. Talwar. Bypassing the embedding: Approximation schemes and compact representations for low dimensional metrics. In *Proc. of 36th ACM Symp. on Theory of Computing (STOC)*, 2004.

Distributed Computing with Imperfect Randomness

Shafi Goldwasser*, Madhu Sudan, and Vinod Vaikuntanathan**

MIT CSAIL, Cambridge MA 02139, USA
{shafi, madhu, vinodv}@theory.csail.mit.edu

Abstract. Randomness is a critical resource in many computational scenarios, enabling solutions where deterministic ones are elusive or even provably impossible. However, the randomized solutions to these tasks assume access to a source of unbiased, independent coins. Physical sources of randomness, on the other hand, are rarely unbiased and independent although they do seem to exhibit somewhat imperfect randomness. This gap in modeling questions the relevance of current randomized solutions to computational tasks. Indeed, there has been substantial investigation of this issue in complexity theory in the context of the applications to efficient algorithms and cryptography.

In this paper, we seek to determine whether imperfect randomness, modeled appropriately, is "good enough" for distributed algorithms. Namely can we do with imperfect randomness all that we can do with perfect randomness, and with comparable efficiency ? We answer this question in the affirmative, for the problem of Byzantine agreement. We construct protocols for Byzantine agreement in a variety of scenarios (synchronous or asynchronous networks, with or without private channels), in which the players have imperfect randomness. Our solutions are essentially as efficient as the best known randomized agreement protocols, despite the defects in the randomness.

1 Introduction

Randomization has proved useful in many areas of computer science including probabilistic algorithms, cryptography, and distributed computing. In algorithm design, randomness has been shown to reduce the complexity requirments for solving problems, but it is unclear whether the use of randomization is inherently necessary. Indeed, an extensive amount of research in the complexity theoretic community these days is dedicated to de-randomization: the effort of replacing random string by deterministic "random-looking" strings.

The case of using randomness within the field of distributed computing is, in contrast, unambiguous. There are central distributed computing problems for which it is provably impossible to obtain a deterministic solution, whereas

---

* This work was supported in part by NSF CNS-0430450, a Minerva Grant 8495, and a Cymerman-Jakubskind award.
** This work was supported in part by NSF CNS-0430450.

P. Fraigniaud (Ed.): DISC 2005, LNCS 3724, pp. 288–302, 2005.

efficient randomized solutions exist. The study of one such problem, the *Byzantine Agreement* problem is the focus of this paper.

Byzantine Agreement: Randomized versus Deterministic Protocols
The problem of Byzantine Agreement (BA) defined by Pease, Shostak and Lamport [18] is for n players to agree on a value, even if some t of them are faulty. Informally, for any set of initial values of the players, a BA protocol should satisfy the following: (1) *Consistency:* All non-faulty players agree on the same value. (2) *Non-triviality:* If all the players started with some value v, they agree on v at the end of the protocol. The faulty players might try to force the non-faulty players to disagree. The good players, in general, do not know who the faulty players are. A BA protocol should ensure that the good players agree, even in the presence of such malicious players.

The possibility of BA depends crucially on the model of communication among the players. When the players communicate via a synchronous network with point-to-point channels, there are $(t+1)$-round deterministic BA protocols (one in which no player tosses coins) even in the presence of $t < \frac{n}{3}$ faults [16]. A lower bound of $t + 1$ communication rounds is known for every deterministic protocol. When the players communicate via an asynchronous network, the celebrated result of Fischer, Lynch and Paterson [15] shows that BA is impossible to achieve even in the presence of a single faulty player.

Yet, Ben-Or [2] in 1983 showed how to achieve Byzantine agreement in an asynchronous network tolerating a linear number of faults via a randomized protocol with expected exponential round complexity. More efficient randomized protocols in asynchronous as well as synchronous networks followed, some of which (due to [19,4,11,14,13,5]) assume the existence of private communication channels between pairs of participants (or alternatively cryptographic assumptions), and some do not require secret communication (notably Chor-Coan [6]).

To summarize these works, both synchronous and asynchronous BA can be achieved via a randomized protocol in expected $O(1)$ number of rounds tolerating an optimal number of faults, assuming private channels of communication exist. Without any secret communication requirements, for $t < n/3$ a randomized protocol exists for synchronous BA using $O(\frac{t}{\log n})$ rounds [1], whereas the best asynchronous BA protocol still requires exponential number of rounds [2,4].

What type of Randomness is Available in the Real World? The common abstraction used to model the use of randomness by a protocol (or an algorithm), is to assume that each participant's algorithm has access to its own source of unbiased and independent coins. However, this abstraction does not seem to be physically realizable. Instead, physical sources are available whose outcome seem only to be "somewhat random".

---

[1] Subsequent to this work, we learned that, in as yet unpublished work, Ben-Or and Pavlov [3] construct an $O(\log n)$ round BA protocol in the full-information model. We note that the results in this paper apply to [3], giving us an $O(\log n)$-round BA protocol in the full-information model, when the players have a block source each, and the sources of different players are independent.

This gap between available physical sources and the abstract model has been addressed starting with the work of von Neumann [23] and Elias [12] which deal with sources of independent bits of unknown bias. In more recent works, sources of dependent bits were modeled by Santha-Vazirani [21], Chor-Goldreich [7], and finally Zuckerman [24] who presented the *weak random source* generalizing all previous models.

Informally, for a weak random source, no sequence of bits has too high a probability of being output. A weak random source is a *block source* [7] if this is guaranteed for every output block (for a block size which is a parameter of the source) regardless of the values of the previous blocks output. Namely, whereas a general weak random source guarantees some minimum amount of entropy if sampled exactly once, a block source guarantees a minimum amount of entropy each time a sample is drawn (where a sample corresponds to a block).

Two natural questions arise. (1) Can weak random sources be used to extract a source of unbiased and independent coins? (2) Even if not, can weak random sources be used within applications instead of perfect random sources, with the same guarantee of correctness and complexity?

The first question was addressed early on, in conjuction with introducing the various models of imperfect randomness. It was shown that it is impossible to extract unbiased random coins with access to a single weak random source [21,7,24]. Researchers went on to ask (starting with Vazirani [22]) whether, given two (or more) weak random sources (all independent from each other), extraction of unbiased random bits is possible. Indeed, it was shown [22,7,24] that two sources suffice. Whereas original works focus on in-principle results, recent work by Barak, Impagliazzo, and Wigderson [1] and others focuses on constructive protocols.

The second question is the type we will we focus on in this work. In the context of probabilistic algorithms, it was shown early on in [7,24] that a single weak random source can be used to replace a perfect source of randomness for any BPP algorithm. Very recently, Dodis et al [10,9], asked the same question in the context of cryptographic protocols. Namely, is it possible for cryptographic appplications (e.g. encryption, digital signatures, secure protocols) to exist in a world where participants each have access to a *single* weak source of randomness? Surprisingly, they show that even if these sources are independent of each other, many cryptographic tasks such as encryption and zero-knowledge protocols are *impossible*.

We thus are faced with a natural and intriguing question in the context of distributed computing:ss Are weak random sources suffiently strong to replace perfect random sources within randomized distributed computing protocols ? This is the starting point of our research.

The Choice of our Randomness Model. The model of randomness we assume in this work is that each player has its own weak source (or block source) that is independent of the sources of all the other players, as was assumed in the work of [9] in the context of cryptographic protocols. We feel that this model is a natural starting point for the study of randomness in distributed computation. We note however that there is a spectrum of models that may be assumed, and one such alternative is discussed in section 1 on future directions.

Our Results. We focus on the problem of achieving consensus in a complete network of n participants t of which can be malicious faults as defined by [18]. We address the settings of synchronous and asynchronous networks, and the cases of private channels (when each pair of participants have a secret communication channel between them) and of a full information network (when no secrecy is assumed for any communication). We note that by the results of Dodis et al. [9], making cryptographic assumptions is doomed for failure.

We will show,

1. In the case of *block sources*: how to obtain the best bounds of fault-tolerance and round complexity currently achieved by randomized distributed protocols. Assuming private channels, we show for both synchronous and asynchronous networks an $O(1)$ expected round protocol for $t < \frac{n}{3}$ faults (matching [14,5]). In the full-information model, we show for synchronous networks an $O(\frac{t}{\log n})$ expected round protocol for $t < \frac{n}{3}$ (matching [6]) and a $O(2^n)$ expected round protocol for $t < \frac{n}{3}$ (matching [4]).
2. In the case of *general weak sources*: We assume private channels. For synchronous networks, we show an $O(1)$ expected round protocol for $t < \frac{n}{3}$ faults (matching [14]). For asynchronous networks, we get an $O(1)$ expected rounds protocol for $t < \frac{n}{5}$. We leave open the question of finding a BA protocol in the full information model where each player has a general weak source.

Our Methods. To achieve our results, we build in various ways on top of the existing distributed algorithms [14,6,2,4]. In general, we follow a 2-step *Extract and Simulate* approach to designing such BA protocols. We utilize first $O(1)$ rounds for a pre-processing protocol, in which the parties interact with each other so that at the end, a large number of them obtain a private uniformly random string. The randomness so obtained is used to run existing randomized BA protocols.

We construct various extraction protocols, in which the players interact to obtain unbiased and independent random bits. The problem that we will need to overcome is naturally that when a player receives a sample from another player (which may be faulty), he cannot assume that the sample is good and not constructed to correlate with other samples being exchanged. We construct extraction protocols that work *even if* some of the players contribute bad inputs which may depend on samples they have seen sent by honest players (in the case of full information protocols).

As building blocks, we will use the extractors of [24,7,20] as well as the *strong extractors* of [8,20]. A strong extractor ensures that the output of the extraction is random even if one is given *some* of the inputs to the extractor. Our procedures will guarantee that a certain fraction of the non-faulty players obtain perfectly unbiased and independent coins. However, this will not necessarily be the case for the *all* the non-faulty players, and thus one may fear that now when running existing randomized BA protocols with perfect randomness only available to some of the non-faulty players, the fault-tolerance of the final protocol may go down. Luckily this is not the case, due the following interesting general observation.

When we analyze the current usage of randomness in [14,6], we find on closer look that one may distinguish between how many non-faulty players truly need to have access to perfectly unbiased and independent sources of random coins, and how many non-faulty players merely need to follow the protocol instructions. The number of non-faulty players which need to have access to perfect coins is drastically lower than the total number of non-faulty players. In the case of [14], it suffices for $t + 1$ players to posses good randomness whereas we need all the $n - t$ non-faulty players to follow the protocol to prove correctness and expected $O(1)$ termination. In the case of [6] it suffices for $(\frac{1}{2} + \delta)n$ (for arbitrarily small constant $\delta > 0$) players to possess good randomness.

Future and Related Work. Two questions are left open when each player has a general weak source (rather than a block source): (1) How to achieve BA in the full information model, and (2) How to achieve optimal fault-tolerance in the case of asynchronous networks in the private channels model. We currently achieve $O(1)$ rounds for $t < n/5$.

Models of randomness other than what we chose to focus on in this paper may have been assumed. The one we find particularly appealing is where each player has a weak random source, but the sources are correlated. Namely, the only guarantee is that the randomness sampled by player i has a large min-entropy even conditioned on the values for random strings sampled by all other players. The model considered in this paper is a first approximation to this more general model. We have obtained some partial results in this model [17].

It is of great interest to study the possibility of other tasks in distributed computing, such as leader election and collective coin-flipping, when the players have imperfect randomness. We briefly note that the results in this paper can be used to show the possibility of both these tasks, in the model where the players have independent block sources.

2   Definitions and the Model

The Network, Communication, Fault and Randomness Models. We let n denote the total number of players in the system and t the number of faulty players. We consider various models of communication between the players. In all cases, the n players form a fully-connected communication graph. i.e, each player i can send to every other player j a message in one step. In the *private channels* model, the communication between players i and j is invisible to all the players but i and j. In contrast, in the *full-information model*, the communication between any two players is publicly visible.

We consider synchronous and asynchronous communication in the network. In the former case, each processor has access to a global clock, and communication is divided into rounds. Messages sent in a round are received in the beginning of the next round, and the network ensures reliable message delivery. In the case of asynchronous communication, however, the only guarantee is that the messages sent are *eventually* received by the recipient. Messages can be arbitrarily re-ordered, and arbitrarily delayed.

We consider Byzantine faults in this paper. Byzantine players can deviate arbitrarily from the prescribed protocol, and co-ordinate with each other so as to mislead the good players into disagreement. We *do not* assume that the Byzantine players are computationally bounded. The coalition of Byzantine players is informally referred to as the adversary. We allow the adversary to be *rushing*. i.e, the adversary can see all the messages sent by the good players in a round r, before deciding what to send in round r.

Each player has his own source of (imperfect) randomness, and the sources of different players generate mutually independent distributions.

Weak Random Sources. Let U_k denote the uniform distribution on k bits. If X is a random variable which has a distribution D, then we write $X \sim D$. The distance between distributions D_1 and D_2 (denoted by $\Delta(D_1, D_2)$) is $\frac{1}{2}\sum_a |\Pr_{X_1 \sim D_1}[X_1 = a] - \Pr_{X_2 \sim D_2}[X_2 = a]|$. When $\Delta(D_1, D_2) \leq \epsilon$, we say that D_1 and D_2 are ϵ-close.

A source of randomness X of length k is simply a random variable that takes values in $\{0, 1\}^k$. If X is not uniformly distributed, we say that the source X is a weak random source. The randomness contained in a source is usually measured in terms of its *min-entropy*. A source X of k bits has min-entropy δk, if for every $a \in \{0, 1\}^k$, $\Pr[X = x] \leq 2^{-\delta k}$. In this case, we call X a (k, δ)-source.

Definition 1. *A (k, δ)-source (or a (k, δ)-weak source) is a random variable X that takes values in $\{0, 1\}^k$ such that for any $x \in \{0, 1\}^k$, $\Pr[X = x] \leq 2^{-\delta k}$.*

A block source is a sequence of random variables $X_1, X_2, \ldots$ such that each X_i (of length k bits) has min-entropy δk, even if conditioned on any realization of the other blocks. This corresponds to sampling multiple times from a source of random bits, when we are guaranteed that each sample has *some* new entropy.

Definition 2. *A (k, δ)-block source is a sequence of random variables $X_1, X_2, \ldots$ (each of length k) such that any X_i has a min-entropy of δk conditioned on all the other random variables. That is, $\Pr[X_i = a_i \mid X_1 = a_1, \ldots, X_{i-1} = a_{i-1}, X_{i+1} = a_{i+1}, \ldots] \leq 2^{-\delta k}$.*

We use (X, Y) to denote the joint distribution of the random variables X and Y. In particular, (X, U_m) denotes the joint distribution of X and an independent uniform random variable U_m.

Extractors. Given a (k, δ)-source X, our first attempt would be to extract "pure randomness" from X. That is, to construct a deterministic function $Ext : \{0, 1\}^k \rightarrow \{0, 1\}^m$ (for some $m > 0$) such that *for any* (k, δ)-source X, $\Delta(Ext(X), U_m)$ is small. But, it is easy to show that this task is impossible in general. Thus it is natural to ask if one can extract uniform randomness given *two independent* (k, δ)-sources. Chor-Goldreich [7] answered this in the affirmative for the case when $\delta > \frac{1}{2}$. More recently, Raz [20] showed this for the case when one of the two sources has min-entropy at least $\frac{k}{2}$ and the other has min-entropy at least $\log k$. Below, we formally define the notion of a deterministic two-source extractor, which is a key tool in our constructions.

Definition 3. *A function $Ext : (\{0,1\}^k)^2 \rightarrow \{0,1\}^m$ is a (k,δ)* **two-source extractor** *if for any (k,δ)-source X_1 and any independent (k,δ)-source X_2, $Ext(X_1, X_2)$ is ϵ-close to U_m.*

A strong two-source extractor is one in which the output of the extractor is independent of each of the inputs separately. More formally,

Definition 4. *A function $Ext : (\{0,1\}^k)^2 \rightarrow \{0,1\}^m$ is a (k,δ)* **two-source strong extractor** *if for any (k,δ)-source X_1 and any independent (k,δ)-source X_2, the distributions $(Ext(X_1, X_2), X_i)$ and (U_m, X_i) are ϵ-close, for $i \in \{1,2\}$.*

Dodis and Oliveira [8] show that some well-known constructions of two-source deterministic extractors indeed yield two-source *strong* extractors. Raz [20] shows how to construct very general two-source *strong* extractors.

3   Extracting Randomness in a Network

Each player participating in a randomized distributed protocol is traditionally assumed to have a uniformly distributed string that is independent of the random strings of the other players. In addition, some protocols assume that the randomness of each player is *private*. i.e, the faulty players have no information on the randomness of the good players. There is no guarantee on the behavior of the protocol if the players use a weak random source or if the players have public randomness.

Our goal would be to run a distributed extraction protocol among the players such that the good players help each other extract a uniform random string collectively from their (mutually independent) weak random sources, even in the presence of some malicious parties. The malicious colluding parties could each contribute an arbitrary string, possibly correlated with what they see in the network, as input to the extraction protocol.

One of the building blocks in our randomness extraction *protocols* is a multi-source extractor whose output is random even if an arbitrary subset of the input sources do not have any min-entropy, but all the sources are independent. We call this a (κ, τ)-immune extractor.

Definition 5. *Let $X_1, X_2, \ldots, X_{\kappa+1}$ be (k,δ)-block sources. A function Ext that takes as input a finite number of blocks from each of the $\kappa + 1$ block sources is called a (κ, τ)-immune (k,δ)-extractor if for any block sources $X_1, X_2, \ldots,$ $X_{\kappa+1}$ such that (i) X_1 is a (k,δ)-source, (ii) at least $\kappa - \tau$ among the κ sources $X_2, \ldots, X_{\kappa+1}$ are (k,δ) sources, and (iii) the X_i's are mutually independent, $Ext(X_1, X_2, \ldots, X_{\kappa+1})$ is ϵ-close to U_m.*

In the above definition, we are guaranteed that the τ "bad" sources (those which do not have any randomness) are independent of the $\kappa + 1 - \tau$ "good" sources. We might need to deal with worse situations. In particular, the τ bad sources could be **dependent** on some of the "good" sources. A (κ, τ)-strongly immune extractor extracts uniform randomness even in this adversarial situation.

Definition 6. *Let $X_1, X_2, \ldots, X_{\kappa+1}$ be (k, δ)-block sources. A function Ext that takes as input a finite number of blocks from each of the $\kappa + 1$ block sources is called a (κ, τ)-**strongly-immune** (k, δ)-**extractor** if for any block sources $X_1, X_2, \ldots, X_{\kappa+1}$ such that (i) X_1 is a (k, δ)-source independent of all other X_i, and (ii) at least $\kappa - \tau$ among the κ sources $X_2, \ldots, X_{\kappa+1}$ are (k, δ)-sources and are mutually independent, $Ext(X_1, X_2, \ldots, X_{\kappa+1})$ is ϵ-close to U_m.*

Some distributed protocols might require the players to have private randomness. But, if the players are connected by non-private channels, most of the inputs to the extraction protocols are publicly visible. In this case, the output of the extraction protocol might depend on the values that were publicly transmitted and is thus not private. We need to construct (κ, τ)-strongly immune *strong* extractors to cope with this situation. The constructions are as given below.

I-*Ext*: A $(t, t - 1)$-immune extractor.

Inputs: Let *Ext* be any (k, δ) two-source extractor. Let $X_1^2, X_1^3, \ldots, X_1^{t+1}$ denote t distinct blocks of the (k, δ)-block source X_1. Let $X_2, \ldots, X_{t+1}$ be one block each from the t other sources.
I-$Ext(\{X_1^i\}_{i=2}^{t+1}, X_2, \ldots, X_{t+1}) = \bigoplus_{i=2}^{t+1} Ext(X_1^i, X_i)$.

Theorem 1. *I-Ext is a $(t, t - 1)$-immune extractor, assuming that Ext is a (k, δ)-two source extractor.*

Proof (Sketch). At least one of the sources (say X_j, $2 \le j \le t + 1$) has min-entropy δk and X_j is independent of all the X_1^i ($i = 2, \ldots, t + 1$). Also, X_1^j has min-entropy δk conditioned on all the blocks $X_1^{j'}$ ($j' \ne j$). That is, the distribution of $(X_1^j | X_1^{j'} = x_1^{j'})$ has min-entropy at least δk. Therefore, $Ext(X_1^j | (X_1^{j'} = x_1^{j'}), X_j)$ is ϵ-close to U_m. Consider any $j' \ne j$. The joint distributions $(X_1^j | X_1^{j'}, Y)$ and $(X_1^{j'}, Z)$ are independent. Thus, $Ext(X_1^{j'}, X_{j'})$ is independent of $Ext(X_1^j, X_j)$, for all $j' \ne j$. This shows that $\bigoplus_{i=2}^{t} Ext(X_1^i, X_i)$ is close to U_m.

Theorem 2. *There exists a $(t, t - 1)$-strongly immune strong extractor SI-Ext.*

Proof (Sketch). In the construction of I-*Ext*, using a two-source strong extractor (for instance, those of [8,20]) in the place of *Ext* gives us SI-*Ext*. We prove the theorem for the case when $t = 2$. The proof for $t > 2$ follows quite easily from this proof.

Let the distributions under consideration be $X = (X^1, X^2), Y$ and Z. Here, the distributions Y and Z could be dependent, but both are independent of X. At least one of Y and Z have min-entropy δk. W.l.o.g, this is Y. Then, since X^1 has min-entropy δk conditioned on $X^2 = x^2$, $Ext((X^1 | X^2 = x^2), Y)$ is ϵ-close to U_m.

Let $D_1 \stackrel{def}{=} Ext((X^1 | X^2 = x^2), Y)$ and let $D_2 \stackrel{def}{=} Ext(X^2, Z)$. We know that $[D_1, Y] \approx [U_m, Y]$ and since $Z = f(Y)$,

$$[D_1, Y, Z] \approx [U_m, Y, Z].$$

We also know that

$$[D_1, X^2] \approx [U_m, X^2],$$

since D_1 is the result of extracting from $(X^1 | X^2 = x^2)$ and Y, both of which are independent of X^2. Since X^2 and Z are independent, and so are X^2 and Y,

$$[D_1, X^2, Y, Z] \approx [U_m, X^2, Y, Z].$$

Therefore,

$$[D_1, X^2, Y, Z, Ext(X^2, Z)] \approx [U_m, X^2, Y, Z, Ext(X^2, Z)].$$

Note that the last component of this distribution is precisely D_2. Thus, D_1 is random, given D_2, Y, Z and X^2. Thus $[D_1 \oplus D_2, X^2, Y, Z] \approx [U_m, X^2, Y, Z]$. In particular, this means $[D_1 \oplus D_2, Y, Z] \approx [U_m, Y, Z]$, which is the definition of the extractor being strong. $\square$

Fact 1. *Suppose X_1, X_2 and Y are random variables, and Z is a random variable such that Z is independent of X_1 and X_2. If $(X_1, Y) \approx (X_2, Y)$, then $(X_1, f(Y, Z)) \approx (X_2, f(Y, Z))$.*

4   Byzantine Agreement Protocols with Block Sources

In this section, we show how to construct randomized Byzantine agreement (BA) protocols that work even when the players have access to block sources (resp. general weak sources), using the extraction protocols of the previous section. Our transformations are fairly generic and they apply to a large class of known randomized BA protocols.

The protocol Synch-PC-Extract ensures that, in the presence of at most t faults, at least $2\lfloor \frac{n}{2} \rfloor - 2t$ good players get private random strings. The protocol Asynch-Extract, on the other hand, ensures that *all* the good players get private random strings, at the end of the protocol.

Theorem 3 (Synchronous, Private Channels). *If $n \geq 3t + 2$, then there exists a BA protocol that runs in expected $O(1)$ rounds tolerating t faults, assuming the players are connected by a synchronous network with private channels, and have (k, δ) block-sources with $\delta > \frac{1}{2}$.*

Protocol Synch-PC-Extract

Group the players $P_1, P_2, \ldots, P_n$ into pairs $(p_1, p_2), \ldots, (p_{n-1}, p_n)$. Let Ext be an (n, δ) two-source extractor. (Note: Assume for simplicity that n is even. If not, add a dummy player.)

Each player P_i does the following:

  - If i is even, sample a k-bit string X_i from the source, and send it to P_{i-1}.
  - If i is odd, sample a k-bit string X_i from the source, and receive a k-bit string X_{i+1} from P_{i+1}. Compute an m-bit string $R_i \leftarrow Ext(X_i, X_{i+1})$. Send to P_{i+1} the first $\frac{m}{2}$ bits of R_i and store the remaining bits.

Protocol Asynch-Extract

Each player p_i does the following: (Note: Ext is either a $(t+1, t)$-immune extractor or a $(t+1, t)$-strongly immune strong extractor).
- Wait to receive $t+1$ strings $Y_1, Y_2, \ldots, Y_{t+1}$ from $t+1$ different players.
- Sample blocks $X_1^1, X_1^2, \ldots, X_1^{t+1}$ from the random source.
- Compute and Store $R_i \leftarrow Ext(\{X_1^j\}_{j=1}^{t+1}, Y_1, Y_2, \ldots, Y_{t+1})$.

Protocol Synch-FI-Extract

Group the players into 4-tuples $(p_1, p_2, p_3, p_4), \ldots, (p_{n-3}, p_{n-2}, p_{n-1}, p_n)$. Let SI-$ext$ be a $(3, 2)$-strongly immune strong extractor. (Note: Assume for simplicity that n is a multiple of four. If not, add at most two dummy players.)
Each player p_i does the following: (Assume that p_i is in a 4-tuple with p_{i+1}, p_{i+2} and p_{i+3}.)
- Samples six blocks X_1^j $(j = 1, \ldots, 6)$ from its random source.
- Send X_1^j to p_{i+j} (for $j = 1, \ldots, 3$). Store X_1^j $(j = 4, \ldots, 6)$.
- Receive k-bit strings Y_j from p_{i+j} $(j = 1, \ldots, 3)$.
- Compute $R_i \leftarrow$ SI-$ext(\{X_1^4, X_1^5, X_1^6\}, Y_1, Y_2, Y_3)$ and store R_i.

Proof. In the first round, the players run the protocol Synch-PC-Extract. Let R_i denote the output of player i after running Synch-PC-Extract. Now, the players run the BA protocol guaranteed by Lemma 1 with player i using R_i as randomness.

There are at least $\lfloor \frac{n}{2} \rfloor - t \geq \lfloor \frac{t}{2} \rfloor + 1$ pairs such that both the players in the pair are good. In each pair, the players extract uniform and independent random strings. Thus, there are at least $2(\lfloor \frac{t}{2} \rfloor + 1) \geq t + 1$ players at the end of the protocol with m-bit strings that are ϵ-close to uniform. Because of the private channels assumption, the inputs used to compute R_i are invisible to the adversary, and therefore, the randomness extracted is private. Now, invoke Lemma 1 to complete the proof.

Lemma 1. *If $n \geq 3t + 1$, then there exists a BA protocol that runs in expected $O(1)$ rounds tolerating t faults in a synchronous network with private channels, even if only $t + 1$ (out of $n - t$) good players have private randomness.*

Proof. The protocol of Feldman and Micali [14] is such a BA protocol. Refer to Appendix A for a proof sketch.

Theorem 4 (Synchronous, Full-Information Model). *If $n \geq 3t + 1$, then there exists a BA protocol that runs in expected $O(\frac{t}{\log n})$ rounds tolerating t faults, assuming the players are connected by a synchronous network with non-private channels, and have (k, δ) block sources with $\delta > \frac{1}{2}$.*

Proof. In the first round, the players run the protocol Synch-FI-Extract. Using the randomness so obtained, run the BA protocol guaranteed by Lemma 2.

Consider the set of 4-tuples of players such that at most two players in the 4-tuple are bad. There are at least $\lfloor \frac{n}{4} \rfloor - \lfloor \frac{t}{3} \rfloor \geq \lfloor \frac{5t}{12} \rfloor$ such tuples. In each such pair, the good players extract uniform and independent random strings, since there are at least two good players in such a 4-tuple and Ext is a $(3, 2)$-*strongly immune* extractor. There are at least $4\lfloor \frac{5t}{12} \rfloor \geq \frac{5}{9}n = (\frac{1}{2} + \Theta(1))n$ players at the end of the protocol with m-bit strings that are ϵ-close to uniform. Moreover, the random strings R_i of these players are private, since Ext is a strong extractor. Now, invoke Lemma 2 to complete the proof.

Lemma 2. *If $n \geq 3t+1$, there exists a BA protocol that runs in expected $O(\frac{t}{\log n})$ rounds tolerating t faults in a synchronous network with non-private channels, even if only $(\frac{1}{2} + \delta)n$ good players have private randomness (for some $\delta > 0$).*

Proof. The protocol of Chor and Coan [6] is such a BA protocol. Refer to Appendix B for a proof sketch.

Theorem 5 (Asynchronous Network). *If $n \geq 3t + 1$, then there exist BA protocols that tolerate t faults in an asynchronous network, when the players have (k, δ) block-sources with $\delta > \frac{1}{2}$, and*

- *run in $O(1)$ rounds, with private channels, and*
- *run in $O(2^n)$ rounds, with non-private channels.*

Proof (Sketch).
In the private channels case: In the first round, the players run the protocol Asynch-Extract with a $(t + 1, t)$-immune extractor in the place of Ext. Let R_i denote the output of player i after running Asynch-Extract. Now, the players run the $O(1)$-round BA protocol of [5], with player i using R_i as the randomness to the [5] protocol.

Each player p_i gets $t + 1$ strings, eventually. This is because $n \geq 2t + 1$ and there are at most t faulty players. At least one of the $t + 1$ strings is "good". i.e, it comes from a (k, δ) block-source which is independent from p_i's source. By the $(t + 1, t)$-immunity of Ext, this means that the output R_i of player i is ϵ-close to uniform. Further, the output R_i of p_i is private, informally because one of the inputs to Ext is unknown to the faulty players.
In the non-private channels case: The players run the protocol Asynch-Extract with a $(t + 1, t)$-strongly immune strong extractor in the place of Ext.

4.1   The Case of General Weak Sources

The statement of Theorem 3 is true even when the players have a general weak source. This is informally because, the extractor uses at most one sample from each source.

Theorem 6 (Asynchronous, Private Channels). *If $n \geq 5t + 2$, then there exists a BA protocol that runs in expected $O(1)$ rounds tolerating t faults, assuming the players are connected by an asynchronous network with private channels, and have weak sources with min-entropy rate $\delta \geq \frac{1}{2}$.*

Proof. The protocol used in the proof of Theorem 3, with the following slight modification, suffices to prove this. The change is that, each player, after receiving a string from its partner in a pair, sends a message indicating that the extraction protocol is complete. When player i receives such a message from $n - 2t$ players, he stops the extraction protocol and sets $R_i = \phi$. Each player eventually receives such a message from $n - 2t$ players, since at least $n - 2t$ players are in pairs in which both the players are good. When a player i receives such a message, it knows that at least $n - 4t$ players have indeed extracted uniform randomness. Since $n - 4t \geq t + 1$, we are done.

References

1. Boaz Barak, Russell Impagliazzo, and Avi Wigderson. Extracting randomness using few independent sources. In *FOCS*, pages 384–393, 2004.
2. Michael Ben-Or. Another advantage of free choice: Completely asynchronous agreement protocols (extended abstract). In *PODC*, pages 27–30, 1983.
3. Michael Ben-Or and Elan Pavlov. Byzantine agreement in the full-information non-adaptive model. *unpublished manuscript*.
4. Gabriel Bracha. An asynchronous [(n-1)/3]-resilient consensus protocol. In *PODC*, pages 154–162, 1984.
5. Ran Canetti and Tal Rabin. Fast asynchronous byzantine agreement with optimal resilience. In *STOC*, pages 42–51, 1993.
6. Benny Chor and Brian A. Coan. A simple and efficient randomized byzantine agreement algorithm. *IEEE Trans. Software Eng.*, 11(6):531–539, 1985.
7. Benny Chor and Oded Goldreich. Unbiased bits from sources of weak randomness and probabilistic communication complexity. *FOCS*, pages 429–442, 1985.
8. Yevgeniy Dodis and Roberto Oliveira. On extracting private randomness over a public channel. In *RANDOM-APPROX*, pages 252–263, 2003.
9. Yevgeniy Dodis, Shien Jin Ong, Manoj P, and Amit Sahai. On the (im)possibility of cryptography with imperfect randomness. In *FOCS*, pages 196–205, 2004.
10. Yevgeniy Dodis and Joel Spencer. On the (non)universality of the one-time pad. In *FOCS*, pages 376–, 2002.
11. Cynthia Dwork, David B. Shmoys, and Larry J. Stockmeyer. Flipping persuasively in constant time. *SIAM J. Comput.*, 19(3):472–499, 1990.
12. P. Elias. The efficient construction of an unbiased random sequence. *Ann. Math. Statist.*, 43(3):865–870, 1972.
13. Paul Feldman. Asynchronous byzantine agreement in expected constant number of rounds. *unpublished manuscript*.
14. Pesech Feldman and Silvio Micali. An optimal probabilistic protocol for synchronous byzantine agreement. *SIAM J. Comput.*, 26(4):873–933, 1997.
15. Michael J. Fischer, Nancy A. Lynch, and Mike Paterson. Impossibility of distributed consensus with one faulty process. In *PODS*, pages 1–7, 1983.
16. Juan A. Garay and Yoram Moses. Fully polynomial byzantine agreement for $>$ processors in $+ 1$ rounds. *SIAM J. Comput.*, 27(1):247–290, 1998.
17. Shafi Goldwasser and Vinod Vaikuntanathan. Distributed computing with imperfect randomness part II. *manuscript, in preparation*.
18. M. Pease, R. Shostak, and L. Lamport. Reaching agreement in the presence of faults. *Journal of the ACM.*, 27:228–234, 1980.

19. Michael O. Rabin. Randomized byzantine generals. *FOCS*, pages 403–409, 1983.
20. Ran Raz. Extractors with weak random seeds. *STOC*, to appear, 2005.
21. M. Santha and U. V. Vazirani. Generating quasi-random sequences from slightly-random sources. In *FOCS*, pages 434–440, Singer Island, 1984.
22. Umesh V. Vazirani. Towards a strong communication complexity theory or generating quasi-random sequences from two communicating slightly-random sources (extended abstract). In *STOC*, pages 366–378, 1985.
23. J. von Neumann. Various techniques for use in connection with random digits. In *von Neumann's Collected Works*, volume 5, pages 768–770. Pergamon, 1963.
24. David Zuckerman. General weak random sources. In *FOCS 1990*, pages 534–543, 1990.

Appendix A – Proof of Lemma 1

We describe the salient features of Feldman-Micali protocol for Byzantine Agreement in a network with private channels, tolerating $t < \frac{n}{3}$ faulty players.

The protocol consists of three building blocks: a graded broadcast protocol, an $n/3$-resilient verifiable secret-sharing protocol and an oblivious common-coin protocol. The graded broadcast protocol is deterministic. The graded VSS protocol of Feldman-Micali [14] has the property that the Sharing protocol is randomized, and the only instructions in the protocol are executed by the dealer h. The share-verification and recovery are deterministic. Therefore,

Lemma 3. *If $n \geq 3t + 1$, there exists an $O(1)$-round protocol, which is a t-resilient graded Verifiable Secret-Sharing (VSS) protocol, assuming only that the dealer has randomness.*

Definition 7 (Oblivious Common Coin). *Let P be a fixed-round protocol in which each player x has no input and is instructed to output a bit r_x. We say that P is an oblivious common coin protocol with fairness p and fault-tolerance t if for all bits b, for every set of t players who are corrupted, $\Pr[\forall$ good players i, $r_i = b]$ $\geq p$. We refer to an execution of P as a coin. The coin is unanimously good if $r_i = b$ for every good player i.*

Lemma 4. *If $n \geq 3t + 1$, there exists an $O(1)$-round oblivious coin protocol, which assumes only that $t + 1$ good players have randomness.*

Proof. The Oblivious Coin protocol of Feldman-Micali [14] is given below.
Protocol Oblivious Common Coin

1. (for every player i): For $j = 1, \ldots, n$, randomly and independently choose a value $s_{ij} \in [0, \ldots, n - 1]$. (Note: We will refer to s_{ij} as the secret assigned to j by i.)
   Concurrently run Share and Graded-Verify (of a VSS protocol) n^2 times, once for each pair $(h, j) \in [1 \ldots n]^2$, wherein h acts as a dealer, and shares s_{hj}, the secret assigned by h to j. Let $verification_i^{hj}$ be player i's output at the end of Graded-Verify for the execution labeled (h, j).

2. (for every player i): Gradecast the value

$$(verification_i^{1i}, verification_i^{2i}, \ldots, verification_i^{ni}).$$

3. (for every player i): for all j, if
   (a) in the last step, you have accepted player j's gradecast of a vector $e_j \in \{0, 1, 2\}^n$,
   (b) for all h, $|verification_i^{hj} - e_j[h]| \leq 1$, and
   (c) $e_j[h] = 2$ for at least $n - t$ values of h,
   then set $player_{ij} = ok$, else set $player_{ij} = bad$.
4. (for every player i): Recover all possible secrets.
   Concurrently run Recover on all the n^2 secrets shared. Denote by $value_i^{hj}$ your output for execution (h, j). If $player_{ij} = bad$, set $SUM_{ij} = bad$, else set

$$SUM_{ij} = \{ \sum_{h \text{ such that } e_j[h]=2} value_i^{hj} \} \bmod n.$$

If for some player j, $SUM_{ij} = 0$, output $r_i = 0$, else output $r_i = 1$.

We now sketch the proof that the above protocol is an Oblivious Common Coin protocol, assuming at least $t + 1$ good players have uniform randomness, and at most t players are faulty. This follows from the following series of observations.

- In step 3(a) of the protocol, all the good players that accept the gradecast of a player i receive the same vector e_i, even if it player i is bad. This means, every good player i computes SUM_{ij} as a sum of the same set of values.
- If SUM_{ij} is not set to bad, all the addenda of SUM_{ij} had $e_j[h] = 2$, which means $verification_i^{hj} \geq 1$ (by Step 3(b) of the above protocol). This in turn means, by the property of graded VSS, that there is a unique secret corresponding to the $(h, j)^{th}$ execution of Share, which can be recovered. Thus, for every player j (who may be malicious), there exists a value γ such that, for any good player i, SUM_{ij} is either γ or bad.
- Moreover, if $SUM_{ij} \neq bad$, then SUM_{ij} is a sum of at least $n - t$ values (by Step 3(c) of the above protocol). At least one of the $n - t$ values is shared by a good player who has randomness (since there are at least $t + 1$ of them). Thus, since all the values shared are independent [2], SUM_{ij} is either set to bad or a random number γ.
- Given this, we can prove that the coin is sufficiently common and sufficiently random. The proof proceeds identically to that of [14]. More precisely, we can prove that for any bit b, $\Pr[\forall \text{ good players } i, r_i = b] \geq min(e^{-1}, 1 - e^{-2/3})$.

Lemma 5 ([14]). *Given an oblivious-coin protocol as a black-box, there is a deterministic protocol that achieves BA in $O(1)$ rounds.*

---

[2] It turns out that this statement is not precise, and has to be proven by a more careful simulation argument, for which we refer the reader to [14].

Appendix B – Proof of Lemma 2

The Chor-Coan protocol for BA in a full-information network is given below. The players are divided into fixed disjoint groups of size g. The ith group consists of the set of players $\{p_{(i-1)g+1}, \ldots, p_{ig}\}$. For any player p_i, let $\mathsf{GROUP}(p_i)$ denote the group that p_i belongs to. The protocol proceeds in phases where, in each phase, the players try to reach agreement on their values. In each phase, one of the groups is said to be *active*. The purpose of the players in the active group is (among other things) to toss coins and send it to all the other players.

1. For $e = 1$ *to* ∞, each player p_i does the following: (Note: e is the current phase.)
   (a) Sends to every player the message $(e, \mathsf{Phase}_1, b_i)$.
   (b) Receive messages from every other player of the form $(e, \mathsf{Phase}_1, *)$.
   (c) If for some v, there are $\geq n - t$ messages of the form (e, Phase_1, v), then set $b_i \leftarrow v$, else set $b_i \leftarrow$ "?"
   (d) If $\mathsf{GROUP}(p_i) \equiv e \ (mod \ \lfloor \frac{n}{g} \rfloor)$ then set $coin \leftarrow b$, else set $coin \leftarrow 0$ {Note : b is a random bit}
   (e) Send to every player the message $(e, \mathsf{Phase}_2, b_i, coin)$.
   (f) Receive messages of the form $(e, \mathsf{Phase}_2, c, coin)$ from every player.
       { Note: Let $\mathsf{NUM}(c)$ be the number of messages received that contain c. }
   (g) If $\mathsf{NUM}(c) \geq n - t$ for some bit c, **decide** c.
   (h) Else, if $\mathsf{NUM}(c) \geq t + 1$ and $\mathsf{NUM}(c) > \mathsf{NUM}(\bar{c})$, set $b_i \leftarrow c$.
   (i) Else, set $b_i \leftarrow$ majority of the $coin_j$'s from the group x, where $x \equiv e (mod \ \lfloor n/g \rfloor)$.

Proof of Lemma 2. The following properties of the protocol are easily verified: (a) If a player p_i decides at the end of a phase, all players decide by the end of the next phase. (b) If a player sets $b_i \leftarrow c$ at the end of a phase (instruction h, above), then no player p_j sets $b_j \leftarrow \bar{c}$. Given this, it is easy to see that agreement is reached when all the remaining players (ones who set b_i to be the coin-toss from a group) set b_i to c (in instruction i). It remains to analyze the expected number of rounds in which this event happens.

Set the size of a group to be $g = 2m = \log n$. Call a group e *good* if more than $m + 1$ players in the group are non-faulty. Call a coin-toss good if at least $m + 1$ good players in a group tossed the same coin (with a fixed value – 0 or 1). It is clear that $\Pr[\text{coin-toss of a group } e \text{ is good} \mid e \text{ is a good group}] \geq \frac{1}{2^{m+1}}$. Now, lets analyze how many bad groups there can be. There are at most $t < (\frac{1}{2} - \epsilon)n$ players who have no randomness, and these players can make at most $\frac{t}{m+1} < (\frac{1}{2} - \epsilon)\frac{2n}{\log n} = (1 - 2\epsilon)\frac{n}{\log n}$ groups bad. Since there are $\frac{n}{\log n}$ groups in total, the number of good groups is at least $\frac{2\epsilon n}{\log n}$.

The protocol terminates as soon as there is a good coin-toss. The expected number of good groups that have to toss coins before they get a good coin is precisely $2^{m+1} \leq 2\sqrt{n}$. The probability that a good coin is not formed after $n^{3/4}$ groups tossing coins is negligible, by a Chernoff Bound. Thus, the expected number of rounds to each agreement is $\frac{2t}{\log n} + n^{3/4} + O(1)$.

Polymorphic Contention Management

Rachid Guerraoui[1], Maurice Herlihy[2,*], and Bastian Pochon[1]

[1] School of Computer and Communication Sciences, EPFL
[2] Brown University and Microsoft Research Cambridge

Abstract. In software transactional memory (STM) systems, a contention manager resolves conflicts among transactions accessing the same memory locations. Whereas atomicity and serializability of the transactions are guaranteed at all times, the contention manager is of crucial importance for guaranteeing that the system as a whole makes progress.

A number of different contention management policies have been proposed and evaluated in the recent literature. An empirical evaluation of these policies leads to the striking result that there seems to be no "universal" contention manager that works best under all reasonable circumstances. Instead, transaction throughput can vary dramatically depending on factors such as transaction length, data access patterns, the length of contended vs. uncontended phases, and so on.

This paper proposes *polymorphic contention management*, a structure that allows contention managers to vary not just across workloads, but across concurrent transactions in a single workload, and even across different phases of a single transaction. The ability to mix contention managers or to change them on-the-fly provides performance benefits, but also poses number of questions concerning how a contention manager of a given class can interact in a useful way with contention managers of different, possibly unknown classes. We address these questions by classifying contention managers in a hierarchy, based on the cost associated with each contention manager, and present a general algorithm to handle conflict between contention managers from different classes. We describe how our polymorphic contention management structure is smoothly integrated with nested transactions in the SXM library.

1   Introduction

Because it is getting harder and harder to make processors run faster, chip manufacturers are focusing on *multicore* architectures, in which multiple processors (cores) communicate directly through shared hardware caches [6]. The next generation of processors will provide increased concurrency instead of increased clock speed, and programming languages and APIs will need to exploit this increased parallelism.

The limitations of conventional synchronization techniques, based on locks and condition variables [1] are well-known [11,10]. Coarse-grained locks, which

---

* Supported by NSF grant 0410042 and by grants from Intel Corporation and Sun Microsystems.

P. Fraigniaud (Ed.): DISC 2005, LNCS 3724, pp. 303–323, 2005.

protect relatively large amounts of data, simply do not scale. Threads block one another even when they do not really interfere, and the lock itself becomes a source of memory contention. Fine-grained locks are more scalable, but they are difficult to use effectively and correctly. In particular, they introduce substantial software engineering problems, as the conventions associating locks with objects become more complex and error-prone. Locks also cause vulnerability to thread failures and delays: if a thread holding a lock is delayed by a page fault, or context switch, other running threads may be blocked.

An alternative to locking is to synchronize by light-weight in-memory *transactions*, an approach called *transactional memory*. A transaction [2] is a finite sequence of memory reads and writes executed by a single thread. Transactions are atomic [19]: each transaction either commits (it takes effect) or aborts (its effects are discarded). Transactions are serializable [14]: they appear to take effect in a one-at-a-time order. (Unlike database transactions, we are not concerned here with backing up changes to non-volatile memory.)

Software transactional memory (STM) systems have been the focus of much recent research [7,10,8,16,17]. Most of these systems guarantee a relatively weak progress property called *freedom from obstruction* [9]: if a transaction runs long enough without overlapping a conflicting transaction, then it will commit. Obstruction-freedom does not rule out livelock or starvation, so stronger progress properties are typically provided "out-of-band" by a user-provided module called a *contention manager*. Roughly speaking, if transaction A is about to take a step that will cause a synchronization conflict with transaction B, then A consults its contention manager to decide whether to proceed, thus causing B to abort, or else to back off for a bounded duration, giving B a chance to finish.

Contention managers affect liveness, not safety. The most natural way to evaluate a contention manager is by its *throughput*, the number of transactions committed per unit of time. A bad transaction manager provides low throughput, but cannot produce unsafe results (except perhaps by throwing unexpected exceptions).

A number of different contention management policies have been proposed [5,10,16,17]. In contrast with a recent publication [17], a striking result of our evaluation (discussed in more details below) is that there seems to be no "universal" contention manager that works best under all reasonable circumstances. Instead, transaction throughput can vary dramatically depending on factors such as transaction length, data access patterns, length of contended vs. uncontended phases, and so on. We expect this uncertainty to be even more drastic in large scale concrete applications.

Figure 1 illustrates how contention manager performance depends on context. The figure features contention managers that have recently appeared in the literature (we give more details on these later in the paper). The two scenarios illustrated differ in the contention pattern among conflicting transactions. Both scenarios use a red-black tree data structure in which a number of threads insert and remove elements. The number of transactions committed within a

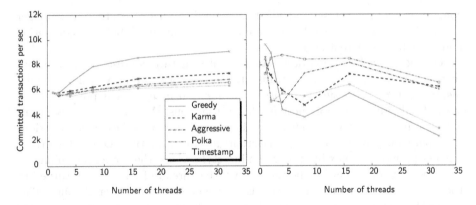

Fig. 1. Comparison of various contention management policies under low (left) and high (right) contention scenarios

constant time period of one second, under various contention management policies, is depicted, with respect to a number of threads ranging from 1 to 32. The scenario on the left reduces contention by making each thread executes a time-delay loop at the end of every transaction. The scenario on the right exhibits a contention-intensive scenario, in which threads continuously insert and remove elements from the red-black tree. Elements are taken from a small set of 256 integers to force contention to happen within the tree. Benchmarks were run on a 4-processor Intel Xeon machine with hyperthreading turned on.

When situations such as those of Figure 1 *simultaneously* appear within a single application, the application benefits from associating distinct contention managers to different groups of transactions, according to the situation encountered by each particular group. The diversity of contention managers within a single application may also be motivated by the change, over the lifetime of the application, of parameters affecting the throughput of committed transactions, for instance the number of threads or the number of tables in a database. In this case, running transactions with a default contention manager from some time on, may lead to conflicts with transactions that are still running with the previous default contention manager and have not yet committed.

We propose *polymorphic contention management*, a structure that allows contention managers to vary not just across workloads, but across concurrent transactions in a single workload, and even across different phases of a single transaction. The ability to mix contention managers or to change them on-the-fly provides performance benefits, but also poses number of questions concerning how one contention manager of a given class[1] can interact in a useful way with contention managers of different, possibly unknown classes. We introduce a hierarchy of contention manager classes, based on the cost associated with each

---

[1] Throughout the paper, the notion of "contention manager class" is to be taken in the object-oriented sense, i.e., a set of instances implementing the same contention manager policy.

contention manager class, and identify general groups of contention manager classes. We present a general algorithm to handle contention between contention managers from different classes.

Our polymorphic contention management structure is presented in the context of SXM, a new software transactional memory library which we implemented in C#. SXM supports distinct contention management policies at the level of individual, possibly nested [13], transactions. We associate transactions with methods in SXM, which makes it natural to isolate nested transactions from parents, and concurrent transactions from one another. Our polymorphic scheme promotes a flexible programming style where the contention manager of a nested transaction can be interactive: the thread of control is returned to the application after the transaction is aborted a certain number of times. This allows the application for possibly changing at runtime the contention manager of the transaction (e.g., if the number of threads increases). The full code of SXM is available on the web for further experimentation [15].

The remainder of the paper is organized as follows. Section 2 gives an overview of elements of SXM that are needed to describe our polymorphic contention management structure. Section 3 explains in more details contention management in SXM and compares different contention managers. Section 4 discusses the mixing of contention managers. Section 5 describes how to associate a contention manager with a transaction in SXM. Section 6 presents the implementation of SXM in C#, including a postprocessor approach to declaring transactions. Section 7 discusses related work.

2   Overview of SXM

Before describing our polymorphic structure, we provide here a short overview of our transaction model, illustrated in Figure 2, and an example of a program using our SXM library. In Section 6, we will give more details about the implementation of SXM and the polymorphic contention management scheme in C#.

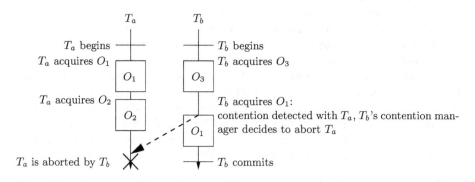

Fig. 2. T_b is attacking victim transaction T_a

2.1 Transactions

We consider a system made of n threads. Each thread executes independently of other threads, and follows a program assigned to it. Beside normal code, a thread may execute *transactions* [2]. A transaction is a basic unit of computation that appears to take place atomically [19] to every other transaction (thread). When a thread finishes a transaction, the transaction may either *commit*, and every modification performed during the transaction instantaneously takes place, or *abort*, in which case no modification is effectively performed.

We consider an object-based memory model. In this model, threads share objects. Within a transaction, a thread accesses *transactional objects*. A transactional object is an object supporting additional methods, for being accessed from within a transaction. Roughly speaking, every transactional object supports a *clone* operation. When a thread executes within a transaction, the thread works on a *copy* of the transactional object, obtained using the clone method. When the thread obtains a copy of the transactional object to work on, we say the thread *acquires* the transactional object. Upon completion, the transaction atomically commits every modification done on every copy acquired, to the original transactional object. If the transaction fails to commit, the thread may restart the transaction.

2.2 Contention Managers

A transaction T_a may fail to commit because another transaction T_b has accessed the same transactional object O, invalidating the copy T_a has obtained. When T_b acquires O, T_b detects a conflict with T_a. At this point however, it is not clear whether T_b, which we call the *attacking* transaction, should abort T_a, which we call the *victim* transaction, or whether T_b should just wait and give more time to T_a to finish. It is possible that T_a never commits if it is always aborted by other transactions. Hence the choice of mediating conflicts among transactions with a *contention manager*.

More precisely, a contention manager instance is associated with each transaction. In case of a conflict, the contention manager of the attacking transaction decides, possibly based on the computation of the transactions, which of the attacking or the victim transaction should abort. On the one hand, a transaction that has aborted many times should be given a change to commit, and thus should not be aborted too easily. On the other hand, a transaction may be blocked, e.g. waiting for swapped-out data to be swapped in, and aborting the blocked transaction in favor of others may lead to better throughput. Clearly, the contention manager is crucial to the performance of a STM system.

By eventually aborting any conflicting transaction if called sufficiently many times, a contention manager may easily ensure *freedom from obstruction* [9], a relatively weak liveness guarantee. More sophisticated contention management policies ensure stronger liveness guarantees [5,16].

2.3   Transactions and Contention Management in SXM

In SXM, the transaction invocation tree is mapped onto the method invocation tree, through a few programming conventions, following the current "library" approach of SXM. Section 6.3 describes an alternative postprocessor approach to declare transactions in SXM.

A transaction is explicitly constructed from a method and the transactional objects must be marked with the Atomic attribute and support the ICloneable interface. We assume here that a particular contention manager has been chosen and specified elsewhere, and we explain how this is effectively achieved in Section 3.

Figure 3 depicts a simple example of a counter in SXM. There are two classes, Application and Counter. The class Application represents the application class, and defines a method Increment, to be run as a transaction. The class Counter implements ICloneable and is marked with Atomic: hence instances of Counter are transactional objects, and may be accessed through the C# property inc, defined in Counter. (We use properties instead of methods because properties make an explicit distinction between get and set accesses, that we respectively associate with read and write accesses. This allows for distinguishing, within a transaction, objects that are accessed read-only, i.e. through a get property, or read-write, i.e. through set property).

The body of the Increment method consists in accessing a single transactional object, counter, instantiated from the class Counter, by invoking the increment property on it. The Main method declares a transaction corresponding to the Increment method, in three steps (line numbers refer to Figure 3):

```
 1: class Application
 2:    Counter counter;         // Transactional object

 3:    public Application()
 4:       this.counter =
                (obtain a fresh Counter instance);     1: // Class representing transactional objects
                                                       2: [Atomic]
 5:    // Increment will be run as transaction         3: class Counter : ICloneable
 6:    public void Increment()                         4:    private int balance;
 7:       this.counter.increment;
                                                       5:    public Counter(int balance)
 8: static public void Main(string argv[ ])            6:       this.balance = balance;
 9:    // Create the application
10:    Application application = new Application();     7:    public object Clone()
                                                       8:       return new Counter(this.balance);
11:    // Create a delegate
12:    Delegate delegate = new                          9: // Property that increments the balance
          SXMDelegate(application.Increment);          10:    property int increment
                                                       11:       set
13:    // Create the transaction                       12:          balance = balance + 1;
14:    SXMAction incrementAction =
          SXMAction.Create(delegate);
15:    ...
16:    // Run the transaction
17:    incrementAction.Run();
```

Fig. 3. Example of a counter in SXM

1. Create first a delegate, representing the method to run as a transaction (line 6, second column). (A delegate is a C# feature that represents a kind of type-safe pointer on a method.)
2. Create a transaction, represented as an instance of SXMAction, from this delegate (line 8, second column).
3. Launch the transaction by invoking the Run method on the SXMAction instance (line 11, second column). (In a real application, running the transaction would obviously occur within a new thread.)

3   Specifying a Contention Manager

3.1   Contention Management Methods

Every transaction is associated with a particular contention manager, where the task of the contention manager is to resolve conflicts encountered with other transactions. The contention manager resolves conflicts based on the computation performed by its associated transaction. In this sense, the contention manager is informed by its associated transaction of the evolution of the computation.

A contention manager exports *notification* and *feedback* methods: notification methods enable the transaction to inform the contention manager of its computation, whereas *feedback* methods enable the contention manager to inform the transaction of what to do in specific situations.

Notification methods include methods such as BeginTransaction, Transaction-Committed, TransactionAborted, as well as methods to indicate an attempt in acquiring a transactional object (OpenReadAttempt and OpenWriteAttempt), and success in acquiring a transactional object (OpenReadSucceeded and OpenWrite-Succeeded).

A feedback method is invoked by a transaction on its own contention manager, in situations where the expertise of the contention manager is needed. We consider two feedback methods:

- The method ResolveConflict is invoked on the contention manager of a transaction whenever a conflict is detected with another transaction. Roughly speaking, the contention manager of the attacking transaction may decide in this case, according to its specific contention management policy (we give examples in the next section), whether to abort the victim transaction, or whether to send to sleep the attacking transaction and give more time to the victim transaction to finish.
- The method ShouldBegin is invoked on the contention manager of a transaction whenever the transaction (re)starts. This method returns whether the transaction should wait, or whether it may start. In a typical contention manager implementation, ShouldBegin blocks the transaction, based on its specific contention management policy, yielding in favor of other threads. The contention manager sends the transaction to sleep until it is appropriate for the transaction to start.

3.2 Examples of Contention Managers

Several contention managers have been defined in the literature [5,16,17]. The Aggressive contention manager systematically aborts the victim transaction. The Polite contention manager exponentially backs off for a fixed number of attempts, and eventually aborts the conflicting transaction. The Randomized contention manager aborts the victim transaction with some probability p, and waits with probability $1 - p$. Greedy and Timestamp contention managers associate a timestamp to a transaction when it is run for the first time. The idea is that an old transaction (one with a lower timestamp) has priority over a young one (one with a higher timestamp). In case of conflict, if the victim has a higher timestamp, it is aborted. With Greedy, if the victim transaction is waiting, then the attacking transaction aborts it; otherwise, the attacking transaction waits, until the victim either commits, aborts, or waits. With Timestamp, if the attacking transaction is not older than the victim, the attacking transaction then waits for a series of fixed intervals. After attempting half the number of intervals, the contention manager of the attacking transaction flags the victim as possibly defunct. After attempting the full number of intervals, if the victim has the defunct flag set, the contention manager of the attacking transaction aborts the victim; meanwhile, if the victim transaction performs any transaction-related operation, its contention manager resets the defunct flag. Karma and Polka contention managers increase the priority of a transaction whenever the transaction successfully acquires a transactional object. When two transactions are in conflict, the attacking transaction makes a number of attempts equal to the difference among priorities of both transaction, with a constant backoff between each attempt (Karma), or with an exponential random backoff between successive attempts (Polka). The Eruption contention manager also maintains the number of transactional objects successfully acquired, denoted *objs*, and gives to a transaction an initial priority of *zero*. In case of conflict, if the victim transaction has a higher priority than the attacking one, the contention manager of the attacking transaction adds *objs* to the priority of the victim transaction, and then sends the attacking transaction to sleep for an exponential random backoff. Otherwise, the contention manager aborts the victim transaction. The idea behind the Eruption contention manager is to increase the priority of the transaction behind which other transactions are waiting.

Figure 4 illustrates, following the example of Section 2, how we create a transaction from the Increment method, and associate with this transaction a Greedy contention manager [5].

```
1: static public void Main(string argv[ ])
2:     Application application = new Application();
3:     Delegate delegate = new SXMDelegate(application.Increment);
4:     SXMAction incrementAction = SXMAction.Create(delegate,typeof(Greedy));
5:     ...
6:     incrementAction.Run();
```

Fig. 4. Specifying a contention manager

3.3   Benchmarks

The benchmarks in this section provide some guidelines for choosing adequate contention managers in different parts of a given concurrent application. In fact, a programmer is encouraged to experiment with different contention management policies, especially since safety is not impacted.

Figures 1 and 5 show the number of committed transactions in a constant period of one second with respect to the number of threads, ranging from 1 to 32, with different contention management policies and in three different scenarios. Figure 1 depicts, on the left, a red-black tree application with low contention among transactions and, on the right, a red-black tree application with high contention among transactions. Figure 5 depicts a red-black forest application, a data structure made of fifty red-black trees, in which threads continuously insert and remove elements, in either one or all trees on a random basis; the length distribution of the transactions produced which a red-black forest exhibits a high variance.

As conveyed by the left part of Figure 1, when there is no contention among transactions at the end of the computation, for various length of uncontented periods, and transactions are approximately of the same size, the Greedy contention manager [5] provides the best throughput. Intuitively, this is because Greedy does not maintain costly data structures for assigning priority to transactions. On the other hand, the right part of Figure 1 shows that Karma [16] and Polka [17] provide a better throughput in a contention-intensive scenario. This might be explained by the fact that the priority assigned to transactions, though more costly to update, reveals itself a good estimator of the intuition that a transaction that has performed a lot of work should have a higher priority than a transaction that has performed less work.

In Figure 5(a), transactions are of irregular length, and the best contention management policies seem uncertain. More precisely, it highly varies depending on the number of threads (we come back to this in Section 4).

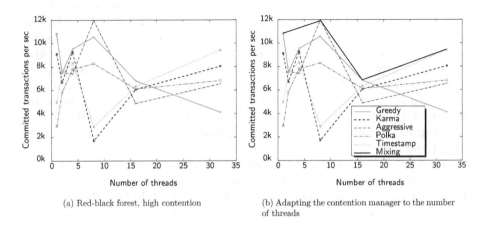

(a) Red-black forest, high contention

(b) Adapting the contention manager to the number of threads

Fig. 5. Red-black forest application

4   Polymorphic Contention Management

4.1   Mixing Contention Managers

In SXM, each transaction may be associated with a distinct contention manager class. Obviously, we would like to associate with each transaction within an application the contention manager for which the best throughput is obtained. This is not necessarily the same contention manager class for all (groups of) transactions.

Figure 5(b) shows the throughput of committed transactions per seconds when the contention manager associated with any new transaction adapts to the current number of threads, within the same application.

To illustrate this situation, consider a server responding to client requests over the Internet, designed such that each client is served by a different thread within the server. Consider that at some point, a high number of clients simultaneously send a request to the server. The number of threads within the application is then high, and the application benefits from switching the default contention manager to be used for any new transaction, to one that is efficient with a high number of threads. When the number of clients later decreases, the number of threads on the server decreases. The application then benefits from switching the default contention manager to one that is efficient with a low number of threads.

A programmer may also want to implement her own contention managers, for the purpose of her application. On the other hand, she might also want to use a contention manager that already exists for other transactions.

Clearly, addressing the conflict resolution (a priori) by considering every possible pair of contention managers in the ResolveConflict method is simply not possible. In the following, we discuss how that can be done in a dynamic manner.

4.2   Coping with Diversity

When two or more contention manager classes are mixed within a single application, two conflicting transactions are not necessarily associated with the same contention manager class. Consider for example a transaction T_a managed by a Greedy contention manager denoted M_a and a transaction T_b, attacking T_a, managed by a Karma contention manager denoted M_b. In the ResolveConflict method, M_b needs to decide whether to abort the victim transaction T_a, monitored by M_a. Although M_b has a reference to M_a, M_b does not know the dynamic type of M_a (Greedy). In fact, M_a is available to M_b as a reference of type IContentionManager, a simple interface implemented by all contention manager implementations in SXM.

To cope with the diversity of contention managers, the easiest policy we may imagine is that any contention manager immediately aborts a conflicting transaction managed by a different contention manager. In fact, this is the behavior of the Aggressive contention manager [16]. In this case, any contention manager is an Aggressive contention manager in face of a contention manager of an unknown class.

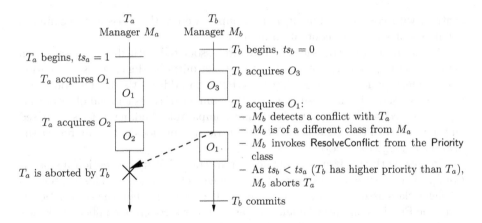

Fig. 6. T_b is attacking victim transaction T_a with a contention manager of a different class

Rank	Contention manager	Data structures
0	IContentionManager	—
1	Aggressive, Polite	—
2	Greedy, Killblocked	Birthdate
3	(Published)Timestamp	Birthdate, variable
4	Kindergarten	List of transactions
5	Karma, Polka, Eruption	List of objects

(column a: ranks 0–1, column b: ranks 2–3, column c: ranks 4–5)

Fig. 7. A hierarchy of contention managers

Fig. 8. Nesting transactions

We classify contention managers in a hierarchy. The hierarchy is based on the cost associated to each contention manager, from the less costly ones (those that do not use any bookkeeping) to the most costly ones (those that maintain much information about the current transaction, the other transactions, etc.). The hierarchy is shown in Figure 7, and includes the contention managers defined in [5] and [16].

More precisely, Figure 7 depicts three general groups of contention managers: (a) ad-hoc contention managers which always adopt the same strategy independently of the computation of transactions, (b) contention managers which base their decision on information local to transactions, and (c) contention managers which base their decision on the computation and previous interactions of transactions. This is reflected in the implementation of the contention managers by (a) no variable at all, (b) simple data structures, and (c) complex data structures. Because contention managers in group b maintain simpler data structures and less bookkeeping than contention managers in group c, but, at the same time, base their decisions on elements of the computation of the transaction, in contrast with contention managers in group a, we use this class as the common denominator among all contention managers.

Furthermore, two transactions that are associated with distinct contention managers were probably not planned to conflict initially. Hence using contention management policies such as Karma or Polka to address the conflict does not really make sense in this case, because the number of transactional objects that have been accessed so far is probably not comparable. Making a decision based on the number of objects acquired by each transaction does not really reflect the priority among transactions.

To cope with this issue, we defined an abstract Priority contention manager, from which every concrete contention manager class inherits. This contention manager class associates a priority to every transaction, when the transaction is run. The Priority contention manager class exports a concrete conflict resolution ResolveConflict method, based on this priority.

Consider the scenario depicted in Fig. 6, where a transaction T_b attacks a transaction T_a, and denote by M_a (resp. M_b) the contention manager of T_a (resp. T_b), and by ResolveConflict$_a$ (resp. ResolveConflict$_b$) the original Resolve-Conflict of contention manager M_a (resp. M_b). When the SXM library detects the conflict, it invokes the ResolveConflict on M_b. Within the method, the conflict resolution algorithm now works as follows:

1. If M_b and M_a are of the same class, or M_b is of a superclass of M_a, then apply ResolveConflict$_b$ between T_a and T_b.
2. If M_b and M_a are of incomparable classes, then apply the ResolveConflict method as defined by the Priority contention manager, between T_a and T_b.

We use the priority and conflict resolution algorithm of the Greedy contention manager as the common priority and conflict resolution algorithm of the Priority contention manager. The Greedy contention manager records the time at which a transaction starts for the first time. When two transactions conflicts, these timestamps are used as priority, with the idea that older transactions have higher priority than recent transactions. Consider a victim transaction T_a and a transaction T_b attacking T_a. We associate timestamp ts_a (resp. ts_b) with T_a (resp. T_b). The ResolveConflict method of the Greedy contention manager proceeds as follows (recall that T_b is attacking T_a):

1. If $ts_a > ts_b$ (T_a was started more recently than T_b) or T_a is waiting, then abort T_a.
2. Otherwise, wait until T_a commits, aborts or starts waiting. (If T_a starts waiting, then see Rule 1.)

5   Associating Contention Managers with Transactions

In Section 3 we pointed out how a particular contention manager may be associated with a transaction at the top level. We go one step further, and allow for decomposing a transaction into nested transactions (following the method invocation tree), and associating different contention managers within the same top level transaction. We discuss now the issues behind nesting transactions and explain how each nested transaction may be associated with a distinct contention manager.

5.1   Issues Behind Nesting Transactions

In SXM, the transaction boundaries are mapped on the method boundaries. Consider an application where a method A invokes a method B. In the application, we declare transaction T_a (resp. T_b) associated with method A (resp. B). There are two possibilities for running transaction T_b:

1. T_b runs within transaction T_a.
2. T_b runs as a separate transaction nested in T_a.

Running transaction T_b as a nested transaction (possibility 2) is more costly than running T_b within T_a (possibility 1), since it requires creating a fresh transaction state. (We give more details on what it takes to create a transaction in Section 6.) To illustrate the usefulness of possibility 2, assume that before invoking T_b, T_a performs a long computation consuming a lot of resources. If a conflict is encountered when executing T_b with a third transaction T_c, we would prefer restarting T_b without restarting T_a. In this case, it is convenient to run T_b as a separate transaction, which may be aborted and restarted separately from T_a. In this case, T_a is not impacted by the conflict encountered by T_b, and the execution of T_a may resume when T_b eventually commits.

Whether one approach is more appropriate than the other depends on the context. Hence we consider both approaches, as either one may be appropriate in different situations: our SXM library provides the programmer with the possibility, for every transaction, to choose which approach to use. When creating a transaction from a method, the programmer may specify, using a boolean parameter, whether the transaction should run within its parent transaction, or as a nested transaction. Figure 9 shows the syntax for declaring a transaction which should be nested in a parent transaction.

In terms of contention management, SXM defines on the one hand notification methods specific to the case where a transaction is run within another transaction, for instance to inform the contention manager about the depth of the transaction. On the other hand, when running a transaction T_b nested in a transaction T_a, SXM enables to associate with T_b a contention manager that is distinct from the contention manager of T_a.

Whereas the implementation of possibility 1 is trivial and only requires declaring additional notification methods, the implementation of possibility 2 is more involved. With possibility 2, if T_b aborts, our SXM library restarts it, without impacting T_a, whereas if T_b reaches completion without aborting, then T_b returns the thread of execution to T_a. When T_b terminates, T_b cannot really commit, because its parent transaction T_a is not finished yet, and may still be aborted later on. If T_b commits, and T_a is later aborted, we would have to roll back the changes of T_b, which is cumbersome.

```
1: static public void Main(string argv[ ])
2:    Application application = new Application();
3:    bool runAsNestedTransaction = true;
4:    Delegate delegate = new SXMDelegate(application.Increment);
5:    SXMAction incrementAction = SXMAction.Create(delegate,typeof(Greedy),runAsNestedTransaction);
6:    ...
7:    incrementAction.Run();
```

Fig. 9. Specifying nested transaction semantics

```
1: class Nesting                              1: public void ParentMethod()
2:    static SXMAction parentAction;          2:    ...
3:    static SXMAction childAction;           3:    // Repeat while nested transaction aborts
                                              4:    while true do
4:    static public void Main(string[ ] argv) 5:       try
5:       Interactive.ManagerType = typeof(Aggressive);  6:          childAction.Run();
6:       Nesting example = new Nesting();     7:          break;
7:       Delegate parent = new               8:       catch InteractiveException
              SXMDelegate(example.ParentMethod);  9:          ...
8:       Delegate child = new                10:          // Associate another manager
              SXMDelegate(example.ChildMethod);  11:          // with child transaction if it aborts
9:       parentAction = SXMAction.Create(parent,  12:          childAction.ManagerType = typeof(Karma);
              typeof(Interactive));          13:          ...
10:       childAction = SXMAction.Create(child,
              typeof(Greedy),true);          14: public void ChildMethod()
11:       ...                                15:    ...
12:       parentAction.Run();
```

Fig. 10. The Interactive contention manager

In SXM, when any nested transaction finishes, the parent transaction inherits the objects acquired by the nested transaction, as shown in Figure 8. When the parent transaction later commits, all the objects it has acquired, included those inherited from nested transactions, are committed. (We give more details on the actual implementation of nested transactions in Section 6.)

5.2   Interactive Contention Management

As part of resolving a conflict among two conflicting transactions, a contention manager may perform several actions: abort the victim transaction, backoff for a random or exponential time, access data structures for bookkeeping, change the priority of the attacking or of the victim transaction, etc.

SXM features the Interactive contention manager, that returns the thread of execution to the parent transaction (or to the executing thread if already at the top level), as soon as a nested transaction aborts. This allows for defining more complex schemes, for instance trying an alternative transaction in case of the first transaction aborts (similarly to the orElse construct of [7]). This is key to dynamically changing the contention manager of the nested transaction, if one feels that another contention manager would then perform better.

The Interactive contention manager is parametrized with another contention manager, as the Interactive contention manager does not feature any contention management policy on its own. Figure 10 depicts an example of the Interactive contention manager. In this example, a parent transaction is associated with the Interactive contention manager (line 9), which was previously parametrized with the Aggressive contention manager (line 5), and a nested transaction is associated with the Greedy contention manager (line 10). The nested transaction is created in such a way it will be run as a separate transaction by SXM (line 10). In case the nested transaction aborts, the Interactive contention manager throws an exception. In the exception handler (line 8, second column), the parent transaction assigns another contention manager class to the nested transaction (line 12, second column), before restarting it (while loop at line 4, second column). When the nested transaction succeeds, the parent transaction may resume its execution.

6   Implementation of SXM in C#

In SXM, when a transaction invokes an operation on a transactional object, a synchronization code is transparently executed before the operation is effectively performed. This synchronization code is generated and added to the program at runtime, using the reflexive API of C#. Roughly speaking, this code allows for detecting conflicts among transactions, upon acquiring a transactional object. In this section, we give more details on implementation issues in SXM.

6.1   Transactional Object Structure

For an object to be transactional, its class is marked with the Atomic attribute and implements the ICloneable interface. Get properties within this class are (implicitly) considered as *read* operations, whereas set properties are (implicitly) considered as *write* operations. The fields of an Atomic class are declared private, so that they are not accessible from the outside of the object by accident, preventing the transaction abstraction from being broken.

To create a transactional object in a program, maybe in a transaction, a thread uses a *transactional object factory*, SXMObjectFactory. Behind the scenes, a transactional object of class Type is represented by an instance of class TX_Type, which inherits from Type. Class TX_Type is created at runtime by the SXMObjectFactory, which is given class Type as a parameter, and return class TX_Type. As TX_Type inherits from Type, instances of class TX_Type returned by the factory may be referenced as instances of class Type, hence a full transparency for the programmer.

An instance of class TX_Type has a single field, denoted stmObject, of type SynchState.[2] Roughly speaking, the instance of class SynchState supports the methods necessary for acquiring a copy of the object. The SynchState object references a Locator object. A Locator references in its turn an XState instance and two instances of class Type. An XState object represents the state of the transaction, and may have three values: ACTIVE, COMMITTED or ABORTED.

---

[2] The SynchState object corresponds to the TMObject in the DSTM system of [10].

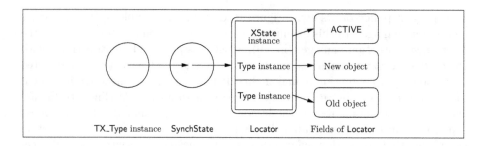

Fig. 11. Transactional object structure

When a fresh XState instance is created for a transaction, it is in the ACTIVE state. In a Locator instance, the XState instance corresponds to the state of the transaction which acquired the transactional object the most recently.

Initially, the SynchState instance referenced by TX_Type, references a Locator instance containing the COMMITTED transaction state, and the original version of the transactional object is referenced by the new object. Figure 11 illustrates the structure of a transactional object.

When a transaction attempts to invoke a method on the transactional object, the transaction really invokes the method with the same signature on the TX_Type instance. (Recall that each instance of a class marked with the Atomic attribute is created from the SXMObjectFactory, which returns instances of class TX_Type.)

TX_Type declares the same properties, with the same signature, as Type. The body of a get (resp. set) property in class TX_Type adds synchronization code before calling the original get (resp. set) property. More precisely, it is implemented as follows:

1. An invocation of OpenRead (resp. OpenWrite) method on stmObject object is performed. Roughly speaking, this encapsulates the steps necessary to obtain a fresh copy of the object, and to make sure no other transaction has a copy of the object. Corresponding to the contention management policy, this means to either abort a conflicting transaction, or to send its transaction to sleep for some time.
2. The original get (resp. set) property of class Type is invoked on the copy returned, and the result is returned to the user (resp. the copy is modified with the given value).

For instance, consider a linked list data structure. A list is composed of zero or more nodes, represented by class Node. A node contains two fields, a integer element, representing the value stored in the node, and a reference next, on the next node in this list. Both fields are accessed through get (resp. set) properties, which only return the value in the field (resp. set the field with the new value). Node is shown in Figure 12(a) and TX_Node generated from Node at runtime through the SXMObjectFactory is shown in Figure 12(b).

```
1:  [Atomic]
2:  class Node : ICloneable
3:     private Node next;
4:     private int element;

5:     public Node(Node next, int element)
6:        this.next = next;
7:        this.element = element;

8:     public object Clone()
9:        return new Node(this.next,this.element);

10:    property Node Next
11:       get
12:          return this.next;
13:       set
14:          this.next = value;

15:    property int Element
16:       get
17:          return this.element;
18:       set
19:          this.element = value;
```

```
1:  class TX_Node : Node
2:     private SynchState stmObject;

3:     public TX_Node() : base()
4:        this.stmObject = new SynchState(this);

5:     property Node Next
6:        get
7:           Node target = stmObject.OpenRead();
8:           return target.Next;
9:        set
10:          Node target = stmObject.OpenWrite();
11:          target.Next = value;

12:    property int Element
13:       get
14:          Node target = stmObject.OpenRead();
15:          return target.Element;
16:       set
17:          Node target = stmObject.OpenWrite();
18:          target.Element = value;
```

(a) Class Node   (b) Class TX_Node, generated from Node at runtime

Fig. 12. Classes Node and TX_Node

We discuss the OpenWrite method, the OpenRead method works in an analogous way.

In OpenWrite, a reference to the Locator installed in the SynchState instance is obtained first. In the Locator, we may read the status (i.e., the XState field) of the transaction that most recently updated the object, to determine which of the old or new object is the current version of the object: if the status of the transaction is COMMITTED, then the new version is the current version, whereas if the status is ACTIVE or ABORTED, then the old object is the current version.

We instantiate a fresh Locator object, with an ACTIVE status field, and a clone of the current version of the object (as determined above) referenced the *old* object (recall that the object supports the ICloneable interface).

If the state of the last transaction that updated the object is ACTIVE, we are in presence of a conflict. In this case, the transaction calls ResolveConflict on its contention manager. If the contention manager decides to abort the other transaction, it atomically swaps the status of the other transaction, from ACTIVE to ABORTED. The contention manager may otherwise decides to wait for some time, and retry from the beginning of the OpenWrite method.

After aborting any conflicting transaction, the transaction atomically updates the SynchState instance (with compare-and-swap) to install the newly created Locator in place of the previous Locator.

At last, the transaction commits by atomically swapping its state from ACTIVE to COMMITTED. If this succeeds, all the new versions of the objects accessed by the transaction become the current versions. Committing fails if another transaction has already swapped the state to ABORTED.

The OpenRead method implementation differs from the OpenWrite method implementation, in that two transactions *reading* the same transactional objects do not conflict with each other.

Note that the indirection induced by the SynchState instance is not strictly necessary. In fact, we could program the full OpenRead and OpenWrite methods directly within TX_Type. However, this would require to write the full body of OpenRead and OpenWrite at runtime by using the C# reflection API. For the sake of simplicity, we introduce this extra object indirection.

6.2   Transaction Structure

Upon running a transaction, by invoking the Run method of the SXMAction object, SXM creates a new transaction state (a fresh XState instance in the ACTIVE state), and associates this new transaction state instance with the new transaction. The transaction state is then later available, when the transaction later acquires transactional object (through OpenRead and OpenWrite methods).

When a transaction starts, a depth counter is incremented. A *zero* value corresponds to the transaction at the top level. If the depth is more than *zero*, then the parameter provided by the programmer is used to determined whether to run the transaction as a nested transaction and associate with it a new contention manager instance, or to run the transaction within the parent transaction. SXM then invokes the transactional method by simply invoking the delegate. When the delegate returns, SXM tries to atomically commit the modifications (by swapping the state of the transaction from ACTIVE to COMMITTED). If the transaction fails to commit, then SXM creates a fresh XState instance, associates this instance with the transaction, and invokes the delegate once again.

If a nested transaction aborts, this means that its state object has been swapped from ACTIVE to ABORTED. However, the parent transaction, which does not share its state with nested transactions, is not affected. Hence SXM only restarts the nested transaction.

If the nested transaction ends without aborting, the parent transaction inherits the objects accessed by the nested transaction. To achieve this, SXM modifies, one after another, the Locator objects referencing the transactional objects accessed by the nested transaction. The modification consists in changing the transaction state reference, from the nested transaction state, to the parent transaction state (for which we keep a reference within the nested transaction).

- If SXM notices that, after having modified the Locator of every transactional object accessed by the nested transaction, the transaction state of the nested transaction has status ABORTED, then SXM aborts the parent transaction (it atomically swaps the state of the parent transaction from ACTIVE to ABORTED), and then restarts the parent transaction from the beginning.
- If SXM succeeds in modifying each Locator object of the transactional objects acquired by the nested transaction, without the nested transaction being aborted, then SXM returns the thread of execution to the parent transaction, which may continue executing. In this case, every transactional object

```
1:  class Application                         1:  [Atomic]
2:      Counter counter;                      2:  class Counter
                                              3:      private int balance;
3:      public Application()
4:          this.counter = new Counter();     4:      property int increment
                                              5:          set
5:      [Transactional(Greedy,true)]          6:              balance = balance + 1;
6:      public void Increment()
7:          this.counter.increment;

8:      static public Main(string[ ] argv)
9:          Application application = new Application();
10:         application.Increment();
```

Fig. 13. A postprocessing approach to an example of a counter in SXM

modified by the nested transaction now references the parent transaction in its Locator object.

When the parent transaction ends, SXM tries to commit the transaction by atomically swapping its state from ACTIVE to COMMITTED. This signals, for each transactional object modified by the transaction and now including the objects inherited from nested transactions, that the new object is the current version of the transactional object. If SXM fails to commit (indicating contention with another transaction), SXM restarts the parent transaction from the beginning.

6.3 Postprocessor Approach to Declaring Transactions

SXM could also be ported as an extension of the CIL postprocessor. CIL is the common intermediate language emitted by the C# compiler. More precisely, we propose extensions to the postprocessor for declaring transactional methods in SXM.

The Transactional attribute marks methods that are transactional. The transaction starts when the method begins and ends when the method ends. As before, the Atomic class attribute marks the shared objects that may be accessed by transactional methods. (The ICloneable interface is implemented automatically with the Atomic attribute.)

Figure 13 revisits the example of the counter, implemented in SXM with postprocessing extensions. The class Application defines a transactional method Increment, which acts on an instance of the Counter class. The Counter class is declared with the Atomic attribute.

To specify which contention manager type to use with a transaction, the programmer may give a parameter to the Transactional attribute. The programmer may also specify, with a parameter to the Transactional attribute, whether a transaction should be executed as a nested transaction (true), or within the parent transaction (false), in case the transaction is run as a nested transaction.

7   Concluding Remarks

In [10], Herlihy et al. proposed a dynamic software transaction memory (DSTM) system in Java for transactions accessing a set of objects not fixed or known in advance. In DSTM, a single contention manager class is used to monitor all transactions.

Harris and Fraser described in [7] a transaction scheme resembling conditional critical regions (CCR). They also proposed a simple form of nesting transactions, where committing a transaction occurs only when the top-level transactions returns. The contention manager is fixed, and a transaction that encounters a conflict systematically aborts, after waiting for the conflicting transaction to finish.

Harris et al. proposed in [8] a STM system in Concurrent Haskell, in which transactions are declared using an atomic block. Transactions can be composed while preserving the atomicity of the composition. Contention management was not discussed.

Scherer and Scott compared in [16] many contention managers, considering various kind of metrics for prioritizing transactions. They elected one (Polka) as the best contention manager and did not consider the question of integrating different contention managers within a single application when the concurrency pattern varies over the life of the application. Taking into account alternative contention managers (Greedy [5]) as well as different load situations led us to revisit the "universality" of Polka, and introduce our polymorphic structure.

The way transactions are nested and mapped to method boundaries in SXM resembles that of Argus [12]. Argus introduced object wrappers called *guardians*. A guardian object is similar to a transactional object as defined in this paper, and encapsulates objects to be accessed within a transaction to provide atomicity guarantees. Argus uses a lock-based approach to ensure atomicity of transactions.

Our transaction scheme is more pragmatic than in Argus as it leaves it up to the programmer to decide whether the method invocation runs in a nested transaction or remains within the parent. Moreover, we only pay the price of nesting transaction upon usage. In this sense, our scheme is closer to that of ACS [4]. Contention management was however not factored out neither in Argus nor in ACS, and concurrency control was achieved using locking: when a nested transaction returns, the parent inherits the locks.

Modular concurrency control approaches [3,18,20] considered the semantics of the operations to enable transaction interleaving. High-level atomicity is preserved, independently of the order in which commutative atomic operations are executed. On the other hand, identifying an operation as commutative when it is not, may lead to a violation of safety; whereas safety is always guaranteed in a STM application. In a sense, a contention manager in a STM application extracts a part of concurrency control that is only concerned with progress (and cannot hamper safety).

References

1. E. Dijkstra. Hierarchical ordering of sequential processes. *Acta Informatica*, 1(2):115–138, 1971.
2. J. Gray. A transaction model, automata languages and programming. *Lecture Notes in Computer Science*, 85:282–298, 1980.

3. R. Guerraoui. Atomic object composition. In *ECOOP'94: Proceedings of the European Conference on Object-Oriented Programming*, pages 118–138. Springer-Verlag, 1994.

4. R. Guerraoui, R. Capobianchi, A. Lanusse, and P. Roux. Nesting actions through asynchronous message passing: the ACS protocol. In *ECOOP '92: Proceedings of the European Conference on Object-Oriented Programming*, pages 170–184. Springer-Verlag, 1992.

5. R. Guerraoui, M. Herlihy, and B. Pochon. Toward a theory of contention managers. In *PODC'05: Proceedings of the twenty-fourth annual symposium on Principles of Distributed Computing*. ACM Press, 2005.

6. L. Hammond, B. Nayfeh, and K. Olukotun. A single-chip multiprocessor. *Computer*, 30(9):79–85, 1997.

7. T. Harris and K. Fraser. Language support for lightweight transactions. In *OOP-SLA'03: Proceedings of the eighteenth ACM Conference on Object-Oriented Programming, Systems, Languages, and Applications*, October 2003.

8. T. Harris, S. Marlow, S. Jones, and M. Herlihy. Composable memory transaction. Technical report, Microsoft Research Cambridge, December 2004.

9. M. Herlihy, V. Luchangco, and M. Moir. Obstruction-free synchronization: Double-ended queues as an example. In *ICDCS '03: Proceedings of the twenty-third International Conference on Distributed Computing Systems*, page 522. IEEE Computer Society, 2003.

10. M. Herlihy, V. Luchangco, M. Moir, and W. Scherer. Software transactional memory for dynamic-sized data structures. In *PODC'03: Proceedings of the twenty-second annual symposium on Principles of distributed computing*, pages 92–101. ACM Press, 2003.

11. M. Herlihy and J. Moss. Transactional memory: architectural support for lock-free data structures. In *ISCA'93: Proceedings of the twentieth Annual International Symposium on Computer Architecture*, pages 289–300. ACM Press, 1993.

12. B. Liskov. Distributed programming in argus. *Communication of ACM*, 31(3):300–312, 1988.

13. J. E. Moss. *Nested Transactions: An Approach to Reliable Distributed Computing*. PhD thesis, MIT, 1981.

14. C. Papadimitriou. The serializability of concurrent database updates. *Journal of the ACM*, 26(4):631–653, 1979.

15. Microsoft Research. *C# software transactional memory*. http://research.microsoft.com/research/downloads/default.aspx.

16. W. Scherer and M. Scott. Contention management in dynamic software transactional memory. In *Workshop on Concurrency and Synchronization in Java Programs*, July 2004.

17. W. Scherer and M. Scott. Advanced contention management for dynamic software transactional memory. In *PODC'05: Proceedings of the twenty-fourth annual symposium on Principles of Distributed Computing*. ACM Press, 2005.

18. P. Schwarz and A. Spector. Synchronizing shared abstract types. *ACM Transactions on Computer Systems*, 2(3):223–250, 1984.

19. W. Weihl. *Specification and Implementation of Atomic Data Types*. PhD thesis, MIT, 1984.

20. W. Weihl. Local atomicity properties: modular concurrency control for abstract data types. *ACM Transactions on Programming Languages and Systems*, 11(2):249–282, 1989.

Distributed Transactional Memory for Metric-Space Networks*

Maurice Herlihy and Ye Sun

Brown University, Providence, RI 02912-1910 USA

Abstract. Transactional Memory is a concurrent programming API in which concurrent threads synchronize via transactions (instead of locks). Although this model has mostly been studied in the context of multiprocessors, it has attractive features for distributed systems as well. In this paper, we consider the problem of implementing transactional memory in a network of nodes where communication costs form a metric. The heart of our design is a new cache-coherence protocol, called the Ballistic protocol, for tracking and moving up-to-date copies of cached objects. For constant-doubling metrics, a broad class encompassing both Euclidean spaces and growth-restricted networks, this protocol has stretch logarithmic in the diameter of the network.

1 Introduction

Transactional Memory is a concurrent programming API in which concurrent threads synchronize via *transactions* (instead of locks). A transaction is an explicitly delimited sequence of steps to be executed atomically by a single thread. A transaction can either *commit* (take effect), or *abort* (have no effect). If a transaction aborts, it is typically retried until it commits. Support for the transactional memory model on multiprocessors has recently been the focus of several research efforts, both in hardware [13, 16, 32, 36, 38, 42] and in software [14, 15, 17, 23, 31, 33, 41].

In this paper, we propose new techniques to support the transactional memory API in a *distributed* system consisting of a network of nodes that communicate by message-passing with their neighbors. As discussed below, the transactional memory API differs in significant ways from prior approaches to distributed transaction systems, presenting both a different high-level model of computation and a different set of low-level implementation issues. The protocols and algorithms needed to support distributed transactional memory require properties similar to those provided by prior proposals in such areas as cache placement, mobile objects or users, and distributed hash tables. Nevertheless, we will see that prior proposals typically fall short in some aspect or another, raising the question whether these (often quite general) proposals can be adapted to meet the (specific) requirements of this application.

---

* Supported by NSF grant 0410042 and by grants from Intel Corporation and Sun Microsystems

P. Fraigniaud (Ed.): DISC 2005, LNCS 3724, pp. 324–338, 2005.

Transactions have long been used to provide fault-tolerance in databases and distributed systems. In these systems, data objects are typically immobile, but computations move from node to node, usually via remote procedure call (RPC). To access an object, a transaction makes an RPC to the object's home node, which in turn makes tentative updates or returns results. Synchronization is provided by *two-phase locking*, typically augmented by some form of deadlock detection (perhaps just timeouts). Finally, a *two-phase commit protocol* ensures that the transaction's tentative changes either take effect at all nodes or are all discarded. Examples of such systems include Argus [28] and Jini [44].

In distributed transactional memory, by contrast, transactions are immobile (running at a single node) but objects move from node to node. Transaction synchronization is *optimistic*: a transaction commits only if, at the time it finishes, no other transaction has executed a conflicting access. In recent software transactional memory proposals, a *contention manager* module is responsible for avoiding deadlock and livelock. A number of contention manager algorithms have been proposed and empirically evaluated [12, 17, 22]. One advantage of this approach is that there is no need for a distributed commit protocol: a transaction that finishes without being interrupted by a synchronization conflict can simply commit.

These two transactional models make different trade-offs. One moves control flow, the other moves objects. One requires deadlock detection and commit protocols, and one does not. The distributed transactional memory model has several attractive features. Experience with this programming model on multiprocessors [17] suggests that transactional memory is easier to use than locking-based synchronization, particularly when fine-grained synchronization is desired. Moving objects to clients makes it easier to exploit locality. In the RPC model, if an object is a "hot spot", that object's home is likely to become a bottleneck, since it must mediate all access to that object. Moreover, if an object is shared by a group of clients who are close to one another, but far from the object's home, then clients must incur high communication costs with the home.

Naturally, there are distributed applications for which the transactional memory model is not appropriate. For example, some applications may prefer to store objects at dedicated repositories instead of having them migrate among clients. In summary, it would be difficult to claim that either model dominates the other. The RPC model, however, has been thoroughly explored, while the distributed transactional memory model is novel.

To illustrate some of the implementation issues, we start with a (somewhat simplified) description of hardware transactional memory. In a typical multiprocessor, processors do not access memory directly. Instead, when a processor issues a read or write, that location is loaded into a processor-local *cache*. A native *cache-coherence* mechanism ensures that cache entries remain consistent (for example, writing to a cached location automatically locates and *invalidates* other cached copies of that location). Simplifying somewhat, when a transaction reads or writes a memory location, that cache entry is flagged as transactional. Transactional writes are accumulated in the cache (or write buffer), and are not written back to memory while the transaction is active. If another thread invalidates a transactional entry, that transaction is aborted and restarted. If a transaction finishes without having had any of its entries invalidated, then the transaction commits by marking its transactional entries as valid or as dirty, and allowing the dirty entries to be written back to memory in the usual way.

In some sense, modern multiprocessors are like miniature distributed systems: processors, caches, and memories communicate by message-passing, and communication latencies outstrip processing time. Nevertheless, there is one key distinction: multiprocessor transactional memory designs extend built-in cache coherence protocols already supported by modern architectures. Distributed systems (that is, nodes linked by communication networks) typically do not come with such built-in protocols, so distributed transactional memory requires building something roughly equivalent.

The heart of a distributed transactional memory implementation is a distributed *cache-coherence* protocol. When a transaction attempts to access an object, the cache-coherence protocol must locate the current cached copy of the object, move it to the requesting node's cache, invalidating the old copy. (For brevity, we ignore shared, read-only access for now.)

We consider the cache-coherence problem in a network in which the cost of sending a message depends on how far it goes. More precisely, the communication costs between nodes form a *metric*. A cache coherence protocol for such a network should be *location-aware*: if a node in Boston is seeking an object in New York City, it should not send messages to Australia.

In this paper, we propose the *Ballistic* distributed cache-coherence protocol, a novel location-aware protocol for metric space networks. The protocol is hierarchical: nodes are organized as clusters at different levels. One node in each cluster is chosen to act as leader for this cluster when communicating with clusters at different levels. Roughly speaking, a higher-level leader points to a leader at the next lower level if the higher-level node thinks the lower-level node "knows more" about the object's current location.

The protocol name is inspired by its communication patterns: when a transaction requests for an object, the request rises in the hierarchy, probing leaders at increasing levels until the request encounters a downward link. When the request finds such a link, it descends, following a chain of links down to the cached copy of the object.

We evaluate the performance of this protocol by its *stretch*: each time a node issues a request for a cached copy of an object, we take the ratio of the protocol's communication cost for that request to the optimal communication cost for that request. We analyze the protocol in the context of *constant-doubling metrics*, a broad and commonly studied class of metrics that encompasses low-dimensional Euclidean spaces and growth-restricted networks [1, 2, 9, 11, 21, 24, 25, 26, 34, 37, 40, 43]. (This assumption is required for performance analysis, not for correctness.) For constant-doubling metrics, our protocol provides amortized $O(\log Diam)$ stretch for non-overlapping requests to locate and move a cached copy from one node to another. The protocol allows only bounded overtaking:

when a transaction requests an object, the Ballistic protocol locates an up-to-date copy of the object in finite time. Concurrent requests are synchronized by *path reversal*: when two concurrent requests meet at an intermediate node, the second request to arrive is "diverted" behind the first.

Our cache-coherence protocol is *scalable* in the number of cached objects it can track, in the sense that it avoids overloading nodes with excessive traffic or state information. Scalability is achieved by overlaying multiple hierarchies on the network and distributing the tracking information for different objects across different hierarchies in such a way that as the number of objects increases, individual nodes' state sizes increase by a much smaller factor.

The contribution of this paper is to propose the first protocol to support distributed transactional memory, and more broadly, to call the attention of the community to a rich source of new problems.

2   Related Work

Many others have considered the problem of accessing shared objects in networks. Most related work focuses on the *copy placement* problem, sometimes called *file allocation* (for multiple copies) or *file migration* (for single copy). These proposals cannot directly support transactional memory because they provide no ability to combine multiple accesses to multiple objects into a single atomic unit. Some of these proposals [5, 8] compare the online cost (metric distance) of accessing and moving copies against an adversary who can predict all future requests. Others [4, 30] focus on minimizing edge congestion. These proposals cannot be used as a basis for a transactional cache-coherence protocol because they do not permit concurrent write requests.

The Arrow protocol [39] was originally developed for distributed mutual exclusion, but was later adapted as a distributed directory protocol [10, 18, 19]. Like the protocol proposed here, it relies on path reversal to synchronize concurrent requests. The Arrow protocol is not well-suited for our purposes because it runs on a fixed spanning tree, so its performance depends on the stretch of the embedded tree. The Ballistic protocol, by contrast, "embeds itself" in the network in a way that provides the desired stretch.

The Ballistic cache-coherence protocol is based on hierarchical clustering, a notion that appears in a variety of object tracking systems, at least as early as Awerbuch and Peleg's mobile users [7], as well as various location-aware distributed hash tables (DHTs) [2, 20, 21, 37, 40]. Krauthgamer and Lee [25] use clustering to locate nearest neighbors. Talwar [43] uses clustering for compact routing, distance labels, and related problems. Other applications include location services [1, 26], animal tracking [9], and congestion control ([11]). Of particular interest, the routing application ([43]) implies that the hierarchical construct we use for cache coherence can be obtained for free if it has already been constructed for routing. Despite superficial similarities, these hierarchical constructions differ from ours (and from one another) in substantial technical ways.

To avoid creating directory bottlenecks, we use random hash ids to assign objects to directory hierarchies. Similar ideas appear as early as Li and Hudak [27]. Recently, location-aware DHTs (for example, [2, 20, 21, 37, 40]) assign objects to directory hierarchies based on object id as well. These hierarchies are randomized. By contrast, Ballistic provides a *deterministic* hierarchy structure instead of a randomized one. A deterministic node structure provides practical benefits. The cost of initializing a hierarchical node structure is fairly high. Randomized constructions guarantee good behavior in the expected case, while deterministic structures yield good behavior every time.

While DHTs are also location aware, they typically manage immutable immovable objects. DHTs provide an effective way to locate an object, but it is far from clear how they can be adapted to track mobile copies efficiently. Prior DHT work considers the communication cost of publishing an object to be a fixed, one-time cost, which is not usually counted toward object lookup cost. Moving an object, however, effectively requires republishing it, so care is needed both to synchronize concurrent requests and to make republishing itself efficient.

There have been many proposals for *distributed shared memory* systems (surveyed in [35]), which also present a programming model in which nodes in a network appear to share memory. None of these proposals, however, support transactions.

3   System Overview

Each node has a *transactional memory proxy* module that provides interfaces both to the application and to proxies at other nodes. An application informs the proxy when it starts a transaction. Before reading or writing a shared object, it asks the proxy to *open* the object. The proxy checks whether the object is in the local cache, and if not, calls the Ballistic protocol to fetch it. The proxy then returns a *copy* of the object to the transaction. When the transaction asks to commit, the proxy checks whether any object opened by the transaction has been *invalidated* (see below). If not, the proxy makes the transaction's tentative changes to the object permanent, and otherwise discards them.

If another transaction asks for an object, the proxy checks whether it is in use by an active local transaction. If not, it sends the object to the requester and invalidates its own copy. If so, the proxy can either surrender the object, aborting the local transaction, or it can postpone a response for a fixed duration, giving the local transaction a chance to commit. The decision when to surrender the object and when to postpone the request is a policy decision. Nodes must use a globally-consistent *contention management* policy that avoids both livelock and deadlock. A number of such policies have been proposed in the literature [12, 17, 22]. Perhaps the simplest is to assign each transaction a timestamp when it starts, and to require that younger transactions yield to older transactions. A transaction that restarts keeps its timestamp, and eventually it will be the oldest active transaction and thus able to run uninterrupted to completion.

The most important missing piece is the mechanism by which a node locates the current copy of an object. As noted, we track objects using the Ballistic cache coherence protocol, a hierarchical directory scheme that uses path reversal to coordinate concurrent requests. This protocol is a distributed *queuing* protocol: when a process joins the queue, the protocol delivers a message to that process's *predecessor* in the queue. The predecessor responds by sending the object (when it is ready to do so) back to the successor, invalidating its own copy.

For read sharing, the request is delivered to the last node in the queue, but the requester does not join the queue. The last node sends a read-only copy of the object to the requester and remembers the requester's identity. Later, when that node surrenders the object, it tells the reader to invalidate its copy. An alternative implementation (not discussed here) can let read requests join the queue as well.

4   Hierarchical Clustering

In this section we describe how to impose a hierarchical structure (called the *directory* or *directory hierarchy*) on the network for later use by the cache coherence protocol.

Consider a metric space of diameter $Diam$ containing n physical nodes, where $d(x, y)$ is the distance between nodes x and y. This distance determines the cost of sending a message from x to y and vice-versa. Scale the metric so that 1 is the smallest distance between any two nodes. Define $N(x, r)$ to be the radius-r neighborhood of x in the metric space.

We select nodes in the directory hierarchy using any distributed maximal independent set algorithm (for example, [3, 6, 29]). We construct a sequence of connectivity graphs as follows:

- At level 0, all physical nodes are in the connectivity graph. They are also called the level 0 or *leaf* nodes. Nodes x and y are connected if and only if $d(x, y) < 2^1$. $Leader^0$ is a maximal independent set of this graph.
- At level ℓ, only nodes from $leader^{\ell-1}$ join the connectivity graph. These nodes are referred to as level ℓ nodes. Nodes x and y are connected in this graph if and only if $d(x, y) < 2^{\ell+1}$. $Leader^\ell$ is a maximal independent set of this graph.

The construction ends at level L when the connectivity graph contains exactly one node, which is called the *root* node. $L \leq \lceil \log_2 Diam \rceil + 1$ since the connectivity graph at level $\lceil log_2 Diam \rceil$ is a complete graph.

The *(lookup) parent* set of a level ℓ node x is the set of level $\ell + 1$ nodes within distance $10 \cdot 2^{l+1}$ of x. In particular, the *home parent* of x is the parent closest to x. By construction, home parent is at most distance $2^{\ell+1}$ away from x. The *move parent* set of x is the subset of parents within distance $4 \cdot 2^{l+1}$ of x.

A directory hierarchy is a layered node structure. Its vertex set includes the level-0 through level-L nodes defined above. Its edge set is formed by drawing edges between parent child pairs as defined above. Edges exist only between neighboring level nodes. Figure 1 illustrates an example of such a directory

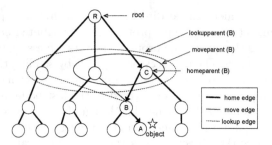

Fig. 1. Illustration of a directory hierarchy

hierarchy. Notice that nodes above level 0 are logical nodes simulated by physical nodes.

We use the following notation:

- $home^\ell(x)$ is the level-ℓ home directory of x. $home^0(x) = x$. $home^i(x)$ is the home parent of $home^{i-1}(x)$.
- $moveProbe^\ell(x)$ is the move-parent set of $home^{\ell-1}(x)$. These nodes are probed at level ℓ during a move started by x.
- $lookupProbe^\ell(x)$ is the lookup-parent set of $home^{\ell-1}(x)$. These nodes are probed at level ℓ during a lookup started by x.

5   The Cache-Coherence Protocol

For now, we focus on the state needed to track a single cached object, postponing the general case to Sect. 6. Each non-leaf node in the hierarchy has a *link* state: it either points to a child, or it is *null*. If we view non-*null* links as directed edges in the hierarchy, then they always point down. Intuitively, when the link points down, the parent "thinks" the child knows where the object is.

Nodes process messages sequentially: a node can receive a message, change state, and send a message in a single atomic step. We provide three operations. When an object is first created, it is *published* so that other nodes can find it. (As discussed briefly in the conclusions, an object may also be republished in response to failures.) A node calls *lookup* to locate the up-to-date object copy without moving it, thus obtaining a read-only copy. A node calls *move* to locate and move the up-to-date object copy, thus obtaining a writable copy.

1. publish(): An object created at a leaf node p is published by setting each $home^i(p).link = home^{i-1}(p)$, leaving a single directed path from root to p, going through each home directory in turn.

   For example, Figure 1 shows an object published by leaf A. A's home directories all point downwards. In every quiescent state of the protocol, there is a unique directed path from the root to the leaf where the object resides, although not necessarily through the leaf node's home directories.

2. lookup(): A leaf q started a lookup request. It proceeds in two phases. In the first *up phase*, the nodes in $lookupProbe^\ell(q)$ are probed at increasing levels until a non-*null* downward link is found. At each level ℓ, $home^{\ell-1}(q)$ initiates a sequential probe to each node in $lookupProbe^\ell(q)$. The ordering can be arbitrary except that the home parent of $home^{\ell-1}(q)$, which is also $home^\ell(q)$, is probed last. If the probe finds no downward links at level ℓ, then it repeats the process at the next higher level.

   If, instead, the probe discovers a downward link, then downward links are followed to reach the leaf node that either holds the object or will hold the object soon. When the object becomes available, a copy is sent directly to q.

3. move(): The operation also has two phases. In the up phase, the protocol probes the nodes in $moveProbe^\ell(q)$ (not $lookupProbe^\ell(q)$), probing $home^\ell(q)$ last. Then $home^\ell(q).link$ is set to point to $home^{\ell-1}(q)$ before it repeats the process at the next higher level. (Recall that probing the home parent's link and setting its link are done in a single atomic step.)

   For the down phase, when the protocol finds a downward link at level ℓ, it redirects that link to $home^{\ell-1}(q)$ before descending to the child pointed to by the old link. The protocol then follows the chain of downward links, setting each one to null, until it arrives at a leaf node. This leaf node either has the object, or is waiting for the object. When the object is available, it is sent directly to q.

Figure 2 shows the protocol pseudocode for the up phase and down phase of lookup and move operations. As mentioned, each node receives a message, changes state, and sends a message in a single atomic step.

5.1 Cache Responsiveness

A cache-coherence protocol needs to be responsive so that an operation issued by any node at any time is eventualy completed. In the Ballistic protocol, overtaking can happen in satisfying concurrent writes: A node B may issue a write operation at a later (wall clock) time than a node A, and yet B's operation may be ordered first if B is closer to the object. Nevertheless, we will show that such overtaking can occur only during a bounded window in time. Therefore, a write operation eventually completes. That a read operation eventually completes follows.

Two parameters are used in proving that a write operation completes. The first parameter T_E, the maximum enqueue delay, is the time it takes for a move request to reach its predecessor. This number is network-specific but finite, since a request never blocks in reaching its predecessor. The other parameter is T_O, the maximum time it takes for an object to travel from one requester to its successor, also finite. T_O includes the time it takes to invalidate existing read-only copies before moving a writable copy. T_O also includes the delay the contention manager sets before responding to a conflicting successor request.

A node has at most one outstanding move request at any time. By invariant analysis, the successor ordering established by the Ballistic protocol never forms a cycle. These two jointly establish that a move request cannot be overtaken by any move request generated more than $n \cdot T_E$ later.

```
// search (up) phase, d is requesting node's home directory
void up(node* d, node* request) {
  node* parent = null;
  iterator iter = LookupParent(d);      // home parent ordered last
  [iterator iter = MoveParent(d);]      // (move only,) a different set
  for (int i=0; i<sizeof(iter); i++) {
    parent = iter.next();
    // --transfer control to next parent in probe set--
    if (parent.link != null) {          // found link
      node* oldlink = parent.link;      // remember link
      [parent.link = d;]                // (move only,) redirect link
      // --transfer control to oldlink instead of going back to d--
      down(oldlink, request);           // start down phase
      break;
    }
    // --transfer control back to d except if current parent is home parent--
  }
  // no links seen,  in the middle of probing home parent now
  // control already at home parent, will not go back to d
  [parent.link = d;]      // (move only,) add link to reverse path
  up(parent, request);    // probe at next level from home parent
}

// trace (down) phase, following links starting from d
void down(node* d, node* request) {
  if (d is leaf) {                  // end of link chain, predecessor found
    d.succ = request;
    return;
  }
  node* oldlink = d.link;    // remember link
  [d.link = null;]           // (move only,) link erased after taken
  // --transfer control to oldlink--
  down(oldlink, request);    // move down
}
```

Fig. 2. Pseudocode for lookup and move operations, lines in "[ ]" are for moves only

Theorem 1 (Finite write response time). *Every move request is satisfied within time $n \cdot T_E + n \cdot T_O$ from when it is generated.*

5.2   Implementing Serializable Transactions

Recall from Sect. 3 that an object is opened before being read or written. Creating a new writable copy invalidates existing read-only copies and writable copies, and creating a new read-only copy downgrades any existing writable copy to a read-only copy. This provides one-copy consistency for each object.

A transaction accesses multiple objects using the Ballistic cache-coherence protocol. Acceses to multiple objects appear to happen instantaneously. As discussed in Sect. 3, this is achieved by letting the local transactional memory proxy watch for conflicting accesses.

5.3   Performance

The Ballistic cache coherence protocol works in any network, but our performance analysis focuses on constant-doubling metrics. A metric is a *constant-doubling metric* if there exists a constant dim, such that each radius-r neighborhood can be covered by at most 2^{dim} radius-$\frac{r}{2}$ neighborhoods. This focus is not overly restrictive. Constant-doubling networks (and even stronger models such as growth-restricted or Euclidean space networks) arise often in practice and are common in the literature (for example, [1, 2, 9, 11, 21, 24, 25, 26, 34, 37, 40, 43]).

In the performance analysis, we consider only the case when move requests do not overlap.

The protocol's *work* is the communication cost of an operation. For publish, we count the communication cost of adding links on the publishing leaf's home parent path. For move and lookup, we count the communication cost of finding the leaf node that will eventually send back the up-to-date object copy.

The protocol's *distance* for a move or lookup operation is the cost of communicating directly from the requesting node to its destination (which is the metric distance between these two nodes).

The protocol's *stretch* is the ratio of the work to the distance. The communication cost of replying to the requesting node can be ignored since the message is sent directly via the underlying routing protocol.

Constant-doubling metrics have the following properties.

1. **Bounded Link Property:** The metric distance between a level-ℓ child and its level-$(\ell + 1)$ parent is less than or equal to $c_b \cdot 2^\ell$, for some constant c_b.
2. **Constant Expansion Property:** Any node has no more than a constant number of lookup parents and lookup children.
3. **Lookup Property:** For any two leaves p and q, let p^ℓ be any of p's level-ℓ ancestors by following move parents only. If $p^\ell \notin lookupProbe^\ell(q)$, then the metric distance beteween p and q is at least $c_l \cdot 2^\ell$ for some constant c_l.
4. **Move Property:** If $p^\ell \notin moveProbe^\ell(q)$, then the metric distance between p and q is at least $c_m \cdot 2^\ell$ for some constant c_m.

Theorem 2. *The publish operation has work $O(Diam)$.*

A lookup request that overlaps with one or more move requests is "chasing" a moving object. We relax the above definition of distance for such a lookup request to be the metric distance from the source of the lookup request to the farthest object location during the interval of this lookup.

Theorem 3. *The stretch for a* lookup *operation is constant.*

Informally, due to the lookup property of constant-doubling metrics, the location of an object (indicated by downward links) is marked at well-known places to direct lookup requests along a low-stretch path.

For move, we are interested in the *amortized* work and distance across a sequence of object movements.

Theorem 4. *If an object has moved a combined distance of d since its initial publication, the amortized* move *stretch is* $O(\min\{\log_2 d, L\})$.

Informally, due to the move property of constant-doubling metrics, the frequency of updating a level-ℓ link is proportional to the cumulative distance moved divided by 2^ℓ.

The stretch results hold when move requests do not overlap. Move requests that concurrently probe overlapping parent sets may "miss" one another. The protocol is still correct, because the requests will eventually meet, but perhaps at a higher level. If this particular race condition can be avoided, then the stretch results in this section still apply when there are overlapping move requests.

6   Support for Multiple Objects

In this section, we provide load-balanced support for multiple objects. Load-balanced solutions are given for growth-restricted networks. *Growth-restricted* is slightly more restrictive than constant doubling: there exists a constant which bounds the ratio between the number of nodes in $N(x, 2r)$ and the number of nodes in $N(x, r)$ for arbitrary node x and arbitrary radius r. The multiple object solution works correctly for any metrics, but without provable load results. Load-balancing in the more general metrics is hard due to the possible "non-smooth" population change when moving between neighboring areas or when expanding size of area under inspection. There is a load-balancing multiple object solution for *static* objects in the more general constant-doubling metrics, which is beyond the scope of this paper.

A physical node which stores information about an object is subject to two kinds of load: it stores state, and it must respond to requests. Moreover, since multiple logical nodes can be mapped to a single physical nodes, a physical node may be subject to loads for multiple logical nodes. We now consider how to balance these loads.

If multiple objects share a single directory, then physical nodes which simulate logical nodes higher in the common hierarchy will bear a greater load. Instead, the load can be more evenly shared by letting different objects use different directory structures mapped onto the physical nodes.

Each object chooses a directory to use based on a random hash *id* between 0 and $n - 1$, where n is the number of physical nodes, assumed to be a power of 2 without loss of generality. In load analysis, we assume that each leaf node (physical node) stores up to m objects and each leaf node generates up to r

requests. We also assume that applications generate a uniform load in the following sense: each request is for an object with a random id located at a random node. Moreover, we assume these conditions continue to hold even after objects have moved around.

Intuitively, nodes low in the hierarchy will have light loads, since they handle requests originating from or ending in a small neighborhood and store links for objects located in a small neighborhood. At higher levels, we "perturb" the directory structure for each object to avoid overloading any particular node.

Here is how the multiple directories are built:

1. Find a base directory as in Sect. 4.
2. Using this directory as a skeleton, n overlapping replacement directories are built. Each is *isomorphic* to the base directory. A level-ℓ node in any replacement directory is at most distance 2^ℓ away from the corresponding level-ℓ node in the base directory. By the triangle inequality, the cost of a mapped level-ℓ edge in the replacement directory is still bounded by a constant factor of 2^ℓ.

We next describe how to construct a replacement directory for a given object id by describing how to map a level-ℓ node A in the base directory. Define $h(A, \ell) = \lfloor \log_2 |N(A, 2^\ell)| \rfloor$. Then a subset of $2^{h(A,\ell)}$ physical nodes are selected (arbitrarily) from $N(A, 2^\ell)$. Each of these $2^{h(A,\ell)}$ nodes is assigned a unique $h(A, \ell)$-bit label and plays the role of A in the directory for any object whose id has this label as a prefix. Obviously, each chosen node is responsible for $\frac{1}{2^{h(A,\ell)}}$ portion of object ids.

Theorem 5. *Stretch results for the base directory carry over to the replacement directory with a constant factor increase.*

Theorem 6. *In growth-restricted networks, each physical node x has $O(\log Diam)$ child degree and parent degree in the multiple directory structure.*

Theorem 7. *In growth-restricted metrics, the expected non-null link storage load at each physical node x is $O(m \cdot \log Diam)$. This expectation is taken over a uniform object id distribution.*

Theorem 8. *In growth-restricted metrics, the expected request handling load at each physical node x is $O(r \cdot \log Diam)$. This expectation is taken over a uniform request distribution.*

7   Discussion

Distributed transactional memory has fault-tolerance properties comparable to distributed transactions under the RPC model. A complete discussion of fault-tolerance is beyond the scope of this paper, but here is an overview of the principal issues. A reliable protocol should be used to pass a cached object from one node's cache to another's, to ensure that the sender invalidates its local copy only if the receiver actually receives the object.

Naturally, if the node holding an object crashes, that object will become unavailable (just as in the RPC model). It is sensible to back up long-lived objects on non-volatile storage so they will become available again when the node recovers. The directory information used by the Ballistic protocol can be treated as soft state, in the sense that it can be regenerated if it is lost. One can detect that part of the directory has been lost if the root sends periodic ping messages down the chain to the object's current location. If a node holding an object fails to receive a ping for too long, then it can republish the object, routing around any failed nodes in the former path, in much the same way that routing protocols rebuild broken paths.

We have assumed a static physical network. When nodes can enter or leave the physical network, it may be necessary to rerun the maximal independent set protocol to rebuild the hierarchy. Distributed maximal independent set algorithms typically limit changes to the area around the affected nodes.

References

[1] Ittai Abraham, Danny Dolev, and Dahlia Malkhi. Lls: a locality aware location service for mobile ad hoc networks. In *DIALM-POMC*, pages 75–84, 2004.

[2] Ittai Abraham, Dahlia Malkhi, and Oren Dobzinski. Land: stretch $(1 + \epsilon)$ locality-aware networks for dhts. In *Proceedings of the fifteenth annual ACM-SIAM symposium on Discrete algorithms*, pages 550–559, 2004.

[3] N. Alon, L. Babai, and A. Itai. A fast and simple randomized parallel algorithm for the maximal independent set problem. *J. Algorithms*, 7:567–583, 1986.

[4] Friedhelm Meyer auf der Heide, Berthold Vöcking, and Matthias Westermann. Caching in networks (extended abstract). In *Proceedings of the eleventh annual ACM-SIAM symposium on Discrete algorithms*, pages 430–439, 2000.

[5] Baruch Awerbuch, Yair Bartal, and Amos Fiat. Competitive distributed file allocation. In *STOC '93: Proceedings of the twenty-fifth annual ACM symposium on Theory of computing*, pages 164–173, 1993.

[6] Baruch Awerbuch, Lenore J. Cowen, and Mark A. Smith. Efficient asynchronous distributed symmetry breaking. In *Proceedings of the twenty-sixth annual ACM symposium on Theory of computing*, pages 214–223, 1994.

[7] Baruch Awerbuch and David Peleg. Concurrent online tracking of mobile users. In *SIGCOMM '91: Proceedings of the conference on Communications architecture & protocols*, pages 221–233, 1991.

[8] Yair Bartal, Amos Fiat, and Yuval Rabani. Competitive algorithms for distributed data management (extended abstract). In *STOC '92: Proceedings of the twenty-fourth annual ACM symposium on Theory of computing*, pages 39–50. ACM Press, 1992.

[9] M. Demirbas, A. Arora, T. Nolte, and N. Lynch. A hierarchy-based fault-local stabilizing algorithm for tracking in sensor networks. In *8th International Conference on Principles of Distributed Systems (OPODIS)*, 2004.

[10] M. J. Demmer and M. P. Herlihy. The arrow directory protocol. In *12th International Symposium on Distributed Computing*, 1998.

[11] Matthias Grünewald, Friedhelm Meyer auf der Heide, Christian Schindelhauer, and Klaus Volbert. Energy, congestion and dilation in radio networks. In *Proceedings of the 14th ACM Symposium on Parallel Algorithms and Architectures*, 10 - 13 August 2002.

[12] R. Guerraoui, M. Herlihy, and B. Pochon. Toward a theory of transactional contention managers. In *Proceedings of the tenty-fourth annual symposium on Principles of distributed computing*, 2005. To appear.

[13] Lance Hammond, Vicky Wong, Mike Chen, Ben Hertzberg, Brian D. Carlstrom, John D. Davis, Manohar K. Prabhu, Honggo Wijaya, Christos Kozyrakis, and Kunle Olukotun. Transactional memory coherence and consistency. In *Proceedings of the 31st Annual International Symposium on Computer Architecture*, June 2004.

[14] Tim Harris and Keir Fraser. Language support for lightweight transactions. In *Proceedings of the 18th ACM SIGPLAN conference on Object-oriented programing, systems, languages, and applications*, pages 388–402, 2003.

[15] Tim Harris, Simon Marlow, Simon Peyton Jones, and Maurice Herlihy. Composable memory transactions. In *Principles and Practice of Parallel Programming*, 2005. To appear.

[16] Maurice Herlihy, Victor Luchangco, and Mark Moir. Obstruction-free synchronization: Double-ended queues as an example. In *Proceedings of the 23rd International Conference on Distributed Computing Systems (ICDS)*, pages 522–529, May 2003.

[17] Maurice Herlihy, Victor Luchangco, Mark Moir, and William N. Scherer, III. Software transactional memory for dynamic-sized data structures. In *Proceedings of the twenty-second annual symposium on Principles of distributed computing*, pages 92–101. ACM Press, 2003.

[18] Maurice Herlihy, Srikanta Tirthapura, and Roger Wattenhofer. Competitive concurrent distributed queuing. In *Proceedings of the twentieth annual ACM symposium on Principles of distributed computing*, pages 127–133, 2001.

[19] M.P. Herlihy and S. Tirthapura. Self-stabilizing distributed queueing. In *Proceedings of 15th International Symposium on Distributed Computing*, October 2001.

[20] Kirsten Hildrum, Robert Krauthgamer, and John Kubiatowicz. Object location in realistic networks. In *Proceedings of the sixteenth annual ACM symposium on Parallelism in algorithms and architectures*, pages 25–35, 2004.

[21] Kirsten Hildrum, John D. Kubiatowicz, Satish Rao, and Ben Y. Zhao. Distributed object location in a dynamic network. In *Proceedings of the Fourteenth ACM Symposium on Parallel Algorithms and Architectures*, pages 41–52, August 2002.

[22] W. N. Scherer III and M. L. Scott. Contention management in dynamic software transactional memory. In *PODC Workshop on Concurrency and Synchronization in Java Programs*, July 2004.

[23] Amos Israeli and Lihu Rappoport. Disjoint-access-parallel implementations of strong shared memory primitives. In *Proceedings of the thirteenth annual ACM symposium on Principles of distributed computing*, pages 151–160, 1994.

[24] David R. Karger and Matthias Ruhl. Finding nearest neighbors in growth-restricted metrics. In *Proceedings of the thiry-fourth annual ACM symposium on Theory of computing*, pages 741–750. ACM Press, 2002.

[25] Robert Krauthgamer and James R. Lee. Navigating nets: simple algorithms for proximity search. In *SODA '04: Proceedings of the fifteenth annual ACM-SIAM symposium on Discrete algorithms*, pages 798–807. Society for Industrial and Applied Mathematics, 2004.

[26] Jinyang Li, John Jannotti, Douglas S. J. De Couto, David R. Karger, and Robert Morris. A scalable location service for geographic ad hoc routing. In *Proceedings of the 6th annual international conference on Mobile computing and networking*, pages 120–130. ACM Press, 2000.

[27] Kai Li and Paul Hudak. Memory coherence in shared virtual memory systems. *ACM Trans. Comput. Syst.*, 7(4):321–359, 1989.

[28] Barbara Liskov. Distributed programming in argus. *Commun. ACM*, 31(3):300–312, 1988.

[29] Michael Luby. A simple parallel algorithm for the maximal independent set problem. *SIAM J. Comput.*, 15(4):1036–1055, 1986.

[30] B. Maggs, F. Meyer auf der Heide, B. Vöcking, and M. Westermann. Exploiting locality for data management in systems of limited bandwidth. In *FOCS '97: Proceedings of the 38th Annual Symposium on Foundations of Computer Science*, pages 284–293. IEEE Computer Society, 1997.

[31] V. J. Marathe, W. N. Scherer III, and M. L. Scott. Design tradeoffs in modern software transactional memory systems. In *7th Workshop on Languages, Compilers, and Run-time Support for Scalable Systems*, October 2004.

[32] Jos F. Martnez and Josep Torrellas. Speculative synchronization: applying thread-level speculation to explicitly parallel applications. In *Proceedings of the 10th international conference on architectural support for programming languages and operating systems (ASPLOS-X)*, pages 18–29. ACM Press, 2002.

[33] Mark Moir. Practical implementations of non-blocking synchronization primitives. In *Proceedings of the sixteenth annual ACM symposium on Principles of distributed computing*, pages 219–228. ACM Press, 1997.

[34] E. Ng and H. Zhang. Predicting internet network distance with coordiantes-based approaches. In *Proceedings of IEEE Infocom*, 2002.

[35] B Nitzberg and V. Lo. Distributed shared memory: a survey of issues and algorithms. *Computer*, 24(8):52–60, 1991.

[36] Jeffrey Oplinger and Monica S. Lam. Enhancing software reliability with speculative threads. In *Proceedings of the 10th international conference on architectural support for programming languages and operating systems (ASPLOS-X)*, pages 184–196. ACM Press, 2002.

[37] C. Greg Plaxton, Rajmohan Rajaraman, and Andrea W. Richa. Accessing nearby copies of replicated objects in a distributed environment. In *ACM Symposium on Parallel Algorithms and Architectures*, pages 311–320, 1997.

[38] Ravi Rajwar and James R. Goodman. Transactional lock-free execution of lock-based programs. In *Proceedings of the 10th international conference on architectural support for programming languages and operating systems (ASPLOS-X)*, pages 5–17. ACM Press, 2002.

[39] Kerry Raymond. A tree-based algorithm for distributed mutual exclusion. *ACM Trans. Comput. Syst.*, 7(1):61–77, 1989.

[40] Antony I. T. Rowstron and Peter Druschel. Pastry: Scalable, decentralized object location, and routing for large-scale peer-to-peer systems. In *Middleware 2001*, pages 329–350, 2001.

[41] Nir Shavit and Dan Touitou. Software transactional memory. In *Proceedings of the fourteenth annual ACM symposium on Principles of distributed computing*, pages 204–213. ACM Press, 1995.

[42] Janice M. Stone, Harold S. Stone, Phil Heidelberger, and John Turek. Multiple reservations and the Oklahoma update. *IEEE Parallel and Distributed Technology*, 1(4):58–71, November 1993.

[43] Kunal Talwar. Bypassing the embedding: algorithms for low dimensional metrics. In *STOC '04: Proceedings of the thirty-sixth annual ACM symposium on Theory of computing*, pages 281–290, 2004.

[44] Jim Waldo and Ken Arnold, editors. *The Jini Specifications*. Jini Technology Series. Pearson Education, 2000.

Concise Version Vectors in WinFS

Dahlia Malkhi[1] and Doug Terry[2]

[1] Microsoft Research Silicon Valley and
The Hebrew University of Jerusalem, Israel
[2] Microsoft Research Silicon Valley

Abstract. Conflicts naturally arise in optimistically replicated systems. The common way to detect update conflicts is via version vectors, whose storage and communication overhead are *number of replicas* × *number of objects*. These costs may be prohibitive for large systems.

This paper presents *predecessor vectors with exceptions* (PVEs), a novel optimistic replication technique developed for Microsoft's WinFS system. The paper contains a systematic study of PVE's performance gains over traditional schemes. The results demonstrate a dramatic reduction of storage and communication overhead in normal scenarios, during which communication disruptions are infrequent. Moreover, they identify a cross-over threshold in communication failure-rate, beyond which PVEs loses efficiency compared with traditional schemes.

1 Introduction

Consider an information system, such as an e-mail client, that is composed of multiple data objects, holding folders, files and tags. Data may be replicated in multiple sites. For example, a user's mailbox may reside at the server, on the user's office and home workstations, and on a PDA. The system allows concurrent, optimistic updates to its objects from distributed locations, without communication or centralized control. So for example, the user might hop on the plane with a copy of her mailbox on a laptop and edit various parts of it while disconnected; she may introduce changes on a PDA, and so on. At some point, when connecting between these components, she wishes to synchronize versions across replicas, and be alerted to any conflicts generated.

This problem model arises naturally within the scope of Microsoft's WinFS project, whose aim is to provide peer-to-peer weakly consistent replicated storage facilities. The problem model is fundamental in distributed systems, and numerous replication methods exist to tackle it. However, the applications that are aimed for by the WinFS team mandate taking scale more seriously than ever before. In particular, e-mail repositories, log files, and databases can easily reach millions of objects. Hence, communicating even a single bit per object (*e.g.*, a 'dirty' bit) in order to be able synchronize replicas might simply be too costly.

In this paper, we present a precise description and correctness proof of the replica reconciliation and conflict detection mechanism inside Microsoft's WinFS. We name the scheme *predecessor vectors with exceptions* (PVE). We

P. Fraigniaud (Ed.): DISC 2005, LNCS 3724, pp. 339–353, 2005.

produce a systematic study of the performance gains of PVE, and provide a comparison with traditional optimistic replication scheme. The results demonstrate a substantial reduction in storage and communication overhead associated with replica synchronization, in most normal cases. In conditions that allow (most) synchronizations to complete without communication breaks, a pair of replicas needs only communicate a constant number of bits per replica in order to detect discrepancies in replicas' states. Moreover, they need to maintain only a single counter per object in order to determine versions ordering and alert to any conflict. Our study also demonstrates the "cut-off" point in the communication fault-rate, beyond which the PVE technique becomes less attractive than the alternatives.

In order to understand the efficiency leap offered by the PVE scheme, let us review the most well known alternative. Version Vectors (VVs) [1] are traditionally used in optimistic replication systems in order to find which replica has more updated object states, as well as to detect conflicting versions. Per object version vectors were pioneered in Locus [1], and subsequently employed in various optimistic replication systems, e.g., [2,4,3].

The version vector for a data object is an array of size R, where R is the number of replicas in the system. Each replica has a pair $\langle \text{replica}, \text{counter} \rangle$ in the vector, indicating the latest counter value introduced on the object by the replica. For example, suppose that we have three replicas, A, B, and C. An object is initialized with VV $(\langle A, 0 \rangle, \langle B, 0 \rangle, \langle C, 0 \rangle)$. An update to the object initiated at replica A increments A's component, and so generates version $(\langle A, 1 \rangle, \langle B, 0 \rangle, \langle C, 0 \rangle)$. Later, B may obtain the new version from A and store it, and produce another update on the object. The newer object state receives version $(\langle A, 1 \rangle, \langle B, 1 \rangle, \langle C, 0 \rangle)$. And so on.

A version vector V *dominates* another vector W if every component of V is no less than W; V *strictly dominates* W, if it dominates W and one component is greater. Due to optimism, there may be objects on different replicas whose version vectors are incomparable by the domination relation; this corresponds to conflicting versions, indicating that simultaneous updates were introduced to the object at different replicas. For example, continuing the scenario above, suppose that all replicas have version $(\langle A, 1 \rangle, \langle B, 1 \rangle, \langle C, 0 \rangle)$ in store. Now proceed to have diverging updates on the object simultaneously by A and C. These generate VVs $(\langle A, 2 \rangle, \langle B, 1 \rangle, \langle C, 0 \rangle)$ and $(\langle A, 1 \rangle, \langle B, 1 \rangle, \langle C, 1 \rangle)$, respectively, which are conflicting as neither one dominates the other.

Consider a system with N objects replicated across R replicas. Further, consider the synchronization between two replicas whose views of the object space differs in q objects. The VV scheme is designed for synchronizing replicas object by object, and incurs the following costs.

1. Store a version-vector per object, incurring a storage overhead of $\widetilde{O}(N \times R)$ bits space; [1]

---

[1] For simplicity of notation, the notation $\widetilde{O}(\cdot)$ indicates the same complexity order as $O(\cdot)$ up to logarithmic factors of N and R, which may be required to code any single value in our settings.

2. Communicate information that allows the two replicas to determine which objects one should send the other, and to detect conflicts. A naive implementation sends all N version vectors, incurring a communication overhead of $\widetilde{O}(N \times R)$. If the replicas store logs of recent updates, and maintain additional information about the position known to other replicas in the log, they may bring the cost down close to $\widetilde{O}(q \times R)$, which is the lowest possible communication overhead with the VV scheme.

These cost measures and their analysis are made more precise later in the paper. Note that even for moderate numbers of replicas R, storing $N \times R$ values is a substantial burden when N is large, and moreover, communicating between $\widetilde{O}(q \times R)$ to $\widetilde{O}(N \times R)$ overhead bits may be prohibitive.

In WinFS, the goal is to quickly synchronize heavy-volume servers, each carrying large magnitudes of objects. In situations where communication distuptions are not the norm, the innovative PVE mechanism in WinFS that reconciles replica discrepancies brings down costs a considerable amount. It needs $\widetilde{O}(R)$ information bits to determine replica's differences, *i.e.*, the equivalence of communicating **one** version vector. In addition, per object meta-information storage and communication is in most cases constant (one counter). Table 1 in Section 5 contains a summary of these complexities. In the remainder of this paper, we describe the foundations of the PVE replication protocol, and compare is against VVs.

The contributions of this paper are as follows. First, we give a precise and detailed formulation of the PVE replica reconciliation protocol employed in WinFS. We note that the full design and the architecture of the WinFS system is the result of a large team effort, and is beyond the scope of this paper. Second, we develop a performance model capturing the cost measures of interest to us, and quantify the performance gains of the PVE scheme, as compared with known methods. Third, we evaluate these measures via simulation under complex system conditions with increasing communication failures rates. This evaluation reveals a cut-off point that characterizes the benefit area of the PVE scheme over traditional version vectors.

2 Problem Statement

In this section, we begin with the precise specification of our problem. Later sections provide a rigorous treatment of the solution.

The system consists of a collection of data objects, potentially numerous. Each object might be quite small, *e.g.*, a mail entry or even a status word. Objects are replicated on a set of hosts. Each host may locally introduce updates to every object, without any concurrency control. These updates create a partial ordering of object versions, where updates that sequentially follow one another are causally related, but non-related updates exist and are *conflicting*.

Our focus is on distributed systems in which updates overwrite previous versions. The alternative would be database or journal systems, in which the history of updates on an object is stored and applied at every replica. State-based storage saves storage and computation, and is suitable for the kind of information systems that WinFS aims for, *e.g.*, a user's Outlook files, where updates may be numerous. In state-based systems only the most recent version of any object needs to be sent. Nevertheless, it is worth noting that the method presented in this paper can work with (minor) appropriate modifications for log-based replication systems. For brevity, we omit this from discussion in this paper.

The goal is to provide a lightweight replica-reconciliation and conflict detection mechanism. The mechanism should provide two communicating replicas with the means to detect precedence ordering on object versions that they hold, and detect any conflicts in them. With this mechanism, they can bring each other up-to-date or report conflicts.

More precisely, we now describe objects, versions, and causality. An object is identified uniquely by its name. Objects are instantiated with versions, where an object instance has the following fields:

name: the unique identifier.
version: a pair $\langle replica\ id, counter \rangle$.
predecessors: a set of preceding versions (including the current version).
data: application-specific opaque information.

Because versions uniquely determine objects' instances, we simply refer to any particular instance by its version. There may be multiple versions with the same object name. We say that these are versions of the same object.

There is a partial, causal ordering among different versions of the same object. When a replica A creates an instance of an object o with version v, the set W of versions that are previously known by replica A on o *causally precedes* version v. In notation, $W \prec v$. For every version $w \in W$, we likewise say that w *causally precedes* v; in notation, $w \prec v$. Causality is transitive.

Since the system permits concurrent updates, the causality relation is only a partial order, i.e., multiple versions might follow any single version. When two versions do not follow one another, they are *conflicting*. I.e., if $w \nprec v \wedge v \nprec w$, then v and w are conflicting.

It is desirable to detect and resolve conflicts, either automatically (when application specific conflict resolution code is available) or by alerting the user and solving manually. In either case, a resolution of conflicting versions is a version that causally follows both. For example, here is a conflict and its resolution: $v_0 \prec v \prec w$; $v \nprec u$; $u \nprec v$; $v_0 \prec u \prec w$.

New versions override previous ones, so we are generally only interested in the most recent version available; versions that causally precede it are obsolete and carry no valuable information. This simple rule is complicated by the fact that multiple conflicting versions may exist, and we are interested in all of them until they can be resolved.

2.1   Performance Measures

This paper is concerned with mechanisms that facilitate synchronization of different replicas. The challenge is to bring the storage and communication costs associated with replica reconciliation (significantly) down. More precisely, we focus on two performance measures:

Storage is the total number of overhead bits stored in order to preserve version ordering.

Communication is (i) the total number of bits communicated between two replicas in order to determine which updates are missing by one that the other has, and (ii) any overhead data that is transferred along with objects' states in order to determine precedence/conflicts.

3 Overview of the PVE Method

This section provides an informal overview of the PVE scheme. Later sections provide a more formal description and a proof of correctness.

The PVE scheme works as follows. An object version is a pair ⟨replica, counter⟩. Instead of using separate counters for distinct objects, the scheme uses one per-replica counter to enumerate the versions that the replica generates on all objects (the counter is across all objects). For example, suppose that replica A first introduces an update to object o_1, and second to o_2. The versions corresponding to o_1 and to o_2 will be $\langle A, 1 \rangle$, $\langle A, 2 \rangle$, respectively. Note that versions are **not** full vectors, as in the traditional VV scheme described in the Introduction.

Each object has, in addition to its version, a predecessor set that captures the versions that causally precede the current one. Predecessor sets are captured in PVE using version vectors, though we will show momentarily that in most cases, PVE can replace these vectors with a null pointer. In order to distinguish these vectors from the traditional version vectors, we call them *predecessor vectors*. A predecessor vector (PV) contains one version, the latest, per replica. When a replica A generates a new object version, the PV associated with the new version contains the latest versions known by A on the object from each other replica. For example, suppose we have three replicas, A, B, and C. A new object starts with a zeroed predecessor vector $(\langle A, 0 \rangle, \langle B, 0 \rangle, \langle C, 0 \rangle)$. Consider the two versions generated by replica A above on o_1 and o_2, $\langle A, 1 \rangle$ and $\langle A, 2 \rangle$, respectively. When A creates these versions, no other versions are known on either o_1 or o_2, hence the PV of $\langle A, 1 \rangle$ is $(\langle A, 1 \rangle, \langle B, 0 \rangle, \langle C, 0 \rangle)$, and the PV of $\langle A, 2 \rangle$ is $(\langle A, 2 \rangle, \langle B, 0 \rangle, \langle C, 0 \rangle)$. A (causally) subsequent update to o_1 by replica B creates version $\langle B, 1 \rangle$, with predecessors $(\langle A, 1 \rangle, \langle B, 1 \rangle, \langle C, 0 \rangle)$. This PV represents the latest versions known by B on object o_1.

The formal definition capturing the per-replica scheme with predecessor vectors scheme are given below.

Definition 1 (Per-Replica Counter).

Let X be a replica. The versions generated by replica X on objects are the ordered sequence $\{\langle X, i \rangle\}_{i=1,2,\dots}$.

Definition 2 (Predecessor Vectors).

Let $X_1, ..., X_R$ be the set of replicas. A predecessors vector (PV) is an R-array of tuples of the form $(\langle X_1, i_1 \rangle, ..., \langle X_R, i_R \rangle)$.

A predecessors vector $(\langle X_1, i_1 \rangle, ..., \langle X_R, i_R \rangle)$ dominates another vector $(\langle X_1, j_1 \rangle, ..., \langle X_R, j_R \rangle)$ if $i_k \geq j_k$ for $k = 1..R$, and it strictly dominates if $i_\ell > j_\ell$ for some $1 \leq \ell \leq R$.

By a natural overload of notation, we say that a predecessor vector $(\langle X_1, i_1 \rangle, ..., \langle X_R, i_R \rangle)$ dominates a version $\langle X_k, j_k \rangle$ if $i_k \geq j_k$; strict domination follows accordingly with strong inequality.

The reader should first note that despite the aggregation of multiple-object versions using one counter, the predecessor version vectors can express precedence relations between versions of the same object. For example, in the scenario above, version $\langle A, 1 \rangle$ precedes $\langle B, 1 \rangle$, and is indeed dominated by the PV associated with version $\langle B, 1 \rangle$. Moreover, PVs do not create false conflicts. The reason is that incomparable predecessor vectors conflict only if they belong to the same object. So for example, suppose that continuing the scenario above, replica A introduces version $\langle A, 3 \rangle$ to object o_1 with predecessors $(\langle A, 3 \rangle, \langle B, 1 \rangle, \langle C, 0 \rangle)$; and simultaneously, replica C introduces version $\langle C, 1 \rangle$ on o_2, with the corresponding PV $(\langle A, 2 \rangle, \langle B, 0 \rangle, \langle C, 1 \rangle)$. These versions would be conflicting had they belonged to the same object, but are fine since they are never compared against each other.

Hence, comparing different versions for the same object is now possible as in the traditional use of version vectors. Namely, the same domination relation among predecessor vectors and versions, though these may contain replica-counters pertaining to different objects, can determine precedence and conflicts of updates to the same object.

Reducing the Overhead. So far we have not introduced any space savings over traditional VVs, though. The surprising benefit of aggregate PVs is as follows. Let $X.knowledge$ denote the component-wise maximum of the PVs of all the versions held by a replica X. The performance savings stems from the following fact: In order to represent ordering relations of **all** the versions X stores for all objects, it suffices for replica X to store only $X.knowledge$. Knowledge aggregates the predecessor vectors of all objects, and is used instead of per-object PV. More specifically, knowledge replaces PVs as follows.

- No PV is stored per object at all. The only vector stored by a replica is its aggregate *knowledge* vector.
- In order for A to determine which versions in its store are more up-to-date than B's store, B simply needs to send $B.knowledge$ to A. Using the difference between $A.knowledge$ and $B.knowledge$, A can determine which versions it should send B.
- Then, having determined the q relevant newer versions, A sends these versions with (only) a single version counter each, plus to send (once) A's *knowledge* vector.

The reader should be concerned at this point that information is lost concerning the ability to tell version precedence. We now demonstrate why this is not the case. When two replicas, A and B, wish to compare their latest versions of the same object o, say $\langle r, n_r \rangle$ and $\langle s, n_s \rangle$ respectively, they simply compare these against $A.knowledge$, $B.knowledge$. If $A.knowledge$ dominates $\langle s, n_s \rangle$, then the version currently held by A for object o, namely $\langle r, n_r \rangle$, strictly succeeds $\langle s, n_s \rangle$. And vice versa. If none of these knowledge vectors dominates the other version, then these are conflicting versions.

Going back to the scenario built above, replica A has in store the following: $o_1.version = \langle A, 3 \rangle$; $o_2.version = \langle A, 2 \rangle$; $knowledge = (\langle A, 3 \rangle, \langle B, 1 \rangle, \langle C, 0 \rangle)$. Replica C stores the following: $o_1.version = \langle B, 1 \rangle$; $o_2.version = \langle C, 1 \rangle$; $knowledge = (\langle A, 2 \rangle, \langle B, 1 \rangle, \langle C, 1 \rangle)$. When comparing their versions for object o_1, A and C will find that A's version is more recent, and when comparing their versions of object o_2, they will find C's version to be the recent one.

The result is that storage overhead in WinFS is $\widetilde{O}(N + R)$, instead of $\widetilde{O}(N \times R)$. More dramatically, the communication overhead associated with synchronization is reduced. The communication overhead of sending $knowledge$ is $\widetilde{O}(R)$, and the total communication overhead associated with synchronizing replicas is $\widetilde{O}(q + R)$.

Dealing with Disrupted Synchronization. Synchronization among two replicas may fail to complete due to network disruption. One way of coping with this is to abort incomplete synchronization procedures; then no further complication to the above scheme is needed.

However, in reality, due to large volumes that may need to be synchronized, aborting a partially-completed synchronization may not be desirable (and in fact, may create increasingly larger and larger synchronization demands, that might become less and less likely to complete). The aggregate knowledge method above introduces a new source of difficulty due to incomplete synchronizations. Let us demonstrate this problem. When replica A receives an object's new version from another replica B, that object does not carry a specific PV. Suppose that before synchronizing with B, the highest version A stores from B on any object is $\langle B, 10 \rangle$. If B sends $\langle B, 14 \rangle$, then clearly versions $\langle B, 11 \rangle$, $\langle B, 12 \rangle$, and $\langle B, 13 \rangle$ are missing in A's knowledge, hence there are "holes".

It is tempting to try to solve this by a policy that mandates sending all versions from one replica in an order that respects their generation order. In the above scenario, send $\langle B, 11 \rangle$ before $\langle B, 14 \rangle$, unless that version has been obsoleted by another version. Then, when $\langle B, 14 \rangle$ is received, A would know that it must already reflect $\langle B, 11 \rangle$, $\langle B, 12 \rangle$, and $\langle B, 13 \rangle$.

Unfortunately, this strategy is impossible to enforce, as illustrated in the following scenario. Object o_1 receives an update from replica A, with version $\langle A, 1 \rangle$, and PV $(\langle A, 1 \rangle, \langle B, 0 \rangle, \langle C, 0 \rangle)$. Meanwhile, object o_2 is updated by B, its version is $\langle B, 1 \rangle$, with PV $(\langle A, 0 \rangle, \langle B, 1 \rangle, \langle C, 0 \rangle)$. Replica A and B synchronize and exchange their latest updates. Subsequently, object o_1 is updated at replica B with version $\langle B, 2 \rangle$ and PV $(\langle A, 1 \rangle, \langle B, 2 \rangle, \langle C, 0 \rangle)$; and object o_2 is updated at replica A with version $\langle A, 2 \rangle$ and PV $(\langle A, 2 \rangle, \langle B, 1 \rangle, \langle C, 0 \rangle)$. The orderings between all versions is as follows:

$o_1 : [\langle A, 1 \rangle; \mathrm{PV} = (\langle A, 1 \rangle, \langle B, 0 \rangle, \langle C, 0 \rangle)] \prec [\langle B, 2 \rangle; \mathrm{PV} = (\langle A, 1 \rangle, \langle B, 2 \rangle, \langle C, 0 \rangle)]$
$o_2 : [\langle B, 1 \rangle; \mathrm{PV} = (\langle A, 0 \rangle, \langle B, 1 \rangle, \langle C, 0 \rangle)] \prec [\langle A, 2 \rangle; \mathrm{PV} = (\langle A, 2 \rangle, \langle B, 1 \rangle, \langle C, 0 \rangle)]$

Then Replica B synchronizes with replica A, sending it all of its recent updates. Replica A now stores: $o_1.version = \langle B, 2 \rangle$; $o_2.version = \langle A, 2 \rangle$; $knowledge = (\langle A, 2 \rangle, \langle B, 2 \rangle, \langle C, 0 \rangle)$.

Now suppose that replica C, which has been detached for a while, comes back and synchronizes with replica A. During this synchronization, only the most recent versions of objects o_1 and o_2 are sent to replica C. In this scenario, there is simply no way to prevent holes: Replica C may first obtain o_1's recent version, i.e., $\langle B, 2 \rangle$, and then have its communication cut. Then version $\langle B, 1 \rangle$ (which happens to belong to o_2) is missing. A similar situation occurs if replica C obtains o_2's recent version first and is then cut.

It is worth noting that although seemingly we don't care about the missing, obsoleted versions, we cannot ignore them. If the subsequent versions are lost from the system for some reason, inconsistency may result. For example, in the first case above, the missing o_2 version $\langle B, 1 \rangle$ is subsumed by a later version $\langle A, 2 \rangle$. However, if replica C simply includes $\langle B, 2 \rangle$ in its knowledge vector, and replica A crashes such that $\langle A, 2 \rangle$ is forever lost from the system, C might never obtain the latest state of o_2 from replica B.

The price paid in the PVE scheme for its substantial storage and communication reduction is the need to maintain information about such exceptions. In the above scenario, replica C will need to store *exception* information as follows. First, $C.knowledge$ will contain $(\langle A, 0 \rangle, \langle B, 2 \rangle, \langle C, 0 \rangle)$ with an *exception* $\langle eB, 1 \rangle$. [2]

Definition 3 (PVs with Exceptions).

A predecessors vector with exceptions *(PVE) is an R-array of tuples of the form* $(\langle X_1, i_1 \rangle \langle eX_1, i_{j_1} \rangle \langle eX_1, i_{j_{k_1}} \rangle, ..., \langle X_R, i_R \rangle \langle eX_R, i_{j_R} \rangle \langle eX_1, i_{j_{k_R}} \rangle)$.

A version $\langle X_k, j_k \rangle$ *is dominated by a predecessors vector* X *with exceptions as above if* $i_k \geq j_k$, *and* j_k *is not among the exceptions in the k'th position in* X.

A predecessors vector with exceptions X *dominates another vector* Y *if the respective PVs without the exceptions dominate, and no exception included* X *is dominated by* Y.

Second, we require that a replica maintain explicit PV for every new version it obtains via a partial synchronization. These explicit PVs may be omitted only if the replica's knowledge dominates them. Continuing the scenario above, we demonstrate a subtle chain of events which necessitates this additional overhead.

---

[2] An alternative form of exception is to store $(\langle A, 0 \rangle, \langle B, 0 \rangle, \langle C, 0 \rangle)$ with a 'positive exception' $\langle eB, 2 \rangle$. The two alternatives result in different storage load under different scenarios, positive exceptions being preferable under long synchronization gaps. For simplicity, we use negative exceptions in the description here, although the method employed in WinFS uses positive exceptions.

Consider the information stored at replica C after partial synchronization: $o_1.version = \langle B, 2 \rangle$; $o_2.version = \bot$; $knowledge = (\langle A, 0 \rangle, \langle B, 2 \rangle \langle eB, 1 \rangle, \langle C, 0 \rangle)$. Suppose that A synchronizes with C and sends it update $\langle A, 1 \rangle$ on o_1. This update clearly does not follow $\langle B, 2 \rangle$ (the current version of o_1 held by C), but according to C's knowledge, neither is it succeeded by it – a conflict! The problem, of course, is that C's knowledge no longer dominates version $\langle A, 1 \rangle$.

Only at the end of the synchronization procedure, the knowledge of the sending replica is merged with the knowledge of the receiving replica. At that point, knowledge at the receiving replica will clearly dominate all of the versions it received during synchronization, and their PV may be omitted. But if synchronization is cut in the middle, some of these PVs must be kept, until such time when the replica's knowledge again dominates them.

In our performance analysis and comparison with other methods, we take into account this cost and measure its effect. Note that, it is incurred only due to communication disruptions that prevent synchronization procedures from completing. Our simulations vary the number of such disruptions from small to aggressively high.

4   Causality-Based Replica Reconciliation

In this section, we begin to provide the formal treatment of the PVE replica reconciliation mechanism. Our approach builds the description in two steps. First, we give a generic set-oriented method for replica reconciliation, and define the properties it requires. Second, in the next section, we instantiate the method with the PVE concise predecessor vectors scheme.

The key enabler of replica synchronization is a mechanism for representing sets of versions, through which precedence ordering can be captured. To this end, replicas store the following information concerning causality. First, replica r maintains information about the entire set of versions it knows of, represented in $r.knowledge$. Second, each version v stored at replica r contains in $v.predecessors$ a representation of the entire set of causally preceding versions. More specifically, we require the maintenance of a set $r.knowledge$ per replica r, and $v.predecessors$ per version v, as follows.

Definition 4 (The Knowledge Invariant). *For every replica r, and version v, we require r to maintain a set $r.knowledge$, such that if $v \in r.knowledge$ then replica r stores version v or a version w such that $v \prec w$.*

Definition 5 (The Predecessors Invariant). *For every object instances v and w, we require r to maintain a set $w.predecessors$ such that $v \in w.predecessors$ if and only if $v \prec w$.*

Given the above two requirements, it should be possible to determine if a version is included in a replica's storage; and if one version precedes another or they conflict.

4.1   A Synchronization Framework

We now give a two-way asymmetric, conflict detection framework that uses *knowledge* and *predecessors*. The protocol is composed of a requestor that contacts a server, and obtains all the versions in the server's knowledge. These versions are integrated into the requestor's storage, and raise conflict alarms where needed.

The synchronization protocol is a one-way protocol between a requesting host and a serving host. It makes use of the conflict causality representation as follows:

---

1. Requestor r sends server s its knowledge set $r.knowledge$.
2. Server s responds with the following:
   (a) For every object o it stores, for which $o.version \notin r.knowledge$, it sends o
3. For every version o received by from s, requestor r does the following:
   (a) For every object w in store, such that $w.name == o.name$:
       if $o \in w.predecessors$ then ignore o and stop;
       else if $w.version \in o.predecessors$ then delete w;
       else alert conflict.
   (b) Insert $o.version$ into $r.knowledge$.
   (c) Integrate $o.predecessors$ into $r.knowledge$.
   (d) store o

Fig. 1. A generic framework for using causality information

However, for our purposes, representing the full *knowledge* and *predecessors* sets is too costly. The challenge is to represent causality in a space-efficient manner, suitable for very large object sets, and moderate-size replica sets, while maintaining the invariants. The detailed solution follows in the next section.

4.2   Concise Version Vectors

The key to our novel conflict-detection technique is to transform the *predecessors* sets into different sets that can be represented more efficiently.

We first require the following technical definition:

Definition 6 (Extrinsic). *Let o be some object, $o.predecessors$ its predecessor set. Let S be a set of versions. We denote by $S\mid_{o.name}$ the reduction of S to versions pertaining to object $o.name$ only. S is called* extrinsic *to o if $S\mid_{o.name} == o.predecessors$.*

The surprising storage saving is derived in PVE from the following realization. For any object o, we can use an extrinsic set to o in place of *predecessors* throughout the protocol. In particular, when a replica's knowledge set is extrinsic to a predecessors set, it may be used in its place; the main storage savings is derived from using an empty set to denote (by convention) the replica's knowledge set, and avoid repeated storage of it. The following rule is the root of the PVE storage and communication savings:

Property 1. At any point in the protocol, any *predecessors* set may be replaced with an extrinsic set. By convention, an empty *predecessors* set indicates the replica's *knowledge* set.

We are now ready to introduce the PVE novel conflict detection scheme, which considerably reduces the size of representations of predecessor versions in normal cases.

Versions and Predecessor Vectors. The scheme uses the per-replica counter defined in Definition 1, that enumerates updates generated by the replica on all objects. Hence, a replica r maintains a local counter c. When replica r generates a version on an object o, it increments the local counter and creates version $\langle r, c \rangle$ on object o. Predecessors are represented using the PVEs as defined in Definition 3.

Knowledge. A replica r maintains in $r.knowledge$ a PVE representing all the versions it knows of. Inserting a new version $\langle s, n_s \rangle$ into $r.knowledge$ is done by updating the highest version seen by s to $\langle s, n_s \rangle$, and possibly inserting exceptions if there are holes between n_s and the previous highest version from s.

Object Predecessors. As already mentioned, an empty ($\perp$) *predecessors* set is used whenever $r.knowledge$ is extrinsic to an object's predecessors. In all other cases, *predecessor* contains a PVE, describing the set of causally preceding versions on the object.

Generating a New Version. When a replica r generates a new update on an object o, the new version $\langle r, c \rangle$ is inserted into $r.knowledge$ right away. Then, if $o.predecessor$ is $\perp$, nothing needs to be done to it. Implicitly, this means that the versions dominated by $r.knowledge$ causally precede the new version. If $o.predecessors$ is not empty, then the new version is inserted to $o.predecessors$ without exceptions. Implicitly this means that the set of versions that were dominated by the previous $o.predecessors$ causally precede the new update.

Merging Knowledge. During synchronization, the knowledge vector of a sender s is merged into the knowledge vector of the receiver r. The goal of the merging is to produce a vector that represents a union of all the versions included in $r.knowledge$ and $s.knowledge$, and replace $r.knowledge$ with it. For example, merging $s.knowledge = (\langle A, 3 \rangle, \langle B, 5 \rangle \langle eB, 4 \rangle, \langle C, 6 \rangle)$ into $r.knowledge = (\langle A, 7 \rangle \langle eA, 6 \rangle, \langle B, 3 \rangle \langle eB, 2 \rangle, \langle C, 1 \rangle)$ yields $(\langle A, 7 \rangle \langle eA, 6 \rangle, \langle B, 5 \rangle \langle eB, 4 \rangle, \langle C, 6 \rangle)$.

Synchronization. Space saving using empty predecessors requires caution in maintaining the extrinsic nature of predecessor sets throughout the synchronization protocol.

First, suppose that a requestor r receives from a server s a version v with an extrinsic $v.predecessors$ set. It is incorrect to merge $v.predecessors$ into the $r.knowledge$ set right away, since $v.predecessors$ may contain versions of objects different from v that r does not have. Hence, only v itself can be inserted into $r.knowledge$.

Second, consider the state of $r.knowledge$ at the end of its synchronization with s. Every version v sent by s has been inserted into $r.knowledge$. However, there may be some versions, e.g., $w \prec v$, which $r.knowledge$ does not contain. s does not explicitly send w, because it is included in $v.predecessors$. But since

1. Requestor r sends server s its knowledge set $r.knowledge$.
2. Server s responds with the following:
   (a) **It sends** $s.knowledge$.
   (b) For every object o it stores, for which $o.version \notin r.knowledge$, it sends o. If $s.knowledge$ is not extrinsic to $o.predecessors$, s sends $o.predecessors$ (otherwise, leave $o.predecessors$ empty).
3. For every version o received from s, requestor r does the following:
   (a) For every object w in store, such that $w.name == o.name$:
       if $o.version \in w.predecessors$ **or** $w.predecessors == \bot$ **and** $o.version \in r.knowledge$ then ignore o and stop;
       else if $w.version \in o.predecessors$ **or** $o.predecessors == \bot$ **and** $w.version \in s.knowledge$ then delete w;
       else alert conflict.
   (b) store o
   (c) **If** $o.predecessors == \bot$, **then unless** $r.knowledge$ **is extrinsic to** $s.knowledge$ **set** $o.predecessors = s.knowledge$.
   (d) **For every object** w **in store, such that** $w.name == o.name$ **(these must be conflicting versions), if** $w.predecessors = \bot$ **then set** $w.predecessors = r.knowledge$.
   (e) Insert $o.version$ into $r.knowledge$.
4. **Merge** $s.knowledge$ **into** $r.knowledge$.
5. **(Lazily) go through versions** v **such that** $v.predecessors \neq \bot$, **and if** $r.knowledge$ **is extrinsic to** $v.predecessors$ **then set** $v.predecessors = \bot$.

Fig. 2. Using extrinsic predecessors; modifications from the generic framework indicated in boldface

predecessor sets are not merged into $r.knowledge$, it may be left not containing w. To address this, at the end of an uninterrupted synchronization with s, the requestor r merges $s.knowledge$ into $r.knowledge$.

Third, should synchronization ever be disrupted in the middle, a requestor r may be left with $r.knowledge$ lacking some versions. This happens if a version v was incorporated into $r.knowledge$, but some preceding version $w \prec v$ has not been merged in.

As a consequence, in a future synchronization request, say with s', r may (inefficiently) receive w from s'. Hence, r checks if it can discard w by testing whether w is contained in $v.predecessors$ (and if yes, r also inserts w into $r.knowledge$ for efficiency). Figure 2 below describes the full PVE synchronization protocol.

4.3 Properties

The following properties are easily derived from the two invariants given in Definition 4 and Definition 5. In the full paper, we provide proof that the protocol above maintains these invariants.

Safety: Every conflicting version received by a requestor is detected.

Non-triviality: Only true conflicts are alerted.

Liveness: at the end of a complete execution of a synchronization procedure, for all objects the requestor r stores versions that are identical, or that causally follow, the versions stored by server s .

5 Performance

Storage overhead associated with precedence and conflict detection comprises of two components. The per replica *knowledge* vector contains aggregate information about all known versions at the replica. In typical, faultless scenarios, the PVE scheme requires $\tilde{O}(R)$ space per replica for the *knowledge* representation. By comparison, the VV scheme has no aggregate information on a replica's knowledge.

Additional storage overhead stems from precedence vectors. In our scheme, in faultless scenarios there is one version counter per object, incurring a space of $\tilde{O}(N)$. By comparison, in faultless scenarios, the VV scheme keeps $\tilde{O}(R \times N)$ storage, i.e., one version vector per object.

The fault-free (lower-bound) storage overhead for PVE and VV are summarized in Table 1.

When failures occur, the overhead of VV remains unchanged, but the PVE scheme may gradually suffer increasing storage overheads. There are two sources of additional complexity. The first is the need to keep exceptions in the knowledge, the second is the explicit version vectors (and their corresponding exceptions) kept for versions which the replica's knowledge does not dominate. In theory, neither of these components has any strict upper bound. These formal upper bounds are also summarize in Table 1 below. Below we provide simulation results that demonstrate storage growth in the PVE scheme relative to failure rates.

The communication overhead associated with synchronization also has two parts. First, a sender and a receiver need to determine which objects have versions yet unknown to the receiver. In the PVE scheme, this is done by conveying the receiver's knowledge vector to the sender. The faultless overhead here is $\tilde{O}(R)$; the upper bound is again theoretically unbounded.

Denote from now on the number of object versions that the sender determines it has to send to the receiver by q. The second component of the communication overhead is the extra precedence information associated with these q objects. In faultless runs of the PVE scheme, this information consists of one counter (the version counter) per object. Hence, the overhead is $\tilde{O}(q)$. In case of faults, as before the knowledge vector might contain an unbounded number of exceptions, and additionally, some objects may have explicit version vectors (and their exceptions) associated with them. Hence, there is no formal upper bound on the synchronization overhead. Here again, our simulation studies relate this complexity with the fault rate.

As for the VV scheme, the only way to convey knowledge of the latest versions held by a replica is by explicitly listing all of them, which requires $\tilde{O}(N \times R)$ bits. Therefore, in realistic deployments of VV, the server may keep a log of version

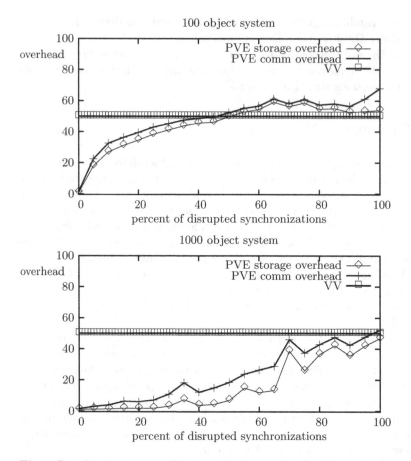

Fig. 3. Per-object storage and communication overheads with varying communication failure frequency, with $N = 100$ objects (top) $N = 1000$ objects (bottom)

vectors of all the objects that received updates since the last synchronization with the requestor, and sends only the VVs associated with these objects. The complexity will be between $\widetilde{O}(q \times R)$ and $\widetilde{O}(N \times R)$.

In face of communication faults, replicas using the PVE method might accumulate over time both knowledge exceptions, and versions that require explicit predecessors. There is no simple formula that describes how frequently are exceptions accrued, as this depends on a variety of parameters and exact causal ordering.

In order to evaluate the effect of communication disruptions on storage in our scheme, we conducted several simple simulations. We ran $R = 50$ replicas, generating version updates to objects at random. The number of objects varied between $N = 100$ and $N = 1000$. Every 100 total updates, a synchronization round was carried out in a round-robin manner: Replica 1 served updates to 2, replica 2 served 3, and so on, up to replica R sending updates back to 1. This was repeated 100 times. A failure-probability variable $pfail$ controlled the chances of

Table 1. Lower and Upper Bounds Comparison of PVE with the version-vector scheme

	Version vectors	PVE
storage l.b.	$\widetilde{O}(N \times R)$	$\widetilde{O}(N + R)$
storage u.b	$\widetilde{O}(N \times R)$	unbounded
comm l.b.	$\widetilde{O}(q \times R)$	$\widetilde{O}(q + R)$
comm u.b.	$\widetilde{O}(N \times R)$	unbounded

a communication disruption within every pairwise synchronization. We measured the resulting average communication and storage overhead. These are depicted in Figure 3 for three cases, 100, 1000 and 10000 objects. We normalize the overhead to per-object overhead. For reference, the per object storage overhead in standard VVs is exactly $R = 50$. The best achievable communication overhead with VVs is also $R = 50$, and is depicted for reference.

The figure clearly indicates a tradeoff in the PVE scheme. When communication disruptions are reasonably low, PVE storage and communication overhead is substantially reduced compared with the VV scheme, even for a relatively small number of objects. As failure rate increases, the number of exceptions in aggregate vector rises, and the total storage used for knowledge and for predecessor sets increases. The point at which the per-object amortized overhead passes that of a single VV depends on the number of objects, and for quite moderate size systems (1K objects) the cut-off point is beyond 90 percent communication disruption rate.

Acknowledgements

The protocol described in this paper was designed by the the Microsoft WinFS product team, including Doug Terry. We especially acknowledge Irena Hudis and Lev Novik for pushing the idea of concise version vectors. Harry Li, Yuan Yu, and Leslie Lamport helped with the formal specification of the replication protocol and the proof of its correctness.

References

1. D. S. Parker (Jr.), G. J. Popek, G. Rudisin, A. Stoughton, B. J. Walker, E. Walton, J. M. Chow, S. Kiser D. Edwards, and C. Kline. Detection of mutual inconsistency in distributed systems. *IEEE Transactions on Software Engineering*, 9(3):240–247, May 1983.
2. T. W. Page (Jr.), R. G.. Guy, J. S. Heidemann, D. H. Ratner, P. L. Reiher, A. Goel, G. H. Kuenning, and G. Popek. Perspectives on optimistically replicated peer-to-peer filing. *Software – Practice and Experience*, 11(1), December 1997.
3. R. Ladin, B. Liskov, L. Shrira, and S. Ghemawat. Providing high availability using lazy replication. *ACM Transactions on Computer Systems*, 10(4):360–391, 1992.
4. D. H. Ratner. *Roam: A Scalable Replication System for Mobile and Distributed Computing*. PhD thesis, 1998. UCLA Technical report UCLA-CSD-970044.

Adaptive Software Transactional Memory*

Virendra J. Marathe, William N. Scherer III, and Michael L. Scott

Department of Computer Science,
University of Rochester,
Rochester, NY 14627-0226
{vmarathe, scherer, scott}@cs.rochester.edu

Abstract. Software Transactional Memory (STM) is a generic synchronization construct that enables automatic conversion of correct sequential objects into correct *nonblocking* concurrent objects. Recent STM systems, though significantly more practical than their predecessors, display inconsistent performance: differing design decisions cause different systems to perform best in different circumstances, often by dramatic margins. In this paper we consider four dimensions of the STM design space: (i) *when* concurrent objects are acquired by transactions for modification; (ii) *how* they are acquired; (iii) what they look like when not acquired; and (iv) the non-blocking semantics for transactions (lock-freedom vs. obstruction-freedom). In this 4-dimensional space we highlight the locations of two leading STM systems: the DSTM of Herlihy et al. and the OSTM of Fraser and Harris. Drawing motivation from the performance of a series of application benchmarks, we then present a new *Adaptive* STM (ASTM) system that adjusts to the offered workload, allowing it to match the performance of the best known existing system on every tested workload.

1   Introduction

Traditional lock-based concurrent systems are prone to several important problems including deadlock, priority inversion, convoying, and lack of fault tolerance. Coarse grain locks are not scalable, and algorithms based on fine grain locks are notoriously difficult to write. Ad-hoc nonblocking implementations of concurrent objects avoid the semantic problems of locks and can match or exceed the performance of fine grain locking, but are at least as difficult to write.

Ideally, one would like a mechanism that provides the convenience of coarse grain locks without their semantic or performance problems. Toward this end, Herlihy [6] was the first to suggest automatically converting sequential code to correct nonblocking concurrent code. Inspired in part by hardware proposals for multiword atomic primitives [9, 20], subsequent researchers developed more sophisticated constructions [1, 11, 15, 19, 21], but these suffer from various practical problems: Most impose time or space overheads too high for real-world systems. Some require unrealistic atomic primitives. Many support only static collections of objects and/or static transactions (in which the set of objects to be accessed is known in advance).

---

* This work was supported in part by NSF grant numbers EIA-0080124, CCR-9988361, and CCR-0204344, by DARPA/AFRL contract number F29601-00-K-0182, and by financial and equipment grants from Sun Microsystems Laboratories.

P. Fraigniaud (Ed.): DISC 2005, LNCS 3724, pp. 354–368, 2005.

Recent software transactional memory (STM) systems have overcome most of these problems [2, 3, 5, 8]: They employ atomic primitives like compare-and-swap (CAS) and load-linked/store-conditional (LL/SC), which are widely supported by current multiprocessors. They support dynamic collections of objects and dynamic transactions. Their space overheads are modest. Finally, their performance overheads are low enough to outperform coarse-grain locks in important cases, and to provide an attractive alternative to even well-tuned fine-grain locks when convenience, fault tolerance, and clean semantics are considered. Those of us working in the field envision a day when STM mechanisms are embedded in compilers for languages like Java and C#, providing nonblocking implementations of synchronized methods "for free".

STM systems may be either word- or object-based, depending on the granularity at which data is modified. We focus on the latter, which appear particularly well suited to object-oriented languages such as Java and C#. The two leading object-based STMs are currently the DSTM of Herlihy et al. [8] and the OSTM of Fraser and Harris [2, 3]. In prior work [13], we undertook a preliminary comparison of these systems. Among other things, we found that DSTM outperforms OSTM by as much as an order of magnitude on write-dominated workloads, while OSTM outperforms DSTM by as much as a factor of two on read-dominated workloads. We attribute much of the difference to the choice of acquire semantics (discussed in Sections 2 and 3.1) and to indirect object access in DSTM, which imposes an extra cache miss on the typical read access.

In the current paper we discuss four principal design decisions for object-based STM, encompassing (i) *when* concurrent objects are acquired by transactions for modification (*eager* vs. *lazy* acquire); (ii) *how* they are acquired (per-object or per-transaction metadata); (iii) what they look like to readers when not currently acquired (level of indirection); and (iv) the type of nonblocking semantics (lock-free vs. obstruction-free). Our taxonomy enhances previous [3, 13] understandings of DSTM and OSTM performance by locating these systems within the four-dimensional design space. By clarifying the performance implications of design dimensions, the taxonomy has also allowed us to develop an *Adaptive* STM system (ASTM) that automatically adapts its behavior to the offered workload, allowing it to closely approximate the performance of the best existing system in every scenario we have tested.

As background, Section 2 outlines a common usage pattern and API for object-based STM. Section 3 presents our characterization of the STM design space and locates DSTM and OSTM within it. Section 4 describes three variants of ASTM, all of which revisit design decisions at run time based on the offered workload. The first two variants adapt along dimensions (ii) and (iii) above; the third adds simultaneous adaptation along dimension (i). Experimental results, presented in Section 5, show ASTM to be competitive with the better of OSTM and DSTM across all execution scenarios, making it highly attractive for general-purpose use.

2 STM Usage

STM transactions provide nonblocking concurrent access to one or more shared *transactional objects*. Transactions typically proceed through the following four phases with respect to any given object:

Open: makes the object available to the transaction. A transaction cannot access an unopened object, but objects may be concurrently opened by multiple transactions.

Acquire: asserts the transaction's *ownership* of the object. An object can be acquired by only one transaction at a time. Any other transaction that subsequently attempts to acquire the object must detect and resolve the conflict. The conflict resolution method determines whether the STM is lock-free [2, 3] or obstruction-free [5, 8]. Acquire is not typically a separate operation. DSTM [8] implements it as part of the open operation (*eager acquire*). OSTM [2, 3] implements it as part of the commit operation (*lazy acquire*).

Commit: attempts to atomically effect all changes to acquired objects made by the current transaction. Typically, this is done by using a compare-and-swap (CAS) or store-conditional instruction to update the status field in a *transaction descriptor* accessible to all competing transactions. (Without loss of generality we assume the use of CAS in the remainder of this paper.) This CAS serves as the linearization point [10] of the transaction.

Release: cleans up metadata associated with a transaction after it commits or aborts. DSTM introduced the concept of *early release* [8], which allows a transaction to relinquish an accessed object prior to committing. Early release reduces the window of contention in which multiple transactions are transiently dependent on a particular object, but it requires the programmer to exploit application-specific knowledge to ensure that transactions are consistent and linearizable.

In our STM experiments (Section 5) we employ a uniform API for beginning, validating, committing, and aborting transactions; and for accessing objects in read-only or read-write modes. Details can be found in the technical report version of this paper [14].

3   STM Design Space

In this section we discuss four key dimensions in the STM design space. We also present a brief comparison of DSTM and OSTM in light of them.

3.1   Eager vs. Lazy Acquire

Transactions acquire objects when first accessed under eager acquire semantics, but at commit time under lazy acquire semantics. Eager acquire allows a transaction to detect contention earlier; this enables a doomed transaction to abort instead of performing useless work. Eager acquire also makes it easier to ensure consistency: If every conflict is resolved when first detected, then an unaborted transaction can be sure that its objects are mutually consistent as of the most recent open operation. With lazy acquire, by contrast, the obvious approach requires a transaction to maintain a private list of opened objects, and to re-verify the entire list when opening another. This approach imposes total overhead quadratic in the number of opened objects. An alternative is to "sandbox" transactional code to catch and recover from memory and arithmetic faults, and to impose a limit on execution time as heuristic protection against infinite loops. In some cases it may be safe to execute with inconsistent data, in which case no verification overhead is required, but this requires application-specific knowledge.

On the other side of the tradeoff, lazy acquire can greatly shrink the window wherein transactions see each other as contenders and may be unnecessarily aborted or delayed. In particular, with lazy acquire transaction A will never be aborted by transaction B if B itself aborts before A attempts to commit.

3.2 Metadata Structure

A transactional object typically wraps an underlying data object; i.e. it contains a pointer through which the data object can be referenced. Two different means of acquiring such an object appear in current object-based STM systems: (i) an acquirer makes the transactional object point to the transaction descriptor; and (ii) the acquirer makes the transactional object point to an *indirection object* that contains pointers to the transaction descriptor and to old and new versions of the data object. Option (i) allows conflicting transactions to see all of their competitors' metadata, but makes object release expensive: A released object cannot be left in an acquired state (where it points to a descriptor), because subsequent accesses would have to search the descriptor's write list to find a current version. Additionally, maintaining descriptors for previous committed and aborted transactions would constitute potential space overhead quadratic in the total number of objects. Instead, a *cleanup* operation must update transactional objects to point directly to the current data object, at the cost of an extra CAS per object.

Cleanup can be omitted entirely with per-object metadata, at the cost of $2\times$ overhead in space. Alternatively, a lightweight cleanup phase might "zero out" pointers to obsolete data objects, making them available for garbage collection. An attractive intermediate option is to omit the cleanup phase, but allow readers to clean up obsolete data objects incrementally.

3.3 Indirection in Object Referencing

As noted in the previous subsection, cleanup is essential with per-transaction metadata. It is optional with per-object metadata. If performed, it provides readers with direct access to the data objects of currently unacquired transactional objects. If not performed, it will tend to induce an extra cache miss for every object opened in read-only mode. The consequent slower reads have a significant impact on overall throughput for read-dominated workloads [13].

3.4 Lock-Freedom vs. Obstruction-Freedom

Lock-free concurrent objects guarantee that at least one thread makes progress in a bounded number of time steps. Obstruction-freedom [7] admits the possibility of livelock, but tends to lead to substantially simpler code: Lock-free STM systems typically arrange to acquire objects in some global total order. They also perform *recursive helping*, in which transaction A performs transaction B's operations on its behalf when A detects a conflict with B. Lock-freedom is most naturally implemented with lazy acquire and sorting; without them a transaction might discover the need to open an object that precedes some other already-opened object in the global total order.

Arbitration among competing transactions in an obstruction-free system is handled "out of band" by a separate *contention manager* [8]. With the right manager, one can obtain high probabilistic—or even strict—guarantees of progress [4, 17, 18].

3.5   Placing DSTM and OSTM

DSTM is obstruction-free, whereas OSTM is lock-free. Transactional objects in DSTM point to an indirection *locator* object, which in turn contains pointers to the most recent acquirer's transaction descriptor and to old and new versions of the data. The acquirer's status determines which version of an object is valid: the new version is valid only when the acquirer has COMMITTED. An unacquired transactional object in OSTM points directly to the appropriate version of the data. As we shall see, this difference in object referencing results in poor performance for DSTM in read-dominated workloads.

OSTM is lock-free; hence, it uses lazy acquire. DSTM uses eager acquire. For write access, DSTM acquires objects by swapping in a new locator; OSTM acquires objects by making them point directly to the transaction descriptor. Neither DSTM nor OSTM acquires objects accessed in read-only mode. Rather, both systems maintain a private *read list*, which they revalidate on every open operation. OSTM must also validate its write list on every open. These bookkeeping, sorting, validation, and cleanup overheads cause OSTM to perform poorly in write-dominated workloads. DSTM has no cleanup phase, but it arranges for readers, at open time, to "zero out" fields in locators that point to obsolete data objects, thus making them available to the garbage collector.

In our STM design space, DSTM can be summarized as the point ⟨eager acquire, per-object metadata, indirect object referencing, obstruction-free⟩; OSTM maps to ⟨lazy acquire, per-transaction metadata, direct object referencing, lock-free⟩. In the following section we describe our ASTM system. It adapts across dimensions (i) and (iii) of the design space: ⟨eager OR lazy acquire, per-object metadata, direct OR indirect object referencing, obstruction-free⟩.

4   Adaptive Software Transactional Memory

As noted in Section 3, and as demonstrated in preliminary experiments [13], the location of an STM system in the design space plays a key role in its algorithmic complexity and performance. The fact that different systems perform best in different circumstances raises the question: Is it possible to adapt among multiple design points to obtain a "best-of-both-worlds" STM system that performs well in all scenarios? We address this question with our ASTM design.

4.1   Basic ASTM Design

In our experiments to date we have yet to identify a workload in which lock freedom provides a performance advantage over obstruction freedom. Given the design flexibility and algorithmic simplifications enabled by obstruction freedom, together with the success of practical contention managers in avoiding livelock problems [18], we have adopted obstruction freedom for ASTM.

Figure 1 depicts a *Transactional Memory Object (TMObject*, borrowed from DSTM terminology*) in ASTM. By default, TMObjects point directly to data objects. A reader transaction does not acquire a TMObject. Instead, it maintains a private read list and guarantees transaction consistency by re-validating the objects on that list at each new open operation. Reads by a transaction are thus *invisible* to other transactions in the system. A writer transaction, on the other hand, acquires a TMObject by installing an indirection object. Borrowing again from DSTM, we refer to this indirection object as a *locator*. Figure 1 illustrates the object acquisition process. ASTM locators, like those of DSTM, contain three pointers: one for the acquirer's transaction descriptor, and one each for old and new versions of the data object. Before acquiring an object a writer instantiates a new locator and a new version of the data object, which it copies from the most recently committed version, found in the current TMObject. The writer then acquires the target TMObject by using an atomic CAS to swing it to the new locator.

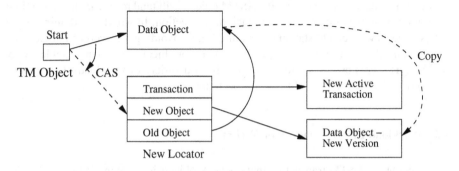

Fig. 1. Acquiring a previously unacquired object

A transaction may be in any of three states: ACTIVE, ABORTED, or COMMIT-TED. With contention, a writer's acquire attempt may fail, or it may find an ACTIVE transaction's locator in the TMObject. The contention manager is invoked to determine which transaction should proceed. If the contention manager indicates that transaction *A* should abort its competitor *B*, *A* attempts to do so by CASing *B*'s descriptor's state from ACTIVE to ABORTED. Otherwise the current transaction retries the acquire (possibly after waiting for some time to let its competitor complete execution). Once all operations for a transaction are complete, it is committed upon successfully changing the descriptor state from ACTIVE to COMMITTED. Immediately prior to committing, a transaction must perform one final validation of objects on its private read list.

A TMObject that points directly to a data object is said to be in the *unacquired* state; a TMObject that points to a locator is in the *acquired* state. If TMObjects were to remain in the acquired state after a writer completes, then subsequent reads would suffer indirection overhead, as described in Section 3.3. To spread the overhead of cleanup over time, and to avoid it entirely when the subsequent access is a write, we leave the work to readers. A reader that finds an object in the acquired state with a transaction that is either COMMITTED or ABORTED first converts the object to the unacquired

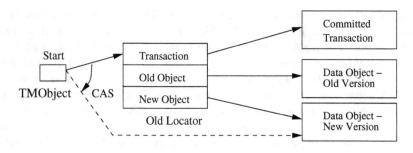

Fig. 2. Cleanup while opening an acquired object in read mode

state. Figure 2 illustrates this conversion. A reader detects contention when an acquired TMObject's locator refers to an ACTIVE transaction.

In workloads dominated by reads, ASTM objects will tend to stay in the unacquired state, improving performance through lack of indirection. In workloads dominated by writes, objects will tend to stay in the acquired state, avoiding the overhead of cleanup. Additionally, ASTM uses eager acquire by default for objects opened in writable mode. ASTM thus seems positioned to perform well for a variety of workloads. Our experimental results (Section 5) confirm this expectation.

4.2   Workload Effect: Readers vs. Writers

As in DSTM, an ASTM transaction that opens N objects in write mode requires $N + 1$ CASes: N to acquire the objects, and one to commit. However, subsequent readers may perform up to N CASes to return the objects to an unacquired state. For write-dominated workloads, these cleanup CASes are rare.

With a roughly uniform mix of reads and writes, transactions that include reads are likely to perform several cleanup CASes. In this case, TMObjects could repeatedly flip between acquired and unacquired states. Readers would become slower, due both to the extra level of indirection in acquired TMObjects and to the extra CASes needed to revert objects from the acquired to unacquired states. These CASes could also interfere with writers, slowing them down as well. As the results in Section 5 will show, however, overall system throughput for ASTM is always competitive with the better existing STM. We attribute this primarily to the division of labor between reads and writes, and to the use of eager acquire: Compared to DSTM, we avoid an extra level of indirection for unacquired objects; compared to OSTM, the benefits of eager acquire significantly outweigh the performance lost from flipping transactional object states.

In the best case, an individual transaction may find all its objects unacquired and incur no indirection overhead. In the worst case, it may find all its objects acquired. In addition to indirection overhead, it would then incur the costs of cleanup for objects opened in read mode plus contention-induced slowdown for writes. In Section 5, we assess benchmarks with transactions that fall in several points on the read-write spectrum. We intend to continue exploring reader-writer tradeoffs as future research.

4.3 Lazy ASTM

As described so far, ASTM uses eager acquire for objects opened in write mode. Suppose that transaction A detects a conflict with B when attempting to open some object of mutual interest. If A is doomed to fail, detecting the conflict early may allow it to abort, and avoid unnecessary work. Similarly, if B is doomed to fail, A has the opportunity to kill it right away. As noted in Section 3, however, the tradeoff can go the other way. We cannot in general be sure which transaction(s) might eventually succeed. In an obstruction-free system like ASTM, the contention manager simply makes an informed guess. If A waits for—or aborts itself in favor of—B, and B fails to commit, we have incurred a significant cost. Similarly, if A aborts B but then itself fails to commit, the work of B was wasted. Either way, this cost could have been avoided if A had delayed its acquire. Even if A rightly kills B, it is possible that B would have detected an inconsistency and aborted itself soon after, suggesting that we may have wasted the overhead of contention management.

To evaluate these tradeoffs, we have developed a lazy variant of ASTM that acquires no objects until commit time. Like the default Eager ASTM, Lazy ASTM uses contention management; both are obstruction-free. Lazy acquire reduces the window in which transactions may see each other as competitors.

As in Eager ASTM, each TMObject in Lazy ASTM can be in the acquired or unacquired state. Readers perform cleanup as necessary. Writers, on the other hand, do not eagerly acquire target TMObjects. Instead, a transaction maintains a private *write list* in its descriptor, in addition to the read list. This write list is revalidated (as is the read list) when opening each new transactional object. Essentially, a transaction remains invisible to other transactions until commit time. As a result, several transactions may open the same object in write mode at the same time. At commit time, a transaction attempts to acquire the TMObjects in its write list by swapping in pointers (using CAS) to newly created locators, each corresponding to the respective TMObject. The CAS will fail if any other transaction has modified the object in-between. But where OSTM sorts objects and uses recursive helping to guarantee lock-freedom, ASTM traverses the write list unsorted and relies on the contention manager to arbitrate conflicts.

4.4 Adapting to Acquire Semantics

Transactions that are doomed to fail tend to detect contention late in their lifetime with lazy acquire, after doing a lot of wasted work. On the other hand, with eager acquire, doomed transactions can interfere with other transactions, delaying or aborting them. Unfortunately there is no way in general to distinguish between these scenarios. In fact, our experiments so far seem to suggest that the tradeoffs largely "cancel out": Though eager acquire is usually a little faster, neither dramatically outperforms the other in most cases. This suggests to us that eager acquire is usually preferable, in order to avoid the bookkeeping complexity of maintaining write lists.

In one specific case, however, our experimental results (Section 5) reveal a significant advantage for lazy acquire: transactions that access a large number of objects in read-only mode, that perform early release on many of these (thereby reducing the window of contention with other potentially conflicting transactions), and that access only a few objects in write mode. A common example is a reader transaction that uses early release incrementally while following a linked path through a data structure. Such a transaction may suffer delays if it encounters objects eagerly acquired by writers. Lazy acquire significantly reduces contention windows for this workload.

The next logical step in our quest for adaptivity in ASTM is to dynamically select an object acquisition strategy. From our observations on the synergy between lazy acquire and early release, we invoke a history-based heuristic for a transaction to adapt to the better acquire strategy (eager or lazy) based on observations made by past transactions. The final version of our system ("Full ASTM") defaults to eager acquire, since this provides the best performance in most cases (details in Section 5). We maintain rolling averages for percentages of writes and of early releases that follow at least one write across transactions executed by a thread. So long as the percentage of writes is below a threshold w and the percentage of early releases exceeds another threshold r, subsequent transactions use lazy acquire; otherwise they use eager acquire.

Our heuristic assumes that transactions will tend to behave similarly to those recently completed. It also reflects the quadratic cost of incremental validation: Even a modest number of writes will result in overhead significant enough to overcome the benefits from reduced contention windows in lazy acquire / early release. In our experiments, we have set the early release threshold r at 50% and the write access threshold w at 25%. Limited experimentation with other values suggests that results are largely insensitive to the exact percentage used.

As in Eager ASTM, readers clean up transactional objects if necessary, and writers use indirection objects (DSTM-style locators). Full ASTM remains obstruction-free; it requires contention management.

5   Experimental Results

In this section we provide a detailed empirical analysis of the main aspects of the STM system design space addressed in this paper: acquire semantics, acquire methodology, object referencing style, and progress guarantees. We present experimental results for a variety of concurrent data structures to assess the extent to which ASTM successfully adapts to the offered workload. We use DSTM and OSTM as a baseline against which to compare our results.

Experiments were conducted on a 16-processor SunFire 6800, a cache-coherent multiprocessor with 1.2GHz UltraSPARC III processors. The testing environment was Sun's Java 1.5 beta 1 HotSpot JVM, augmented with a JSR166 update from Doug Lea [12]. We measured throughput over a period of 10 seconds for each benchmark, varying the number of worker threads from 1 to 48. Results were averaged over a set of six test runs. In all experiments, we use the Polka contention manager [18] for DSTM and for all three variants of ASTM (Eager, Lazy, Full); Scherer and Scott report this manager to be both fast and stable. We perform incremental revalidation in all systems for all benchmarks, rechecking the consistency of previously opened objects when opening anything new.

5.1   Write-Dominated Workloads

In DSTM and Eager ASTM, objects opened in write mode are immediately acquired, and the transaction is free to forget the original transactional objects. Validation, moreover, is trivial: If the transaction descriptor is still `ACTIVE`, all objects opened in write mode are consistent. Because they acquire objects lazily, OSTM and Lazy ASTM must maintain a write list in addition to the read list, and must revalidate objects on *both* lists incrementally. ASTM defaults to eager acquire mode, but when it switches to lazy acquire mode, it incurs the same write list maintenance and validation overhead as OSTM and Lazy ASTM.

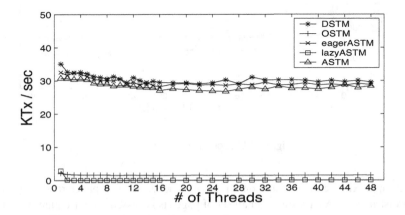

Fig. 3. IntSet performance results

In write-dominated workloads, OSTM and Lazy ASTM suffer significantly from the bookkeeping and incremental validation overhead for maintaining write lists for transactions. DSTM and Eager ASTM, however, do not incur these overheads. Our strategy of having ASTM acquire objects eagerly by default enables ASTM to remain in eager acquire mode for write-dominated transactions. To assess the impact of this design choice, Figure 3 shows STM performance results on the IntSet benchmark. IntSet maintains a sorted list of integers ranging between 0...255 (the range has been restricted in all benchmarks to deliberately increase contention). Concurrent threads continuously insert and delete nodes in the list. A transaction opens all visited nodes in write mode. DSTM, Eager ASTM and ASTM all perform comparably: an order of magnitude better than OSTM and Lazy ASTM. Experiments with modified versions of the code (not shown here) reveal that most of the overhead in OSTM and Lazy ASTM comes from extra bookkeeping; the remainder comes from incremental validation and sorting (in OSTM). Notice that Lazy ASTM livelocks (drops from low throughput to essentially none) when we move from one to two processors.

Figure 4 shows performance results for the LFUCache benchmark [17]. This program uses a priority queue heap to simulate cache replacement in an HTTP web proxy via the least-frequently used (LFU) algorithm [16]. The LFU replacement policy assumes that the most frequently accessed pages are most likely to be accessed next. A transaction typically reads a page, increments its frequency count, and rearranges the heap (if necessary).

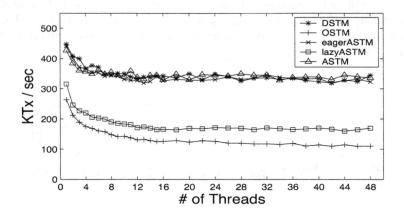

Fig. 4. LFUCache performance results

To approximate the demand on a real web cache, we pick pages randomly from a Zipf distribution. As a result, a small set of pages is accessed most frequently; transactions are essentially write-dominated (for page i, the cumulative probability of selection is $p_c(i) \propto \sum_{0<j\leq i} 1/j^2$). DSTM, Eager ASTM and ASTM perform comparably. Lazy ASTM suffers from bookkeeping overhead; OSTM additionally incurs overhead from sorting and recursive helping.

5.2 Read-Dominated Workloads

As discussed in Section 3, the style in which unacquired objects are referenced has a considerable impact on read performance. DSTM uses indirection objects (locators), while OSTM arranges for unacquired transactional objects to point to data objects directly. All three ASTM variants adapt their object referencing style to the underlying workload. We illustrate this facet of ASTM's performance relative to OSTM and DSTM using two read-dominated benchmarks: IntSetRelease (another sorted list of integers), and RBTree (a concurrent red-black tree).

IntSetRelease is a highly concurrent IntSet variant in which transactions open objects in read mode and release them, early, while moving down the list. Once found, the nodes to be updated are upgraded to write mode. DSTM performs the worst due to indirection overhead. ASTM and Eager ASTM perform the best, with Lazy ASTM and OSTM incurring minor overheads from bookkeeping (both) and sorting (OSTM). Even though most objects are typically released early, writes always occur at the very end of a transaction. For this reason, ASTM tends to remain in eager acquire mode.

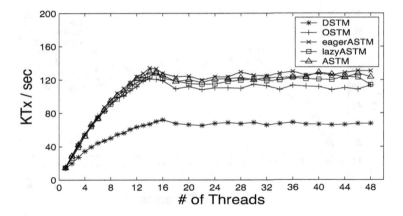

Fig. 5. IntSetRelease performance results

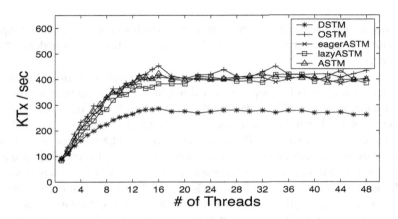

Fig. 6. RBTree performance results

RBTree is a concurrent red-black (balanced) search tree. As in the linked-list bench-marks, threads repeatedly perform randomized insertions and deletions. A transaction typically opens objects in read mode as it searches down the tree for the right place to perform an insertion or deletion. Subsequently, it upgrades to write mode only those nodes that are needed to rebalance the tree. Performance results appear in Figure 6. All the ASTMs and OSTM perform comparably well. Since no early releases are in-volved in transactions, ASTM remains in eager acquire mode. Since most nodes are never upgraded to write mode, DSTM yields the lowest throughput.

5.3 Conflict Window

Although lazy object acquisition leads to bookkeeping and validation overheads, it helps reduce the window of contention between transactions. As per our discussion in

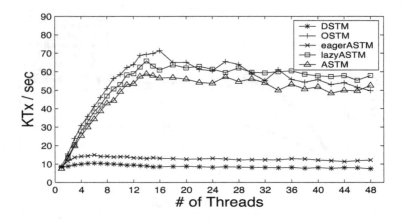

Fig. 7. RandomGraphList performance results

Section 4.3, early release can lead to a situation in which lazy acquire might be expected to significantly outperform eager acquire. We see this situation in the RandomGraphList benchmark.

RandomGraphList represents a random undirected graph as a sorted linked list in which each node points to a separate sorted neighbor list. To increase contention, we restrict the graph size to 256 nodes, numbered 0...255. Transactions randomly insert or delete a node. For insertions, transactions additionally select a small randomized neighbor set for the target node. Transactions traverse the adjacency list (using read and early release as in IntSetRelease) to find the target node. They then read and update that node's neighbor list, together with the neighbor list of each of its new neighbors.

Transactions are very long in RandomGraphList. With eager acquire, the window of conflict is very large. Figure 7 shows STM throughputs for RandomGraphList. Lazy acquire is a clear winner, with throughput more than a factor of five higher than that of eager acquire. With eager acquire, reader transactions encounter unnecessary contention with writer transactions (for objects that would be released early anyway), leading to virtually serialized access to the main node list. DSTM bears the additional indirection overhead and hence performs the worst. Here, synergy between lazy acquire and early release significantly reduces the number of read-write conflicts. Eager ASTM performs a little better than DSTM, but significantly worse than Lazy ASTM. Lazy ASTM lags a little behind OSTM up to 16 threads; since data access patterns are random (due to random neighbor sets), transactions in Lazy ASTM apparently livelock on each other for a while before someone makes progress. OSTM, being lock-free, does not suffer from this delay. After 16 threads though, the overhead of recursive helping in OSTM causes reduction in its throughput. ASTM follows Lazy ASTM's performance curve, and is more or less competitive with both OSTM and Lazy ASTM. Because ASTM defaults to eager acquire mode, the first few transactions use eager acquire and are consequently very slow. Thereafter, ASTM switches to lazy acquire mode and starts catching up with Lazy ASTM and OSTM.

6   Concluding Remarks

The possibility of automatically converting sequential code to concurrent code has made STM an attractive topic of research, and recent work [2, 3, 5, 8] has brought it to the verge of practical utility. Much will now depend on the constants: Is the overhead relative to lock-based code small enough to be outweighed by the (clear and compelling) semantic and software engineering benefits?

In this paper we have presented a detailed analysis of the design space of modern STMs, identifying four key dimensions of STM system design. Various choices in this space lead to varied performance tradeoffs. Consequently no single STM performs the best (or comparably) in all possible scenarios. Our analysis has led us to create a new STM system that adapts to the offered workload, yielding throughput comparable to the best existing system in all scenarios we have tested. The object acquisition methodology, adaptive object referencing style, and obstruction-free nature of ASTM have been carefully selected to give maximum throughput in all cases. We have also demonstrated the feasibility of adapting acquire semantics via simple history-based heuristics.

Although our analysis of the STM design space is fairly exhaustive, another design dimension remains unexplored: tradeoffs in *visible* vs. *invisible* reads [17, 18]. Preliminary results from our exploration of read strategies (not shown here) suggest that adapting between the two may improve performance. We also forsee future work in greater exploration of execution scenarios that favor eager or lazy acquire semantics. Finally, we will strive to find ever better adaptation heuristics.

Acknowledgments

We are grateful to Sun's Scalable Synchronization Research Group for donating the SunFire machine and for providing us with a copy of their DSTM code.

References

[1] G. Barnes. A Method for Implementing Lock-Free Shared Data Structures. In *Proc. of the 5th Ann. ACM Symp. on Parallel Algorithms and Architectures*, pages 261–270, 1993.

[2] K. Fraser. Practical Lock-Freedom. Technical Report UCAM-CL-TR-579, Cambridge University Computer Laboratory, Feb. 2004.

[3] K. Fraser and T. Harris. Concurrent Programming without Locks. *Submitted for publication*, 2004.

[4] R. Guerraoui, M. P. Herlihy, and B. Pochon. Toward a Theory of Transactional Contention Managers. In *Proc. of 24th Ann. ACM Symp. on Principles of Distributed Computing*, July 2005.

[5] T. Harris and K. Fraser. Language Support for Lightweight Transactions. In *Proc. of 18th Ann. ACM Conf. on Object-Oriented Prog., Sys., Langs., and Apps.*, Oct. 2003.

[6] M. P. Herlihy. A Methodology for Implementing Highly Concurrent Data Structures. In *Proc. of the 2nd ACM Symp. on Principles & Practice of Parallel Prog.*, Mar. 1990.

[7] M. P. Herlihy, V. Luchangco, and M. Moir. Obstruction Free Synchronization: Double-Ended Queues as an Example. In *Proc. of 23rd Intl. Conf. on Distributed Computing Sys.*, pages 522–529, May 2003.

[8] M. P. Herlihy, V. Luchangco, M. Moir, and W. N. Scherer III. Software Transactional Memory for Dynamic-sized Data Structures. In *Proc. of 22nd Ann. ACM Symp. on Principles of Distributed Computing*, July 2003.

[9] M. P. Herlihy and J. E. B. Moss. Transactional Memory: Architectural Support for Lock-Free Data Structures. In *Proc. of the 20th Ann. Intl. Symp. on Computer Architecture*, pages 289–300, May 1993.

[10] M. P. Herlihy and J. M. Wing. Linearizability: a Correctness Condition for Concurrent Objects. *ACM Trans. on Prog. Langs. and Sys.*, 12(3):463–492, 1990.

[11] A. Israeli and L. Rappoport. Disjoint-Access-Parallel Implementations of Strong Shared Memory Primitives. In *Proc. of the 13th Ann. ACM Symp. on Principles of Distributed Computing*, pages 151–160, 1994.

[12] D. Lea. Concurrency JSR-166 Interest Site. http://gee.cs.oswego.edu/dl/concurrency-interest/.

[13] V. J. Marathe, W. N. Scherer III, and M. L. Scott. Design Tradeoffs in Modern Software Transactional Memory Systems. In *Proc. of 14th Workshop on Langs., Compilers, and Run-time Support for Scalable Sys.*, Oct. 2004.

[14] V. J. Marathe, W. N. Scherer III, and M. L. Scott. Adaptive Software Transactional Memory. Technical Report TR 868, Dept. of Computer Science, University of Rochester, May 2005.

[15] M. Moir. Transparent Support for Wait-Free Transactions. In *Proc. of the 11th Intl. Workshop on Distributed Algorithms*, pages 305–319. Springer-Verlag, 1997.

[16] J. T. Robinson and M. V. Devarakonda. Data Cache Management Using Frequency-Based Replacement. In *Proc. of the 1990 ACM SIGMETRICS Conf. on Measurement and Modeling of Computer Sys.*, pages 134–142, 1990.

[17] W. N. Scherer III and M. L. Scott. Contention Management in Dynamic Software Transactional Memory. In *Proc. of Workshop on Concurrency and Synchronization in Java Progs.*, pages 70–79, July 2004.

[18] W. N. Scherer III and M. L. Scott. Advanced Contention Management in Dynamic Software Transactional Memory. In *Proc. of 24th Ann. ACM Symp. on Principles of Distributed Computing*, July 2005.

[19] N. Shavit and D. Touitou. Software Transactional Memory. In *Proc. of 14th Ann. ACM Symp. on Principles of Distributed Computing*, pages 204–213, Aug. 1995.

[20] J. M. Stone, H. S. Stone, P. Heidelberger, and J. Turek. Multiple Reservations and the Oklahoma Update. *IEEE Parallel and Distributed Technology*, 1(4):58–71, Nov. 1993.

[21] J. Turek, D. Shasha, and S. Prakash. Locking without Blocking: Making Lock Based Concurrent Data Structure Algorithms Nonblocking. In *Proc. of the 11th ACM Symp. on Principles of Database Sys.*, pages 212–222, 1992.

Optimistic Generic Broadcast

Piotr Zieliński

University of Cambridge,
Computer Laboratory
piotr.zielinski@cl.cam.ac.uk

Abstract. We consider an asynchronous system with the Ω failure detector, and investigate the number of communication steps required by various broadcast protocols in runs in which the leader does not change. Atomic Broadcast, used for example in state machine replication, requires three communication steps. Optimistic Atomic Broadcast requires only two steps if all correct processes receive messages in the same order. Generic Broadcast requires two steps if no messages conflict. We present an algorithm that subsumes both of these approaches and guarantees two-step delivery if all conflicting messages are received in the same order, and three-step delivery otherwise. Internally, our protocol uses two new algorithms. First, a Consensus algorithm which decides in one communication step if all proposals are the same, and needs two steps otherwise. Second, a method that allows us to run infinitely many instances of a distributed algorithm, provided that only finitely many of them are different. We assume that fewer than a third of all processes are faulty ($n > 3f$).

1 Introduction

State machine replication [7] is a common way of increasing fault-tolerance of client-server systems. As opposed to centralized systems, where clients send requests to a single server, in this approach, each request is broadcast to a group of servers. In order for this approach to work, client requests must be delivered to all the servers in the same order. The broadcast primitive that ensures this property is called Uniform Atomic Broadcast[1].

We consider an asynchronous system with the Ω leader oracle [3], and investigate the number of communication steps required by various broadcast protocols in runs in which the leader does not change. Atomic Broadcast is expensive in the sense that it requires three communication steps: one for the client request to reach the servers and two for the servers to agree on the order of the requests [4,10,12]. Two approaches have been proposed in the literature to deal with this problem: Optimistic Atomic Broadcast and Generic Broadcast.

---

[1] "Uniform" abstractions offer guarantees to all processes as opposed to only correct ones. All abstractions considered in this paper are uniform, so from now on we will omit this word from abstraction names.

P. Fraigniaud (Ed.): DISC 2005, LNCS 3724, pp. 369–383, 2005.

Algorithm	no conflicting messages	all messages same order	conflicting messages same order	general scenario
Chandra and Toueg [3]	3	3	3	3
Opt. Atomic Broadcast [14]	4	2	4	4
Generic Broadcast [16]	2	4	4	4
This paper	2	2	2	3

Fig. 1. Latency degree comparison of several broadcast algorithms

Optimistic Atomic Broadcast [14] takes advantage of the fact that in many networks messages tend to arrive at different processes in the same order. Protocols implementing this primitive are able to deliver messages in two communication steps as long as all processes receive messages in the same order.

Generic Broadcast [1,16] achieves better efficiency by introducing a binary conflict relation on messages, requiring only that conflicting messages are delivered in the same order by all processes. For example, two "read" requests or any two requests operating on unrelated objects are non-conflicting and can be delivered in different orders.

In this paper, we present an algorithm that implements both of these approaches at the same time. Optimistic Generic Broadcast, as we call it, guarantees message delivery in two communication steps if all correct processes receive all *conflicting* messages in the same order. When this condition does not hold, all messages are delivered within three communication steps. Both of these latencies match the respective lower bounds [10,16]. Our algorithm requires that fewer than a third of all processes are incorrect ($n > 3f$), which is necessary to deliver messages in two steps [15].

Fig. 1 gives a short comparison of several algorithms. We consider four scenarios: without conflicting messages, with correct processes receiving *all* messages in the same order, with correct processes receiving *conflicting* messages in the same order, and with no restrictions. For each of these scenarios, Fig. 1 shows the number of communication steps required to deliver messages, formally known as *latency degree* [17]. The comparison shows that our algorithm is, in terms of latency, strictly better than the other protocols. This remains true even if we ignore the third column, which is specific to our algorithm.

Our Generic Broadcast protocol uses a new Consensus algorithm. If the leader is correct and does not change, this algorithm decides in one communication step if all proposals are the same, and in two steps otherwise. In the literature, algorithms have been proposed that satisfy only the first condition [2], only the second condition [3,9,11,17], or both but the first only for the privileged value [6]. To the best of our knowledge, the Consensus algorithm presented in this paper is the first to meet both conditions fully.

The paper is structured in the following way. Section 2 introduces our asynchronous system model, and gives precise definitions of Consensus, Atomic Broadcast, and Generic Broadcast. Sections 3 and 4 describe our Optimistic

Generic Broadcast algorithm. Section 5 presents the implementation of One-Two Consensus. Finally, Section 6 shows how to implement infinitely many Consensus instances at the same time, which is used by our Generic Broadcast algorithm. Correctness of the presented algorithms is only argued informally; for rigorous proofs, see the extended version of this paper [18].

2   System Model

Our system model consists of n processes, out of which at most f can fail by crashing. We assume that less than a third of the processes are faulty $(n > 3f)$. Processes communicate through asynchronous reliable channels. In other words, there is no time limit on message transmission time, and messages between correct processes never get lost.

We assume that each process is equipped with an unreliable leader oracle Ω, which eventually outputs the same correct leader at all correct processes. The extended version of this paper [18] shows that Ω is the weakest failure detector that allows us solve (Optimistic) Generic Broadcast in an asynchronous system, provided at least one pair of messages conflict. In the special case when no messages conflict, Generic Broadcast becomes identical to Uniform Reliable Broadcast [8].

In the Consensus problem, processes submit proposals and are required to eventually agree on one of them. Formally, we require the following properties:

Uniform Validity. If a process decides on x, then some process proposed x.
Uniform Agreement. No two processes decide differently.
Termination. If all correct processes propose, then they eventually decide.

In Atomic Broadcast, processes broadcast messages, which are delivered by all processes in the same order. Formally [5],

Validity. If a correct process broadcasts a message m, then all correct processes will eventually deliver m.
Uniform Agreement. If a process delivers a message m, then all correct processes eventually deliver m.
Uniform Integrity. For any message m, every process delivers m at most once, and only if m was previously broadcast.
Uniform Total Order. If some process delivers message m' after message m, then every process delivers m' only after it has delivered m.

Generic Broadcast is identical to Atomic Broadcast, except that only conflicting messages must be delivered in the same order:

Uniform Partial Order. If some process delivers message m' after message m conflicting with m', then every process delivers m' only after it has delivered m.

The notion of conflict is captured by a binary conflict relation on the set of all possible messages, which is a parameter of the problem [16]. For example, one might consider a relation on *read* and *write* requests in which all pairs of messages conflict unless both of them are *reads*. We assume that the conflict relation and therefore the (infinite) set of all possible messages are both known to all processes in advance.

3   Basic Generic Broadcast Algorithm

We say that a run is *stable* if the (correct) leader output by the Ω failure detector is the same at all correct processes and never changes. In this section, we will present a simplified version of our Generic Broadcast algorithm, which is correct in stable runs with correct senders but might not make progress in other runs. In Section 4, we will show how to extend this algorithm to obtain a fully correct Generic Broadcast implementation.

3.1   Partial Order on Messages

Our algorithm operates by making processes agree on the delivery order of each pair of conflicting messages. More precisely, processes cooperate in building a partial order "$\rightarrow$" on conflicting messages and deliver messages in any order consistent with this partial order. For any two messages m and m', relation $m \rightarrow m'$ requires m to be delivered before m'. Since non-conflicting messages can be delivered in any order, the relation "$\rightarrow$" is defined only for pairs of messages $\{m, m'\}$ that conflict. For these, we expect that eventually either $m \rightarrow m'$ or $m' \rightarrow m$.

The following diagram shows an example with four messages. All pairs of messages conflict, except for m_2 and m_3, which can be delivered in different orders by different processes.

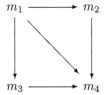   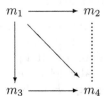

Processes deliver messages in any order consistent with the partial order "$\rightarrow$". In the first example, "$\rightarrow$" is defined for all pairs of conflicting messages. Processes can deliver the four messages in one of two orders m_1, m_2, m_3, m_4 or m_1, m_3, m_2, m_4, both consistent with "$\rightarrow$". Messages m_2 and m_3 can be delivered in different orders by different processes; this does not violate the Partial Order property because these messages do not conflict.

In the second example, the relation between conflicting messages m_2 and m_4 is not known (yet). As a result, none of them can be delivered. However, whatever the order of m_2 and m_4 will be, one of the orders: m_1, m_3, m_2, m_4 and m_1, m_3, m_4, m_2 will be consistent with "$\rightarrow$". These two orders share a common prefix m_1, m_3, so messages m_1 and m_3 can be delivered straight away.

```
1   when receive(m) do
2       for all possible non-received messages m' conflicting with m do
3           first_{m,m'}.propose(m)
4   when first_{m,m'}.decide(m) do
5       set m → m'
6   when m is undelivered and
7           m → m' for all undelivered messages m' conflicting with m do
8       deliver(m)
```

Fig. 2. Basic Generic Broadcast algorithm

Another way of looking at the delivery process is realizing that m_1 can be delivered because $m_1 \to m$ for all $m \neq m_1$. After m_1 has been delivered, we can deliver m_3 because $m_3 \to m$ for all undelivered m's conflicting with m_3. Conflicting messages m_2 and m_4 will be delivered only when their order is known.

3.2   Basic Algorithm

In our algorithm, processes agree on the partial order "$\to$" by using Consensus to agree on the delivery order of every pair of conflicting messages. In other words, for each *unordered* pair $\{m, m'\}$ of conflicting messages, we use a separate instance of Consensus. In each such instance $first_{m,m'}$, each process p proposes the message m or m' that arrived at p first.

The resulting partial order is built based on decisions of the Consensus instances $first_{m,m'}$. If the instance decides on m, then m is deemed to be the first message of the two ($m \to m'$). Hence, if the instance $first_{m,m'} = first_{m',m}$ decides on m', then $m' \to m$. Messages are delivered in an order consistent with "$\to$". Section 4 will explain why cycles do not appear in stable runs, and explain how to deal with them in other runs.

The basic algorithm is shown in Fig. 2. Senders broadcast their messages using ordinary broadcast. When a process receives a message m, it proposes m to instances $first_{m,m'}$ for all messages m' conflicting with m that have not been received (yet). In other words, the process proposes m to precede all such messages m' in the delivery order. An undelivered message m is delivered once $m \to m'$ holds for all possible undelivered messages m' conflicting with m.

Since the set of all messages is usually infinite, the $receive(m)$ action involves executing infinitely many instances of Consensus. Section 6 will show how to accomplish this with finite resources. Until then, we will stick with the "infinite" version of the algorithm because it is easier to understand.

The algorithm satisfies Uniform Integrity and Uniform Partial Order. For the former, we assume the existence of an artificial message $\bot$, which is never sent and conflicts with all other messages. Therefore, delivering any message m requires $m \to \bot$, which means that some process must have proposed m to $first_{m,\bot}$, so some process must have broadcast m.

To prove Uniform Partial Order, we will assume, to derive a contradiction, that conflicting messages m and m' are delivered in different orders at different processes. This would mean that $m \to m'$ at one of the processes, and $m' \to m$ at another, which is impossible by the Uniform Agreement property of the underlying Consensus.

3.3 Delivery Latency

In this section, we will explain why, in stable runs, the basic algorithm delivers all messages in three communication steps. We will also see that if, in addition, all conflicting messages arrive at all correct processes in the same order, then all these messages are delivered in two communication steps.

We assume that the underlying Consensus algorithm satisfies the following two properties:

C1: In stable runs in which all correct processes propose the same value, the decision is made one communication step after all correct processes proposed.

C2: In stable runs, all correct processes decide on the value proposed by the leader two communication steps after the leader proposed (even if other processes have not proposed).

Section 5 presents a Consensus algorithm with these properties.

Any message broadcast by a correct process is received by the leader in one communication step. Property **C2** ensures that the order is decided two communication steps later, giving three communication steps in total for delivery latency. If all correct processes receive conflicting messages in the same order, then they propose the same order to Consensus instances. Therefore, Property **C1** implies that decision will be made in one communication step, giving two communication steps in total for delivery latency.

4   Full Generic Broadcast Algorithm

Before presenting the full version of the algorithm, we will highlight two main problems with the basic version in unstable runs.

4.1   Cycles

Cycles in the relation "$\to$" built by the basic algorithm lead to a deadlock. In stable runs, cycles do not appear because Property **C2** ensures that "$\to$" reflects the linear order of message reception at the leader. In unstable runs, however, different parts of the "$\to$" relation might have been proposed by different processes.

As an example, consider a system with three processes p_1, p_2, p_3. Each of these processes receives three messages m_1, m_2, m_3 in a different order:

$$p_1 : m_1, m_2, m_3 \qquad \text{executes } first_{m_1, m_2}.propose(m_1),$$
$$p_2 : m_2, m_3, m_1 \qquad \text{executes } first_{m_2, m_3}.propose(m_2),$$
$$p_3 : m_3, m_1, m_2 \qquad \text{executes } first_{m_3, m_1}.propose(m_3).$$

If all of the above proposals become decisions, then the cycle

$$m_1 \to m_2 \to m_3 \to m_1$$

will be formed, and as a result none of these messages will ever be delivered.

To cope with cycles, we introduce the notion of blocked messages. We say that a message is *blocked* if it belongs to a cycle, or it is a successor of a blocked message. In our example, all three messages are blocked, and any message m_4 with, say, $m_2 \to m_4$ would be blocked as well. Obviously, blocked messages will never be delivered by the basic algorithm. In the full version of the algorithm, we will sometimes deliver blocked messages to break cycles and avoid deadlocks.

4.2 Faulty Senders

Another problem with the basic algorithm are faulty senders. If a sender crashes, then its messages might reach only a subset of the correct processes. For Consensus instances, this means that not all the correct processes propose, and therefore it can happen that only some of the correct processes decide. Since these decisions are directly related to message deliveries, the Uniform Agreement property might be violated.

A common solution to this problem is to make processes rebroadcast every received message, thereby implementing Non-Uniform Reliable Broadcast [7]. Thus, if a correct process receives a message, then all correct processes will. As a result, all correct processes will propose, decide, and deliver the message.

Therefore, to ensure Uniform Agreement, it is sufficient to guarantee that every delivered message has been received by at least one correct process. For this reason we introduce the notion of a process "seeing" a message. We say that a process *sees* a message m if it has received, in some instance of Consensus, a message containing m. Recall that a message is delivered only if at least one Consensus instance decided on it. Since the decision of any Consensus instance must have been seen by at least one *correct* process [18], every delivered message has been seen by a correct process, which is exactly what we need.

The problem discussed here could also be solved by making the senders use Uniform Reliable Broadcast [8]. This abstraction, however, requires two communication steps, which would slow our algorithm down by one step.

4.3 Algorithm

Fig. 3 shows the full version of our algorithm. To resolve cycles and be able to deliver blocked messages, we use an auxiliary Atomic Broadcast protocol. The latency of this Atomic Broadcast protocol affects only unstable runs because cycles cannot appear in stable ones.

A process reacts only to messages m received for the first time. It rebroadcasts m to other processes using both ordinary broadcast and also Atomic Broadcast. The rationale behind the former is to ensure that if one correct process receives a message, then eventually all correct processes will. As mentioned before,

```
1    when receive(m) do
2      if m is received for the first time then
3        broadcast(m)
4        abcast(m)
5        for all possible non-received messages m' conflicting with m do
6          first_{m,m'}.propose(m)
7    when see(m) do
8      receive(m)
9    when first_{m,m'}.decide(m) do
10     set m → m'
11   when m is undelivered and
12     m → m' for all undelivered messages m' conflicting with m do
13     deliver₁(m)
14   task cycle-resolution is
15     repeat forever
16       wait until abdeliver(m)
17       see(m)
18       wait until m has been delivered or
19               all undelivered messages conflicting with m are blocked
20       if m has not been delivered yet then
21         deliver₂(m)
```

Fig. 3. Full Generic Broadcast algorithm

Atomic Broadcast is used to resolve cycles. Finally, as in the basic version, the process executes $first_{m,m'}.propose(m)$ for all possible messages m' conflicting with m that were not received before m. The order "$\rightarrow$" is constructed in the same way as in the basic version.

In the full version, messages can be delivered either normally or during cycle resolution. To distinguish these two kinds of deliveries, we call the former 1-delivery, and the latter 2-delivery. Messages are 1-delivered in exactly the same way as in the basic version.

If a process has seen a message, it behaves as if it had received it. The decision of any Consensus instance must have been seen by at least one *correct* process. Therefore, any 1-delivered message has been seen by a correct process, who broadcast it, so that all correct processes would eventually receive that message and propose it to some Consensus instances. This property is vital for Uniform Agreement.

The cycle resolution task loops over messages delivered by the underlying Atomic Broadcast protocol. For each such message m, the task executes $see(m)$ and waits until one of the two conditions holds. If m has already been delivered, then the loop goes to the next iteration. Otherwise, if all undelivered messages conflicting with m are blocked, then m is delivered. The rationale behind this strategy is that, since none of the blocked messages can be 1-delivered, it is safe to deliver m, thereby, possibly, breaking the cycle. The use of Atomic Broadcast ensures that the messages m chosen to break cycles are the same at different processes.

To show that lines 18–19 always terminate, we must prove that all never-blocked messages m' conflicting with m will eventually be delivered. Since m' is not blocked, the graph of paths $m' \leftarrow m_1 \leftarrow \cdots \leftarrow m_k$ of undelivered messages does not contain cycles, and forms a tree rooted at m'. The leaves of this tree will be successively 1-delivered, resulting eventually in 1-delivery of m'.

4.4   Example

Both m_1 and m_3 can be 1-delivered because the only message conflicting with them (m_2) is their successor. Messages m_1 and m_3 can be delivered in any order; this does not violate Partial Order because they do not conflict. Assume that, at the same time, the *cycle-resolution* task abdelivers m_1. Since the only message conflicting with it (m_2) is blocked by the cycle $m_2 \rightarrow m_4 \rightarrow m_5 \rightarrow m_2$, message m_1 is 2-delivered if it has not been 1-delivered yet.

After m_1 and m_3 have been delivered, no other message can be 1-delivered, because all messages are blocked. If now the cycle resolution task abdelivers m_2, then since all undelivered messages conflicting with it (m_4, m_5) are blocked, m_2 is 2-delivered. This delivery breaks the cycle, and now all undelivered messages conflicting with m_4 (i.e., m_5 and m_6) are its successors, so m_4 is 1-delivered. Conflicting messages m_5 and m_6 cannot be delivered until the processes agree on their order. If, for example, $m_5 \rightarrow m_6$, then message m_5 will be 1-delivered, followed by m_6.

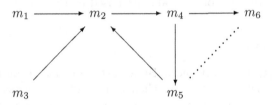

5   One-Two Consensus

Our Generic Broadcast algorithm uses One-Two Consensus shown in Fig. 4. This algorithm uses three underlying Consensus instances: 1, 2, and L. When a process p proposes x, it first broadcasts the pair (x, p), and then uses instance 1 to propose x, instance 2 to propose the pair (x, p), and instance L to propose the current output of its leader oracle Ω. Instances 1 and L make a decision in one communication step, provided that all correct processes propose the same value. We achieve this by using the algorithm by Brasileiro et al. [2], which requires $n > 3f$. Instance 2 decides in two communication steps, however, it requires only the correct leader to have proposed. This can be implemented with the Paxos algorithm [11].

```
1   when propose(x) by process p do
2       broadcast(x, p)
3       propose₁(x)
4       propose₂(x, p)
5       proposeₗ(l) where l is the leader output by Ω

6   task decide at process p is
7       wait until decideₗ(l)
8       wait until one of the conditions is true and decide on x
9           condition 1: decide₁(x) and receive(x, l)
10          condition 2: decide₂(x, l)
11          condition 3: decide₁(x) and decide₂(y, q) with q ≠ l
```

Fig. 4. One-Two Consensus

When process p wants to decide, it first waits until instance L decides on some leader l. In stable runs, in which the output of Ω is the same at all correct processes, this should happen within one communication step. Then, process p waits until one of the three conditions in Fig. 4 holds. The first two conditions correspond to instances 1 and 2 deciding on the value proposed by the leader. If all correct processes propose the same value, then the first condition will hold in one communication step. If the leader is correct, then the second condition will hold in two communication steps. The third condition is a fall-back designed for unstable runs; processes adopt the decision from instance 1, provided that instance 2 did not decide on the value proposed by the leader.

5.1   Thriftiness

Aguilera et al. [1] define a Generic Broadcast algorithm to be *thrifty* if it uses the underlying oracle (here Ω) only when some conflicting messages are received. Our algorithm is not thrifty; the one-two step Consensus described above uses Ω in all cases. To make our algorithm thrifty, we need a Consensus algorithm that, if all correct processes propose the same value, decides in one step, *without* using Ω. This property is a stronger version of **C1**, which we call **C1**[*].

The algorithm by Brasileiro et al. [2] satisfies **C1**[*]; it decides in one step if all correct processes propose the same value, without using Ω, otherwise it starts an underlying Consensus algorithm. This means that it does not satisfy **C2**; if correct processes propose different values, it may take three steps to decide, instead of two. For our Optimistic Generic Broadcast algorithm this means four steps in general stable runs instead of three. In terms of latency, such an algorithm is still strictly better than both Generic Broadcast [1,13,16] and Optimistic Atomic Broadcast [14], however might be slower than the one proposed by Chandra and Toueg [3] (Fig. 1).

Guerraoui and Raynal [6] proved that no Consensus algorithm based on Ω can be both configuration-efficient and oracle-efficient, which in our case implies

---

1   $\mathcal{I}$ is the family of disjoint sets of virtual instances, initially empty

2   **when** receive event e tagged with the set I_e **do**

3   **for each** $I \in \mathcal{I}$ **do**

4   split I into $I \cap I_e$ and $I \setminus I_e$

5   create a new physical instance A_I for $I = I_e \setminus \bigcup \mathcal{I}$, and add I to $\mathcal{I}$

6   eliminate empty sets from $\mathcal{I}$

7   **for each** $I \in \mathcal{I}$ **do**

8   **if** $I \cap I_e \neq \emptyset$ **then**

9   send the event e to instance A_I

Fig. 5. Emulating infinitely many virtual instances

that Properties $\mathbf{C1}^*$ and $\mathbf{C2}$ cannot hold at the same time. This observation makes us conjecture that no thrifty Generic Broadcast algorithm can achieve the latencies from the bottom row in Fig. 1.

The underlying Atomic Broadcast protocol, employed by our algorithm to break cycles, also uses Ω [3]. However, in the absence of conflicting messages, cycles cannot be created. Therefore, instead of processes performing $abcast(m)$ immediately after receiving m (as in Fig. 3), they can defer it until they have received some conflicting messages. This modification prevents the algorithm from using Atomic Broadcast if no conflicting messages are received.

6   Handling Infinitely Many Instances

Our Generic Broadcast algorithm uses infinitely many Consensus instances. This section explains how to implement an infinite number of *virtual instances* of a distributed algorithm using only finitely many *physical instances* at every process. As we will see, this is possible provided that there are only finitely many *different* virtual instances. For example, in our Generic Broadcast algorithm from Fig. 3, a process proposes *the same* message m to an infinite number of instances of Consensus.

Let us start with finitely many virtual instances, and denote these by i_1, $i_2, \ldots, i_k$. The usual approach is to tag any event (a message or a function call) with the identifier of the instance. Each process runs k physical instances of the algorithm. Every event tagged with i_k is directed to the k-th instance, and every event produced by the k-th instance is tagged with i_k. In this case, virtual and physical instances are the same, so this method can be used only with finitely many virtual instances.

To implement an infinite number of virtual instances, some of them must share a single physical instance. Algorithm in Fig. 5 maintains a family $\mathcal{I}$ of disjoint sets of virtual instances, initially empty. Each element $I \in \mathcal{I}$ is a set of virtual instances that share a single physical instance denoted as A_I. All events generated by A_I are tagged with the set I.

When an event tagged with a set of virtual instances I_e arrives, the process does the following. First, if some virtual instances sharing the same physical instance start to differ, the physical instance is cloned. This is done by splitting elements $I \in \mathcal{I}$ into $I \cap I_e$ and $I \setminus I_e$, so that every element of $\mathcal{I}$ is either a subset of I_e or disjoint with it. When such a split happens, the physical instance A_I is replaced with two new instances $A_{I \cap I_e}$ and $A_{I \setminus I_e}$, both identical to A_I. Also, a new physical instance is created for $I_e \setminus \bigcup \mathcal{I}$ to ensure that every virtual instance corresponds to some physical instance; in other words, we want to make sure that for each $i \in I_e$ there is $I \in \mathcal{I}$ with $i \in I$. Finally, the event is sent to all physical instances corresponding to any virtual instances in I_e.

6.1   Representing Sets

The above method can be used to execute an infinite number of Consensus instances at the same time, provided that we can represent infinite sets of instances in a finite form. For use in the algorithm from Fig. 5, the families of representable sets must be closed under subtraction and intersection. Closeness under set union is not necessary; $I_e \setminus \bigcup \mathcal{I}$ can be computed by iteratively subtracting elements of $\mathcal{I}$ from I_e. In this section, we will briefly present such representations for some families of sets useful in our Generic Broadcast algorithm.

Border sets. Finite sets can be trivially represented by listing their elements. The family of *border sets* contains all sets that are either finite (F) or are complements of finite sets ($\overline{F}$). For example, the set $\overline{\{m_1, m_2\}}$ consists of all messages except for m_1 and m_2. The representation of a border set consists of the finite set F and a flag indicating whether the set is F or $\overline{F}$. The family of border sets is closed under negation and intersection (which implies subtraction):

$$F_1 \cap F_2 = F_1 \cap F_2, \qquad\qquad F_1 \cap \overline{F_2} = F_1 \setminus F_2,$$
$$\overline{F_1} \cap F_2 = F_2 \setminus F_1, \qquad\qquad \overline{F_1} \cap \overline{F_2} = \overline{F_1 \cup F_2}.$$

M-sets. How can we use border sets to represent sets such as "the set of all non-received messages conflicting with m"? Of course, that depends on the conflict relation. It is often the case that messages can be divided into a small number of categories (e.g., "read" and "write"), such that conflict properties of messages are determined by the categories they belong to. Consider a system with k categories $C_1, \ldots, C_k$, where C_i is the set of all messages in the i-th category. For any border sets $B_1, \ldots, B_k$ satisfying $B_i \subseteq C_i$, we define a *m-set*

$$\langle B_1, \ldots, B_k \rangle = B_1 \cup \cdots \cup B_k$$

to be the set containing all messages from sets $B_1, B_2, \ldots, B_k$.

As an example consider a system with two categories: "read" and "write"; any two requests conflict unless they are both reads. Assume that requests w_1, w_2, r_1, and r_2 have been received. The set of all non-received requests conflicting with r_2 is $\langle \emptyset, \overline{\{w_1, w_2\}} \rangle$, that is, no read requests and all possible write requests except for w_1 and w_2.

The family of m-sets is closed under subtraction and intersection:

$$\langle B_1, \ldots, B_k \rangle \cap \langle B_1', \ldots, B_k' \rangle = \langle B_1 \cap B_1', \ldots, B_k \cap B_k' \rangle,$$
$$\langle B_1, \ldots, B_k \rangle \setminus \langle B_1', \ldots, B_k' \rangle = \langle B_1 \setminus B_1', \ldots, B_k \setminus B_k' \rangle.$$

Sets of message pairs. In our Generic Broadcast algorithm, each Consensus instance is identified by an unordered pair of messages. By $\{m, M\}$ we denote the set of pairs containing m and one element of the m-set M:

$$\{m, M\} = \{\, \{m, m'\} : m' \in M \,\}$$

For example, M can be the set of all possible non-received messages m' conflicting with a given message m. Consider the $receive(m)$ routine from our Generic Broadcast algorithm in Fig. 3. We can replace infinitely many invocations of $first_{m,m'}.propose(m)$ with a single $first_{m,M}.propose(m)$. The family of sets $\{m, M\}$ can be used in the algorithm from Fig. 5 because it is closed under intersection and subtraction (we assume $m \neq m'$):

$$\{m, M\} \cap \{m, M'\} = \{m, M \cap M'\},$$
$$\{m, M\} \setminus \{m, M'\} = \{m, M \setminus M'\},$$
$$\{m, M\} \cap \{m', M'\} = \begin{cases} \{m, \{m'\}\} & \text{if } m \in M' \text{ and } m' \in M, \\ \{m, \emptyset\} & \text{otherwise,} \end{cases}$$
$$\{m, M\} \setminus \{m', M'\} = \begin{cases} \{m, M \setminus \{m'\}\} & \text{if } m \in M' \text{ and } m' \in M, \\ \{m, M\} & \text{otherwise.} \end{cases}$$

7   Conclusion

We presented a new algorithm that solves the Generic Broadcast problem, in which conflicting messages must be delivered in the same order by all processes. In stable runs, our algorithm delivers messages in three communication steps. If all conflicting messages are received by all correct processes in the same order, then all messages are delivered within two communication steps. In terms of latency degree [17], this algorithm is strictly better than any proposed so far [1,3,13,14,16], and matches several lower bounds [10,15,16]. Although we implicitly assumed that only the main n processes are allowed to broadcast messages, our model can easily be extended to allow external processes to broadcast as well.

In our algorithm, for each pair of conflicting messages, processes use Consensus to agree on their order. Messages are delivered in any order consistent with the agreed partial order. In unstable runs, circular dependencies can occur, and these are broken using Atomic Broadcast. The abstract formulation of the algorithm uses infinitely many instances of Consensus at the same time. Since there are only finitely many *different* instances, this can be emulated with finite resources, as we show in this paper. The new underlying Consensus algorithm uses one-step [2] and two-step [11] algorithms to decide in one communication step if all proposals are the same, and in two otherwise (in stable runs).

Although our Generic Broadcast algorithm is optimal in terms of latency degree, its message and computation complexities may still be prohibitive. Therefore, we see our contribution in the lower-bound matching algorithm. Further research will be required to optimize it for practical applications.

References

1. Marcos Kawazoe Aguilera, Carole Delporte-Gallet, Hugues Fauconnier, and Sam Toueg. Thrifty Generic Broadcast. *Lecture Notes in Computer Science*, 1914: 268–282, 2000.
2. Francisco Brasileiro, Fabíola Greve, Achour Mostefaoui, and Michel Raynal. Consensus in one communication step. *Lecture Notes in Computer Science*, 2127:42–50, 2001.
3. Tushar Deepak Chandra and Sam Toueg. Unreliable failure detectors for reliable distributed systems. *Journal of the ACM*, 43(2):225–267, 1996.
4. Bernadette Charron-Bost and André Schiper. Uniform Consensus is harder than Consensus. Technical Report DSC/2000/028, Swiss Federal Institute of Technology (EPFL), Lausanne, Switzerland, May 2000.
5. Xavier Défago, André Schiper, and Péter Urbán. Total order broadcast and multicast algorithms: Taxonomy and survey. *ACM Computing Surveys*, 36(4):372–421, 2004.
6. Rachid Guerraoui and Michel Raynal. The information structure of indulgent Consensus. Technical Report PI-1531, IRISA, April, 2003.
7. Vassos Hadzilacos and Sam Toueg. Fault-tolerant broadcast and related problems. In Sape Mullender, editor, *Distributed Systems*, chapter 5, pages 97–146. ACM Press, New York, 2nd edition, 1993.
8. Vassos Hadzilacos and Sam Toueg. A modular approach to fault-tolerant broadcasts and related problems. Technical Report TR94-1425, 1994.
9. Michel Hurfin and Michel Raynal. A simple and fast asynchronous consensus protocol based on a weak failure detector. *Distributed Computing*, 12(4):209–223, 1999.
10. Idit Keidar and Sergio Rajsbaum. On the cost of fault-tolerant Consensus when there are no faults. *ACM SIGACT News*, 32, 2001.
11. Leslie Lamport. Paxos made simple. *ACM SIGACT News*, 32(4):18–25, December 2001.
12. Leslie Lamport. Lower bounds on Consensus. Unpublished note, March 2002.
13. Fernando Pedone and André Schiper. Handling message semantics with Generic Broadcast protocols. *Distributed Computing*, 15(2):97–107, 2002.
14. Fernando Pedone and André Schiper. Optimistic Atomic Broadcast: a pragmatic viewpoint. *Theoretical Computer Science*, 291(1):79–101, 2003.
15. Fernando Pedone and André Schiper. On the inherent cost of Generic Broadcast. Technical Report IC/2004/46, Swiss Federal Institute of Technology (EPFL), May 2004.
16. Fernando Pedone and André Schiper. Generic Broadcast. In *Proceedings of the 13th International Symposium on Distributed Computing (DISC'99)*, 1999.

17. André Schiper. Early Consensus in an asynchronous system with a weak failure detector. *Distributed Computing*, 10(3):149–157, April 1997.
18. Piotr Zieliński. Optimistic Generic Broadcast. Technical Report 638, Computer Laboratory, University of Cambridge, July 2005. `http://www.cl.cam.ac.uk/TechReports/UCAM-CL-TR-638.html`.

Space and Step Complexity Efficient Adaptive Collect

Yehuda Afek and Yaron De Levie

School of Computer Science,
Tel-Aviv University, Israel 69978

Abstract. Space and step complexity efficient deterministic adaptive to total contention collect algorithms are presented. One of them has an optimal $O(k)$ step and $O(n)$ space complexities, but restrict the processes identifiers size to $O(n)$. Where n is the total number of processes in the system and k is the total contention, the total number of processes active during the execution. Unrestricting the name space increases the space complexity to $O(n^2)$ leaving the step complexity at $O(k)$. To date all deterministic adaptive collect algorithms that we are aware of are either nearly quadratic in their step complexity or their memory overhead is exponential in n.

1 Introduction

In most asynchronous read/write shared memory algorithms each of n processes has its own dedicated register into which it writes new information it has. To collect the information written by others a process reads all the other registers. Obviously, this implementation of a collect operation is wait-free but not adaptive. An implementation of a high level operation is adaptive if the step complexity of the operation is a function of the actual number of processes active rather than n the total number of processes in the system. Three measures of the number of active processes have been defined [AAF+99], *total contention*, *interval contention*, and *point contention*. In an algorithm that is adaptive to *total contention* the step complexity of a high level operation is a function only of the *total number of different processes that have been active in the algorithm execution before this operation terminates*[1].

Following [AKWW] the focus of this paper are adaptive to total contention collect algorithms that are efficient both in space and step complexities. To date all the deterministic adaptive collect algorithms that we are aware of [AKWW, AFG02, MA95, AF03, AST99] are either exponential in space complexity or nearly quadratic in the step complexity (see Table 1).

---

[1] In *interval contention* the step complexity of a high level operation is a function only of the *total number of different processes that are active during the specific operation sub-execution interval*. In *point contention* the step complexity of a high level operation is a function only of the *maximum number of different processes that are simultaneously active at some point during the operation sub-execution interval*.

P. Fraigniaud (Ed.): DISC 2005, LNCS 3724, pp. 384–398, 2005.

In this paper *deterministic* collect algorithms are presented. The first is an $O(n^3)$ space $O(k)$ adaptive step complexity algorithm (§ 4.1). Where n is the total number of processes in the system, k is the total contention of an operation and $\{1 \ldots N\}$ is the processes identifiers name space. The second algorithm (§ 4.2) reduces the space complexity to $O(n)$ for the price of increasing the step complexity to $O(k \log \log k)$ and restricting the identifiers size of processes to $O(n)$ (i.e., $N = O(n)$). The $O(k)$ steps $O(n)$ space algorithm (§ 4.3) is an extension of the second algorithm. Finally we remove the restriction on the name space from the third algorithm and obtain an $O(n^2)$ space and $O(k)$ step complexity unrestricted name space collect algorithm (also in § 4.3).

Table 1. Results summary. Section 5 algorithms are slightly less efficient than Subsection 4.3 algorithm but much simpler.

Ref & assumptions	Step complexity		Space complexity
	1-st Store by a process	Collect	
[AFG02] *Unrestricted*	$O(k)$	$O(k)$	$O(2^n)$
[AKWW] *Unrestricted*	$O(k/\delta)$	$O(k^2/\delta \log n)$	$O(n^{2+\delta})$
Subsection 4.3 $N = O(n)$	$O(\min(k, n^{3/8}))$	$O(k)$	$O(n)$
Subsection 4.3 *Unrestricted*	$O(k)$	$O(k)$	$O(n^2)$
Section 5 $N = O(n)$	$O(\min(k, \sqrt{n}))$	*if* $(k \leq n^{1/3})$ *then* $O(k)$ *else* $O(\min(n, k \log k))$	$O(n)$
Section 5 *Unrestricted*	$O(k)$	*if* $(k \leq n^{2/3})$ *then* $O(k)$ *else* $O(k \log k)$	$O(n^2)$
[AKWW] *Randomized* $N = O(n)$	$O(k)$	$O(k)$	$O(n^{1.5})$

In [AKWW], Attiya et al. provided a *randomized* $O(n^{1.5})$ space collect algorithm whose expected step complexity is $O(k)$ while assuming that N is of size $O(n)$. (This assumption could be relaxed also in this *randomized* algorithm by using the Moir-Anderson [MA95, AF98] renaming algorithm, resulting in a $O(n^2)$ space complexity and worst case step complexity of $O(k^4)$ (instead of $O(k^2)$), but remaining with linear expected step complexity.)

In [AFK04] Attiya, Fich and Kaplan prove that any $O(f(k))$-adaptive to total contention one-shot collect algorithm requires at least $\Omega(f^{-1}(n))$ multi-writer registers. That is, if the adaptive step complexity is $O(k)$ then the algorithm requires at least $\Omega(n)$ multi-writer registers. Hence, the deterministic algorithms presented in [AKWW, AFG02] still leave a large gap between the corresponding space complexity upper and lower bounds. In this paper we close the gap when the identifiers size of processes is restricted to $O(n)$ ($N = O(n)$), and the gap has been substantially reduced when N is unrestricted.

In [AF03, AST99] collect algorithms that adapt to point contention are given. Being point contention adaptive these algorithms assume that the register size is $O(n)$ times larger than the register size in the algorithms discussed above.

All algorithms in this paper use a new collect building block, called *Telescopic Watermark Collect* (*TWC*), that has the following two properties: $O(N^{1.5})$ space complexity, and $O(k)$ step complexity if the identifier size of an incoming process is at most quadratic in the number of processes that have accessed the building block so far. To derive from this collect object the first algorithm, which is an $O(n^3)$ space, $O(k)$ steps collect, processes in their first *store* operation go through an adaptive (also in the output name space) MA-renaming ($n \times n$)-matrix (see Figure 2(b))). Then, the new *id* a process obtains from the MA-renaming is used as the *id* with which the process performs a *store* operation in a TWC in which $N_{TWC} = n^2$ (i.e., of (n^3) space). Notice that in this algorithm there is no restriction on the identifiers size of participating processes.

To reduce the space complexity of this algorithm we use a smaller size TWC object and a smaller size MA-renaming matrix. However, such smaller structures may not have room for all n processes. That is, when k the total number of processes that participate in the collect is large enough, processes may fail to obtain a new id from the MA-renaming, or may not fit into the smaller TWC structure. For such processes we either apply recursive divide and conquer or, add a backup structure whose step complexity may be worse but is used only when it is guaranteed that k is above a certain threshold, such as $k > n^{1/4}$ or $n^{1/3}$ and spending that many steps would not hurt the adaptive-linearity of the algorithm.

The model used in the paper is given in Section 2. Preliminary building blocks used in our algorithms are described in Section 3. The linear step linear space algorithm is constructed in Section 4 via a sequence of constructions. In Section 5 we present two additional algorithms with a much simpler presentation and space complexities as efficient as the above, but with a slightly less efficient step complexity ($k \log k$ instead of k). Finally in Section 6 concluding remarks are provided. Due to space limitation some proofs and the code have been omitted from this extended abstract and can be found at [AD].

2   Model

Following [AFG02, AKWW], here is a brief description of the model. We use the standard asynchronous shared-memory model of computation. A system consists of n processes, $p_1, ..., p_n$, communicating by reading and writing to atomic shared registers. Each process has a unique identifier from the name space $\{1, ..., N\}$.

An algorithm is $f(k)$ adaptive to total contention if there is a non-decreasing function f such that the step complexity of each of its operations is $O(f(k))$, where k is the total number of different processes that have been active since the beginning of the algorithm execution up to the end of the operation execution.

A *collect algorithm* provides two operations *store* and *collect*. A *store(val)* operation by process p_i sets *val* to be the latest value for p_i. A *collect* operation returns a view, a set of values, one for each processor such that, $V[p_i]$ the value for process p_i, is the last value stored by p_i before the *collect* has started or concurrently with the *collect* operation. And the view returned by a *collect* operation C_l that completely follows another *collect* operation C_e is at least as updated as C_e. That is each $V[p_i]$ of C_l is the same or a later value that was written by p_i.

3   Algorithms Preliminaries and Building Blocks

As described in the Introduction each of our algorithms is constructed from a collection of building blocks (structures). In its first *store* operation a process traverses a sequence of these structures until it captures a node in one of the structures and uses the register associated with that node as its dedicated register for the rest of the algorithm execution. In each subsequent invocation of *store* a process updates directly the register it has captured in the first invocation. Therefore, in the following algorithms we mostly describe and analyze the *capture* and *collect* operations. In a *collect* operation a process scans the relevant portions of the data structures that were traversed during the preceding store operations, and collects the information found in all the captured registers.

In all our algorithms, in its first invocation of a *store* operation a process goes (in the *capture* procedure) through several structures and may go through a renaming process several times. Each time taking the previously obtained *id* and generating a newer *id* either by going through a renaming algorithm or by some other arithmetics. In all these algorithms when process p_j starts the first *store* operation it assigns its original *id* into a variable called $name_j$. As it renames itself the *id* in id_j may change while going from one building block to the next, but $name_j$ always holds the original name of the process. In each building block the parameter N denotes the largest *id* that any process may access this building block with. The parameter n denotes the maximum number of processes that may access the object or building block.

A key building block used in all our algorithms is the *Telescopic Watermark Collect* object (TWC). In this section we provide a step wise construction of the Telescopic Watermark object from smaller building blocks, which are: *Watermark Collect* (WC), and *Divided Watermark Collect* (DWC).

Notation:

- A process p_j accesses each of the building blocks WC, DWC, and TWC with input parameters $name_j$ and id_j. Each of these building blocks takes a parameter N, e.g., $TWC(N)$, which is the largest *id* a process may access this building block with. Copies of the building block are later generated with different values of N.
- Each of the collect algorithms in Sections 4 and 5 is denoted by (*steps, space*) − *Collect*, indicating this algorithm has *steps* step complexity and

space space complexity. E.g., (k, n^2)-Collect denotes an $O(k)$ step $O(n^2)$ space adaptive collect algorithm.

3.1   Watermark Collect(N)

Assume that magically we have an adaptive renaming oracle that renames the processes as they access it with numbers in the range $1, \ldots, f(k)$ where k is the total number of processes that have showed up so far, e.g., $f(k) = 2k - 1$. Then if f is linear, a (n, k)-Collect algorithm is simple to obtain by giving each process a register in an $O(n)$ size array of registers indexed by the new *id* (call it *index*) a process has obtained. To ensure that a *collect* operation scans only the "occupied" portion of the array we "watermark" the array with a corresponding array of flags. In its first *store* operation a process sets all the flags in the array from the entry that corresponds to the register it has captured in the array until the first flag.

The Watermark Collect is basically that. The most suitable renaming we found is the AF-renaming (Attiya Fouren) *Reflectors Network* - that provides a $(2k - 1)$-renaming in $O(N)$ steps and $O(N^2)$ space [AF98], which are thus the complexities of the Watermark Collect. We append the renaming object with an array A each entry of which consists of three registers *name*, *value* and *flag* (see Figure 1(a)). In the *capture* operation (called by the first invocation of the *store* operation) a process p_j uses its id_j to rename itself to obtain a new *id*, called index. It then captures register $A[index]$ and sets all the flags in $A[index].flag, A[index - 1].flag, \ldots, A[1].flag$. To collect the values stored in the Watermark Collect a process sweeps through the array A from $A[1]$ to the first un-set Flag entry, reading all the values associated with these entries. Clearly the store operation takes $O(N)$ steps (due to the renaming cost), the collect takes $O(k)$ steps and the space complexity is $O(N^2)$ (again due to the Reflectors Network in the AF renaming).

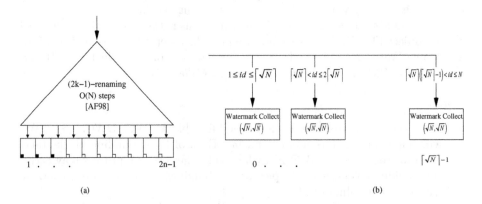

(a)   (b)

Fig. 1. (a) Watermark Collect(n, N) (b) Divided Watermark Collect(N) constructions

Notice that replacing the AF-renaming in this construction with any $O(k)$-renaming algorithm with $O(k)$ step complexity and $O(S)$ space complexity results in an $O(k)$ steps collect algorithm with $O(n + S)$ space complexity.

3.2   Divided Watermark Collect(N)

The main problem with the Watermark Collect is the high cost of a *store* operation and of space, due to the AF-renaming. On the other hand, the cost of the *collect* operation is $O(k)$. As a first step in alleviating this issue we reduce the cost of the *store* operation on the account of increasing the cost of the *collect* operation until they are both $O(\sqrt{N})$. At the same time we also reduce the space complexity. This is achieved by using smaller size Watermark Collect objects and assigning processes to the different Watermark Collects according to their ids. Specifically, the Divided Watermark Collect is constructed from a sequence of $\lceil \sqrt{N} \rceil$ Watermark Collects($\lceil \sqrt{N} \rceil$), which results in a $O(\sqrt{N})$ steps store and $O(k + \sqrt{N})$ collect with $O(N^{1.5})$ space.

In its *capture* operation a process p_j such that, $i\lceil \sqrt{N} \rceil < id_j \leq (i+1)\lceil \sqrt{N} \rceil$ invokes the *capture* method of the i'th Watermark Collect object with input parameters $(name_j, id_j \ mod \ \lceil \sqrt{N} \rceil)$ (see Figure 1(b)). To perform a *collect*, a process collects the values from all the $\lceil \sqrt{N} \rceil$ Watermark Collects as was described above.

3.3   Telescopic Watermark Collect(N)

To turn the non-adaptive Divided Watermark Collect into an adaptive collect we assume that the *ids* with which processors enter the object are adaptive. That is we assume that magically each process arrives with an *id* in the range $1, \ldots, f(k)$ where k is the total number of processes that have showed up so far, e.g., $f(k) = k^2$ (if MA-renaming is used). We then construct a sequence of increasing in size Divided Watermark Collect objects and send processes with small *ids* to small DWC objects. In this way the step complexity of the *store* operation is a function of the complexity of the DWC that is used. For example, if a process with $id = t$ accesses a $DWC(O(t))$ then its store step complexity (in the corresponding DWC) is $O(\sqrt{t})$. Since $t = O(k^2)$ (assuming $f(k) = k^2$) the resulting step complexity is $O(k)$. To collect the values from this sequence of DWC objects structure we associate with each DWC a flag (similar to the flags in the Watermark object). The flag of a DWC is set if any process stored a value to any DWC of equal or larger size. In the *collect* operation a process collects the values from all the DWCs whose flag is set (until the first one whose flag is not set).

That is, the Telescopic Watermark Collect object consists of a telescopic sequence of increasing in size DWC collect objects, each twice the size of the previous one. The first one is for constant name space C and the last is for name space N. I.e., there are $\approx \log N$ DWC's(see Figure 2(a)). Finally, another array, called sweep array, of size $\approx \log N$, is used to hold the flag registers associated with each DWC.

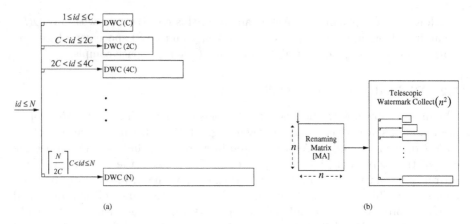

Fig. 2. (a) Telescopic Watermark Collect(N) (b) Unrestricted Name Space (k, n^3)-Collect constructions

In its *capture* operation (called by the first *store* operation) a process uses its *id* to decide into which DWC it stores its value. A process with $id \leq C$ selects the first one, where as with $2^{i-1}C < id \leq 2^i C$ selects the i'th DWC (see Figure 2(a)). The process also sets the flags in the Sweep Array according to the DWC it has selected. To perform a *collect*, a process collects from the smallest DWC until the first DWC whose flag is not set. On each such DWC the *collect* will be as described in subsection 3.2.

The Telescopic Watermark Collect thus consumes $O(N^{1.5})$ space and provides $O(k)$ step complexity if the size of the *id* of any incoming process is at most quadratic in the number of processes that have accessed this building block before this process finishes. The space complexity is dominated by the space requirement of the largest DWC(N), which is $\sqrt{N}$ Watermark collects each consuming (by the AF-renaming in it) $O(N)$ space.

Lemma 1. *The* Telescopic Watermark Collect *provides $O(k)$ step complexity if the size of the id of any incoming process is at most quadratic in k.*

4   Stepwise Construction of Linear Step and Linear Space Collect Algorithm

4.1   Unrestricted Name Space (k, n^3)-Collect

As was described above a straightforward method to construct a collect object from the TWC is to frontend a TWC(n^2) with a Moir Anderson adaptive $O(k^2)$-renaming matrix [AF98, MA95], which takes $O(k)$ steps and $O(n^2)$ space. We thus derived an $O(k)$ steps collect with $O(n^3)$ space (see the construction in Figure 2(b)).

4.2 Restricted Name Space $(k \log \log k, n)$-Collect

Consider a MA-renaming $(n^{1/4} \times n^{1/4})$ matrix followed by a $\mathrm{TWC}(n^{1/2})$. As long as $k \leq n^{1/4}$ this construction provides an $O(n)$ space collect structure that requires $O(k)$ steps for both *store* and *collect* operations. If $k > n^{1/4}$ then processes may fail to obtain a name in the MA-renaming in their capture procedure. In this event a special flag associated with this MA-renaming is set and these processes are then recursively divided into $n^{1/4}$ groups each of at most $n^{3/4}$ processes (see Figure 3). I.e., a process with id_j such that, $i\lceil n^{3/4}\rceil < id_j \leq (i+1)\lceil n^{3/4}\rceil$ (where in this case id_j is the *name* with which the process started), enters group i and replaces its id_j with $id_j \bmod \lceil n^{3/4}\rceil$. In each group we repeat the above recursively. E.g., in the first level of the recursion, each group is of size at most $n^{3/4}$, and contains MA-renaming $(n^{\frac{3}{4}\cdot\frac{1}{4}} \times n^{\frac{3}{4}\cdot\frac{1}{4}})$ matrix followed by a $\mathrm{TWC}(n^{\frac{3}{8}})$. Processes in a group in the first level that fail to obtain a name in the MA-renaming $(n^{\frac{3}{16}} \times n^{\frac{3}{16}})$ matrix are then recursively divided into $n^{\frac{3}{4}\cdot\frac{1}{4}}$ groups, each of size $n^{\frac{3}{4}\cdot\frac{3}{4}}$. This divide and conquer step is repeated recursively $O(\log_{\frac{4}{3}}(\log_q n))$ times, getting at the bottom $O(n)$ groups each capable of containing a constant number $q \geq 2$ of processes. In each such group at the bottom level there is a constant size array, where each process captures the entry indexed by the id with which it had entered this level.

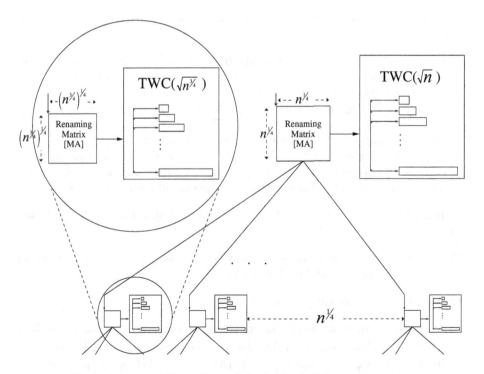

Fig. 3. Restricted Name Space $(k \log \log k, n)$-Collect construction

In a collect operation a process essentially performs a DFS on the flagged portion of the tree of groups and in each such flagged group it performs a collect. I.e., if the group is not at the bottom level it performs the collect on the corresponding TWC of the group, otherwise it performs the collect on the corresponding constant size array. A collect on the array simply requires going through all the entries of the array collecting all the values from the captured entries.

Lemma 2. *At level i there are $n^{1-(3/4)^i}$ groups each capable of containing at most $n^{(3/4)^i}$ processes.*

Observation 1. *At each level, a process may belong only to one group while trying to capture a node.*

Observation 2. *if $k \leq n^{1/4}$ all the processes capture a node in the first group.*

Lemma 3. *The store operation in the first invocation takes $O(\min(k, n^{1/4}))$ steps.*

Definition 1. k_G *is the number of processes that enter the MA-renaming associated with group G while trying to capture a node.*

Definition 2. S_i *is the set: $\{G \mid G$ is a group at level i s.t., $k_G > 0\}$.*

Lemma 4. *The collect operation on all the groups in S_i $(i = 1 \ldots \log \log n)$, takes $O(k)$ steps.*

Proof. In case level $i < \log \log n$ (not the bottom level), the collect operation on the TWC associated with group $G \in S_i$ takes $O(k_G)$ steps. This follows Lemma 1 and the fact that the identifiers size of processes that enter the TWC in this group is $\leq k_G^2$. Due to Observation 1, $\sum_{G \in S_i} k_G = k$, and therefore, the step complexity of the collect operation on all the groups in S_i is $O(k)$.

In case $i = \log \log n$ (bottom level), the collect operation on a group takes $O(1)$ steps. Due to observation 1, there are no more than k groups in S_i. Therefore, the step complexity of the collect operation on all the groups in S_i is $O(k)$.

Lemma 5. *The total number of groups the collect operation visits is $O(k \log \log n)$.*

Corollary 1. *The collect operation takes $O(k)$ steps if $k \leq n^{1/4}$ (Observation 2), and $O(k \log \log n) = O(k \log \log k)$ otherwise.*

Lemma 6. *The space complexity is $O(n)$.*

Proof. Each group G at level i (except the bottom level) contains two data structures, MA-Renaming and TWC. The MA-Renaming is a $(n^{(\frac{3}{4})^i})^{\frac{1}{4}} \times (n^{(\frac{3}{4})^i})^{\frac{1}{4}}$ matrix and therefore consumes $O((n^{(\frac{3}{4})^i})^{\frac{1}{2}})$ space. The TWC is for processes with identifiers of size at most $(n^{(\frac{3}{4})^i})^{\frac{1}{2}}$ and therefore consumes $O(((n^{(\frac{3}{4})^i})^{\frac{1}{2}})^{1.5}) =$

$O(n^{(\frac{3}{4})^{i+1}})$ space. Hence, the space required by each group at level i is dominated by the TWC and is thus $O(n^{(\frac{3}{4})^{i+1}})$.

At level i there are $n^{1-(\frac{3}{4})^i}$ groups (lemma 2). Therefore, in each level except the bottom level, the space complexity of all the groups together is

$$O(n^{(\frac{3}{4})^{i+1}}) \cdot n^{1-(\frac{3}{4})^i} = O(n^{1-\frac{1}{4} \cdot (\frac{3}{4})^i}).$$

Following Lemma 2 there are $\log_{\frac{4}{3}}(\log_q n)$ levels where q is the size of the group at the bottom level which is ≥ 2. Therefore the total space complexity of the construction in all the levels except the bottom one is

$$O\left(\sum_{i=0}^{\log\log(n)-1} n^{1-\frac{1}{4} \cdot (\frac{3}{4})^i} \right).$$

We claim (the proof is omitted from this extended abstract) that the above summation is $< 15n$

Clearly the space required by the groups at the bottom level is $O(n)$ □

4.3   Restricted Name Space (k, n)-Collect

In the last algorithm we achieved $(k \log \log k, n)$-collect assuming a restricted name space $(N = O(n))$. Whereas the store step complexity of that algorithm is already $O(k)$, the step complexity of the collect is $O(k \log \log k)$. The complexity of the collect would have been linear in k if (1) in each visited group G the number of steps spend is linear in the number of processes k'_G that have entered G's TWC in the *capture* procedure, and (2) the number of groups visited by a collect is $O(k)$. Neither (1) nor (2) are satisfied in the $(k \log \log k, n)$-collect described above but with some modifications it will satisfy them.

Notation: Let TWC_G be the TWC in group G, k'_G the total number of processes which have entered TWC_G in the *capture* procedure, and n_G the maximum number of processes which may enter group G.

To satisfy point (1) above we ensure that any process which captures a node in a TWC_G has identifier of size at most $O(k'^2_G)$. The first $n_G^{1/4} \times n_G^{1/4}$ MA-renaming matrix does not provide this, since it is possible that more than $n_G^{1/4}$ processes reach this MA-renaming but only a few of them obtain a new name. And their new name sizes may be in the order of $n_G^{1/2}$. To this end, a second $n_G^{1/4} \times n_G^{1/4}$ MA-renaming matrix is inserted before the TWC_G such that each process that obtained a name in the first $n_G^{1/4} \times n_G^{1/4}$ MA-renaming matrix goes through this second renaming matrix of the same size (see Figure 4). Lets distinguish between two cases, $k'_G \leq n_G^{1/4}$ and $k'_G > n_G^{1/4}$. In the former each process obtains a new identifier of size $O(k'^2_G)$ in the second renaming matrix. In the Latter these processes obtain "good enough" identifiers in the first MA-renaming. Still, a process which did not obtain a name in the second MA-renaming may not enter the TWC with the identifier it got from the first MA-renaming, since another process might have gotten the same id from the second MA-renaming. Therefore, in this case we add to this identifier a $n_G^{1/4}$ offset and enlarge the TWC to a $TWC_G(2n_G^{1/2})$ such that it accommodates this new identifier size. All these changes do not affect the *collect* operation which remain unchanged.

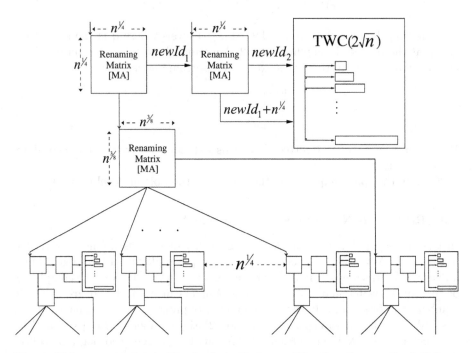

Fig. 4. This construction is Fig. 3 after all the modifications to get (k,n)-Collect. Processes that obtain a new name in a MA-renaming exit the matrix on the right, processes that fail exit at the bottom.

To satisfy Point (2) above we ensure that when a *collect* operation goes down one level from group G it visits only one child group unless at least $\Omega(n_G^{3/8})$ processes entered group G in their *capture* procedure. In the capture procedure at any group G, a process that fails to obtain a name in the first MA-renaming goes through yet another third MA-renaming matrix of size $n_G^{3/8} \times n_G^{3/8}$ (see Figure 4). A process that does not get a new id in the third MA-renaming continues as usual to one of the $n_G^{1/4}$ groups, not before it turns on a flag indicating that these groups are being used (which means that $k_G > n_G^{3/8} \gg n_G^{1/4}$, k_G is the number of processes which visit group G). If a process does get a new id it goes down into a new child group of G, of the same size as the other child groups, and continues in the same way it would have done in any of the other child groups. The only change in the *collect* operation is that when it goes down to the next level its path is divided only if $k_G > n_G^{3/8}$ (instead of $k_G > n_G^{1/4}$).

These two changes improve the step complexity of the collect to $O(k)$ while asymptotically, not affecting the space complexity.

Lemma 7. *The* store *operation takes* $O(\min(k, n^{3/8}))$ *steps.*

Lemma 8. *The collect operation in a visited* TWC_G *takes* $O(k'_G)$ *steps if* $k'_G > 0$, $O(1)$ *otherwise.*

Lemma 9. *The total number of groups the collect operation visits is* $O(k)$.

Proof. The lemma is proved by showing that each process that performs *capture* (out of the k processes) is responsible for $O(1)$ groups that the *collect* visits.

We assign all the groups visited by a collect operation to the different processes that perform capture. The assignment is such that a capturing process maybe assigned many fractions of groups, however the assignment completely covers all the groups. The lemma is proved by showing that the sum of all fractions assigned to a capturing process is $O(1)$.

1. The root group is assigned to the first process that starts executing the capture procedure.
2. A process which enters Group G is assigned $O(n_G^{-\frac{1}{8}})$ out of the $n_G^{\frac{1}{4}}+1$ groups that G is divided into.

To prove that the assignment completely covers all the groups visited by a *collect* operation we distinguish between two cases. Whether the *collect* visits all the child groups of G, or visits just one child group of G. In the former more than $n_G^{\frac{3}{8}}$ capturing processes entered G covering all the child groups since $n_G^{\frac{3}{8}} \cdot O(n_G^{-\frac{1}{8}}) = O(n_G^{\frac{1}{4}})$. In the latter more than $n_G^{\frac{1}{4}}$ capturing processes entered G covering the child group since $n_G^{\frac{1}{4}} \cdot n_G^{-\frac{1}{8}} = n_G^{\frac{1}{8}} > 1$.

To complete the proof note that the sum of assignments each capturing process receives is at most

$$1 + \sum_{i=0}^{\log\log(n)-1} n^{-\frac{1}{8}(\frac{3}{4})^i}$$

The proof that this expression < 31 is omitted from this extended abstract. $\square$

Corollary 2. *The collect operation takes* $O(k)$.

Unrestricted case: This algorithm has an unrestricted name space variant by simply sending a process in the capture procedure first through a MA-renaming $(n \times n)$ matrix and using the obtained *id* as the *id* with which it enters the above algorithms. The structure of each algorithm is then initiated for n^2 processes, i.e., replace n with n^2 in the above. This results in (k, n^2)-Collect unrestricted name space algorithm.

5   Simple Linear Space and Nearly Linear Step Collect Algorithm

In this section we provide two considerably simpler algorithms which are built from three basic building blocks, a *Telescopic Watermark Collect(N)* (Section 3.3), an *IDs Tree(N)*, and the *Moir Anderson renaming matrix* as suggested in [MA95, AF98].

The *IDs Tree(N)* data structure (which is used with different values of N) is a balanced binary tree with N leaves. With each internal node we associate a register - Flag. The leaf nodes of the IDs Tree are the nodes that processes attempt to capture in the first invocation of a *store* operation, and with each leaf node a $< value ; name >$ pair of registers is associated. The leaf nodes of each IDs Tree are arranged in an array indexed by processes id's. To capture a leaf-node in a *store* operation a process accesses that node (without contention, it is the only process with that id) and then marks the flags along the path from this leaf-node to the root of the tree. To *collect* the values stored in an IDs Tree a process performs a DFS traversal of the flagged portion of the tree. Clearly the *store* operation on the IDs Tree takes $O(\log N)$ steps and the *collect* operation takes $O(min(k \log(N), N))$ steps. The space complexity is $O(N)$.

Restricted Name Space (k log k, n)-Collect. In the *capture* operation (see Figure 5(a)) called by the first invocation of the *store* operation a process first tries to obtain a new id with the MA adaptive renaming matrix of size $n^{1/3} \times n^{1/3}$. If it obtains a new name then it runs with it in a TWC($n^{2/3}$). Otherwise it runs with its *name*, the original id, in an IDs Tree(n).

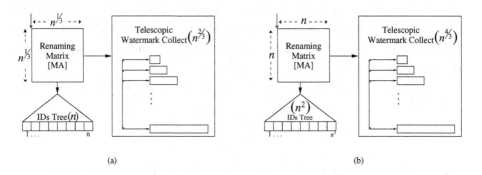

(a)   (b)

Fig. 5. (a) Restricted Name Space ($k \log k$, n)-Collect (b) Unrestricted Name Space ($k \log k$, n^2)-Collect constructions

To perform a *collect*, a process collects from both the TWC($n^{2/3}$) and the IDs Tree(n). Thus a $(min(k \log k, n), n)$-collect algorithm has been obtained.

Unrestricted Name Space (k log k, n^2)-Collect. An unrestricted name space variant of the above is obtained using the same ideas and following the structure depicted in Figure 5(b).

6   Concluding Remarks

While for processes with identifiers of size $O(n)$, an optimal $O(n)$ space $O(k)$ step complexity collect algorithm has been presented, it is still open to find an algorithm with such complexities for the unrestricted name space case.

A major theme of this paper is the relations between adaptive renaming algorithms and adaptive collect algorithms. Clearly replacing the MA-renaming by a more efficient, in both space and step, renaming algorithm would induce a more efficient, in space, collect algorithm for the unrestricted name space case.

Many renaming and collect algorithms work in the same method as the algorithms in this paper, of capturing a node in a network of nodes [MA95, AF98, AFG02]. In the renaming algorithms the total number of nodes is the name space of the new names, each node represents a new *id*. In the collect on the other hand, the number of nodes relates to the space complexity and does not necessarily effect the other qualities of the algorithm.

The algorithms in this paper combine a linear-adaptive step complexity renaming algorithm which is not optimal in the space of new names (MA-renaming), with an optimal renaming algorithm which is not adaptive in the step complexity (AF-renaming). By cascading these two algorithms we made the step complexity of the latter effectively adaptive. Still this is not useful for a linear adaptive renaming algorithm, but because in the first store operation of the collect it is only necessary to capture a unique node and not a unique number, this is enough to get a linear collect algorithm.

The adaptive collect algorithms presented in Section 4.3 may be used to construct an adaptive atomic snapshot algorithm by carefully modifying Afek et al. [AAD+93]. The resulting atomic snapshot algorithm runs in $O(k^2)$ steps and $O(n)$ multi-writer registers if the name space is restricted ($N = O(n)$) and with $O(n^2)$ multi-writer registers if the name space is unrestricted.

Acknowledgements. We would like to thank Hagit Attiya and the DISC-05 anonymous referees for helpful comments.

References

[AAD+93]   Yehuda Afek, Hagit Attiya, Danny Dolev, Eli Gafni, Michael Merritt, and Nir Shavit. Atomic snapshots of shared memory. *J. ACM*, 40(4):873–890, 1993.

[AAF+99]   Yehuda Afek, Hagit Attiya, Arie Fouren, Gideon Stupp, and Dan Touitou. Long-lived renaming made adaptive. In *PODC '99: Proceedings of the eighteenth annual ACM symposium on Principles of distributed computing*, pages 91–103, New York, NY, USA, 1999. ACM Press.

[AD]   Yehuda Afek and Yaron De Levie. Space and step complexity efficient adaptive collect. http://www.cs.tau.ac.il/~afek/papers/collect.pdf.

[AF98]   Hagit Attiya and Arie Fouren. Adaptive wait-free algorithms for lattice agreement and renaming (extended abstract). In *PODC '98: Proceedings of the seventeenth annual ACM symposium on Principles of distributed computing*, pages 277–286, New York, NY, USA, 1998. ACM Press.

[AF03]   Hagit Attiya and Arie Fouren. Algorithms adapting to point contention. *J. ACM*, 50(4):444–468, 2003.

[AFG02]   H. Attiya, A. Fouren, and E. Gafni. An adaptive collect algorithm with applications. *Distributed Computing*, 15(2):87–96, 2002.

[AFK04]   Hagit Attiya, Faith Ellen Fich, and Yaniv Kaplan. Lower bounds for adaptive collect and related objects. In *PODC '04: Proceedings of the twenty-third annual ACM symposium on Principles of distributed computing*, pages 60–69, New York, NY, USA, 2004. ACM Press.

[AKWW]   Hagit Attiya, Fabian Kuhn, Mirjam Wattenhofer, and Roger Wattenhofer. Efficient adaptive collect using randomization. In *Distributed algorithms*, pages 159–173. Also in DISC '04: 18th International Symposium on Distributed Computing.

[AST99]   Yehuda Afek, Gideon Stupp, and Dan Touitou. Long-lived adaptive collect with applications. In *FOCS '99: Proceedings of the 40th Annual Symposium on Foundations of Computer Science*, pages 262–272, 1999.

[MA95]   Mark Moir and James H. Anderson. Wait-free algorithms for fast, long-lived renaming. *Science of Computer Programming*, 25(1):1–39, 1995.

Observing Locally Self-stabilization in a Probabilistic Way

Joffroy Beauquier, Laurence Pilard, and Brigitte Rozoy

Laboratoire de Recherche en Informatique - CNRS,
Université Paris-Sud - Bât. 490 91405,
Orsay Cedex, France
beauquier@lri.fr - (0)1.69.15.67.96
pilard@lri.fr (0)1.69.15.66.34
rozoy@lri.fr (0)1.69.15.66.09

Regular Track

Abstract. A self-stabilizing algorithm cannot detect by itself that stabilization has been reached. For overcoming this drawback Lin and Simon introduced the notion of an external observer: a set of processes, one being located at each node, whose role is to detect stabilization. Furthermore, Beauquier, Pilard and Rozoy introduced the notion of a local observer: a single observing entity located at an unique node. This entity is not allowed to detect false stabilization, must eventually detect that stabilization is reached, and must not interfere with the observed algorithm.

We introduce here the notion of probabilistic observer which realizes the conditions above only with probability 1. We show that computing the size of an anonymous ring with a synchronous self-stabilizing algorithm cannot be observed deterministically. We prove that some synchronous self-stabilizing solution to this problem can be observed probabilistically.

1 Introduction

The notion of self-stabilization was introduced by Dijkstra [Dij74]. He defined an algorithm as self-stabilizing when "regardless of its initial state, it is guaranteed to arrive at a legitimate state in a finite number of steps". Such a property is very desirable for any distributed algorithm, because after any unexpected perturbation modifying the memory state, the algorithm eventually recovers and returns to a legitimate state, without any outside intervention.

Dijkstra's notion of self-stabilization, which originally had a very narrow scope of application, is proving to encompass a formal and unified approach to fault-tolerance under a model of transient failures for distributed algorithms [Dol00, Tel94].

It has been objected to the self-stabilizing approach that 1) a self-stabilizing algorithm only eventually recovers, involving that during some time the behaviour is not correct, 2) a process can never know whether or not the algorithm is stabilized [Dol00].

P. Fraigniaud (Ed.): DISC 2005, LNCS 3724, pp. 399–413, 2005.

There is little that you can do against the first point because it is inherently bounded to the very definition of self-stabilization.

The only studies dealing with the second issue are the important paper by Lin and Simon [LS92] and the paper [BPR04]. Obviously, no detection of stabilization from the inside is possible since any local variable used for that purpose could be corrupted. Meanwhile it is perfectly feasible to detect stabilization from the outside (for instance and although it is just a theoretical remark, when a bound on the number of steps before stabilization is known, simply by counting). "From the outside" can be replaced by "from the inside but using stable memory" (memory not subject to failures).

By restricting their attention to ring networks, Lin and Simon in [LS92] propose a new model, in which it is meaningful to say that a process knows that the ring is stable. This model introduces the notion of a distributed observer, located at each node of the network. This observer is responsible for detecting stabilization and does not influence the self-stabilizing protocol. As the observer involves, at each node, the presence of a stable memory, such a distributed observer is suited only for small local area networks, in which strong security and reliability can be ensured. It is unrealistic for large or heterogeneous networks.

In [BPR04], a local observer has been introduced. This local observer is located at only one node of the network, then only one node has to dispose of some stable memory. The local observer is responsible for detecting stabilization and does not influence the self-stabilizing protocol. In [BPR04], it is proven that if there exists a synchronous self-stabilizing distributed solution for some problem in a distinguished network, then there exists a synchronous self-stabilizing distributed solution, not necessarily the same, for the same problem, that can be observed by a local observer.

In this paper, we raise the question of determining whether or not the stabilization detection is feasible by a local observer in an anonymous and synchronous network. We prove that there exists a self-stabilizing algorithm for some problem P, for which there is no deterministic observation. Then we introduce the notion of local and probabilistic observer and we prove that such an observer can detect the stabilization of another self-stabilizing algorithm solving P.

The plan of the paper is the following. First, we describe the distributed systems and we introduce the formal definition of a local and probabilistic observer. Then, we prove that the problem of determining the size of a synchronous, anonymous and one-way ring cannot be observed by a local deterministic observer. Next, we introduce a self-stabilizing algorithm which computes the size of a synchronous, anonymous and one-way ring. Finally, we prove that this algorithm can be observed by a local and probabilistic observer.

2   Model

In this section, we define a distributed algorithm and we state what it means for a distributed algorithm to be self-stabilizing. We use the classical model for distributed algorithms of [Tel94] and the notion of a local observer of [BPR04].

We recall the definition of a deterministic observer and we define a probabilistic observer.

Distributed algorithm. A distributed algorithm $\mathcal{A} = (C, A)$ is an automaton, where C is the set of all states (called *configurations*) of $\mathcal{A}$ and A is the set of all transitions (called *actions*) of $\mathcal{A}$. An execution of $\mathcal{A}$, noted $e = c_1 a_1 c_2 a_2 \ldots$ is a maximal sequence of configurations and actions of $\mathcal{A}$ such that c_{i+1} is reached from c_i by the execution of the action a_i. The sequence is maximal if it is either infinite, or it is finite but no action of $\mathcal{A}$ is enabled in the last configuration. All computations considered in this paper are assumed to be maximal.

An algorithm $\mathcal{A}$ is self-stabilizing for a specification $\mathcal{SP}$ if and only if there exists a sub-set $\mathcal{C_L}$ of the set of the configurations of $\mathcal{A}$ such that: (i) every execution of $\mathcal{A}$ contains at least one configuration in $\mathcal{C_L}$, (ii) every execution of $\mathcal{A}$ with an initial configuration in $\mathcal{C_L}$ verifies $\mathcal{SP}$ and $\mathcal{C_L}$ is closed. We call $\mathcal{C_L}$ the set of legitimate configurations of $\mathcal{A}$.

We use the definition of a probabilistic self-stabilizing algorithm defined in [BGJ99].

A probabilistic algorithm $\mathcal{A}$ is self-stabilizing for a specification $\mathcal{SP}$ if and only if there exists a sub-set $\mathcal{C_L}$ of the set of the configurations of $\mathcal{A}$ such that: (i) the probability for an execution to reach a configuration in $\mathcal{C_L}$ is equal to 1, (ii) the probability for an execution from a configuration in $\mathcal{C_L}$ to stay in $\mathcal{C_L}$ is equal to 1.

Observer. As it is described in [BPR04], an observer has the following features. (1) The observer is *located at a process of the network*. If the network is anonymous, the location of the observer is arbitrary. (2) The observer is not allowed to detect stability with any information *depending on the network* (for instance the size). (3) The observer *cannot interfere with the algorithm*, which means that the executions of the algorithm are the same with or without the observer. (4) The observer is *not subject to any type of corruption*. (5) The observer observes the behavior of the local process (sequential sequence of instructions) and tries to *match part of this behavior with some predefined sequences*. (6) The announcement of the stabilization obeys some *safety* and *liveness* conditions.

The observer can be viewed as a mechanism having a predetermined set of sequences of actions as a parameter. The mechanism observes the local behavior of a process and continuously tries to match one of its sequences to the observed behavior. As soon as a matching is performed, the observer *announces* the stablilization.

The observer must satisfy three conditions :

1. Safety. The observer does not *announce* if the algorithm is not stabilized.
2. Liveness. Once the algorithm is stabilized, the observer eventually *announces*.
3. Non-interference. The executions of the algorithm are the same with or without the observer.

Definition 21 (Deterministic observer). *If $\mathcal{A}$ is a self-stabilizing algorithm and $\mathcal{O}$ a deterministic observer of $\mathcal{A}$, we have: (safety) as long as $\mathcal{A}$ is not* *stabilized, $\mathcal{O}$ returns false, and (liveness) once $\mathcal{A}$ is stabilized, $\mathcal{O}$ eventually returns* true. *We say that $\mathcal{A}$ is an* observable *algorithm.*

The deterministic and probabilistic observers have different safety and liveness conditions. A probabilistic observer is defined with a parameter α.

Definition 22 (Probabilistic observer). *If $\mathcal{A}$ is a self-stabilizing algorithm and $\mathcal{O}_\alpha$ a probabilistic observer of $\mathcal{A}$, we have: (liveness) the observer announces eventually the stabilization with probability 1; (safety) $\forall \varepsilon \in]0, 1], \exists \alpha$ used by the observer: $Proba(correct\ announcement\ by\ \mathcal{O}_\alpha) > 1 - \varepsilon$.*

In the safety property, ε is the margin of error of the announcement. For each margin of error ε allowed for the announcement, there exists a value of the parameter α such that the probability for a false announcement is less than ε. α is used to compute predetermined sequences of the observer. Intuitively the smaller ε is, the higher α is.

3   Impossibility Result with a Deterministic Observer

In [BPR04], the following result has been proven: for any problem pb in a synchronous and distinguished (presence of a leader) network, we have: if there exists a self-stabilizing algorithm $\mathcal{A}$ solving pb, then there exists a self-stabilizing algorithm $\mathcal{B}$ solving pb and which is observable in a deterministic way. In this section, we raise the following question: does the result remain true if the network is anonymous? For this purpose, we present a synchronous and anonymous problem which cannot be observed in a deterministic way. This problem is the computation of the size of a synchronous, anonymous and one-way ring. (Synchronous means that a computation proceeds by rounds. In each round, each process is activated. Anonymous means that processes are indistinguishable: no id's, same code).

Theorem 31. *Let $\mathcal{A}$ be a self-stabilizing algorithm computing the size of a synchronous, anonymous and one-way ring. There is no deterministic observer for $\mathcal{A}$.*

Proof.
Proof by contradiction.
Let $\mathcal{O}bs$ be a deterministic observer of $\mathcal{A}$. Let R be a ring and n be the size of R. We execute $\mathcal{A}$ and $\mathcal{O}bs$ on R. $\mathcal{O}bs$ is located at an arbitrary process of the ring. Let P_0 be this process. For the need of the proof, the processes of R are named as follows: for all i in $[0, n-1]$, P_i is the successor of $P_{(i+1)\bmod n}$.
Let $State_{P_i}$ be the local state of the process $P_i \in R$ at the initial round ($State_{P_i}$ includes all messages contained in the input channel of P_i).
Let e be an execution of $\mathcal{A}$ and $\mathcal{O}bs$ on R, from the configuration: $State_{P_0}, \ldots,$ $State_{P_{n-1}}$. Let r be the round of e where $\mathcal{O}bs$ announces the stabilization.

Now, let R' be a ring and n' be the size of R' such that $n' \geq r+1$ and $n' \neq n$. We execute $\mathcal{A}$ and $\mathcal{O}bs$ on R'. $\mathcal{O}bs$ is located at an arbitrary process of the ring. Let P'_0 be this process. For the need of the proof, the processes of R are named as follows: for all i in $[0, n-1]$, P'_i is the successor of $P'_{(i+1) \bmod n}$.

Let e' be an execution of $\mathcal{A}$ and $\mathcal{O}bs$ on R', with this initialization:
$$\forall i \in [0, n'-1] : State_{P'_{i \bmod n}} = State_{P_i}.$$

We say that $P_i \in R$ is the *associate* of $P'_j \in R'$ if and only if $i = j \bmod n$. For instance, P_0 is the associate of P'_0 and P'_{2n}, if it exists. If P is the associate of P', then P and P' have the same initialization in e and in e'.

If $\mathcal{A}$ is deterministic and since the ring is one-way then all actions executed by a process at a round depend only on the local states of P and of its predecessor. Thus, the observer sees exactly the same actions in P_0 and P'_0 during the first r rounds of e and e'.

If $\mathcal{A}$ is probabilistic, then all actions executed by a process at a round also depend on probabilistic choices in the execution e. In this case, we choose e' such that all probabilistic choices in e are the same than in e'. Thus, the observer sees exactly the same actions in P_0 and P'_0 during the first r rounds of e and e'.

$\mathcal{O}bs$ announces during the round r in e, so $\mathcal{O}bs$ announces during the round r in e'. But the size of R is different from the size of R', thus $\mathcal{O}bs$ makes a false announcement in e'. Therefore $\mathcal{O}bs$ is not an observer for $\mathcal{A}$.

$\square$

4   Positive Result with a Probabilistic Observer

Let pb be the problem of computing the size of a synchronous, anonymous and one-way ring. We proved in section 3, that if $\mathcal{A}$ is a self-stabilizing algorithm solving pb, then it cannot exist any deterministic observer for $\mathcal{A}$. We introduce in this section a self-stabilizing algorithm $\mathcal{RS}$ solving pb and observable in a probabilistic way. In the first part, we describe this algorithm, then its probabilistic observer.

4.1   The Algorithm

In the sequel we note n the size of the ring.

Specification of the Algorithm

The algorithm is probabilistic as it is defined in [BGJ99] and verifies the following specification $\mathcal{SP}$: (i) each process knows eventually the size of the ring with probability 1, and (ii) a process that knows the size of the ring does not modify this value with probability 1.

The variable $size_P$ of a process P contains the current ring size value estimated by P. The legitimate configurations $\mathcal{C_L}$ of $\mathcal{RS}$ are the configurations of $\mathcal{RS}$ in which: $\forall P, size_P = n$. An execution e of $\mathcal{RS}$ satisfies the specification $\mathcal{SP}$ if and only if e has a suffix containing only legitimate configurations.

Let E be the set of all executions of $\mathcal{RS}$, e be an element of E and r_e be a round of e. Let P be a process and let $size_P(r_e)$ be the value of $size_P$ at round r_e.

Convergence : the probability for an execution to reach a legitimate configuration is equal to 1: $\forall e \in E, \mathrm{Proba}(\forall P : size_P(r_e) = n) \xrightarrow{\ r_e \ \to \ +\infty\ } 1$;

Correctness : the probability for an execution from a legitimate configuration to stay in a legitimate configuration is equal to 1:
$\forall e \in E, \mathrm{Proba}(\forall r'_e > r_e, \forall P : size_P(r'_e) = n) \xrightarrow{\ r_e \ \to \ +\infty\ } 1$

Description of the Algorithm

The ring is anonymous, then all processes in the ring execute the same program. Processes communicate by token passing.

When creating a token T, process P assigns a **period of life** to T in $life_T$. Then P saves this period in $life_P$. Now P has to wait the end of this period for creating another token. To do this, the process has a counter cpt_P such that: at the begining of each round, cpt_P is incremented by 1 and, when the process creates a new token, cpt_P is reset to 0. Thus, when $cpt_P \geq life_P$, the period of life of the last token created by P is over. Furthermore, every time P creates a token, the assigned period of life of the token is incremented by 1.

A process also assigns to each created token T a **counter** cpt_T which is initialized to 1. Moreover, at each round, if T is transmitted, then its counter is incremented by 1. A process relays all tokens which have not exhausted their periods of life ($cpt_T < life_T$). Thus, eventually all token disappears and eventually two distincts tokens created by P cannot be in the ring at the same round.

Finally, a process assigns to a token a **color**. The process randomly chooses the color between black and white (equiprobability) and stores this color in $color_P$.

In summary, the variables of a process are:

1. $color_P$: the color of the last token created by P;
2. cpt_P: the number of rounds since P has created its last token. At a round, if P creates a token, then cpt_P is reset to 0, elsewhere cpt_P is incremented by 1;
3. $life_P$: the period of life of the last token created by P. When P creates a token, $life_P$ is incremented by 1;
4. $size_P$: the size of the ring computed by P. $size_P$ is the output variable of the algorithm.

The variables of a token $Token(color_T, cpt_T, life_T)$ are:

1. $color_T$: the color of the token (constant during the life of T);
2. cpt_T: the number of processes visited by the token. cpt_T is initialized to 1, then is incremented by 1 at each round (this variable also counts the number of rounds since T has been created);
3. $life_T$: the period of life of the token (constant during the life of T).

Computation of the size of the ring. Between two token creations, a process analyses all tokens that it receives. Each token received by P is either recognized or not. A token is recognized by P if and only if $color_P = color_T$ and $cpt_P = cpt_T$. "P recognizes a token T" means that T is possibly the last token created by P.

In order to compute the size of the ring, a process P has two arrays: $S_P[\,]$ and $F_P[\,]$ in which P counts respectively the number of recognized and not recognized tokens among those received. More precisely, if P receives and recognizes a token T such that $cpt_T = i$, then P *marks a success in* i, i.e. P executes the action $S_P[i] := S_P[i] + 1$. Otherwise, if P receives but does not recognize a token T such that $cpt_T = i$, then P *marks a failure in* i, i.e. P executes the action $F_P[i] := F_P[i] + 1$.

Finally, a process P computes the size of the ring in $size_P$:

$$size_P := \inf\left\{ i > 0 : \frac{S_P[i]}{S_P[i] + F_P[i]} \geq 0.9 \right\}$$

Figure 1 contains the algorithm executed by processes. Each round a process executes the procedure *Compute-Size()*.

Informal Explanation of the Algorithm

Example 1. Figure 2 shows an example of execution. Let r be a round and P be a process creating a token T at round r. Let us suppose that the value of $life_P$ is 11 at round $r-1$ and that P chooses black for T. Thus, at round r, P initializes its variables: $color_P := \bullet$; $cpt_P := 0$; $life_P := 12$ and P creates $T(\bullet, 0, 12)$. According to the algorithm $\mathcal{RS}$, T is transmitted if and only if $cpt_T < life_T$. Thus T circulates around the ring until round $r+12$.

At round $r+5$, P receives T with $cpt_T = cpt_P = 5$ and $color_T = color_P = \bullet$. Thus, at round $r+5$, P marks a success in 5. At round $r+10$, P receives T for the second time with $cpt_T = cpt_P = 10$ and $color_T = color_P = \bullet$. Thus, at round $r+10$, P marks a success in 10.

At round $r+12$, Q_2 receives T with $cpt_T = life_T$. Thus Q_2 does not transmit T. T disappears from the ring. During all the token circulation, $life_P$ and $life_T$ remains constant, thus during all the token circulation, $life_P = life_T$. Thus, when T disappears, P knows that fact and then, if P does not receive any token during the round, creates a new token.

We call *real-token* a token created by the execution of the function *Create-Token()* and *false-token* a token resulting from a bad initialization.

We note $S_P[i](r)$, the value of the variable $S_P[i]$ at round r. We note $S_P[i]$, the value of the variable $S_P[i]$ at the current round. We use the same notation for all variables.

In the sequel k denotes a strictly positive integer.

Ratio for multiples of the size. If a process P receives a real-token T with $cpt_T = n$, then T has performed one complete circulation around the ring.

Procedure Create-Token() =

$\text{color}_P :=$ uniformly at random choice in {white, black}
$\text{cpt}_P := 0$
$\text{life}_P := \text{life}_P + 1$
Send Token(color_P, 1, life_P) to the successor of P

Procedure Compute-Size() =

$\text{cpt}_P := \text{cpt}_P + 1$
$m_P :=$ value of the received channel of P

Part 1: P receives a token T.
if $m_P = \text{Token}(\text{color}_T, \text{cpt}_T, \text{life}_T)$ **then**
    (1) P marks a success or a failure
    if $\text{cpt}_P = \text{cpt}_T \wedge \text{color}_P = \text{color}_T$ **then** $S_P[\text{cpt}_T] := S_P[\text{cpt}_T] + 1$
                                                  else $F_P[\text{cpt}_T] := F_P[\text{cpt}_T] + 1$

    (2) P updates size_P.
$$\text{size}_P := \inf \left\{ i > 0 : \frac{S_P[i]}{S_P[i] + F_P[i]} \geq 0.9 \right\}$$

    (3) If T does not reach its period of life, then P transmits T,
    (4) else if the last token created by P has disappeared then P creates a new token.
    if $\text{cpt}_T < \text{life}_T$
        then Send Token(color_T, $\text{cpt}_T + 1$, life_T) to successor of P
        else if $\text{cpt}_P \geq \text{life}_P$ **then** Create-Token()

Part 2: P does not receive any token.
    if the last token created by P has disappeared then P creates a new token.
else if $\text{cpt}_P \geq \text{life}_P$ **then** Create-Token()

Fig. 1. The algorithm

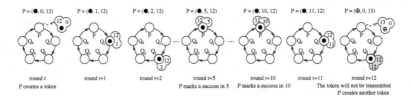

Fig. 2. Behaviours of successes and failures for multiples of the size ($\oplus$ represents the white color)

Thus T has been created by P, $\text{color}_P = \text{color}_T$ and $\text{cpt}_P = \text{cpt}_T$ when P receives T (for the first time). Then P recognizes T. In the same way, if a process P receives a real-token T with $\text{cpt}_T = kn$, then T has performed k entire traversals of the ring. Thus T has been created by P, $\text{color}_P = \text{color}_T$ and

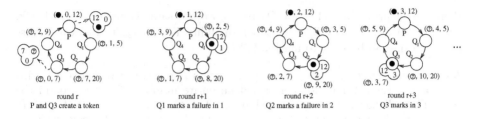

round r
P and Q3 create a token

round r+1
Q1 marks a failure in 1

round r+2
Q2 marks a failure in 2

round r+3
Q3 marks in 3

Fig. 3. Behaviours of successes and failures for not multiples of the size ($\circlemath{?}$ represents black or white)

$cpt_P = cpt_T$ when P receives T (for the kth time). P recognizes T. Thus, if a process P receives a token T such that $cpt_T = kn$, then:

(i) either T is a real-token, then T has been created by P, $color_P = color_T$ and $cpt_P = cpt_T$, and then P marks a success in cpt_T;

(ii) or T comes from a bad initialization of the system; T is a false-token.

Note that in the ring, there are at most n false-tokens, because the capacity of a channel is 1. Moreover, cpt_T is incremented by 1 at each round. Thus for each token T and for all $j \geq 1$, $cpt_T = j$ is true during at most one round in an execution. Therefore P marks something in j at most one time for each false-token and so P marks in kn at most n times during an execution. Thus, P marks at most n failures in kn during an execution.

P creates an infinite number of tokens. Each of them are recognized by P when they return to P after an entire traversal of the ring. Thus, P marks an infinite number of successes in n. Furthermore, we have seen that P marks at most n failures in n. Thus, for all process P we have:

$$\lim_{r \to +\infty} \left(\frac{S_P[n](r)}{S_P[n](r) + F_P[n](r)} \right) = 1 \geq 0.9$$

Example 2. Figure 3 shows the same execution as in figure 2, but considers the behavior of several processes. At round r, P creates a token T.

Suppose that Q_3 creates a token T' at round r, with $life_{T'} = 7$. Suppose that Q_1, Q_2 and Q_4 do not create any token at round r. At round r, we have: $Q_1=(\circlemath{?}, 1, 5)$, $Q_2=(\circlemath{?}, 7, 20)$, $Q_3=(\circlemath{?}, 0, 7)$ and $Q_4=(\circlemath{?}, 2, 9)$. We will see that Q_1, Q_2 and Q_4 mark failures when they receive T, but not necessarily Q_3.

For a sake of clarity, starting from round $r+1$, figure 3 only shows the token T created by P.

At round $r+1$, process Q_1 receives T with $cpt_T \neq cpt_{Q_1}$ Thus whatever the color of Q_1 is, Q_1 marks a failure in 1. Note that $cpt_T \neq cpt_{Q_1}$ is due to the fact that P and Q_1 have not created their last token at the same round. In the same way, at round $r+2$, process Q_2 receives T with $cpt_T \neq cpt_{Q_2}$. Thus whatever the color of Q_2 is, Q_2 marks a failure in 2. At round $r+3$, process Q_3 receives T with $cpt_T = cpt_{Q_3}$. This equality is due to the fact that P and Q_3 have created their last token at the same round. Now, the color of Q_3 determines if Q_3 marks a success or a failure when it receives T. If $color_{Q_3} = \bullet$, then Q_3 marks a success in 3, else a failure. Note that, when Q_3 created its last token, there was a probability $1/2$ for Q_3 to choose the same color as P, i.e. black. Thus, when Q_3 receives T, there is a probability $1/2$ for Q_3 to mark a success and the same probability to mark a failure.

Ratio for not multiples of the size. If a process P receives a real-token T with $cpt_T \neq kn$, then T has not performed an entire number of turns around the ring. Then T has not been created by P. Let $Q \neq P$ be the creator of T. When P receives T: either $color_P \neq color_T$ and thus P does not recognize T, or $color_P = color_T$ and thus P recognizes T if and only if $cpt_T = cpt_P$. P and Q choosing their color independently, the probability of having $color_P = color_T$ is equal to $1/2$. Thus, when P receives a token T such that cpt_T is not a multiple of n, we have:

$$\text{Proba}(P \text{ marks a success in } cpt_T) \leq \text{Proba}(P \text{ marks a failure in } cpt_T)$$

Thus, for all process P and $\forall i \in \mathbb{N}^{*+}$ such that i is not a multiple of n, we have:

$$\text{Proba}\left(\frac{S_P[i](r)}{S_P[i](r) + F_P[i](r)} \geq 0.9 \right) \xrightarrow{r \to +\infty} 0$$

Conclusion. Let us recall that a process P computes the size of the ring in its variable $size_P$:

$$size_P := \inf\left\{ i > 0 : \frac{S_P[i]}{S_P[i] + F_P[i]} \geq 0.9 \right\}$$

Then the ratio allows us to distinguish between the multiples of the size and the other values. Indeed, only multiples of the size have a ratio value greater than or equal to 0.9. On the other hand, the *inf* allows us to choose the smallest multiple.

4.2   Proof of the Algorithm

In the proof, we use the following notation: $R_P[i] = \dfrac{S_P[i]}{S_P[i] + F_P[i]}$

Progression of Each Process

Lemma 41. *Let P be a process. For each round r and for each $l \geq 1$: if $cpt_P(r) = life_P(r) = l$, then $\exists r' \geq r$ such that $life_P(r') = l + 1$,*

Proof.
By contradition.

Let r_0 be the first round during which the ring does not contain any false token. Note that all tokens have a bounded life, thus eventually all false tokens disappear.

Let P be a process such that $cpt_P(r_0) = life_P(r_0) = l$. Let us suppose that $\forall r \geq r_0, life_P(r) = life_P(r_0)$. If P never created any token from the round r_0, P has necessarily received a token at each round after round r_0. Since all tokens eventually disappear, there exists at least one process in the ring which creates an infinite number of tokens. Let $\mathbb{P}_\infty$ be the set of processes which create an infinite number of tokens and let $\mathbb{P}_{\not\infty}$ be the set of processes which create a finite number of tokens. $1 \leq |\mathbb{P}_\infty| \leq n - 1$ and $1 \leq |\mathbb{P}_{\not\infty}| \leq n - 1$.

Let $r_1 \geq r_0$ be the last round where a process in $\mathbb{P}_{\not\infty}$ creates a token.

If $Q \in \mathbb{P}_\infty$, Q creates an infinite number of tokens, thus we have:

$\forall i, \exists r_Q \geq r_1, \forall r \geq r_Q : life_Q(r) > i$

$\Rightarrow \exists r_Q \geq r_1, \forall r \geq r_Q : life_Q(r) > n^n + 1$

$\Rightarrow \exists r \geq r_1, \forall r' \geq r, \forall Q \in \mathbb{P}_\infty : life_Q(r') > n^n + 1$

Let $r_2 \geq r_1$ be a round such as : $\forall r \geq r_2, \forall Q \in \mathbb{P}_\infty : life_Q(r) > n^n + 1$

Between rounds r_2 and $r_2 + n^n$, we have: $\forall P \in \mathbb{P}_\infty$, P does not create any token, and $\forall Q \in \mathbb{P}_\infty$, Q has created at most one token.

But $|\mathbb{P}_\infty| \leq n - 1$.

Thus, between rounds r_2 and $r_2 + n^n$, there exists a sequence of n rounds in which no token is created and at most $n - 1$ tokens circulate in the ring.

Therefore, during this sequence of n rounds, there exists at least one round during which P does not receive any token, and then, during this round, P creates a token. Contradiction.

$\square$

Corollary 41. $\forall P$ *a process:*

1. $\forall i \in \mathbb{N}^{*+}$, *P creates an infinite number of tokens T such that* $life_T \geq i$
2. $\forall i \in \mathbb{N}^{*+}$, *P receives an infinite number of tokens T such that* $cpt_T = i$.

Ratio for Multiples of the Size

Theorem 41. $\forall i \in \mathbb{N}^{*+}$ *such that i is a multiple of n, we have:*

$$\lim_{r \to +\infty} R_P[i](r) = 1$$

Proof.

Let $i = kn$, with $k \in \mathbb{N}^{*+}$.

If P receives a token T such that $cpt_T = i$, then either (i) T is a false-token, then P can mark a failure in i, or (ii) T is a real-token, then P is the creator of T and P marks a success in i.

(i) As the ring contains at most n false-tokens, P marks at most n failures in i.

(ii) Lemma 41 involves that each process sends an infinite number of tokens with an increasingly large value of period of life. Thus, P marks an infinite number of successes in i.

Thus: $\forall i = kn, \lim_{r \to +\infty} R_P[i](r) = 1$

$\square$

Ratio for Not-multiples of the Size

Lemma 42. $\forall i \in \mathbb{N}^{*+}$ *such as i is not a multiple of n, we have: when P receives a token T such as* $cpt_T = i$: *Proba(P marks a success in i) $\leq$ Proba(P marks a failure in i)*

Proof.

Let $i \in \mathbb{N}^{*+}$ be not multiple of n.

When P receives a false-token T such as $cpt_T = i$:

Proba($color_P = color_T$) = Proba($color_P \neq color_T$) = $\frac{1}{2}$, and

Proba($cpt_P = cpt_T$) $\leq$ Proba($cpt_P \neq cpt_T$)

Thus, Proba(P marks a success in i) $\leq$ Proba(P marks a failure in i)

If P receives a real-token T such as $cpt_T = i$, then T has been created for i rounds by the process $Q \neq P$. Let r be the round where Q created T.

Case (i): If P has created a token T' at round r, then when P receives T, we have: $\text{Proba}(cpt_P = cpt_T = i) \leq 1$, and

$\text{Proba}(color_P = color_T) = \text{Proba}(color_P \neq color_T) = \frac{1}{2}$

Thus, $\text{Proba}(P$ marks a success in $i) \leq \text{Proba}(P$ marks a failure in $i)$

Case (ii): If P has not created a token at round r, then when P receives T, we have: $cpt_P \neq cpt_T$. Thus, $\text{Proba}(P$ marks a success in $i) \leq \text{Proba}(P$ marks a failure in $i)$. $\qquad\square$

Theorem 42. $\forall i \in \mathbb{N}^{*+}$ *such as i is not a multiple of n, we have:*

$$Proba\,(R_P[i](r) \geq 0.9) \xrightarrow{\ r\ \rightarrow\ +\infty\ } 0$$

Proof Outline.

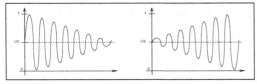

Fig. 4. Variance

According to lemma 42, if i is not a multiple of n, then the probability for P to mark a failure in i is greater than the probability for P to mark a success in i. Thus the average value of $R_P[i](r)$ is smaller than or equal to 0.5. But the average value is not sufficient to conclude. Indeed, the average value of the two functions draw in the figure 4 is 0.5, but the variance value of the first function is 0 while the variance value of the second function is $+\infty$. Intuitively, if the ratio is of the form of the first function then the theorem is true, else the theorem is false. Note that, if $R_P[i](r) = 1/2 = 0.5$, then P has marked one success among two marks, and only 8 consecutive successes are enough to set $R_P[i](r)$ above 0.9. But, if $R_P[i](r) = 500/1000 = 0.5$, then P has marked 500 successes among 1000 marks, and 4000 consecutive successes must be marked by P in order to increase $R_P[i](r)$ above 0.9. Thus, when time passes, it is more and more difficult to have $R_P[i](r)$ greater than 0.9.

Using a technique similar to the proof of Bienaymé-Tchebycheff inequality, we prove that $\text{Proba}(R_P[i](r) \geq 0.9) \leq \frac{1}{8.(0,4)^3.N^2}$. The detailed proof, is left for the complete version of the paper.

Theorem 43. $\forall i \in \mathbb{N}^{*+}$ *such as i is not a multiple of n, we have:*

$$Proba\,(\forall r' \geq r : R_P[i](r') \geq 0.9) \xrightarrow{\ r\ \rightarrow\ +\infty\ } 0$$

Proof Outline. We use a similar argument as for theorem 42. The detailed proof is left for the complete version of the paper.

Conclusion

Theorem 44 (Convergence). *Let E be the set of all possible executions of $\mathcal{RS}$, e be an element of E and r be a round of e.*

$$Proba(\forall \text{ process } P : size_P(r) = n) \xrightarrow{\ r\ \rightarrow\ +\infty\ } 1$$

Proof Outline. This theorem results from theorems 41 and 42. We compute a finite multiplication of probabilities to obtain this result. The detailed proof is left for the complete version of the paper.

Theorem 45 (Correctness). *Let E be the set of all possible executions of $\mathcal{RS}$, e be an element of E and r be a round of e.*

$$Proba\left(\forall r' \geq r, \forall\ process\ P : size_P(r') = n\right) \xrightarrow{\ r\ \rightarrow\ +\infty\ } 1$$

Proof Outline. This theorem results from theorems 41 and 43. We also compute a finite multiplication of probabilities to obtain this result.

The proof is based on the fact that $\left(\sum^\infty \frac{1}{N^2}\right) \sim \frac{1}{N}$. The detailed proof is left for the complete version of the paper.

4.3 The Observer

In the sequel, we do not make the predefined sequences of the observer explicit (for the sake of simplicity) but we rather describe in a informal way what the observer tries to match. The transcription of this informal observation into formal sequences is straightforward.

Behaviour of the Observer. The observer has two arrays: $S_{\mathcal{O}bs}[\,]$ and $F_{\mathcal{O}bs}[\,]$. $\forall i \geq 1$, $S_{\mathcal{O}bs}[i]$ and $F_{\mathcal{O}bs}[i]$ are initialized to 0. If P is the observed process, then the observer counts in these arrays the number of modifications that P executes in $S_P[\,]$ and $F_P[\,]$. Let $s_P[i]$ and $f_P[i]$ be the initial values of $S_P[i]$ and $F_P[i]$ respectively. Note that the observer considers neither $s_P[i]$, nor $f_P[i]$.

Let n be the size of the ring. If a process P receives a false-token T such that $cpt_T = n$, then P can mark a failure in n when it receives T, for instance if $color_T \neq color_P$. But P can receive at most n false-tokens like that, because a ring of size n can contain at most n false-tokens at the initialization. On the other hand, if P receives a real-token T such that $cpt_T = n$, then P is the creator of T, then P marks a success in n. Thus: $\forall r \geq 0, F_P[n](r) \leq f_P[n] + n$.

Since the counter of a token is incremented by 1 at each round, all false-tokens which cause a failure in n will arrive during the first n rounds. Then, for the value i, the observer does not count the first i tokens that arrived at P. For that the observer has a counter $count_{\mathcal{O}bs}$. This counter is initialized to 0 and is incremented by 1 at each round.

Let P be the observed process. The observer executes:

(a) At each round, $count_{\mathcal{O}bs} := count_{\mathcal{O}bs} + 1$
(b) $\forall i \geq 1$, P marks a success in i and $count_{\mathcal{O}bs} > i \Rightarrow S_{\mathcal{O}bs}[i] := S_{\mathcal{O}bs}[i] + 1$
(c) $\forall i \geq 1$, P marks a failure in i and $count_{\mathcal{O}bs} > i \Rightarrow F_{\mathcal{O}bs}[i] := F_{\mathcal{O}bs}[i] + 1$

The observer announces the stabilization if and only if $size_P$ is such that:

1. $F_{\mathcal{O}bs}[size_P] = 0$ and
2. $\forall i < size_P : F_{\mathcal{O}bs}[i] > 0$ and
3. $S_{\mathcal{O}bs}[size_P] \geq size_P + \alpha$, where α depends on ε.

We have: $F_{\mathcal{O}bs}[n] = 0$ is always true. Thus, if $size_P > n$, the second condition is never satisfied. Therefore, the observer cannot announce if $size_P > n$.

If $size_P < n$, the probability for $F_{\mathcal{O}bs}[size_P]$ to satisfy the first condition decreases as the number of $size_P$ tests increases. The third condition forces the observer to wait for $size_P$ to be sufficiently tested before announcing.

Proof of the observer.

Theorem 46. $\forall \varepsilon \in [0, 1[, \exists \alpha : Proba(\text{false announcement by } \mathcal{O}bs_\alpha) \le \varepsilon$

Proof.

Let $Prob = \text{Proba(false announcement)} \le \sum_{i=1}^{+\infty} \text{Proba(false announcement on } i)$
Let T be a false token. From round $n+1$, if T circulates the ring, then $cpt_T > n$.
Thus P never marks any failure in n from round $n+1$. Moreover, according to (a) and (c), the observer only counts the failures marked by P in n from round $n+1$. Therefore, $F_{\mathcal{O}bs}[n] = 0$ is always true. Then if $size_P > n$ the second condition is never satisfied. Therefore, the observer cannot announce if $size_P > n$ and we have:

if $i > n$, then Proba(false announcement on i) $= 0$
$\Rightarrow Prob \le \sum_{i=1}^{n-1} \text{Proba(false announcement on } i)$
If $i < n$ then Proba(false announcement on i)
$\quad \le \text{Proba}(F_{\mathcal{O}bs}[i] = 0, \text{ with } i \text{ having been tested at least } i + \alpha \text{ times})$
$\quad \le \left(\frac{1}{2}\right)^{i+\alpha}$ (according to the lemma 42)

So, we have:

$$Prob \le \sum_{i=1}^{n-1} \left(\frac{1}{2}\right)^{i+\alpha} = \left(\frac{1}{2}\right)^\alpha * \sum_{i=1}^{n-1} \left(\frac{1}{2}\right)^i \le \left(\frac{1}{2}\right)^\alpha$$

By choosing $\alpha \ge -\frac{\log \varepsilon}{\log 2}$, we obtain: Proba(false annoucement) $\le \varepsilon$ □

Theorem 47. *The observer eventually announces the stabilization with probability 1.*

Proof.

According to theorem 45, we have: $\text{Proba}\left(\forall r' \ge r, \forall P : size_P(r') = n\right) \xrightarrow{r \to +\infty} 1$
Let us prove that: Proba(observer announces on n) $\xrightarrow{r \to +\infty} 1$
First condition: $F_{\mathcal{O}bs}[n] = 0$.
$\quad$ (*) $F_{\mathcal{O}bs}[n] = 0$ is always true.
Second condition: $\forall i < n : F_{\mathcal{O}bs}[i] > 0$
$\quad$ According to corollary 41, $\forall i \in \mathbb{N}^{*+} : i < n$, P receives an infinite number of tokens T such that $cpt_T = i$. Moreover, according to theorem 42, if P receives a token T such that $cpt_T < n$, then the probability for P to mark a success in cpt_T is less than the probability for P to mark a failure in cpt_T. Therefore:
$\quad$ (**) $\text{Proba}(\forall i < n : F_{\mathcal{O}bs}[i](r) > 0) \xrightarrow{r \to +\infty} 1$
Third condition: $S_{\mathcal{O}bs}[n] \ge n + \alpha$

According to corollary 41, P creates at least $2n+\alpha$ tokens with a period of life $\geq n$, thus: P marks at least $2n+\alpha$ successes in n and the observer marks at least $n+\alpha$ successes in n. Therefore:

(***) eventually, $(S_{\mathcal{O}bs}[n] \geq n+\alpha)$

According to (*), (**) and (***), we have:

$$\text{Proba(observer announces on } n) \xrightarrow{\ r \to +\infty\ } 1$$

Thus the observer eventually announces the stabilization with probability 1.

$\square$

5   Conclusion

In this paper, we introduce the notion of a local and probabilistic observer for self-stabilizing algorithms. Our result is that, if the network is uniform and synchronous, then some problems having a self-stabilizing solution do not have any self-stabilizing solution that can be observed by a local and deterministic observer, but have a self-stabilizing solution that can be observed by a local and probabilistic observer. Computing the size of the ring is not only a particular example, but the first step for extending the probabilistic observation to a larger class of problems. The reason why is that, once the size is known for sure (in fact almost sure), it is easier to observe self-stabilizing snapshots, leading to the observation of more complex stabilizations.

References

[BGJ99]   J. Beauquier, M. Gradinariu, and C. Johnen. Randomized self-stabilizing and space optimal leader election under arbitrary scheduler on rings. Technical Report 99-1225, Universite Paris Sud, 1999.

[BPR04]   Joffroy Beauquier, Laurence Pilard, and Brigitte Rozoy. Observing locally self-stabilization. *Journal of High Speed networks*, 2004.

[Dij74]   Edsger W. Dijkstra. Self-stabilizing systems in spite of distributed control. *Communications of the ACM*, 17(11):643–644, nov 1974.

[Dol00]   Shlomi Dolev. *Self-Stabilization*. MIT Press, Cambridge, MA, 2000.

[LS92]   Chengdian Lin and Janos Simon. Observing self-stabilization. In Maurice Herlihy, editor, *Proceedings of the 11th Annual Symposium on Principles of Distributed Computing*, pages 113–124, Vancouver, BC, Canada, August 1992. ACM Press.

[Tel94]   Gerard Tel. *Introduction to Distributed Algorithms*. Cambridge Uni Press, Cambridge, 1994.

Asymptotically Optimal Solutions for Small World Graphs

Michele Flammini[1], Luca Moscardelli[1], Alfredo Navarra[1],
and Stephane Perennes[2]

[1] Department of Computer Science, University of L'Aquila, Italy
{flammini, moscardelli, navarra}@di.univaq.it
[2] MASCOTTE project, I3S-CNRS/INRIA/Univ. Nice, Sophia Antipolis, France
Stephane.Perennes@sophia.inria.fr

Abstract. We consider the problem of determining constructions with
an asymptotically optimal oblivious diameter in small world graphs under the Kleinberg's model. In particular, we give the first general lower
bound holding for any monotone distance distribution, that is induced
by a monotone generating function. Namely, we prove that the expected
oblivious diameter is $\Omega(\log^2 n)$ even on a path of n nodes. We then focus on deterministic constructions and after showing that the problem
of minimizing the oblivious diameter is generally intractable, we give
asymptotically optimal solutions, that is with a logarithmic oblivious
diameter, for paths, trees and Cartesian products of graphs, including
d-dimensional grids for any fixed value of d.

1 Introduction

A generic graph G is said to represent a Small-World when each node can "easily
and quickly" reach any other one using just local information or, in other words,
if the resulting "oblivious" diameter is polylogarithmic in the number of the
involved nodes. In the literature such a property is also known as "six degrees of
separation" coming from Miligram's experiments [12,15], that showed an average
distance of six hops between any two USA citizens in delivering mails. Recently
such a property has been extensively studied and formalized by the Kleinberg's
works formalizing the so-called "small-world phenomena" [9,7,8]. The relevance
of such a topic results from its numerous applications in social, natural and
peer-to-peer networks [1,13,14,16], where the common property is the partial
knowledge of the environment and the wish of sharing information.

In the Kleinberg's model, a two dimensional square mesh is augmented by
the random addition of one directed outgoing arc or "long link" per node. Thus,
besides its four adjacent nodes in the mesh, a generic node x has a further
neighbor y chosen with probability $P_x[y] = \frac{1}{H_x dist^2(x,y)}$, where $dist(x,y)$ is the
Manhattan distance between x and y in the mesh and $H_x = \sum_{y \neq x} \frac{1}{dist^2(x,y)}$ is
a normalizing coefficient. As a consequence, the closer y is from x, the higher
is the probability to have the long link (x,y). Kleinberg proposed a greedy algorithm for routing on the augmented graph that at each step always chooses

P. Fraigniaud (Ed.): DISC 2005, LNCS 3724, pp. 414–428, 2005.

the link (eventually the long one) whose endpoint is closest to the target node according to the original distances without long links. He proved an $O(\log^2 n)$ expected number of hops performed by such an algorithm for connecting every source-destination pair. Starting from such results, considerable effort has been then devoted in investigating several variants of the original model in terms of network topology, number and probability distribution of the long links, starting knowledge of each node and so forth (see for instance [3,5,4,10,11]).

1.1 Related Work

The basic Kleinberg's model [9] was extensively studied in the recent years due to its applications and characterizations of several environments. For instance such a model was used to generate search protocols in peer-to-peer networks [16] and to evaluate the World Wide Web diameter [1].

In [5] and independently in [10] is proved the tightness of Kleinberg's results for $n \times n$ mesh networks, that is, the greedy routing algorithm performs $\Theta(\log^2 n)$ hops to connect any pair of nodes, while the diameter of the network is $\Theta(\log n)$. In [10], the authors also extend their results to the case in which each node of the grid has the additional knowledge of the long links of the $\log n$ closest ones, obtaining $O(\log^{\frac{3}{2}} n)$ steps for the 2-dimensional case and $O(\log^{1+\frac{1}{d}} n)$ in the general d-dimensional model. The $O(\log^{1+\frac{1}{d}} n)$ bound is also achieved in [5] by an oblivious greedy algorithm.

A nice characterization of small-world graphs is given in [11], where a limit separating small-world from "large-world" graphs is defined. Namely, considering a d-dimensional grid and a probability distribution of the long links according to the inverse power r of the covered distance, the authors showed a poly-log expected diameter when $d < r < 2d$, but polynomial when $r > 2d$. They also presented a framework to construct classes of small-world graphs with $\Theta(\log n)$ expected diameter.

In [4], *treewidth* aspects and their relations with social networks are considered. Informally, the treewidth of a graph represents the "distance" of its structure from a tree. Its relevance is given by the fact that many classes of graphs have a bounded treewidth, like for instance trees, outer-planar graphs and series-parallel graphs, and many NP-hard problems can be polynomially solved when restricted to bounded treewidth graphs. In [4] an almost tight upper bound of $O(\log^2 n)$ on the expected diameter is provided for any graph G of n nodes with bounded treewidth. For the lower bound, in fact, an $\Omega(\frac{\log^2 n}{\log \log n})$ holds on directed rings of n nodes [2].

1.2 Our Contribution

In this paper we consider the problem of determining constructions with an asymptotically optimal oblivious diameter in small world graphs under the Kleinberg's model.

In particular, we give the first general lower bound holding for any non increasing distance distributions, that is induced by a non increasing generating function. Namely, we prove that the expected oblivious diameter is $\Omega(\log^2 n)$ even on a path of n nodes. Such a result is particularly relevant because, as shown in [9,11], only highly decreasing distance distributions are expected to have good performances. However, we extend the lower bound also to non decreasing distance distributions, thus including all the monotone ones.

Even if our results are related to the ones in [2], there are two major differences. First of all, the expected oblivious diameter investigated in this paper is a slightly different measure from the expected delivery time of [2], which according to Kleinberg's model is the average delivery time between all the source-destination pairs. As a consequence, while our lower bound is higher than the one of [2] and is obtained by exploiting a novel and unrelated approach, it does not directly apply to the expected delivery time. Moreover, our results hold for undirected paths and the ones in [2] for directed rings.

We then focus on deterministic constructions. We show that unfortunately the problem adding at most k outgoing long links per node so as to minimize the oblivious diameter is generally intractable. We then give asymptotically optimal solutions, that is with a logarithmic oblivious diameter, for paths, trees and Cartesian products of graphs, including d-dimensional grids for any fixed value of d. Clearly, our upper bounds hold also for the expected delivery time considered by the previous authors.

The paper is organized as follows. In the next section we introduce the basic notation and definitions. Section 3 deals with the general lower bound for distance distributions. In Section 4 we prove the intractability of the oblivious diameter minimization problem and in Section 5 we give the above mentioned asymptotically optimal deterministic construction for the different topologies. Finally, in Section 6, we give some conclusive remarks and discuss some open questions.

2   Definitions

We model a network as a symmetric digraph $G = (V, A)$ of n nodes in which $V = \{1, \ldots, n\}$. We denote as *short links* all the edges in A. *Small World Graphs (SWG)* are build from G by adding directed long arcs, also called *long links*, that are arbitrary couples in $V \times V$.

Definition 1 (Small World Graph). *Given a digraph $G = (V, A)$ and $\hat{A} \subset V \times V$), $SWG(G, \hat{A})$ is the digraph $H = (V, A \cup \hat{A})$ obtained by adding to G the long links in $\hat{A}$.*

- *For any two nodes $x, y \in V$, $dist(x, y)$ is the distance between x and y, that is, the one in the network G.*
- *The outdegree and the indegree of $SWG(G, \hat{A})$ are always considered to be the ones of the digraph with arc set $\hat{A}$.*

A greedy or *oblivious* algorithm for routing on $SWG(G, \hat{A})$ at each step chooses one of the links, including the long ones, whose endpoint is closest to the target node according to the distances in G.

Definition 2 (Oblivious Routing). *In $SWG(G, \hat{A})$*

- *A path $P = <x_0, x_1, x_2, \ldots, x_k>$ from x_0 to x_k is said to be oblivious if, for any $i \in \{0, 1, 2, \ldots, k-1\}$, $(x_i, x_{i+1}) \in A \cup \hat{A}$ and for any y such that $(x_i, y) \in A \cup \hat{A}$, $dist(x_{i+1}, x_k) \leq dist(y, x_k)$.*
- *The oblivious distance from x to y in $SWG(G, \hat{A})$ is the maximum length of an oblivious path from x to y.*
- *The oblivious diameter $\mathcal{OD}(SWG(G, \hat{A}))$ of $SWG(G, \hat{A})$ is the maximum oblivious distance between two nodes in V.*

Given a network G and an integer $k > 0$, a relevant design goal is that of determining a small world graph $SWG(G, \hat{A})$ with minimum oblivious diameter among the ones with maximum outdegree bounded by k.

Definition 3 (Small World Diameter). *Given an integer $k > 0$, the small world diameter $\mathcal{OD}_k(G)$ of a network G is the minimum oblivious diameter of a small world graph $SWG(G, \hat{A})$ with outdegree k.*

In the basic Kleinberg's model [9] long links are chosen randomly according to given probabilistic distributions. As a consequence, the oblivious diameter of the resulting small world graph is a random variable and we are interested in determining distributions reducing its expected value.

Since any deterministic construction of a small world graph is a particular probabilistic one, we are mostly interested in "truly" random solutions in which long links selecting probabilities of distinct nodes are independent and have a low dependence from the target nodes. This avoids deterministic constructions to appear as special cases.

On this respect, a possible reasonable random distribution is the one in which the probability of a long link depends only on its length.

Definition 4. *A probabilistic distribution is distance generated or is a distance distribution if there exists a function $f : \mathbb{N} \to \mathbb{R}^+$ such that $Pr((x, y) \in \hat{A}) = \frac{f(dist(x,y))}{\sum_{z \in V} f(dist(x,z))}$.*

Notice that the probabilistic distributions on meshes based on the Kleinberg's model [9] are then induced by the family of the functions $f(d) = d^{-\alpha}$.

3   Distance Generated SWG

According to the results shown in [9,11], distance distributions achieving a low oblivious diameter should have the property that the probability of the long links is a highly decreasing function of their length. However, in this section we show that even under such an assumption we cannot hope to have an expected oblivious diameter of an order lower than $\log^2 n$, and that the same holds in the reverse case in which probabilities increase with the distance, even in a simple path P_n of n nodes.

In order to prove the claim, we prove a slightly stronger statement for a broader class of distance distributions. Namely, given a fixed positive number $p \leq 1$, once an outgoing long link at a given node x has been drawn according to the distance distribution, it is installed or added to the graph with a given probability $r_x \leq p$, otherwise it is removed (with probability at least equal to $1-p$), independently of all the other long links. We call the resulting distribution a p-distribution. Our results will then follow as a corollary of the p-distributions ones considering the special case $p = 1$.

In the following we restrict on paths P_n of n nodes with node set $V = \{1, ..., n\}$ and arc set $A = \{(x, x+1), (x+1, x) | 1 \leq x < n\}$. Let L_x be the random variable "length of the long link of x". Given a function $f : \mathbb{N} \to \mathbb{R}^+$, we will always implicitly assume that the probabilities of L_x are given by the distance distribution generated by f, that is $Pr(L_x = d) = a \cdot f(d) / \sum_{y \in V} f(dist(x, y))$, where a is the number of nodes at distance d from x.

The following lemma will be useful for proving the final result.

Lemma 1. *Given a path P_n and a non increasing generating function $f : \mathbb{N} \to \mathbb{R}$, for any two nodes x, y such that $x < y \leq n/2$, $Pr(L_x \leq j) \geq Pr(L_y \leq j)$ for any $j < x$.*

Proof. Since f is not increasing, $Pr(L_x \leq j) = \dfrac{2\sum_{i=1}^{j} f(i)}{2\sum_{i=1}^{x-1} f(i) + \sum_{i=x}^{n-x-1} f(i)} \geq \dfrac{2\sum_{i=1}^{j} f(i)}{2\sum_{i=1}^{y-1} f(i) + \sum_{i=y}^{n-y-1} f(i)} = Pr(L_y \leq k)$. $\qquad\square$

Theorem 1. *For any non increasing function f on a path P_n and any p-distance distribution generated by f, $\mathbb{E}(\mathcal{OD}(SWG(G, \hat{A}))) = \Omega(\min(n, \frac{\log^2(n)}{\sqrt{p}}))$.*

Proof. We show that $\mathbb{E}(\mathcal{OD}(SWG(G, \hat{A}))) \geq k \min(n, \frac{\log^2(n)}{\sqrt{p}})$ with $k = 1/n_0$, where n_0 is a suitably large (constant) number specified in the sequel.

In order to prove the claim, we show that starting from node $n/4$ (from now on called the *S-node*), at least one node in the *destination segment*, that is between $n/4$ and $n/2$, has expected oblivious distance at least $k \min(n, \frac{\log^2(n)}{\sqrt{p}})$.

We divide the proof in three cases.

- $p < \frac{1}{n}$. In this case, the expected oblivious diameter is clearly at least $\frac{n}{8}$, since the probability of maintaining at least one long link between $n/4$ and $n/2$ is lower than $1/2$. Thus the claim holds as $k \leq 1/8$.
- $\frac{1}{n} \leq p < \frac{1}{\log^4 n}$. In this case, since the expected oblivious diameter is at least equal to the expected number of steps needed from $n/4$ to meet the first maintained long link, that is $1/p$, it is sufficient to observe that $\frac{1}{p} = \frac{\log^2 n}{\sqrt{p}} \frac{1}{\log^2 n \sqrt{p}} > \frac{\log^2 n}{\sqrt{p}}$. Thus again the claim holds as $k \leq 1$.
- $p > \frac{1}{\log^4 n}$. In this case we prove the claim by induction on the number of nodes in the path as described in the remaining part of the proof.

As base of the induction we consider a path P_{n_0}, where n_0 is the suitably large integer defining the constant n_0. Clearly the claim for P_{n_0} is true as $k = \frac{1}{n_0}$.

Now, given any $n > n_0$, assuming the claim true for any $P_{n'}$ with $n' < n$, we prove that it holds also for P_n.

For any $i = 2, 3, \ldots, \log n - 4 \log \log n - \log k$, let P^i be the subpath of $\frac{n}{2^i}$ nodes whose S-node, that is the one placed at one fourth of its length, coincides with the one of P_n. In other words, P^i is given by the segment of P_n going from $\frac{n}{4} - \frac{n}{2^{i+2}} + 1$ to $\frac{n}{4} + \frac{3n}{2^{i+2}}$. Clearly, by assumption, each P^i has at least $k \log^4 n \geq k \frac{\log^2 n}{\sqrt{p}}$ nodes.

Any oblivious path going from the S-node of P^i to any of the nodes in its destination segment, that is between nodes $\frac{n}{4}$ and $\frac{n}{4} + \frac{n}{2^{i+2}}$, cannot use any long link starting from P^i and ending outside P^i, or starting before $\frac{n}{4}$, that is at lefthand side of the S-node. Moreover, if p_i is the probability that node $\frac{n}{4}$ has a long link of length at most $\frac{n}{2^i}$, then by Lemma 1 p_i is an upper bound on the probability of having long links of length at most $\frac{n}{2^i}$ for all the nodes in P^i greater than $\frac{n}{4}$, i.e., in the righthand side of its S-node, which is also an upper bound to the probability for such nodes of having a long link falling inside P^i. Considering the long links starting from P^i and ending outside P^i, or starting before $\frac{n}{4}$, as removed, the routing is then performed according to a $(p \cdot p_i)$-distribution.

By the inductive hypothesis, with this induced distribution in P^i, at least one node in the destination segment has expected oblivious distance at least $k \min(\frac{n}{2^i}, \frac{\log^2(|P_i|)}{\sqrt{p \cdot p_i}})$ from the S-node.

If the minimum is $\frac{n}{2^i}$ then $\frac{n}{2^i} \geq \frac{\log^2 n}{\sqrt{p}} > k \frac{\log^2 n}{\sqrt{p}}$ and the claim holds by observing that the S-nodes of P_n and P^i coincide and the destination segment of P^i is contained in the one of P_n.

If $\frac{n}{2^i}$ is not the minimum, it must be $k \frac{\log^2(\frac{n}{2^i})}{\sqrt{p \cdot p_i}} < k \frac{\log^2(|P_n|)}{\sqrt{p}}$, otherwise the claim holds by the same arguments of the previous case. Therefore $\sqrt{p_i} > \frac{\log^2 \frac{n}{2^i}}{\log^2 n} > 1 - \frac{2i}{\log n}$ and $p_i > (1 - \frac{2i}{\log n})^2 > 1 - \frac{4i}{\log n}$. So the probability $\overline{p_i}$ that from the S-node there exists a long link longer than $\frac{n}{2^i}$ is $1 - p_i < \frac{4i}{\log n}$.

Being this true for every $i = 2, 3, \ldots, \log n - 4 \log \log n - \log k$, let us denote by $g(n)$ the highest expected number of steps needed in P_n to reach a node in its destination segment from its S-node, or analogously the expected length of the longest oblivious path from the S-node to one of the nodes in the destination segment. We can recursively calculate $g(n)$ using the inductive hypothesis on shorter paths in the following way.

We distinguish the cases in which either there exists a long link starting from the S-node (with probability at most p) or we are forced to move on a short link (with probability at least $1 - p$).

- If there exist a long link starting from the S-node, denoting by L its length we distinguish four subcases.
  - The long link is toward a node to the left of the S-node: we move through a short link and recurse on the path of length $n - 4$ having the node $\frac{n}{4} + 1$ as its S-node.
  - $L \leq \frac{n}{8}$: we move along the long link and we recurse on the path of length $n - 4L$ having the node $\frac{n}{4} + L$ as its S-node.

- $\frac{n}{8} < L \le \frac{n}{2}$: we move along a short link and recurse on the path of length $2L - 4$ having the node $\frac{n}{4} + 1$ as its *S-node*.
- $L > \frac{n}{2}$: we move along a short link and recurse on the path of length $n - 4$ having the node $\frac{n}{4} + 1$ as its *S-node*.

- If we are forced to move through a short link, we recurse on the path of length $n - 4$ having the node $\frac{n}{4} + 1$ as its *S-node*.

Notice that in all the cases the destination segment of the shorter path on which we recurse is included in the one of P_n. Then,

$$g(n) \ge 1 + (1 - p)g(n - 4) + p\left(\sum_{l=2}^{\frac{n}{8}} Pr(L = l)g(n - 4l) + \right.$$
$$\left. + \sum_{l=\frac{n}{8}+1}^{\frac{n}{2}} Pr(L = l)g(2l - 4) + \sum_{l=\frac{n}{2}+1}^{n} Pr(L = l)g(n - 4)\right) \ge$$
$$\ge 1 + (1 - p)g(n - 4) + p\sum_{l=2}^{\frac{n}{8}} Pr(L = l)g(n - 4l) + p\sum_{l=\frac{n}{8}+1}^{n} Pr(L = l)g\left(\frac{n}{8}\right) \ge$$
$$\ge 1 + (1 - p)g(n - 4) + p\sum_{i=4}^{\log n - 1} Pr\left(\frac{n}{2^i} < L \le \frac{n}{2^{i-1}}\right)g\left(n - \frac{4n}{2^{i-1}}\right) +$$
$$+ p \cdot Pr\left(L > \frac{n}{8}\right)g\left(\frac{n}{8}\right).$$

The last term of the above inequality is minimized when the probabilities multiplying the terms with the lower arguments of g, that is $Pr(L > \frac{n}{8})$ and $Pr(\frac{n}{2^i} < L \le \frac{n}{2^{i-1}})$ for the lowest values of i, are maximized. Recalling that $Pr(L > \frac{n}{2^i}) = \overline{p_i} < \frac{4i}{\log n}$ for every $i = 2, 3, \ldots, \log n - 4 \log \log n - \log k$, pushing probabilities as much as possible to such terms, it can be easily shown that the last term of the above inequality is minimized when $Pr(L > \frac{n}{8}) = 12/\log n$ and $Pr(\frac{n}{2^i} < L \le \frac{n}{2^{i-1}}) = 4/\log n$ for i between 4 and $\frac{\log n}{4}$. This actually holds only if we consider intervals of L for which we previously bounded $\overline{p_i}$, that is if $\frac{\log n}{4} < \log n - 4 \log \log n$, that can be obtained by setting n_0 to a suitably large integer such that $\frac{\log n_0}{4} < \log n_0 - 4 \log \log n_0$. Therefore, $g(n) \ge$

$$1 + (1 - p)g(n - 4) + p\sum_{i=4}^{\frac{\log n}{4}}\left(\frac{4}{\log n}g\left(n - \frac{4n}{2^{i-1}}\right)\right) + p\frac{12}{\log n}g\left(\frac{n}{8}\right).$$

By the inductive hypothesis, since $k \le \frac{1}{110}$, it is then possible to show that

$$g(n) \ge 1 + k\frac{\log^2 n}{\sqrt{p}}.$$

$\square$

An analogous proof obtained by considering as *S-node* node $\frac{n}{2}$ shows the following theorem.

Theorem 2. *For any non decreasing function f on a path P_n and any p-distance distribution generated by f, $\mathbb{E}(\mathcal{OD}(SWG(G, \hat{A}))) = \Omega(\min(n, \frac{\log^2(n)}{\sqrt{p}}))$.*

4 Complexity Results

Starting from the results shown in the previous section, we now focus on the determination of efficient deterministic constructions minimizing the oblivious diameter.

Unfortunately, the resulting optimization problem is generally intractable.

Theorem 3. *Given a graph G and an integer $k > 0$, deciding if $\mathcal{OD}_k(G) \leq 2$ is an NP-complete problem.*

Proof. Let us first observe that the decision problem belongs to the class NP. In fact, given a graph $G = (V, A)$ and a $SWG(G, \hat{A})$, it is possible to compute in polynomial time the length of all the oblivious paths connecting a node $u \in V$ to a generic node $z \in V$. For this task for every $v \in V - \{z\}$ let us define F_v as the set of all the adjacent nodes reachable from v through an oblivious path directed to z. Then, for every $v \in V$, let $g_z(v) = \max\{g_z(w) + 1 | w \in F_v\}$ be the length of the longest oblivious path from v to z. Clearly $g_z(z) = 0$, while $g_z(v)$ for any other node $v \in V$ can be computed in an incremental way such that at the i-th step, the oblivious distances of all the nodes at distance at most i in G from z are evaluated. Thus, in at most $|V|$ steps all the $g_z(v)$ can be computed for all the nodes $v \in V$. The oblivious diameter of $SWG(G, \hat{A})$ will then be $OD(SWG) = max_{u,z \in V}\{g_z(u)\}$.

In order to prove the NP-completeness of the problem, we provide a polynomial time reduction from the *Minimum Set Cover* problem (MSC) (known to be NP-complete; see [6]). In this problem we have a universe set $U = \{u_1, \ldots, u_m\}$ of m elements, a family $\{S_1, \ldots, S_f\}$ of f subsets of U and an integer $k \leq f$; we want to decide if there exist k subsets $S_{j_1}, \ldots, S_{j_k}$ that cover U, i.e., such that $\bigcup_{i=1}^{k} S_{j_i} = U$.

Starting from an instance I_{MSC} of MSC, we construct a Small World Graph $H = (V, A \cup \hat{A})$ with oblivious diameter at most equal to 2 if and only if I_{MSC} admits a cover of k subsets.

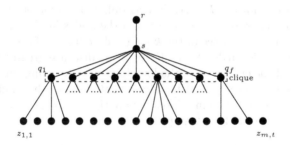

Fig. 1. The reduction graph of Theorem 3

Let $t = k^2 + k + 1$ and $G = (V, A)$, with $V = \{r\} \cup \{s\} \cup V_1 \cup V_2$ and $A = \{(r, s), (s, r)\} \cup A_1 \cup A_2 \cup A_3$ (see Figure 1),
$V_1 = \{q_i \mid i = 1, \ldots, f\}$,
$V_2 = \{z_{j,h} \mid j = 1, \ldots, m \wedge h = 1, \ldots, t\}$,
and
$A_1 = \{(s, q_i), (q_i, s) \mid i = 1, \ldots, f\}$,
$A_2 = \{(q_i, q_j) \mid i = 1, \ldots, f \wedge j = 1, \ldots, f \wedge i \neq j\}$,
$A_3 = \{(q_i, z_{j,h}), (z_{j,h}, q_i) \mid u_j \in S_i \wedge h = 1, \ldots, t\}$.

Informally, in the reduction graph, each subset S_i corresponds to the subgraph induced by node q_i and all the nodes $z_{j,h}$ such that $u_j \in S_i$ that are connected to q_i.

The idea underlying our construction is that, in order to obtain an oblivious diameter equal to 2, the only way is to put k long links in $\hat{A}$ from $r \in V$ to the k nodes q_i associated to the subsets of the cover, and the same for each node in V_2.

Assume there are k covering sets $S_{l_1}, \ldots, S_{l_k}$, we show that there exists a $SWG(G, \hat{A})$ having oblivious diameter at most 2. First of all, notice that node s is at distance at most 2 from all the other nodes and the same holds for all the nodes in V_1, since there is a clique between them (the arcs in A_2). Moreover, node r is at distance at most 2 from node s and from all the nodes in V_1. Finally, the nodes in V_2 are at distance at most 2 from s and all the nodes in V_1.

It remains to show that it is possible to choose at most k long links per node in such a way that the oblivious distance from node r to the nodes in V_2, from every node in V_2 to node r and between any couple of nodes in V_2, is at most 2.

Let us consider $\hat{A} = \hat{A}_1 \cup \hat{A}_2 \cup \hat{A}_3$ with
$\hat{A}_1 = \{(r, q_{l_i}) \mid 1 \leq i \leq k\}$,
$\hat{A}_2 = \{(z_{j,h}, q_{l_i}) \mid 1 \leq j \leq m \wedge 1 \leq h \leq t \wedge 1 \leq i \leq k\}$ and
$\hat{A}_3 = \{(q_i, r) \mid 1 \leq i \leq f\}$.

The oblivious path between r and the nodes in V_2 is of length 2 since its first arc is a long link in $\hat{A}_1$ whose endpoint is adjacent to the destination. Similarly, the oblivious path between two nodes in V_2 is of length 2 since its first arc is a long link in $\hat{A}_2$. The oblivious path between a node in V_2 and r is of length 2 since its second arc is a long link in $\hat{A}_3$.

In order to conclude the proof, it remains to show that if there are no k covering sets, then no $SWG(G, \hat{A})$, having oblivious diameter at most 2, exists. Consider the oblivious paths between r and the nodes in V_2. Since there are no k covering sets, for any choice of the k long links outgoing from r, after the first move there must exist at least t nodes in V_2 at distance greater than 1 from s and from each of the endpoints of the long links of r. Recalling that $t > (k+1)k$, since from s and from each of such endpoints at most k other nodes at distance grater than 1 can be reached in a further step, there must exist at least one node in V_2 that is not reachable in 2 steps from r.   □

5   Deterministic Results for Specific Topologies

In this section we show that truly random constructions cannot achieve the performance of deterministic ones on basic topologies such as paths, trees and Cartesian products of graphs, including d-dimensional grids.

5.1   Paths

We give a slightly more general deterministic construction for node weighted paths that will be useful both for unweighted paths, that is with uniform weights, and for trees.

Let P_n^w be a path of $n > 1$ nodes with weights $w_x \geq 1$, $w_x \in \mathbb{Z}$, associated to nodes $x \in \{1, 2, \ldots, n\}$, and let $W = \sum_{x=1}^{n} w_x$.

Let $\mathcal{W} = \{W_1, W_2, \ldots, W_{\lceil \log_2 W \rceil}\}$ be a partition of the set $\{1, 2, \ldots, W\}$ such that $W_i = \{z | \frac{W}{2^i} \leq z < \frac{W}{2^{i-1}}\}$ for all $i = 1, 2, \ldots, \lceil \log_2 W \rceil$.

In case of maximum outdegree at most equal to 1, we perform the deterministic construction in the following way.

Let u be the first node of the path such that $\sum_{x=1}^{u} w_x \geq \frac{W}{2}$. We assign a long link from node 1 to node u and from node $u + 1$ to node n, plus their opposite ones from u to 1 and from n to $u + 1$, respectively. Let those four links be considered of level 1. We now recursively consider the subpaths $[2, \ldots, u - 1]$ and $[u + 2, \ldots, n - 1]$, assigning for each of them four long links of level 2 in the same way, that is, dividing the current subpath in two weight-balanced portions. The long links are assigned till at most the $\lceil \log W \rceil$-th level is reached. Let us say that a node is of level i if it is the end-point of a long link of level i (by construction it cannot be the endpoint of long links of different levels).

Lemma 2. *In the above construction an oblivious path from a node x with weight $w_x \in W_i$ to a node y with weight $w_y \in W_j$ has length at most $4(i+j-1)$.*

Proof. First of all, it is easy to check that a node with weight in W_i is of level at most i. In fact, after assigning the long links of level i, the recursive construction is applied to subpaths consisting of nodes whose weights sum is less than $\frac{W}{2^i}$, so that no node with weight in W_i can exist in them. Thus, a long link to each node in W_i must be assigned before applying the recursive construction after level i. Clearly such a long link is of level at most i.

Let us now consider a generic source-destination pair (x, y) and let $w_x \in W_i$ and $w_y \in W_j$ be the weights of x and y, respectively. In order to prove that the oblivious path $\mathcal{OP}_{x,y}$ from x to y is bounded by $4(i + j - 1)$, we need to show the following properties:

1) The difference between the levels of two consecutive nodes in $\mathcal{OP}_{x,y}$ is at most 1.

2) The maximum number of consecutive nodes of the same level in $\mathcal{OP}_{x,y}$ is at most 4.

3) The sequence of the levels met from the source to the destination along $\mathcal{OP}_{x,y}$ determines a particular node z for which the subsequence from the source to z is not increasing while the one from z to the destination is not decreasing. Eventually, z can coincide with the source or with the destination, thus yielding a monotonic function.

In fact, if the above properties hold, since the level of node x is at most i and the one of node y is at most j, the claim holds by observing that $\mathcal{OP}_{x,y}$ meets at most all the levels from i to 1 and then (if $j \geq 2$) from 2 to j, and for each level at most 4 consecutive nodes, so that $|\mathcal{OP}_{x,y}| \leq 4(i + j - 1)$.

To prove 1) it is sufficient to notice that, by construction, the levels of two adjacent nodes of P_n (without considering the long links) differ of at most 1, while two nodes connected by a long link are of the same level.

By construction, the nodes of a given level $i \geq 2$ are included in groups of at most four ones under long links of level $i - 1$ and there are no crossing links. Hence to move from a quadruple of level i to another one of the same level we have to encounter at least two nodes of level $i - 1$. The nodes of level 1 are just 4. Property 2) then follows directly by observing that in no oblivious path a node can appear twice.

In order to prove 3) it is sufficient to show that if a node x_i of level $i = 2, \ldots, \lceil \log_2 W \rceil$ is reached from a node x_{i-1} of level $i - 1$ in $\mathcal{OP}_{x,y}$, than no node of level less than i can appear in the remaining part of $\mathcal{OP}_{x,y}$. As already observed, by construction x_i and at most other three nodes of level i are included under a long link l_{i-1} of level $i - 1$ and there not exist crossing links. Therefore, assuming by contradiction that a node of level smaller than i is reached in the remaining part of $\mathcal{OP}_{x,y}$, it follows that one of the two endpoints of l_{i-1}, say $\check{x}$, has to be reached first. If $\check{x} \equiv x_{i-1}$ the contradiction follows directly by observing that in no oblivious path a node can appear twice. In the other case, it follows since the long link connecting x_{i-1} to $\check{x}$ had to be chosen previously given the obliviousness of the path $\mathcal{OP}_{x,y}$. $\square$

Theorem 4. $\mathcal{OD}_1(P_n) = O(\log n)$.

Proof. The claim is a direct consequence of Lemma 2. In fact, in the special case in which all the weights of the nodes are equal to 1, thus summing up to $W = n$, the levels are at most $\lceil \log_2 n \rceil$ and the length of any oblivious path is bounded by $4(2\lceil \log_2 n \rceil - 1)$ (see Figure 2). $\square$

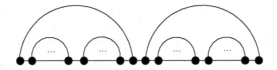

Fig. 2. The deterministic construction for the path

We now extend these results to the general case in which the maximum outdegree is bounded by a given $k > 0$. The corresponding construction is quite similar to the previous one.

Let $W = \{W_1, W_2, \ldots, W_{\lceil \log_{2k} W \rceil}\}$ be a partition of the set $\{1, 2, \ldots, W\}$ such that for all $i = 1, 2, \ldots, \lceil \log_{2k} W \rceil$, $W_i = \{z | \frac{W}{(2k)^i} \leq z < \frac{W}{(2k)^{i-1}}\}$.

Let $u_0 = 0$, and having determined $u_0, \ldots, u_{j-1}$, let $u_j, j = 1, \ldots, 2k - 1$, be the first node of the path such that $\sum_{x=u_{j-1}+1}^{u_j} w_x \geq \frac{W}{2k}$. Finally, let $u_{2k} = n$. Notice that u_0 does not correspond to any node of the path, but it has been set to 0 to simplify the description of the construction. We assign two pairwise opposite long links between $u_j + 1$ and nodes $u_{j+1}, \ldots, u_{\min\{j+k, 2k\}}$ for $j = 0, \ldots, 2k - 1$. Let those links be considered of level 1. We now recursively consider the subpaths $[u_j + 2, \ldots, u_{j+1} - 1]$ for $j = 0, \ldots, 2k - 1$, assigning to each of them long links of level 2 in the same way, that is, dividing the current subpath in $2k$ weight-balanced portions. The long links are assigned till at most the $\lceil \log_{2k} W \rceil$-th level is reached. Again, a node is said of level i if it is the end-point of a long link of level i.

Arguments similar to the ones for outdegree 1 prove the following claims.

Lemma 3. *In the above construction the oblivious path from a node x with weight $w_x \in W_i$ to a node y with weight $w_y \in W_j$ has length at most $4(i+j-1)$.*

Theorem 5. $\mathcal{OD}_k(P_n) = O(\log_k n)$.

5.2   Trees

We now present a deterministic construction having outdegree 1 for trees based on their standard separation property. Namely, it is possible to determine a *heavy path* $(u_1, \ldots, u_h)$ starting from the root $r = u_1$ and descending at each step in one of the subtrees having largest cardinality, till reaching a leaf. Let U_j, $j = 1, \ldots, h$, be the set of the sons of u_j not equal to u_{j+1}. As it can be easily checked, the deletion of the heavy path separates the tree into several subtrees with roots in U_j, $j = 1, \ldots, h$. Each of such subtrees has size at most equal to the half of the one of the original tree.

On the heavy path we apply the outdegree 1 construction for weighted paths shown in the previous subsection, assigning to each node u_j a weight equal to the total number of nodes in the subtrees rooted at nodes in U_j plus 1.

In each subtree we recursively do the same construction.

Theorem 6. *For a tree T with n nodes $\mathcal{OD}_1(T) = O(\log n)$.*

Proof. Let the eccentricity $e(n)$ of a tree of n nodes be the maximum length of an oblivious path starting from the root of the tree to one internal node and vice versa, according to the above construction. We first show that $e(n) = O(\log n)$.

Consider an oblivious path between the root and a generic node x of the tree. By construction, considering the heavy path determined from the root, it is easy to check that if x belongs to a subtree rooted at a node in U_j, node u_j of the heavy path must be a node of the oblivious path from the root to x. By Lemma 2, the length of the oblivious path from the root to u_j depends on the weight w_j of u_j. More precisely, if i is the maximum value such that $w_j < \frac{n}{2^{i-1}}$, such a length is bounded by $4i$.

The same arguments hold for the oblivious path from x to the root, which must step through u_j.

Thus, for $i \geq 1$, the following recursive inequality holds: $e(n) \leq 4i + 1 + e\left(\frac{n}{2^{\max\{1,i-1\}}}\right)$, where the addition of 1 is due to the oblivious step from u_j to the appropriate subtree with root in U_j, while the maximum between 1 and $i - 1$ below the last factor is due to the fact that such a subtree has size at most $w_j < \frac{n}{2^{i-1}}$ and according to the standard separation property of the tree at most equal to $n/2$. It is easy to check how such inequality implies $e(n) \leq 10 \log n + 10 = O(\log n)$.

If we consider now the oblivious diameter of the deterministic construction, it is easy to see that it is at most twice $e(n/2)$ plus the oblivious diameter of a

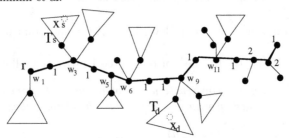

Fig. 3. The *heavy path* and the associated weights

heavy path (generated from the root or recursively in one of the subtrees). In fact, for any source-destination pair (x_s, x_d), there must exist a minimal subtree $\bar{T} \subseteq T$ (eventually the whole tree) generated during the construction containing both x_s and x_d. Consider the heavy path of $\bar{T}$ and let $\bar{u}_s$ and $\bar{u}_d$ the two nodes such that $\bar{U}_s$ and $\bar{U}_d$ include the roots of the subtrees containing x_s and x_d, respectively. The oblivious path is then obtained by the concatenation of the oblivious ones from x_s to $\bar{u}_s$, from $\bar{u}_s$ to $\bar{u}_d$ and from $\bar{u}_d$ to x_d.

Since the maximum sum of the node weights of the heavy path of $\bar{T}$ is at most n, by Lemma 2 the oblivious distance of $\bar{u}_s$ and $\bar{u}_s$ is $O(\log n)$.

Therefore, $\mathcal{OD}_1(T) \leq 2 + 2e\left(\frac{n}{2}\right) + O(\log n) = O(\log n)$.   □

5.3   Cartesian Products

Given any two digraphs $G_1 = (V_1, A_1)$ and $G_2 = (V_2, A_2)$, the Cartesian product of G_1 and G_2, denoted as $G_1 \square G_2$, is a digraph having $|V_2|$ rows or horizontal components and V_1 columns or vertical components. Routing along each row is done according to G_1 and in each column according to G_2. More precisely, $G_1 \square G_2$ has node set $\{(x, y)\} | x \in V_1, y \in V_2\}$ and arc set $\{((x, y), (x, y')) | (y, y') \in A_2\} \cup \{((x, y), (x', y)) | (x, x') \in A_1\}$.

Lemma 4. *For every two digraphs* G_1 *and* G_2, $\mathcal{OD}_{k_1+k_2}(G_1 \square G_2) = \mathcal{OD}_{k_1}(G_1) + \mathcal{OD}_{k_2}(G_2)$.

Proof. We use along each row (resp. column) the same construction with outdegree k_1 (resp. k_2) for G_1 (resp. G_2). Clearly, this yields outdegree at most $k_1 + k_2$. The lemma then follows by observing that the oblivious paths from a node (x, y) to another node (x', y') in $G_1 \square G_2$ are all and only the ones alternating in all the possible ways horizontal and vertical moves according to the oblivious paths from x to x' in G_1 and from y to y' in G_2, so that $\mathcal{OD}_{k_1+k_2}(G_1 \square G_2) = \mathcal{OD}_{k_1}(G_1) + \mathcal{OD}_{k_2}(G_2)$.   □

As far as we restrict to Cartesian products of paths, it is also possible to obtain deterministic constructions having outdegree equal to 1. Consider in fact the $n \times n$ grid resulting from the product $P_n^2 \equiv P_n \square P_n$ of two paths of n nodes. The idea is to alternate the nodes of the grid for vertical and horizontal movements according to the long links of our deterministic construction withoutdegree 1 for

$P_{\lfloor\frac{n}{2}\rfloor}$ in a chessboard like fashion, thus obtaining at each node of the grid either horizontal or vertical long links. Thus, for any odd (resp. even) row the odd (resp. even) nodes represent a horizontal copy of $P_{\lfloor\frac{n}{2}\rfloor}$ and for any odd (resp. even) column the even (resp. odd) nodes represent a vertical copy.

By extending such a construction to d-dimensional grids P_n^d, that is to Cartesian products of d paths of n nodes, it is possible to prove the following lemma (details will appear in the full version of the paper).

Theorem 7. *Given any integer $d \geq 2$, $\mathcal{OD}_1(P_n^d) = O(d^2 \log N)$, where $N = n^d$ is the number of nodes of P_n^d.*

Again such a construction is asymptotically optimal, that is with an oblivious diameter logarithmic in the total number of nodes, for the most significant cases of grids having a constant number of dimensions.

6 Conclusion and Future Work

We have given the first general lower bound on the expected oblivious diameter holding for any monotone distance distribution. Moreover, after showing the intractability of the problem in the deterministic case, we have given asymptotically optimal constructions for paths, trees and Cartesian products of graphs, including d-dimensional grids for any fixed value of d.

Many problems are left open. First of all, even if as proved in the literature only non increasing distance distributions are expected to yield a low oblivious diameter, can our lower bound be extended to completely arbitrary distance distributions?

Moreover, the lower bound concerns only path topologies, that is one-dimensional grids. Although it is intuitively clear that the oblivious diameter can only get worse in higher dimensional grids due to the possibility of having long links changing many dimensions at the same time, for such topologies we don't have a formal proof yet.

Another worth investigating issue is that of determining randomized or deterministic constructions always achieving a polylogarithmic oblivious diameter when at most a polylogarithmic number of outgoing long links per node are allowed.

Is there a construction achieving an $O(\log_k n)$ oblivious diameter for trees in case of at most k outgoing long links per node?

It would be also interesting to give asymptotically optimal deterministic solutions for broader classes of networks, like for instance for grids having a non constant number of dimensions.

An important final remark is that, differently from the classical problem of determining bounded degree graphs with a minimum diameter, in the considered specific small world graphs deterministic constructions seem to be more effective than probabilistic ones. Is this true in general, that is when there is no restriction on the topology?

References

1. ADAMIC, L. A. The Small World Web. In *Proc. of the 3rd European Conference on Research and Advanced Technology for DIGITAL LIBRARIES (ECDL)* (1999), vol. 1696, Lecture Notes in Computer Science, Springer-Verlag, pp. 443–452.

2. ASPNES, J., DIAMADI, Z., AND SHAH, G. Fault-tolerant routing in peer-to-peer systems. In *Proc. of the 21st annual symposium on Principles of distributed computing (PODC)* (2002), ACM Press, pp. 223–232.

3. BARRIERE, L., FRAIGNIAUD, P., KRANAKIS, E., AND KRIZANC, D. Efficient routing in networks with long range contacts. In *Proc. of the 15th International Conference on Distributed Computing (DISC)* (2001), Springer-Verlag, pp. 270–284.

4. FRAIGNIAUD, P. A new perspective on the small-world phenomenon: Greedy routing in tree-decomposed graphs. In *Proceedings of the 13th Annual European Symposium on Algorithms (ESA)* (2005, to appear).

5. FRAIGNIAUD, P., GAVOILLE, C., AND PAUL, C. Eclecticism shrinks even small worlds. In *Proc. of the 23rd annual ACM symposium on Principles of distributed computing (PODC)* (2004), ACM Press, pp. 169–178.

6. GAREY, M., AND JOHNSON, D. *Computers and Intractability: A Guide to the Theory of NP-Completeness.* W.H. Freeman and Co., 1979.

7. KLEINBERG, J. Small-world phenomena and the dynamics of information. In *Proc. of the 14th Advances in Neural Information Processing Systems (NIPS)* (2001).

8. KLEINBERG, J. The Small-World Phenomenon and Decentralized Search. *SIAM News 37*, 3 (2004).

9. KLEINBERG, J. M. The small-world phenomenon: an algorithm perspective. In *Proc. of the 32nd ACM Symposium on Theory of Computing (STOC)* (2000), pp. 163–170.

10. MARTEL, C., AND NGUYEN, V. Analyzing Kleinberg's (and other) small-world models. In *Proc. of the 23rd Annual ACM SIGACT-SIGOPS Symposium on Principles of Distributed Computing (PODC)* (2004), pp. 179–188.

11. MARTEL, C., AND NGUYEN, V. Analyzing and characterizing small-world graphs. In *Proc. of the 16th Annual ACM-SIAM Symposium on Discrete Algorithms (SODA)* (2005), pp. 311–320.

12. MILGRAM, S. The small world problem. *Psychology Today 2* (1967), 60–67.

13. WALSH, T. Search in a small world. In *Proc. of the 16th International Joint Conference on Artificial Intelligence (IJCAI)* (1999), pp. 1172–1177.

14. WANG, X. F., AND CHEN, G. Complex networks: small-world, scale-free, and beyond. *IEEE Circuits and Systems Magazine 3*, 1 (2003), 6–20.

15. WATTS, D. J., AND STROGATZ, S. H. Networks, Dynamics and Small-World Phenomenon. *American Journal of Sociology 105*, 2 (1999), 493–527.

16. ZHANG, H., GOEL, A., AND GOVINDAN, R. Using the small-world model to improve freenet performance. *SIGCOMM Computer Communication Review 32*, 1 (2002), 79–79.

Deciding Stability in Packet-Switched FIFO Networks Under the Adversarial Queuing Model in Polynomial Time *, **

Maria J. Blesa

ALBCOM Research Group,
Dept. Llenguatges i Sistemes Informàtics,
Universitat Politècnica de Catalunya,
Ω-213 Campus Nord, E-08034 Barcelona, Spain
mjblesa@lsi.upc.edu

Abstract. In spite of the importance of the FIFO protocol and the research efforts invested in obtaining results for it, deciding whether a given (packet-switched) network is stable under FIFO has remained an open question for several years. In this work, we address the general case of this problem and try to characterize the property of stability under FIFO in terms of network topologies. Such a characterization provides us with the family of network topologies that, under the FIFO protocol, can be made unstable by some adversarial traffic pattern. We show that the property of stability under FIFO is decidable in polynomial time.

1 Introduction

Since the emergence of computer networks, protocols were used for the establishment of ordered communications among computers. Communication takes place at different levels: low level protocols define for example the bit- and byte-ordering, their transmission, and the error detection and correction of the bit stream; high level protocols deal for example with the data packet formatting, the packet routing and the packet scheduling.

In this paper, we are interested in this latter functionality, in which the *protocol* (also called *scheduling policy*) determines the order in which the packets requiring to cross a link are scheduled to be forwarded. Most scheduling protocols aim at moving information across a network in an efficient and reliable manner. This often requires congestion and flow control, error detection and correction, and handshaking to coordinate the information transfer. Most network communication protocols are implemented as part of the operating system on the computers wishing to communicate. The *first-in-first-out* (FIFO) protocol is

---

* Partially supported by EU Programmes under contract numbers IST-2001-33116 (FLAGS), IST-2004-15964 (AEOLUS), COST-295 (DYNAMO), and by the Spanish CICYT projects TIC-2001-4917-E and TIC-2002-04498-C05-03 (TRACER).
** The reader is addressed to an extended technical report version of the paper in [6], for details on the proofs of the theorems.

P. Fraigniaud (Ed.): DISC 2005, LNCS 3724, pp. 429–441, 2005.

still one of the most popular, important and effective scheduling policies, in spite of its simplicity. The FIFO protocol schedules queued packets according to a *local criterion* in which the highest priority is given to the packet that has arrived first in the queue. This locality property makes the FIFO protocol easy to be implemented.

Appropriate models to study networking systems that implement specific communication protocols are needed. Those models could help us to understand better the dynamics of nowadays' communication networks, and therefore to detect and overcome the conditions leading to undesirable negative effects, as well as helping on their further prevention. One of those undesirable negative effects is the lack of stability.

Stability refers to the fact that the number of packets in the system remains bounded (by a bound that can be a function of the system parameters, but not dependent on time) as the system dynamically evolves in time. Stability is studied in relation to the three main components modeling a synchronous communication system $(\mathcal{G}, \mathcal{A}, \mathcal{P})$: the network $\mathcal{G}$, the traffic pattern defined by $\mathcal{A}$, and the protocol $\mathcal{P}$. *Networks* are modeled by directed graphs in which the nodes represent the hosts, and the arcs represent the links between those hosts. The *traffic pattern* controls where and how packets join the system and, optionally, defines their trajectory. The protocols considered are usually greedy.[1]

A strongest notion of stability is that of *universal stability*. Universal stability can be addressed from the network or from the protocol point of view. A network $\mathcal{G}$ is universally stable if, for any protocol and any traffic pattern, the resulting system is stable. A protocol $\mathcal{P}$ is universally stable if, for any network and any adversary the resulting system is stable.

According to the classification introduced in [3], we will also differentiate and refer to the property of stability in the case in which packets follow *simple paths* as *simple-path stability*, leaving then the term *stability* to refer to the case in which packets follow *paths*.[2]

The Adversarial Queueing Theory (AQT) model proposed by Borodin et al. [7] has become an important model to study stability issues in packet-switched communication networks. These models have been shown to be good theoretical frameworks for describing the traffic pattern in both connectionless networks (such as the Internet) and short-term connection networks, as well as connection-oriented networks (such as ATM networks). Adversarial models allow to analyze the system in a worst-case scenario, since they have replaced traditional stochastic arrival assumptions in the traffic pattern by worst-case inputs. The AQT model

---

[1] (Store and forward)greedy protocols are those forwarding a packet across a link e whenever there is at least one packet waiting to traverse e. At each time step, only one packet from those waiting is forwarded through the link; the rest are kept in a queue at the link. Greedy protocols are also called work-conserving protocols.

[2] We consider a *path* through a digraph a traversal of consecutive vertices along a sequence of arcs, in which repeated vertices (but no arcs) within the path are permissible. When there are no repeated vertices in the path (and therefore no arcs either), then it is called a *simple path*.

considers the time evolution of a packet-routing network as a game between an adversary, which produces the traffic pattern, and a queueing policy. The system is considered to be *synchronous*. At each time step the adversary may inject a set of packets to some of the nodes. In the case of static routing, the adversary specifies the route that every injected packet must traverse before arriving to its destination. When arriving to destination, packets are considered to disappear from the system. If more than one packet wishes to cross an edge e at the same time step, then the queueing policy chooses exactly one of these packets. The remaining packets wait in the queue. This game then advances to the next time step. The goal of the adversary is to try to prevent the protocol from guaranteeing load and delay bounds. On the contrary, the main goal of the model is to study conditions for stability of the network under different protocols.

In order not to trivially overload the system and in order to be able to guarantee delay bounds, it is necessary to restrict the traffic arriving to the network. The constraints on the traffic pattern must ensure that, over long periods of time, the maximum traffic injected in a link is roughly the amount of traffic that the link can forward. Two parameters (r, b) constraint an adversary in the AQT model, where $b \geq 0$ is the *burstiness* and $0 < r < 1$ is the *injection rate*. Let $N_e(I)$ be the number of packets injected by the adversary in a time interval I, whose path require to traverse a particular edge e. The adversary must obey the following (leaky-bucket) constraint:

$$N_e(I) \leq \lceil r|I| \rceil + b. \tag{1}$$

Recent research on stability has mainly considered the AQT model and has put special interest in the FIFO protocol (see, e.g., [7,4,8,17,18,9,5,19]).

Our motivations and contributions. Universal stability of networks is a non-trivial property; since it is a predicate quantified over all protocols and adversaries, it might at first appear that it is not a decidable property. One of the deepest results in the context of network stability in the adversarial queueing model establishes that, to the contrary, this is not the case [4]. The question of characterizing networks that are universally stable, and algorithmically recognizing such networks, naturally arises next. This question was also recently answered in [3] by fully characterizing the property under different network representation and considering different restrictions on the packet trajectories. Moreover, in the same work it is shown that deciding universal stability of networks requires polynomial time.

Concerning the protocol point of view, it is known that FTG, NFS, SIS and LIS are universally stable, while FIFO, LIFO, NTG and FFS are not [4].[3] For those

---

[3] The protocol *last-in-first-out* (LIFO) gives priority to the packet which entered the queue the latest. Concerning injection times, *shortest-in-system* (SIS) gives priority to the packet introduced last into the system, while *longest-in-system* (LIS) gives it to the one that has been in the system the longest. Concerning the distance to the destination, *nearest-to-go* (NTG) assigns highest priority to the packet that is closest to its destination and FTG (Furthest To Go) to the packet that is farthest. Similarly, *nearest-from-source* (NFS) and *farthest-from-source* (FFS) consider the distance to the source.

queueing polices which are not universally stable, a weaker notion of stability is addressed, that of the *stability under a protocol*. Here the problem is to *decide which networks are stable, and which are not, under a fixed queuing policy $\mathcal{P}$. In the best case, a characterization of stability under the protocol $\mathcal{P}$ can be obtained.* To the best of our knowledge, only two results are known in this sense: Deciding stability under the NTG-LIS[4] and FFS protocols is polynomially solvable and it is, moreover, equivalent to deciding universal stability of networks [3,1].

In this paper *we address the problem of deciding stability under the* FIFO *protocol*. In spite of the importance of this property and this protocol, the aspects concerning its decidability and complexity were still, since some years, an open question in the area. In this work, *we show that the property of stability under* FIFO *is decidable in polynomial time* and do a step forward towards the characterization of the property.

Taking the characterization of (network) universal stability as starting reference [3], and using similar techniques as the ones we used there, we propose two characterizations of the stability under FIFO. These characterizations are composed by two candidate sets of forbidden subdigraphs. One of them is actually the characterization of the property. The eligibility of one or the other candidate set as the decisive characterization depends on the stability of the digraph $\mathcal{U}_1$ (see Figure 1). In the case that $\mathcal{U}_1$ is unstable under FIFO, the characterization would be the same as the characterization of the digraphs that are universally stable [3]. This would have some nice implications since, in the case this holds, a digraph would be universally stable if and only if it is stable under FIFO. In spite of the simplicity of the network topology in $\mathcal{U}_1$, some important questions about it remain still open nowadays. One of these particular questions is concerned with its stability under the FIFO protocol.

Organization. The paper is organized as follows. In Section 2 we introduce some preliminaries of the work; this includes a review of the results existing in the literature which are concerned with stability under FIFO, and also the notation used in the forthcoming of the paper. In Section 3, the family of digraphs which are stable under FIFO are presented. Also in this section, the family of digraphs which are not stable are introduced by its minimal representants. The property of stability under FIFO is characterized in Section 4 in terms of those unstable minimal representants. In the same section, a polynomial-time algorithm is given for deciding the property of stability under the FIFO protocol. The work concludes in Section 5, where some open questions as well as some possible extensions of the work are pointed out.

2   Preliminaries

The *first-in-first-out* (FIFO) greedy protocol is probably one of the most commonly used scheduling protocols. FIFO is used in many contexts in computer environments, either internally (e.g., in operating systems to process I/O device

---

[4] The protocol NTG-LIS works as NTG, but solves ties using the LIS protocol.

interruptions or information exchange between processes) or externally (e.g., as communication protocol for information exchange between computers). One of its main advantages, specially when implementing it, is that its criterion to schedule packets is completely based on simple local properties. In the FIFO protocol, highest priority is given to the packet that has arrived first in the queue. Observe that, when two packets arrive to the queue at the same time then they have to be queued in some order, which we will assume that is decided *arbitrarily* by the adversary.

2.1 Previous Results on FIFO in the AQT Model

Due to its relevance, much attention has been put on the study of stability conditions in AQT under the FIFO protocol. Already the pioneering work of Borodin et al. [7] showed that ring topologies are not stable under FIFO for the extreme injection rate $r = 1$. It is however of higher interest to find bounds when adversaries work in underloaded conditions, i.e., when their injection rate $r < 1$. Thus, the consecutive improvement of the lower bounds for instability under FIFO was one of the research subjects in the last years. As time and research advanced, this lower bound was dropping from $r \geq 0.85$ [4], to $r \geq 0.84$ [11], $r \geq 0.8357$ [8], $r \geq 0.771$ [17], $r \geq 0.749$ [16], and finally to $r > 0.5$ [19]. A step further was done recently, when FIFO was shown to be unstable at arbitrarily low rates [5,15]. The existence of a network-dependent upper bound was shown in [8], which was recently generalized to $r \leq 1/d$ [19,9], where d is the length of the longest route traversed by any packet.

However, as we have pointed out before, the aspects concerning its decidability and complexity were still, since some years, an open question in the area.

2.2 Digraph Subdivision Operations

We use standard graph terminology to denote the following digraphs: directed k-cycles, *acyclic* digraphs, and *unicyclic* digraphs. A directed k-cycle is a directed (simple) cycle with k vertices, where $k \geq 2$. We say that two directed (simple) cycles are *embedded* when they share one or more edges, and they are *collar-chained* when they only share one vertex but no edges (e.g., in Figure 1, the two cycles in digraph $\mathcal{U}_2$ are collar-chained, while the multiple cycles in the other digraphs are embedded). A unicyclic digraph is a digraph that contains only one (simple) cycle.

We will characterize the property of stability under FIFO in terms of a family of forbidden subdigraphs. To this aim, we first need to identify the families of digraphs which are stable under this protocol. Then the simplest digraphs which are not stable should be identified. The family of the digraphs which are not stable under FIFO will be then defined by iteratively applying *subdivision operations* to those simplest digraphs. We consider the following subdivision operations:

- The *subdivision of an arc* (u, v) in a digraph $\mathcal{G}$ consists in the addition of a new vertex w and the replacement of (u, v) by (u, w) and (w, v).

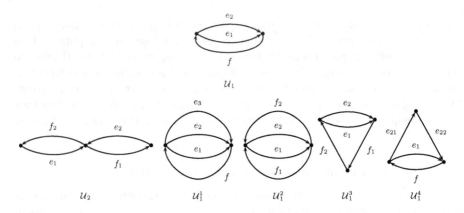

Fig. 1. Minimum forbidden subdigraphs characterizing stability under FIFO. The two candidate sets to consider are either $\{\mathcal{U}_1, \mathcal{U}_2\}$ or $\{\mathcal{U}_1^1, \mathcal{U}_1^2, \mathcal{U}_1^3, \mathcal{U}_1^4, \mathcal{U}_2\}$; the former would characterize the stability under FIFO in the case that $\mathcal{U}_1$ is not stable under that protocol, while the latter would characterize it in the case that $\mathcal{U}_1$ is stable under FIFO.

– The *subdivision of a 2-cycle* (u, v), (v, u) in a digraph $\mathcal{G}$ consists in the addition of a new vertex w and the replacement of (u, v), (v, u) by the arcs (u, w), (w, u), (v, w) and (w, v).

Then, given a digraph $\mathcal{G}$, we will denote as $\mathcal{E}(\mathcal{G})$ the family of digraphs formed by $\mathcal{G}$ and all the digraphs obtained from $\mathcal{G}$ by successive arc or 2-cycle subdivisions. Note that, a strongly connected digraph remains so when applying arc or 2-cycle subdivisions to it. In the following, we will be using digraphs and networks as synonyms. All the digraphs considered in this paper are strongly connected and they may have multiple edges (arcs) but no loops.[5] Since we deal with static routing, a packet transmitted over those digraphs follows a predefined (and non-changing) *path*. To keep lighter the notation, a path is specified by the sequence of its edges or by the concatenation of sub-paths. Moreover, the names used to denote the digraphs and their edges correspond to the ones depicted in Figure 1.

3   Stability of Digraphs Under FIFO

In this section, we show which digraphs are stable under FIFO as well as those simplest digraphs which are not stable under this protocol. By applying subdivision operations to those simplest unstable digraphs the whole family of digraphs which are not stable under FIFO will be determined.

In the following lemma, we enounce the known property that the instability of any of the subdigraphs of a digraph produces automatically instability in the graph.

---

[5] Multiple edges share the same pair of different endpoints. The endpoints of a loop is the same vertex.

Lemma 1 ([4]). *If H is a subdigraph of G and H is unstable, then G is also unstable.*

This property is maintained when acyclically connecting digraphs which are stable under FIFO. Given two digraphs $\mathcal{G}_1$ and $\mathcal{G}_2$, let us denote as $\mathcal{G}_{1\to2}$ the family of digraphs formed by joining $\mathcal{G}_1$ and $\mathcal{G}_2$ with arcs that go only from $\mathcal{G}_1$ to $\mathcal{G}_2$.

Lemma 2. *If digraphs $\mathcal{G}_1$ and $\mathcal{G}_2$ are stable under FIFO, then so is any digraph $\mathcal{G} \in \mathcal{G}_{1\to2}$.*

Proof. Assume that the adversary working against $\mathcal{G}$ has rate r and burstiness b. Any packet injected into $\mathcal{G}_1$ by this adversary will get out of $\mathcal{G}_1$ within a bounded number of time steps t_1, because $\mathcal{G}_1$ is stable under FIFO. Some of the packets leaving $\mathcal{G}_1$ might join $\mathcal{G}_2$. Let us consider a time interval of t_2 steps starting right after the t_1 time steps mentioned before. The packets joining $\mathcal{G}_2$ during that t_2 time steps must have been introduced in the system during the last $t_1 + t_2$ steps; moreover, there are at most $r(t_1 + t_2) + b$ of those packets.

We want to show that all the packets coming from $\mathcal{G}_1$ together with the packets injected directly in $\mathcal{G}_2$ could have been generated by an adversary working only against $\mathcal{G}_2$. Consider that such an adversary has rate $1 > r' > r$ and burstiness $b' \geq b$. During any interval $t \geq t_2$, the total amount of packets introduced into $\mathcal{G}_2$ would be $r't + b'$. In order for those packets to be generated by the mentioned adversary, it must hold that $r't + b' = r't + b' - ((r' - r)t_2 + b' - rt_1 - b)$, which holds when considering $t_2 = rt_1/(r' - r)$. ∎

As a consequence of Lemmas 1 and 2 we can state the following:

Theorem 1. *A digraph $\mathcal{G}$ is stable under FIFO if and only if all its strongly connected components are stable under FIFO.*

All directed acyclic graphs[6] and (isolated) directed cycles on any number of vertices are known to be universally stable [7,4], thus being also stable under the FIFO protocol. Let us re-write these known properties as Lemma 3.

Lemma 3 ([7,4]). *All acyclic digraphs and k-cycles (where $k \geq 2$) are stable under FIFO.*

Observe that an uniclycic digraph $\mathcal{G}$ can be seen as composed by a k-cycle, and different lines connected acyclically to it. By extension, every digraph with more than one cycle can be seen as an acyclic connection of two stable subdigraphs if any two cycles are neither collar-chained nor embedded. In this case, the cycles are acyclically connected by directed non-empty paths. The following lemmas can be stated as a consequence of Lemmas 2 and 3.

Lemma 4. *All unicyclic digraphs are stable under FIFO.*

---

[6] Note that this includes directed *trees* and *multi-trees*, i.e., directed trees with single arcs and multi-arcs.

Lemma 5. *All digraphs with more than one cycle in which any pair of cycles are neither collar-chained nor embedded are stable under* FIFO.

In a strongly connected digraph, every vertex can be accessed from any other vertex of the digraph. Note that all the directed acyclic digraphs as well as all the digraphs formed by acyclic connections are not strongly connected. However, in the context of communication networks strongly connected topologies are of highest interest. Beyond the directed cycle and unicyclic digraphs, the next networks to consider are then the digraphs $\mathcal{U}_1$ and $\mathcal{U}_2$ depicted in Figure 1, which are the smallest non-unicyclic strongly connected digraphs, i.e., the smallest strongly-connected digraphs with more than one cycle. Observe that $\mathcal{U}_1$ is the smallest network that has two embedded cycles, and that $\mathcal{U}_2$ is the smallest network that has two collar-chained cycles. In the following, we show that neither the digraph $\mathcal{U}_2$, nor any of its extensions, are stable under FIFO.

Lemma 6. *The digraphs in $\mathcal{E}(\mathcal{U}_2)$ are not stable under* FIFO.

However, it remains still an open question (as it was already pointed out in [3]) whether the digraph $\mathcal{U}_1$ is stable under FIFO. Instead, let us consider the digraphs $\mathcal{U}_1^1$, $\mathcal{U}_1^2$, $\mathcal{U}_1^3$ and $\mathcal{U}_1^4$ depicted in Figure 1, which are the next strongly connected digraphs to consider after $\mathcal{U}_1$ (in terms of their size). Digraphs $\mathcal{U}_1^1$ and $\mathcal{U}_1^2$ are obtained from $\mathcal{U}_1$ when considering multi-edges, while digraphs $\mathcal{U}_1^3$ and $\mathcal{U}_1^4$ are obtained from $\mathcal{U}_1$ when subdividing arcs. The digraphs that result from 2-cycle subdivisions of $\mathcal{U}_1$ contain $\mathcal{U}_2$ as a subdigraph, and so they can be made unstable under the FIFO protocol. Although no result concerning the stability of $\mathcal{U}_1$ under FIFO is known, we show in the following that neither digraphs $\mathcal{U}_1^1$, $\mathcal{U}_1^2$, $\mathcal{U}_1^3$ or $\mathcal{U}_1^4$, nor any of their extensions are stable under FIFO.

Lemma 7. *The digraphs in $\mathcal{E}(\mathcal{U}_1^1) \cup \mathcal{E}(\mathcal{U}_1^2) \cup \mathcal{E}(\mathcal{U}_1^3) \cup \mathcal{E}(\mathcal{U}_1^4)$ are not stable under* FIFO.

However, a quite high injection rate ($r \geq 0.929$, see appendix) is needed to produce instability in this networks, which indicates that, although possible, it is not "easy" to make a system unstable under FIFO with these underlying topologies.

Observe that, by considering the family of digraphs composed by $\mathcal{U}_2, \mathcal{U}_1^1, \mathcal{U}_1^2, \mathcal{U}_1^3, \mathcal{U}_1^4$ and their extensions, the only digraphs which are not included are those which have as subdigraph a digraph in

$$\mathcal{E}(\mathcal{U}_1) \setminus \left\{ \mathcal{E}(\mathcal{U}_2) \cup \mathcal{E}(\mathcal{U}_1^1) \cup \mathcal{E}(\mathcal{U}_1^2) \cup \mathcal{E}(\mathcal{U}_1^3) \cup \mathcal{E}(\mathcal{U}_1^4) \right\},$$

i.e., those whose strongly connected components are exactly $\mathcal{U}_1$. If $\mathcal{U}_1$ is stable under FIFO, then those digraphs are also because of Lemma 2; if $\mathcal{U}_1$ is not stable under FIFO, then those digraphs can be made also unstable but, in this case, they would not be the smallest forbidden subdigraphs because they contain $\mathcal{U}_1$.

4   Characterizing Stability Under FIFO

In this section two candidate sets of forbidden subdigraphs are proposed for the characterization of the stability under FIFO. The choice of the right candidate

---

Algorithm 1 : Stability under FIFO   (sup. $\mathcal{U}_1$ is not stable under FIFO)

INPUT: A strongly connected digraph $\mathcal{G} = (V, E)$

compute a (any) directed k-cycle $C = (e_1 \ldots e_k)$ of $k \geq 2$ vertices, and let

    $C_V \leftarrow \{v \mid \exists e \in C : e = (v, u)\} \subseteq V$ (set of vertices of the cycle C)

    $C_E \leftarrow \{e \mid e \in C\} \subseteq E$ (set of arcs of the cycle C)

if $\mathcal{G}$ does not have a directed k-cycle of $k \geq 2$ vertices **then**

    return YES

else

    Let $\mathcal{G}' = (V, E \setminus C_E)$ be the digraph resulting after removing from $\mathcal{G}$ the arcs in C

    if there are two different vertices $u, v \in C_V$ connected in $\mathcal{G}'$ by a directed path

    then

        return NO

    else

        return YES

    end if

end if

---

has a penchant for one subset or the other depending on the stability of $\mathcal{U}_1$. Whatever the decisive characterization is, we can state the stability under FIFO can be decided in polynomial time.

Theorem 2. *If the digraph $\mathcal{U}_1$ is not stable under FIFO, then any digraph $\mathcal{G}$ is stable under FIFO if and only if it does not contain as subdigraph a digraph from $\mathcal{E}(\mathcal{U}_1) \cup \mathcal{E}(\mathcal{U}_2)$. Otherwise, if the digraph $\mathcal{U}_1$ is stable under FIFO, then any digraph $\mathcal{G}$ is stable under FIFO if and only if it does not contain as subdigraph a digraph from $\mathcal{E}(\mathcal{U}_1^1) \cup \mathcal{E}(\mathcal{U}_1^2) \cup \mathcal{E}(\mathcal{U}_1^3) \cup \mathcal{E}(\mathcal{U}_1^4) \cup \mathcal{E}(\mathcal{U}_2)$.*

Proof. If the digraph $\mathcal{U}_1$ is not stable under FIFO then, according to Theorem 6 and the fact that the instability of a subdigraph implies the instability of the whole digraph, no digraph $\mathcal{G}$ containing as subdigraph a digraph from $\mathcal{E}(\mathcal{U}_1) \cup \mathcal{E}(\mathcal{U}_2)$ is not stable. If $\mathcal{G}$ does not contain as subdigraph a digraph from $\mathcal{E}(\mathcal{U}_1) \cup \mathcal{E}(\mathcal{U}_2)$ then all its strongly connected components must consist of at most one simple directed cycle. Therefore, $\mathcal{G}$ is stable under FIFO according to Lemma 3 and Theorem 1.

If the digraph $\mathcal{U}_1$ is stable under FIFO then, according to Lemmas 6 and 7, together with the fact that the instability of a subdigraph implies the instability of the whole digraph, no digraph $\mathcal{G}$ containing as subdigraph a digraph from $\mathcal{E}(\mathcal{U}_1^1) \cup \mathcal{E}(\mathcal{U}_1^2) \cup \mathcal{E}(\mathcal{U}_1^3) \cup \mathcal{E}(\mathcal{U}_1^4) \cup \mathcal{E}(\mathcal{U}_2)$ is stable. If, on the contrary, $\mathcal{G}$ does not contain as subdigraph a digraph from that set, then all its strongly connected components either consist of at most one simple directed cycle (and then, according to Lemma 3 and Theorem 1, $\mathcal{G}$ would be stable under FIFO), or they contain as a subdigraph the digraph $\mathcal{U}_1$ (which here we have assumed that is stable under FIFO). ∎

This result, when put in relation with Lemmas 3, 4, 5, 6, and 7, can be stated in terms of digraphs' properties.

Algorithm 2 : Stability under FIFO (sup. $\mathcal{U}_1$ is stable under FIFO)

INPUT: A strongly connected digraph $\mathcal{G} = (V, E)$

compute a (any) directed k-cycle $C = (e_1 \dots e_k)$ of $k \geq 2$ vertices, and let

$\quad C_V \leftarrow \{v \mid \exists e \in C : e = (v, u)\} \subseteq V$ (set of vertices of the cycle C)

$\quad C_E \leftarrow \{e \mid e \in C\} \subseteq E$ (set of arcs of the cycle C)

if $\mathcal{G}$ does not have a directed k-cycle of $k \geq 2$ vertices **then**
$\quad$ **return** YES
else
$\quad$ Let $\mathcal{G}' = (V, E \setminus C_E)$ be the digraph resulting after removing from $\mathcal{G}$ the arcs in C
$\quad$ **if** there are two different vertices $u, v \in C_V$ connected in $\mathcal{G}'$ by a directed path
$\quad$ **then**
$\quad\quad$ $P \leftarrow$ such a directed path connecting $u \in C_V$ and $v \in C_V$ in $\mathcal{G}'$
$\quad\quad$ **if** $|C_V| = k > 2$ **then**
$\quad\quad\quad$ **return** NO
$\quad\quad$ **else if** $|P| > 1$ **or** there is another directed path $P' \neq P$ in $\mathcal{G}'$ between two
$\quad\quad$ different vertices in C_V **then**
$\quad\quad\quad$ **return** NO
$\quad\quad$ **end if**
$\quad$ **end if**
$\quad$ compute the strongly connected components of $\mathcal{G}'$
$\quad$ **if** a strongly connected component of $\mathcal{G}'$ contains a directed k-cycle of $k \geq 2$
$\quad$ vertices **then**
$\quad\quad$ **return** NO
$\quad$ **else**
$\quad\quad$ **return** YES
$\quad$ **end if**
end if

Corollary 1. *If the digraph $\mathcal{U}_1$ is not stable under FIFO, then a strongly connected digraph $\mathcal{G}$ is stable under FIFO if and only if $\mathcal{G}$ has just a directed k-cycle (on any $k \geq 2$). Otherwise, if the digraph $\mathcal{U}_1$ is stable under FIFO, then a strongly connected digraph $\mathcal{G}$ is stable under FIFO if and only if $\mathcal{G}$ has just a directed k-cycle (on any $k \geq 3$) or a 2-cycle with at most one multi-edge.*

Then, instead of detecting the proposed forbidden subdigraphs by means of subdigraph homeomorphism (which would be NP-complete [10]), the stability of digraphs under FIFO can be decided in polynomial time by detecting the proposed forbidden subdigraphs in terms of the digraphs' properties outlined in Lemmas 4, and 5, and Corollary 1.

Theorem 3. *The stability under FIFO of a given digraph can be decided in polynomial time.*

Proof. Algorithms 1 and 2 check stability under FIFO of a given strongly connected digraph $\mathcal{G}$ according to Lemmas 4, and 5, and Corollary 1. Both algorithms run in polynomial time. Algorithm 1 would be applied in the case that

$\mathcal{U}_1$ is not stable under FIFO, while Algorithm 2 would be applied in the case that $\mathcal{U}_2$ is stable under FIFO.

According to Theorem 1, the strongly connected components of the digraph need to be computed first. Thus the result follows by combining the computation of the strongly connected components of the given digraph (with complexity $O(|V| + |E|)$ using Tarjan's algorithm [20] based on depth-first search –DFS–) either with Algorithm 1 or Algorithm 2.   ∎

5   Conclusions, Remarks, Open Questions and Further Work

In spite of the importance of the FIFO protocol and the research efforts invested in obtaining results for it, deciding whether a given network is stable under FIFO was still an open question. We have addressed this problem and tackled the general case, i.e., the decidability and complexity of stability under the FIFO protocol, and . In this work, we have shown that the property of stability under FIFO is decidable in polynomial time.

We wanted to identify which network topologies determine that a system under FIFO is (or is not) stable and then, be able to provide a characterization of the property. Taking the characterization of (network) universal stability as starting reference, we have proposed an (open) characterization of the stability under FIFO (see Theorem 2). The characterization is composed by two candidate sets of forbidden subdigraphs. The eligibility of one or the other candidate set as the decisive characterization depends on the stability of the digraph $\mathcal{U}_1$ (see Figure 1). In the case that $\mathcal{U}_1$ is unstable under FIFO, the characterization would be defined by $\mathcal{U}_1$ and $\mathcal{U}_2$, and it would be the same as the characterization of the digraphs that are universally stable [3]. This would have some nice implications since, in the case this holds, a digraph would be universally stable if and only if it is stable under FIFO. In the case that $\mathcal{U}_1$ is stable under FIFO, the characterization would be defined by $\mathcal{U}_2$, $\mathcal{U}_1^1$, $\mathcal{U}_1^2$, $\mathcal{U}_1^3$, and $\mathcal{U}_1^4$.

Some important questions remain still open concerning the stability under FIFO, being of course the most important one that of finding out *whether $\mathcal{U}_1$ can be made unstable under* FIFO , which would establish the decisive characterization.

In the same way as we proceeded in this work, other variants of stability can be tackled. Different variants can be defined according to the constraints on the packet trajectory and, as it was shown in [3], this influences strongly the characterization of the stability properties. Keeping the representation of the network as a directed graph, we can consider also the property of *simple-path* stability under FIFO. *The characterization of this property is also an open question nowadays.* A first step to it would be to study what is the behaviour of the smallest digraphs which are known not to be universally stable, when the system schedules the packets according to the FIFO policy. Those digraphs are exactly the ones depicted in Figure 2, which characterize the universal stability of networks [3]. The following lemma states the simple-path instability under FIFO of the digraphs in $\mathcal{E}(\mathcal{S}_3) \cup \mathcal{E}(\mathcal{S}_4)$.

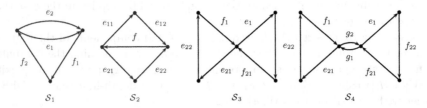

Fig. 2. Minimum forbidden subdigraphs characterizing simple-path universal stability [3]. The digraphs S_3 and S_4 will belong to the set of forbidden subdigraphs characterizing the property of simple-path stability under FIFO. In order to know which digraphs complete that characterization, the stability under FIFO of the digraphs S_1 and S_2, their extensions, and the digraphs with the same basic topology but multi-edges, need to be studied.

Lemma 8. *The digraphs in $\mathcal{E}(S_3) \cup \mathcal{E}(S_4)$ are not simple-path stable under* FIFO.

This is a first step into the characterization of the property of simple-path stability under FIFO, however the simple-path stability of the digraphs in $\mathcal{E}(S_1) \cup \mathcal{E}(S_2)$, together with other digraphs which do not contain any digraph in $\mathcal{E}(S_3) \cup \mathcal{E}(S_4)$ as a subdigraph, have to be deeply studied before converging to a characterization of the property.

The characterization of stability (and variants) under protocols other than FIFO are still also an open question in this topic. To the best of our knowledge, only the characterization of stability (and variants) under FFS and NTG-LIS are additionally known [1,3]. Establishing the characterization of the stability under LIFO would be of higher interest, because this protocol is gaining popularity in the last years due to the discovery of the significant quality improvement on the performance of interactive real-time services, such as IP telephony and IP teleconferencing [12,13,14].

Acknowledgments

The author would like to thank the unknown referees for their comments and suggestions.

References

1. C. Àlvarez, M. Blesa, J. Díaz, A. Fernández, and M. Serna. The complexity of deciding stability under FFS in the adversarial model. *Information Processing Letters*, 90(5):261–266, 2004.
2. C. Àlvarez, M. Blesa, J. Díaz, A. Fernández, and M. Serna. Adversarial models for priority-based networks. *Networks*, 45(1):23–35, 2005.
3. C. Àlvarez, M. Blesa, and M. Serna. A characterization of universal stability in the adversarial queueing model. *SIAM Journal on Computing*, 34(1):41–66, 2004.

4. M. Andrews, B. Awerbuch, A. Fernández, J. Kleinberg, T. Leighton, and Z. Liu. Universal stability results for greedy contention–resolution protocols. *Journal of the ACM*, 48(1):39–69, 2001.

5. R. Bhattacharjee, A. Goel, and Z. Lotker. Instability of FIFO at arbitrarily low rates in the adversarial queueing model. *SIAM Journal on Computing*, 34(2):318–332, 2004.

6. Blesa, M.J.: Deciding Stability under FIFO in the Adversarial Queuing model in polynomial time. Research Report LSI-05-3-R, Dept. Llenguatges i Sistemes Informàtics, UPC (2005). URL www.lsi.upc.edu/dept/techreps/techreps.html

7. A. Borodin, J. Kleinberg, P. Raghavan, M. Sudan, and D. Williamson. Adversarial queueing theory. *Journal of the ACM*, 48(1):13–38, 2001.

8. J. Díaz, D. Koukopoulos, S. Nikoletseas, M. Serna, P. Spirakis, and D. Thilikós. Stability and non-Stability of the FIFO Protocol. In *13th annual ACM Symposium on Parallel Algorithms and Architectures* (SPAA'01), pages 48–52, 2001.

9. J. Echagüe, V. Cholvi, and A. Fernández. Universal stability results for low rate adversaries in packet switched networks. *IEEE Communication Letters*, 7(12):578–580, 2003.

10. S. Fortune, J. Hopcroft, and J. Wyllie. The directed subgraph homeomorphism problem. *Theoretical Computer Science*, 10(4):111–121, 1980.

11. A. Goel. Stability of networks and protocols in the adversarial queueing model for packet routing. *Networks*, 37(4):219–224, 2001.

12. M. Hamdi. LCFS queuing for real-time audio-visual services in packet networks. In *IEEE International Workshop on Audio-Visual Services over Packet Networks* (AVSPN'97), 1997.

13. M. Hamdi, R. Noro, and J.-P. Hubaux. *Fresh Packet First* scheduling for voice traffic in congested networks. Technical Report SSC034, Computer Science Department, Swiss Federal Institute of Technology (EPFL), 1997.

14. M. Hamdi. *Fresh Packet First* scheduling for interactive services in the Internet. in *4th International Conference on Information Systems Analysis and Synthesis* (ISAS'98). 1998.

15. D. Koukopoulos, M. Mavronicolas, and P. Spirakis. FIFO is unstable at arbitrarily low rates (even in planar networks). *Electronic Colloquium on Computational Complexity*, 10(16), 2003.

16. D. Koukopoulos, S. Nikoletseas, and P. Spirakis. The range of stability for heterogeneous and FIFO queueing networks. *Electronic Colloquium on Computational Complexity*, TR01-099, 2001.

17. D. Koukopoulos, S. Nikoletseas, and P. Spirakis. Stability behavior of FIFO protocol in the adversarial queueing model. In A. K. Y. Manolopoulos, S. Evripidou, editor, *8th Panhellenic Conference on Informatics* (PCI'2001), volume 2563 of *Lecture Notes in Computer Science*, 2001. Springer-Verlag.

18. D. Koukopoulos, S. Nikoletseas, and P. Spirakis. Stability issues in heterogeneous and FIFO networks under the adversarial queueing model. In *8th International Conference on High Performance Computing* (HIPC'01), volume 2228 of *Lecture Notes in Computer Science*, pages 3–14, 2001. Springer-Verlag.

19. Z. Lotker, B. Patt-Shamir, and A. Rosén. New stability results for adversarial queuing. *SIAM Journal on Computing*, 33(2):286–303, 2004.

20. R.E. Tarjan. Depth first search and linear graph algorithms. *SIAM Journal on Computing*, 1(2):146–160, 1972.

Compact Routing for Graphs Excluding a Fixed Minor

(Extended Abstract)

Ittai Abraham[1], Cyril Gavoille[2], and Dahlia Malkhi[3]

[1] School of Computer Science and Engineering,
The Hebrew University of Jerusalem, Jerusalem, Israel
`ittaia@cs.huji.ac.il`
[2] Laboratoire Bordelais de Recherche en Informatique,
University of Bordeaux, Bordeaux, France
`gavoille@labri.fr`
[3] School of Computer Science and Engineering,
The Hebrew University of Jerusalem, Jerusalem, Israel,
and Microsoft Research, Silicon Valley Center
`dalia@microsoft.com`

Abstract. This paper concerns compact routing schemes with arbitrary node names. We present a compact name-independent routing scheme for unweighted networks with n nodes excluding a fixed minor. For any fixed minor, the scheme, constructible in polynomial time, has constant stretch factor and requires routing tables with poly-logarithmic number of bits at each node.

For shortest-path labeled routing scheme in planar graphs, we prove an $\Omega(n^{\epsilon})$ space lower bound for some constant $\epsilon > 0$. This lower bound holds even for bounded degree triangulations, and is optimal for polynomially weighted planar graphs ($\epsilon = 1/2$).

1 Introduction

Consider a distributed network of nodes connected via a network in which each node has an arbitrary network identifier. A routing scheme allows any source node to route messages to any destination node, given the destination's network identifier. The fundamental trade-offs in compact routing schemes is between the *space* used to store the routing table on each node and the *stretch* factor of the routing scheme, the maximum ratio over all pairs between the length of the route induced by the scheme and the length of a shortest-path between the same pair.

The trivial solution to routing on shortest paths (stretch factor 1) is for each node to store a routing table with $\Omega(n)$ entries that contains the next hop of an all pairs shortest-path algorithm. This solution is very expensive as it requires each node to store $\Omega(n \log n)$ bits. Thus, network designers are faced with two conflicting goals: reduce both the stretch factor and the size of the routing tables.

P. Fraigniaud (Ed.): DISC 2005, LNCS 3724, pp. 442–456, 2005.
© Springer-Verlag Berlin Heidelberg 2005

In this paper we assume a network with arbitrary node names. This model is called the *name-independent* model because the designer of the routing scheme has no control over node names. So node names cannot encode any topological awareness, like for instance the X, Y-coordinates in a geographic network. This routing problem may appear daunting: In order to route to a node, we must first somehow gain knowledge about its location in the network, but, in order to have some guarantees on the stretch factor, we must do so without exceeding too much the distance to the target.

A weak variant of this fundamental problem is called *labeled routing*. In this version of the problem, the designer of a solution may pick node names that contain (bounded size) information about their location in the network. This variant is useful in many aspects of network theory, but less so in practice: Knowledge of the labels needs to be disseminated to all potential senders, as these labels are not the addresses by which nodes of an *existing* network, e.g., an IP network, are known. Furthermore, if the network may admit new joining nodes, all the labels may need to be re-computed and distributed to any potential sender. Finally, various recent applications pose constraints on nodes addresses that cannot be satisfied by existing labeled routing schemes. E.g., Distributed Hash Tables (DHTs) require nodes names in the range $[1, n]$, or ones that form a binary prefix.

There is a subtle distinction between a *designer-port* model and a *fixed-port* model. In the *fixed-port* model (also known as the adversarial port model) the names of outgoing links, or ports, from each node may be arbitrarily chosen by an adversary from the set $\{1, \ldots, n\}$. In the *designer-port* model they may be determined by the designer of the routing scheme. Our routing scheme applies to the fixed-port model.

In this paper we are interested in the design of fixed-port name-independent compact routing schemes with low space and stretch, typically with $O(1)$ stretch and $\widetilde{O}(1)$ memory per node[1]. Unfortunately, it is known that, even for the labeled variant, any routing scheme of stretch $O(k)$ applying on all graphs requires $\Omega(n^{1/k})$ bit memory in the worst-case [32,36]. Identifying large realistic families of networks supporting low stretch and memory name-independent routing schemes is a wide open question. Here, we restrict our attention to families of graphs excluding a fixed minor, so including all families closed under taking minors (by The Minor Theorem of Robertson & Seymour). For instance, it includes all graphs of bounded treewidth or bounded genus.

A graph H is a *minor* of G if H is a subgraph of a graph obtained by a series of edge contractions[2] of G. The study of graphs excluding a fixed minor has lead to fundamental graph theory results. In the context of routing, several natural classes of networks can be defined by their forbidden minor. Among them are *trees* [27] (excluding K_3) and *series parallel* networks [18] (excluding K_4) that

---

[1] The notation $\widetilde{O}(\cdot)$ indicates complexity similar to $O(\cdot)$ up to poly-logarithmic factors.

[2] The *contraction* of the edge e with endpoints u, v is the replacement of u and v with a single node whose incident edges are the edges other than e that were incident to u or v [37].

capture many network backbone structures, and *planar graphs* (excluding K_5 or $K_{3,3}$) that capture the structure of two dimensional maps.

1.1 Related Work

The space-stretch trade-off has been extensively studied under various models and extensions. We refer the reader to Peleg's book [30] and to the surveys of Gavoille and Peleg [20,22] for comprehensive background.

There is a large body of work on special families of graphs. For the labeled model: graphs with bounded treewidth [31], bounded chordality [14,15,16] (i.e., graphs for which every induced cycle is bounded), and more recently, graphs (or metrics) with bounded doubling dimension [10,24,33,34] (i.e., graphs for which any radius-$2r$ ball can be covered by a bounded number of radius-r balls). For the name-independent model: trees [1,27], graphs with bounded growth dimension [5]. Observe that planar graphs are not captured by any of these families.

No low memory and stretch name-independent routing schemes are known for planar graphs, however several schemes have been proposed for this family for the labeled variant.

Surprisingly, for stretch 1, the complexity of the size of the routing tables is not known. The best scheme up to date has been proposed by Lu [28]: the node labels range in $[1, n]$, the routing tables are of $7.181n + o(n)$ bits (per node), and each routing decision takes $O(\log^{2+\epsilon} n)$ bit operations for every fixed $\epsilon > 0$. Earlier, it was proved that, actually, genus-g graphs support $n \log g + O(n)$ bit routing tables [21], that provides $8n + o(n)$ bits in the planar case. They also showed in [21] that if each node is forced to route along a shortest-path tree fixed by an adversary, then any routing scheme requires $\Omega(n)$ bits in the worst-case (this actually extends to $\Omega(n \log r)$ bits for a $K_{r,n-r}$, so setting $r = 2$ for planar). However, if the designer of the scheme has freedom to optimize the routes among those of equal costs, then only the $\Omega(\sqrt{n})$ bit lower bound for trees applies [17]. Furthermore, this lower bound concerns only schemes that assign node labels in $[1, n]$ exactly. Better results exist for some particular subclass of planar graphs. In [12], it is proved that quadrangulations[3] where all inner nodes have degree at least 4 (these include the subgraphs of a grid bounded by a circuit) have a labeled routing scheme with $O(\deg(v) \log n)$ bit memory for each node v. For other particular plane graphs, namely the non-positively curved plane graphs, a labeled $O(\log^2 n)$ bit routing scheme exists [11].

To summarize, if poly-log node labels are allowed, then no trivial lower bound on the memory is known for the shortest-path labeled routing scheme problem in general planar graphs, whereas $O(n)$ is the upper bound [21,28].

The situation is however quite different if routing schemes with stretches > 1 are considered. For instance routing in Euclidian plane graphs[4] is investigated in [8,9]. It is shown that plane triangulations having the diamond property (which

---

[3] I.e., plane graphs where all the inner faces are of length 4.
[4] I.e., a planar graphs embedded in the plane whose edges are weighted by the Euclidean distance between their endpoints.

is the case for classical triangulations as the Delaunay, greedy and minimum-weight triangulations) have a constant stretch labeled routing scheme where node labels are the coordinates and the memory requirement of each node v consists only in the coordinates of v and of its neighbors, therefore is $O(\deg(v) \log n)$ bits. The same results hold for all plane graphs possessing both the diamond property and the good convex polygon property. For general planar graphs, Frederickson and Janardan have presented in [19] two schemes. The first one achieve $O(n^{4/3} \log n)$ bits in total (the sum of the routing table size over all the nodes), stretch 3, and uses $O(\log n)$ bit node labels. The second one uses $O((1/\epsilon)n^{1+\epsilon} \log n)$ bit in total, for every fixed $\epsilon > 0$, stretch 7, and $O((1/\epsilon) \log n)$ bit node labels. Recently, Thorup [35] improves the stretch bound thanks to an extension of his *distance oracles* for planar graphs. He obtained a labeled routing scheme with stretch $1 + \epsilon$ in which for a fixed $\epsilon > 0$, routing tables and node labels have $O((1/\epsilon) \log^2 n)$ bits. For Euclidean metrics, Hassin and Peleg show in [25] a labeled scheme with $O(\log n)$ out going edges per node, $O(\log n)$-hop routes, and $1 + \epsilon$ stretch. The out degree is further reduced to a constant by Abraham and Malkhi [4].

1.2   Our Contributions

Our first contribution is a name-independent routing schemes for unweighted graphs excluding a fixed minor. We prove the following.

Theorem 1. *For every n-node unweighted graph excluding a fixed $K_{r,r}$ minor, there is a polynomial time constructible name-independent routing scheme with constant stretch factor, in which every node v requires routing tables of $\widetilde{O}(1)$ bits and $O(\log^2 n/\log\log n)$-bit headers.*

The general result follows since graphs excluding a $K_{r,r}$ minor exclude K_{r+1} minor and thus exclude any fixed graph H on $r + 1$ nodes. Note that the result was not known even for trees, i.e., $H = K_3$. For $H = K_{3,3}$, it is important to observe that the $\widetilde{O}(1)$ memory $1 + \epsilon$ stretched labeling routing scheme of Thorup [35] for planar graphs cannot be extended to name-independent scheme since in that case a stretch of 3 at least is required if less than $\Omega(n \log n)$ bits are used [3].

Our scheme is based on a cover for graphs excluding a $K_{r,r}$ minor which is a novel variant of the Klein, Plotkin, and Rao [26] partitioning algorithm. While the scheme in [26] gives a partition algorithm with weak diameter bounds, no information is given about the structure of the short paths that bound the diameter. Our covering algorithm gives an explicit structure to the short paths formed. This explicitness may be of independent interest and is presented in Section 3. Moreover, we show how to utilize this structure for an efficient routing scheme in Section 4.

Our second contribution is a lower bound. As said previously in the introduction, no (trivial) lower bounds are known for stretch 1 labeled routing schemes in planar graphs. Based on the distance labeling lower bound of [23], we prove in Section 5 an $\Omega(n^\epsilon)$ lower bound on the label length (the length of the local routing tables plus the node label length). This bound holds even in the quite simple case: a bounded degree triangulation.

Theorem 2. *Every shortest-path labeled routing scheme on polynomially weighted n-node planar graphs of bounded degree requires a total label length (the length of all the routing tables and node labels in the graph) of $\Omega(n^{1+1/2})$ bits. Moreover, the (maximum) label length is $\Omega(n^{1/4})$ for some weighted bounded degree triangulations. For unweighted planar graphs, the two bounds are respectively $\Omega(n^{1+1/3})$ and $\Omega(n^{1/6})$.*

Observe that there is a labeled scheme using only $\widetilde{O}(\sqrt{n})$ bit node labels for weighted[5] graphs of treewidth $O(\sqrt{n})$ [31] (thus including planar graphs). So, in a sense Theorem 2 is optimal. However, no shortest-path routing scheme is known to achieve $\widetilde{O}(\sqrt{n})$ routing tables but with $\widetilde{O}(1)$ node labels.

1.3   Outline of Techniques

Awerbuch and Peleg introduced *sparse covers* [6] in order to build a hierarchal routing scheme for general graphs [7]. Their scheme is based on tree covers with geometrically increasing radii. Typically each node of the graph belongs to $O(kn^{1/k})$ trees of the cover, where $k \geq 1$ is a parameter. For each radius ρ and source node s, the ball of radius ρ centered at s is contained in some trees of radius $O(k\rho)$. Roughly speaking, the routing task for s consists in seeking the target t in each tree it belongs to. However, this high level description hides many difficulties to implement, and tree routing plays an important role [6,7,1].

The situation for graphs excluding a fixed minor is quite different. It is currently an open question to design a sparse cover for such graphs with trees (or clusters) of strong radius $O(\rho)$ so that each node belongs to $O(1)$ such clusters. Klein, Plotkin, Rao [26] achieve sparse covers in which clusters have only *weak-diameter* $O(\rho)$, i.e., the shortest paths between any two nodes of a cluster can go outside the cluster itself. For our application, it means that a node v might potentially be involved, for the routing between many pairs of nodes, in several clusters that do not contain v. Therefore the naive approach of using [7] with a cover based on [26] may require $\Omega(n)$ nodes to participate in routing for $\Omega(n)$ clusters and hence require $\Omega(n^2)$ bits in total.

Instead, we present a novel partitioning algorithm for graphs excluding a $K_{r,r}$ minor for constant r. Our cover borrows from [26] but has some subtle differences. Using a new analysis we prove explicit properties on the structure of short paths between nodes in the same cluster. Our decomposition creates a set of clusters and trees, such that each node belongs to a constant number of clusters and trees. For every u, v of a same cluster, we construct a path connecting them of length $O(\rho)$ that is "well-structured". It decomposes in at most r particular subpaths, called *tail-connections*: each tail-connection is an upward path towards a root of one tree and a downward path on another tree (see Section 3).

---

[5] With polynomial edge weights.

Given this partition, we create an intricate rooted tree for each cluster that takes advantage of the cover properties. Finally, we present a single-source routing scheme in the fixed-port model in order to route on these trees. Our scheme uses the unweighted designer-port construction of [1,2] in a non-trivial manner over several overlapping trees in order to route efficiently both inside and outside of the cluster, and some recent results from graph minor theory [13] (see Section 4).

Due to space constrains some proofs of this extended abstract have been moved in the full version.

2   Preliminaries

Consider an unweighted connected graph $G = (V, E)$ with n nodes. Each node has an arbitrary unique network identifier consisting of polylog(n) bits. Using standard hashing techniques it is possible to generalize the model and assume nodes have arbitrarily long unique labels.

For a set of nodes $U \subseteq V$, let $G[U]$ be the subgraph induced by U. Given a subgraph $H \subset G$, let $d_H(u, v)$ denote the length of a shortest path in H from u to v. Given $v \in V$, let $d_H(v, U) = \min_{u \in U} d_H(u, v)$, and let $B_H(v, \rho) = \{u \in H \mid d_H(u, v) \leq \rho\}$. We denote by $\operatorname{diam}(H) = \max_{u,v \in H} d_H(u, v)$ the (strong) diameter of H, and $\deg_H(v)$ the degree of v in H.

For an index $j \geq 0$ and a rooted tree T with root $\tau \in T$ let $C(T, j) = \{v \in T \mid j\rho \leq d_T(v, \tau) < (j + 1)\rho\}$, specifically in our construction we will use j's such that either $j \in \mathbb{N}$ or $j + 1/2 \in \mathbb{N}$.

Let T be a tree with root τ, a node $v \in T$, and a number k. The *tail* of v of length k on T, denoted by $\operatorname{tail}(T, v, k)$, is the path of length $\min\{k, d_T(v, \tau)\}$ from v towards τ on T.

For a node $\tau \in G$, let $\operatorname{BFS}(G, \tau)$ be a breadth-first search tree of G rooted at τ. Let $r \in (N)$ be a parameter, and let $R = \{1, 2, \ldots, r\}$.

Definition 1. *(Tail-connected) Given a parameter $\rho \in \mathbb{N}$, cluster $H \subseteq G$, and a collection of rooted trees $\mathcal{T}$, two nodes $u, v \in H$ are tail-connected if there are trees $T_1, T_2 \in \mathcal{T}$ such that $\operatorname{tail}(T_1, u, (r + 2)\rho + 1)$ and $\operatorname{tail}(T_2, v, (r + 2)\rho + 1)$ intersect.*

Definition 2. *(r-Tail-Connected) Nodes $u, v \in H$ are r-tail-connected if there exists $2r - 2$ nodes $u = x_1, x_2, \ldots, x_{2r-1}, x_{2r-2} = v \in H$ (not necessarily distinct) such that for any even i, $d_H(x_i, x_{i+1}) \leq 1$, and for any odd i, x_i, x_{i+1} are tail-connected.*

3   The Weak Diameter Cover

Theorem 3. *For every graph $G = (V, E)$ excluding a $K_{r,r}$ minor, and parameter $\rho > 0$, there exists a polynomial algorithm that constructs a collection of connected components $\mathcal{H}_\rho$ and a collection of trees $\mathcal{T}_\rho$ such that:*

1. *(Cover) For every $v \in V$, there exists $H \in \mathcal{H}_\rho$ such that $B_G(v, \rho/4) \subseteq H$.*
2. *(Sparse clusters) For every $v \in V$, $|\{H \in \mathcal{H}_\rho \mid v \in H\}| \leq 2^r$.*
3. *(Sparse trees) For every $v \in V$, $|\{T \in \mathcal{T}_\rho \mid v \in T\}| \leq 2^{O(r \log r)}$.*
4. *(Weak diameter) For every $H \in \mathcal{H}_\rho$, and every $u, v \in H$, the nodes u, v are r-tail-connected with trees in $\mathcal{T}_\rho$.*

The rest of the section is devoted to the proof of Theorem 3. We first describe a *partitioning algorithm* of a graph G that depends on a parameter $\rho > 0$. It returns a cluster H and implicitly graphs G_i, H_i and trees T_i, for $i \in R$.

Actually, in order to create a partition of the graph into clusters, we apply this algorithm for all possible choices of indices $j_i \geq 0$ (see also the proof of Theorem 3).

Partitioning algorithm: Initially $H_1 = G_1 = G$. Given G_i and H_i set a root $\tau_i \in H_i$ and choose an index j_i. Let $T_i = \mathrm{BFS}(G_i, \tau_i)$. Let H_{i+1} be a connected component of the subgraph graph induced by the nodes

$$H_i \cap C(T_i, j_i)$$

Let G_{i+1} be the connected component of

$$G_i \cap \bigcup_{\ell \in \{j_i - i, \ldots, j_i, \ldots, j_i + i\}} C(T_i, \ell)$$

that contains H_{i+1}. If $i = r$ then return $H = H_{i+1}$ and stop. Otherwise repeat.

For the analysis it will be convenient to use the following notation: for all $u \in G_i$ and $i \in R$, let $\mathrm{tail}_i(u) = \mathrm{tail}(T_i, u, (i+1)\rho + 1)$.

Lemma 1. *Let H be the graph returned after the partitioning algorithm and assume that $j_i > r + 1$ for each $i \in R$. Let $X \subseteq H$ be any r nodes of H. If for each $x \neq x' \in X$ and $i, i' \in R$ the tails $\mathrm{tail}_i(x)$ and $\mathrm{tail}_{i'}(x')$ are pairwise disjoint then G contains a $K_{r,r}$ minor.*

Proof. In order to show that G contains a $K_{r,r}$ minor we construct two sets, each one containing, r connected subgraphs, each subgraph called hereafter left or right super node. The super nodes are chosen to be pairwise disjoint and such that each left-right pair of super nodes are connected by an edge with one endpoint in each super node. Then, by contracting all the edges of all the super nodes, and then keeping theses nodes and the left-right edges, it will prove that G has a $K_{r,r}$ minor.

For $x \in X$, let $L_x = \bigcup_{i \in R} \mathrm{tail}_i(x)$. The left super nodes of the $K_{r,r}$ will be the sets $\{L_x \mid x \in X\}$. Observe that each left super node indeed induces a connected subgraph and that theses super nodes are pairwise disjoint by the assumption.

For the right super nodes, for all $i \in R$ let U_i denote the subtree of T_i formed by the paths from each $x \in X$ to τ_i the root of T_i. The right super nodes will be the V_i for $i \in R$, where $V_i = U_i \setminus \bigcup_{x \in X} \mathrm{tail}_i(x)$. Observe that each V_i induces a

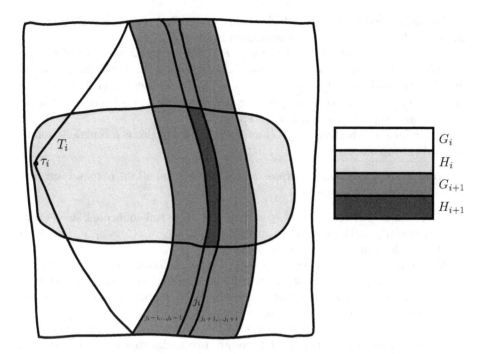

Fig. 1. A schematic drawing of one stage in the algorithm. Note that the paths of T_i from τ_i to nodes in H_{i+1} may use some nodes in G_i outside H_i.

connected subtree of G. Since $j_i > r+1$ for all $i \in R$ and $X \subseteq H_{i+1} \subseteq C(T_i, j_i)$ then $|\mathrm{tail}_i(x)| = (i+1)\rho + 1$ hence $d_{G_i}(X, V_i) > i\rho$ for all $i \in R$.

The super edges will be the edges in T_i connecting each V_i with each $\mathrm{tail}_i(x) \in L_x$ for each $i \in R, x \in X$. Since all tails, for distinct $x \in X$, are disjoint, we are left only with showing that all V_i's are pairwise disjoint and disjoint from all the tails.

To do so, we prove that for every $x \in X$ and $i \in R$, the path on T_i from x to τ_i is disjoint from V_j and $\{\mathrm{tail}_j(y) \mid y \in X \setminus \{x\}\}$ for all $i < j$. Seeking a contradiction, assume that for some $x \in X$ and $i \in R$ the path on T_i from x to τ_i intersects some node $v \in G_j$ which is part of another super node (either $v \in V_j \subseteq G_j$ or $v \in \mathrm{tail}_j(y) \subseteq G_j$ for $y \neq x$) for some $i < j$.

Recall that $d_{G_j}(x, V_j) > j\rho$. To arrive to a contradiction we will show that: (1) $v \in V_j$, (2) the path P on T_i from x to v has length $\leq (i+1)\rho$, (3) by induction, that for $i \leq \ell \leq j$ we have $P \subseteq G_\ell$. For $\ell = j$ this is a contradiction since $i < j$ and it implies that $d_{G_j}(x, v) \leq j\rho$.

Observe that $v \in G_j \subseteq \bigcup_{\ell \in \{j_i - i, \ldots, j_i, \ldots, j_i + i\}} C(T_i, \ell)$. Since T_i is a BFS tree then the path from x to the root τ_i on T_i can intersect v only if $v \in \bigcup_{\ell \in \{j_i - i, \ldots, j_i\}} C(T_i, \ell)$ hence $d_{T_i}(x, v) \leq (i+1)\rho$. This completes the first induction base for $\ell = i$ of (3). This also implies that the path P must be a sub-path of $\mathrm{tail}_i(x)$ and that length of P is at most $(i+1)\rho$, proving (2). Since the tails are disjoint by assumption, it must be that $v \in V_j$, proving (1).

For the second base $\ell = i+1$ observe that $v \in G_{i+1}$ and T_i is a BFS tree so the path P on T_i from x to v is contained inside G_{i+1}.

Assume $P \subseteq G_\ell$ for $i < \ell < j$ we prove $P \subseteq G_{\ell+1}$. Since $x \in H_{\ell+1} \subseteq C(T_\ell, j_\ell)$ and $G_{\ell+1}$ is the connected component that contains x inside the subgraph induced by the nodes $G_\ell \cap \bigcup_{m \in \{j_\ell - \ell, \ldots, j_\ell, \ldots, j_\ell + \ell\}} C(T_\ell, m)$ then $d_{G_\ell}(x, G_\ell \setminus G_{\ell+1}) > \ell\rho \geq (i+1)\rho$. Hence a path in G_ℓ from x to v of length $\leq (i+1)\rho$ does not leave $G_{\ell+1}$. This completes the inductive step.

Hence for $\ell = j$ we have $P \subseteq G_j$ and $|P| \leq (i+1)\rho$ this is a contradiction to $d_{G_j}(x, V_j) > j\rho$ since $i < j$. $\square$

Lemma 2. *If G has no $K_{r,r}$ minor and $j_i > r+1$ for all $i \in R$ then every two nodes of H are r-tail-connected.*

Proof. Fix $u, v \in H$. If $d_H(u, v) \leq r$ then u, v are r-tail-connected since every node is trivially tail-connected to itself. Let $u = x_1, x_2, \ldots, x_{t-1}, x_t = v$ be a shortest path from u to v on H for some $t > r$.

We recursively define a set of nodes $y_1, \ldots, y_r$ as follows. Let $y_1 = u$. Given $y_1, \ldots, y_i$ let y_{i+1} be the node x_ℓ with highest index ℓ such that y_i and $x_{\ell-1}$ are tail-connected. Hence for any index $\ell \leq m \leq t$ node y_i and x_m are not tail connected. Observe that this process can create at most r nodes $y_1, \ldots, y_r$ until v is reached. Suppose v is not reached at stage $r-1$ and consider the set $y_1, \ldots, y_{r-1}, v$ then from Lemma 1 there are two nodes that are tail-connected in this set. But by the construction of the sequence only y_{r-1} and v can be tail-connected. $\square$

Proof (of Theorem 3). Creating the cover is done by running the partition algorithm in the following manner. Note that the output of the partition algorithm (a cluster H and implicitly for each $i \in R$ graphs G_i, H_i, trees T_i) depends only on the choice of the roots $\tau_1, \ldots, \tau_t$ of the trees, the indices $j_1, \ldots, j_t$, and the choice of connected components $H_1, \ldots, H_t$. We fix a consistent choice of roots. Each time a root τ_i is to be chosen from subgraph H_i, we choose it as the node with minimal lexicographic order among the nodes in H_i.

The sets $\mathcal{H}_\rho$ and $\mathcal{T}_\rho$ consist of all the clusters H and trees T_i for all possible choices of connected components and all possible choices of indices $j_1, \ldots, j_r$ such that for each $i \in R$ either $j_i \in \mathbb{N}$ or $j_i + 1/2 \in \mathbb{N}$.

Property 1. *(Cover).* It follows from the simple observation that for any $v \in G$ and tree BFS tree T spanning G with root τ there must exist some integer $j \in \mathbb{N}$ such that either $B_G(v, \rho/4) \subset C(T, j)$ or $B_G(v, \rho/4) \subset C(T, j+1/2)$. Then, given any v, we construct by induction a sequence of indices $j_1, \ldots, j_i$ such that $B_G(v, \rho/4) \subseteq H_{i+1}$, and thus, for $i = t$, returning a cluster $H \in \mathcal{H}_\rho$ containing $B_G(v, \rho/4)$.

Property 2. *(Sparse clusters).* Due to the fact that for every $i \in R$, $j_i \in \mathbb{N}$ or $j_i + 1/2 \in \mathbb{N}$, then a node belongs of at most 2^{i-1} graphs H_i. This is true since for each graph H_i that v belongs to, it belongs to at most two graphs of type H_{i+1}. Hence the number of clusters a node belongs to is at most 2^r.

Property 3. *(Sparse trees).* For each graph G_i that v belongs to, it belongs to at most $2i+1$ graphs G_{i+1} due to the use of $2i+1$ stripes in the definition of G_{i+1}.

Hence for each $i \in R$, by simple induction, a node belongs to $\prod_{1 \le j \le i} 2j + 1 \le (2i + 1)!!$ graphs G_i. Therefore a node belongs to at most $\sum_{i \in R} (2i + 1)!! = 2^{O(r \log r)}$ trees by summing over all G_{i+1} for all $i \in R$.

Property 4. *(Weak diameter).* When $j_i > r + 1$ for each $i \in R$ this follows directly from Lemma 2. If there is some $i \in R$ for which $j_i \le r + 1$ then any two nodes in H are tail-connected via tree T_i.   □

4   Name-Independent Routing Scheme for Weak Diameter Cover

Theorem 1. *For every n-node unweighted graph excluding a fixed $K_{r,r}$ minor, there is a polynomial time constructible name-independent routing scheme with constant stretch factor, in which every node v requires routing tables of $\widetilde{O}(1)$ bits and $O(\log^2 n / \log \log n)$-bit headers.*

The key ingredient of our routing scheme is the following lemma:

Lemma 3. *Let $\mathcal{H}, \mathcal{T}$ be the set of clusters and trees obtained from the cover algorithm with parameter ρ on a graph excluding a fixed $K_{r,r}$ minor. There exists an error-reporting name-independent routing scheme such that*

1. *Each node v stores $\widetilde{O}(1)$ bits per tree of $\mathcal{T}$ it belongs to.*
2. *Each node v stores $\widetilde{O}(1)$ bits per cluster of $\mathcal{H}$ it belongs to.*
3. *For any $H \in \mathcal{H}$ and $s, t \in H$, searching for t from s in H will find t at cost $O(\rho)$.*
4. *For any $H \in \mathcal{H}$ and $s \in H, t \notin H$, searching for t from s in H will cost $O(\rho)$ until an error report is sent back to s.*

Lemma 3 is proven by constructing for every $H \in \mathcal{H}$ a rooted tree T_H. Consider first the case that H has a strong diameter of $O(\rho)$. Hence T_H can simply be a spanning BFS tree of H. In this case we can use the following result for single-source tree routing on unweighted trees on graphs excluding a fixed minor.

Lemma 4. *Let F be a forest (i.e., a set of disjoint trees) of an n-node graph G excluding a fixed minor. Then there exists polynomial time constructible scheme with $\widetilde{O}(1)$ bit routing tables for each $v \in G$ such that for each tree $T \in F$ there is a name-independent single-source error-reporting routing scheme on T (in the fixed port model) with cost $O(\mathrm{diam}(T))$.*

The construction and proof of Lemma 4 is an extension of the scheme in [1,2] with results from graph minor theory [13] that imply that graphs excluding a fixed minor have constant arboricity. The *arboricity* [29] of a graph G is the minimum number of forests into which the edges of G can be partitioned. In the full version we show in the proof of Lemma 4 how to utilize this fact, for routing on any tree $T \in F$ which is a subgraph of G, in order to bound the routing table size when converting from the designer ports used in [1] to the standard fixed port model.

However, H may not have a small strong diameter so routing outside the cluster must occur. At a high level, the idea of the construction is as follows. According to the partition algorithm, the route between every pair of nodes x, y in H is a route containing at most r pairs of intersecting tails, with at most a single edge from one pair to the next.

In the following we sketch the main ideas for the case of $r = 3$. The high level idea is to build a tree T_H that will span H but will also go outside H. The root of T_h is an arbitrary node $r_1 \in H$. The diameter of T_H will be $O(\rho)$. Each branch may leave H once or twice along tail-connected paths (for the case of $r = 3$).

More specifically, when stepping outside H, we only do it along tail-connected paths, which are composed of two parts: Going upward in some tree T_k, and then downward on some tree T_ℓ. Consider in T_H the case where we have a branch containing $u \rightsquigarrow w \rightsquigarrow v$, such that u and v belong to H, the left $\rightsquigarrow$ stands for a path on tree T_k and the right $\rightsquigarrow$ stands for a path on T_ℓ, and w is a node in the intersection between the two tail paths, $w \in T_k \cap T_\ell$. We collapse the each of the paths $\rightsquigarrow$ into a single edge, entering and leaving a *virtual node* which we denote by $\langle u, k, \ell, z \rangle$ where $z = d_{T_k}(u, w)$.

We build a rooted tree T_H, a set of clusters $\mathcal{M} = \{M(x) \mid x \in H\}$, and a data structure $\{S(x) \mid x \in H\}$ with the following properties:

1. T_H spans H, i.e., $H \subseteq T_H$
2. The nodes of $T_H \setminus H$ are *virtual nodes*. A real node x may have children that are virtual nodes of the form $\langle x, k, \ell, z \rangle$ where $x \in H, k, \ell \in R, z \in O(\rho)$.
3. A virtual node in T has only real children.
4. Each three node path in T, $x \rightarrow v \rightarrow u$, where v is a virtual node $\langle x, k, \ell, z \rangle$, corresponds to a tail-connection between x and u formed by trees $x \in T_k, u \in T_\ell$ and the intersection node $w \in T_k \cap T_\ell$ such that $d_{T_k}(x, w) = z$.
5. By expanding each three node path in T, $x \rightarrow v \rightarrow u$, where v is a virtual node, to its corresponding path in G, the diameter of the this graph is $O(\rho)$.
6. For each node x with virtual children there exists a set of nodes $M(x) \subset H$ such that: (1) $|M(x)| \leq \rho$. (2) $G[M(x)]$ is connected. (3) For every $x, y \in H$, $M(x) \cap M(y) = \varnothing$.
7. For each node x with virtual children, the data structure $S(x)$ of $o(\log^2 n)$ bits contains routing information that allows reaching any node of $M(x)$ at cost $O(\rho)$.

Now suppose we have built the tree. There remains the problem of building a name-independent scheme for it. A useful result here would be the single-source name-independent scheme we have presented in [1] (Lemma 4). This would give us stretch $O(1)$ with $\tilde{O}(1)$ memory per node. However, it cannot be employed easily, since some nodes in T_H are outside the cluster H, and may not maintain specific information about T_H (or else, they might need to maintain information about too many trees). Additionally, nodes in T_H may have neighbors outside T_H, which prevents us from using the result in [1] directly.

The solution we develop emulates the virtual tree of T_H. We need to address three issues.

1. Each (regular) node v must distinguish its neighbors in T_H from any other neighbors it may have in G. The solution is based on having bounded arboricity. We use a partition of the edges into a constant number of forests. This allows nodes to store only $\tilde{O}(1)$ bits of information about all their children in the tree.
2. Each node u must recognize its virtual children, and be able to route to them. To solve this, first note that for any u, there are $O(\rho)$ possible combinations of trees T_k, T_ℓ and nodes w along upward tails within distance $O(\rho)$. Therefore, u utilizes $O(\rho)$ virtual children. We allocate for u a set of ρ nodes, denoted $M(u)$, each of which emulates one virtual child. So whenever an algorithm on T_H calls to use a path from u to w, we first search a node within $M(x)$ that emulates w. Then obtain the necessary information from it and route back to u. This side-track information lookup incurs a cost of $O(\rho)$ hops. Then we use this information to simply route on T_k toward w.
3. The emulation of a virtual node w must be able to reach any child v of w in T_H. The route is along the tree T_ℓ. Our solution is to define for T_H a subtree of T_ℓ that contains H, as well as all nodes in T_ℓ within distance $O(\rho)$ from H. To be more precise, we define a forest $F(\ell, j)$ which is the subgraph of T_ℓ that spans a constant $O(r)$ number of consecutive levels $C(T_\ell, \cdot)$. Let $j = j_\ell$ be the index that generated H_ℓ. The diameter each tree in $F(\ell, j)$ is $O(\rho)$ hence we can route on the tree T in $F(\ell, j)$ that contains both w and v. Using the single-source name-independent scheme of [1] on $T \in F(\ell, j)$, node w can route to v via the root of the tree $T \in F(\ell, j)$ at a cost of $O(\rho)$.

We now go back to describe the construction of the tree T_H. We start by choosing a root r_1 arbitrarily. The first component of the tree T_H is simply a BFS tree of a set C_1 containing all nodes reachable within H via length 8ρ paths from r_1.

In the next step, we bring in nodes $r_2, r_3, \ldots$ that have distance greater than 8ρ from T_H, and are tail-connected with r_1. We do not include in the tree all the nodes along the tails from r_1 to r_i. Rather, we define a virtual node $\langle r_1, k, \ell, z \rangle$, that records the name T_k of the tree of the upward tail, the name T_ℓ of the tree of the downward tail, and the distance z upward on T_k of the intersection with T_ℓ. The virtual node is added to the tree, as well as the edges $(r_i, \langle r_1, k, \ell, z \rangle)$, $(\langle r_1, k, \ell, z \rangle, r_i)$. We also add all nodes with paths of length 4ρ in H from r_i. We then set $T_H = \bigcup_i C_i$. In order to store node r_1's virtual children information, we designate as $M(r_1)$ the ρ closest nodes to r_2.

In the next step, we bring in one at a time nodes r_i that are at distance at least 8ρ from T_H, and that are tail connected to some node x in T_H. For each such node x, we repeat the process for r_1 above. Finally, we insert into T_H all remaining nodes, which must be at distance at most $O(\rho)$ within H.

Due to space constrains the construction for general r and the proof of Lemma 4, Lemma 3 and Theorem 1 will appear in the full version.

5   Lower Bounds

Theorem 2. *Every shortest-path labeled routing scheme on polynomially weighted n-node planar graphs of bounded degree requires a total label length (the length of all the routing tables and node labels in the graph) of $\Omega(n^{1+1/2})$ bits. Moreover, the (maximum) label length is $\Omega(n^{1/4})$ for some weighted bounded degree triangulations. For unweighted planar graphs, the two bounds are respectively $\Omega(n^{1+1/3})$ and $\Omega(n^{1/6})$.*

Let us consider the problem of labeled routing in planar graphs along shortest-path. To strengthen our lower bound we assume that the routing table and the node label of any target t are merged into a single routing label, denoted by $L(G,t)$ for a graph G. So in this model, the routing decision in the source s is taken with full knowledge of $L(G,s)$ and $L(G,t)$. Observe that in this model, we make no assumptions on headers (rewritable and of arbitrary length). We also assume the designer-port model, i.e., the designer can permute the port numbers in order to optimize the maximum label length, however the ports of v must range in $\{1, \ldots, \deg(v)\}$.

Our proof is based on the planar graph construction of [23]. This graph, denoted G_k for some parameter k, was used to prove lower bounds for *distance labeling schemes* in planar graphs. For this labeling problem each node of a graph receives a label such that distances between any two nodes can be computed from their labels only. There is no general relation between both labeling problems, routing and distance, and thus a lower bound on distance labeling cannot be applied to labeled routing as a black box. Nethertheless, in the full version we show how to adapt the G_k construction to force a costly routing decision.

References

1. I. Abraham, C. Gavoille, and D. Malkhi, *Routing with improved communication-space trade-off*, in $18^t h$ International Symposium on Distributed Computing (DISC), vol. 3274 of Lecture Notes in Computer Science, Springer, Oct. 2004, pp. 305–319.
2. ——, *Routing with improved communication-space trade-off*, Tech. Report RR-1330-04, LaBRI, University of Bordeaux 1, 351, cours de la Liberation, 33405 Talence Cedex, France, July 2004.
3. I. Abraham, C. Gavoille, D. Malkhi, N. Nisan, and M. Thorup, *Compact name-independent routing with minimum stretch*, in $16^t h$ Annual ACM Symposium on Parallel Algorithms and Architecture (SPAA), ACM PRESS, June 2004.
4. I. Abraham and D. Malkhi, *Compact routing on euclidian metrics*, in Proceedings of the twenty-third annual ACM symposium on Principles of distributed computing (PODC), ACM Press, 2004, pp. 141–149.
5. I. Abraham and D. Malkhi, *Name independent routing for growth bounded networks*, in $17^t h$ Annual ACM Symposium on Parallel Algorithms and Architecture (SPAA), ACM Press, July 2005. To appear.
6. B. Awerbuch and D. Peleg, *Sparse partitions*, in 31th Annual IEEE Symposium on Foundations of Computer Science (FOCS), IEEE Computer Society Press, Oct. 1990, pp. 503–513.

7. B. AWERBUCH and D. PELEG, *Routing with polynomial communication-space trade-off*, SIAM J. Discret. Math., 5 (1992), pp. 151–162.

8. P. BOSE and P. MORIN, *Competitive online routing in geometric graphs*, Theoretical Computer Science, 324 (2004), pp. 273–288.

9. ——, *Online routing in triangulations*, SIAM Journal on Computing, 33 (2004), pp. 937–951.

10. H.T.-H. CHAN, A. GUPTA, B.M. MAGGS, and S. ZHOU, *On hierarchical routing in doubling metrics*, in $16^t h$ Symposium on Discrete Algorithms (SODA), ACMSIAM, Jan. 2005.

11. V.D. CHEPOI, F.F. DRAGAN, and Y. VAXES, *Distance and routing labeling schemes for non-positively curved plane graphs*, Journal of Algorithms, (2004). To appear.

12. V.D. CHEPOI and A. ROLLIN, *Interval routing in some planar quadrangulations*, in $8^t h$ International Colloquium on Structural Information & Communication Complexity (SIROCCO), Carleton Scientific, June 2001, pp. 89–104.

13. M. DEVOS, G. DING, B. OPOROWSKI, D.P. SANDERS, B. REED, P.D. SEYMOUR, and D. VERTIGAN, *Excluding any graph as a minor allows a low tree-width 2-coloring*, Journal of Combinatorial Theory, Series B, 91 (2004), pp. 25–41.

14. Y. DOURISBOURE, *Compact routing schemes for bounded tree-length graphs and for k-chordal graphs*, in $18^t h$ International Symposium on Distributed Computing (DISC), vol. 3274 of Lecture Notes in Computer Science, Springer, Oct. 2004, pp. 365–378.

15. Y. DOURISBOURE and C. GAVOILLE, *Improved compact routing scheme for chordal graphs*, in $16^t h$ International Symposium on Distributed Computing (DISC), vol. 2508 of Lecture Notes in Computer Science, Springer, Oct. 2002, pp. 252–264.

16. F.F. DRAGAN and I. LOMONOSOV, *On compact and efficient routing in certain graph classes*, in $15^t h$ Annual International International Symposium on Algorithms and Computation (ISAAC), vol. 3341 of Lecture Notes in Computer Science, Springer, Dec. 2004, pp. 402–414.

17. T. EILAM, C. GAVOILLE, and D. PELEG, *Compact routing schemes with low stretch factor*, Journal of Algorithms, 46 (2003), pp. 97–114.

18. P. FLOCCHINI and F.L. LUCCIO, *Routing in series parallel networks.*, Theory Comput. Syst., 36 (2003), pp. 137–157.

19. G.N. FREDERICKSON and R. JANARDAN, *Efficient message routing in planar networks*, SIAM Journal on Computing, 18 (1989), pp. 843–857.

20. C. GAVOILLE, *Routing in distributed networks: Overview and open problems*, ACM SIGACT News - Distributed Computing Column, 32 (2001), pp. 36–52.

21. C. GAVOILLE and N. HANUSSE, *Compact routing tables for graphs of bounded genus*, in $26^t h$ International Colloquium on Automata, Languages and Programming (ICALP), vol. 1644 of LNCS, Springer, July 1999, pp. 351–360.

22. C. GAVOILLE and D. PELEG, *Compact and localized distributed data structures*, Journal of Distributed Computing, 16 (2003), pp. 111–120. PODC 20-Year Issue.

23. C. GAVOILLE, D. PELEG, S. PÉRENNÈS, and R. RAZ, *Distance labeling in graphs*, Journal of Algorithms, 53 (2004), pp. 85–112.

24. A. GUPTA, R. KRAUTHGAMER, and J.R. LEE, *Bounded geometries, fractals, and low-distortion embeddings*, in $44^t h$ Annual IEEE Symposium on Foundations of Computer Science, IEEE Computer Society Press, Oct. 2003, pp. 534–543.

25. Y. HASSIN and D. PELEG, *Sparse communication networks and efficient routing in the plane*, Distributed Computing, 14 (2001), pp. 205–215.

26. P. KLEIN, S.A. PLOTKIN, and S. RAO, *Excluded minors, network decomposition, and multicommodity flow*, in $25^t h$ Annual ACM Symposium on Theory of Computing (STOC), ACM Press, 1993, pp. 682–690.

27. K.A. LAING, *Brief announcement: name-independent compact routing in trees*, in $24^t h$ Annual ACM Symposium on Principles of Distributed Computing (PODC), ACM Press, 2004, pp. 382–382.

28. H.-I. LU, *Improved compact routing tables for planar networks via orderly spanning trees*, in $8^t h$ Annual International Computing & Combinatorics Conference (COCOON), vol. 2387 of LNCS, Springer, Aug. 2002, pp. 57–66.

29. C.S.J. NASH-WILLIAMS, *Edge-disjoint spanning trees of finite graphs*, J. London Math. Soc, 36 (1961), pp. 445–450.

30. D. PELEG, *Distributed Computing: A Locality-Sensitive Approach*, SIAM Monographs on Discrete Mathematics and Applications, 2000.

31. ——, *Proximity-preserving labeling schemes*, Journal of Graph Theory, 33 (2000), pp. 167–176.

32. D. PELEG and E. UPFAL, *A trade-off between space and efficiency for routing tables*, Journal of the ACM, 36 (1989), pp. 510–530.

33. A. SLIVKINS, *Distance estimation and object location via rings of neighbors*, in $24^t h$ Annual ACM Symposium on Principles of Distributed Computing (PODC), ACM Press, July 2005. To appear. Also appears as Cornell CIS technical report TR2005-1977.

34. K. TALWAR, *Bypassing the embedding: Algorithms for low dimensional metrics*, in $36^t h$ Annual ACM Symposium on Theory of Computing (STOC), June 2004, pp. 281–290.

35. M. THORUP, *Compact oracles for reachability and approximate distances in planar digraphs*, in $42^n d$ Annual IEEE Symposium on Foundations of Computer Science (FOCS), IEEE Computer Society Press, Oct. 2001, pp. 242–251.

36. M. THORUP and U. ZWICK, *Compact routing schemes*, in $13^t h$ Annual ACM Symposium on Parallel Algorithms and Architectures (SPAA), ACM Press, July 2001, pp. 1–10.

37. D.B. WEST, *Introduction to Graph Theory (second edition)*, Prentice Hall, 2001.

General Compact Labeling Schemes for Dynamic Trees

Amos Korman

Department of Computer Science and Applied Mathematics,
The Weizmann Institute of Science, Rehovot, 76100 Israel
`amos.korman@weizmann.ac.il`

Abstract. An F- labeling scheme is composed of a *marker* algorithm for labeling the vertices of a graph with short labels, coupled with a *decoder* algorithm allowing one to compute $F(u,v)$ of any two vertices u and v directly from their labels. As applications for labeling schemes concern mainly large and dynamically changing networks, it is of interest to study *distributed dynamic* labeling schemes.

A general method for constructing labeling schemes for dynamic trees was previously developed in [28]. This method is based on extending an existing *static* tree labeling scheme to the dynamic setting. This approach fits many natural functions on trees, such as distance, routing, nearest common ancestor etc.. The resulted dynamic schemes incur overheads (over the static scheme) on the label size and on the communication complexity. In particular, all their schemes yield a multiplicative overhead factor of $\Omega(\log n)$ on the label sizes of the static schemes. Following [28], we develop a different general method for extending static labeling schemes to the dynamic tree settings. Our method fits the same class of tree functions. In contrast to the above paper, our trade-off is designed to minimize the label size on expense of communication.

Informally, for any k we present a dynamic labeling scheme incurring multiplicative overhead factors (over the static scheme) of $O(\log_k n)$ on the label size and $O(k \log_k n)$ on the amortized message complexity. In particular, by setting $k = \sqrt{n}$, we obtain dynamic labeling schemes with asymptotically optimal label sizes and sublinear amortized message complexity for the routing and the nearest common ancestor functions.

1 Introduction

Motivation: Global information maintenance using local data structures plays an extensive role in the areas of distributed computing and communication networks. Its goal is to cheaply store useful information about the network and make it readily and conveniently accessible. This is particularly significant when the network is large and geographically dispersed, and information about its structure must be accessed from various local points in it.

Recently, a number of studies focused on a *localized* network representation method based on assigning a (hopefully short) *label* to each vertex, allowing one to infer information about any two vertices *directly* from their labels, without

P. Fraigniaud (Ed.): DISC 2005, LNCS 3724, pp. 457–471, 2005.

using *any* additional information sources. Such labeling schemes have been developed for a variety of information types, including vertex adjacency [8, 7, 21], distance [29, 26, 19, 18, 16, 22, 34, 10, 2], tree routing [13, 35], flow and connectivity [25], tree ancestry [5, 6, 24], nearest common ancestor in trees [3] and various other tree functions, such as center, separation level, and Steiner weight of a given subset of vertices [30]. See [17] for a survey.

By now, the basic properties of localized labeling schemes for *static* (fixed topology) networks are reasonably well-understood. In most realistic contexts, however, the typical setting is highly dynamic, namely, the network topology undergoes repeated changes. Therefore, for a representation scheme to be practically useful, it should be capable of reflecting online the current up-to-date picture in a dynamic setting. Moreover, the algorithm for generating and revising the labels must be *distributed*, in contrast with the sequential and centralized label assignment algorithms described in the above cited papers.

The dynamic models investigated in this paper concern the *leaf-dynamic* tree model in which at each step a leaf can be added to or removed from the tree and the *leaf-increasing* tree model in which the only topological event that may occur is that a leaf joins the tree. We present a general method for constructing dynamic labeling schemes which is based on extending existing *static* tree labeling schemes to the dynamic setting. This approach fits a number of natural tree functions, such as routing, nearest common ancestor relation and distance. Such an extension can be naively achieved by calculating the static labeling from scratch after each topological change. Though this method yields a good label size, it may incur a huge communication complexity. Another naive solution would be that each time a leaf u is added as a child of an existing node v, the label given to u is the label of v concatenated with $F(u,v)$. Such a scheme incurs very little communication but the label sizes may be huge.

Before stating the results included in this paper, we list some previous related works.

Related works: Static labeling schemes for routing on trees were investigated in [13]. For the *designer port* model, in which each node can freely enumerate its incident ports, they show how to construct a static routing scheme using labels of at most $O(\log n)$ bits on n-node trees. In the *adversary port* model, in which the port numbers are fixed by an adversary, they show how to construct a static routing scheme using labels of at most $O(\frac{\log^2 n}{\log \log n})$ bits on n-node trees. They also show that the label sizes of both schemes are asymptotically optimal. Independently, a static routing scheme for trees using $(1 + o(1)) \log n$ bit labels was introduced in [35] for the designer port model. A static labeling scheme for the nearest common ancestor relation on trees (which includes in particular the ancestry relation) was developed in [3] using labels of $O(\log n)$ bits on n-node trees.

In the *sequential* (non-distributed) model, dynamic data structures for trees have been studied extensively (e.g., [32, 9, 20, 4]). For comprehensive surveys on dynamic graph algorithms see [12, 15].

Labeling schemes for the ancestry relation in the leaf-dynamic tree model were investigated in [11]. They assume that once a label is given to a node it remains unchanged. Therefore, the issue of updates is not considered even for the non distributed setting. For the above model, they present a labeling scheme that uses labels of $O(m)$ bits, where m is the number of nodes added to the tree throughout the dynamic scenario. They also show that this bound is asymptotically tight. Other labeling schemes are presented in the above paper assuming that clues about the future topology of the dynamic tree are given throughout the scenario.

The study of dynamic distributed labeling schemes was initiated by [28]. Dynamic distributed distance labeling schemes on trees were investigated in [28] and [27]. In [28] they present a dynamic labeling scheme for distances in the leaf-dynamic tree model with message complexity $O(\sum_i \log^2 n_i)$, where n_i is the size of the tree when the i'th topological event takes place. The protocol maintains $O(\log^2 n)$ bit labels, when n is the current tree size. This label size is proved in [19] to be asymptotically optimal even for the static (unweighted) trees scenario.

In [27] they develop two β-approximate distance labeling schemes (in which given two labels, one can infer a β-approximation to the distance between the corresponding nodes). The first scheme applies to the *edge-dynamic* tree model, in which the vertices of the tree are fixed but the (integer) weights of the edges may change (as long as they remain positive). The second scheme applies to the *edge-increasing* tree model, in which the only topological event that may occur is that an edge increases its weight by one.

In scenarios where at most m topological events occur, the message complexities of the first and second schemes are $O(m \Lambda \log^3 n)$ and $O(m \log^3 n + n \log^2 n \log m)$, respectively, where Λ is some density parameter of the tree. The label size of both schemes is $O(\log^2 n + \log n \log W)$ where W denotes the largest edge weight in the tree. This label size is shown in [19] to be asymptotically optimal even for the static weighted trees scenario.

The study of methods for extending static labeling schemes to the dynamic setting was also initiated in [28]. There, they assume the designer port and consider two dynamic tree models, namely, the leaf-increasing and the leaf-dynamic tree models. Their approach fits a number of natural functions on trees, such as distance, routing, nearest common ancestor relation etc.. Their resulted dynamic schemes incur overheads (over the static scheme) on the label sizes and on the communication complexity. Specifically, given a static F-labeling scheme π for trees , let $\mathcal{LS}(\pi, n)$ be the maximum number of bits in a label given by π to any vertex in any n-node tree, and let $\mathcal{MC}(\pi, n)$ be the maximum number of messages sent by π in order to assign the static labels in any n-node tree. Assuming $\mathcal{MC}(\pi, n)$ is polynomial[1] in n, the following dynamic schemes

---

[1] The actual requirement is that the message complexity is bounded above by some function f which satisfies $f(a + b) \geq f(a) + f(b)$ and $f(\alpha \cdot n) = \Theta(f(n))$ for any constant $\alpha > 0$. These two requirements are satisfied by most natural relevant functions, such as $c \cdot n^\alpha \log^\beta n$, where $c > 0$, $\alpha \geq 1$ and $\beta > 0$. For simplicity, we assume $\mathcal{MC}(\cdot, n)$ itself satisfies these requirements.

are derived. For the leaf-increasing tree model, they construct a dynamic F-labeling scheme π^{inc}. The maximum label given by π^{inc} to any vertex in any n-node tree is $O(\log n \cdot \mathcal{LS}(\pi, n))$ and the number of messages sent by π^{inc} is $O(\log n \cdot \mathcal{MC}(\pi, n))$. In the case where n_f, the final number of nodes in the tree, is known in advance, they construct a dynamic F-labeling scheme with label size $O\left(\frac{\log n_f \log n}{\log \log n_f} \cdot \mathcal{LS}(\pi, n)\right)$ and message complexity $O\left(\frac{\log n}{\log \log n_f} \cdot \mathcal{LS}(\pi, n_f)\right)$. For the leaf-dynamic tree model, they construct two dynamic F-labeling schemes. Let n_i be the size of the tree when the i'th topological event takes place. The first dynamic F-labeling scheme has label size $O(\log n \cdot \mathcal{LS}(\pi, n))$ and message complexity $O\left(\sum_i \log n_i \cdot \frac{\mathcal{MC}(\pi, n_i)}{n_i}\right) + O(\sum_i \log^2 n_i)$ and the second dynamic F-labeling scheme has label size $O\left(\frac{\log^2 n}{\log \log n} \cdot \mathcal{LS}(\pi, n)\right)$ and message complexity $O\left(\sum_i \frac{\log n_i}{\log \log n_i} \cdot \frac{\mathcal{MC}(\pi, n_i)}{n_i}\right) + O(\sum_i \log^2 n_i)$.

Our contribution: Following [28], we present a different method for constructing dynamic labeling schemes. Our method is also based on extending existing static labeling schemes to the dynamic setting. However, our resulted dynamic schemes incur a different trade-off between the overhead factors on the label sizes and the message communication. In comparison to [28], our trade-off gives better performances for the label size on expense of communication. Our approach fits the same class of tree functions as described in [28]. The following results apply for both the designer port model and the *adversary port* model in which the port numbers are fixed by an adversary. Given a static F-labeling scheme π for trees, let $\mathcal{LS}(\pi, n)$ and $\mathcal{MC}(\pi, n)$ be as before. Let $k(x)$ be a reasonable[2] sublinear function of x. For the leaf-increasing tree model, we construct the dynamic F-labeling scheme $\mathrm{SDL}^{k(x)}$. Consider any scenario on a dynamically growing tree such that the final number of nodes in the tree is n. The maximum label given by $\mathrm{SDL}^{k(x)}$ to any vertex in the tree is $O(\log_{k(n)} n \cdot \mathcal{LS}(\pi, n))$, and the number of messages used by $\mathrm{SDL}^{k(x)}$ is $O(k(n) \log_{k(n)} n \cdot \mathcal{MC}(\pi, n))$.

For the leaf-dynamic tree model, we construct the dynamic F-labeling scheme $\mathrm{DL}^{k(x)}$ with the following complexities. The maximum label given by $\mathrm{DL}^{k(x)}$ to any vertex in any n-node tree is $O(\log_{k(n)} n \cdot \mathcal{LS}(\pi, n))$ and the number of messages used by $\mathrm{DL}^{k(x)}$ is $O\left(\sum_i k(n_i)(log_{k(n_i)} n_i)\frac{\mathcal{MC}(\pi, n_i)}{n_i}\right) + O(\sum_i \log^2 n_i)$, where n_i is the size of the tree when the i'th topological event takes place. We note that by setting $k(n) = \sqrt{n}$, we obtain dynamic labeling schemes with asymptotically the same label size as the static ones and sublinear amortized message complexity. In particular, we get non dynamic labeling schemes with sublinear amortized message complexity and asymptotically optimal label size for the routing and the nearest common ancestor functions.

---

[2] We require that both $k(x)$, $\log_{k(x)} x$ and $\frac{k(x)}{\log_{k(x)} x}$ are not decreasing functions. The above requirement is satisfied by most natural sublinear functions such as $\alpha x^\epsilon \log^\beta x$, $\alpha \log^\beta \log x$ etc..

Paper outline: We start with preliminaries in Section 2. In Section 3 we present the FSDL_p^k schemes which will be used in section 4, where we introduce the dynamic labeling schemes for the leaf-increasing and the leaf-dynamic tree models. In section 5 we discuss how to reduce the external memory used for updating and maintaining the labels.

2   Preliminaries

Our communication network model is restricted to tree topologies. The network is assumed to dynamically change via vertex additions and deletions. It is assumed that the *root* of the tree, r, is never deleted. The following types of topological events are considered.

Add-leaf: A new vertex u is *added* as a child of an existing vertex v. Subsequently, v is informed of this event.

Remove-leaf: A leaf of the tree is *deleted*. Subsequently, the leaf's parent is informed of this event. We consider two types of dynamic models. Namely, the *increasing-dynamic* tree model in which the only topological event that may occur is of type add-leaf, and the *leaf-dynamic* tree model in which both types of topological events may occur. For simplicity, we assume that initially the tree consists of a single vertex, namely, its root.

Incoming and outcoming links from every node are identified by so called *port-numbers*. When a new child is added to a node v, the corresponding ports are assigned a unique port-number, in the sense that no currently existing two ports of v have the same port-number. We consider two main variations, namely, the *designer port* model and the *adversary port* model. The former allows each node v to freely enumerate its incident ports while the latter assumes that the port numbers are fixed by an adversary.

Our Method is applicable to any function F such that for every two vertices u and v in the tree the following condition is satisfied.

(C1) For every vertex w, such that w is on the path between u and v, $F(u,v)$ can be calculated in polynomial time from $F(u,w)$ and $F(w,v)$.

In particular, our method can be applied to the nearest common ancestor relation and the labeling for routing, thereby extending static labeling schemes such as those of [3, 13, 35] to the dynamic setting. We further assume, for simplicity of presentation, that F is symmetric, i.e., $F(u,v) = F(v,u)$. A slight change to the suggested protocols handles the more general case, without affecting the asymptotic complexity results.

A *labeling scheme* $\pi = \langle \mathcal{M}_\pi, \mathcal{D}_\pi \rangle$ for a function F on pairs of vertices of a tree is composed of the following components:

1. A *marker* algorithm $\mathcal{M}_\pi$ that given a tree, assigns labels to its vertices.
2. A polynomial time *decoder* algorithm $\mathcal{D}_\pi$ that given the labels $L(u)$ and $L(v)$ of two vertices u and v, outputs $F(u,v)$.

In this paper we are interested in distributed networks where each vertex in the tree is a processor. This does not affect the definition of the decoder algorithm of the labeling scheme since it is performed locally, but the marker algorithm changes into a *distributed marker protocol*.

Let us first consider static networks, where no changes in the topology of the network are allowed. For these networks we define *static* labeling schemes, where the marker protocol $\mathcal{M}$ is initiated at the root of a tree network and assigns static labels to all the vertices once and for all.

We use the following complexity measures to evaluate a static labeling scheme $\pi = \langle \mathcal{M}_\pi, \mathcal{D}_\pi \rangle$.

1. *Label Size*, $\mathcal{LS}(\mathcal{M}_\pi, n)$: the maximum number of bits in a label assigned by $\mathcal{M}_\pi$ to any vertex on any n-vertex tree.
2. *Message Complexity*, $\mathcal{MC}(\mathcal{M}_\pi, n)$: the maximum number of messages sent by $\mathcal{M}_\pi$ during the labeling process on any n-vertex tree. (Note that messages can only be sent between neighboring vertices).

We assume that the static labeling scheme assigns unique labels. For any static labeling scheme, this additional requirement can be ensured at an extra additive cost of at most n to $\mathcal{MC}(n)$ and $\log n$ to $\mathcal{LS}(n)$.

Example 1. The following is a possible static labeling scheme STATDFS for the ancestry relation on trees based on the notion of interval schemes ([33], cf. [31]). Given a rooted tree, simply perform a depth-first search starting at the root, assigning each vertex v the interval $I(v) = [a, b]$ where a is its DFS number and b is the largest DFS number given to any of its descendants. The corresponding decoder decides that v is an ancestor of w iff their corresponding intervals, $I(v)$ and $I(w)$, satisfy $I(v) \subseteq I(w)$. It is easy to verify that this is a correct labeling scheme for the ancestry relation. Clearly, $\mathcal{MC}(\text{STATDFS}, n) = O(n)$ and $\mathcal{LS}(\text{STATDFS}, n) = O(\log n)$.

Labeling schemes for routing are presented in [13]. They consider both the designer port model and the adversary port model. The schemes of [13] are designed as a sequential algorithm, but examining the details reveals that these algorithms can be easily transformed into distributed protocols. In the designer port model, we get a static labeling scheme for routing with label size and communication complexity similar to those of the STATDFS static labeling scheme. In the adversary port model we get a static labeling scheme for routing with linear communication and $O(\frac{\log^2 n}{\log \log n})$ label size. The label sizes of both schemes are asymptotically optimal.

The dynamic labeling schemes involve a marker protocol $\mathcal{M}$ which is activated after every change in the network topology. The protocol $\mathcal{M}$ maintains the labels of all vertices in the underlying graph so that the corresponding decoder algorithm will work correctly. We assume that the topological changes occur serially and are sufficiently spaced so that the protocol has enough time to complete its operation in response to a given topological change before the occurrence of the next change.

We distinguish between the label $\mathcal{M}(v)$ given to each node v to deduce the required information in response to online queries, and the additional external storage $Memory(v)$ at each node v, used during updates and maintenance operations. For certain applications (and particularly routing), the label $\mathcal{M}(v)$ is often kept in the router itself, whereas the additional storage $Memory(v)$ is kept on some external storage device. Subsequently, the size of $\mathcal{M}(v)$ seems to be a more critical consideration than the total amount of storage needed for the information maintenance.

For the leaf-increasing tree model, we use the following complexity measures to evaluate a dynamic labeling scheme $\pi = \langle \mathcal{M}_\pi, \mathcal{D}_\pi \rangle$.

1. *Label Size*, $\mathcal{LS}(\mathcal{M}_\pi, n)$: the maximum size of a label assigned by the marker protocol $\mathcal{M}_\pi$ to any vertex on any n-vertex tree in any dynamic scenario.
2. *Message Complexity*, $\mathcal{MC}(\mathcal{M}_\pi, n)$: the maximum number of messages sent by $\mathcal{M}_\pi$ during the labeling process in any scenario where n is the final number of vertices in the tree.

Finally, we consider the leaf-dynamic tree model, where both additions and deletions of vertices are allowed. Instead of measuring the message complexity in terms of the maximal number of nodes in the scenario, for more explicit time references, we use the notation $\bar{n} = (n_1, n_2, \ldots, n_t)$ where n_i is the size of the tree immediately after the i'th topological event takes place. For simplicity, we assume $n_1 = 1$ unless stated otherwise. The definition of $\mathcal{LS}(\mathcal{M}_\pi, n)$ remains as before, and the the definition of the message complexity changes into the following.

Message Complexity, $\mathcal{MC}(\mathcal{M}_\pi, \bar{n})$: the maximum number of messages sent by $\mathcal{M}_\pi$ during the labeling process in any scenario where n_i is the size of the tree immediately after the i'th topological event takes place.

3   The Finite Semi-Dynamic F-Labeling Schemes FSDL_p^k

In this section, we consider the leaf-increasing tree model. Given a static F-labeling scheme $\pi = \langle \mathcal{M}_\pi, \mathcal{D}_\pi \rangle$, we first fix some integer k and then, for each integer $p \geq 1$, we recursively define a dynamic scheme FSDL_p^k which acts on growing trees and terminates at some point. Each dynamic scheme FSDL_p^k is guaranteed to function as a dynamic F-labeling scheme as long as it operates. Scheme FSDL_p^k may terminate only when n, the number of nodes in the current tree, is at least k^p. Moreover, the overheads (over π) of Scheme FSDL_p^k are $O(p)$ on the label size and $O(p \cdot k)$ on the communication complexity. These schemes are used in the next section as building blocks for our dynamic F-labeling schemes. We start with the following definition.

A *finite semi-dynamic F-labeling scheme* is a dynamic F-labeling scheme that is applied on a dynamically growing tree T and terminates at some point. I.e., the root can be in one of two states, namely, 0 or 1, where initially, the root is in state 1 and when the root changes its state to 0, the scheme is considered to be terminated. The requirement from a finite semi-dynamic F-labeling scheme is that until the root changes its state to 0, the scheme operates as a dynamic F-labeling scheme. For a finite semi-dynamic F-labeling scheme, $\mathcal{S}$, let $\mathcal{TS}(\mathcal{S})$ be the minimum number of vertices in the tree at the time $\mathcal{S}$ terminates. Assuming $\mathcal{TS}(\mathcal{S}) \geq n$, the complexities $\mathcal{LS}(\mathcal{S}, n)$ and $\mathcal{MC}(\mathcal{S}, n)$ are defined in the same manner as they are defined for dynamic labeling schemes.

Let $\pi = \langle \mathcal{M}_\pi \mathcal{D}_\pi \rangle$ be a static F-labeling scheme such that $\mathcal{MC}(\pi, n)$ is polynomial in n (see footnote 1). Fix some integer $k > 1$. We now describe for each integer $p \geq 1$, the finite semi-dynamic F-labeling scheme $\mathrm{FSDL}_p^k = \langle \mathcal{M}_p, \mathcal{D}_p \rangle$.

Our dynamic schemes repeatedly engage the marker protocol of the static labeling scheme, and use the labels it produces to construct the dynamic labels. In doing so, the schemes occasionally apply to the already labeled portion of the tree a *reset* operation (defined below) invoked on some subtree T' rooted at r'.

Sub-protocol Reset(T')

- r' initiates broadcast and convergcast (see [29]) in order to calculate $n(T')$, the number of vertices in T'.
- r' invokes the static labeling scheme π on T'.

We describe the finite semi-dynamic F-labeling schemes FSDL_p^k in a recursive manner. It will follow from our description that Scheme FSDL_p^k terminates immediately after some Sub-protocol Reset is invoked on the current tree, T. We start by describing FSDL_1^k.

Scheme FSDL_1^k

- Whenever a new node joins T, it sends a signal to r instructing it to invoke Sub-protocol Reset(T). (Recall that in this sub-protocol, r calculates the value $n(T)$ which is the current number of nodes in T).
- If $n(T) \geq k$ then r changes it state to 0 and the scheme terminates.

Clearly FSDL_1^k is a finite semi-dynamic F-labeling scheme.

Given the finite semi-dynamic F-labeling scheme $\mathrm{FSDL}_{p-1}^k = \langle \mathcal{M}_{p-1}, \mathcal{D}_{p-1} \rangle$, we now describe the scheme $\mathrm{FSDL}_p^k = \langle \mathcal{M}_p, \mathcal{D}_p \rangle$.

Scheme FSDL_p^k

1. We first initiate FSDL_{p-1}^k at r. At some point during the scenario, (after some application of Sub-protocol Reset(T)), the root is supposed to change its state to 0 in order to terminate Scheme FSDL_{p-1}^k. Instead of doing so, we proceed to step 2.
2. Let T_0 be the tree at the time the last application of Sub-protocol Reset was applied. Let $n(T_0)$ be the number which was calculated in the first step of that sub-protocol and let $\mathcal{M}_\pi(u)$ be the static label given to $u \in T_0$ in the second step of that sub-protocol.
3. If $n(T_0) \geq k^p$ then r changes its state to 0 and the scheme terminates. Otherwise we continue.

4. r broadcasts a signal to all the vertices in T_0 instructing each vertex u to invoke Scheme FSDL_{p-1}^k on T_u, the future subtree rooted at u. Let $\text{FSDL}_{p-1}(u) = \langle \mathcal{M}_{p-1}^u, \mathcal{D}_{p-1} \rangle$ denote the scheme FSDL_{p-1}^k which is invoked by u. (Recall that Scheme FSDL_{p-1}^k is initiated on trees with initial size 1, therefore each vertex u ignores its current neighbors in T_0 and applies Scheme $\text{FSDL}_{p-1}^k(u)$ only on itself and its future descendants).
5. For each vertex w, let u be the vertex in T_0 such that $w \in T_u$. The label given to w by the marker is composed of three fields as follows. $\mathcal{M}_p(w) = \langle \mathcal{M}_\pi(u), F(u, w), \mathcal{M}_{p-1}^u(w) \rangle$.
6. For a vertex z and $i \in \{1, 2, 3\}$, let $L_i(z)$ denote the i'th field of $L(z)$. Given two labels $L(x)$ and $L(y)$ of two vertices x and y, the decoder $\mathcal{D}_p$ operates as follows.

   – If $L_1(x) = L_1(y)$ (which means that x and y belong to the same subtree T_u for some $u \in T_0$) then $\mathcal{D}_p$ outputs $\mathcal{D}_{p-1}(L_3(x), L_3(y))$.
   – If $L_1(x) \neq L_1(y)$ then this means that $x \in T_u$ and $y \in T_v$ where both u and v belong to T_0. Furthermore, u is on the path from x to v and v is on the path from x to y. Therefore $F(x, u) = L_2(x)$, $F(u, v) = \mathcal{D}_\pi(L_1(x), L_1(y))$ and $F(v, y) = L_2(y)$. The decoder proceeds using Condition (C1) on F.

7. If at some point during the scenario, some vertex $u \in T_0$ is supposed to terminate $\text{FSDL}_{p-1}(u)$ by changing its state to 0, then instead of doing so, it sends a signal to the root r which in turn invokes Sub-protocol $\text{Reset}(T)$. We proceed by going back to step 2.

By induction it is easy to show that Scheme FSDL_p^k is indeed a finite semi-dynamic F-labeling scheme. It follows directly from step 3 of Scheme FSDL_p^k that $\mathcal{TS}(\text{FSDL}_p^k) \geq k^p$.

Lemma 1. – $\mathcal{LS}(\text{FSDL}_p^k, n) \leq O(p \cdot \mathcal{LS}(\pi, n))$.
– $\mathcal{MC}(\text{FSDL}_p^k, n) \leq 5pk \cdot \mathcal{MC}(\pi, n)$.

Proof. The existence of a static F-labeling scheme π with labels of at most $\mathcal{LS}(\pi, n)$ bits implies that for any two vertices u and v in any n-node tree, $F(u, v)$ can be encoded using $O(\mathcal{LS}(\pi, n))$ bits. This can be done by simply writing the labels of the two vertices. The first part of the lemma follows by induction. We now turn to prove the second part of the lemma using induction on p.
Since $\mathcal{MC}(\pi, a) \geq a$ for every $a \geq 1$, it follows that for $p = 1$, $\mathcal{MC}(\text{FSDL}_1^k) \leq 5k \cdot \mathcal{MC}(\pi, n)$. Assume now that $\mathcal{MC}(\text{FSDL}_p^k) \leq 5pk \cdot \mathcal{MC}(\pi, n)$. Let us now consider FSDL_{p+1}^k. We distinguish between two types of messages sent by Scheme FSDL_{p+1}^k during the dynamic scenario. The first type of messages consists of the messages sent in the different applications of Scheme FSDL_p^k. The second type of messages consists of the broadcast messages in step 4 of Scheme FSDL_{p+1}^k and the messages resulted from the applications of step 7 of Scheme FSDL_{p+1}^k

(which correspond to sending a signal to the root and applying Sub-protocol Reset). Let us first bound from above the number of messages of the first type. Recall that Scheme FSDL_{p+1}^k initially invokes Scheme FSDL_p^k until the latter is supposed to terminate. If at this point Scheme FSDL_{p+1}^k does not terminate, then each vertex on the current tree invokes Scheme FSDL_p^k on its future subtree until one of these schemes is supposed to terminate. Again, if at this point Scheme FSDL_{p+1}^k does not terminate, then each vertex on the current tree invokes Scheme FSDL_p^k on its future subtrees, on so forth. Note that the different applications of FSDL_p^k act on disjoint sets of edges and since we assume that $\mathcal{MC}(\pi, (a+b)) \geq \mathcal{MC}(\pi, a) + \mathcal{MC}(\pi, b)$ is satisfied for every $a, b \geq 1$ (see footnote 1), we get (by our induction hypothesis) that the number of messages of the first type is at most $5pk \cdot \mathcal{MC}(\pi, n)$.

Since $\mathcal{TS}(\text{FSDL}_p^k) \geq k^p$, we get that if step 2 of Scheme FSDL_{p+1}^k was applied i times, then the number of nodes in the tree is at least ik^p. Therefore, by step 3 of Scheme FSDL_{p+1}^k we get that step 2 of Scheme FSDL_{p+1}^k can be applied at most k times. Using the fact that $\mathcal{MC}(\pi, a) \geq a$ for every $a \geq 1$, the total number of messages of type 2 sent by FSDL_{p+1}^k is therefore at most $5k\mathcal{MC}(\pi, n)$. Altogether, we get that the number of messages sent by FSDL_{p+1}^k during the dynamic scenario is at most $5pk \cdot \mathcal{MC}(\pi, n) + 5k \cdot \mathcal{MC}(\pi, n) = 5(p+1)k \cdot \mathcal{MC}(\pi, n)$. The second part of the lemma follows.   ∎

4   The Dynamic F-Labeling Schemes

Let $\pi = \langle \mathcal{M}_\pi \mathcal{D}_\pi \rangle$ be a static F-labeling scheme such that $\mathcal{MC}(\pi, n)$ is polynomial in n (see footnote 1) and let $k(x)$ be a sublinear function (see footnote 2). We first construct the dynamic F-labeling scheme $\text{SDL}^{k(x)}$ for the leaf-increasing tree model and then show how to transform it to our dynamic F-labeling scheme $\text{DL}^{k(x)}$ which is applicable in the leaf-dynamic tree model.

4.1   The Dynamic F-Labeling Scheme $\text{SDL}^{k(x)}$

We now describe our dynamic F-labeling scheme $\text{SDL}^{k(x)}$ in the leaf-increasing tree model. Throughout the scheme $\text{SDL}^{k(x)}$, we invoke the schemes FSDL_p^k for different parameters k and p.

Scheme $\text{SDL}^{k(x)}$

1. Invoke Scheme $\text{FSDL}_1^{k(1)}$.
2. Recall that while invoking Scheme FSDL_p^k, just before this scheme is supposed to terminate, Sub-protocol $\text{Reset}(T)$ is invoked in which n', the number of nodes in T, is calculated. For such n', let p' be such that $k(n')^{p'} \leq n' < k(n')^{p'+1}$. Let $p = p' + 2$ and let $k = k(n')$. Instead of terminating the above scheme, we proceed to step 3.

3. r invokes Scheme FSDL_p^k (with the parameters defined in the previous step) while ignoring step 1 of this scheme. I.e., we start directly in step 2 of Scheme FSDL_p^k.

   At some point, Scheme FSDL_p^k is supposed to terminate. Instead of terminating it, we proceed by going back to step 2 of Scheme $\mathrm{SDL}^{k(x)}$.

The proof of the following theorem appiers in the full version of this paper.

Theorem 1. $\mathrm{SDL}^{k(x)}$ *is a dynamic F-labeling scheme for the leaf-increasing tree model, satisfying the following properties.*

- $\mathcal{LS}(\mathrm{SDL}^{k(x)}, n) \leq O(\log_{k(n)} n \cdot \mathcal{LS}(\pi, n))$.
- $\mathcal{MC}(\mathrm{SDL}^{k(x)}, n) \leq O(k(n)(\log_{k(n)} n)\mathcal{MC}(\pi, n))$.

4.2 The Dynamic F-Labeling Scheme $\mathrm{DL}^{k(x)}$

In this section we show how to use $\mathrm{SDL}^{k(x)}$ in order to get the dynamic F-labeling scheme $\mathrm{DL}^{k(x)}$ which applies to the leaf-dynamic tree model. The details are omitted from this abstract.

Naively running $\mathrm{SDL}^{k(x)}$ in the leaf-dynamic tree model while ignoring deletions may result in a large label size relative to the size of the current tree. In order to overcome this difficulty, we use the same method as used in [28]. Informally, our scheme $\mathrm{DL}^{k(x)}$ invokes $\mathrm{SDL}^{k(x)}$ while ignoring deletions completely. In addition, our scheme $\mathrm{DL}^{k(x)}$ invokes a sub-protocol for counting topological events (using a technique inspired by [1]) until the number of topological events becomes $\Theta(n)$. We then execute $\mathrm{SDL}^{k(x)}$ from scratch. The number of messages that the above sub-protocol uses in order to count the topological changes is $O(\sum_i \log n_i)$ when n_i is the number of vertices in the tree when the i'th topological event takes place. We therefore get the following theorem.

Theorem 2. $\mathrm{DL}^{k(x)}$ *is a dynamic F-labeling scheme for the leaf-dynamic tree model, satisfying the following properties.*

- $\mathcal{LS}(\mathrm{DL}^{k(x)}, n) \leq O(\log_{k(n)} n \cdot \mathcal{LS}(\pi, n))$.
- $\mathcal{MC}(\mathrm{DL}^{k(x)}, \bar{n}) \leq O\left(\sum_i k(n_i)(\log_{k(n_i)} n)\frac{\mathcal{MC}(\pi, n_i)}{n_i}\right) + O(\sum_i \log^2 n_i)$.

By setting $k(x) = \sqrt{n}$, we get the following corollary.

Corollary 1. − *In the leaf-dynamic tree model, there exists a dynamic F-labeling scheme with the same asymptotic label size as π and sublinear amortized message complexity.*
- *In the leaf-dynamic tree model, there exist dynamic labeling schemes for the nearest common ancestor relation and for the routing function (both in the designer port model and in the adversary port model) using asymptotically optimal label sizes and sublinear message complexity.*

5   External Memory Complexity

Throughout this section some details are omitted from this abstract. We distinguish between three types of memory bits used by a node v. The first type consists of the bits in the label $\mathcal{M}(v)$ given to v by the marker algorithm. The second type consists of the memory bits used by the static algorithm π in order to calculate the static labels. The third type of bits, referred to as the *external memory* bits, consists of the additional external storage used during updates and maintenance operations by the dynamic labeling scheme. As mentioned before, for certain applications (and particularly routing), the label $\mathcal{M}(v)$ seems to be a more critical consideration than the total amount of storage needed for the information maintenance. In addition, the second type of memory bits are used by the static algorithm π only when it is invoked which is done infrequently. We note that one can construct static labeling schemes for all the above mentioned functions (i.e., routing in the designer port model, routing in the adversary port model, nearest common ancestor and distance) using linear message complexity and asymptotically optimal label size. Moreover, at any vertex, the number of memory bits used by these static algorithms is asymptotically the same as the label size. The details concerning these static labeling schemes appear in the full version of this paper.

In the following discussion, we try to minimize the number of external memory bits used by our dynamic schemes. Let us first describe the need for these memory bits.

Consider either Scheme $\mathrm{DL}^{k(x)}$ or Scheme $\mathrm{SDL}^{k(x)}$ for some function $k(x)$. At any time during the scenario, there exist some k', such that all the schemes of the form FSDL_l^k that are currently being invoked, are such that $k = k'$ and $l \leq \log_{k'} n$, where n is the current number of nodes in the tree. Let $p = \log_{k'} n$. For each $l \leq p$, each scheme FSDL_l^k that is currently being invoked acts on a different subtree of T. Therefore, a node v may participate at the same time in different schemes FSDL_l^k for different l's (actually, it can participate in at most one scheme FSDL_l^k for each $l \leq p$). As a result, each vertex v must know which of its edges correspond to each subtree T_l, the subtree containing v on which Scheme FSDL_l^k is invoked. Naively storing this information at v may incur $\Omega(p \cdot n)$ bits of memory. Note that v's communication in Scheme FSDL_l^k is done either by communicating with its parent or by communicating with all its children in T_l. Let E_l be the port numbers (at v) corresponding to the edges connecting v to its children in T_l. It is therefore enough to ensure that v is able to detect which of its port numbers is in E_l. We first consider our schemes in the designer port model, and then discuss them in the adversary port model.

5.1   External Memory in the Designer Port Model

In the designer port model, in order to reduce the memory used at each node, we exploit the fact that the tree T_l is a subtree of T_{l+1}. This is done as follows. Each node v enumerates its ports from 1 to its degree so that the following is maintained. For each $i = 1, 2 \cdots p$, there exist an integer a_i and a function ϕ_i

such that ϕ_i is a one to one and onto function from $\{1, 2 \cdots a_i\}$ to E_l. In other words, v enumerates its port numbers so that the port numbers from 1 to a_i correspond to the edges connecting v to its children in T_l. Therefore, in order to know the port numbers in E_l, v needs only to store the a_i's. This costs $O(p \log n)$ memory bits and we therefore obtain the following lemma.

Lemma 2. *In the designer port model, for any execution of Scheme* $\mathrm{DL}^{k(x)}$ *or Scheme* $\mathrm{SDL}^{k(x)}$ *the maximal number of external memory bits used by a vertex in any n-node tree is bounded from above by* $O(\log_{k(n)} n \cdot \log n)$.

5.2   External Memory in the Adversary Port Model

We first remark that in [28], the designer port model is assumed. Since port numbers are used in the labels given by the dynamic schemes of [28], applying their scheme in the adversary port model may affect the label sizes of the schemes. Specifically, let $\tau(n)$ be the maximum port number given by the adversary to any node in any n-node tree, taken over all scenarios. Then the upper bound on the label sizes of the general schemes proposed in [28] changes from $O(d \log_d n \cdot \mathcal{LS}(\pi, n))$ to $O(d \log_d n \cdot (\mathcal{LS}(\pi, n) + \log \tau(n)))$ (see Lemma 4.12 of [28]).

In contrast, applying our schemes in the adversary port model may only affect the external memory complexities. As discussed before, it is enough to guarantee that each node v knows for each $l < p$ which of its port numbers is in E_l. The strategy we propose is that node v distributes the relevant information to its children in T and collects it back when needed. Let u_i be the child of v corresponding to the i'th smallest port number of v. Let p_i^l be the i'th smallest port number of v in E_l and let $j(p_i^l)$ be such that p_i^l leads to $u_{j(p_i^l)}$.

In the leaf-increasing tree model, for each i, node u_i keeps a table, denoted $Table(u_i)$, containing p fields. Each field l in this table contains $j(p_i^l)$. If node v wants to communicate with its children in T_l, it must collect the corresponding port numbers. This is done by inspecting its children in T one by one starting by u_1, u_2, etc.. Note that v can identify u_i, as it is a local computation at v to find out which of its ports has the i'th smallest port number. By inspecting the l'th field in u_i's table, v is able to detect which of its ports leads to its i'th smallest edge in E_l. Since the number of nodes v needs to inspect is the same as the number of its children in T_l then this inspection does not affect the asymptotic message complexity of the scheme. Since the number of bits in each table $Table(u_i)$ is at most $O(p \cdot \log n)$, we obtain the following lemma.

Lemma 3. *In the adversary port model and the leaf-increasing tree model, the maximal number of external memory bits used by a vertex in Scheme* $\mathrm{SDL}^{k(n)}$ *is bounded from above by* $O(\log_{k(n)} n \cdot \log n)$.

In the leaf-dynamic model, where deletions are allowed, several difficulties may be encountered while trying to apply the strategy proposed above. The details are omitted from this abstract and appear in the full version of this paper, where we obtain the following lemma.

Lemma 4. *Assuming the adversary port model and the leaf-dynamic tree model, the maximal number of external memory bits used by a vertex in Scheme* $\mathrm{DL}^{k(x)}$ *is bounded from above by* $O(\log_{k(n)} n \cdot \log \tau(n))$.

References

[1] Y. Afek, B. Awerbuch, S.A. Plotkin and M. Saks. Local management of a global resource in a communication. *J. of the ACM* **43**, (1996), 1–19.

[2] S. Alstrup, P. Bille and T. Rauhe. Labeling schemes for small distances in trees. In *Proc. 14th ACM-SIAM Symp. on Discrete Algorithms*, Jan. 2003.

[3] S. Alstrup, C. Gavoille, H. Kaplan and T. Rauhe. Nearest Common Ancestors: A Survey and a new Distributed Algorithm. *Theory of Computing Systems* **37**, (2004), 441–456.

[4] S. Alstrup, J. Holm and M. Thorup. Maintaining Center and Median in Dynamic Trees. In *Proc. 7th Scandinavian Workshop on Algorithm Theory*, July. 2000.

[5] S. Abiteboul, H. Kaplan and T. Milo. Compact labeling schemes for ancestor queries. In *Proc. 12th ACM-SIAM Symp. on Discrete Algorithms*, Jan. 2001.

[6] S. Alstrup and T. Rauhe. Improved Labeling Scheme for Ancestor Queries. In *Proc. 19th ACM-SIAM Symp. on Discrete Algorithms*, Jan. 2002.

[7] M.A. Breuer and J. Folkman. An unexpected result on coding the vertices of a graph. *J. of Mathematical Analysis and Applications* **20**, (1967), 583–600.

[8] M.A. Breuer. Coding the vertexes of a graph. *IEEE Trans. on Information Theory*, IT-12:148–153, 1966.

[9] R. Cole and R. Hariharan. Dynamic LCA Queries on Trees. In *Proc. 10th ACM-SIAM Symp. on Discrete Algorithms*, 235–244, 1999.

[10] E. Cohen, E. Halperin, H. Kaplan and U. Zwick. Reachability and Distance Queries via 2-hop Labels. In *Proc. 13th ACM-SIAM Symp. on Discrete Algorithms*, Jan. 2002.

[11] E. Cohen, H. Kaplan and T. Milo. Labeling dynamic XML trees. In *Proc. 21st ACM Symp. on Principles of Database Systems*, June 2002.

[12] D. Eppstein, Z. Galil and G. F. Italiano. Dynamic Graph Algorithms. In *Algorithms and Theoretical Computing Handbook*, M. J. Atallah, ed., CRC Press, 1999, chapter 8.

[13] P. Fraigniaud and C. Gavoille. Routing in trees. In *Proc. 28th Int. Colloq. on Automata, Languages & Prog.*, LNCS 2076, pages 757–772, July 2001.

[14] P. Fraigniaud and C. Gavoille. A space lower bound for routing in trees. In *Proc. 19th Symp. on Theoretical Aspects of Computer Science*, Mar. 2002.

[15] J. Feigenbaum and S. Kannan. Dynamic Graph Algorithms. In *Handbook of Discrete and Combinatorial Mathematics*, CRC Press, 2000.

[16] C. Gavoille and C. Paul. Split decomposition and distance labelling: an optimal scheme for distance hereditary graphs. In *Proc. European Conf. on Combinatorics, Graph Theory and Applications*, Sept. 2001.

[17] C. Gavoille and D. Peleg. Compact and Localized Distributed Data Structures. *J. of Distributed Computing* **16**, (2003), 111–120.

[18] C. Gavoille, M. Katz, N.A. Katz, C. Paul and D. Peleg. Approximate Distance Labeling Schemes. In *9th European Symp. on Algorithms*, Aug. 2001, Aarhus, Denmark, SV-LNCS 2161, 476–488.

[19] C. Gavoille, D. Peleg, S. Pérennes and R. Raz. Distance labeling in graphs. In *Proc. 12th ACM-SIAM Symp. on Discrete Algorithms*, pages 210–219, Jan. 2001.

[20] J. Holm, K. Lichtenberg and M. Thorup. Poly-logarithmic deterministic fully-dynamic algorithms for connectivity, minimum spanning tree, 2-edge, and biconnectivity. *J. of the ACM* **48(4)**, (2001), 723–760.

[21] S. Kannan, M. Naor, and S. Rudich. Implicit representation of graphs. In *Proc. 20th ACM Symp. on Theory of Computing*, pages 334–343, May 1988.

[22] H. Kaplan and T. Milo. Short and simple labels for small distances and other functions. In *Workshop on Algorithms and Data Structures*, Aug. 2001.

[23] H. Kaplan and T. Milo. Parent and ancestor queries using a compact index. In *Proc. 20th ACM Symp. on Principles of Database Systems*, May 2001.

[24] H. Kaplan, T. Milo and R. Shabo. A Comparison of Labeling Schemes for Ancestor Queries. In *Proc. 19th ACM-SIAM Symp. on Discrete Algorithms*, Jan. 2002.

[25] M. Katz, N.A. Katz, A. Korman and D. Peleg. Labeling schemes for flow and connectivity. In *Proc. 19th ACM-SIAM Symp. on Discrete Algorithms*, Jan. 2002.

[26] M. Katz, N.A. Katz, and D. Peleg. Distance labeling schemes for well-separated graph classes. In *Proc. 17th Symp. on Theoretical Aspects of Computer Science*, pages 516–528, February 2000.

[27] A. Korman and D. Peleg. Labeling Schemes for Weighted Dynamic Trees. In *Proc. 30th Int. Colloq. on Automata, Languages & Prog.*, Eindhoven, The Netherlands, July 2003, Springer LNCS.

[28] A. Korman, D. Peleg and Y. Rodeh. Labeling schemes for dynamic tree networks. *Theory of Computing Systems* **37**, (2004), 49–75.

[29] D. Peleg. Proximity-preserving labeling schemes and their applications. In *Proc. 25th Int. Workshop on Graph-Theoretic Concepts in Computer Science*, pages 30–41, June 1999.

[30] D. Peleg. Informative labeling schemes for graphs. In *Proc. 25th Symp. on Mathematical Foundations of Computer Science*, volume LNCS-1893, pages 579–588. Springer-Verlag, Aug. 2000.

[31] D. Peleg. *Distributed Computing: A Locality-Sensitive Approach*. SIAM, 2000.

[32] D. D. Sleator and R. E. Tarjan. A data structure for dynamic trees. *Journal of Computer and System Sciences* **26(1)**, (1983), 362–391.

[33] N. Santoro and R. Khatib. Labelling and implicit routing in networks. *The Computer Journal* **28**, (1985), 5–8.

[34] M. Thorup. Compact oracles for reachability and approximate distances in planar digraphs. *J. of the ACM* **51**, (2004), 993–1024.

[35] M. Thorup and U. Zwick. Compact routing schemes. In *Proc. 13th ACM Symp. on Parallel Algorithms and Architecture*, pages 1–10, Hersonissos, Crete, Greece, July 2001.

The Dynamic And-Or Quorum System

Uri Nadav[1] and Moni Naor[2]

[1] Dept. of Computer Science Tel-Aviv University
[2] Dept. of Computer Science and Applied Mathematics, The Weizmann Institute

Abstract. We investigate issues related to the probe complexity of the And-Or quorum system and its implementation in a dynamic environment. Our contribution is twofold: We first analyze the algorithmic probe complexity of the And-Or quorum system, and present two optimal algorithms. The first is a non-adaptive algorithm with $O(\sqrt{n} \log n)$ probe complexity, which matches a known lower bound. The second is an adaptive algorithm with a probe complexity that is linear in the cardinality of a quorum set ($O(\sqrt{n})$), and requires at most $O(\log \log n)$ rounds. To the best of our knowledge, all other adaptive algorithms with same parameters (load and probe complexity) require $\theta(\sqrt{n})$ rounds.

Our second contribution is presenting the 'dynamic And-Or' quorum system - an adaptation of the above quorum system to a dynamic environment, where processors join and leave the network. It is based on a dynamic overlay network that emulates the De-Bruijn network and maintains the good properties of the quorum system(e.g.,load and availability). The algorithms suggested for the maintenance of these dynamic data structures are strongly coupled with the dynamic overlay network. This fact enables the use of gossip protocols which saves in message complexity and keeps the protocols simple and local. All these qualities make the 'dynamic And-Or' an excellent candidate for an implementation of dynamic quorums.

1 Introduction and Motivation

Quorum systems (QS) serve as a basic tool providing a uniform and reliable way to achieve coordination between processors in a distributed system. Quorum systems are defined as follows: A set system is a collection of sets $\mathcal{S} = \{S_1, \ldots, S_m\}$ over an underlying universe $U = \{u_1, \ldots, u_n\}$. A set system is said to satisfy the *intersection property*, if every two sets $S, R \in \mathcal{S}$ have a nonempty intersection. Set systems with the intersection property are known as *quorum systems* and the sets in such a system are called quorums.

We are interested in two aspects of quorum systems that arise from peer-to-peer environments, where processors are loosely coupled and may join and leave the network at will:

1. The setting in which the quorum operates is often dynamic, and should accommodate changes in the quorum system over time. We address the problem of designing a quorum system that is fit for a scalable and dynamic environment where processors leave and join at will.

P. Fraigniaud (Ed.): DISC 2005, LNCS 3724, pp. 472–486, 2005.

2. In a dynamic setting a global view of the system is usually hard to maintain and is therefore not assumed. We are interested in solutions which use local algorithms for the maintenance of the QS i.e., ones in which the input for a processor only comes from its local view of its neighbors in the network.

This paper deals with the And-Or quorum system, presented by Naor and Wool[16]. We examine the And-Or system both in a static environment where the set of processors is fixed, and in a dynamic and scalable environment. We conclude that it is very suitable for implementation in a dynamic setting.

1.1 Definitions and Preliminaries

The *load* on a system of processors, as defined in [16], captures the probability of accessing the busiest processor. An *access strategy* μ, for a quorum system $\mathcal{Q}$, is a probability distribution over the quorums in $\mathcal{Q}$, i.e. $\sum_{Q \in \mathcal{Q}} \mu(Q) = 1$. An access strategy can be thought of as a method for choosing a quorum. The load $\mathcal{L}(i)$ induced by a strategy on a processor $i \in U$ is the probability that processor i is chosen by the strategy, i.e. $\mathcal{L}(i) = \Pr_\mu[i \in Q]$. The load of a strategy μ is $\mathcal{L}(\mu) = \max_{i \in U} \mathcal{L}(i)$. For a quorum system $\mathcal{Q}$, the load $\mathcal{L}(\mathcal{Q})$ is the minimum load induced by a strategy, over all strategies. Let $c(\mathcal{Q})$ denote the size of the smallest quorum in $\mathcal{Q}$. Naor and Wool prove in [16] the following lemma:

Lemma 1 ([16]). *The load of a quorum system $\mathcal{Q}$ is at least* $max\{\frac{1}{c(\mathcal{Q})}, \frac{c(\mathcal{Q})}{n}\}$ *which implies that* $\mathcal{L}(\mathcal{Q}) \geq \frac{1}{\sqrt{n}}$.

We assume that processors may temporarily fail(halt). The failure of a processor occurs with some fixed probability p and is independent from failures of other processors in the network (Random faults model). A quorum is said to be alive if all of its elements are alive (non-faulty), and dead otherwise. The *availability* of a quorum system $\mathcal{Q}$ is measured by the global failure probability F_p which is the probability that all quorums in $\mathcal{Q}$ are dead. This failure probability measures how resilient the system is.

The availability measure tells us about the probability of a quorum set to survive in the random-fault model, but tells us nothing about the complexity of finding a live quorum. The probe complexity of a quorum system captures the number of probes required for finding a live quorum (cf. [5],[18]). We use the same probing model defined in [18], where a user learns the state of a processor with a single probe (by sending a message and waiting a timeout period for the reply) i.e., faults are detectable. It is also assumed that the state of a processor does not change while the system is being probed. A lower bound on the algorithmic probe complexity of a non-adaptive algorithm, as a function of the load was given in [15]:

Theorem 1 ([15]). *Let $\mathcal{Q}$ be a quorum system over a universe of processors U with load $\mathcal{L} = \mathcal{L}(\mathcal{Q})$. Assume that each element in U fails with some fixed probability $p \leq \frac{1}{2}$. Let $X \subset U$ be a predefined set of elements (that corresponds to a non-adaptive algorithm) s.t.,*

$$\Pr[X \, contains \, a \, live \, quorum] \geq \frac{1}{2},$$

then

$$|X| \geq \frac{1}{2\log(1/p)+1} \frac{\log(1/4\mathcal{L})}{\mathcal{L}}.$$

In particular if $\mathcal{L} = O(\frac{1}{\sqrt{n}})$ then $|X| = \Omega(\sqrt{n}\log n)$.

A *non-adaptive* algorithm for finding a live quorum decides on which processors to probe prior to gaining any knowledge as to which processors failed. Such algorithms are attractive since they could be executed in parallel. An *adaptive* algorithm on the other hand, can act in a number of rounds, such that in each round the probe results of prior rounds are known.

1.2   Quorum System for P2P and Dynamic Environments

Recently, peer-to-peer applications gained enormous popularity, which led to an extensive research on dynamic distributed data structures on overlay networks. Most of the attention was put on dynamic hash tables (c.f [10][14][19][20][21]). In these constructions data items are divided locally and on the fly between active processors in the network. An overlay network is built up dynamically, as processors join and leave the network.

The design of quorum systems for a dynamic environment raises two problems:

Integrity: When processors join or depart the system the quorum sets should be modified. The integrity of the system is preserved in two aspects: First, the intersection property must hold. Second, the adaptation should keep the properties of the quorum system e.g., load and availability.

Locality: Even if the set of quorums is well defined, it is required of a user to actually know the quorum structure in order to choose a quorum. In a dynamic system a global view of the system is hard to maintain and is therefore not assumed. The users of the quorum system are the processors themselves. When a processor selects a quorum it has no knowledge of the complete quorum structure and only has access to its close neighborhood.

We combine techniques from works on dynamic overlay networks together with the And-Or quorum system and come up with a design that provides high scalability and locality while preserving other measurements of quality from classic research of quorum systems.

1.3   Related Work

Peleg and Wool defined the availability of quorum systems in [17] and studied the availability of some quorum system classes. In [18] Peleg and Wool studied the complexity of finding a live quorum or evidence for the lack of, in an adversarial-fault model. In this model crash faults are assumed to be detectable, and a probe action to a processor is assumed to have $O(1)$ complexity. In [5] Hassin and Peleg analyzed the probe complexity of several systems in the random-fault model. Bazzi [3] introduced the term *'cost of failures'*. Given a network implementation and an algorithm for finding a live quorum, the cost of failures measures the average communication overhead caused by encountering a faulty processor. In [15] Naor and Wieder defined the *Algorithmic probe complexity* as the actual time and message complexity required for finding a live quorum.

In [16] Naor and Wool presented both the *Paths* quorum system and the *And-Or* system, and showed that they both have asymptotically optimal load and availability. In [15], Naor and Wieder suggested an adaptation of *Paths* in a dynamic environment and showed that it maintains the optimal load and availability of the original system. Malkhi et al [11] suggested a relaxation for quorum systems in which the intersection of two quorums is only required with some high probability. It was shown that such a relaxation results in a dramatic improvement in the resilience of the system. Abraham and Malkhi [2] introduced the *'dynamic ϵ-intersecting system'* which is an adaptation of the ϵ-intersecting system for a dynamic environment.

In [13] we have shown an embedding of the *'And-Or tree'* structure over the *'Distance-Halving'* overlay network [14], which served as a fault-tolerant storage system. We use the same embedding here for the construction of a dynamic quorum system. In quorum systems the major design goal is to ensure intersection between quorums, whereas in storage systems, files reconstruction serves as the main target. The intersection property of quorum-systems is necessary but not sufficient for this matter. We wish to emphasize this difference in goals which leads to entirely different algorithms and analyses. We also emphasize the fact that the fault-model in [13] is adversarial, in contrast with a random-fault model analyzed in this paper.

1.4   Results and Paper Organization

This paper is divided into two parts. In the first part, we analyze the algorithmic probe complexity of the *And-Or* quorum system (Section 2). We show a non-adaptive algorithm for finding a live quorum with $O(\sqrt{n}\log n)$ probe complexity. This matches a lower bound of Naor and Wieder [15]. We further show an adaptive algorithm with a probe complexity of $O(\sqrt{n})$, which is optimal (up to constants). Thus combined with the results in [16] the *And-Or* system is shown to have an excellent balance between many somewhat contradictory measures of quality.

The *'Paths'* quorum system was already shown to achieve optimal load, availability [16], and algorithmic probe complexity [15]. The adaptive algorithm for paths requires $O(\sqrt{n})$ probes as in our case. However, it requires $\theta(\sqrt{n})$ rounds, whereas our algorithm only requires $O(\log\log n)$ rounds. To the best of our knowledge, no other algorithm with similar parameters works as fast. Our algorithm also achieves early stopping in the case of no faults. Our contribution is therefore twofold: First, our adaptive algorithm works very fast. Second, the analysis is kept simple in contrast with the results in [16][15] which require heavy tools from percolation theory.

We should note however that the *Paths* quorum system has a better availability than And-Or, in the sense that it remains available for every failure probability $p < \frac{1}{2}$. In contrast, it was shown in [16] that the And-Or has the same asymptotic behavior, but for $p < p_c$, where p_c is a constant strictly less than $\frac{1}{2}$.

In the second part of this paper (Section 4) we present and analyze *'dynamic And-Or'*, a construction for a dynamic and scalable quorum system which could be viewed as a dynamic adaptation of the And-Or system. We show that the dynamic And-Or keeps the optimal load, availability and probe complexity of the And-Or system.

The remainder of this paper is organized in the following way. In Section 2 we present the optimal adaptive and non-adaptive algorithms for finding a live quorum in the random-fault model. Section 3 analyzes the And-Or quorum system on a balanced binary tree which is incomplete. This structure is a step towards the adaptation of the And-Or for a dynamic environment, which is presented in Section 4. Section 4 then presents two different implementations of the And-Or system in a dynamic environment. Finally, our conclusions and open questions are presented in Section 5. We note that all proofs are omitted from this version due to lack of space.

2 The And-Or Quorum System

We recall the construction of the *'And-Or'* quorum system presented in [16]. Consider a complete binary tree of height h, rooted at *root*, and identify the 2^h leaves of the tree with systems processors. We define two collections of subsets over the set of processors, using the following recursive definitions:

(i) For a leaf v, ANDset$(v) = $ ORset$(v) = \big\{\{v\}\big\}$.
(ii) ANDset$(v) = \big\{S \cup R \,|\, S \in $ ORset$(v.left) \wedge R \in $ ORset$(v.right)\big\}$.
(iii) ORset$(v) = $ ANDset$(v.left) \cup $ ANDset$(v.right)$

The And-Or quorum system is then composed of the collections ANDset$(root)$ and ORset$(root)$. A natural recursive procedure can be used to generate a set $S \in $ ANDset$(root)$. The procedure visits nodes of the tree, beginning at the root and propagating downwards. It considers the nodes of the tree as AND/OR gates (on even/odd levels). When visiting an AND gate it continues to both its children, and when visiting an OR gate one of its children is chosen. The leaves visited by the procedure form S. A similar procedure generates a set $R \in $ ORset$(root)$. The And-Or structure induces the following properties:

Lemma 2 (from [16]). *Consider a complete binary tree of height h rooted at root. Let $S \in $ ANDset$(root)$ and $R \in $ ORset$(root)$ then $|S \cap R| = 1$, $|R| = 2^{\lfloor \frac{h}{2} \rfloor}$ and $|S| = 2^{\lfloor \frac{h+1}{2} \rfloor}$.*

Lemma 2 states that each set $S \in $ ANDset$(root)$ intersects each set $R \in $ ORset$(root)$. This property is used to define the *'And-Or'* quorum system: A quorum in the And-Or system is any set $Q = S \cup R$ where S is a member of ANDset($root$) and R is a member of ORset($root$). For a binary tree T we denote the set of quorums with AndOr(T). The load of the And-Or system was shown to be optimal $(O(\frac{1}{\sqrt{n}}))$ in [16].

The And-Or system was shown to have a failure probability F_p which exponentially decays in n. For $p \leq \frac{1}{4}$ it was shown in [16] that F_p(AndOr) $\leq$ $\exp(-\Omega(\sqrt{n}))$.

2.1   A Non-adaptive Algorithm

We now show a non-adaptive algorithm for choosing a live quorum in the And-Or quorum system. The probe complexity of this algorithm is $O(\sqrt{n}\log n)$ which matches the lower bound of Theorem 1.

Let r be the root of a complete binary tree. We introduce the notion of ANDset collection on internal nodes of the tree, in level h, denoted ANDset(r, h):

Definition 1 (ANDset(r, h)). *Let T be a binary tree rooted at r with h levels. Let T' be the same tree, where all the nodes in level $h+1$ or above are truncated, and the nodes of level h serve as leaves. Then* ANDset(r, h) *equals the collection* ANDset(r) *as defined on T'.*

The non-adaptive algorithm uniformly picks a set $R \in$ ANDset(r, h) where

$$h = \lfloor \log n - 2 \log \log n \rfloor.$$

All processors which are descendants of nodes in R are then chosen. The cardinality of such a set follows from Lemma 2.

Lemma 3. *The cardinality of a set of processors S chosen by the non-adaptive algorithm is $O(\sqrt{n}\log n)$.*

Observation 1 follows directly from the definition of the recursive procedure for selecting a member of ANDset(r):

Observation 1. *Let S be a member of* ANDset(r) *then there exists a set $R \in$* ANDset(r, h) *and a collection $\{S_v : v \in R, S_v \in$ ANDset(v)$\}$ such that:*

$$S = \cup_{v \in R} S_v.$$

From the high availability property of the And-Or, and from Observation 1 it follows that a live member of ANDset(r) is contained in the probed set, with high probability[1] .

Theorem 2 (Non-adaptive Probe Complexity). *Let S denote the set of processors chosen as described above, then S contains a live set from the collection* ANDset(r) *w.h.p .*

In a similar way a subset of processors that contains a live member of ORset(r) can be chosen. Joining such a set with a live member of ANDset(r) yields a live quorum in the And-Or quorum system.

---

[1] By "with high probability" (w.h.p.), we mean "with probability at least $1 - O(n^{-\alpha})$ for some constant $\alpha > 0$, for a system with n processors."

2.2   An Adaptive Algorithm

We present an adaptive algorithm for finding a live quorum for the And-Or system which requires $\theta(\sqrt{n})$ probes. By an adaptive algorithm we mean an algorithm that probes several subsets of processors, in a number of rounds. The algorithm is assumed to send all messages (probes) in a specific round prior to getting any reply from any of the processors that are probed in this round. Answers from probed processors are returned before some timeout, after which the algorithm decides which processors to probe in the next round. The number of rounds therefore determines the time complexity of the algorithm so it is desired to have as small as possible number of rounds.

Our algorithm requires w.h.p. only $O(\log \log n)$ rounds. Naor and Wieder presented in [15] an adaptive algorithm for the Paths quorum system with a $\theta(\sqrt{n})$ probe complexity, however, their solution requires $\theta(\sqrt{n})$ rounds.

As in the non-adaptive case, it is sufficient to show how to find a live member of ANDset($root$). A live member of ORset($root$) can be found in a similar way. To adaptively find a live member of ANDset($root$), the algorithm first picks an arbitrary set $S \in$ ANDset($root$) and probe its members. If S turns out to be alive then the algorithm may finish. Otherwise, the set is being 'corrected', by replacing the choices that turned out to be *dead*, in the following way.

Let parent(v) denote the internal node in the tree which is the parent of v. To correct a choice of a *dead* processor $v \in S$, the leaves in the subtree $v' = $ parent(v) are probed. If the newly probed processors contain a live member of ANDset(v') then the algorithm can finish. Otherwise, the last step is recursively repeated with parent(v'). This process runs in parallel for each faulty processor $v \in S$. Following from Observation 1, when all processes stop, the probed elements contain a live member of ANDset(r). If a live member exists, then by the time all the process reach the root of the tree, this live member is found. Algorithm 1 describes this process more formally.

We turn to the analysis of the probe complexity of the adaptive algorithm. Step 2 of Algorithm 1 finds for each $v \in S$ its lowest ancestor v', for which a live member in ANDset(v') exists. Note that if v is alive then $v' = v$. Denote

---

Algorithm 1 Adaptive Find Live Quorum

Input: Oracle access to the state of processors (*live* or *dead*).

Output: A live member of ANDset(r) (or *'fail'* in case none was found).

1. Probe the members of some set $S \in$ ANDset($root$).
2. For each $v \in S$ which is *dead*, do the following:
   (a) Set $v' = $ parent(v)
   (b) Probe all leaves of v'
   (c) While the leaves in the subtree v' do not contain a live member of ANDset(v'), set $v' \leftarrow$ parent(v') and go back to stage 2b.
   (d) Add the members of the live set to S.

by h_v the distance from v to this v'. h_v determines the number of rounds for each process. The number of rounds of the algorithm is $max_{v \in S}\{h_v\}$. Lemma 4 states that the expected height h_v is constant and that w.h.p. for all $v \in S$, $h_v \leq 2 \log \log n$:

Lemma 4. *Let $v \in S$, then* $E[h_v] = O(1)$, *and moreover,*

$$\Pr[\bigwedge_{v \in S} h_v \leq 2 \log \log n] = 1 - O(\frac{1}{\sqrt{n}}),$$

where the probability is taken over the occurrence of faults.

This guarantees that the number of rounds is at most $2 \log \log n$. To show $O(\sqrt{n})$ probe complexity, we need to prove there is a concentration around $E[h_v]$ w.h.p . The variables h_v are not independent since the trees may intersect, and therefore Chernoff inequality cannot be directly applied. This problem is addressed through dividing the random variables h_v into a logarithmic number of sets, such that within each set, all variables are independent.

Theorem 3. *The number of elements probed by the adaptive algorithm is w.h.p. $O(\sqrt{n})$. The number of rounds required in Step 2c of the algorithm is w.h.p. at most $2 \log \log n$.*

Early Stopping. We showed that a live quorum can be found in the And-Or quorum system when each processor fails with some constant probability p, in time $\theta(\log \log n)$ w.h.p . It is desirable that in a different fault model, for example when the failure probability of a processor is $o(1)$, the running time will shorten, namely, achieving early stopping of the algorithm. When no faults occur at all, the adaptive algorithm finds a live quorum in a single round. When the failure probability is $O(\frac{1}{n^c})$ for some constant $c > 0$, then w.h.p. no subtree generated in the adaptive algorithm grows to a height of more than a constant. It can be shown in this case that w.h.p. the number of steps required from the algorithm is a constant.

3   The And-Or Quorum System on a Balanced Binary Tree

Till now we have discussed the And-Or quorum system in the case the And-Or structure is defined over a complete binary tree. In Section 4 we present two ways of maintaining a binary tree over a dynamic environment of processors which is incomplete. In such a case the definition of the recursive structures, ANDset(*root*) and ORset(*root*) remains well defined. Lemma 2 can be extended to show that the intersection property is maintained, so the AndOr(*root*) structure is a quorum system. However, the load, availability and probe complexity of the new system are no longer guaranteed to be optimal as in the original And-Or

system. To maintain the optimal properties of the And-Or we restrict ourselves
to balanced trees.

A family of trees is a set of trees $\{T_i\}_{i=1}^{\infty}$ such that T_i has i leaves.

Definition 2 (Balanced Tree). *A family $\{T_i\}_{i=1}^{\infty}$ of trees is said to be balanced
if the following holds:*

- *Each node in the tree is either a leaf or has two children.*
- *There exists a constant $c \geq 0$ s.t. for each tree T_i, the difference between the
  levels of the leaves is bounded by c.*

Theorem 4 states that the And-Or on balanced trees maintains optimal
asymptotic load and availability.

Theorem 4. *Let T be a tree in a balanced family of trees with n leaves. Let
$\mathcal{Q} = \text{AndOr}(T)$ be the And-Or quorum system defined on T. The load of $\mathcal{Q}$ is
$\mathcal{L}(\mathcal{Q}) = O(\frac{1}{\sqrt{n}})$. Also, when the processors fail independently with probability
$p < p_c$, for a constant p_c that depends only on the balance factor c, the global
fail probability is:*

$$F_p(\text{AndOr}(T)) \leq \exp(-O(\sqrt{n})).$$

4 The Dynamic And-Or Quorum System

In this section we present an adaptation of the Balanced And-Or quorum system over a dynamic network. We present two implementations: The first is on
top of the Identity-Management scheme [12]. In this scheme a balanced binary
tree structure is maintained over the active processors in the network and the
embedding of the quorum system is straightforward. The second is on top of the
distance-halving network, which emulates the De-Bruijn network in a dynamic
environment (see [4,6] for other dynamic implementations of this network). In
this network, communication lines correspond to edges of a binary tree, so that
this implementation saves in the message complexity of finding a quorum.

For the entire section, we make the following simplifying assumption: An underlying layer takes care of concurrent operations of Join/Depart/'Use Quorum',
so that the network implementation gets these operations sequentially (where
'Use Quorum' is an operation that sends a message to all the members of a
quorum). We refer the reader to [9] where techniques for achieving concurrency
in peer-to-peer networks are introduced.

4.1 A Dynamic And-Or Quorum System Using the
      Identity-Management Scheme

The first implementation of the And-Or quorum system in a dynamic environment uses the Identity-Management scheme presented by Manku [12]. In this
scheme a balanced binary tree, with the active processors acting as its leaves,
is maintained at all times, as processors join and depart from the system. The

binary tree structure defines the hosts' identities. Only leaf nodes of the tree correspond to a processor's identity. The internal nodes of the tree are conceptual. The sequence of 0s and 1s along the path from the root to a leaf node constitutes the identity of that leaf. The Identity-Management scheme keeps the tree structure balanced such that at each moment, all leaves are at one of three bottom levels of the tree. This balanced tree is used as a balanced And-Or tree, which was shown in Section 3 to generate a quorum system with optimal properties.

As was mentioned in Section 1.2, a dynamic environment raises two design issues of *integrity* and *locality*. To maintain *integrity* when the tree structure changes, all the quorums in use that are no longer legitimate quorums, must be modified. In the Identity-Management scheme there are two distributed algorithms that change the tree structure, one for joining a processor and one for processor departure. The algorithms for modifying quorums during join/depart are simple and are left for a full version of this paper.

To address the issue of locality we show how a processor can send messages to a random quorum without any knowledge of the tree structure. We use the fact that for each processor with identity x, level $|x| - 2$ is guaranteed to be complete. Details are left for a full version of this paper.

4.2 A Dynamic And-Or Quorum System over the Distance Halving Network

We now describe an adaptation of the balanced And-Or quorum system of Section 3 to a dynamic environment over the distance halving (DH) network of Naor and Wieder [14]. This implementation in contrast to the one of Section 4.1, strongly couples the quorum system with the dynamic network edges, saving in communication complexity of algorithms for selecting a quorum.

We use the same embedding of a binary tree over the DH-network, that we defined in [13]. We briefly repeat the description of the DH-network and of the binary tree embedding in it. The key idea behind most constructions of distributed hash tables, is to partition a (continuous) range of keys (denoted I) among the participating processors in the network. In our case I is the interval $[0, 1)$. Denote by $\boldsymbol{x}$ a set of n points in I. The point x_i serves as the identity of the ith processor, in a network of n processors. The points of $\boldsymbol{x}$ divide I into n segments. Define the segment of x_i to be $s(x_i) = [x_i, x_{i+1})$ $(i = 1, \ldots, n-1)$ and $s(x_n) = [x_n, 1) \cup [0, x_1)$. In the DH-network, each processor u_i is associated with the segment $s(x_i)$. If a point y is in $s(x_i)$ we say that u_i covers y. Notice that each point $y \in I$ is covered by exactly one processor. When data is written to y it is being stored in the processor that covers y, and remains stored in a single processor throughout the lifetime of the DH-network.

For a set $S \subset I$ and an identities vector $\overrightarrow{x}$, we denote by $\mathrm{CP}_{\overrightarrow{x}}(S)$ the set of processors that cover the points in S, i.e., $\mathrm{CP}_{\overrightarrow{x}}(S) \triangleq \{p_i | \exists s \in S, s \in s(x_i)\}$. In case $\overrightarrow{x}$ is clear from context we omit it and simply write $\mathrm{CP}(S)$.

We recall the construction of the DH-network from [14]. We first define the DH-graph $G_c = (E_c, V_c)$. The vertex set of G_c is the unit interval I. The edge set of G_c is defined by the following functions:

$$\ell(y) \triangleq \frac{y}{2}, \; r(y) \triangleq \frac{y+1}{2},$$

where $y \in I$, and ℓ and r abbreviates 'left' and 'right' respectively. The edge set of G_c is then

$$E_c \triangleq \{(y, \ell(y)), (y, r(y)) | \; y \in I\}.$$

We denote by $parent(x)$ the function that returns the parent of a point $x \in I$ in the DH-graph i.e., $parent(x) = \begin{cases} 2x, & x < \frac{1}{2}, \\ 1 - 2x, & x \geq \frac{1}{2}. \end{cases}$ A pair of processors (u_i, u_j) are connected if there exists an edge (y, z) in the DH-graph, such that $y \in s(x_i)$ and $z \in s(x_j)$.

To implement the And-Or system on a DH-network we identify an embedding of a binary tree on the DH-graph. The $\ell(\cdot)$ and $r(\cdot)$ functions induce an embedding of a complete binary tree on every point x in I, in a natural way. The left child of a point x is $\ell(x)$ and the right child is $r(x)$.

An important parameter of the DH-network studied in [14] is the ratio between the largest and smallest cells induced by a composition. More formally:

Definition 3 (From [14]). *The* smoothness *of* $\overrightarrow{x}$ *denoted by* $\rho(x)$ *is defined to be* $\max_{i,j} \frac{|x_i|}{|x_j|}$. *If* $\rho(x)$ *is a constant independent of* n *we say that* $\overrightarrow{x}$ *is smooth.*

The smoothness of a network is maintained by the join/depart algorithms, in which processors choose their identities. Several methods for achieving smoothness are described in [7,10,12,1,14]. In the following dynamic adaptation of the And-Or system we assume both the network is kept smooth at all times, with a constant factor ρ, and that each processor has an approximation of $\log n$ (up to an additive factor). The Identity Management scheme [12] achieves a smoothness factor $\rho = 4$. In this scheme a node can also approximate the value of $\log n$ up to an additive constant of ± 2.

The Dynamic And-Or Quorum System Based on a Smooth Distance Halving Network. We first assume that at any moment, each processor has a local variable $l = \lceil \log n \rceil$, where n is the number of currently active processors in the network. Similar methods can be used when only an approximation of l within an additive constant is available.

The set of quorums is defined using an embedding of a binary tree T in the DH-graph, rooted in an arbitrary fixed point $r \in I$ with depth l. A set $S \in \text{ANDset}(r)$ is a set of points in I and so are sets in $\text{ORset}(r)$. Note that T has between n and $2n$ leaves. A quorum set is defined as the set of processors that cover a quorum (of points in I) in $\text{AndOr}(T)$, i.e.,

$$Q = \{S \cup R | \; S = \text{CP}(S'), R = \text{CP}(R'), S' \in \text{ANDset}(r), R' \in \text{ORset}(r)\}.$$

Observation 2. *For any identities vector assignment* $\overrightarrow{x}$, $\mathcal{Q}$ *is a quorum system.*

When $\overrightarrow{x}$ is smooth each processor covers at most a constant number of leaves, which guarantees $\mathcal{Q}$ posses of an $O(\frac{1}{\sqrt{n}})$ load:

Theorem 5. *Let* $\mathcal{Q}$ *be the dynamic And-Or quorum system as defined above. If* $\overrightarrow{x}$ *is smooth then the load* $\mathcal{L}(\mathcal{Q}) = O(\frac{1}{\sqrt{n}})$.

Quorum Selection Through Gossip and Adaptation to Network Updates. The fact that the edges of the And-Or tree correspond to real communication lines of the DH-network enables a gossip based protocol which saves in message complexity. The dynamic And-Or presented in Section 4.1, requires that a message be sent to each of the processors selected. Let r denote the expected number of routing hops per message. r is typically logarithmic in the number of processors [1,14,20,21]. If a message is sent to m processors, the number of messages actually sent is blown to rm. In the And-Or system based on the DH-network, messages can percolate through the nodes that cover the tree in a similar manner to the recursive procedure for choosing a member of the ANDset collection (see Section 2). In this manner the total number of messages sent is less than $2\sqrt{n}$.

To keep a quorum consistent with the changing tree structure, it is necessary to modify the quorums in use as the network evolves. Each processor p, maintains a local variable $S(p)$ which is the set of all leaves (points in I), which are members of a quorum in use, and are covered by p. p updates $S(p)$ whenever one of the following events occur: First, when l, the local approximation of the height of the And-Or tree changes. Second, when the segment covered by p shrinks/grows, as a result of neighbor join/depart.

When l increases, each leaf x in the tree splits into $\ell(x), r(x)$. When l decreases, x becomes parent(x). p updates $S(p)$, by 'passing' all members $x \in S(p)$ to either $\ell(x)$ or $r(x)$ or parent(x) in a manner that resembles the gossip protocol. In the case where the segment covered by p changes, p either inserts new leaves into $S(p)$ or deletes leaves in $S(p)$ which are no longer covered by it, and passes them to the new processors that cover them. Note that each update to this distributed data structure, can be done by sending a messages via a single edge in the DH-network.

Analyzing the Availability and Probe Complexity of the Dynamic And-Or. In the dynamic And-Or environment we say a point $x \in I$ is alive if and only if the processor that covers it is alive. Otherwise it is said to be dead. A subset of points in I is said to be alive iff all its members are alive. Note that a live quorum of processors in the dynamic And-Or exists, iff a live quorum (of points) exists on the embedded And-Or structure.

In the And-Or system the analysis of F_p was kept relatively simple due to the fact that the failure probabilities of two disjoint subtrees are independent. In the dynamic case however, though processors fail independently, the failure of leaves in the tree is not independent. The status of two leaves is dependent only if they are covered by the same processor. In a smooth network each processor covers at most a constant number of leaves in the embedded tree, so the event that a leaf fails depends on at most a constant number of other such events.

Due to this limited dependency, we can use the technique of domination by product measure which was introduced by Liggett et al.[8], and was used by Naor and Wieder in [15] in a similar context. The intuition behind this technique is that the above configuration is very similar to a configuration where each processor covers exactly one leaf, in which case leaves fail independently of each other and the availability analysis is as in the classic network.

The following theorem ensures high availability for the dynamic And-Or:

Theorem 6. *There exists a constant $p_c > 0$ such that for every $p \le p_c$, the failure probability of the dynamic And-Or quorum system over a smooth DH-network is $F_p = \exp(-\theta(\sqrt{n}))$.*

We now turn to discuss probe complexity in the dynamic case. We use essentially the same algorithms described in Section 2, but here we first select a set of leaves and then use the set of processors that cover them. The analysis here is more complicated. The events that leaves in different subtrees contain live sets are no longer independent since two points in disjoint trees can be covered by the same processor.

We need to show that the non-adaptive algorithm applied to the dynamic case finds a live quorum w.h.p., in order to attain $O(\sqrt{n}\log n)$ probe complexity. The proof of Theorem 2 used the fact that for $p \le \frac{1}{4}$, an And-Or quorum system on a subtree of height $2\log\log n$ has a failure probability $F_p \le \frac{1}{n}$. Theorem 6 for the dynamic And-Or stated that for p small enough, the same applies.

Theorem 7. *There exists a constant $p_c > 0$ s.t., when the failure probability $p \le p_c$, then the set of processors chosen by the non-adaptive algorithm (Section 2), contains a live quorum w.h.p . This set is of size $O(\sqrt{n}\log n)$.*

The adaptive algorithm for the dynamic case also works in the same way as in the classic case. Again, Theorem 6 can be used to show that the local subtrees generated in step 2c of Algorithm 1, have an expected constant height. Hence, on average the algorithm probes $\theta(\sqrt{n})$ processors. However, unlike in the classic case, here there is dependency between the height of different subtrees, so Chernoff bound cannot be used to bound the probability of large deviation. Following the Markov inequality, the probability for $\omega(\sqrt{n})$ probes cannot be a constant. Hence, with probability $1 - o(1)$, the number of probes required is $\theta(\sqrt{n})$. However, we did not show this happens with probability $1 - n^{-\alpha}$, $\alpha > 0$. Therefore, bounding the probe complexity of the adaptive algorithm with a bound lower than $O(\sqrt{n}\log n)$ remains an open problem.

4.3   Comparing with Other Dynamic Quorum Constructions

Comparing with other dynamic constructions of quorum systems, the *dynamic And-Or* system holds some advantages. Most of these advantages were already stated and are summarized in Table 1. A major advantage of the dynamic And-Or lays in the strong coupling between the combinatorial structure of the And-Or and the overlay network structure. For example, in the *Dynamic Paths*[15], whenever a processor joins or departs from the system a local computation of a Voronoi diagram is required. In the dynamic And-Or, join/depart events only require the insertion/deletion of a constant number of values to a set.

It was shown in [17] that for every quorum system, the global failure probability $F_p \overset{n\to\infty}{\to} 1$, when $p > \frac{1}{2}$. A 'critical failure probability' is the maximum p, for which the system is available i.e., for which F_p converges to 0 as n goes to infinity. It was shown in [15] that the critical probability for *'Dynamic Paths'* is $\frac{1}{2}$. The critical value for the And-Or system is $\alpha = \frac{3-\sqrt{5}}{2} < \frac{1}{2}$. The best failure probability p for which we have shown availability in the Dynamic And-Or, is a constant greater than 0, but strictly less than α. The actual critical value remains unknown, but in any case the 'Dynamic Paths' achieves a better result in this criteria.

Table 1. A comparison between the dynamic And-Or, the dynamic Paths and the dynamic probabilistic quorum system

	Dynamic And-Or	Dynamic Paths[15]	Dynamic PQS[2]
Load	$\theta(\frac{1}{\sqrt{n}})$	$\theta(\frac{1}{\sqrt{n}})$	$\theta(\frac{\sqrt{\log n}}{\sqrt{n}})$
Failure Probability	$e^{-\Omega(\sqrt{n})}$	$e^{-\Omega(\sqrt{n})}$	$e^{-\Omega(n)}$
Adaptive Algorithmic PC	$O(\sqrt{n})$	$O(\sqrt{n})$	$O(\sqrt{n}\log n)$
Number of rounds	$\theta(\log\log n)$	$\theta(\sqrt{n})$	1
Critical p	$0 < p_c \leq \frac{1}{4}$	$\frac{1}{2}$	-

5   Conclusions and Open Questions

We have shown that the And-Or quorum system has an adaptive algorithm for finding a live quorum, that operates in $\log\log n$ rounds and has a $O(\sqrt{n})$ probe complexity. Is there a quorum system with an optimal load for which there is an adaptive algorithm that works in a constant number of rounds (and the same probe complexity)? Recall that Naor and Wieder showed a lower bound on the probe complexity as a function of the load for non-adaptive algorithms (Theorem 1). This can be viewed as a lower bound on single round algorithms. A more general goal would be to extend this lower bound for adaptive algorithms with an arbitrary number of rounds. A milestone would be to prove the optimality of our algorithm for finding a live quorum in the And-Or system, or to find an algorithm with better probe complexity.

In Section 4 we showed that most of the good properties of the And-Or quorum system are maintained in the dynamic implementation over the DH-network. We showed that the algorithmic probe complexity of our adaptive algorithm is $O(\sqrt{n})$ on expectation and even with probability $1 - o(1)$. However, showing the probe complexity is $O(\sqrt{n})$ w.h.p. remains open as well.

Acknowledgements

We would like to thank Ilan Gronau for thoroughly reading this paper, and Udi Wieder and the anonymous referees for their useful comments.

References

1. I.Abraham, B.Awerbuch, Y.Azar, Y.Bartal, D.Malkhi, and E.Pavlov. A generic scheme for building overlay networks in adversarial scenarios. *IPDPS*, 2003.
2. I.Abraham ,D.Malkhi. Probabilistic quorums for dynamic systmes. *DISC*, 2003.
3. R. Bazzi. Planar quorums. *Distributed Algorithms, WDAG*, 1996.
4. P.Fraigniaud, P.Gauron. An overview of the content-addressable network d2b. *PODC*, 2003.
5. Y.Hassin, D.Peleg. Average probe complexity in quorum systems. *PODC* 2001.
6. M. F. Kaashoek, D. R. Karger. Koorde: A simple degree-optimal distributed hash table. *IPTPS*, 2003.
7. D. Karger, M. Ruhl. Simple efficient load balancing algorithms for peer-to-peer systems. *SPAA* 2004.
8. T. Liggett, R. Schonmann, and A.Stacey. Domination by product measures. *The Annals of Probability*, 25(1) 1997.
9. N.Lynch, D.Malkhi, and D.Ratajczak. Atomic data access in distributed hash tables. *IPTPS*, 2002.
10. D.Malkhi, M.Naor, and D.Ratajczak. Viceroy: A scalable and dynamic emulation of the butterfly. *PODC*, 2002.
11. D.Malkhi, M.Reiter, and R.Wright. Probabilistic quorum systems. *PODC*, 1997.
12. G. S. Manku. Balanced binary trees for ID management and load balance in distributed hash tables. *PODC*, 2004.
13. U.Nadav, M.Naor. Fault-tolerant storage in a dynamic environment. *DISC*, 2004.
14. M.Naor, U.Wieder. Novel architectures for p2p applications: the continuous-discrete approach. *SPAA*, 2003.
15. M.Naor, U. Wieder. Scalable and dynamic quorum systems. *PODC*, 2003.
16. M.Naor, A.Wool. The load, capacity, and availability of quorum systems. *SIAM Journal on Computing*, 27(2), 1998.
17. D.Peleg, A.Wool. The availability of quorum systems. *Inf. Comput.*, 123(2), 1995.
18. D.Peleg , A.Wool. How to be an efficient snoop, or the probe complexity of quorum systems. *SIAM Journal on Discrete Mathematics*, 15(3), 2002.
19. S.Ratnasamy, P.Francis, M.Handley, R.Karp, and S.Shenker. A scalable content addressable network. *Proc ACM SIGCOMM*, 2001.
20. I.Stoica, R.Morris, D.Karger, F.Kaashoek, and H.Balakrishnan. Chord: A scalable Peer-To-Peer lookup service for internet applications. *ACM SIGCOMM Conference*, 2001.
21. B.Y. Zhao and J. Kubiatowicz. Tapestry: An infrastructure for fault-tolerant wide-area location and routing. Technical Report UCB CSD 01-1141, University of California at Berkeley, 2001.

Brief Announcement: Byzantine Clients Rendered Harmless

Barbara Liskov[1] and Rodrigo Rodrigues[2]

[1] MIT Computer Science and Artificial Intelligence Laboratory, Cambridge MA, USA
[2] INESC-ID / Instituto Superior Técnico, Lisbon, Portugal

1 Introduction

The original work on quorum systems assumed that servers fail benignly, by crashing or omitting some steps. More recently, researchers have developed techniques that enable quorum systems to provide data availability in the presence of arbitrary (Byzantine) faults [6]. Earlier work provides correct semantics despite server (i.e., replica) failures and also handles some of the problems of Byzantine clients [1,2,4,6, 9].

This paper describes the first protocols to handle all problems caused by Byzantine clients. Our protocols ensure that bad clients cannot interfere with good clients. Bad clients cannot prevent good clients from completing reads and writes, nor can they cause good clients to see inconsistencies. In addition bad clients that have been removed from operation can leave behind at most a bounded number of "lurking" writes that could be done on their behalf by a colluder.

2 BFT-BC Protocol

The initial Byzantine quorum algorithm [6] uses a group of $3f + 1$ replicas to survive f failures. Quorums are of size $2f + 1$, which ensures that any two quorums intersect in at least one non-faulty replica. Each replica maintains a copy of the data object, along with an associated timestamp, and a client signature that authenticates the data and timestamp.

Writes require two phases. First, the client contacts a quorum to obtain the highest timestamp produced so far. The client then picks a timestamp higher than this, signs the new value and timestamp, and proceeds to the second phase where the new value is stored at a quorum of replicas. A replica allows write requests only from authorized clients and overwrites what is stored only if the timestamp in the request is greater than what it already has.

Reads usually require a single phase where the client queries a quorum of replicas and returns the value with the highest timestamp (provided the signature is correct). An extension of this protocol [7] requires a second phase that writes back the highest value read to a quorum (this ensures atomic semantics for reads).

P. Fraigniaud (Ed.): DISC 2005, LNCS 3724, pp. 487–489, 2005.

This protocol is not designed to handle Byzantine-faulty clients, which can damage the system in several ways: associate different values with the same timestamp; carry out the protocol partially, e.g., install a modification at just one replica; choose a very large timestamp and exhaust the timestamp space; or issue a large number of write requests and hand them off to a colluder who will run them after the bad client has been removed from the system (the colluder could be one of the replicas, or a completely separate machine).

To avoid these problems, we must limit what bad clients can do. But we must also allow good clients to make progress, in spite of bad clients that might collude with one another and/or with bad replicas.

The reason bad clients can do these bad things is that replicas act independently. Replicas could collaborate to carry out client requests, but this would change the Byzantine quorum approach into a state machine replication approach [3]. Our goal is to find a solution that preserves the spirit, efficiency, and simplicity of Byzantine quorums, while avoiding problems caused by bad clients.

We have developed two protocols that accomplish this goal: a protocol that requires 3 phases for writes, and an optimized protocol that usually requires only 2 phases. In both cases reads are done as above.

Our protocols use the client as a way of informing replicas about what other replicas are doing. This communication takes the form of "proofs", collections of $2f + 1$ statements signed by different replicas, that vouch for a particular client action. Clients collect proofs as they carry out steps of the protocol and present them in later steps to show that what they are doing is permitted.

In the first step of our 3-phase write protocol, a client reads the current timestamp from a quorum of replicas. Each reply now includes a "prepare proof", which vouches for the legality of what is being returned. The client then selects the reply with the largest timestamp, and produces a timestamp one larger than this.

In step 2, the client sends prepare requests to all replicas; these requests include the new timestamp and a hash of the value it wants to write, the prepare proof it obtained in step 1, plus a "write proof" that shows it completed its previous write (or null if this is its first write). Replicas record prepare requests and allow only one prepare per client for a write that hasn't happened yet; a replica uses the write proof to ensure it is up to date with respect to this client. In addition the replica checks that the timestamp is one greater than that in the prepare proof. If the replica accepts the request it sends a prepare certificate for the requested timestamp and hash.

The client waits for a quorum of certificates: thus it collects a prepare proof. In step 3 it sends this proof together with the value it wants to write to all replicas. Replicas carry out the request if the proof is valid and the new value matches the hash in the proof. In this case, the replica returns a write certificate containing the new timestamp. The client collects a quorum of these certificates and thus obtains the write proof it will use the next time it writes.

This protocol ensures that a bad client must write the same timestamp and value at all replicas. In addition it prevents a bad client from preparing a number of writes in advance, which could be carried out by a colluder after it has left the system. A further point is that good clients cannot be obstructed by bad ones since they can use the largest timestamp they get in step 1 for either a read or write.

This protocol isn't as efficient as the base Byzantine quorum protocol because of the prepare step. In a separate technical report[5] we present an optimized protocol that merges phases 1 and 2 and does writes in only two phases most of the time.

3   Discussion

Our protocols are more efficient than those proposed previously. Furthermore they enforce stronger constraints on the behavior of bad clients: we handle all problems handled by previous protocols plus we limit the number of lurking writes that a bad client can leave behind after it has left the system.

In addition we provide stronger safety and liveness guarantees than previous protocols: in particular read operations cannot return null values, and reads terminate in a constant number of rounds (at most two), independently of the behavior of concurrent writers.

Our use of prepare proofs is what enables us to ensure liveness, since this allows a client to complete a read using information it received from just one replica. No previous protocol for Byzantine clients uses this technique. As a result most protocols can only ensure that a read will return the result of the latest write in a constant number of rounds provided there are no concurrent writes.

References

[1] R. Bazzi and Y. Ding. Non-skipping timestamps for byzantine data storage systems. In *Distributed Computing, 18th International Conference, DISC 2004*, pages 405–419, Oct. 2004.

[2] C. Cachin and S. Tessaro. Optimal resilience for erasure-coded byzantine distributed storage. Technical Report RZ 3575, IBM Research, Feb. 2005.

[3] M. Castro and B. Liskov. Practical Byzantine Fault Tolerance. In *Proc. 3rd OSDI*, Feb. 1999.

[4] G. Goodson, J. Wylie, G. Ganger, and M. Reiter. Efficient byzantine-tolerant erasure-coded storage. In *Proc. of the International Conference on Dependable Systems and Networks*, June 2004.

[5] B. Liskov and R. Rodrigues. Byzantine clients rendered harmless. Technical Report MIT-LCS-TR-994 and INESC-ID TR-10-2005, July 2005.

[6] D. Malkhi and M. Reiter. Byzantine Quorum Systems. *Journal of Distributed Computing*, 11(4):203–213, 1998.

[7] D. Malkhi and M. Reiter. Secure and scalable replication in phalanx. In *Proc. 17th SRDS*, Oct. 1998.

[8] D. Malkhi, M. Reiter, and N. Lynch. A Correctness Condition for Memory Shared by Byzantine Processes. Unpublished manuscript, Sept. 1998.

[9] J. Martin, L. Alvisi, and M. Dahlin. Minimal Byzantine storage. Technical Report TR-02-38, University of Texas at Austin, Department of Computer Sciences, Aug. 2002.

Brief Announcement: Reliably Executing Tasks in the Presence of Malicious Processors

Antonio Fernández[1], Chryssis Georgiou[2], Luis López[1], and Agustín Santos[1]

[1] LADyR, GSyC, Universidad Rey Juan Carlos, Móstoles, Spain
[2] Dept. of Computer Science, University of Cyprus, CY-1678 Nicosia, Cyprus

Problem and Motivation. The demand for processing large amounts of data has increased over the last decade. As traditional one-processor machines have limited computational power, distributed systems consisting of multitude of cooperating processing units are used instead. An example of such a massive distributed cooperative computation is the SETI@Home project [5]. As the search for extraterrestrial intelligence involves the analysis of gigabytes of raw data that a fixed-size collection of machines would not be able to effectively carry out, the data are distributed to millions of voluntary machines around the world. A machine acts as a server and sends data (aka tasks) to these client computers, which they process and report back the result of the task computation. This gives rise to a crucial problem: how can we prevent malicious clients from damaging the outcome of the overall computation?

In this work we abstract this problem in the form of a distributed system consisting of a master fail-free processor and a collection of processors (workers) that can execute tasks; worker processors might act maliciously. Since each task returns a value, we want the master to accept only correct values with high probability. Furthermore, we assume that the service provided by the workers is not free (as opposed to the SETI@Home project). For each task that a worker executes, the master computer is charged with a work-unit. Therefore, considering a single task assigned to several workers, our goal is to have the master computer to accept the correct value of the task with high probability, with the smallest possible amount of work. We explore two ways of bounding the number of faulty processors and evaluate an algorithm that the master can run. Our preliminary analytical results show that it is possible to obtain high probability of correct acceptance with reasonable amount of work.

Prior/Related work. The problem we consider in this work can be viewed as a special case of the voting problem [1] where a deciding agent decides on a value based on values generated and sent by processing nodes; the goal is for the agent to reach the correct decision with high probability. The voting problem has been considered in the presence of malicious voters (e.g., [6]), and optimal strategies have been identified that maximize the probability of correct decision. However, to the best of our knowledge, no prior work involving malicious voters consider minimizing the amount of work while restricting the probability of incorrect decisions of the voting procedure.

Do-All is the abstract problem of having a collection of processors to cooperatively perform a collection of independent tasks in the presence of failures [2]. This problem has been widely studied the last two decades in a variety of computation and failure models. Recently, this problem was studied under Byzantine processors [4]. Although

P. Fraigniaud (Ed.): DISC 2005, LNCS 3724, pp. 490–492, 2005.

the idea of executing tasks in the presence of malicious nodes is the same, the model and the problem we consider in this work are different.

Model and Algorithm. We assume there is a *master* processor M which has a task that has to be executed. This task returns a value, which M wants to reliably obtain. M is not capable of executing the task itself, so a set P of n (powerful) processors (called *workers*), $P = \{1, ..., n\}$, is made available to M. We assume that the workers might fail, and their faulty behavior is not restricted (e.g., send incorrect value, do not send any value, etc). We want to minimize the (expected) number of workers that have to run the task in order to obtain a failure probability of no more than ρ. The workers are continuously waiting for M to give them a task to execute, they execute a task if they are assigned one, and return the computed value. However, processors can be slow, and messages can get lost or arrive late. In order to introduce these assumptions in the model, we consider that there is a known probability d of M receiving the reply from a given worker on time. We also consider two types of known bounds on the number of faulty processors. We either assume that (i) there is a fixed bound $f < n/2$ on the maximum number of processors that can fail, or (ii) there is a probability $p < 1/2$ of any processor to be faulty.

We explore the following algorithm. First M chooses uniformly at random a subset S from the set P. We consider two ways to do so: either M defines a probability q and chooses each worker with that probability or it fixes a value s and chooses exactly s workers. Then, M sends the task to the processors in S and waits T time for the replies (T is a value set by M based on the value of d). M has a threshold τ and accepts as correct any value v received from at least τ workers within time T. If there is no such value, the algorithm has failed (it is repeated). Note that the (expected) work of an execution of this algorithm is exactly the (expected) size of the set S.

Using Chernoff bounds we show that our algorithm guarantees a failure probability of no more than ρ for: (a) $q = \frac{3(\ln 2 - \ln \rho)}{(1-2p)^2 npd}$ and $\tau = 2np(1 - p)qd$ when we use parameters p and q, with expected work $E[|S|] = nq$, (b) $s = \lceil \frac{3(\ln 2 - \ln \rho)}{(1-2p)^2 pd} \rceil$ and $\tau = 2sp(1 - p)d$ when we use parameters p and s, with work $|S| = s$, (c) $q = \frac{3(\ln 2 - \ln \rho)n^2}{(n-2f)^2 fd}$ and $\tau = \frac{2f(n-f)qd}{n}$ when we use parameters f and q, with expected work $E[|S|] = nq$, and (d) $s = \lceil \frac{3(\ln 2 - \ln \rho)n^3}{(n-2f)^2 fd} \rceil$ and $\tau = \frac{2f(n-f)sd}{n^2}$ when we use parameters f and s, with work $|S| = s$. (For $p < 1/6$ the values for $p = 1/6$ should be used. For $f < n/6$ the values for $f = n/6$ should be used.) More details can be found in [3].

References

1. D. Blough and G. Sullivan. A comparison for voting strategies for fault-tolerant distributed systems. In *SRDS'90*, pp.136–145, 1990.
2. C. Dwork, J. Halpern, and O. Waarts. Performing work efficiently in the presence of faults. *Siam J. on Computing*, 27(5):1457–1491, 1998.
3. A. Fernández, C. Georgiou, L. López, and A. Santos. Reliably executing tasks in the presence of malicious processors. Technical Report, 2005. (http://gsyc.info/publicaciones/tr.)

4. A. Fernández, C. Georgiou, A. Russell, and A. Shvartsman. The Do-All problem with Byzantine processor failures. *Theoretical Computer Science*, 333(3):433–454, 2005.
5. E. Korpela, D. Werthimer, D. Anderson, J. Cobb, and M. Lebofsky. SETI@Home:Massively distributed computing for SETI. *Computing in Science and Engineering*, 3(1):78–83, 2001.
6. M. Paquette and A. Pelc. Optimal decision strategies in Byzantine environments. In *SIROCCO'04*, pp.245–254, 2004.

Brief Announcement:
Obstruction-Free Step Complexity:
Lock-Free DCAS as an Example

Faith Ellen Fich[2,*], Victor Luchangco[1], Mark Moir[1], and Nir Shavit[1]

[1] Sun Microsystems Laboratories
[2] University of Toronto

We propose *obstruction-free step complexity*, a new complexity measure for non-blocking algorithms. We believe that this measure provides a more pragmatic quantification of nonblocking algorithms than previous measures, providing better guidance for designers of practical nonblocking algorithms.

In our opinion, the main shortcoming of existing complexity measures for non-blocking algorithms is that they are targeted towards worst-case behavior in worst-case scenarios, and say little about behavior in more common cases. This is true for the *sensitivity* measure of Attiya and Dagan [1], and the *d-local step complexity* of Afek et al. [2]. These measures are directed at evaluating the behavior of algorithms under contention, i.e., when concurrent operations actively interfere with each other's progress. However, in practice, a well-designed system manages contention so that it does not impact performance too greatly. Thus, these previous measures do not evaluate the behaviour that is likely to be observed.

For *any* nonblocking algorithm, be it wait-free, lock-free or obstruction-free, the *obstruction-free step complexity* of the algorithm is the maximum over all reachable states of the number of steps required for any operation to complete if the process executing the operation runs alone from that state.[1]

Obstruction-free step complexity is targeted towards a more pragmatic evaluation of the performance of nonblocking algorithms in real-world applications, and is based on the assumption, evidenced by numerous technical papers, that performance in uncontended cases is more important in many practical settings than worst-case performance under contention. Moreover, by far the most common approach to dealing with contention is backoff, in which contended cases are essentially turned into uncontended ones by delaying contending operations; other contention management approaches behave similarly. This suggests that even for applications and systems in which contention is significant, it is important to design algorithms that perform well while there is no contention. In particular, if operations complete quickly as soon as contention subsides, then contention management techniques such as backoff will be more effective, and

---

* The research of Faith Ellen Fich was financially supported by the Natural Sciences and Engineering Research Council of Canada and the Scalable Synchronization Research Group of Sun Microsystems, Inc.

[1] Algorithms that can take an unbounded number of steps even in the absence of contention have unbounded obstruction-free step complexity.

P. Fraigniaud (Ed.): DISC 2005, LNCS 3724, pp. 493–494, 2005.

will produce progress more quickly. This is the motivation behind our proposed complexity measure.

Because the obstruction-free step complexity of an algorithm bounds the number of steps that a process takes when running alone from an *arbitrary* reachable state, even one in which other processes may be in the midst of executing the algorithm, it evaluates how amenable an algorithm is to contention management strategies such as backoff.

It is important to distinguish obstruction-free step complexity from an alternative measure, which we call *completely contention-free step complexity*: the maximum number of steps any process takes if it runs alone from a "quiescent" state (i.e., a state in which no process is in the midst of executing the algorithm). This measure provides no insight into how amenable the algorithm is to contention management. In particular, a lock-based algorithm may have very low completely contention-free complexity, but a process that stops while holding a lock can prevent all the other processes from making progress indefinitely, and no contention management can help in this case.

Taking an approach similar to that of [1,2], we use obstruction-free step complexity to evaluate nonblocking implementations of multilocation synchronization operations from unary ones. One difficulty in designing such algorithms is deciding what an operation should do when it discovers that another operation is already accessing a location it wants to access. One option is to "abort" the competing operation, causing the aborted operation to retry; another is to "help" that operation complete. Aborting operations excessively can compromise lock-freedom, as multiple operations can repeatedly abort each other. On the other hand, if an operation always helps the competing operation, long chains can form such that one operation must recursively help all the operations in the chain, even if none of them are actively interfering.

In particular, we consider implementations of double-compare-and-swap from compare-and-swap, and present the first algorithm with *constant* obstruction-free step complexity. All previous lock-free algorithms use the recursive-helping technique and therefore do not have constant obstruction-free step complexity. To achieve constant obstruction-free step complexity, our algorithm introduces a novel approach, which carefully helps only enough to ensure lock-freedom, while avoiding long helping chains. Note that our result does not contradict the separation result of [1], which considered the worst-case step complexity of *wait-free* algorithms over *all* executions: our algorithm is only lock-free, and the obstruction-free step complexity measure focuses only on the uncontended case.

References

1. Attiya, H., Dagan, E.: Improved implementations of binary universal operations. J. ACM **48** (2001) 1013–1037
2. Afek, Y., Merritt, M., Taubenfeld, G., Touitou, D.: Disentangling multi-object oeprations. In: Proceedings of the 16th Annual ACM Symposium on Principles of Distributed Computing. (1997) 111–120

Brief Announcement: Communication-Efficient Implementation of Failure Detector Classes ◇$\mathcal{Q}$ and ◇$\mathcal{P}$ *

Mikel Larrea and Alberto Lafuente

The University of the Basque Country,
20018 San Sebastián, Spain
{mikel.larrea, alberto}@si.ehu.es

1 Introduction

Several algorithms implementing failure detector classes ◇$\mathcal{Q}$ and ◇$\mathcal{P}$ have been proposed in the literature. The algorithm proposed by Chandra and Toueg in [2] uses a heartbeat mechanism and all-to-all communication to detect faulty processes. The algorithms proposed by Aguilera et al. in [1] and by Larrea et al. in [4] use heartbeats too, and rely on a leader-based approach. On the other hand, the algorithm proposed by Larrea et al. in [3] uses a polling —or query/reply— mechanism on a ring arrangement of processes. The leader-based and the ring-based algorithms are more efficient than the all-to-all algorithm regarding the number of messages exchanged (linear vs. quadratic). Compared to polling, the heartbeat mechanism reduces the number of messages to the half. Therefore, a heartbeat *and* ring-based algorithm should outperform the former ones.

We consider a finite set Π of n processes, $\Pi = \{p_1, p_2, \ldots, p_n\}$. Every pair of processes is connected by a unidirectional, reliable and FIFO communication link. Processes can fail by crashing, without recovery. We consider that processes are arranged in a logical ring. The functions $pred(p)$ and $succ(p)$ respectively denote the predecessor and the successor of a process p in the ring. Concerning timing assumptions, we consider the model of partial synchrony proposed in [2].

2 The Algorithm

Fig. 1 presents the algorithm, which is based on the periodical sending of heartbeat messages among processes in the ring. As a consequence, its cost in terms of the number of messages periodically exchanged is linear. Regarding the number of links that carry messages, the proposed algorithm is communication-efficient, i.e., it eventually uses only n links to carry messages. Note that this number is optimal for implementing either ◇$\mathcal{Q}$ or ◇$\mathcal{P}$ in a failure-free scenario. Intuitively, every process must periodically inform that it is still alive by sending a message, which gives us the minimum number of n links.

* Research partially supported by the Spanish Research Council (MCyT), under grants TIC2001-1586-C03-01 and TIN2004-07474-C02-02, the Basque Government, under grant S-PE04UN19, and the Gipuzkoa Provincial Council, under grant OF-846/2004.

P. Fraigniaud (Ed.): DISC 2005, LNCS 3724, pp. 495–496, 2005.

Every process p executes the following:

$pred_p \leftarrow pred(p)$ {*p's estimation of its nearest correct predecessor in the ring*}
$succ_p \leftarrow succ(p)$ {*p's estimation of its nearest correct successor in the ring*}
$L_p \leftarrow \emptyset$ {L_p *provides the properties of* $\Diamond \mathcal{Q}$}
$G_p \leftarrow \emptyset$ {G_p *provides the properties of* $\Diamond \mathcal{P}$}
for all $q \in \Pi$:   {$\Delta_p(q)$ *is the duration of p's time-out interval for q*}
      $\Delta_p(q) \leftarrow$ default time-out interval

cobegin

|| *Task 1:* **repeat periodically**
      send (p-is-alive, G_p) to $succ_p$

|| *Task 2:* **repeat periodically**
      if p did not receive ($pred_p$-is-alive, $-$) from $pred_p$
                during the last $\Delta_p(pred_p)$ ticks of p's clock **then**
            $L_p \leftarrow L_p \cup \{pred_p\}$ {*p suspects $pred_p$ has crashed*}
            $G_p \leftarrow G_p \cup \{pred_p\}$
            $pred_p \leftarrow pred(pred_p)$
            send ($START\_sending\_heartbeats, p$) to $pred_p$

|| *Task 3:* **when** receive (q-is-alive, G_q) for some q
      if $q \in L_p$ **then**   {*p was erroneously suspecting q*}
            $L_p \leftarrow L_p - \{succ(pred_p), \ldots, q\}$
            $\Delta_p(q) \leftarrow \Delta_p(q) + 1$
            send ($START\_sending\_heartbeats, q$) to $pred_p$
            $pred_p \leftarrow q$
      if $q = pred_p$ **then**
            $G_p \leftarrow (G_q - \{p\}) \cup L_p$
            $succ_p \leftarrow$ p's nearest process following the ring $\notin G_p$

|| *Task 4:* **when** receive ($START\_sending\_heartbeats, new\_succ$)
      $succ_p \leftarrow new\_succ$

|| *Task 5:* **repeat periodically**
      if $succ_p \neq succ(p)$ **then**
            send (p-is-alive, G_p) to $succ(p), \ldots, pred(succ_p)$

coend

Fig. 1. A heartbeat-based ring implementation of $\Diamond \mathcal{Q}$ and $\Diamond \mathcal{P}$

References

1. M. Aguilera, C. Delporte-Gallet, H. Fauconnier, and S. Toueg. Stable leader election. In *Proceedings of the 15th International Symposium on DIstributed Computing (DISC'2001)*, pages 108–122, Lisbon, Portugal, October 2001. LNCS 2180, Springer-Verlag.
2. T. D. Chandra and S. Toueg. Unreliable failure detectors for reliable distributed systems. *Journal of the ACM*, 43(2):225–267, March 1996.
3. M. Larrea, S. Arévalo, and A. Fernández. Efficient algorithms to implement unreliable failure detectors in partially synchronous systems. In *Proceedings of the 13th International Symposium on DIstributed Computing (DISC'99)*, pages 34–48, Bratislava, September 1999. LNCS 1693, Springer-Verlag.
4. M. Larrea, A. Fernández, and S. Arévalo. Eventually consistent failure detectors. *Journal of Parallel and Distributed Computing*, 65(3):361–373, March 2005.

Brief Announcement: Optimal Resilience for Erasure-Coded Byzantine Distributed Storage

Christian Cachin[1] and Stefano Tessaro[2,*]

[1] IBM Research, Zurich Research Laboratory, CH-8803 Rüschlikon, Switzerland
[2] ETH Zurich, Department of Computer Science, CH-8092 Zürich, Switzerland

Summary. We consider distributed storage systems implemented by a set of n servers and accessed by a possibly unbounded set of clients, for reading and writing data. Servers and clients communicate by exchanging messages over a fully connected asynchronous network. This model is suitable for heterogeneous and wide-area networks, and, furthermore, avoids timing assumptions, which may otherwise become a vulnerability of the system. We consider Byzantine failures and assume that up to t servers and any number of clients may deviate from the protocol in an arbitrary way.

The problem of implementing a storage system can be formalized as the problem of simulating a multiple-writer multiple-reader read/write register by the servers. Atomicity is the strongest consistency condition for registers, requiring every execution to appear sequential, and it is the one considered here.

Previous fault-tolerant simulations of registers in a message-passing environment are based on replication of data (see e.g. [5,1]). An approach that wastes less resources is based on information dispersal [6] and erasure coding. Here, the data is split into blocks such that each server stores exactly one block, and the information stored at the honest servers is enough to reconstruct the original data. Keeping the dispersed blocks consistent in the presence of failures is not trivial, however. However, most prior solutions for information dispersal in the Byzantine-failure model do not support concurrent access to the stored data. Only the recent protocol of Goodson et al. [4] addresses this question and ensures atomic semantics, but requires $t < \frac{n}{4}$ and still allows malicious clients to write inconsistent data to the servers; a potentially expensive repair protocol is used to recover from such "poisonous writes." Cachin and Tessaro [2] introduce verifiable information dispersal where the servers run a protocol to prevent that inconsistent information is stored by malicious clients. Verifiable information dispersal eliminates the need for a recovery operation and requires only $t < \frac{n}{3}$, but is limited to a single writer and does not allow for concurrent updates.

The challenge with using erasure coding in the concurrent setting is that no server stores the entire data, and in order to read correctly, a client must receive data blocks belonging to the same data item from multiple servers. A possible way for keeping track of multiple concurrently written versions of the data is provided by (logical) timestamps: Whenever a new data item is written, it receives a higher timestamp. Malicious parties, however, may be able to mount

---

* Work done at IBM Research, Zurich Research Laboratory.

P. Fraigniaud (Ed.): DISC 2005, LNCS 3724, pp. 497–498, 2005.

a denial-of-service attack by making timestamps arbitrarily large. Bazzi and Ding [1] considered this problem and solved it by introducing so-called non-skipping timestamps, where the value of every timestamp is bounded by the number of writes that have been executed previously in the system and where no timestamp value can be "skipped." Their solution supports the Byzantine failure of $t < \frac{n}{4}$ servers.

Results. We provide a new fault-tolerant simulation of an atomic register for data that is not self-verifying [5]. In particular, this is the first protocol for storage-efficient distributed simulation of a multiple-writer multiple-reader read/write register that provides atomic semantics and optimal resilience, i.e., tolerates the failure of up to one third of the servers and of an arbitrary number of clients. It follows the "listeners' pattern" proposed by Martin et al. [5], but uses asynchronous verifiable information dispersal [2] and asynchronous reliable broadcast for tolerating Byzantine clients. Our protocol improves the storage and communication efficiencies of Martin et al.'s protocol for the simulation of atomic registers [5] and improves the resilience and the storage complexity of Goodson et al.'s solution for erasure-encoded storage [4], and avoids potentially expensive recovery operations. Like some of the previous work, our protocol uses interaction among the servers. Additionally, we provide an improved implementation of non-skipping timestamps based on threshold signatures [7] that withstands the Byzantine failure of clients and of up to one third of the servers. The key management is much easier than in previous solutions: We require only the public key of the service to be stored at the clients, but no client keys at the servers. The details of our protocol can be found in the full version [3].

References

1. R. Bazzi and Y. Ding, "Non-skipping timestamps for Byzantine data storage systems," in *Proc. 18th International Conference on Distributed Computing (DISC 2004)* (R. Guerraoui, ed.), vol. 3274 of *Lecture Notes in Computer Science*, pp. 405–419, 2004.
2. C. Cachin and S. Tessaro, "Asynchronous verifiable information dispersal," in *Proc. 24th Symp. on Reliable Distributed Systems (SRDS 2005)*, Oct. 2005.
3. C. Cachin and S. Tessaro, "Optimal resilience for erasure-coded Byzantine distributed storage," Research Report RZ 3575, IBM Research, Feb. 2005.
4. G. R. Goodson, J. J. Wylie, G. R. Ganger, and M. K. Reiter, "Efficient Byzantine-tolerant erasure-coded storage," in *Proc. International Conference on Dependable Systems and Networks (DSN-2004)*, pp. 135–144, 2004.
5. J.-P. Martin, L. Alvisi, and M. Dahlin, "Minimal Byzantine storage," in *Proc. 16th International Conference on Distributed Computing (DISC 2002)* (D. Malkhi, ed.), vol. 2508 of *Lecture Notes in Computer Science*, pp. 311–325, Springer, 2002.
6. M. O. Rabin, "Efficient dispersal of information for security, load balancing, and fault tolerance," *Journal of the ACM*, vol. 36, no. 2, pp. 335–348, 1989.
7. V. Shoup, "Practical threshold signatures," in *Advances in Cryptology: EUROCRYPT 2000* (B. Preneel, ed.), vol. 1087 of *Lecture Notes in Computer Science*, pp. 207–220, Springer, 2000.

Brief Announcement: Agreement Among Unacquainted Byzantine Generals *

Michael Okun

School of Computer Science, The Hebrew University of Jerusalem
mush@cs.huji.ac.il

Background. The Byzantine Agreement (BA) problem introduced by Pease, Shostak and Lamport in [1] is one of the central problems in distributed computing. It was extensively studied under various timing, topology, authentication and failure assumptions. In previous works it was assumed that the network topology is known to the processors in advance, i.e., every processor has an a priori knowledge of the true unique identifier of the processor to which it is connected by each of its communication channels (see Fig. 1a).

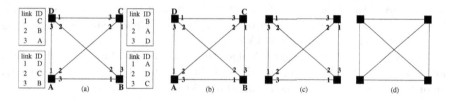

Fig. 1. A system with 4 processors: (a) the standard model, (b) without topology information, (c) anonymous model, (d) anonymous model without port awareness

This work deals with the BA problem when this assumption is relaxed. First, we consider the case in which each processor has a unique identifier, but the processors start without knowing the identifiers of the processors or the identifiers of the links between the processors (see Fig. 1b). In this case there are several reasonable models, all of which assume that each message carries an id of the sender. The models vary according to the ways in which a faulty processor may corrupt the id field in its messages. Specifically, we consider the following models:

($\mathcal{I}_1$) A message sent by any processor always includes its unique true id. In this case a faulty processor can prevent a correct processor p from directly learning about its id iff it sends no messages to p throughout the whole BA protocol.

($\mathcal{I}_2$) A faulty processor may send messages with different ids, not necessarily its own, however it cannot use an id belonging to a correct processor. This implies that "identity theft" is not allowed in this model.

* This research was supported by Israeli Council for Higher Education and by Sally Berg foundation.

P. Fraigniaud (Ed.): DISC 2005, LNCS 3724, pp. 499–500, 2005.

($\mathcal{I}_3$) A faulty processor may include any id in its messages, even that of correct processors, i.e., it is able to "fake" messages of correct processors.

In addition, we consider the case in which there are no identifiers at all (anonymous processors). Two types of anonymous networks are examined:

($\mathcal{A}_1$) The processors are port aware: each processor has an internal labeling of its communication channels, which allows it to distinguish between messages arriving via different channels (see Fig. 1c).

($\mathcal{A}_2$) The processors are port unaware: each processor receives all its messages through a single mailbox, and cannot associate a message with the link through which it was received (see Fig. 1d).

We note that the above five models form a strict hierarchy, in the sense that each model is the result of further relaxation of its predecessor.

Results. The BA problem has no deterministic solution in the $\mathcal{A}_2$ model even in the presence of a single faulty processor. This can be shown by a simple valency argument. On the other hand, Ben-Or's randomized algorithm can be used to achieve BA with probability 1 (whenever the number of faulty processors, f, is less than $1/3$ of the total number of processors, n). These characteristics of $\mathcal{A}_2$ are similar to the asynchronous BA case.

For $\mathcal{A}_1$ we found an efficient BA algorithm that runs in at most $6f+1$ rounds, for $n > 3f$ [2]. It is based on the ideas of the Srikanth-Toueg (and similar) BA algorithms, though some non-trivial adaptations were required.

Finding the exact number of rounds required for achieving BA in the various models seems to be a much harder problem. The difficulty is that the Exponential Information Gathering algorithms (which are the only known algorithms for the standard BA that work in the optimal number of rounds), if at all, can be used only for $\mathcal{I}_1$.

In the $\mathcal{I}_2$ model BA can be achieved in $f + 1$ rounds. The proof of this (tight) upper bound is non-constructive, and is based on several new techniques [3]. Further model relaxations increase the number of rounds: in $\mathcal{I}_3$, even for $f = 1$, a relatively simple chain-argument shows that 3 rounds are required. However, it is still not clear if the additional round is also necessary for higher values of f.

Finding the exact number of rounds required for BA in the $\mathcal{A}_1$ model, or even proving a sufficiently tight upper bound is also an open problem.

References

[1] M. Pease, R. Shostak, L. Lamport, Reaching Agreement in the Presence of Faults, *J. ACM* 27(2) (1980) 228-234.

[2] M. Okun, A. Barak, On Anonymous Byzantine Agreement, Leibniz Center TR 2004-2, School of Computer Science, The Hebrew University, 2004, submitted for publication.

[3] M. Okun, On the Round Complexity of Byzantine Agreement Without Initial Set-Up, 2005, submitted for publication.

Brief Announcement:Subscription Propagation and Content-Based Routing with Delivery Guarantees

Yuanyuan Zhao, Sumeer Bhola, and Daniel Sturman

IBM T.J.Watson Research Center
{yuanyuan, sbhola, sturman}@us.ibm.com

Abstract. Subscription propagation enables efficient content-based routing in publish/subscribe systems and is a challenging problem when it is required to support reliable delivery in networks with redundant routes. We have designed a generic model and a highly-asynchronous algorithm accomplishing these goals. Existing algorithms can be interpreted as different encodings and optimizations of the generic algorithm and hence their correctness can be derived from the generic algorithm.

1 Introduction and Related Works

A content-based publish/subscribe system consists of publishers that generate messages and subscribers that register interest in all future messages matching a predicate. The system, implemented as a network of routing brokers, is responsible for routing published messages to interested subscribers. Information providers and consumers are decoupled, since publishers need not be aware of which subscribers receive their messages, and subscribers need not be aware of the sources of the messages they receive.

Subscription propagation is a mechanism of propagating subscribers' interest throughout the broker network. It allows brokers to filter out and withhold from sending messages to parts of the network where there are no interested subscribers. This functionality is hence very important for efficiency and scalability of content-based pub/sub systems. However, the task of designing a subscription propagation algorithm is greatly challenged by several factors, especially: 1) clients' requirement of strong service guarantees such as reliable in-order, gapless delivery; 2) the existence of multiple routing paths between publishers and subscribers; 3) communication asynchrony, especially asynchrony among multiple redundant paths; 4) failures.

As a result, most previous work on subscription propagation [1,2,3] did not provide a solution that guarantees the correctness of content-based routing and hence is not capable of supporting reliable delivery in the presence of failures and multiple paths. We think this situation is due to lack of understanding of the fundamentals of the subscription propagation problem. There is no coherent theory of how subscription propagation algorithms should work in general. As a result, designing subscription propagation algorithms typically becomes isolated activities each dealing with different situations.

P. Fraigniaud (Ed.): DISC 2005, LNCS 3724, pp. 501–502, 2005.

2   Our Contributions

We have studied the structure of the subscription propagation problem and its interaction with content-based routing, reliable delivery and redundant routes and
defined a general model for subscription propagation and content-based routing.
We present the model in the context of a redundant routing tree where each tree
node can contain multiple brokers and each edge can contain multiple broker-
broker links. The model utilizes constructs that are inherently asynchronous and
fault tolerant. For example, it uses subscription and conjunction sets where sets
operations can inherently tolerate message duplication and re-ordering. Under
this model, we define the correctness criteria of subscription propagation and
content-based routing and a set of sufficient conditions for supporting reliable
delivery. These sufficient conditions, such as *eventual montonicity*, allow designing of highly-asynchronous algorithms.

Using the formal model, we construct a generic asynchronous subscription
propagation and content-based routing algorithm. The algorithm supports reliable delivery in the presence of multiple routing paths, broker and link failures,
and communication asynchrony without requiring expensive distributed agreement between redundant paths. It provides high network availability and efficiency by allowing data message routing to choose any of the redundant paths.
The generic algorithm is further refined to utilize subscription aggregation.

Many existing algorithms can be interpreted as specializations of the generic
algorithm under different circumstances. For instance, algorithms that assume
FIFO links and single routing paths can optimize the size of subscription state
maintained at a broker. For the algorithms described in [5], the virtual time
vectors can be viewed as an optimization that reduces space consumption but
restricts when subscription changes can be applied. The correctness attribute of
the generic algorithm applies to these algorithms.

A detailed description of this work is available in [4].

References

1. A. Carzaniga, D. Rosenblum, and A. Wolf. Design and evaluation of a wide-area
   event notification service. ACM Transactions on Computer Systems, 19(3):332383,
   August 2001.
2. G. Cugola, E. D. Nitto, and A. Fuggetta. The jedi event-based infrastructure and
   its application to the development of the opss wfms. IEEE Transactions on Software
   Engineering, 27(9):827850, September 2001.
3. P. Triantafillou and A. Economides. Subscription summarization: A new paradigm
   for efficient publish/subscribe systems. In Proceedings of the 24th International
   Conference on Distributed Computing Systems (ICDCS04), 2004.
4. Y. Zhao, S. Bhola, and D. Sturman. A general algorithmic model for subscription
   propagation and content-based routing with delivery guarantees. Technical report,
   RC23669, IBM Research, 2005.
5. Y. Zhao, D. Sturman, and S. Bhola. Subscription propogation in highly-available
   publish/subscribe middleware. In ACM/IFIP/USENIX 5th International Middleware Conference (Middleware 2004).

Brief Announcement: Asynchronous Verifiable Information Dispersal

Christian Cachin[1] and Stefano Tessaro[2,*]

[1] IBM Research, Zurich Research Laboratory, CH-8803 Rüschlikon, Switzerland
[2] ETH Zurich, Department of Computer Science, CH-8092 Zürich, Switzerland

Summary. We consider the distribution of data by a client among a set of n storage servers, of which up to t might be faulty exhibiting arbitrary, i.e., *Byzantine*, behavior. The goal is to ensure that clients can always recover the stored data correctly, independently from the behavior of faulty servers or other, faulty clients. An inefficient solution is based on replication such that every server keeps a copy of the data. The classic alternative is *information dispersal* (IDA): using an *erasure code*, the data is split into blocks such that each server holds exactly one block and only a subset of the blocks is needed in order to reconstruct the data.

A protocol for information dispersal based on IDA tolerating Byzantine servers has been proposed by Garay et al. [4]. It relies on *synchronous* networks, which are adequate for tightly coupled clusters but unrealistic for geographically distributed or heterogeneous systems. An *asynchronous* system model is more appropriate for such settings.

In this paper, we introduce the notion of *verifiability* for information dispersal in *asynchronous* networks with a computationally bounded adversary. Intuitively, verifiability means that whenever the honest servers accept to store some data, then the data is also consistent and no two distinct honest clients can reconstruct different data. This notion of verifiability originates in the related context of secret sharing [3,1].

We propose a new scheme for asynchronous verifiable information dispersal that is also storage- and communication-efficient and achieves optimal resilience $t < \frac{n}{3}$. The scheme, called AVID, integrates an asynchronous reliable broadcast protocol with erasure coding and achieves communication complexity $\mathcal{O}(n|F|)$ bits for storing a file F, which is an order of magnitude more efficient than what results from the previously known approach, which needs $\mathcal{O}(n^2|F|)$ bits. The storage blow-up of the scheme is asymptotically optimal.

Several optimizations are presented for lowering the storage requirements, including one that uses error-*correcting* codes, called AVID-ECC, and one using reliable broadcast, called AVID-RBC. One of the optimized schemes leads directly to a communication-efficient protocol for asynchronous reliable broadcast with Byzantine faults, which communicates only $\mathcal{O}(n|m|)$ bits instead of $\mathcal{O}(n^2|m|)$ for broadcasting a large message m. We also consider how to provide *confidentiality* for the stored data such that it can only be read by authorized users. All details can be found in the full version [2].

* Work done at IBM Research, Zurich Research Laboratory.

P. Fraigniaud (Ed.): DISC 2005, LNCS 3724, pp. 503–504, 2005.
© Springer-Verlag Berlin Heidelberg 2005

Comparison. Garay et al. [4] propose a synchronous information dispersal scheme without Byzantine clients. It is based on a *gateway*, through which clients access the servers. The gateway broadcasts the file to all servers and every server applies an information dispersal algorithm to compute its block. An inefficient asynchronous dispersal protocol results from replacing the gateway by a Byzantine-fault-tolerant reliable broadcast protocol. The resulting scheme, which we call *asynchronous GGJR*, satisfies our verifiability property, but has communication blow-up $\Theta(n^2)$.

An asynchronous solution for erasure-coded storage tolerating also Byzantine client failures has recently been proposed by Goodson et al. [5]. Here, inconsistently written data can only be detected at read-time; the content of the storage system is then rolled back to restore the data to the last correctly written data. The major drawback of this approach is that retrieving data can be very inefficient in the case of several failed write operations, and that consistency depends on correct clients. The protocol requires $t < \frac{n}{4}$.

The following table summarizes the performance of the schemes. Our main scheme achieves better storage blow-up and tolerates more corrupted servers than the protocol of Goodson et al. [5], which has a better (i.e., constant) communication blow-up, but does not provide verifiability. Obtaining verifiability is what seems to cause an increase by a factor of $\Theta(n)$ in the communication complexity.

Scheme	Model	Storage Blow-up	Comm. Blow-up
GWGR [5]	$t < \frac{n}{4}$, no verifiability	$\frac{n}{n-3t} + o(1)$	$\mathcal{O}(1)$
asynchronous GGJR	$t < \frac{n}{3}$, verifiability	$\frac{n}{n-t} + o(1)$	$\Theta(n^2)$
AVID (this paper)	$t < \frac{n}{3}$, verifiability	$\frac{n}{n-2t} + o(1)$	$\mathcal{O}(n)$
AVID-RBC (this paper)	$t < \frac{n}{3}$, verifiability	$\frac{n}{n-t} + o(1)$	$\mathcal{O}(n)$
AVID-ECC (this paper)	$t < \frac{n}{4}$, verifiability	$\frac{n}{n-3t}$	$\mathcal{O}(n)$

References

1. C. Cachin, K. Kursawe, A. Lysyanskaya, and R. Strobl, "Asynchronous verifiable secret sharing and proactive cryptosystems," in *Proc. 9th ACM Conference on Computer and Communications Security (CCS)*, pp. 88–97, 2002.
2. C. Cachin and S. Tessaro, "Asynchronous verifiable information dispersal," in *Proc. 24th Symp. on Reliable Distributed Systems (SRDS 2005)*, Oct. 2005.
3. P. Feldman, "A practical scheme for non-interactive verifiable secret sharing," in *Proc. 28th IEEE Symposium on Foundations of Computer Science (FOCS)*, pp. 427–437, 1987.
4. J. A. Garay, R. Gennaro, C. Jutla, and T. Rabin, "Secure distributed storage and retrieval," *Theoretical Computer Science*, vol. 243, no. 1–2, pp. 363–389, 2000.
5. G. R. Goodson, J. J. Wylie, G. R. Ganger, and M. K. Reiter, "Efficient Byzantine-tolerant erasure-coded storage," in *Proc. International Conference on Dependable Systems and Networks (DSN-2004)*, pp. 135–144, 2004.

Brief Announcement: Towards a Theory of Self-organization

E. Anceaume[1], X. Defago[2], M. Gradinariu[1], and M. Roy[3]

[1] IRISA, Rennes, France
{anceaume, mgradina}@irisa.fr
[2] JAIST and PRESTO, JST, Japan
defago@jaist.ac.jp
[3] LAAS-CNRS, Toulouse, France
roy@laas.fr

Self-organization is an evolutionary process in which the effects of the environment are minimal; i.e., where the development of new, complex structures primarily takes place in and throughout the system itself. Natural phenomena, living forms, or social systems (e.g., growing crystals, cells aggregation, ant colonies) are examples of self-organizing systems in which a global order of the system emerges from local interactions. In the newly emerging fields of distributed systems (p2p, ad-hoc networks, sensor networks, cooperative robotics), self-organization has become one of the most desired properties. The major feature of all recent scalable distributed systems is their extreme dynamism in terms of structure, content, and load. In peer-to-peer systems, self-organization is handled through protocols for node arrival and departure, based either on a fault-tolerant overlay network, such as in CAN, Chord, Pastry, or on a localization and routing infrastructure [2]. In ad-hoc networks, self-organizing solutions have been designed to cluster ad-hoc nodes [4]. Self-organizing algorithms have also been developed to arrange mobile robots into predefined geometric patterns (e.g., [3]).

Informal definitions for self-organization, or the related self* properties (e.g., self-configuration, self-healing or self-reconfiguration) have been proposed previously [4]. Zhang and Arora [4] propose the concepts of self-healing and self-configuration in wireless ad-hoc networks.

The correctness proofs for self-organizing systems should be based on a well-founded theoretical model that can capture the dynamic behavior of these systems. Hence, the characterization of the self-organizing aspects of these systems cannot solely focus on the non-dynamic periods since they may be absent or very short. Moreover, defining self-organization as a simple convergence process towards a stable predefined set of admissible configurations is inadequate for two reasons. First, it may be impossible to clearly characterize the set of admissible configurations since, in dynamic systems, a configuration should include the state of some key parameters that have a strong influence on the dynamicity of the system. These parameters can seldom be quantified a priori (e.g., the status of batteries in sensor networks, or the data stored within p2p systems). Second, due to the dynamic behavior of nodes, it may happen that no execution of the system converges to one of the predefined admissible configurations.

P. Fraigniaud (Ed.): DISC 2005, LNCS 3724, pp. 505–506, 2005.

We propose a formal specification of the self-organization notion. Our specification is based on the locality principle, i.e., the fact that interactions and knowledge are both limited in scope. We formalize this idea [1], leading first to the notion of *local self-organization*. Intuitively, a locally self-organizing system should reduce the entropy of the system in the neighborhood of each node. For example, a locally self-organizing p2p system forces components to be adjacent to components that improve, or at least maintain, some property or evaluation criterion. We then formalize the notion of *self-organization* by imposing the system to be locally self-organizing at all its nodes, and by ensuring that despite its dynamicity, the system entropy progressively decreases. That is, self-organization strongly relies on the local self-organization property, and on the behavior of the system during the connection/disconnection actions. According to this behavior, the system guarantees different levels of self-organization, namely, the weak and the strong self-organization. The weak self-organization is defined in terms of two properties. The *weak liveness* property says that either (1) infinitely often, there are static fragments, i.e., sequences of configurations with no connections/disconnections, during which the knowledge of the system enriches, or (2) all processes have reached a stable state. The *safety* property states that, during all static fragments, system knowledge does not decrease. The weak self-organization definition applies to static fragments. Nothing is guaranteed during dynamic ones (i.e., sequences of configurations in which connections/disconnections occur). For instance, the weak liveness does not forbid processes to reset their neighbors lists after each connection/disconnection. To prevent the system from "collapsing" during dynamic fragments, *strong self-organization* specifies a stronger property guaranteeing that for all the processes of which the neighborhood is unchanged, information is maintained. Specifically, this ensures the existence of a non-empty group of processes for which local information has been maintained between the end of a static fragment and the beginning of the subsequent one. The second contribution of this work is a case study. Using our framework we prove the weak self-organization of Pastry and CAN, two well known peer-to-peer overlays.

Future investigation focuses on the design of a probabilistic extension of our model motivated by the fact that connection/disconnection actions are well-modeled by probabilistic laws.

References

1. E. Anceaume, X. Defago, M. Gradinariu, and M. Roy. Towards a theory of self-organization. Technical Report 1694, IRISA, 2005.
2. Stephanos Androutsellis-Theotokis and Diomidis Spinellis. A survey of peer-to-peer content distribution technologies. *ACM Comput. Surv.*, 36(4):335–371, 2004.
3. I. Suzuki and M. Yamashita. Distributed anonymous mobile robots: formation of geometric paterns. *SIAM Journal of Computing*, 28:1347–1363, 1999.
4. H. Zhang and A. Arora. Gs3 : Scalable self-configuration and self-healing in wireless networks. *Proc. of the 21st Annual ACM Symposium on Principles of Distributed Computing (PODC'02)*, pages 58–67, 2002.

Brief Announcement:
Timing Games and Shared Memory

Zvi Lotker[1], Boaz Patt-Shamir[2], and Mark R. Tuttle[3]

[1] CWI
lotker@cwi.nl
[2] Tel Aviv University
boaz@eng.tau.ac.il
[3] HP Labs
mark.tuttle@hp.com.

Abstract. We model a simple problem in advertising as a strategic timing game, and consider continuous and discrete versions of this game. For the continuous game, we completely characterize the Nash equilibrium for two players. For the discrete game, we give an efficient algorithm to compute the Nash equilibrium for n players.

We consider a model with a single shared register, a stream of readers arriving at a constant rate in the interval $[0, 1]$, and a set of writers that each write to the register one time. We interpret the value of the register as an advertisement, the readers as customers, and the writers as advertisers. The register represents any public space such as an ad on a web page or an entry in a system directory. The register's value might be a link to a web site or a pointer to some service, resource, or product. Since the advertiser's goal is to maximize the number of customers seeing its ad, and since the customers arrive at a constant rate, this is equivalent to maximizing the length of time the ad is in the register before it is overwritten by another ad. Since each advertiser can write its ad to the register only once, when should it write?

We model this problem as a non-cooperative, complete-information strategic game, a game we call the *publicity game*. The publicity game is a symmetric game with n players, each player i chooses a number $x_i \in [0, 1]$, and the payoff to player i is the distance from x_i to the next point. Formally, given the choices $x_1, \ldots, x_n$ of the players, we define $\operatorname{bigger}(i) = \{x_j \mid x_j \geq x_i \text{ and } j \neq i\}$ and $\operatorname{next}(i) = \min \operatorname{bigger}(i)$. The payoff for player i is defined by

$$u_i(x_1, x_2, \ldots, x_n) = \begin{cases} \operatorname{next}(i) - x_i & \text{if } \operatorname{bigger}(i) \neq \emptyset \\ 1 - x_i & \text{otherwise} \end{cases}$$

Note that if two players happen to choose the same value, the payoff to both of them is 0. We consider other payoffs to colliding players in the full paper.

Our publicity game is a new variant of "timing games" like "War of Attrition" [2,3,5], but our payoffs do not change with time as in that game, and the work of Baye *et al.* [1] is also related to some of our results for the two-player game. Our game superficially resembles the Hotelling location games [4], but these games either are zero-sum or they involve pricing, and are fundamentally different.

P. Fraigniaud (Ed.): DISC 2005, LNCS 3724, pp. 507–508, 2005.
© Springer-Verlag Berlin Heidelberg 2005

The publicity game has only mixed-strategy equilibria:

Theorem 1. *There is no equilibrium of pure strategies for the publicity game.*

It is not hard to bound the game value of symmetric equilibria:

Theorem 2. *If v is a symmetric equilibrium value for the publicity game with n players, then $1/(n+1) < v < 1/n$.*

In fact, as we now show, we can compute this game value quite accurately, and prove it is unique.

We cannot compute the game value for n players exactly, but we can find a closed form for the special case of two players.

Theorem 3. *There is a Nash equilibrium for the two-player publicity game defined by*

$$f_1(x) = \begin{cases} \frac{1}{1-x} , & \text{if } 0 \le x \le 1 - \frac{1}{e} \\ 0 , & \text{otherwise} \end{cases}$$

This equilibrium in unique up to a set of points in $[0,1]$ of measure zero, and the expected payoff for each player is $\frac{1}{e}$.

We can approximate the game value for n players if we restrict attention to a discrete version of the publicity game that restricts players to choosing one of the $k+1$ points $\left\{0, \frac{1}{k}, \frac{2}{k}, \ldots, 1\right\}$. In the full paper, we give an algorithm EQUILIBRIUM(n, k, ϵ) that approximates the symmetric equilibrium value v to within ϵ by doing a binary search for v and inductively computing the probabilities the symmetric equilibrium assigns to the discrete points in the unit interval.

Theorem 4. *There is a unique symmetric equilibrium to the discrete publicity game, and* EQUILIBRIUM(n, k, ϵ) *computes the equilibrium value to within ϵ.*

This algorithmic approach to finding the equilibrium for the n-player game is interesting, because the differential equations that characterize the equilibria to general n-player games are often quite hard to solve.

This paper is a first step toward understanding the effect of delayed actions on the outcome of timely games. These games arise naturally in many situations such as recommendation systems and other economic systems. To this end, we have defined and analyzed a simple game we called the publicity game. To the best of our knowledge, this is the first time this game is explicitly addressed.

References

1. M. R. Baye, D. Kovenock, and C. de Vries. A general linear model of contests. Mimeo, 1998. Unpublished manscript available from http://www.nash-equilibrium.com/baye/Contests.pdf.
2. D. Fudenberg and J. Tirole. *Game Theory*. MIT Press, 1991.
3. K. Hendricks, A. Weiss, and C. Wilson. The war of attrition in continuous time with complete information. *International Economic Review*, 29(4):663–680, Nov. 1988.
4. H. Hotelling. Stability in competition. *Economic Journal*, 39:41–57, 1929.
5. J. Maynard Smith. The theory of games and the evolution in animal conflicts. *Journal of Theoretical Biology*, 47:209–221, 1974.

Brief Announcement: A Lightweight Group Mutual k-Exclusion Algorithm Using Bi-k-Arbiters

Yu-Chen Kuo and Huang-Chen Lee

Department of Computer and Information Science, Soochow University,
100 Taipei, Taiwan, ROC
yckuo@cis.scu.edu.tw

Abstract. In this paper, we propose a bi-k-arbiter quorum structure for the group mutual k-exclusion problem in distributed systems. We design a lightweight group mutual k-exclusion algorithm adopting the bi-k-arbiter to solve the group mutual k-exclusion problem. Adopting bi-k-arbiters, the concurrent processes accessing to the same resource could use the lightweight quorum to reduce the message complexity.

Extended Abstract

The mutual exclusion problem is a problem to guarantee that concurrent processes accessing to a shared resource must execute in a mutually exclusive way. In [3], Joung introduced the group mutual exclusion, which is an extension of mutual exclusion problem while exploring concurrency. In the group mutual exclusion problem, there are m resources and it allows more than one process to access the same resource, simultaneously. The processes accessing to a same resource constitute a group. However, if two groups request to access different resources at the same time, only one group is allowed. The group mutual k-exclusion problem [5] is an extension of the group mutual exclusion problem. It allows that at most k groups can access k different resources at the same time.

In the past, numerous solutions for the group mutual exclusion problem had been proposed [1-5]. Among them, the quorum-based approach [3] is an important algorithm to solve the problem. It utilized m-group [3] quorum structure to achieve the group mutual exclusion. Informally, a quorum is a set of some processes in a system. The system may have some quorums that could constitute a type of quorum structure, such as m-groups or k-arbiters [4], etc. Each quorum structure is used to solve a particular problem.

An m-group is a list $(C_1, C_2, ..., C_m)$ of m quorum sets, each of which is used to control the access of one of m resources. In an m-group, $\forall Q_i \in C_i$ must intersect $\forall Q_j \in C_j$, $1 \leq i,j \leq m$. In the quorum-based group mutual exclusion algorithm adopting m-groups, a process requesting to access a resource i is required to obtain the permission from every member of a quorum $Q_i \in C_i$. Due to the intersection property (viz., $\forall Q_i \in C_i$ intersects $\forall Q_j \in C_j$, $1 \leq i,j \leq m$), no two processes access to different resources can be proceeded at the same time.

In this paper, we propose a *bi-k-arbiter* quorum structure, extended from k-arbiters [4], to solve to the group mutual k-exclusion problem. An ordered pair $B = (C, L)$,

P. Fraigniaud (Ed.): DISC 2005, LNCS 3724, pp. 509–510, 2005.
© Springer-Verlag Berlin Heidelberg 2005

where C and L contain complete quorums Q^c and lightweight quorums Q^l of U, respectively, is a bi-k-arbiter under U if B satisfies the following properties:

1. **Complete Quorum Intersection Property**: $\forall Q_1^c, Q_2^c, ..., Q_{k+1}^c \in C, \bigcap_{1 \le i \le k+1} Q_i^c \ne \varnothing$.

2. **Lightweight Quorum Intersection Property**: $\forall Q_i^l \in L$ and $\forall Q_j^c \in C, Q_i^l \cap Q_j^c \ne \varnothing$.

3. **Quorum Containing Property**: $\forall Q_i^l \in L, \exists Q_j^c \in C$ such that $Q_i^l \subset Q_j^c$.

4. **Complete Quorum Minimality Property**: $\forall Q_i^c, Q_j^c \in C, Q_i^c \not\subset Q_j^c$.

5. **Lightweight Quorum Minimality Property**: $\forall Q_i^l, Q_j^l \in L, Q_i^l \not\subset Q_j^l$.

For example, let $C=\{\{1,2,3,4,5,6\},\{1,2,3,7,8,9\},\{1,4,5,7,8,10\},\{2,4,6,7,9,10\}, \{3,5,6,8,9,10\}\}$ constructed from the *binomial*(5, 2)-*arbiter* [4] and $L=\{\{1,2,3\}, \{2,4,6\}, \{3,5,6\}, \{4,7,10\}\}$. It is not hard to verify that $B=(C, L)$ is a bi-2-arbiter under $U=\{1,2,3,4,5,6,7,8,9,10\}$ and $k=2$.

Intuitively, a bi-k-arbiter can be applied to develop the lightweight group mutual k-exclusion algorithm as follows: A process A requesting to access a resource i is required to obtain the permission of a quorum $Q^c \in C$. However, A will first try to collect the permission of a lightweight quorum $Q^l \in L$. If there is a process B which had collected the permission of a complete quorum $Q^c \in C$ and access the resource i already, then due to the lightweight quorum intersection property, we observe that $Q^c \cap Q^l \ne \varnothing$. Thus, A can be granted by some node in Q^c to access the resource i, immediately. The message complexity of A can be reduced. Otherwise, if no such B exists, by the quorum containing property, A will continue to collect the permission from $Q^c - Q^l$ (for some $Q^c \in C$ and $Q^l \subset Q^c$) until a complete quorum is obtained. On the other hand, if there are $k+1$ groups of processes requesting to access $k+1$ resources, due to the complete quorum intersection property, those $k+1$ complete quorums must have at least one common member. The common member will be the arbiter to reject the lowest priority (ordered by the timestamp) request. The group mutual k-exclusion problem could be solved. Furthermore, since the bi-k-arbiter is extended from the k-arbiter, the bi-k-arbiter inherits the property of k-arbiters [4] that it allows a process to request more than one resource in a single request message. The message complexity could further be reduced when a process requests more than one resource at a time.

References

1. R. Atreya, N. Mittal: A distributed group mutual exclusion algorithm using surrogate-quorums, Technical Report (2003), The University of Texas at Dallas
2. J. Beauquier, S. Cantarell, A. K. Datta, F. Petit: Group mutual exclusion in tree networks, Journal of Information Science and Engineering, Vol. 19, No 3 (2003) 415-432
3. Y.-J. Joung: Quorum-based algorithms for group mutual exclusion, IEEE Transactions on Parallel and Distributed Systems, Vol. 14, No. 5 (2003) 463-476
4. Y.-C. Kuo: A simple scheme to construct k-arbiters with uniform quorum sizes, Journal of the Chinese Institute of Engineers, Vol. 26, No. 5(2003),709-714
5. K. Vidyasankar: A simple group mutual l-exclusion algorithm, Information Processing Letters, Vol. 85(2003),79-85

Brief Announcement: Could Any Graph Be Turned into a Small-World?

Philippe Duchon[1], Nicolas Hanusse[1],
Emmanuelle Lebhar[2], and Nicolas Schabanel[2]

[1] LABRI, University of Bordeaux, Bordeaux, France
{duchon, hanusse}@labri.fr
[2] LIP, École Normale Supérieure de Lyon, Lyon, France
{elebhar, nschaban}@ens-lyon.fr

1 Introduction

In the last decade, effective measurements of real interaction networks have revealed specific unexpected properties. Among these, most of these networks present a very small diameter and a high clustering. Furthermore, very short paths can be efficiently found between any pair of nodes without global knowledge of the network (i.e., in a decentralized manner) which is known as the small-world phenomenon [1]. Several models have been proposed to explain this phenomenon [2,3]. However, Kleinberg showed in [4] that these models lack the essential *navigability* property: in spite of a polylogarithmic diameter, decentralized routing requires the visit of a polynomial number of nodes in these models.

He proposed a navigable model defined as a grid augmented by additional random links according to a specific distribution. This raised an essential question to capture the small-world phenomenon: are there only specific graph metrics that can be turned into small-worlds by the addition of shortcuts? We show that the navigability property is not specific to the grid topology, and that a wide family of graphs can be turned into navigable small-worlds by the addition of one random link per node. In a second step, we try to catch the dimensional phenomenon showing that if two independent graphs can be augmented into two navigable small-worlds then their cartesian product can also be (e.g. any product of arbitrary length tori). In all the following, we consider infinite graphs, but our definitions and results apply as well to families of finite graphs (see [5]).

Turning graphs into small-worlds. In the following, an *underlying metric* δ_H of a graph G is the metric given by a spanning connected subgraph H, and $b_{H,\mathbf{u}}(r)$ is the number of nodes at distance $\leq r$ from $\mathbf{u}$ in H. Also, a routing algorithm for a graph H, augmented by random links, is said *decentralized* if it only uses δ_H and the knowledge of the nodes it has previously visited as well as their neighbors; crucially, it can only visit nodes that are neighbors of previously visited nodes. Definition 1 is inspired by the work of Kleinberg [4].

Definition 1. *A graph H augmented by random links is a* navigable small-world *if there exists a decentralized algorithm that, for any two nodes $\mathbf{u}$ and $\mathbf{v}$, computes a path, using the underlying metric δ_H, from $\mathbf{u}$ to $\mathbf{v}$ in the augmented graph by*

P. Fraigniaud (Ed.): DISC 2005, LNCS 3724, pp. 511–513, 2005.

visiting an expected number of nodes bounded by a polylogarithmic function of $b_{H,\mathbf{v}}(\delta_H(\mathbf{u}, \mathbf{v}))$.

Kleinberg showed in [4] that adding one random link according to a harmonic distribution whose exponent equals the dimension of the regular $n \times \cdots \times n$ grid, turns the grid into a navigable small-world. But this approach fails for instance on unbalanced $n \times m$ grids (with $m \gg n$), since the "dimension" varies with the distance: balls of small radius grow like r^2 but larger balls grow like $r^{1+\epsilon(r)}$, where $\epsilon(r) \to 0$ as r grows.

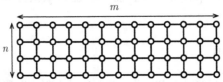

It appears that defining the random link distribution in terms of ball growth in the original base graph, rather than in terms of distance between nodes, allows to generalize Kleinberg's process to a wide class of graphs. Precisely, we say that a bounded degree infinite graph H (resp., family of finite graphs $\mathcal{H}$) is an α-*moderate growth graph* if the size of the ball centered on each node $\mathbf{u}$ of H (resp., of $H \in \mathcal{H}$) can be written as $b_{H,\mathbf{u}}(r) = r^{d_\mathbf{u}(r)}$, where the "apparent dimension from $\mathbf{u}$", $d_\mathbf{u}(r)$, verifies: $\frac{\partial d_\mathbf{u}(r)}{\partial r} \le \frac{\alpha}{r \ln r}$.

This class includes all graphs with non-increasing "apparent dimension" $d_\mathbf{u}(r)$ (e.g., unbalanced grids). Thanks to the regularity of ball growth in this class, adding one random link of length r according to $1/(b_{H,\mathbf{u}}(r) \log^{1+\epsilon} r)$ yields navigable small-worlds. Our theorem below covers graphs whose balls grow like $r^{O(\log \log r)}$ or slower, and, in particular, all known Cayley graphs (since the existence of groups of intermediate growth, between polynomial and $e^{\sqrt{r}}$, is still open). We also show that the cartesian product of two moderate growth graphs can be turned into a small-world, even though it may not belong to the class itself. This reveals that the small-world phenomenon of a network may rely on multiple underlying structures.

Theorem 1. *Any α-moderate growth infinite graph H (resp., family of graphs $\mathcal{H}$), augmented by one long range link per node $\mathbf{u}$, pointing to a random node $\mathbf{v}$ at distance r with probability proportional to $\frac{1}{b_{H,\mathbf{u}}(r) \log^q r}$, for any $q > 1$, is a navigable small-world. any pair of nodes at distance ℓ from each other is $O(\ln^{1+q+\alpha \ln 5} \ell)$.*

Given any two moderate growth graphs, their cartesian product G augmented by one long range link per node $\mathbf{u}$, pointing to a random node $\mathbf{v}$ at distance r with probability proportional to $\frac{1}{b_{G,\mathbf{u}}(r) \log^{q'} r}$, for all $q' > q_0$, for some constant $q_0 > 0$, is a navigable small-world.

References

1. Milgram, S.: The small world problem. Psychology Today **61** (1967)
2. Watts, D., Strogatz, S.: Collective dynamics of small-world networks. Nature **393** (1998)

3. Newman, M.E.J., Watts, D.J.: Scaling and percolation in the small-world network model. Phys. Rev. **60** (1999) 7332–7342
4. Kleinberg, J.: The small-world phenomenon: an algorithmic perspective. In: Proceedings of the 32nd ACM Symp. on Theory of Computing (STOC). (2000) 163–170
5. Duchon, P., Hanusse, N., Lebhar, E., Schabanel, N.: Could any graph be turned into a small world? To appear in Theoretical Computer Science special issue on Complex Networks (2005) Also available as Research Report LIP-RR2004-62.

Brief Announcement:
Papillon: Greedy Routing in Rings

Ittai Abraham[1], Dahlia Malkhi[2], and Gurmeet Singh Manku[3]

[1] Hebrew University of Jerusalem
ittaia@cs.huji.ac.il
[2] Hebrew University of Jerusalem and Microsoft Research
dalia@microsoft.com
[3] Google
manku@google.com

Abstract. We construct the first n-node degree-d ring-based network with worst-case GREEDY routes of length $\Theta(\log n / \log d)$ hops.

We study GREEDY routing over uni-dimensional metrics[1] defined over n nodes lying in a ring. GREEDY routing in graph (V, E) with distance function $\delta : V \times V \to \mathcal{R}^+$ entails the following decision: Given target node t, node u with neighbors $N(u)$ forwards a message to $v \in N(u)$ such that $\delta(v, t) = \min_{x \in N(u)} \delta(x, t)$. The distance metric we use over n nodes placed in a circle is the clockwise-distance between pairs of nodes (the full paper contains a similar study of the absolute-distance metric):

$$\delta_{clock}(u, v) = v - u \text{ if } v \geq u, \; n + v - u \text{ otherwise.}$$

Let Δ_{clock} denote the worst-case GREEDY route length with δ_{clock}. $\overline{\Delta}_{clock}$ denotes the average GREEDY route length over all-pairs.

Summary of results. We construct a family of network topologies, the *Papillon*[2], in which GREEDY routes are asymptotically optimal. Papillon has GREEDY routes of length $\Delta_{clock} = \Theta(\log n / \log d)$ hops in the worst-case when each node has d out-going links. Papillon is the first construction that achieves asymptotically optimal worst-case GREEDY routes.

Upon further investigation, two properties of Papillon emerge: (a) GREEDY routing does not send messages along shortest paths, and (b) Edge congestion with GREEDY routing is not uniform – some edges are used more often than others. We exhibit the first property by identifying routing strategies that result in paths shorter than those achieved by GREEDY routing. In fact, one of these strategies guarantees uniform edge-congestion.

---

[1] The principles of this work can be extended to higher dimensional spaces. We focus on one-dimension for simplicity.

[2] Our constructions are variants of the well-known butterfly family, hence the name Papillon.

P. Fraigniaud (Ed.): DISC 2005, LNCS 3724, pp. 514–515, 2005.

The Papillon network. The intuitive idea of the Papillon construction is as follows. Nodes are arranged in m levels, where $n = \kappa^m m$. A node at level i has links to nodes one level down (wrapping at zero). Level-i links cover nodes between the current node, and distance roughly κ^i hops away, where hops are counted by the logical ordering of the nodes on the ring, and cut the distance to the target to roughly $\kappa^{(i-1)}$. In essence, Papillon is a geometric analogue of the bitonic butterfly network.

The reason that greedy routing works on Papillon is the following. So long as the current node's level i is too small, i.e., the distance to the target is more than κ^i, any link followed serves simply to go down the levels until we wrap at level zero and reach level $m - 1$. When the current level i is large enough, i.e., the distance to the target is at most κ^i, then one of the level links cuts the distance to κ^{i-1}. In this manner, eventually the target is reached.

$\mathcal{P}_{clock}(\kappa, m)$ *is a directed graph for any* $\kappa, m \geq 1$. *Let* $n = \kappa^m m$. *Let* $\ell(u) \equiv (m - 1) - (u \bmod m)$. *Each node has* κ *links. For node* u, *these links are to nodes* $(u + x) \bmod n$, *where* $x \in \{1 + im\kappa^{\ell(u)} \mid i \in [0, \kappa - 1]\}$.

Theorem 1. *For* $\mathcal{P}_{clock}(\kappa, m)$, $\Delta_{clock} \leq 3m - 2$ *and* $\overline{\Delta}_{clock} \leq 2m - 1$.

Putting $d = \kappa$, we obtain that in an n-node, degree-d network, worst-case routes are $\Theta(\log n / \log d)$. Curiously, GREEDY routing is not along shortest paths.

Theorem 2. *There exists a non-GREEDY strategy for* $\mathcal{P}_{clock}$ *with routes of length at most* $2m - 1$. *The average is at most* $1.5m$. *The strategy is congestion-free, with uniform load on edges for all-pairs communication.*

Previous results. With $\Theta(\log n)$ out-going links per node, several graphs over n nodes in a circle support GREEDY routes with $\Theta(\log n)$ GREEDY hops. Deterministic graphs with this property include variants of Chord, and this is also the known lower bound on any uniform graph (i.e., whose link-distances are the same from every node) with distance function $\delta_{clockwise}$. Randomized graphs which trade degree-d with route lengths $\Theta((\log^2 n)/d)$ on average include randomized-Chord and Symphony, with a gap to the known lower bound on uniform randomized network of $\Omega(\frac{\log^2 n}{d \log \log n})$.

Papillon extends the above results by constructing a non-uniform graph with $\Delta_{clock} = \Theta(\log n / \log d)$ in an n-node degree-d network, which is asymptotically optimal. Previously, this tradeoff was achieved on butterfly-like networks only with non-greedy routing (Viceroy, Ulysses, and Mariposa) or by greedy routing assisted with look-ahead. For $d = o(\log n)$, this beats the lower bound on uniform, randomized greedy routing networks (and it meets it for $d = O(\log n)$). In the specific case of $d = \log n$, our greedy routing achieves $O(\log n / \log \log n)$ average route length.

Please see http://arxiv.org/abs/cs.DC/0507034 for further details.

Brief Announcement: An Efficient Long-Lived Adaptive Collect Algorithm*

Burkhard Englert

California State University Long Beach, Dept. of Comp. Engr. & Comp. Science,
Long Beach, CA 90840
englert@cecs.csulb.edu

Abstract. We present a new long-lived, efficient, adaptive collect algorithm. Namely, our algorithm adapts to $\mathcal{K}$-contention - it has the property that if during an operation the interval contention k exceeds a pre-determined constant $\mathcal{K}$ the step complexity is $O(N)$. If, it falls below $\mathcal{K}$, the processors executions will eventually have adaptive step complexity of $O(k^3)$. Moreover, for $\mathcal{K}$ such that $\mathcal{K}^3 \leq N$ our algorithm requires only $O(N^2)$ shared memory registers.

1 Summary

To solve many well known problems such as atomic snapshot or renaming, it is essential that processors are able to gather information about each other. A simple way in which communication can be established is through the use of an array of Single-Writer Multi-Reader (SWMR) registers where each processor has a unique array entry assigned to it. Only a fixed processor is allowed to write to each array location while all processors can read all array entries. To update information about itself a processor writes into its array entry and to collect information about the other processors it reads all entries in an arbitrary order. Such a collect algorithm with step complexity $O(N)$, however, where N is the total number of processors in the system, is possibly inefficient if only few of the N processors are actually participating. This motivated researchers to look for *adaptive* algorithms whose step complexity only depends on the number of the concurrently participating processors.

Motivated by Lamport's MX algorithm [5], many adaptive algorithms have since been designed. Recently, a number of different adaptive collect algorithms were presented [1,2,3,4]. The algorithm by Attiya, Fouren and Gafni [3] for example, has an asymptotically optimal $O(k)$ step complexity, but it is a *one-shot* algorithm and the memory consumption is exponential in N. More recently Attiya, Kuhn, Wattenhofer and Wattenhofer [4] presented a new randomized adaptive collect algorithm with asymptotically optimal step complexity and polynomial memory overhead. For any constant $\gamma > 1$ they also presented a new deterministic collect algorithm with $O(k^2/((\gamma-1)\log n))$ step complexity

---

* An extended abstract of this paper appears in the Proceedings of the DPNA 2005 (IEEE-ICPADS 2005) workshop.

P. Fraigniaud (Ed.): DISC 2005, LNCS 3724, pp. 516–518, 2005.
© Springer-Verlag Berlin Heidelberg 2005

and $O(n^{\gamma+1})/(\gamma - 1)\log n)$ memory complexity. However, their algorithms are *one-shot*, not long-lived and hence adapt only to total contention with respect to shared memory operations. On the other hand the collect algorithm by Afek, Stupp and Touitou [1] is long-lived and adapts to the point contention (and hence to interval contention) k. It is designed for low contention, has step complexity $O(k^3)$ and uses $O(N^3)$ shared memory registers. As a result, if the interval contention k during the execution of a collect is high such that $k^3 >> N$, where N is the number of processors in the system, their algorithm [1] is less efficient than a "straightforward" collect algorithm where processors read all N SWMR registers in any order. Moreover, since such a "naive" algorithm only requires $O(N)$ shared memory cells but the long-lived adaptive collect algorithm by Afek, Stupp and Touitou [1] requires $O(N^3)$ shared memory registers, a significant memory overhead is encountered. In this sense it is very desirable to have an algorithm that itself can "adapt" to low or high (interval) contention.

We call such an algorithm *adaptive to $\mathcal{K}$-contention*. The constant $\mathcal{K}$ can be determined in advance. For example, if, as in [1], the adaptive step complexity is $O(k^3)$, we can let $\mathcal{K}$ be the largest integer such that $\mathcal{K}^3 < N$. Our new algorithm provides a mechanism to switch back and forth between the two approaches solely based on the interval contention a processor encounters.

Our paper makes the following contributions:

- We present a new long-lived adaptive collect algorithm. Previous algorithms [1] were designed for low contention and their performance suffers if the contention encountered exceeds $\mathcal{K}$ such that $\mathcal{K}^3 > N$. Our algorithm is *efficient* since it guarantees that a processor never needs to perform more than $O(N)$ steps in a *collect* operation. Moreover, our algorithm guarantees that if the interval contention k of two successive operations by a processor p is less than $\mathcal{K}$ and the contention of all other operations by other processors that occur or are active between these two operations is also less than $\mathcal{K}$, then the step complexity of the second operation by p is $O(k^3)$.
- Our algorithm introduces a mechanism that allows processors to switch back and forth from operation to operation between reading the registers of all other processors and an adaptive execution.
- Our algorithm requires only $O(N^2)$ shared memory registers (instead of $O(N^3)$ [1]) thereby reducing the memory complexity overhead encountered by long-lived adaptive collect algorithms.

Acknowledgement. We are grateful to Eli Gafni for helpful discussions and comments.

References

1. Y. Afek, G. Stupp and D. Touitou. Long-lived adaptive collect with applications. *Proc. of the 40th Ann. Symp. on Foundations of Computer Science*: 262-272, October 1999.

2. H. Attiya and A. Fouren. Algorithms adaptive to point contention. In *J. ACM*, 50(4): 444-468, July 2003.
3. H. Attiya, A. Fouren and E. Gafni. An adaptive collect algorithm with applications. *Distributed Computing*, 15(2): 87-96, 2002.
4. H. Attiya, F. Kuhn, M. Wattenhofer and R. Wattenhofer. Efficient Adaptive Collect using Randomization. *Proc. 18th Annual Conference on Distributed Computing (DISC)*, 2004.
5. L. Lamport. A fast mutual exclusion algorithm. *ACM Transactions on Computer Systems*, 5(1): 1-11. February 1987.

Author Index

Abraham, Ittai   442, 514
Afek, Yehuda   384
Aiyer, Amitanand   48
Alvizi, Lorenzo   48
Anceaume, Emmanuelle   505
Attiya, Hagit   122, 169

Badishi, Gal   18
Bazzi, Rida A.   48
Beauquier, Joffroy   399
Bhola, Sumeer   501
Blesa, Maria J.   429
Brodsky, Alex   137

Cachin, Christian   497, 503
Chockler, Gregory   152

David, Matei   137
De Levie, Yaron   384
Defago, Xavier   505
Delporte-Gallet, Carole   184
Duchon, Philippe   511

Engelhardt, Kai   229
Englert, Burkhard   516

Fauconnier, Hugues   184
Fernández, Antonio   490
Fich, Faith Ellen   78, 137, 493
Flammini, Michele   414
Freiling, Felix C.   93

Gafni, Eli   63
Gavoille, Cyril   442
Georgiou, Chryssis   490
Goldwasser, Shafi   288
Gradinariu, Maria   505
Guerraoui, Rachid   122, 184, 244, 303

Hanusse, Nicolas   511
Harris, Tim   108
Hendler, Danny   169
Herlihy, Maurice   303, 324
Herzberg, Amir   2, 18

Junqueira, Flavio   3

Keidar, Idit   18
Korman, Amos   457
Kouznetsov, Petr   122
Kuhn, Fabian   273
Kuo, Yu-Chen   509

Lafuente, Alberto   495
Larrea, Mikel   495
Lebhar, Emmanuelle   511
Lee, Huang-Chen   509
Liskov, Barbara   487
López, Luis   490
Lotker, Zvi   507
Luchangco, Victor   78, 493
Lynch, Nancy   152

Malkhi, Dahlia   199, 339, 442, 514
Manku, Gurmeet Singh   514
Marathe, Virendra J.   354
Marzullo, Keith   3
Mitra, Sayan   152
Mittal, Neeraj   93
Mitzenmacher, Michael   1
Moir, Mark   78, 493
Moore, Brad T.   214
Moscardelli, Luca   414
Moscibroda, Thomas   273
Moses, Yoram   229

Nadav, Uri   472
Naor, Moni   472
Navarra, Alfredo   414
Nieberg, Tim   273

Okun, Michael   499
Oprea, Florin   199

Patt-Shamir, Boaz   507
Pelc, Andrzej   260
Penso, Lucia Draque   93
Perennes, Stephane   414

Pilard, Laurence   399
Pochon, Bastian   303
Purcell, Chris   108

Rajsbaum, Sergio   63
Rodrigues, Rodrigo   487
Roy, Matthieu   505
Rozoy, Brigitte   399
Ruppert, Eric   244

Santos, Agustín   490
Schabanel, Nicolas   511
Scherer III, William N.   354
Scott, Michael L.   354
Shavit, Nir   78, 493
Sivilotti, Paolo A.G.   214
Sturman, Daniel   501

Sudan, Madhu   288
Sun, Ye   324

Tauber, Joshua   152
Terry, Doug   339
Tessaro, Stefano   497, 503
Tuttle, Mark R.   507

Vaikuntanathan, Vinod   288
Venkatesan, S.   93
Völzer, Hagen   33

Wattenhofer, Roger   273

Zhao, Yuanyuan   501
Zhou, Lidong   199
Zieliński, Piotr   369

Lecture Notes in Computer Science

For information about Vols. 1–3630

please contact your bookseller or Springer

Vol. 3738: V.R. Syrotiuk, E. Chávez (Eds.), Ad-Hoc, Mobile, and Wireless Networks. XI, 360 pages. 2005.

Vol. 3728: V. Paliouras, J. Vounckx, D. Verkest (Eds.), Integrated Circuit and System Design. XV, 753 pages. 2005.

Vol. 3726: L.T. Yang, O.F. Rana, B. Di Martino, J. Dongarra (Eds.), High Performance Computing and Communcations. XXVI, 1116 pages. 2005.

Vol. 3725: D. Borrione, W. Paul (Eds.), Correct Hardware Design and Verification Methods. XII, 412 pages. 2005.

Vol. 3724: P. Fraigniaud (Ed.), Distributed Computing. XIV, 520 pages. 2005.

Vol. 3718: V.G. Ganzha, E.W. Mayr, E.V. Vorozhtsov (Eds.), Computer Algebra in Scientific Computing. XII, 502 pages. 2005.

Vol. 3717: B. Gramlich (Ed.), Frontiers of Combining Systems. X, 321 pages. 2005. (Subseries LNAI).

Vol. 3715: E. Dawson, S. Vaudenay (Eds.), Progress in Cryptology – Mycrypt 2005. XI, 329 pages. 2005.

Vol. 3714: H. Obbink, K. Pohl (Eds.), Software Product Lines. XIII, 235 pages. 2005.

Vol. 3713: L. Briand, C. Williams (Eds.), Model Driven Engineering Languages and Systems. XV, 722 pages. 2005.

Vol. 3712: R. Reussner, J. Mayer, J.A. Stafford, S. Overhage, S. Becker, P.J. Schroeder (Eds.), Quality of Software Architectures and Software Quality. XIII, 289 pages. 2005.

Vol. 3711: F. Kishino, Y. Kitamura, H. Kato, N. Nagata (Eds.), Entertainment Computing - ICEC 2005. XXIV, 540 pages. 2005.

Vol. 3710: M. Barni, I. Cox, T. Kalker, H.J. Kim (Eds.), Digital Watermarking. XII, 485 pages. 2005.

Vol. 3708: J. Blanc-Talon, W. Philips, D. Popescu, P. Scheunders (Eds.), Advanced Concepts for Intelligent Vision Systems. XXII, 725 pages. 2005.

Vol. 3707: D.A. Peled, Y.-K. Tsay (Eds.), Automated Technology for Verification and Analysis. XII, 506 pages. 2005.

Vol. 3706: H. Fuks, S. Lukosch, A.C. Salgado (Eds.), Groupware: Design, Implementation, and Use. XII, 378 pages. 2005.

Vol. 3703: F. Fages, S. Soliman (Eds.), Principles and Practice of Semantic Web Reasoning. VIII, 163 pages. 2005.

Vol. 3702: B. Beckert (Ed.), Automated Reasoning with Analytic Tableaux and Related Methods. XIII, 343 pages. 2005. (Subseries LNAI).

Vol. 3699: C.S. Calude, M.J. Dinneen, G. Păun, M. J. Pérez-Jiménez, G. Rozenberg (Eds.), Unconventional Computation. XI, 267 pages. 2005.

Vol. 3698: U. Furbach (Ed.), KI 2005: Advances in Artificial Intelligence. XIII, 409 pages. 2005. (Subseries LNAI).

Vol. 3697: W. Duch, J. Kacprzyk, E. Oja, S. Zadrożny (Eds.), Artificial Neural Networks: Formal Models and Their Applications – ICANN 2005, Part II. XXXII, 1045 pages. 2005.

Vol. 3696: W. Duch, J. Kacprzyk, E. Oja, S. Zadrożny (Eds.), Artificial Neural Networks: Biological Inspirations – ICANN 2005, Part I. XXXI, 703 pages. 2005.

Vol. 3695: M.R. Berthold, R. Glen, K. Diederichs, O. Kohlbacher, I. Fischer (Eds.), Computational Life Sciences. XI, 277 pages. 2005. (Subseries LNBI).

Vol. 3694: M. Malek, E. Nett, N. Suri (Eds.), Service Availability. VIII, 213 pages. 2005.

Vol. 3693: A.G. Cohn, D.M. Mark (Eds.), Spatial Information Theory. XII, 493 pages. 2005.

Vol. 3692: R. Casadio, G. Myers (Eds.), Algorithms in Bioinformatics. X, 436 pages. 2005. (Subseries LNBI).

Vol. 3691: A. Gagalowicz, W. Philips (Eds.), Computer Analysis of Images and Patterns. XIX, 865 pages. 2005.

Vol. 3690: M. Pěchouček, P. Petta, L.Z. Varga (Eds.), Multi-Agent Systems and Applications IV. XVII, 667 pages. 2005. (Subseries LNAI).

Vol. 3687: S. Singh, M. Singh, C. Apte, P. Perner (Eds.), Pattern Recognition and Image Analysis, Part II. XXV, 809 pages. 2005.

Vol. 3686: S. Singh, M. Singh, C. Apte, P. Perner (Eds.), Pattern Recognition and Data Mining, Part I. XXVI, 689 pages. 2005.

Vol. 3685: V. Gorodetsky, I. Kotenko, V. Skormin (Eds.), Computer Network Security. XIV, 480 pages. 2005.

Vol. 3684: R. Khosla, R.J. Howlett, L.C. Jain (Eds.), Knowledge-Based Intelligent Information and Engineering Systems, Part IV. LXXIX, 933 pages. 2005. (Subseries LNAI).

Vol. 3683: R. Khosla, R.J. Howlett, L.C. Jain (Eds.), Knowledge-Based Intelligent Information and Engineering Systems, Part III. LXXX, 1397 pages. 2005. (Subseries LNAI).

Vol. 3682: R. Khosla, R.J. Howlett, L.C. Jain (Eds.), Knowledge-Based Intelligent Information and Engineering Systems, Part II. LXXIX, 1371 pages. 2005. (Subseries LNAI).

Vol. 3681: R. Khosla, R.J. Howlett, L.C. Jain (Eds.), Knowledge-Based Intelligent Information and Engineering Systems, Part I. LXXX, 1319 pages. 2005. (Subseries LNAI).

Vol. 3679: S.d.C. di Vimercati, P. Syverson, D. Gollmann (Eds.), Computer Security – ESORICS 2005. XI, 509 pages. 2005.

Vol. 3678: A. McLysaght, D.H. Huson (Eds.), Comparative Genomics. VIII, 167 pages. 2005. (Subseries LNBI).

Vol. 3677: J. Dittmann, S. Katzenbeisser, A. Uhl (Eds.), Communications and Multimedia Security. XIII, 360 pages. 2005.

Vol. 3676: R. Glück, M. Lowry (Eds.), Generative Programming and Component Engineering. XI, 448 pages. 2005.

Vol. 3675: Y. Luo (Ed.), Cooperative Design, Visualization, and Engineering. XI, 264 pages. 2005.

Vol. 3674: W. Jonker, M. Petković (Eds.), Secure Data Management. X, 241 pages. 2005.

Vol. 3673: S. Bandini, S. Manzoni (Eds.), AI*IA 2005: Advances in Artificial Intelligence. XIV, 614 pages. 2005. (Subseries LNAI).

Vol. 3672: C. Hankin, I. Siveroni (Eds.), Static Analysis. X, 369 pages. 2005.

Vol. 3671: S. Bressan, S. Ceri, E. Hunt, Z.G. Ives, Z. Bellahsène, M. Rys, R. Unland (Eds.), Database and XML Technologies. X, 239 pages. 2005.

Vol. 3670: M. Bravetti, L. Kloul, G. Zavattaro (Eds.), Formal Techniques for Computer Systems and Business Processes. XIII, 349 pages. 2005.

Vol. 3669: G.S. Brodal, S. Leonardi (Eds.), Algorithms – ESA 2005. XVIII, 901 pages. 2005.

Vol. 3668: M. Gabbrielli, G. Gupta (Eds.), Logic Programming. XIV, 454 pages. 2005.

Vol. 3666: B.D. Martino, D. Kranzlmüller, J. Dongarra (Eds.), Recent Advances in Parallel Virtual Machine and Message Passing Interface. XVII, 546 pages. 2005.

Vol. 3665: K. S. Candan, A. Celentano (Eds.), Advances in Multimedia Information Systems. X, 221 pages. 2005.

Vol. 3664: C. Türker, M. Agosti, H.-J. Schek (Eds.), Peer-to-Peer, Grid, and Service-Orientation in Digital Library Architectures. X, 261 pages. 2005.

Vol. 3663: W.G. Kropatsch, R. Sablatnig, A. Hanbury (Eds.), Pattern Recognition. XIV, 512 pages. 2005.

Vol. 3662: C. Baral, G. Greco, N. Leone, G. Terracina (Eds.), Logic Programming and Nonmonotonic Reasoning. XIII, 454 pages. 2005. (Subseries LNAI).

Vol. 3661: T. Panayiotopoulos, J. Gratch, R. Aylett, D. Ballin, P. Olivier, T. Rist (Eds.), Intelligent Virtual Agents. XIII, 506 pages. 2005. (Subseries LNAI).

Vol. 3660: M. Beigl, S. Intille, J. Rekimoto, H. Tokuda (Eds.), UbiComp 2005: Ubiquitous Computing. XVII, 394 pages. 2005.

Vol. 3659: J.R. Rao, B. Sunar (Eds.), Cryptographic Hardware and Embedded Systems – CHES 2005. XIV, 458 pages. 2005.

Vol. 3658: V. Matoušek, P. Mautner, T. Pavelka (Eds.), Text, Speech and Dialogue. XV, 460 pages. 2005. (Subseries LNAI).

Vol. 3657: F.S. de Boer, M.M. Bonsangue, S. Graf, W.-P. de Roever (Eds.), Formal Methods for Components and Objects. VIII, 325 pages. 2005.

Vol. 3656: M. Kamel, A. Campilho (Eds.), Image Analysis and Recognition. XXIV, 1279 pages. 2005.

Vol. 3655: A. Aldini, R. Gorrieri, F. Martinelli (Eds.), Foundations of Security Analysis and Design III. VII, 273 pages. 2005.

Vol. 3654: S. Jajodia, D. Wijesekera (Eds.), Data and Applications Security XIX. X, 353 pages. 2005.

Vol. 3653: M. Abadi, L. de Alfaro (Eds.), CONCUR 2005 – Concurrency Theory. XIV, 578 pages. 2005.

Vol. 3652: A. Rauber, S. Christodoulakis, A. M. Tjoa (Eds.), Research and Advanced Technology for Digital Libraries. XVIII, 545 pages. 2005.

Vol. 3651: R. Dale, K.-F. Wong, J. Su, O.Y. Kwong (Eds.), Natural Language Processing – IJCNLP 2005. XXI, 1031 pages. 2005. (Subseries LNAI).

Vol. 3650: J. Zhou, J. Lopez, R.H. Deng, F. Bao (Eds.), Information Security. XII, 516 pages. 2005.

Vol. 3649: W.M. P. van der Aalst, B. Benatallah, F. Casati, F. Curbera (Eds.), Business Process Management. XII, 472 pages. 2005.

Vol. 3648: J.C. Cunha, P.D. Medeiros (Eds.), Euro-Par 2005 Parallel Processing. XXXVI, 1299 pages. 2005.

Vol. 3646: A. F. Famili, J.N. Kok, J.M. Peña, A. Siebes, A. Feelders (Eds.), Advances in Intelligent Data Analysis VI. XIV, 522 pages. 2005.

Vol. 3645: D.-S. Huang, X.-P. Zhang, G.-B. Huang (Eds.), Advances in Intelligent Computing, Part II. XIII, 1010 pages. 2005.

Vol. 3644: D.-S. Huang, X.-P. Zhang, G.-B. Huang (Eds.), Advances in Intelligent Computing, Part I. XXVII, 1101 pages. 2005.

Vol. 3643: R. Moreno Díaz, F. Pichler, A. Quesada Arencibia (Eds.), Computer Aided Systems Theory – EUROCAST 2005. XIV, 629 pages. 2005.

Vol. 3642: D. Ślezak, J. Yao, J.F. Peters, W. Ziarko, X. Hu (Eds.), Rough Sets, Fuzzy Sets, Data Mining, and Granular Computing, Part II. XXIII, 738 pages. 2005. (Subseries LNAI).

Vol. 3641: D. Ślezak, G. Wang, M. Szczuka, I. Düntsch, Y. Yao (Eds.), Rough Sets, Fuzzy Sets, Data Mining, and Granular Computing, Part I. XXIV, 742 pages. 2005. (Subseries LNAI).

Vol. 3639: P. Godefroid (Ed.), Model Checking Software. XI, 289 pages. 2005.

Vol. 3638: A. Butz, B. Fisher, A. Krüger, P. Olivier (Eds.), Smart Graphics. XI, 269 pages. 2005.

Vol. 3637: J. M. Moreno, J. Madrenas, J. Cosp (Eds.), Evolvable Systems: From Biology to Hardware. XI, 227 pages. 2005.

Vol. 3636: M.J. Blesa, C. Blum, A. Roli, M. Sampels (Eds.), Hybrid Metaheuristics. XII, 155 pages. 2005.

Vol. 3634: L. Ong (Ed.), Computer Science Logic. XI, 567 pages. 2005.

Vol. 3633: C. Bauzer Medeiros, M. Egenhofer, E. Bertino (Eds.), Advances in Spatial and Temporal Databases. XIII, 433 pages. 2005.

Vol. 3632: R. Nieuwenhuis (Ed.), Automated Deduction – CADE-20. XIII, 459 pages. 2005. (Subseries LNAI).

Vol. 3631: J. Eder, H.-M. Haav, A. Kalja, J. Penjam (Eds.), Advances in Databases and Information Systems. XIII, 393 pages. 2005.